800 INSTANT POT RECIPES #2020

By Jamie Sutter

Contents

VEGETABLES & SIDE DISHES **12**
1. Indian Urad Dal 13
2. Aromatic Cabbage with Vegetables and Herbs 13
3. Classic Italian Tomato Soup 13
4. Rich Vegan Bowl with Tahini 13
5. Buttery Sautéed Baby Potatoes with Rosemary 14
6. Greek Eggplant with Chickpeas 14
7. Ranch Cauliflower and Ricotta Dip 14
8. Spicy Cream of Broccoli Soup 14
9. Classic Beet Salad with Cheese 15
10. Moroccan-Style Couscous Salad 15
11. Garam Masala Vegetable Sauté 15
12. Spicy and Saucy Rice 15
13. Cauliflower with Greek-Style Sauce 16
14. Green Beans with Garlic and Chives 16
15. Old-Fashioned Vegetable Stew 16
16. Indian Sweet Corn 16
17. Zingy Vegetable Sticks 17
18. Brussels Sprouts with Parmigiano-Reggiano 17
19. Traditional Sweet Onion and Cheese Soup.................17
20. Kamut, Spinach and Celery Bowl 17
21. Grandma's Snow Peas 18
22. Bell Peppers with Balsamic Vinegar 18
23. Root Veggies with Horseradish Mayo 18
24. Winter Vegetables with Orange Butter 18
25. Eggplant with Steamed Eggs and Tomatoes 19
26. 4-Ingredient Saucy Millet 19
27. Swiss Chard with Bacon and Cheese 19
28. Red Lentils with Peppers and Cilantro 19
29. Braised Cabbage with Chanterelle Mushrooms.........20
30. Bucatini with Capers and Olives 20
31. Easy Vegetarian Skewers 20
32. Punjabi Rajma Masala 20
33. Fall Acorn Squash Chowder 21
34. Indian Tamatar Baingan..21
35. Artichoke, Kale and Cheese Dip.....................................21
36. Easy Frijoles Refritos 21
37. Mashed Potatoes with Garlic and Herbs 22
38. Marshmallow-Topped Sweet Potatoes 22
39. Honey-Mustard Glazed Cipollini Onions 22
40. Easy Italian Endive 22
41. Glazed Baby Carrots 23
42. Sriracha Bang Bang Corn 23
43. Classic Mushroom Stroganoff...23
44. Layered Zucchini Casserole 23
45. Potatoes with Cheese and Parsley 24
46. Braised Collard Greens with Bacon 24
47. Thai Tom Kha Gai 24
48. Brussels Sprouts with Romano Cheese 24
49. Kale and Potato Soup 25
50. Vegetables with Halloumi Cheese 25
51. Traditional Provençal Ratatouille 25
52. Refreshing Chickpea Salad 25
53. Bamies Latheres me Domata 26
54. Pancetta Green Beans 26
55. Keto Cauliflower Rice 26
56. Old-Fashioned Cabbage with Ham 26
57. Sweet Potato Puree 27
58. Potato and Broccoli Chowder 27
59. Padma Lakshmi's Yogurt Rice 27
60. Dijon Broccoli Salad with Feta Cheese 27
61. Authentic Italian Caponata 28
62. Paprika Creamed Carrot Mash 28
63. Warm Chickpea Salad 28
64. Creamed Broccoli with Mustard and Seeds 28
65. Roasted Herbed Baby Potatoes 29
66. Mini Sweet Potatoes with Butter 29
67. Mediterranean Tomato Soup with Feta Cheese 29
68. Caramelized Onion and Bacon Tart...............................29
69. Vegetarian Ratatouille Provencale 30
70. Lebanese Zucchini and Garbanzo Bean Bake 30
71. Harvest Vegetables with Barley.......................................30
72. Italian Stuffed Peppers with Mushroom and Sausage ...30
73. Green Artichoke Dipping Sauce 31
74. Balsamic Mayo Potato Wedges 31
75. Romano Eggplant and Wine Sauce 31
76. Cheesy Mashed Cauliflower 31
77. Winter Vegetable and Lentil Stew 32
78. Asian Vegetable Soup..32
79. Cream of Potato Soup 32
80. Belgian Endive with Dijon Sauce 32
81. Vegan Tomato and Zucchini Risotto 33
82. Stuffed Peppers with Cheddar Cheese 33
83. Chana Aloo Masala 33
84. Simple Zucchini Slices with Herbs 33
85. Traditional Greek Fasolakia 34

BEANS, LEGUMES & LENTILS **35**
86. Simple Black Pepper Beans 36
87. Spicy Chickpeas with Herbs 36
88. Black Bean Chili...36
89. Country-Style Black Eyed Peas 36
90. Borlotti Beans with Tomato and Herbs 37
91. Traditional Japanese Kuromame.....................................37
92. Kidney Beans with Carrot and Peppers 37
93. Greek-Style Bean Salad 37
94. Spicy Yellow Lentils with Green Onions 38
95. Perfect Mong Daal Khichri 38
96. Famous Vegan Lentil Tacos 38
97. Easiest Lebanese Mujadara Ever 38
98. Black-Eyed Peas with Bacon 39
99. Herbed Pea Spread 39
100. Japanese-Style Chickpeas 39
101. Farmhouse Split Pea Soup with Ham 39
102. Egyptian Ful Mudammas 40
103. Indian Sorakkai Sambar 40
104. Adzuki Bean Purée 40
105. Rajma with Adzuki Beans 40
106. Baked Beans with Italian sausage..................................41
107. Kidney Bean Soup with Bacon 41
108. French Lentil Salad 41
109. Colorful Lentil and Pepper Salad 41
110. Seafood with Green Lentils 42
111. Country-Style Beans with Sausage 42
112. Portuguese Baked Beans 42
113. Refried Beans with Cheese 42

114. Classic Bean Soup with Herbs 43
115. Authentic Spicy Hummus 43
116. Pinto Beans with Rice and Herbs 43
117. French Du Lentilles du Puy.........................43
118. Black Beans with Tomato and Cilantro 44
119. Classic Lentil Curry 44
120. Rancher's Texas Chili 44
121. Italian-Style Heirloom Beans 44
122. Warm Red Lentil Salad 45
123. Tarragon Green Peas 45
124. Split Pea Sauce 45
125. Authentic Tarka Dhal 45
126. Classic Lentil Gumbo 46

RICE, PASTA & GRAINS 47
127. Brown Rice Risotto with Olives 48
128. Cajun Rice Chowder 48
129. Saucy and Peppery Millet 48
130. Creamed Ziti with Mozzarella 48
131. Japanese-Style Okayu 49
132. Basic Breakfast Oatmeal 49
133. Cremini Mushroom Pilau 49
134. Polenta with Feta Cheese 49
135. Kamut with Sweet Onions 50
136. Amaranth with Eggs and Cheddar Cheese ...50
137. Mom's Barley with Vegetables 50
138. Traditional Spanish Paella 50
139. Tangy Wild Rice Soup 51
140. Pilaf with Petite Peas and Peanuts 51
141. Spanish Rice with Chorizo Sausage 51
142. Tangy Farro Salad 51
143. Authentic Asian Congee 52
144. Pakistani Basmati Rice 52
145. Sweet Couscous with Almonds and Pears ...52
146. Greek Rizogalo with Cinnamon 52
147. Sweet Brioche Bread Pudding 53
148. Rice and Chicken Bake 53
149. Greek-Style Oats 53
150. Basic Japanese Sushi Rice 53
151. Sweet Kamut with Cherries 54
152. Spelt Risotto with Mushrooms and Spinach ...54
153. Barley and Chickpea Salad with Cheese 54
154. Creamed Corn with Cottage Cheese 54
155. Aromatic Amaranth Porridge with Almonds ...55
156. Festive Mac 'n' Cheese 55
157. Spicy and Saucy Bulgur Wheat 55
158. Risotto Salad with Fruits 55
159. Barley, Chicken and Vegetable Soup 56
160. Italian Mushrooms Risotto with Cheese 56
161. Buckwheat Breakfast Bowl 56
162. Shrimp Risotto with Herbs 56
163. Classic Nutty Oatmeal with Banana 57
164. Smoked Salmon and Green Bean Pilau 57
165. Cheesy Polenta with Mushrooms and Olives ...57
166. Italian Chicken and Rice Casserole 57
167. Old-Fashioned Oatmeal with Figs 58
168. Pilaf with Vegetables and Cheese................58
169. Warm Winter Chocolate Oatmeal 58
170. Arroz Estilo Mexicano.................................58
171. Cheese Cilantro Cornbread.........................59
172. Hearty Beef Stew with Rice 59

173. Rustic Pecorino Romano Risotto 59
174. Breakfast Millet Porridge 59
175. Buttery Quinoa Porridge with Scallions 60
176. Old-Fashioned Grits with Cream Cheese 60
177. Rich Barley and Corn Soup 60
178. Three-Grain Porridge with Pepper 60
179. Vanilla Buckwheat Porridge with Fruits 61
180. Cheesy Farro Pilaf with Mushrooms 61
181. Oatmeal Soup with Onions.........................61
182. Movie Night Popcorn 61
183. Herb Buttermilk Cornbread 62
184. Couscous, Chicken, and Vegetable Soup 62
185. Mediterranean-Style Kamut Pilaf 62

PORK 63
186. Country-Style Pork Stew 64
187. Melt-in-Your-Mouth Pork 64
188. Sticky Pulled Pork 64
189. Decadent Pork Chops with Pineapple 64
190. Spicy Pork-Bacon Meatballs 65
191. Sticky St. Louis-Style Ribs 65
192. Macaroni with Pork Sausage and Cheese 65
193. Pork Loin, Sausage with Polenta 65
194. Pulled Pork Taquitos 66
195. Herbed Pork with Winter Vegetables 66
196. Indian Pork Curry 66
197. Pork Sausage and Peppers Casserole 66
198. Braised Ribs with Tomatillos and Beer 67
199. Bourbon-Orange Glazed Ham 67
200. Chinese-Style Spicy Braised Pork 67
201. Ground Pork Goulash with Cheese 67
202. Hawaiian Pork Sandwiches 68
203. Authentic Tacos de Carnitas 68
204. Korean Momofuku Bo Ssam........................68
205. Christmas Pork with Mustard Gravy 68
206. Rustic Pork Pâté 69
207. Perfect Pork Loin Chops 69
208. Pork Sausages with Black Beans 69
209. Marsala Pork and Vegetable Casserole.........69
210. Pork and Mushroom Paprikash 70
211. Perfect Mexican Chile Verde 70
212. Pork and Corn Chowder 70
213. Pork in Creamed Sauce 70
214. Mexican Pork Soup 71
215. Ground Pork Stuffed Peppers with Cheese ...71
216. Orange-Glazed Picnic Shoulder 71
217. Pork Fajita Wraps.......................................71
218. Authentic Tacos with Morita Salsa 72
219. Roasted Pork with Red Wine 72
220. Cajun Sticky Ribs 72
221. Parmesan Meatballs with Marinara Sauce 72
222. Italian Pasta Bolognese with a Twist 73
223. Italian Pork Chops with Cheese 73
224. Neapolitan Pork Ragù 73
225. Pork Sliders with Cholula Sauce 73
226. Thai Green Curry with Pork 74
227. Authentic Venezuelan Pork Arepas..............74
228. Mexican Pork and Hominy Stew (Posole Rojo) ...74
229. Tangy Braised Pork Loin Roast 74
230. Authentic Pork Cassoulet 75
231. Ground Pork Omelet 75

232. Mustard Pork Belly with Herbs 75
233. Cajun Pork and Pepper Casserole 75
234. Macaroni and Cheese with Pork Sausage 76
235. German Pork with Sauerkraut..................................76
236. Smothered Pork Chops with Mustard 76
237. Goan Pork Masala 76
238. Perfect Pulled Pork Sliders 77
239. Pork Romano Meatloaf 77
240. Pork Steak in Red Wine Sauce 77
241. Pork Fajitas with Pico de Gallo 77
242. Perfect Saucissons Provençal 78
243. Glazed Picnic Ham 78
244. Mexican Meatloaf with Salsa 78
245. Spicy Pork Frittata 78
246. Spicy Pork Spare Ribs 79
247. Balsamic Boston Butt 79
248. Asian-Style Pork with Mushrooms 79
249. Old-Fashioned Pork Steaks 79
250. Home-Style Pork Cheeseburgers..............................80
251. Easy BBQ Pork 80
252. Country-Style Pork Ribs 80
253. Pork with Riesling Sauce 80
254. Pork Liver Mousse with Brandy 81
255. Ale-Braised Pork Ham Hock with Herbs 81
256. Japanese Buta Niku No Mushimono...........................81
257. Sticky Pulled Pork with Apples 81
258. Dad's Pork Chops and Potatoes 82
259. Pork Loin with Salsa Sause 82
260. Loin Roast with Cream Cheese Sauce 82
261. Pork and Vegetable Medley 82
262. Creamy Italian-Style Pork with Mushrooms 83
263. Beer-Braised Paprika Ribs 83
264. Pork Cutlets with Ricotta Cheese 83
265. Spare Ribs with Hoisin Sauce 83
266. Chunky Pork Soup with Peppers 84
267. Decadent Pork with Port and Raisins 84
268. Traditional Bosanski Lonac....................................84
269. Pork with Herb-Wine Sauce 84
270. Summer Ribs with Spicy Sauce 85

POULTRY 86
271. Cheesy Loaded Meatloaf 87
272. Chicken with Millet and Green Beans.........................87
273. Farmhouse Beer Turkey Chili 87
274. Chinese-Style Glazed Duck 87
275. Country-Style Chicken Thigh Soup 88
276. Beer-Braised Turkey Drumsticks 88
277. Creamed Taco Chicken Salad 88
278. Sticky Duck in Cherry Sauce...................................88
279. Turkey Fillets with Cremini Mushrooms 89
280. Chicken, Cheese and Pasta Bake 89
281. Stuffed Turkey with Chèvre Cheese 89
282. Chicken Breast and Salsa Casserole 89
283. Mexican Chicken Carnitas 90
284. Japanese Teriyaki Chicken 90
285. Chicken with Cheese Parsley Dip..............................90
286. Ground Turkey Casserole 90
287. Grandma's Chicken Soup 91
288. Duck with Harvest Vegetables 91
289. Greek-Style Chicken-Stuffed Peppers 91

290. Fettuccine with Duck Ragout 91
291. Chicken and Bean Medley 92
292. Chicken Breasts with Vegetables and Herbs 92
293. Classic Chicken Salad with Herbs 92
294. Italian-Style Turkey with Vegetables..........................92
295. Rich Meatball Soup 93
296. Asian-Style Saucy Duck 93
297. Chicken Thigh and Green Bean Soup 93
298. Dijon Herbed Turkey Meatloaf 93
299. Chicken Lasagna with Pepper-Jack Cheese...................94
300. Mediterranean Turkey Salad with Feta Cheese...............94
301. Perfect Chicken Cutlets with Sherry 94
302. Thanksgiving Turkey Breasts 94
303. 4-Cheese Chicken Alfredo 95
304. Skinny Turkey Salad 95
305. Turkey Thighs with Dill-Wine Sauce 95
306. Mexican Taco Meat 95
307. Harvest Vegetable and Chicken Soup 96
308. Fontina Cheese-Stuffed Meatballs 96
309. Chicken Sausage and Cauliflower Chowder 96
310. Chinese-Glazed Chicken Drumsticks 96
311. Spicy Chicken Drumettes 97
312. Indian Duck Masala 97
313. Turkey and Zucchini Casserole 97
314. Roasted Turkey with Mayo and Herbs 97
315. Mediterranean-Style Chicken Drumsticks 98
316. Smothered Chicken Cutlets with Pasta 98
317. Old-Fashioned Turkey and Tomato Soup 98
318. Asian-Style Chicken Drumsticks with Rice 98
319. Turkey Stew with Root Vegetables 99
320. Cheesy Chicken Tenders 99
321. Pinot Grigio Chicken 99
322. Traditional Locrio de Pollo 99
323. Thai Chicken Curry..100
324. Asian-Style Duck Breast 100
325. Decadent Turkey Breasts in Sweet Apricot Sauce 100
326. Duck with Wild Mushrooms and Port Wine 100
327. The Best Chicken Tacos Ever 101
328. French Coq au Vin 101
329. BBQ Meatloaf with Parmesan Cheese 101
330. Chicken Fillets with Cheese and Peppers 101
331. Mexican-Style Chicken Sliders 102
332. Ranch Chicken with Onions 102
333. Sticky Turkey Thighs 102
334. Mexican-Style Turkey Tacos 102
335. Traditional Szechuan Duck.....................................103
336. Italian-Style Turkey and Rice 103
337. Turkey Sandwich with Cheese and Lettuce 103
338. Mexican-Style Turkey and Sausage Meatloaf.................103
339. Duck Salad with Peanut Butter 104
340. Chicken Breasts with Mayo-Cheese Sauce 104
341. Lebanese Tabouli Salad 104
342. Dijon Chicken Meatballs 104
343. Thai-Style Duck Breasts 105
344. Swiss Spicy Turkey Meatballs 105
345. Blood Orange Duck Breast 105
346. Chicken with Port Wine Sauce 105
347. Meatball and Mozzarella Sliders with Tomato Sauce 106
348. Turkey, Herb and Green Bean Chowder 106
349. Chicken Siciliano with Marsala Wine 106

350. Chicken Sloppy Joes 106

BEEF 107
351. Japanese Beef Stew 108
352. Chinese Beef Rump Roast 108
353. Classic Sloppy Joes 108
354. Spicy Thai Beef Salad 108
355. Saucy Delmonico Steak with Cheese 109
356. Beef Goulash Soup 109
357. French-Style Beef Tenderloin 109
358. Spicy Beef Chuck 109
359. Steak Salad with Feta Cheese 110
360. Classic Beef Brisket with Cheese 110
361. Cheeseburger and Tomato Soufflé 110
362. Beef with Vegetables and Port Wine 110
363. Syrah-Braised Beef 111
364. Best-Ever Homemade Tacos 111
365. Rustic Beef Brisket with Vegetables 111
366. Beef with Wontons and Cream Cheese 111
367. Creamed New York Strip 112
368. Harvest Beef Stew 112
369. Classic Beef Stroganoff 112
370. Chunky Hamburger Soup 112
371. Ground Beef, Cheese and Bean Bowl 113
372. Authentic Hungarian Pörkölt 113
373. Ground Beef and Tomato Frittata 113
374. Classic Beef Sandwich 113
375. Boozy and Spicy Short Ribs 114
376. Beef Stew with Muffin Top 114
377. Saucy and Spicy Rump Steak 114
378. Wine Braised-Beef with Cabbage Slaw 114
379. Spanish-Style Pot Roast 115
380. Turkish Doner Kebab 115
381. Basic Korean Bulgogi 115
382. Perfect Ossobuco Milanese 115
383. Winter Short Ribs with Leeks 116
384. Traditional Lavaş with Beef 116
385. Breakfast Cheeseburger Cups 116
386. Pakistani Beef Biryani 116
387. Homemade Philly Cheesesteak Sandwich 117
388. Kheema Pav (Bombay Sloppy Joes) 117
389. Winter Chili with Ground Chuck 117
390. Risotto with Ground Beef 117
391. Filet Mignon with Mushroom Sauce 118
392. Vietnamese Pho Bo 118
393. Rich Taco Meatloaf 118
394. Classic Steak Pepperonata with Red Wine 118
395. Bulgarian Palneni Chushki 119
396. Chianti Beef Mélange 119
397. Roast Beef with Gravy 119
398. Chinese Sirloin Steak 119
399. Perfect Beef Bourguignon 120
400. Beef Sirloin Soup with Potatoes 120
401. Homemade Beef Tacos 120
402. Nana's Steak Soup with Root Vegetables 120
403. Rustic Beef Short Ribs 121
404. Easy Shoulder Roast with Russet Potatoes 121
405. Festive Glazed Chuck Roast 121
406. Corned Beef Brisket 121
407. Spicy Shredded Beef 122

408. Beef Brisket with Riesling Sauce 122
409. Authentic Beef Gulyás 122
410. Romano and Bacon Meatballs 122
411. Winter Stew with Beef and Macaroni 123
412. Peppery Strip Steak with Pine Nuts 123
413. Beef Curry Stew 123
414. Sticky Quinoa Meatballs 123
415. Simple Perfect Enchiladas 124
416. Steak with Spicy Rum Sauce 124
417. Traditional Beef Peperonata 124
418. Beef Stroganoff with Cream Cheese 124
419. Boozy Chuck Roast 125
420. BBQ Pot Roast 125
421. Sticky Spicy Asian Ribs 125
422. Sage Merlot Roast Beef 125
423. Serbian-Style Moussaka with Cheese 126
424. Beef Sausage and Kidney Bean Casserole 126
425. Parmesan Dijon Meatballs 126
426. Steak with Celery and Marinara 126
427. Chinese Wine-Braised Beef 127
428. Sausage and Bean Hotpot 127
429. Roast Beef with Small Potatoes 127
430. Beef and Pinto Bean Wraps 127

LOW CARB 128
431. Ham Bone Soup with Harvest Vegetables 129
432. Home-Style Blueberry Yogurt 129
433. Deviled Eggs with Cottage Cheese 129
434. Mini Frittatas with Bacon and Cheese 129
435. Fake-Out Mac n' Cheese 130
436. Skinny Spinach Muffins 130
437. Eggs with Chanterelles and Mexican Cheese 130
438. Asian Saucy Duck Breast 130
439. Ground Chuck and Tomato Frittata 131
440. Chicken Liver Pate with Wine 131
441. Mustard Beer Braised Chuck Roast 131
442. Aromatic Zucchini Bread 131
443. Italian Pork with Dill-Mushroom Sauce 132
444. Cheese, Zucchini and Bacon Quiche 132
445. Holiday Pork Butt with Leeks 132
446. Deviled Eggs with Avocado and Tomatoes 132
447. Dijon Mustard-Herb Chicken 133
448. Loaded Barbecue Meatloaf Cups 133
449. Rustic Chicken Fingers 133
450. Easy Mini Pizzas 133
451. Pork Loin with Milk and Herbs 134
452. Swiss Chard and Cheese Bake 134
453. Spicy Ground Pork Omelet 134
454. Easy Keto Granola 134
455. Cholula Chicken Wings 135
456. The Best Shirred Eggs Ever 135
457. Mediterranean-Style Chicken Fillets 135
458. Keto Cucumber Canapés 135
459. French-Style Dijon Chicken 136
460. Mini Lasagna Cups 136
461. Festive Herb Chicken 136
462. Savory Cauliflower Crepes 136
463. Thanksgiving Roast Turkey 137
464. Traditional Hungarian Sausage Stew 137
465. Easy Homemade Cheeseburger 137

466. Cheese, Kale and Egg Quiche 137
467. Cod Fish, Herb and Tomato Chowder 138
468. Sloppy Joe Zucchini Boats 138
469. Basic Hamburger Soup 138
470. Cheese Mushroom Pâté 138
471. French-Style Beef Bourguignon 139
472. Keto Cereals with Berries 139
473. Traditional Beef Ragù with Italian Wine 139
474. Summer Berry Cupcakes 139
475. Classic Chicken Veggie Stock 140
476. Italian Keto Balls with Marinara Sauce 140
477. Meat Sauce with Malvasia and Herbs 140
478. Two-Cheese Cauliflower Muffins 140
479. Basic Marinara Sauce 141
480. Ricotta and Chorizo Dipping Sauce 141
481. Classic Bolognese Sauce 141
482. Old Bay Dipping Sauce 141
483. Two-Cheese and Bacon Dip 142
484. Ground Meat and Cheese-Stuffed Peppers 142
485. Hot Pepper Sauce 142
486. Mashed Cauliflower with French Gravy 142
487. Dip de Queso Crema 143
488. Cheese, Zucchini and Herb Quiche 143
489. Greek-Style Deviled Eggs 143
490. Beef Keto Tacos 143
491. Dilled Swiss Cheese Sauce 144
492. Pepper and Cheese Cups 144
493. Hard-Boiled Eggs with Chives 144
494. Cheesy Salmon Keto Fat Bombs 144
495. Ham and Swiss Cheese Muffins 145

SNACKS & APPETIZERS 146
496. BBQ Appetizer Meatballs 147
497. Hot Pizza Dip 147
498. Aromatic Fingerling Potatoes with Herbs 147
499. Polenta with Cream Cheese and Herbs 147
500. Pork Taco Meat with Coleslaw 148
501. Nacho Cheese Sauce 148
502. Basic Hummus Dip 148
503. Two-Cheese Artichoke Dip 148
504. Buttery Button Mushrooms with Herbs 149
505. Corn on the Cob with Chips 149
506. Buffalo Cheese and Chicken Dip 149
507. 4-Ingredient Little Smokies 149
508. Steamed Artichokes with Greek Dip 150
509. Herb Ricotta Hummus 150
510. Mini Stuffed Peppers 150
511. Harvest Vegetable and Tahini Dip 150
512. Garlicky Buttery Shrimp 151
513. Turnip Greens with Sesame Seeds 151
514. Sicilian-Style Chicken Wings 151
515. Spicy BBQ Cocktail Wieners 151
516. Mexican-Style Boozy Ribs 152
517. Aromatic Baby Potato Bites 152
518. Glazed Little Smokies 152
519. Mexican Queso Dip 152
520. Tangy Chicken Wings 153
521. Swiss Cheese and Cauliflower Bites 153
522. Jelly Glazed Meatballs 153
523. Bean, Tomato and Sour Cream Dip 153

524. Chicken Lettuce Wraps 154
525. Shrimp and Salad Skewers 154
526. Maple Glazed Nuts 154
527. Glazed and Dilled Baby Carrots 154
528. Short Ribs with Herbs and Molasses 155
529. Popcorn with A Twist 155
530. BBQ Glazed Ribs 155
531. Minty Fava Bean Dip 155
532. Paprika Mushroom Bites 156
533. Baby Carrots with Sesame Seeds and Raisins 156
534. Dijon-Glazed Sausages 156
535. Butter Mushrooms with Herbs 156
536. Calamari Bites with Herbs and Wine 157
537. Easy Asparagus Bites 157
538. Sweet Potato Bites 157
539. Italian-Style Broccoli with Mayonnaise 157
540. Borani or Kashkeh Bademjoon 158
541. German-Style Krautsalat 158
542. Chicken Nacho Sauce 158
543. Ranch Potato Bites 158
544. Ricotta and Chicken Dipping Sauce 159
545. Zingy Cauliflower Bites with Tahini Sauce 159
546. Broccoli Tots with Colby Cheese 159
547. Sausage and Cheese-Stuffed Mushrooms 159
548. Turkey Cocktail Meatballs 160
549. Easy Buttery Sweet Potatoes 160
550. Creole Boiled Peanuts 160
551. Winter Vegetable Puree 160
552. Dad's Barbecued Wings 161
553. Mixed Vegetable Appetizer 161
554. Buttery Brussels Sprout Bites 161
555. Italian-Style Cauliflower Salad 161
556. Gourmet Spicy Deviled Eggs 162
557. Artichokes with Garlic-Mayo Dip 162
558. Party Chicken Bites 162
559. Decadent Broccoli Salad 162
560. Cajun Meat Dipping Sauce 163
561. Traditional Sofrito Sauce 163
562. Habanero BBQ Almond Popcorn 163
563. Yellow Bean and Tofu Bowl 163
564. Spicy Party Mix 164
565. Candied Baby Carrots 164
566. Perfect Cheeseburger Dip 164
567. Traditional Dijon and Carrot Salad 164
568. Pizza-Style Dipping Sauce 165
569. Apple and Rutabaga Salad 165
570. Smoked Sausage Cheese Dip 165

FISH & SEAFOOD 166
571. Fish en Papillote 167
572. Portuguese Seafood Stew 167
573. Wine-Braised Blue Crab 167
574. Thai-Style Mussels with Beer 167
575. Seafood and Rice Hotpot 168
576. Spanish-Style Spicy Calamari 168
577. Traditional Spicy Gumbo 168
578. Rich Tuna and Green Pea Soup 168
579. Mussels with Wine-Scallion Sauce 169
580. Seafood with Halloumi Cheese and Olives 169
581. Tarragon Tuna Fillets 169

582. Spicy and Saucy Halibut 169
583. Cheesy Cod Fish 170
584. Tilapia with Herb-Mushroom Sauce 170
585. Italian-Style Sole with Vegetables 170
586. Lemony Grouper Filets 170
587. Japanese-Style Pollock Curry 171
588. Tuna with Tangy Butter Sauce 171
589. Saucy Tilapia with Spinach 171
590. Red Snapper in Tomatillo Sauce 171
591. Japanese Teriyaki Salmon 172
592. Hungarian Parikash (Harcsapaprikás) 172
593. Peppery Tilapia Filets 172
594. Creole Fish Stew 172
595. Mix-and-Match Fish Packets 173
596. Sole with Tartar Sauce 173
597. Honey-Orange Sea Bass 173
598. Louisiana-Style Jambalaya 173
599. Old Bay Crab 174
600. Herbed Carp Risotto 174
601. Creamed Crab Salad 174
602. Tuna with Lemon and Eschalot 174
603. Croissants with Salmon Salad 175
604. Ocean Trout with Spring Onions 175
605. Classic Dijon Shrimp Salad 175
606. Haddock with Tomato and Beans 175
607. Authentic Paella Valenciana 176
608. Creamed Codfish with Basmati Rice 176
609. Old Bay Sausage, Prawn and Potato Boil 176
610. Easy Sea Bass Pilau 176
611. Classic Fish Tacos 177
612. Buttery Mackerel with Peppers 177
613. Greek-Style Seafood Bake 177
614. Tandoori Fish Tikka 177
615. Tunisian-Style Couscous 178
616. Sea Scallops in Champagne Sauce 178
617. Spicy Red Snapper Boil 178
618. Vegetable Salmon Skewers 178
619. Codfish and Tomato Casserole 179
620. Halibut Steaks in Chardonnay Sauce 179
621. Spicy Haddock Curry 179
622. Creamy Ham Hock and Seafood Soup 179
623. Buttery Lobster Tails 180
624. Clams with Bacon and Wine 180
625. Parmesan Prawn Dip 180
626. Herb Tomato Shrimp 180
627. Cá Kho Tộ (Caramelized & Braised Fish) 181
628. Festive Salmon with Pesto Sauce 181
629. Codfish with Butter and Scallions 181
630. Prawn, Tomato, and Herb Risotto 181
631. Halibut with Cheese-Mayo Sauce 182
632. Ocean Trout and Noodle Salad 182
633. Italian-Style Stuffed Salmon 182
634. Vermouth Tilapia Medley 182
635. Shrimp with Carrots and Wine 183
636. Classic Parmesan Fish 183
637. Tuna, Asparagus and Tomato Quiche 183
638. Mahi-Mahi Fish with a Twist 183
639. Classic Haddock and Green Beans 184
640. Halibut with Tomatoes and Wine 184

VEGAN **185**
641. Traditional Kongunad Kurma 186
642. Basic Vegan Rice 186
643. Classic Garlicky Kale 186
644. Pepper and Green Pea Stew 186
645. Brussels Sprouts with a Twist 187
646. Mom's Festive Green Beans 187
647. Traditional Milagu Rasam Soup 187
648. Exotic Curried Cabbage 187
649. Punjabi Bhindi Masala 188
650. Nana's Chili with Tortilla Chips 188
651. Chinese-Style Bok Choy 188
652. Spanish Salmorejo with Pepitas 188
653. Colorful Indian Curry 189
654. Classic Homemade Hummus 189
655. Authentic Spanish Pisto 189
656. Italian Tomato Risotto 189
657. Mexican Posole Rojo 190
658. Classic Vegetable, Noodle and Corn Soup 190
659. Kerala-Style Beets 190
660. Spaghetti Squash with Basil-Walnut Pesto 190
661. Farmhouse Vegetable Soup 191
662. Potato and Chanterelle Mushroom Mélange 191
663. Steamed Winter Vegetables 191
664. Cabbage with Tomato and Rice 191
665. Authentic Minestrone Soup 192
666. Thai-Style Rice 192
667. Creole Boiled Peanuts 192
668. Red Kidney Beans with Roasted Peppers 192
669. Lentil Stew with Green Beans 193
670. Mediterranean-Style Zucchini 193

SOUPS, STOCKS & STEWS **194**
671. Provençal Chicken and Kamut Soup 195
672. Classic Russian Borscht (Beet Soup) 195
673. Aromatic Fisherman's Stock 195
674. Thai-Style Vegetable Soup 195
675. Roasted Vegetable and Wine Broth 196
676. Vegetable and Rice Noodle Soup 196
677. Italian Wedding Soup 196
678. Sichuan Pickle and Corn Soup 196
679. Vegetarian Autumn Soup 197
680. Wild Rice Vegetable Soup 197
681. Classic Stroganoff Soup 197
682. Creamy Vegan Soup 197
683. Lentil, Spinach and Carrot Soup 198
684. Codfish Soup in a Bread Bowl 198
685. Easy Polish Bigos 198
686. Vegan Beluga Lentil Stew 198
687. Hearty Beef Potato Stew 199
688. Pork and Sour Cream Stew 199
689. Traditional French Beef Stew (Pot-Au-Feu) 199
690. Japanese Hayashi Raisu 199
691. Basic Brown Stock 200
692. Old-Fashioned Beef Stew 200
693. Paprika Root Vegetable Soup 200
694. Country-Style Pork Broth 200
695. Potato, Cauliflower and Cheese Soup 201
696. Sicilian-Style Fish and Potato Stew 201

697. Mom's Pork Vegetable Soup 201
698. Hearty Irish Burgoo 201
699. Tex-Mex Taco Stew 202
700. Chicken Stew with Olives and Wine 202

DESSERTS **203**
701. Autumn Pumpkin Cake 204
702. Mom's Lemon Cake 204
703. Blood Orange Butter Cake 204
704. Rum Croissant Pudding 204
705. Red Wine Berry Compote 205
706. Mini Lava Molten Cakes 205
707. Vanilla Orange Flan 205
708. Hungarian Golden Pull-Apart Cake 205
709. Traditional Crème Brûlée 206
710. Traditional Budin de Pan 206
711. Pineapple Almond Cake 206
712. Classic Chocolate Brownie 206
713. Banana and Peach Tapioca Pudding 207
714. Chocolate Mini Muffins 207
715. Key Lime Butter Cakes 207
716. American-Style Cheesecake 207
717. Lemon and Blueberry Mousse 208
718. Grandma's Stuffed Apples 208
719. Cinnamon Cherry Crumble 208
720. Cranberry Sweet Risotto 208
721. Indian Kheer with Pistachios 209
722. French Chocolate Chip Custard 209
723. Coconut and Date Pudding 209
724. Farmhouse Apple Cake 209
725. Rich Pudding Cake with Blackberries 210
726. Double Chocolate Fudge 210
727. Vanilla Stewed Fruit 210
728. Cinnamon Roll Pear Pie 210
729. Stewed Bramley Apples with Cranberries 211
730. Vanilla Cupcakes with Cream Cheese Frosting 211
731. Mason Jar Cake 211
732. Chocolate Apricot Cake 211
733. Peanut Butter Penuche 212
734. Autumn Squash and Coconut Mousse 212
735. Golden Key Cake 212
736. Granny's Monkey Bread with Hazelnuts 212
737. Rustic Chocolate and Raisin Cake 213
738. Traditional Bismarck Pancake 213
739. Stuffed Nectarines with Vanilla Yogurt 213
740. Authentic Greek Hosafi 213
741. Vanilla Rice Pudding Dates 214
742. Coconut and Almond Mini Cheesecakes 214
743. Rustic Sponge Cake 214
744. French Soufflé with a Twist 214
745. Orange Butterscotch Pudding 215
746. Mixed Berry and Orange Compote 215
747. Old-Fashioned Pastry Cream 215
748. Streuselkuchen with Peaches 215

749. Fig and Homey Buckwheat Pudding 216
750. Zingy Blueberry Sauce 216
751. Chocolate Almond Custard 216
752. Classic Berry Jam 216
753. Walnut and Cinnamon Butter Cake 217
754. Honey Stewed Apples 217
755. Vanilla Almond Cheesecake 217
756. Greek-Style Compote with Yogurt 217
757. Butterscotch Lava Cakes 218
758. Cinnamon Coffee Cake 218
759. Bourbon Brioche Bread Pudding 218
760. Mexican Pudding (Arroz Con Leche) 218
761. Pumpkin Pudding Chocolate Ganache 219
762. Rich Almond Cheesecake 219
763. Vanilla Bread Pudding with Apricots 219
764. Banana Bread with Coconut 219
765. Mediterranean-Style Carrot Pudding 220
766. Easy Dulce de Leche 220
767. Mango Mug Cake 220
768. Chocolate Coffee Pots de Crème 220
769. Almond Cherry Crumble Cake 221
770. Pull-Apart Dessert with Walnuts 221

MORE INSTANT POT RECIPES **222**
771. Swiss Cheese and Cauliflower Frittata 223
772. Blueberry Butter Sauce 223
773. Breakfast Chocolate Chip Oatmeal 223
774. Spiced Rum Apple Cider 223
775. Fancy Creamed Fruit Salad 224
776. Hibiscus Iced Tea 224
777. Eggs, Cheese and Toast 224
778. Authentic Mexican Horchata 224
779. Rum Banana Bread with Pecans 225
780. Tomato Sauce with Mediterranean Herb 225
781. Blackberry French Toast 225
782. Skinny Homemade Applesauce 225
783. Breakfast Hash Browns 226
784. Red Wine Chicken Ragù 226
785. Jammy Rice Pudding 226
786. Spicy Chorizo Sauce 226
787. Balkan-Style Sponge Cake (Patispanj) 227
788. Kid-Friendly Pear Butter 227
789. Oatmeal with Coconut Milk and Seeds 227
790. Beef Bone and Vegetable Broth 227
791. Double Chocolate Oatmeal 228
792. Chili Bean Sauce 228
793. Sparkling Cranberry Quencher 228
794. Mom's Festive Coulis 228
795. Cinnamon Roll Pear and Pecan Pie 229
796. Dad's Homemade Salsa 229
797. Perfect Mini Cheesecakes 229
798. Indian Masala Sauce 229
799. Giant No-Flip Pancake 230
800. Perfect Homemade Bouillon 230

INTRODUCTION

What is so Fascinating about an Instant Pot?

Wouldn't it be great if you could find a quick and easy way to cook sumptuous dinner every night? Wouldn't it be great if you could make an entire family meal in a single pot? It is perfectly possible when you have a good multi-cooker and an enviable collection of reliable recipes. The Instant Pot is an electric fully-programmable cooker that combines multiple kitchen appliances in one machine; it can improve your cooking and make it much more convenient and healthier. On the other hand, this recipe collection is a good place to start your Instant Pot adventure since we got you covered with the top 800 Instant Pot recipes that are designed to make cooking a more enjoyable experience for everyone! The Instant Pot allows you to cook a wide range of spectacular meals, from appetizers and stews to desserts and casseroles. Whether you tend to bake a festive cake or cook a hearty family soup, this cookbook offers proven strategies on how to maximize the use of your Instant Pot. Home-cooked meals are linked to improved mental and physical health, making the Instant Pot is a must-have in every kitchen. How the Instant Pot does work? Why you might want to begin using the Instant Pot right now?

The Instant Pot is an intelligent, programmable multi-cooker that can cook your food under pressure at high temperature, speeding up the process and producing healthy and delicious meals. Basically, the Instant Pot requires liquid such as water or stock to produce steam inside an inner pot. Then, you should seal the lid and press the right button. That's all folks!

While your Instant Pot has a basic pressure cooker functionality, it can also bake, steam, sauté and make yogurt, using revolutionary heating and cooking system. At first glance it might look complicated. However, once you get familiar with how your Instant Pot works, you will be fascinated by its versatility and convenience. In general terms, the Instant Pot consists of a base unit, removable cooking pot, LCD panel, trivet, condensation collector (a small plastic cup) and an air-tight lid (with the steam vent on the top). The Instant Pot accessories that are sold separately include silicone cupcake liners, egg steamer rack, multi-purpose pan, steamer rack, silicone mini mitts, and so forth. Doubtlessly, the more you use this amazing multi-cooker, the more you will be aware how versatile it is!

The best way to improve your health, lose weight, and feel better is to eat homemade meals. If you think you do not have time to cook, please think twice. The Instant Pot actually promotes inspirational but simple approach to the cooking, producing appealing food combinations, instead of dumping dull ingredients into your stock pot. You can cook almost everything in your Instant Pot; it can fulfill all of your nutritional needs throughout the day. As you probably already know, healthy eating is about consuming well-balanced meals, including five major food groups – vegetables, fruits, grains, dairy, and protein. As a result of technology, with its innovative formula, the Instant Pot forever changed the way we cook and eat. This cookbook will guide you through the process of making delicious meals every day! Remember, no one is born a great cook, we learn by doing!

10 Must Know Instant Pot Tips

- First things first, you should read the user's manual thoroughly to make the most of your Instant Pot. Consult your manual every now and then, even if you are a top-tier chef.

- It may look robust and terrifying, but the Instant Pot has a few safety features so there is no need to worry. They include an anti-block shield, safety lid lock, steam release valve, and overheat protection. New versions have a unique ability to automatically seal the steam release. However, you should stay away from the steam and do not open your Instant Pot near your face. Needless to say, keep the lid sealed until your cooker is completely depressurized; you cannot take a peek. Period. Keep in mind that the sealing ring should be replaced occasionally (every 12-18 months).

- Stick to the rule – add one cup of liquid to the inner pot. Your Instant Pot cannot create the steam without liquid. If you think your meal is too watery in the end, simply add cornstarch slurry or your favorite cream, press the "Sauté" button and wait until your desired consistency is achieved. On the other hand, using too much liquid can leave you with a tasteless mash.

- Although, your Instant Pot cooks without monitoring and stirring, do not leave it unattended when pressure cooking your meal just to be safe.

- Never fill your Instant Pot more than 2/3 of the way, including liquids; when cooking foods that expand such as beans and grains, your Instant Pot shouldn't be more than 1/3 full.

- Just as with a regular cooking, pressure cooking in phases is the best option for many recipes. Cut larger pieces of food into uniform sizes to ensure even cooking. If you tend to pressure cook meat and vegetables at the same time, you can sauté your veggies first, set them aside, and then, pressure cook the meat. Another great possibility is to brown the meat and cook them quickly using the "Manual" setting. Then, you can perform quick pressure release and add the vegetables to the inner pot. You can pressure cook everything for a couple of minutes more for the final stage of cooking.

- Before beginning to cook in your Instant Pot, make sure to read and know the entire recipe. Reading instructions from a professional is always handy since you cannot add ingredients and check your meal later. Some important things to know include the number of servings, cook time, necessary items, food sense, and so forth. In this way, you will know when to add your ingredients, which pressure level to use (high or low), as well as the pressure release method (quick or natural). The wrong pressure release can ruin your meal, too.

  A pro tip: You can double a recipe and freeze the leftovers in single-serve portions. The Instant Pot is the perfect tool for meal prepping and batch cooking. In addition, you will be able to reheat your food in the Instant Pot.

- Undercook rather than overcook. If you are not sure how long to cook something, remember – less is more. You can always cook your food a few minutes longer, but you cannot fix mushy and overcooked meal.

- Pay attention to the cooking temperature; otherwise, your food will dry out or burn. This is the common mistake with the Instant Pot. You can use the "Manual" mode to choose the exact temperature.

- Make sure you buy the right sized Instant Pot, according to the number of people you usually cook for.

How to Use the Instant Pot Buttons

The Instant Pot is top-notch; you will be impressed with how well it can replace your slow cooker, sauté pan, steamer, stock pot, pressure cooker, rice cooker, yogurt maker, and food warmer. It has multiple programs that are controlled by a built-in microprocessor while a user-friendly interface allows you to easily select your desired cooking program and monitor the cooking process.

<u>Manual</u> – this feature allows you to adjust cook time and pressure. This makes it the most utilized function, since you can select parameters according to your recipe.

<u>Soup/Broth</u> – this is an ideal program for hearty soups, home-style broth and sauces. This feature allows your soup to simmer gently without boiling too heavily just like your grandma used to make; it will result in an amazing, soul warming soup.

<u>Meat/Stew</u> – this program cooks tender, juicy and flavorful meat to perfection. Since you can cook inexpensive and though cuts of meat, this genius feature will make your Instant Pot a real game changer!

<u>Bean/Chili</u> – although you do not have to soak your beans the night before, most foodies recommend pre-soaking for a creamier texture.

<u>Slow Cook</u> – you can use this button for slow cooking and gentle simmering. If you want your dinner ready for when you come back home, this is a must do! <u>Sauté</u> – you can sauté or brown items before pressure cooking or you can finish them (thicken the liquid or brown the meat) just as you would in a typical skillet or pot. With its possibilities for searing, sautéing, browning and simmering, this feature will make your Instant Pot even more indispensable in the kitchen!

<u>Rice</u> – with this setting, you'll need to adjust the cook time for white rice: 4-8 minutes, jasmine rice: 4-5 minutes, brown rice: 22-28 minutes, wild rice: 25-30 minutes.

<u>Multigrain</u> – use this program for cooking grains. You should follow a few easy steps: measure out dry ingredients; measure out the exact amount of water; rinse your grains; seal the lid and press the button.

<u>Porridge</u> – this program is best for oatmeal, porridge and congee. It is essential for a non-fuss family breakfast in busy mornings.

<u>Steam</u> – use this program to cook delicate items from vegetables and fruits to fish and seafood. You can use your Instant Pot as a traditional steamer since it has a trivet and steamer rack or basket for steaming.

<u>Yogurt</u> – this is two-step, fully automated program for making yogurt at home. For the best results, milk must reach a minimum of 161 degrees F for 15 seconds.

Cooking is a lifelong adventure. With your Instant Pot and this recipe collection successful pressure cooking is guaranteed. Before you know it, you will be cooking the best family meals and party dinners, making the best memories ever!

VEGETABLES & SIDE DISHES

1. Indian Urad Dal

(Ready in about 45 minutes | Servings 6)

Ingredients

1 ½ cups moong dal
2 cups green beans, fresh
2 garlic cloves, minced
1 teaspoon cilantro, ground
1 teaspoon celery seeds
1 ½ tablespoons olive oil
2 shallots, chopped
1/2 teaspoon ground allspice
1/2 teaspoon smoked paprika
Sea salt and ground black pepper, to your liking
1/2 teaspoon fennel seeds
1/2 teaspoon ground cumin
7 cups water

Directions

Press the "Sauté" button to heat up your Instant Pot. Then, heat olive oil and cook the shallots until just tender.

Now, add the garlic and cook 30 to 40 seconds more or until it is aromatic and slightly browned. Stir in all seasonings; cook until aromatic or 2 minutes more, stirring continuously.

Add the moong dal and water. Secure the lid. Select the "Manual" mode and cook for 17 minutes under High pressure.

Once cooking is complete, use a natural pressure release for 20 minutes; carefully remove the lid.

Season with sea salt and black pepper; add the green beans and secure the lid again. Select the "Manual" mode one more time and cook for 2 minutes under High pressure.

Once cooking is complete, use a quick pressure release; carefully remove the lid. Serve immediately with garlic croutons. Bon appétit!

Per serving: 221 Calories; 4.3g Fat; 34.7g Carbs; 12.8g Protein; 2.1g Sugars

2. Aromatic Cabbage with Vegetables and Herbs

(Ready in about 15 minutes | Servings 4)

Ingredients

1 (1 ½-pound) head of cabbage, cut into wedges
2 carrots, chopped
1 bell pepper, chopped
4 tablespoons olive oil
2 sprigs thyme
2 sprigs rosemary
1 bay leaf
1 ½ cups roasted vegetable broth
1 teaspoon cayenne pepper
Sea salt and ground black pepper, to taste

Directions

Add all ingredients to the inner pot of your Instant Pot. Stir to combine.

Secure the lid. Choose the "Manual" mode and cook for 6 minutes at High pressure. Once cooking is complete, use a quick pressure release; carefully remove the lid.

Ladle into individual bowls and serve warm. Bon appétit!

Per serving: 185 Calories; 13.8g Fat; 15.5g Carbs; 2.5g Protein; 8.2g Sugars

3. Classic Italian Tomato Soup

(Ready in about 30 minutes | Servings 4)

Ingredients

1 pound tomatoes, seeded and chopped
1 tablespoon olive oil
1/2 cup double cream
1/2 teaspoon dried basil
1/2 teaspoon dried oregano
1 tablespoon fresh Italian parsley, roughly chopped
A bunch of scallions, chopped
Sea salt, to taste
1/4 teaspoon freshly ground black pepper
2 carrots, grated
1/2 teaspoon cayenne pepper
1 garlic clove, minced
1 celery, chopped
4 cups roasted-vegetable broth

Directions

Press the "Sauté" button to heat up the Instant Pot. Now, heat the oil; sauté the scallions, garlic, carrot, and celery approximately 5 minutes.

Stir in the tomatoes, broth, salt, black pepper, cayenne pepper, basil, and oregano.

Secure the lid. Select the "Soup" setting; cook for 20 minutes at High pressure. Once cooking is complete, use a natural pressure release; carefully remove the lid.

Fold in the cream and purée the soup with an immersion blender. Serve topped with fresh parsley. Bon appétit!

Per serving: 175 Calories; 11.1g Fat; 12.5g Carbs; 7.7g Protein; 6.7g Sugars

4. Rich Vegan Bowl with Tahini

(Ready in about 10 minutes | Servings 4)

Ingredients

1 pound cauliflower florets
1/3 cup water
2 tablespoons olive oil
1/2 teaspoon sea salt
1 cup vegetable broth
1 clove garlic, pressed
1 tablespoon fresh parsley, finely chopped
4 carrots, sliced
4 medium potatoes, diced
2 tablespoons fresh lime juice
1/4 cup olive oil
1/3 cup tahini

Directions

Place the vegetables, olive oil, salt, and vegetable broth in the inner pot of your Instant Pot.

Secure the lid. Choose the "Manual" mode and cook for 4 minutes at High pressure. Once cooking is complete, use a quick pressure release; carefully remove the lid.

Meanwhile, make the tahini sauce by mixing the remaining ingredients. Serve the warm vegetables with the tahini sauce on the side. Bon appétit!

Per serving: 506 Calories; 32g Fat; 48.5g Carbs; 11.2g Protein; 4.3g Sugars

5. Buttery Sautéed Baby Potatoes with Rosemary

(Ready in about 30 minutes | Servings 4)

Ingredients

1 ½ pounds baby potatoes
3 tablespoons butter, melted
2 garlic cloves, minced
1/2 teaspoon turmeric powder
1/2 teaspoon lime zest, grated
1 cup chicken stock

2 sprigs rosemary, leaves only
2 tablespoons parsley, finely chopped
1/2 teaspoon ginger powder
Coarse sea salt and ground black pepper, to taste

Directions

Press the "Sauté" button to heat up the Instant Pot. Warm the butter and add the garlic, parsley, potatoes, rosemary, ginger, and lime zest.

Sauté the potatoes, turning them periodically, about 8 minutes. Add the stock, turmeric powder, salt, and black pepper.

Secure the lid. Select the "Manual" setting; cook for 12 minutes at High pressure. Once cooking is complete, use a quick pressure release; carefully remove the lid.

Serve warm and enjoy!

Per serving: 220 Calories; 9.2g Fat; 30.4g Carbs; 5g Protein; 1.3g Sugars

6. Greek Eggplant with Chickpeas

(Ready in about 15 minutes | Servings 4)

Ingredients

2 tablespoons olive oil
2 bell peppers, deseeded and diced
2 vine-ripened tomatoes, pureed
16 ounces chickpeas, boiled and rinsed
1 red onion, chopped
1/2 teaspoon ground turmeric
1/2 teaspoon sea salt

2 pounds eggplant, cut into cubes
4 garlic cloves, sliced
1 teaspoon oregano
1 teaspoon basil
1 teaspoon paprika
2 tablespoons sea salt
1/2 teaspoon ground black pepper

Directions

Toss the eggplant with 2 tablespoons of sea salt in a colander. Let it sit for 30 minutes; then squeeze out the excess liquid.

Press the "Sauté" button and heat the olive oil. Now, cook the onion until tender and translucent; add the reserved eggplant, peppers and garlic and continue to cook an additional 2 minutes or until they are fragrant.

Add the remaining ingredients to the inner pot. Stir to combine well.

Secure the lid. Choose the "Manual" mode and cook for 3 minutes at High pressure. Once cooking is complete, use a quick pressure release; carefully remove the lid. Ladle into individual bowls and serve immediately.

Per serving: 342 Calories; 10.4g Fat; 53.4g Carbs; 13.8g Protein; 17.4g Sugars

7. Ranch Cauliflower and Ricotta Dip

(Ready in about 10 minutes | Servings 8)

Ingredients

1 head cauliflower, cut into florets
1 teaspoon Ranch seasoning mix
1 cup Ricotta cheese, at room temperature
1 teaspoon fresh garlic, pressed
1/2 tablespoon fresh rosemary, chopped

1/4 teaspoon ground black pepper, or more to taste
1 cup tomato puree
1/2 cup red onion, chopped
1 teaspoon crushed red pepper
1 tablespoon fresh cilantro, chopped
1 cup mayonnaise
Sea salt, to taste

Directions

Prepare your Instant Pot by adding 1 cup of water and a steamer basket to its bottom.

Arrange the cauliflower florets in the steamer basket.

Secure the lid. Choose the "Manual" mode and Low pressure; cook for 5 minutes. Once cooking is complete, use a quick pressure release; carefully remove the lid.

Add the cauliflower to your food processor; add the remaining ingredients. Process until everything is well incorporated.

Place in your refrigerator until ready to use. Bon appétit!

Per serving: 176 Calories; 13.7g Fat; 7.4g Carbs; 6.5g Protein; 2.8g Sugars

8. Spicy Cream of Broccoli Soup

(Ready in about 15 minutes | Servings 4)

Ingredients

1 pound broccoli florets
12 ounces spinach
1 shallot, finely chopped
2 cloves garlic, minced
1 cup coconut milk
1/2 cup coconut cream
1 teaspoon cayenne pepper

1 piri piri pepper, minced
1/2 teaspoon ground cumin
2 teaspoons sesame oil
Sea salt and ground black pepper, to taste
5 cups vegetable broth, preferably homemade

Directions

Press the "Sauté" button and heat the oil until sizzling. Now, cook the garlic, shallot, pepper, and cumin until they are just softened and aromatic.

Then, stir in the broccoli, broth, salt, black pepper, and cayenne pepper.

Secure the lid. Choose the "Manual" mode and cook for 5 minutes at High pressure. Once cooking is complete, use a quick pressure release; carefully remove the lid.

Afterwards, stir in the spinach, coconut milk, and cream. Seal the lid again and let it sit in the residual heat until the spinach wilts.

Now, puree the soup with an immersion blender and serve warm. Bon appétit!

Per serving: 218 Calories; 10.4g Fat; 19.3g Carbs; 15.4g Protein; 8g Sugars

9. Classic Beet Salad with Cheese

(Ready in about 30 minutes | Servings 6)

Ingredients

1/4 cup extra-virgin olive oil
1/4 cup apple cider vinegar
1 cup goat cheese, crumbled
1 teaspoon yellow mustard
1 ½ pounds red beets
1 teaspoon honey
1 teaspoon cumin seeds
Kosher salt and ground black pepper, to taste

Directions

Add 1 ½ cups of water and beets to your Instant Pot.

Secure the lid. Choose "Manual" mode and High pressure; cook for 25 minutes. Once cooking is complete, use a quick pressure release; carefully remove the lid.

After that, rub off skins; cut the beets into wedges. Transfer them to a serving bowl.

Thoroughly combine the vinegar, mustard, honey, salt, black pepper, cumin seeds, and olive oil. Dress the salad, top with goat cheese and serve well chilled.

Per serving: 222 Calories; 16.1g Fat; 12.9g Carbs; 7.5g Protein; 9.1g Sugars

10. Moroccan-Style Couscous Salad

(Ready in about 10 minutes | Servings 4)

Ingredients

1 pound couscous
1 tablespoon olive oil
2 tablespoons sesame butter (tahini)
2 tablespoons fresh mint, roughly chopped
2 bell peppers, diced
1 cucumber, diced
2 cups vegetable broth
1/4 cup yogurt
1 tablespoon honey
2 tomatoes, sliced
A bunch of scallions, sliced

Directions

Press the "Sauté" button and heat the oil; then, sauté the peppers until tender and aromatic. Stir in the couscous and vegetable broth.

Secure the lid. Choose the "Manual" mode and cook for 2 minutes at High pressure. Once cooking is complete, use a quick pressure release; carefully remove the lid.

Then, stir in the remaining ingredients; stir to combine well and enjoy!

Per serving: 563 Calories; 9.2g Fat; 98g Carbs; 19.6g Protein; 7.3g Sugars

11. Garam Masala Vegetable Sauté

(Ready in about 20 minutes | Servings 6)

Ingredients

1 tablespoon sesame oil
1 tablespoon garam masala
1/2 teaspoon dhania
1/2 teaspoon haldi
1/2 teaspoon ground black pepper
Sea salt, to taste
1/2 teaspoon fresh ginger, grated
2 bell pepper, seeded and sliced
1 red chili pepper, seeded and sliced
1 teaspoon garlic paste
Naan:
2 ½ cups all-purpose flour
1/4 cup vegetable oil
1 egg
1/2 teaspoon salt
2/3 cup warm water
1 tablespoon dry active yeast
1 teaspoon sugar

Directions

Press the "Sauté" button to heat up your Instant Pot. Heat the oil until sizzling. Once hot, sauté the peppers, garlic, ginger, and spices.

Secure the lid. Choose the "Manual" mode and Low pressure; cook for 4 minutes. Once cooking is complete, use a quick pressure release; carefully remove the lid.

Meanwhile, make the naan by mixing the yeast, sugar and 2 tablespoons of warm water; allow it sit for 5 to 6 minutes.

Add the remaining ingredients for naans; let it rest for about 1 hour at room temperature.

Now, divide the dough into six balls; flatten the balls on a working surface.

Heat up a large-sized pan over moderate heat. Cook naans until they are golden on both sides. Serve these naans with the reserved vegetables and enjoy!

Per serving: 319 Calories; 12.7g Fat; 43.5g Carbs; 7.6g Protein; 1.7g Sugars

12. Spicy and Saucy Rice

(Ready in about 30 minutes | Servings 5)

Ingredients

1 medium-sized leek, chopped
1 bell pepper, seeded and finely chopped
2 fresh serrano peppers, seeded and finely chopped
1 teaspoon mustard seeds
1 teaspoon salt
1/2 teaspoon cayenne pepper
1/2 teaspoon freshly ground black pepper
4 cups vegetable stock
2 tablespoons canola oil
2 garlic cloves, minced
1 ½ cups white rice
2 tablespoons fresh parsley leaves, chopped
1/2 tablespoon cumin seeds

Directions

Press the "Sauté" button and heat the oil. Once hot, cook the garlic, leek, and peppers until tender and aromatic.

Add the remaining ingredients and stir to combine.

Secure the lid. Choose the "Rice" mode and cook for 10 minutes. Once cooking is complete, use a natural pressure release for 15 minutes; carefully remove the lid.

Serve in individual bowls and enjoy!

Per serving: 316 Calories; 7.7g Fat; 51g Carbs; 8.9g Protein; 1.3g Sugars

13. Cauliflower with Greek-Style Sauce

(Ready in about 10 minutes | Servings 4)

Ingredients

1 ½ pounds cauliflower, broken into florets
1/2 cup vegetable stock, preferably homemade
1 tablespoon peanut oil
1 tablespoon fresh parsley, chopped
1/2 cup Greek-style yogurt
1 teaspoon curry powder
1 habanero pepper, minced

1 yellow onion, chopped
1 clove garlic, pressed
1 tablespoon fresh cilantro, chopped
Sea salt, to taste
2 tomatoes, puréed
1/2 teaspoon ground black pepper
1/2 teaspoon red pepper flakes

Directions

Press the "Sauté" button to heat up your Instant Pot. Now, heat the oil and sauté the onion for 1 to 2 minutes.

Add the garlic and continue to cook until fragrant.

Stir in the remaining ingredients, except the yogurt; stir to combine well.

Secure the lid. Choose the "Manual" mode and High pressure; cook for 3 minutes. Once cooking is complete, use a quick pressure release; carefully remove the lid.

Pour in the yogurt, stir well, and serve immediately.

Per serving: 121 Calories; 6.6g Fat; 13.4g Carbs; 4.8g Protein; 5.8g Sugars

14. Green Beans with Garlic and Chives

(Ready in about 10 minutes | Servings 4)

Ingredients

1 ½ pounds green beans, trimmed
2 tablespoons olive oil
2 garlic cloves, minced
1 teaspoon cayenne pepper

2 tablespoons fresh chives, chopped
Salt and freshly ground black pepper, to taste

Directions

Press the "Sauté" button and heat the oil until sizzling. Now, sauté the garlic until tender but not browned.

Add the green beans, salt, black pepper, and cayenne pepper to the inner pot. Pour in 1 cup of water.

Secure the lid. Choose the "Manual" mode and cook for 3 minutes at High pressure. Once cooking is complete, use a quick pressure release; carefully remove the lid.

Garnish with fresh chives and serve warm.

Per serving: 117 Calories; 7.2g Fat; 12.6g Carbs; 3.3g Protein; 5.6g Sugars

15. Old-Fashioned Vegetable Stew

(Ready in about 35 minutes | Servings 4)

Ingredients

2 cups white mushrooms, thinly sliced
1 ½ tablespoons cornstarch
1 jalapeno pepper, deveined and chopped
1 leek, chopped
2 carrots, trimmed and chopped
2 tablespoons butter, at room temperature
1 teaspoon garlic, minced

2 sprigs rosemary, leaves picked
3 ripe tomatoes, pureed
1/2 teaspoon ground black pepper
1/2 pound white potatoes, peeled and diced
Sea salt, to taste
2 sprigs thyme, leaves picked
2 ½ cups stock, preferably homemade

Directions

Press the "Sauté" button and melt the butter. Now, sauté the leek and carrots until they are tender, about 3 minutes.

Add the mushrooms, garlic, rosemary, and thyme; cook an additional 3 minutes or until they are aromatic and tender.

Add a splash of homemade stock to deglaze the pan. Add the remaining stock, pureed tomatoes, jalapeno pepper, potatoes, salt, and black pepper.

Secure the lid and choose "Soup" mode. Cook for 20 minutes at High pressure. Once cooking is complete, use a quick release; carefully remove the lid.

Meanwhile, make the cornstarch slurry by whisking 1 ½ tablespoons of cornstarch with 2 tablespoons of water. Add the slurry to the Instant Pot.

Cook the cooking liquid in the residual heat for 5 minutes longer or until it has thickened. Ladle into individual bowls and serve warm. Enjoy!

Per serving: 181 Calories; 7.3g Fat; 24.1g Carbs; 6.1g Protein; 5.1g Sugars

16. Indian Sweet Corn

(Ready in about 10 minutes | Servings 4)

Ingredients

2 tablespoons ghee
1/2 teaspoon chaat masala powder
1/2 teaspoon turmeric powder

2 cups sweet corn kernels, frozen
1/2 teaspoon red chili powder
Himalayan salt and ground black pepper, to taste

Directions

Place all ingredients in the inner pot of your Instant Pot.

Secure the lid. Choose the "Manual" mode and cook for 4 minutes at High pressure. Once cooking is complete, use a quick pressure release; carefully remove the lid.

Serve immediately.

Per serving: 124 Calories; 6.7g Fat; 16.1g Carbs; 2.8g Protein; 3.1g Sugars

17. Zingy Vegetable Sticks

(Ready in about 10 minutes | Servings 6)

Ingredients

1 cup water
1 teaspoon grated orange peel
1 turnip, cut into sticks
1/2 teaspoon baking soda
1 tablespoon agave nectar
2 parsnips, peeled and halved lengthwise

2 carrots, cut into sticks
1/2 teaspoon kosher salt
1/2 teaspoon white pepper, ground
1/2 teaspoon fresh ginger, grated
2 tablespoons sesame oil

Directions

Press the "Sauté" button to heat up your Instant Pot; heat the oil.

Sauté the vegetables until aromatic and tender. Now, add the remaining ingredients and gently stir to combine.

Secure the lid. Choose the "Manual" mode and High pressure; cook for 4 minutes. Once cooking is complete, use a quick pressure release; carefully remove the lid.

Serve warm or at room temperature.

Per serving: 99 Calories; 4.7g Fat; 14.4g Carbs; 1g Protein; 6.7g Sugars

18. Brussels Sprouts with Parmigiano-Reggiano

(Ready in about 15 minutes | Servings 6)

Ingredients

1 ½ pounds Brussels sprouts, trimmed and halved
1/2 cup Parmigiano-Reggiano, grated
1 teaspoon shallot powder
1/2 teaspoon basil

1 teaspoon rosemary
1 teaspoon garlic, minced
1/2 stick butter
Sea salt and red pepper, to taste

Directions

Place 1 cup of water and a steamer basket in the inner pot of your Instant Pot. Place the Brussels sprouts in the steamer basket.

Secure the lid. Choose the "Steam" mode and cook for 3 minutes at High pressure. Once cooking is complete, use a quick pressure release; carefully remove the lid.

Press the "Sauté" button and melt the butter; once hot, cook the basil, rosemary, and garlic for 40 seconds or until aromatic.

Add in the Brussels sprouts, shallot powder, salt, and pepper. Press the "Cancel" button. Scatter the grated parmesan cheese over the Brussels sprouts and serve immediately. Bon appétit!

Per serving: 184 Calories; 15.8g Fat; 10.1g Carbs; 3.9g Protein; 2.5g Sugars

19. Traditional Sweet Onion and Cheese Soup

(Ready in about 35 minutes | Servings 6)

Ingredients

1 loaf French bread, cut into slices and toasted
1 ½ cups Munster cheese, shaved
6 sweet onions, sliced
2 garlic cloves
Kosher salt and ground black pepper, to taste

1 tablespoon granulated sugar
3 tablespoons ghee
5 cups chicken stock, preferably homemade
2 fresh rosemary sprigs
1/2 teaspoon cayenne pepper
1/3 cup sherry wine
1/2 cup water

Directions

Press the "Sauté" button to heat up the Instant Pot. Then, melt the ghee; sauté the onions until translucent, about 5 minutes.

Add the garlic and sauté it for 1 to 2 minutes more. Reduce the heat to low; add the salt, black pepper, cayenne pepper, and white sugar. Continue to cook, stirring frequently, until sweet onions are slightly browned.

Pour in the sherry wine, and scrape off any brown bits from the bottom of your Instant Pot. Now, pour in the water and chicken stock; add rosemary and stir to combine.

Secure the lid. Select the "Manual" setting; cook for 8 minutes under High pressure. Once cooking is complete, use a quick pressure release; carefully remove the lid.

Then, preheat your oven to broil.

Divide the soup among ovenproof bowls; top with toasted bread and shaved Munster cheese; place your soup under the broiler for 5 to 6 minutes, or until the cheese is bubbly. Serve warm and enjoy!

Per serving: 353 Calories; 15.4g Fat; 40.5g Carbs; 15.4g Protein; 20.2g Sugars

20. Kamut, Spinach and Celery Bowl

(Ready in about 20 minutes | Servings 5)

Ingredients

4 tablespoons olive oil
3 cups water
2 cups baby spinach
1 large carrot, cut into sticks
1 celery rib, sliced

1 shallot, finely chopped
1 ½ cups dried kamut
Salt and freshly ground black pepper, to taste
2 tablespoons fresh lime juice

Directions

Add the kamut and water to the inner pot.

Secure the lid. Choose the "Manual" mode and cook for 9 minutes at High pressure. Once cooking is complete, use a quick pressure release.

Add the vegetables, olive oil, salt, and black pepper.

Secure the lid. Choose the "Manual" mode and cook for 3 minutes at High pressure. Once cooking is complete, use a quick pressure release.

Drizzle fresh lime juice over each serving and enjoy!

Per serving: 295 Calories; 12g Fat; 42g Carbs; 8.6g Protein; 5.3g Sugars

21. Grandma's Snow Peas

(Ready in about 10 minutes | Servings 4)

Ingredients

1 pound snow peas, frozen
1/2 teaspoon ground black pepper
1 parsnip, sliced
1 ½ tablespoons coconut oil
1 cup water

1 tablespoon white sugar
Seasoned salt, to taste
2 carrots, sliced
1/2 teaspoon red pepper flakes, crushed

Directions

Add all of the above ingredients to your Instant Pot.

Secure the lid. Select the "Steam" setting; cook for 4 minutes at High pressure. Once cooking is complete, use a quick pressure release; carefully remove the lid.

Transfer everything to a serving dish. Enjoy!

Per serving: 126 Calories; 5.4g Fat; 16.9g Carbs; 3.6g Protein; 8.1g Sugars

22. Bell Peppers with Balsamic Vinegar

(Ready in about 10 minutes | Servings 2)

Ingredients

4 bell peppers, seeded and sliced
1/2 cup court bouillon
2 tablespoons olive oil

2 tablespoons balsamic vinegar
1/2 cup water
Sea salt and ground black pepper, to taste

Directions

Press the "Sauté" button and heat the oil. Once hot, cook the peppers until just tender and fragrant.

Add the salt and black pepper. Pour in the bouillon and water.

Secure the lid. Choose the "Manual" mode and cook for 3 minutes at High pressure. Once cooking is complete, use a quick pressure release.

Drizzle balsamic vinegar over your peppers and serve immediately.

Per serving: 178 Calories; 13.7g Fat; 13.7g Carbs; 2.3g Protein; 8.4g Sugars

23. Root Veggies with Horseradish Mayo

(Ready in about 10 minutes | Servings 4)

Ingredients

1 red onion, sliced
1/4 teaspoon dried dill weed
1/2 teaspoon ground pepper
2 tablespoons fresh parsley
1 celery with leaves, chopped
1 carrot, sliced
1 1/3 cups water
1 teaspoon garlic powder

1/2 teaspoon sea salt
1 turnip, sliced
For the Horseradish Mayo:
1/2 cup mayonnaise
2 teaspoons Dijon mustard
1 tablespoon horseradish, well drained

Directions

Add 1 1/3 cups of water and steamer basket to the Instant Pot.

Arrange the celery, turnip, carrot, and onion in the steamer basket. Season the vegetables with dried dill weed, garlic powder, sea salt, and ground pepper.

Secure the lid and choose the "Manual" mode, High pressure and 3 minutes. Once cooking is complete, use a quick release; remove the lid carefully.

In a mixing bowl, combine the horseradish, mayonnaise, and Dijon mustard. Garnish steamed vegetables with fresh parsley; serve with the horseradish mayo on the side. Bon appétit!

Per serving: 116 Calories; 9.7g Fat; 5.2g Carbs; 2.4g Protein; 2.6g Sugars

24. Winter Vegetables with Orange Butter

(Ready in about 20 minutes | Servings 5)

Ingredients

2 tablespoons orange juice
1 teaspoon orange peel, finely shredded
2 tablespoons cold butter
1 tablespoon maple syrup

1/2 pound yellow beets
1/2 pound red beets
1 pound carrots
Kosher salt and ground black pepper, to taste

Directions

Place 1 cup of water and a steamer basket in your Instant Pot. Place the carrots and beets in the steamer basket.

Secure the lid. Choose the "Steam" mode and cook for 10 minutes at High pressure. Once cooking is complete, use a quick pressure release; carefully remove the lid.

Peel the carrots and beets and reserve; slice them into bite-sized pieces.

Press the "Sauté" button and choose the lowest setting. Cut in butter and add the remaining ingredients.

Drain the carrots and beets and add them back to the inner pot; let them cook until your vegetables are nicely coated with the glaze or about 5 minutes. Bon appétit!

Per serving: 131 Calories; 4.9g Fat; 20.8g Carbs; 2.4g Protein; 13.4g Sugars

25. Eggplant with Steamed Eggs and Tomatoes

(Ready in about 50 minutes | Servings 4)

Ingredients

4 eggs
1 pound eggplant, peeled and cut pieces
1 jalapeño pepper, minced
2 tablespoons butter, at room temperature
1/2 cup scallions, chopped
2 teaspoons salt
1 red bell pepper, chopped
2 ripe tomatoes, chopped
Sea salt, to taste
2 garlic cloves, smashed
1/2 teaspoon freshly ground black pepper

Directions

Toss the eggplant with the salt and allow it to sit for 30 minutes; then, drain and rinse the eggplant.

Press the "Sauté" button to heat up the Instant Pot. Once hot, melt the butter. Stir in the eggplant and cook for 3 to 5 minutes, stirring periodically.

Add the garlic, scallions, peppers, and tomatoes; cook an additional 4 minutes. Season with salt and pepper.

Secure the lid. Select the "Manual" setting; cook for 8 minutes at HIGH pressure. Once cooking is complete, use a quick release; carefully remove the lid. Reserve.

Add 1 cup of water and metal rack to the Instant Pot. Crack the eggs into ramekins; lower the ramekins onto the rack.

Secure the lid. Select the "Steam" setting; cook for 5 minutes under High pressure. Serve with the eggplant mixture on the side. Bon appétit!

Per serving: 235 Calories; 15.8g Fat; 13.5g Carbs; 11.4g Protein; 7.7g Sugars

26. 4-Ingredient Saucy Millet

(Ready in about 45 minutes | Servings 6)

Ingredients

1 cup millet
1 tablespoon olive oil
Sea salt and ground black pepper, to taste
1 pound small-sized tomatoes, halved

Directions

Preheat your oven to 350 degrees F. Place your tomatoes in a roasting pan. Drizzle olive oil over them; season with salt and pepper. Roast for about 35 minutes or until the tomatoes are soft.

Meanwhile, combine the millet with 2 cups of water in the inner pot of your Instant Pot.

Secure the lid. Choose the "Manual" mode and cook for 9 minutes at High pressure. Once cooking is complete, use a natural pressure release for 10 minutes; carefully remove the lid.

Add the roasted tomatoes to the warm millet and serve immediately.

Per serving: 162 Calories; 3.8g Fat; 27.2g Carbs; 4.5g Protein; 2.7g Sugars

27. Swiss Chard with Bacon and Cheese

(Ready in about 15 minutes | Servings 4)

Ingredients

12 ounces Swiss chard, torn into pieces
1 cup Caciocavallo cheese, shredded
1/2 pound Canadian bacon, chopped
Sea salt and ground black pepper, to taste
1/4 cup rose wine
1 teaspoon paprika
1/2 cup vegetable broth
1/4 cup water
1/2 teaspoon dried basil
1/2 teaspoon dried marjoram

Directions

Press the "Sauté" button to heat up your Instant Pot. Once hot, cook the Canadian bacon until crisp; crumble with a fork and set it aside.

Stir in the remaining ingredients, except for Caciocavallo cheese.

Secure the lid. Choose the "Manual" mode and Low pressure; cook for 4 minutes. Once cooking is complete, use a quick pressure release; carefully remove the lid.

Add the Caciocavallo cheese, cover with the lid and allow it to sit for a further 4 minutes or until your cheese is melted. Top each serving with reserved bacon and serve warm.

Per serving: 214 Calories; 12.1g Fat; 5.8g Carbs; 22.1g Protein; 2.4g Sugars

28. Red Lentils with Peppers and Cilantro

(Ready in about 10 minutes | Servings 4)

Ingredients

1 sweet pepper, seeded and chopped
1 habanero pepper, seeded and chopped
1 cup red lentils
1/4 cup fresh cilantro, roughly chopped
1 medium-sized leek, sliced
1 teaspoon garlic, pressed
Kosher salt and ground black pepper, to taste
2 cups water

Directions

Add all ingredients, except for the fresh cilantro, to the inner pot of your Instant Pot.

Secure the lid. Choose the "Manual" mode and cook for 2 minutes at High pressure. Once cooking is complete, use a quick pressure release; carefully remove the lid.

Spoon the lentil mixture into a nice serving bowl. Serve garnished with fresh cilantro and enjoy!

Per serving: 242 Calories; 1g Fat; 47.5g Carbs; 15.1g Protein; 9.3g Sugars

29. Braised Cabbage with Chanterelle Mushrooms

(Ready in about 15 minutes | Servings 4)

Ingredients

1/2 pound Chanterelle mushrooms, thinly sliced
1 pound purple cabbage, cut into wedges
1/2 teaspoon adobo seasoning
3 teaspoons olive oil
1/3 cup Worcestershire sauce
1 teaspoon cayenne pepper

2 red onions, cut into wedges
2 garlic cloves, smashed
1/2 teaspoon ground bay leaf
1/3 teaspoon white pepper
2 tablespoons champagne vinegar
Salt, to taste

Directions

Press the "Sauté" button to heat up the Instant Pot; heat the oil. Once hot, add the mushrooms; cook until they are lightly browned, about 4 minutes.

Add the other ingredients in the order listed above. Gently stir to combine and secure the lid.

Now, choose the "Manual" setting, High pressure and 4 minutes.

Once cooking is complete, use a quick release; remove the lid carefully. Bon appétit!

Per serving: 121 Calories; 3.8g Fat; 20.3g Carbs; 4g Protein; 10.1g Sugars

30. Bucatini with Capers and Olives

(Ready in about 25 minutes | Servings 4)

Ingredients

3/4 pound bucatini pasta
1 tablespoon olive oil
1 tablespoon Italian seasoning blend
1/2 cup black olives, pitted, and thinly sliced
2 garlic cloves, pressed

Coarse salt, to taste
2 tablespoons capers, soaked and rinsed
2 vine-ripened tomatoes, pureed
1 cup water

Directions

Press the "Sauté" button and add the oil. Once hot, cook the garlic until aromatic. Add the black olives, capers, tomatoes, Italian seasoning blend, and salt.

Bring to a boil and turn the Instant Pot to the lowest setting; let the sauce simmer for 10 to 13 minutes. Stir in the bucatini pasta and water.

Secure the lid. Choose the "Manual" mode and cook for 8 minutes at High pressure. Once cooking is complete, use a quick pressure release.

Serve warm and enjoy!

Per serving: 374 Calories; 7.1g Fat; 72.7g Carbs; 7.3g Protein; 1.8g Sugars

31. Easy Vegetarian Skewers

(Ready in about 10 minutes | Servings 4)

Ingredients

8 ounces button mushrooms, whole
2 bell peppers, seeded and diced
2 medium zucchinis, cut into 1-inch slices
2 cups cherry tomatoes
1 head broccoli, broken into florets and blanched

1/2 teaspoon crushed red pepper
1 teaspoon dried oregano
1 teaspoon dried rosemary
1/4 teaspoon ground bay leaves
4 tablespoons olive oil
Fresh juice of 1/2 lemon
Sea salt and ground black pepper, to taste

Directions

Prepare your Instant Pot by adding 1 cup of water and a metal rack to its bottom.

Thread the vegetables onto bamboo or wooden skewers.

Drizzle them with olive oil and fresh lemon juice; add seasonings.

Secure the lid. Choose the "Manual" mode and High pressure; cook for 3 minutes. Once cooking is complete, use a quick pressure release; carefully remove the lid. Bon appétit!

Per serving: 224 Calories; 14.3g Fat; 22.5g Carbs; 6.4g Protein; 13.4g Sugars

32. Punjabi Rajma Masala

(Ready in about 35 minutes | Servings 5)

Ingredients

8 cups water
1/4 teaspoon red curry paste
1/2 teaspoon avocado powder
2 tablespoons canola oil
1 teaspoon ginger garlic paste
1 tablespoon fenugreek, chopped
1 pound red kidney beans
1/2 teaspoon turmeric powder

1 green chili pepper, finely chopped
Sea salt and freshly ground black pepper, to taste
2 small-sized potatoes, peeled and diced
2 tomatoes, pureed
1 onion, finely sliced

Directions

Add the red kidney beans and water to the inner pot of your Instant Pot.

Secure the lid. Choose the "Bean/Chili" mode and cook for 25 minutes at High pressure. Once cooking is complete, use a quick pressure release; carefully remove the lid. Drain and reserve.

Press the "Sauté" button and heat the oil until sizzling. Now, sauté the onion until tender and translucent.

Add the remaining ingredients. Gently stir to combine.

Secure the lid. Choose the "Manual" mode and cook for 4 minutes at High pressure. Once cooking is complete, use a quick pressure release; carefully remove the lid.

Stir the reserved beans into the potato mixture and serve warm. Bon appétit!

Per serving: 406 Calories; 6.2g Fat; 66g Carbs; 24.5g Protein; 1.1g Sugars

33. Fall Acorn Squash Chowder

(Ready in about 25 minutes | Servings 6)

Ingredients

1 ½ pounds acorn squash, shredded

6 ounces cream cheese

1 cup candy onions, chopped

2 bell peppers, deveined and chopped

2 tablespoons ghee, melted

1 carrot, chopped

1 bay leaf

2 cups water

1 garlic clove, minced

4 cups vegetable stock

1 celery, chopped

Directions

Press the "Sauté" button to heat up the Instant Pot; melt the ghee and sauté candy onions, garlic and peppers until they are softened.

Add the remaining ingredients.

Secure the lid. Select the "Soup" setting; cook for 20 minutes at High pressure. Once cooking is complete, use a quick pressure release; carefully remove the lid.

Afterwards, purée the soup with an immersion blender and serve hot. Enjoy!

Per serving: 365 Calories; 23.3g Fat; 32.1g Carbs; 8.8g Protein; 16.8g Sugars

34. Indian Tamatar Baingan

(Ready in about 40 minutes | Servings 4)

Ingredients

1 Kashmiri chili pepper, chopped

4 curry leaves

1 teaspoon cumin seeds

1 pound eggplant, sliced

1 cup water

2 tomatoes, pureed

2 shallots, chopped

1 tablespoon butter

1 tablespoon sea salt

1 tablespoon sesame oil

Directions

Toss the eggplant with sea salt in a colander. Let it sit for 30 minutes; then squeeze out the excess liquid.

Press the "Sauté" button and heat the sesame oil; now sauté the cumin seeds for 30 seconds or until aromatic. Then, cook the shallots for 2 to 3 minutes more or until they have softened.

Then, melt the butter. Now, cook the eggplant until lightly charred. Add the water, chili pepper, tomatoes, and curry leaves to the inner pot.

Secure the lid. Choose the "Manual" mode and cook for 2 minutes at High pressure. Once cooking is complete, use a quick pressure release; carefully remove the lid.

Serve in individual bowls and enjoy!

Per serving: 105 Calories; 6.7g Fat; 11.2g Carbs; 2.1g Protein; 6.6g Sugars

35. Artichoke, Kale and Cheese Dip

(Ready in about 20 minutes | Servings 10)

Ingredients

1 cup cream cheese

1 teaspoon shallot powder

1 teaspoon fennel seeds

1 can (14-ounce) artichoke hearts, drained and roughly chopped

1 cup Colby cheese, shredded

1 teaspoon yellow mustard

2 garlic cloves, minced

1/2 pound kale leaves, fresh or frozen torn into pieces

Sea salt and ground black pepper, to taste

1 cup mayonnaise

Directions

Place 1 cup of water and a metal rack in your Instant Pot.

Then, thoroughly combine all ingredients in a casserole dish that is previously greased with a nonstick cooking spray; cover the casserole dish with a piece of aluminum foil, making a foil sling if needed.

Lower the casserole dish onto the rack.

Secure the lid. Select the "Steam" setting; cook for 10 minutes at High pressure. Once cooking is complete, use a quick pressure release; carefully remove the lid.

Serve with chips or pita wedges. Enjoy!

Per serving: 219 Calories; 19g Fat; 5.5g Carbs; 7.6g Protein; 1.7g Sugars

36. Easy Frijoles Refritos

(Ready in about 1 hour 10 minutes | Servings 6)

Ingredients

8 cups water

1 cup molasses

1 tablespoon Cholula hot sauce

1 teaspoon salt

2 onions, chopped

5 cloves garlic, minced

1 cup ketchup

2 tablespoons olive oil

1 ½ pounds pinto beans, rinsed and drained

2 tablespoons soy sauce

Directions

Place the beans and water in your Instant Pot.

Secure the lid. Choose the "Bean/Chili" mode and cook for 40 minutes at High pressure. Once cooking is complete, use a natural pressure release for 10 minutes; carefully remove the lid. Set aside.

Press the "Sauté" button and heat the oil until sizzling. Now, cook the onion and garlic until tender and fragrant. Add the reserved beans back to the inner pot. Stir in the remaining ingredients.

Secure the lid. Choose the "Manual" mode and cook for 10 minutes at High pressure. Once cooking is complete, use a quick pressure release. Bon appétit!

Per serving: 594 Calories; 5.6g Fat; 114g Carbs; 26.2g Protein; 51.4g Sugars

37. Mashed Potatoes with Garlic and Herbs

(Ready in about 15 minutes | Servings 4)

Ingredients

1 pound Yukon Gold potatoes, peeled and cubed
1/2 teaspoon dried rosemary
Salt and ground black pepper, to taste
2 tablespoons spring garlic, minced
1/3 cup sour cream
1/2 teaspoon dried oregano
1/2 stick butter, softened
1/2 teaspoon paprika
1 cup water
1/4 cup milk

Directions

Add 1 cup of water and steamer basket to the base of your Instant Pot.

Place cubed potatoes in the steamer basket; transfer it to the Instant Pot. Secure the lid. Select the "Manual" mode; cook for 4 minutes under High pressure.

Once cooking is complete, use a quick release; carefully remove the lid.

Meanwhile, heat a pan over a moderate heat. Melt the butter and cook spring garlic until it is tender and aromatic.

Add the milk and scrape up any browned bits with a spatula. Allow it to cool slightly.

In a mixing bowl, mash the cooked potatoes. Add the butter/garlic mixture along with the other ingredients.

Taste, adjust the seasonings and serve warm. Bon appétit!

Per serving: 230 Calories; 14g Fat; 23.3g Carbs; 3.8g Protein; 1.7g Sugars

38. Marshmallow-Topped Sweet Potatoes

(Ready in about 30 minutes | Servings 6)

Ingredients

2/3 cup milk
1 egg, whisked
3/4 cup granulated sugar
7 tablespoons butter softened
1 cup water
6 medium-sized sweet potatoes, peeled and cut into 1-inch pieces
1 teaspoon vanilla paste

Topping:
1 cup mini marshmallows
1/2 cup chopped pecans
3/4 cup brown sugar
1/2 cup all-purpose flour
1/4 teaspoon cinnamon, or to taste
4 tablespoons butter, at room temperature
1/8 teaspoon salt

Directions

Add the sweet potatoes and water to the Instant Pot.

Secure the lid. Choose the "Manual" mode and cook for 8 minutes at High pressure. Once cooking is complete, use a quick pressure release; carefully remove the lid.

Drain the potatoes and transfer them to a mixing bowl. Now, add the granulated sugar, butter, vanilla, milk, and egg to the bowl.

Mash the potatoes using a potato masher or your food processor. Scrape the mashed potatoes into a lightly greased baking dish.

Mix all ingredients for the topping; top your casserole with the pecan/marshmallow mixture. Place a metal trivet and 1 cup of water in the inner pot. Lower the baking dish onto the trivet; make a foil sling if needed.

Secure the lid. Choose the "Manual" mode and cook for 15 minutes at High pressure. Once cooking is complete, use a quick pressure release; carefully remove the lid. Bon appétit!

Per serving: 580 Calories; 28.9g Fat; 77g Carbs; 6.4g Protein; 47.1g Sugars

39. Honey-Mustard Glazed Cipollini Onions

(Ready in about 15 minutes | Servings 4)

Ingredients

3/4 cup roasted vegetable stock
2 bay leaves
2 teaspoons honey
1 ½ pounds Cipollini onions, outer layer eliminated
1 ½ tablespoons corn starch
1 rosemary sprig
1 thyme sprig
Sea salt and ground black pepper, to taste
1 tablespoon mustard

Directions

Add all ingredients to your Instant Pot. Secure the lid and choose the "Steam" mode. Cook for 10 minutes at High pressure.

Once cooking is complete, use a quick release; carefully remove the lid.

Arrange the onions on a serving platter and serve warm. Enjoy!

Per serving: 96 Calories; 0.9g Fat; 19.9g Carbs; 3.4g Protein; 12.1g Sugars

40. Easy Italian Endive

(Ready in about 15 minutes | Servings 4)

Ingredients

1 shallot, sliced
Sea salt and freshly ground pepper, to taste
1 teaspoon cayenne pepper
2 garlic cloves, minced
4 tablespoons Romano cheese, preferably freshly grated
2 pounds endive, coarsely chopped
2 tablespoons extra-virgin olive oil
1 tablespoon Italian seasoning mix
8 ounces Italian dry salami, cut into 1/2-inch chunks
2 tomatoes, chopped
1 cup chicken broth

Directions

Press the "Sauté" button and heat the olive oil until sizzling. Now, cook the Italian salami for 3 minutes; add the shallot and garlic and cook an additional 2 minutes or until they have softened.

Add the endive, tomatoes, spices, and broth to the inner pot.

Secure the lid. Choose the "Manual" mode and cook for 2 minutes at High pressure. Once cooking is complete, use a quick pressure release; carefully remove the lid.

Divide between serving bowls and serve garnished with the grated Romano cheese. Bon appétit!

Per serving: 393 Calories; 26.2g Fat; 21.3g Carbs; 20.4g Protein; 5.6g Sugars

41. Glazed Baby Carrots

(Ready in about 20 minutes | Servings 4)

Ingredients

1 ½ pounds baby carrots
1/4 cup champagne vinegar
3/4 cup water
3 tablespoons ghee
1/2 teaspoon ground white pepper

1/2 teaspoon paprika
2 tablespoons soy sauce
2 tablespoons sesame seeds, toasted
1/2 teaspoon kosher salt
2 teaspoons honey

Directions

Press the "Sauté" button on your Instant Pot. Place all of the above ingredients, except for the carrots and sesame seeds, in your Instant Pot.

Cook this mixture for 1 minute, stirring frequently. Stir in baby carrots.

Secure the lid. Select the "Steam" setting; cook for 10 minutes at High pressure. Once cooking is complete, use a quick pressure release; carefully remove the lid.

Press the "Sauté" button one more time. Let it simmer until the sauce has reduced and thickened. Sprinkle with sesame seeds and serve at room temperature. Enjoy!

Per serving: 175 Calories; 10.3g Fat; 19.4g Carbs; 1.8g Protein; 12.6g Sugars

42. Sriracha Bang Bang Corn

(Ready in about 10 minutes | Servings 5)

Ingredients

5 ears corn on the cob, husked
Sriracha Aioli:
2 tablespoons Sriracha

1/2 cup mayonnaise
1/4 teaspoon sea salt
1 tablespoon lemon juice

Directions

Add 1 cup of water and a metal trivet to the inner pot of your Instant Pot. Place your corn on the trivet.

Secure the lid. Choose the "Manual" mode and cook for 2 minutes at High pressure. Once cooking is complete, use a quick pressure release; carefully remove the lid.

Then, whisk the mayonnaise, lemon juice, Sriracha, and salt until well combined. Serve the warm corn on the cob with the Sriracha aioli on the side. Bon appétit!

Per serving: 207 Calories; 10.2g Fat; 29.5g Carbs; 4.6g Protein; 0g Sugars

43. Classic Mushroom Stroganoff

(Ready in about 45 minutes | Servings 8)

Ingredients

14 ounces brown mushrooms, thinly sliced
1 ripe tomato, seeded and chopped
Sea salt and ground black pepper, to taste
1/2 teaspoon cayenne pepper
1 cup shallots, chopped
2 garlic cloves, minced
1 celery with leaves, chopped

1 bell pepper, seeded and thinly sliced
1 habanero pepper, minced
2 russet potatoes, chopped
1 cup water
2 bay leaves
2 tablespoons olive oil
1 cup vegetable stock
2 tablespoons corn flour, plus 3 tablespoons of water
1/2 teaspoon Hungarian paprika

Directions

Press the "Sauté" button to heat up the Instant Pot. Then, heat the olive oil and sauté the shallot, garlic, potatoes, and celery until they are softened; add a splash of vegetable stock, if needed.

Stir in the mushrooms, water, stock, paprika, cayenne pepper, bay leaves, and tomatoes.

Secure the lid. Select the "Meat/Stew" setting; cook for 35 minutes at High pressure. Once cooking is complete, use a quick pressure release; carefully remove the lid.

Make the slurry by whisking the corn flour with 3 tablespoons of water. Add the slurry back to the Instant Pot and press the "Sauté" button one more time.

Allow it to cook until the liquid has thickened. Discard bay leaves and serve warm.

Per serving: 137 Calories; 3.9g Fat; 23g Carbs; 4.5g Protein; 2.8g Sugars

44. Layered Zucchini Casserole

(Ready in about 20 minutes | Servings 4)

Ingredients

1 pound zucchini, cut into long slices
1 pound ground chuck
1 teaspoon Italian seasoning blend
1 onion, chopped
1 teaspoon cayenne pepper
1 tablespoon canola oil
1 cup tomato puree

1/2 cup Parmesan cheese, grated
1/4 pound Italian sausage, crumbled
2 garlic cloves, minced
1 cup cream cheese
Sea salt and ground black pepper, to taste

Directions

Press the "Sauté" button and heat the oil. Then, cook the ground chuck, sausage, and onion for 3 to 4 minutes; stir in the garlic and cook an additional minute.

In a mixing bowl, thoroughly combine the cheese and seasonings.

Place a layer of the zucchini strips on the bottom of a lightly greased baking pan. Spoon 1/3 of the meat mixture onto the zucchini layer. Place 1/2 of the cheese mixture and tomato puree on the meat layer.

Repeat the layers, ending with a cheese layer. Add 1 cup of water and a metal rack to the inner pot. Lower the baking pan onto the rack.

Secure the lid. Choose the "Manual" mode and cook for 6 minutes at High pressure. Once cooking is complete, use a quick pressure release; carefully remove the lid. Bon appétit!

Per serving: 617 Calories; 45.2g Fat; 29.2g Carbs; 18.4g Protein; 6.7g Sugars

45. Potatoes with Cheese and Parsley

(Ready in about 20 minutes | Servings 6)

Ingredients

1/4 cup extra-virgin olive oil
1 cup Pecorino Romano cheese, grated
1/4 cup Italian flat-leaf parsley, chopped
1/2 teaspoon freshly ground black pepper
3/4 cup beef broth
6 white potatoes, cut into cubes
1/4 cup brown ale
1 teaspoon garlic powder
1 teaspoon oregano, dried
1/2 teaspoon shallot powder
2 sprigs rosemary, leaves picked
Coarse salt, to taste

Directions

Toss the potato cubes with shallot powder, garlic powder, oregano, rosemary, salt, and black pepper.

Press the "Sauté" button and heat the oil. Now, cook the potatoes for 5 minutes, stirring periodically.

Add the broth and brown ale; secure the lid. Choose the "Manual" mode and cook for 9 minutes at High pressure.

Once cooking is complete, use a quick release; carefully remove the lid. Toss the warm potatoes with Pecorino Romano and serve garnished with Italian parsley. Enjoy!

Per serving: 270 Calories; 9g Fat; 38.8g Carbs; 9.2g Protein; 1.6g Sugars

46. Braised Collard Greens with Bacon

(Ready in about 10 minutes | Servings 4)

Ingredients

2 ½ pounds fresh collard greens
4 garlic cloves, chopped
2 cups chicken broth
1/4 cup dry white wine
Kosher salt and ground black pepper, to taste
1 onion, chopped
6 smoked bacon slices, chopped
1 teaspoon paprika
1 bay leaf

Directions

Press the "Sauté" button to preheat your Instant Pot. Then, cook the bacon until crisp and set aside.

Add the remaining ingredients to the inner pot and stir to combine.

Secure the lid. Choose the "Manual" mode and cook for 5 minutes at High pressure. Once cooking is complete, use a quick pressure release; carefully remove the lid.

Serve garnished with the reserved bacon. Bon appétit!

Per serving: 304 Calories; 19.3g Fat; 19.8g Carbs; 17.8g Protein; 2.9g Sugars

47. Thai Tom Kha Gai

(Ready in about 10 minutes | Servings 4)

Ingredients

1/2 cup coconut cream, unsweetened
1/4 teaspoon grated nutmeg
1 pound celery with leaves, chopped
1 (2-inch) piece young galangal, peeled and chopped
1 teaspoon garlic, minced
1/2 cup leeks, chopped
1/2 teaspoon ground bay leaves
1 fresh jalapeño peppers, seeded and finely chopped
4 cups roasted vegetable stock, preferably homemade
1 tablespoon sesame oil
Sea salt and freshly ground black pepper, to taste

Directions

Press the "Sauté" button to heat up your Instant Pot. Heat the sesame oil and sauté the garlic and leeks until tender about 1 minute 30 seconds.

Stir in the celery and galangal; continue to cook for a further 2 minutes.

Next, add the ground bay leaves, jalapeño peppers, stock, salt, black pepper and nutmeg.

Secure the lid. Choose the "Manual" mode and High pressure; cook for 3 minutes. Once cooking is complete, use a quick pressure release; carefully remove the lid.

Then, purée the soup with an immersion blender until smooth and creamy. Return the pureed soup to the Instant Pot; fold in the coconut cream.

Afterwards, press the "Sauté" button. Allow your soup to simmer until thoroughly warmed. Ladle into soup bowls and serve hot. Bon appétit!

Per serving: 200 Calories; 15.9g Fat; 9.5g Carbs; 7.7g Protein; 3.7g Sugars

48. Brussels Sprouts with Romano Cheese

(Ready in about 15 minutes | Servings 4)

Ingredients

1 cup Romano cheese, grated
1/2 teaspoon red pepper flakes
1/2 cup scallions, finely chopped
Salt, to taste
1 ½ pounds Brussels sprouts, trimmed
2 garlic cloves, minced
1/2 teaspoon freshly ground black pepper
3 tablespoons ghee

Directions

Place 1 cup of water and a steamer basket on the bottom of your Instant Pot. Place the Brussels sprouts in the steamer basket.

Secure the lid. Choose the "Steam" mode and High pressure; cook for 5 minutes. Once cooking is complete, use a quick pressure release; carefully remove the lid.

While the Brussels sprouts are still hot, add the ghee, garlic, scallions, salt, black pepper, red pepper, and Romano cheese; toss to coat well and serve.

Per serving: 261 Calories; 16.2g Fat; 20.1g Carbs; 13.2g Protein; 4.1g Sugars

49. Kale and Potato Soup

(Ready in about 20 minutes | Servings 4)

Ingredients

2 cups kale, torn into pieces
2 garlic cloves, minced
2 cups tomato puree
1 cup turnip, chopped
Kosher salt and ground black pepper, to taste
2 medium potatoes, chopped
2 carrots, chopped
5 cups chicken broth
1 onion, chopped
2 teaspoons butter, at room temperature
1 teaspoon dried basil
1 teaspoon dried oregano

Directions

Press the "Sauté" button and melt the butter. Once hot, cook the onion until tender and translucent.

Then, add the garlic and continue to sauté an additional 30 seconds, stirring continuously. Add a splash of chicken broth to deglaze the pan.

Now, stir in the basil, oregano, salt, black pepper, potatoes, carrots, turnip, and tomato puree; stir to combine.

Secure the lid. Choose the "Manual" mode and cook for 5 minutes at High pressure. Once cooking is complete, use a natural pressure release for 10 minutes; carefully remove the lid.

Stir in the kale and seal the lid; let it sit in the residual heat until thoroughly warmed. Adjust the seasonings to taste and serve immediately.

Per serving: 245 Calories; 4.5g Fat; 41g Carbs; 12.5g Protein; 10.9g Sugars

50. Vegetables with Halloumi Cheese

(Ready in about 10 minutes | Servings 4)

Ingredients

1 tablespoon butter
2 rosemary sprigs, leaves picked
1 thyme sprig, leaves picked
8 ounces Halloumi cheese, cubed
1/2 cup Kalamata olives, pitted and halved
1/2 cup dry Greek wine
12 ounces button mushrooms, thinly sliced
1 pepperoncini pepper, minced
1 teaspoon dried basil
2 tomatoes, chopped
1/3 cup water
1/2 pound eggplant, sliced
1/2 pound zucchini, sliced
2 garlic cloves, minced
1/2 cup shallots, chopped
1 tablespoon olive oil

Directions

Press the "Sauté" button to heat up your Instant Pot; heat the olive oil and butter. Cook the garlic and shallots for 1 to 2 minutes, stirring occasionally.

Stir in the mushrooms, pepper, eggplant, and zucchini and continue to sauté an additional 2 to 3 minutes.

After that, add the basil, rosemary, thyme, tomatoes, water, and wine.

Secure the lid. Choose the "Manual" mode and Low pressure; cook for 3 minutes. Once cooking is complete, use a quick pressure release; carefully remove the lid.

Garnish each serving with the cheese and olives; serve warm or at room temperature.

Per serving: 305 Calories; 20.8g Fat; 18.4g Carbs; 15.2g Protein; 10.4g Sugars

51. Traditional Provençal Ratatouille

(Ready in about 40 minutes | Servings 4)

Ingredients

3 sweet peppers, seeded and sliced
1 teaspoon basil
1 teaspoon rosemary
1 pound tomatoes, pureed
4 tablespoons Pinot Noir
1 cup vegetable broth
1 teaspoon oregano
1 tablespoon sea salt
1 pound zucchini, sliced
4 tablespoons extra-virgin olive oil
1 pound eggplant, sliced
2 onions, sliced
4 cloves garlic, pressed
Sea salt and ground red pepper, to taste

Directions

Toss the eggplant with 1 teaspoon of salt in a colander. Let it sit for 30 minutes; then squeeze out the excess liquid. Transfer the eggplant to the inner pot of your Instant Pot.

Add the other ingredients to the inner pot

Secure the lid. Choose the "Manual" mode and cook for 6 minutes at High pressure. Once cooking is complete, use a quick pressure release; carefully remove the lid.

Season to taste with salt and pepper and serve warm. Enjoy!

Per serving: 268 Calories; 15.7g Fat; 26.7g Carbs; 8.4g Protein; 8.1g Sugars

52. Refreshing Chickpea Salad

(Ready in about 45 minutes + chilling time | Servings 6)

Ingredients

1 bay leaf
3 tablespoons extra-virgin olive oil
Sea salt and ground black pepper, to taste
2 cloves garlic, peeled, whole
2 red bell peppers, thinly sliced
2 tablespoons fresh lemon juice
1/4 cup fresh basil, roughly chopped
1 red onion, thinly sliced
1 green bell pepper, thinly sliced
1 ½ cups dry chickpeas, well-rinsed
5 cups water

Directions

Add the chickpeas, water, bay leaf and garlic to the Instant Pot.

Secure the lid. Choose the "Bean/Chili" mode and High pressure; cook for 40 minutes. Once cooking is complete, use a natural pressure release; carefully remove the lid.

Allow the chickpeas to cool completely; then; transfer to a salad bowl. Add the remaining ingredients and stir to combine well. Serve well-chilled and enjoy!

Per serving: 266 Calories; 10.1g Fat; 35.1g Carbs; 10.9g Protein; 7.1g Sugars

53. Bamies Latheres me Domata

(Ready in about 25 minutes | Servings 5)

Ingredients

2 pounds okra
1 tablespoon olive oil
1 cup tomato puree
4 tablespoons tomato ketchup
1 teaspoon fish sauce
Sea salt and ground black pepper, to taste
1 cup chicken stock
1 teaspoon garlic powder
2 shallots, chopped
1 teaspoon turmeric powder
1 teaspoon porcini powder

Directions

Press the "Sauté" button and heat the oil until sizzling. Now, sauté the shallot until tender and fragrant.

Add in the remaining ingredients and gently stir to combine well.

Secure the lid. Choose the "Manual" mode and cook for 5 minutes at High pressure. Once cooking is complete, use a natural pressure release for 15 minutes; carefully remove the lid.

Divide between serving bowls and serve warm. Bon appétit!

Per serving: 162 Calories; 4.5g Fat; 27.8g Carbs; 7.8g Protein; 8.7g Sugars

54. Pancetta Green Beans

(Ready in about 10 minutes | Servings 4)

Ingredients

1 ½ pounds green beans, cut in half
5 ounces pancetta, diced
2 garlic cloves, pressed
1 yellow onion, chopped
1/2 teaspoon dried oregano
1/2 teaspoon dried dill
Kosher salt, to taste
1/4 teaspoon ground black pepper
1/2 teaspoon cayenne pepper
2 tablespoons sesame oil
1 cup water

Directions

Press the "Sauté" button to heat up your Instant Pot. Now, heat the sesame oil and sauté the garlic and onion until softened and fragrant; set it aside.

After that, stir in the pancetta and continue to cook for a further 4 minutes; crumble with a fork and set it aside.

Add the remaining ingredients; stir to combine.

Secure the lid. Choose the "Manual" mode and Low pressure; cook for 3 minutes. Once cooking is complete, use a quick pressure release; carefully remove the lid.

Serve warm, garnished with the reserved onion/garlic mixture and pancetta. Bon appétit!

Per serving: 177 Calories; 12.1g Fat; 9.9g Carbs; 8.8g Protein; 2.3g Sugars

55. Keto Cauliflower Rice

(Ready in about 10 minutes | Servings 3)

Ingredients

2 tablespoons butter
2 tablespoons fresh parsley, roughly chopped
1 ½ pounds cauliflower
Sea salt, to taste
1/2 teaspoon white pepper

Directions

Add the cauliflower florets and 1 cup of water to the inner pot.

Secure the lid. Choose the "Manual" mode and cook for 2 minutes at High pressure. Once cooking is complete, use a quick pressure release.

Stir the salt, pepper, and butter into warm cauliflower rice.

Serve garnished with fresh parsley and enjoy!

Per serving: 127 Calories; 8.3g Fat; 11.7g Carbs; 4.5g Protein; 4.4g Sugars

56. Old-Fashioned Cabbage with Ham

(Ready in about 20 minutes | Servings 4)

Ingredients

1 pound cabbage, shredded
1 cup fully cooked ham, cubed
1 cup double cream
2 garlic cloves, chopped
1 celery rib, chopped
2 bay leaves
1/4 cup fresh chives, chopped
1 ½ tablespoons olive oil
3 ½ cups broth, preferably homemade
Sea salt, to taste
1/2 teaspoon black peppercorns
1 leek, chopped

Directions

Press the "Sauté" button on your Instant Pot; add olive oil. Once hot, cook leeks for 3 minutes or until they are softened.

Stir in the celery and cook for 3 minutes more. Add a splash of broth if needed. Now, add the garlic and cook for 30 seconds more or until it is fragrant.

Add the cabbage, broth, salt, black peppercorns, and bay leaves. Secure the lid.

Choose the "Manual" mode and cook for 3 minutes at High pressure. Once cooking is complete, use a quick release; carefully remove the lid.

Fold in the ham and double cream and continue to cook in the residual heat for 5 minutes longer.

Taste, adjust the seasonings and serve in individual bowls, garnished with fresh chopped chives. Enjoy!

Per serving: 292 Calories; 19.5g Fat; 16.6g Carbs; 14.6g Protein; 7.9g Sugars

57. Sweet Potato Puree

(Ready in about 15 minutes | Servings 6)

Ingredients

2 pounds sweet potatoes, peeled and diced
2 tablespoons fresh parsley leaves, roughly chopped
A pinch of grated nutmeg
1/2 teaspoon cayenne pepper
1 cup water
1 garlic clove, pressed
1/4 cup sour cream
2 tablespoons butter
1 teaspoon sea salt
A bunch of scallions, finely sliced

Directions

Add the sweet potatoes and water to the Instant Pot.

Secure the lid. Choose the "Manual" mode and cook for 8 minutes at High pressure. Once cooking is complete, use a quick pressure release; carefully remove the lid.

Drain the potatoes. Mash the potatoes using a potato masher or your food processor.

Now, add the remaining ingredients and stir well to combine. Enjoy!

Per serving: 179 Calories; 4.9g Fat; 31.3g Carbs; 2.8g Protein; 6.4g Sugars

58. Potato and Broccoli Chowder

(Ready in about 35 minutes | Servings 6)

Ingredients

1 pound broccoli, broken into small florets
2 cups roasted-vegetable stock
Kosher salt, to taste
1 cup sour cream
1 carrot, sliced
3 cups water
1/4 teaspoon ground black pepper
1/4 teaspoon red pepper flakes, crushed
1/2 pound celery, chopped
1/2 cup leeks, chopped
2 potatoes, peeled and diced

Directions

Simply place all of the above ingredients, except for the sour cream, in your Instant Pot.

Secure the lid. Select the "Soup" setting; cook for 30 minutes at High pressure. Once cooking is complete, use a quick pressure release; carefully remove the lid.

Then, puree the soup with an immersion blender. Serve in individual bowls, garnished with a dollop of sour cream. Bon appétit!

Per serving: 193 Calories; 5.5g Fat; 28.6g Carbs; 9.2g Protein; 2.1g Sugars

59. Padma Lakshmi's Yogurt Rice

(Ready in about 25 minutes | Servings 5)

Ingredients

1 ½ cups basmati rice, rinsed
Himalayan salt and ground black pepper, to taste
4 tablespoons grapeseed oil
1 cup full-fat yogurt
1 chili pepper, minced
1 cinnamon stick
1 teaspoon fennel seeds
2 tablespoons fresh dhania (coriander), chopped
8 curry leaves
1 teaspoon fresh ginger, peeled and grated

Directions

Press the "Sauté" button and heat the oil; now sauté the fennel seeds and curry leaves for 30 seconds or until aromatic.

Now, stir in the basmati rice, chili pepper, ginger, cinnamon, salt, and black pepper. Pour in 2 cups of water.

Secure the lid. Choose the "Manual" mode and cook for 4 minutes at High pressure. Once cooking is complete, use a natural pressure release for 15 minutes; carefully remove the lid.

Fluff your rice with a fork and stir in the yogurt. Stir until everything is well combined. Serve garnished with fresh dhania and enjoy!

Per serving: 323 Calories; 11.7g Fat; 49.2g Carbs; 4.5g Protein; 1.2g Sugars

60. Dijon Broccoli Salad with Feta Cheese

(Ready in about 10 minutes | Servings 4)

Ingredients

1 large (1 ½-pound) head broccoli, cut into small florets
1 ½ cups feta cheese, crumbled
1/4 cup extra-virgin olive oil
2 tablespoons parsley leaves, roughly chopped
2 spring garlic stalks, smashed
2 green onions, chopped
1 cup radishes, sliced
Salt and ground black pepper, to taste
1 tablespoon tahini paste
2 tablespoons lemon juice
1 teaspoon Dijon seeds

Directions

Prepare your Instant Pot by adding 1 cup of water and a steamer basket to its bottom.

Place the broccoli in the steamer basket.

Secure the lid. Choose the "Manual" mode and High pressure; cook for 5 minutes. Once cooking is complete, use a quick pressure release; carefully remove the lid.

Afterwards, toss your broccoli with the remaining ingredients. Serve at room temperature with garlic croutons if desired. Enjoy!

Per serving: 302 Calories; 21.1g Fat; 18.2g Carbs; 14.2g Protein; 7.4g Sugars

61. Authentic Italian Caponata

(Ready in about 15 minutes | Servings 4)

Ingredients

1 cup butternut squash, cut into 1/2-inch chunks
1 onion, diced
4 tablespoons Parmigiano-Reggiano cheese, grated
Sea salt and ground black pepper

4 bell peppers, cut into 1/2-inch chunks
2 garlic cloves, minced
4 tablespoons olive oil
1 cup vine-ripened tomatoes, pureed
1 tablespoon Italian seasoning mix

Directions

Press the "Sauté" button and heat the olive oil until sizzling. Now, sauté the onion until tender and translucent.

Stir in the garlic and continue to sauté an additional 30 seconds, stirring frequently.

Stir in the salt, black pepper, butternut squash, peppers, tomatoes, and Italian seasoning mix.

Secure the lid. Choose the "Manual" mode and cook for 4 minutes at High pressure. Once cooking is complete, use a quick pressure release; carefully remove the lid.

Afterwards, scatter the grated cheese over the caponata and serve warm. Bon appétit!

Per serving: 194 Calories; 15.1g Fat; 13.5g Carbs; 3.4g Protein; 5.3g Sugars

62. Paprika Creamed Carrot Mash

(Ready in about 10 minutes | Servings 6)

Ingredients

2 pounds carrots, chopped
1/4 cup heavy cream
Kosher salt, to taste
1 teaspoon paprika

2 tablespoons butter, room temperature
1 teaspoon coriander
1/2 teaspoon ground black
1 cup water

Directions

Add water to the base of your Instant Pot.

Put the carrots into the steaming basket. Transfer the steaming basket to the Instant Pot.

Secure the lid and choose the "Manual" button, High pressure and 3 minutes. Once cooking is complete, use a natural release; remove the lid carefully.

Mash the carrots with a fork or potato masher. Add the butter, paprika, coriander, salt, ground black, and heavy cream.

Taste, adjust the seasonings and serve immediately. Bon appétit!

Per serving: 113 Calories; 6g Fat; 14.6g Carbs; 1.5g Protein; 7.3g Sugars

63. Warm Chickpea Salad

(Ready in about 1 hour | Servings 6)

Ingredients

1 cup chickpeas, rinsed
1 avocado, peeled, pitted, and sliced
Sea salt and ground black pepper, to taste
1/2 cup scallions, sliced
1 cup cherry tomatoes, halved

2 tablespoons fresh lemon juice
1/4 teaspoon curry powder
1 teaspoon sea salt
1 teaspoon baking soda
1 bell pepper, sliced
1/4 cup olive oil

Directions

Add the dry chickpeas to the inner pot; pour in 6 cups of water. Add the sea salt and baking soda.

Secure the lid. Choose the "Manual" mode and cook for 35 minutes at High pressure. Once cooking is complete, use a natural pressure release for 20 minutes; carefully remove the lid.

Drain and transfer to a nice serving bowl. Toss the cooked chickpeas with the other ingredients; toss to combine well. Bon appétit!

Per serving: 190 Calories; 7g Fat; 26.2g Carbs; 8g Protein; 5.1g Sugars

64. Creamed Broccoli with Mustard and Seeds

(Ready in about 10 minutes | Servings 4)

Ingredients

2 tablespoons sesame seeds
1 teaspoon dried parsley flakes
2 tablespoons pepitas
2 garlic cloves, pressed
1 teaspoon Dijon mustard
1 head (1 ½-pound) broccoli, broken into florets
1/2 teaspoon dried oregano

2 tablespoons sunflower seeds
2 tablespoons mayonnaise
2 tablespoons balsamic vinegar
2 tablespoons extra-virgin olive oil
Salt and black pepper, to taste
1/2 teaspoon dried basil

Directions

Add 1 cup of water and a steamer basket to the bottom of your Instant Pot. Place the broccoli florets in the steamer basket.

Secure the lid and choose the "Steam" mode; cook for 6 minutes under High pressure. Once cooking is complete, use a quick release; carefully remove the lid.

While the broccoli is still hot, add the remaining ingredients. Toss to combine and serve at room temperature.

Per serving: 199 Calories; 15.6g Fat; 9.9g Carbs; 8.7g Protein; 2.9g Sugars

65. Roasted Herbed Baby Potatoes

(Ready in about 15 minutes | Servings 4)

Ingredients

1/2 cup roasted vegetable broth

Sea salt and ground black pepper, to taste

2 tablespoons olive oil

1/2 teaspoon paprika

1/2 teaspoon sage

1 ½ pounds baby potatoes, scrubbed

2 garlic cloves, smashed

1/2 cup water

1 teaspoon oregano

1 teaspoon basil

1 teaspoon rosemary

Directions

Pierce the baby potatoes with a fork; place them in the inner pot along with the garlic, broth, and water.

Secure the lid. Choose the "Manual" mode and cook for 10 minutes at High pressure. Once cooking is complete, use a quick pressure release; carefully remove the lid. Drain and reserve.

Press the "Sauté" button and heat the olive oil until sizzling. Now, sauté the seasonings for 30 seconds, stirring frequently. Throw the reserved potatoes into the inner pot.

Cook until they are browned and crisp on all sides. Serve warm.

Per serving: 198 Calories; 7.1g Fat; 30.3g Carbs; 4.1g Protein; 1.3g Sugars

66. Mini Sweet Potatoes with Butter

(Ready in about 35 minutes | Servings 4)

Ingredients

1/4 teaspoon freshly grated nutmeg

2 tablespoons light butter

1 pound whole small sweet potatoes, cleaned

1/4 teaspoon salt

Directions

Add 1 cup of water and a steamer basket to the Instant Pot. Arrange the sweet potatoes in the steamer basket.

Secure the lid and choose the "Steam" mode. Cook for 10 minutes at High pressure. Once cooking is complete, use a natural release for 20 minutes; remove the lid carefully.

Toss the steamed sweet potatoes with salt, nutmeg, and butter. Eat warm. Bon appétit!

Per serving: 154 Calories; 5.9g Fat; 23.5g Carbs; 2.3g Protein; 7.3g Sugars

67. Mediterranean Tomato Soup with Feta Cheese

(Ready in about 30 minutes | Servings 4)

Ingredients

1 (28-ounce) can tomatoes, crushed

1/2 cup double cream

1/2 teaspoon cayenne pepper

1 teaspoon fresh basil, chopped

1/2 cup feta cheese, cubed

2 stalks green garlic, chopped

1 celery stalk, diced

2 carrots, diced

1 cup green onions, chopped

1 teaspoon fresh rosemary, chopped

1 tablespoon olive oil

2 cups vegetable broth

1 tablespoon olive oil

Sea salt and ground black pepper, to your liking

Directions

Press the "Sauté" button and heat 1 tablespoon of olive oil. Sauté the green onions, garlic, celery, and carrots until softened.

Add the vegetable broth, salt, black pepper, cayenne pepper, basil, rosemary, and tomatoes to the inner pot.

Secure the lid. Choose the "Manual" mode and cook for 6 minutes at High pressure. Once cooking is complete, use a natural pressure release for 10 minutes; carefully remove the lid.

Stir in the double cream and seal the lid again; let it sit for 10 minutes more. Ladle into soup bowls; garnish with feta and 1 tablespoon of olive oil. Bon appétit!

Per serving: 245 Calories; 18g Fat; 15g Carbs; 8.3g Protein; 10.1g Sugars

68. Caramelized Onion and Bacon Tart

(Ready in about 40 minutes | Servings 4)

Ingredients

4 slices bacon, chopped

1 teaspoon garlic, minced

1 cup double cream

1/2 cup cream cheese

1/2 cup Monterey-Jack cheese, shredded

1 teaspoon cayenne pepper

1 tablespoon butter

1 onion, thinly sliced

5 eggs

Sea salt and ground black pepper, to taste

Directions

Press the "Sauté" button to preheat your Instant Pot. Then, melt the butter and cook the onions for 15 minutes or until they are golden brown; reserve.

Add the bacon and garlic and cook an additional 2 to 3 minutes. Transfer the onion and bacon to the baking pan.

In a mixing bowl, thoroughly combine the eggs, salt, black pepper, cayenne pepper, double cream, cream cheese. Pour this mixture into the pan.

Secure the lid. Choose the "Porridge" mode. Cook for 20 minutes at High pressure. Once cooking is complete, use a quick release; carefully remove the lid.

Top with the shredded Monterey-Jack cheese; seal the lid and let it sit in the residual heat until thoroughly warmed. Carefully flip onto a serving plate. Bon appétit!

Per serving: 485 Calories; 43.5g Fat; 5.7g Carbs; 18.3g Protein; 4.5g Sugars

69. Vegetarian Ratatouille Provencale

(Ready in about 25 minutes | Servings 4)

Ingredients

1 tablespoon sea salt
1 red chili pepper, seeded and minced
1/2 teaspoon celery seeds
4 cloves garlic, minced
4 sweet peppers, seeded and chopped
2 tomatoes, pureed

1 pound eggplant, cut into rounds
1 cup roasted vegetable broth
3 tablespoons olive oil
1 red onion, sliced
2 tablespoons coriander, chopped
Sea salt and ground black pepper, to taste
1 teaspoon capers

Directions

Toss the eggplant with 1 tablespoon of sea salt; allow it to drain in a colander.

Press the "Sauté" button and heat the olive oil. Sauté the onion until tender and translucent, about 4 minutes.

Add the garlic and continue to sauté for 30 seconds more or until fragrant. Add the remaining ingredients to the inner pot, including the drained eggplant.

Secure the lid. Choose the "Manual" mode. Cook for 7 minutes at High pressure. Once cooking is complete, use a quick pressure release; carefully remove the lid.

Press the "Sauté" button and cook on low setting until the ratatouille has thickened or about 7 minutes. Bon appétit!

Per serving: 231 Calories; 11.1g Fat; 33.1g Carbs; 5.7g Protein; 11.3g Sugars

70. Lebanese Zucchini and Garbanzo Bean Bake

(Ready in about 1 hour | Servings 4)

Ingredients

4 Lebanese zucchinis, trimmed, seeded, cored out
1 (15-ounce) can garbanzo beans, rinsed and drained
1/2 cup natural yogurt, to serve
1/4 cup flat-leaf parsley, chopped
1/4 cup mint, chopped
2 tablespoons olive oil
1 large-sized carrot, grated

1/2 teaspoon cayenne pepper
1/4 cup coriander, chopped
1/2 teaspoon chili powder
1 teaspoon baharat
1/3 cup brown rice, well-rinsed
1 yellow onion, chopped
2 cloves garlic, minced
Sea salt and ground black pepper, to taste

Directions

Cook the rice in a pan according to package directions; drain, season with salt, black pepper, and cayenne pepper; reserve.

Add 1 cup of water and a steamer basket to the Instant Pot. Now, place the zucchini in the steamer basket.

Secure the lid. Choose the "Steam" mode and High pressure; cook for 3 minutes. Once cooking is complete, use a natural pressure release; carefully remove the lid.

Wipe down the Instant Pot with a damp cloth. Press the "Sauté" button and heat the oil until sizzling.

Once hot, cook the onion, garlic, and carrot until they are tender. Add the garbanzo beans, parsley, mint, coriander, chili powder, and baharat; continue to sauté an additional 2 to 3 minutes; add the reserved rice.

Fill each zucchini with the stuffing; serve immediately with natural yogurt. Bon appétit!

Per serving: 360 Calories; 21.6g Fat; 32.4g Carbs; 10.8g Protein; 6.6g Sugars

71. Harvest Vegetables with Barley

(Ready in about 25 minutes | Servings 4)

Ingredients

1 tablespoon olive oil
2 stalks celery, chopped
2 carrots, chopped
4 cups vegetable broth
1 teaspoon red pepper flakes
2 tomatoes, pureed
1 onion, chopped
2 cloves garlic, minced

1 red chili pepper, minced
2 cups water
Sea salt and ground black pepper, to taste
2 sweet peppers, seeded and chopped
1 ½ cups pearled barley

Directions

Press the "Sauté" button and heat the olive oil. Now, sauté the onion until tender and translucent.

Then, stir in the garlic and peppers and cook an additional 3 minutes. Stir in the pearled barley. Pour in water and broth.

Secure the lid. Choose the "Manual" mode. Cook for 15 minutes at High pressure. Once cooking is complete, use a quick pressure release; carefully remove the lid.

Add the remaining ingredients to the inner pot.

Secure the lid. Choose the "Manual" mode. Cook for 5 minutes at High pressure. Once cooking is complete, use a quick pressure release; carefully remove the lid. Bon appétit!

Per serving: 401 Calories; 6.5g Fat; 74.4g Carbs; 14.7g Protein; 5.7g Sugars

72. Italian Stuffed Peppers with Mushroom and Sausage

(Ready in about 25 minutes | Servings 4)

Ingredients

1/2 pound Italian sausage, ground
4 medium-sized bell peppers, cored
1/2 pound button mushrooms, roughly chopped
3/4 cup buckwheat, soaked overnight
1/2 teaspoon red pepper flakes, crushed

1 teaspoon dried basil
1/2 teaspoon mustard seeds
1/2 teaspoon dried oregano
2 (15-ounce) cans tomatoes
1 onion, chopped
1 ½ cups chicken broth
Salt and ground black pepper, to taste
2 cloves garlic, minced

Directions

Press the "Sauté" button to preheat the Instant Pot. Once hot, add olive oil; now, sauté the onion and garlic until tender and aromatic.

Add the Italian sausage and mushrooms; continue to cook an additional 2 minutes; reserve the sausage/mushroom mixture.

Now, add the soaked buckwheat and chicken broth.

Secure the lid. Choose the "Manual" mode and High pressure; cook for 3 minutes. Once cooking is complete, use a natural pressure release; carefully remove the lid.

Add the reserved sausage/mushroom mixture and seasonings; stir to combine well. Stuff the peppers. Wipe down the Instant Pot with a damp cloth.

Add 1 ½ cups of water and metal rack to the Instant Pot. Place the stuffed peppers in a casserole dish; add tomatoes, mustard seeds, and bay leaf. Lower the dish onto the rack.

Secure the lid. Choose the "Manual" mode and High pressure; cook for 10 minutes. Once cooking is complete, use a natural pressure release; carefully remove the lid. Serve warm and enjoy!

Per serving: 478 Calories; 19.7g Fat; 65.6g Carbs; 19.6g Protein; 11.4g Sugars

73. Green Artichoke Dipping Sauce

(Ready in about 15 minutes | Servings 8)

Ingredients

10 ounces artichoke hearts
1 pound fresh or frozen spinach leaves
9 ounces cream cheese
1 cup goat cheese, crumbled
1 onion, chopped

2 cloves garlic, minced
1 cup chicken broth
Sea salt and freshly ground black pepper, to taste
1 teaspoon red pepper flakes
2 tablespoons butter

Directions

Press the "Sauté" button and melt the butter. Then, sauté the onion and garlic until just tender and fragrant.

Then, add the artichoke hearts, broth, salt, black pepper, and red pepper flakes.

Secure the lid. Choose the "Manual" mode and cook for 5 minutes at High pressure. Once cooking is complete, use a quick pressure release; carefully remove the lid.

Add the spinach and cheese to the inner pot; seal the lid and let it sit in the residual heat until thoroughly warmed. Enjoy!

Per serving: 222 Calories; 17.4g Fat; 8.6g Carbs; 9.9g Protein; 2.4g Sugars

74. Balsamic Mayo Potato Wedges

(Ready in about 15 minutes | Servings 6)

Ingredients

2 garlic cloves, pressed
1/2 stick butter, melted
2 tablespoons mayonnaise
2 tablespoons balsamic vinegar
1/2 teaspoon cayenne pepper
1 teaspoon thyme

2 pounds russet potatoes, peeled and diced
1/2 teaspoon mustard powder
1/2 teaspoon sea salt
1/4 teaspoon ground black pepper

Directions

Add a metal rack and 1 cup of water to your Instant Pot. Place the potatoes on the rack.

Secure the lid. Select the "Steam" mode and cook for 10 minutes under High pressure. Once cooking is complete, use a quick pressure release; carefully remove the lid.

Cut your potatoes into wedges and toss them with the remaining ingredients. Serve at room temperature. Bon appétit!

Per serving: 221 Calories; 11.2g Fat; 27.9g Carbs; 3.4g Protein; 1g Sugars

75. Romano Eggplant and Wine Sauce

(Ready in about 10 minutes | Servings 6)

Ingredients

1/2 cup Romano cheese, freshly grated
1 cup white wine
2 tablespoons tahini (sesame butter)
1 pound eggplants, sliced
1 teaspoon oregano

1/2 teaspoon rosemary
1 teaspoon basil
4 garlic cloves, minced
2 tomatoes, chopped
Sea salt and ground black pepper, to taste
2 tablespoons olive oil

Directions

Press the "Sauté" button and heat the olive oil. Then, cook the eggplant slices until they are charred at the bottom. Work with batches.

Add the garlic, tomatoes, wine, and spices.

Secure the lid. Choose the "Bean/Chili" mode and cook for 3 minutes at High pressure. Once cooking is complete, use a quick pressure release; carefully remove the lid.

Press the "Sauté" button again to thicken the cooking liquid. Add the tahini paste and stir to combine. Top with Romano cheese and serve.

Per serving: 147 Calories; 10.4g Fat; 9.3g Carbs; 5.2g Protein; 4.6g Sugars

76. Cheesy Mashed Cauliflower

(Ready in about 20 minutes | Servings 5)

Ingredients

1 cauliflower head
1/2 cup beer
1 ½ cup Colby cheese, shredded
1/2 cup sour cream
2 tablespoons butter

1 ½ tablespoons arrowroot powder
1 teaspoon garlic powder
1/2 teaspoon cayenne pepper
Sea salt and freshly ground black pepper
1 1/3 cups water

Directions

Add 1 1/3 cups of water to your Instant Pot.

Put the cauliflower head into the steaming basket. Transfer the steaming basket to the Instant Pot.

Secure the lid and choose the "Manual" button, High pressure and 5 minutes. Once cooking is complete, use a quick release; carefully remove the lid.

Season the cooked cauliflower with cayenne pepper, salt, and ground black pepper. Mash cooked cauliflower with a potato masher.

Next, melt the butter in a pan that is preheated over moderate heat. Whisk in the arrowroot powder and cook for 40 seconds, stirring continuously.

Gradually pour in the beer, stirring continuously. Add the garlic powder and cook until the sauce has thickened, for 3 to 4 minutes.

Remove from heat and stir in the Colby cheese and sour cream; stir until the cheese has melted. Add the mashed cauliflower and stir until everything is well incorporated. Bon appétit!

Per serving: 297 Calories; 23.6g Fat; 8.9g Carbs; 12.8g Protein; 1.4g Sugars

77. Winter Vegetable and Lentil Stew

(Ready in about 15 minutes | Servings 4)

Ingredients

1 onion, chopped
Kosher salt and ground black pepper, to taste
2 tomatoes, pureed
2 cups vegetable broth
3 cloves garlic, minced
1 parsnip, chopped
2 cups brown lentils

1 sprig thyme, chopped
1 carrot, chopped
1 stalk celery, chopped
1 sprig rosemary, chopped
3 cups Swiss chard, torn into pieces
1 tablespoon olive oil
1 teaspoon basil

Directions

Press the "Sauté" button and heat the oil. Sauté the onion until tender and translucent or about 4 minutes.

Then, stir in the garlic and cook an additional 30 seconds or until fragrant.

Now, stir in the carrot, celery, parsnip, lentils, tomatoes, spices, and broth.

Secure the lid. Choose the "Manual" mode. Cook for 10 minutes at High pressure. Once cooking is complete, use a quick pressure release; carefully remove the lid.

Afterwards, add the Swiss chard to the inner pot. Seal the lid and allow it to wilt completely. Bon appétit!

Per serving: 510 Calories; 7.4g Fat; 84.2g Carbs; 31.5g Protein; 10.3g Sugars

78. Asian Vegetable Soup

(Ready in about 15 minutes | Servings 4)

Ingredients

1 tablespoon light soy sauce
2 tablespoons fresh parsley, roughly chopped
2 tablespoons mijiu (rice wine)
1/2 teaspoon dried dill
1 teaspoon smoked paprika
2 tablespoons sesame oil, softened

2 carrots, trimmed and chopped
Sea salt and freshly ground pepper, to taste
1/2 pound mushroom, sliced
3 cups water
1/2 cup milk
2 shallots, chopped
2 cloves garlic, smashed

Directions

Press the "Sauté" button and heat the oil. Once hot, sweat the shallots and garlic until tender and translucent.

Add the mushrooms and carrots. Season with salt, ground pepper, dill, and paprika. Sauté for 3 more minutes more or until the carrots have softened. Add rice wine to deglaze the pan.

Add the water, milk, and light soy sauce. Secure the lid. Choose the "Manual" function, High pressure and 5 minutes.

Once cooking is complete, use a quick release; carefully remove the lid. Taste, adjust the seasonings and serve in individual bowls, garnished with fresh parsley. Bon appétit!

Per serving: 117 Calories; 8.7g Fat; 7.6g Carbs; 3.4g Protein; 4.6g Sugars

79. Cream of Potato Soup

(Ready in about 25 minutes | Servings 4)

Ingredients

1 pound potatoes, cut into bite-sized pieces
1 cup double cream
1 sweet pepper, deveined and sliced
1 jalapeno pepper, deveined and sliced
3 cups creamed corn kernels

1 sweet onion, chopped
2 garlic cloves, minced
Kosher salt and ground black pepper, to taste
1/2 teaspoon cayenne pepper
4 tablespoons all-purpose flour
4 cups vegetable broth
2 tablespoons butter

Directions

Press the "Sauté" button and melt the butter. Once hot, sauté the sweet onions, garlic, and peppers for about 3 minutes or until they are tender and fragrant.

Sprinkle the flour over the vegetables; continue stirring approximately 4 minutes or until your vegetables are coated.

Add the broth and potatoes and gently stir to combine.

Secure the lid. Choose the "Manual" mode and cook for 5 minutes at High pressure. Once cooking is complete, use a quick pressure release; carefully remove the lid.

Press the "Sauté" button and use the lowest setting. Stir in the creamed corn, double cream, salt, black pepper, and cayenne pepper.

Let it simmer, stirring continuously for about 5 minutes or until everything is thoroughly heated. Taste and adjust the seasonings. Bon appétit!

Per serving: 439 Calories; 20.4g Fat; 56.2g Carbs; 12.8g Protein; 9.3g Sugars

80. Belgian Endive with Dijon Sauce

(Ready in about 6 minutes | Servings 2)

Ingredients

1 pound Belgian endive, halved lengthwise
1/2 cup scallions, chopped
Sea salt and ground black pepper, to taste
1 bay leaf
1 teaspoon Dijon mustard
1 tablespoon soy sauce

1/4 cup champagne vinegar
1 teaspoon lime juice
1/2 teaspoon crushed red pepper flakes
2 tablespoons sesame oil
2 garlic cloves, minced
1 cup water

Directions

Press the "Sauté" button to heat up the Instant Pot; heat the sesame oil. Once hot, cook the garlic and scallions for 40 seconds to a minute or until aromatic.

Add the Belgian endive, vinegar, lime juice, mustard, soy sauce water, red pepper, salt, black pepper, and bay leaf.

Secure the lid. Choose the "Manual" mode and Low pressure; cook for 2 minutes or until tender when pierced with the tip of a knife.

Once cooking is complete, use a quick pressure release; carefully remove the lid. Serve immediately.

Per serving: 203 Calories; 15.6g Fat; 13g Carbs; 4.1g Protein; 2.9g Sugars

81. Vegan Tomato and Zucchini Risotto

(Ready in about 30 minutes | Servings 4)

Ingredients

1 ½ cups long grain white rice
1 green zucchini, cut into thick sliced
1 onion, chopped
2 (12-ounce) cans tomato paste
1 teaspoon Italian seasoning blend
1 bay leaf
2 cups water
2 carrots, thinly sliced
1 tablespoon olive oil
1 teaspoon garlic, chopped
2 teaspoons fresh lime juice
4 cups spinach
Sea salt and ground black pepper, to your liking

Directions

Press the "Sauté" button and heat the oil. Once hot, cook the onion and garlic for 2 to 3 minutes or until just tender and aromatic.

Stir in the rice, water, carrots, zucchini, tomato paste, Italian seasoning blend, salt, black pepper, and bay leaf.

Secure the lid. Choose the "Rice" mode and cook for 10 minutes at Low pressure. Once cooking is complete, use a natural pressure release for 15 minutes; carefully remove the lid.

Add the spinach and press the "Sauté" button. Let it simmer on the lowest setting until wilts. Drizzle lime juice over each portion and serve. Bon appétit!

Per serving: 473 Calories; 4.9g Fat; 98.5g Carbs; 15.1g Protein; 26.2g Sugars

82. Stuffed Peppers with Cheddar Cheese

(Ready in about 10 minutes | Servings 4)

Ingredients

6 ounces Cheddar cheese, grated
2 ounces sour cream
1/2 teaspoon dill, fresh or dried
1/2 white onion, finely chopped
1/2 teaspoon paprika
8 baby bell peppers, seeded and sliced lengthwise
1 tablespoon peanut oil
2 garlic cloves, smashed
Sea salt and ground black pepper, to taste

Directions

Start by adding 1 cup of water and a steamer basket to the Instant Pot.

Then, thoroughly combine all ingredients, except for peppers. Then, stuff the peppers with this mixture.

Arrange the peppers in the steamer basket.

Secure the lid. Choose the "Manual" mode and High pressure; cook for 5 minutes. Once cooking is complete, use a quick pressure release; carefully remove the lid.

Serve immediately and enjoy!

Per serving: 168 Calories; 8.8g Fat; 15.8g Carbs; 8.2g Protein; 8.2g Sugars

83. Chana Aloo Masala

(Ready in about 20 minutes | Servings 4)

Ingredients

1/2 teaspoon cumin seeds
1 cup yogurt
1 tablespoon chickpea flour
2 tomatoes, pureed
1/2 teaspoon chili powder
1 yellow onion, chopped
2 cups green peas
4 curry leaves
3 cups vegetable broth
1/2 teaspoon garam masala
1 tablespoon coriander
1 tablespoon ghee, melted
Sea salt and ground black pepper, to taste

Directions

Press the "Sauté" button and melt the ghee. Once hot, cook the cumin seeds for about 1 minute or until fragrant.

Add the onion and continue sautéing an additional 3 minutes.

Now, stir in the green peas, tomatoes, garam masala, coriander, chili powder, salt, black pepper, curry leaves, and broth.

Secure the lid. Choose the "Manual" mode and cook for 12 minutes at High pressure. Once cooking is complete, use a quick pressure release; carefully remove the lid.

Now, stir in the chickpea flour and let it simmer on the "Sauté" button until the cooking liquid has thickened. Serve in soup bowls with yogurt on the side. Bon appétit!

Per serving: 239 Calories; 9.1g Fat; 29.2g Carbs; 12.6g Protein; 14.9g Sugars

84. Simple Zucchini Slices with Herbs

(Ready in about 10 minutes | Servings 4)

Ingredients

1 ½ pounds zucchini, cut into thick slices
1/3 teaspoon smoked paprika
1/3 teaspoon ground black pepper
1/2 teaspoon dried oregano
1/2 cup water
1/2 cup vegetable broth
1 teaspoon rosemary, fresh or dried
1 ½ tablespoons olive oil
2 garlic cloves, minced
1 teaspoon basil, fresh or dried
Coarse sea salt, to taste

Directions

Press the "Sauté" button to heat up your Instant Pot; heat the olive oil. Once hot, cook the garlic for 1 minute.

Add the remaining ingredients.

Secure the lid. Choose the "Manual" mode and Low pressure; cook for 3 minutes. Once cooking is complete, use a quick pressure release; carefully remove the lid. Bon appétit!

Per serving: 88 Calories; 5.9g Fat; 5.9g Carbs; 5.3g Protein; 0g Sugars

85. Traditional Greek Fasolakia

(Ready in about 15 minutes | Servings 4)

Ingredients

1 ½ pounds fresh green beans

6 ounces Feta cheese, crumbled

1/2 dried dill

4 garlic cloves, chopped

1 teaspoon paprika

1/2 teaspoon dried oregano

1/2 teaspoon dried basil

2 tablespoons olive oil

1 cup bone broth, preferably homemade

2 vine-ripened tomatoes, pureed

Sea salt and freshly ground black pepper, to season

Directions

Press the "Sauté" button and heat the oil. Now, sauté the garlic until it is fragrant but not browned.

Add the other ingredients, except for the feta cheese, to the inner pot; and stir to combine.

Secure the lid. Choose the "Manual" mode and cook for 5 minutes at High pressure. Once cooking is complete, use a quick pressure release; carefully remove the lid.

Ladle into individual bowls and serve with Feta cheese on the side. Enjoy!

Per serving: 237 Calories; 17.5g Fat; 13.7g Carbs; 9.9g Protein; 4.9g Sugars

BEANS, LEGUMES & LENTILS

86. Simple Black Pepper Beans

(Ready in about 35 minutes | Servings 6)

Ingredients

1 teaspoon black peppercorns, to taste
2 tablespoons bouillon granules
2 bay leaves
1 ¼ pounds dry navy beans
6 cups water

Directions

Rinse off and drain navy beans. Place the navy beans, water, bouillon granules, bay leaves, and black peppercorns in your Instant Pot.

Secure the lid. Choose the "Manual" mode and cook at High pressure for 20 minutes.

Once cooking is complete, use a natural release; remove the lid carefully. Bon appétit!

Per serving: 292 Calories; 1.6g Fat; 52.3g Carbs; 19g Protein; 3.6g Sugars

87. Spicy Chickpeas with Herbs

(Ready in about 55 minutes | Servings 4)

Ingredients

2 cups chickpeas
4 cups water
1 thyme sprig
1 large yellow onion, chopped
1 teaspoon mixed peppercorns
2 bay leaves
1/2 whole capsicum, deseeded and chopped
1 tablespoon olive oil
2 cups tomato sauce
1 teaspoon salt
Sea salt, to taste
1 teaspoon baking soda
1 rosemary sprig

Directions

Press the "Sauté" button and heat the olive oil; now, sauté the onion until tender and translucent. Then, add the remaining ingredients and stir to combine.

Secure the lid. Choose the "Bean/Chili" mode and cook for 40 minutes at High pressure. Once cooking is complete, use a natural pressure release for 10 minutes; carefully remove the lid.

Ladle into serving bowls and garnish with fresh chives if desired. Bon appétit!

Per serving: 453 Calories; 11.9g Fat; 68.2g Carbs; 21.5g Protein; 14.1g Sugars

88. Black Bean Chili

(Ready in about 30 minutes | Servings 6)

Ingredients

1 cup leeks, chopped
1 teaspoon cocoa powder, unsweetened
1/2 cup golden raisins
2 garlic cloves, minced
1/2 teaspoon ground bay leaf
1 teaspoon dried basil
1 tablespoon brown sugar
1/4 teaspoon black pepper, or more to taste
1 ½ cups stock, preferably homemade
1 tablespoon chili powder
1/2 teaspoon ground allspice
2 ripe tomatoes, chopped
2 (15-ounce) cans black beans, rinsed and drained
2 tablespoons soy sauce
1/2 teaspoon celery salt
2 tablespoons olive oil
1/2 cup sour cream
1/2 pound ground pork
1/2 pound ground beef

Directions

Press the "Sauté" button to heat up your Instant Pot. Now, heat the olive oil until sizzling.

Cook the ground meat, crumbling it with a spatula, until it is no longer pink; reserve.

Now, stir in the leeks and garlic; cook until they have softened. Now, add chili powder, ground allspice, ground bay leaf, basil, sugar, salt, and pepper. Continue to sauté for 4 minutes more.

Now, deglaze the bottom of the inner pot with the stock. Add the tomatoes, beans, soy sauce, and cocoa powder.

Then, choose the "Manual" button, High pressure and 8 minutes. Once cooking is complete, use a natural release; remove the lid carefully.

Add the raisins and cook in the residual heat for 5 to 6 minutes. Ladle into individual bowls and serve garnished with sour cream.

Per serving: 375 Calories; 20g Fat; 24.2g Carbs; 24.6g Protein; 13.3g Sugars

89. Country-Style Black Eyed Peas

(Ready in about 50 minutes | Servings 6)

Ingredients

2 cups black eyed peas, rinsed
1 tablespoon fresh parsley, chopped
Sea salt and ground black pepper, to taste
2 cups cream of celery soup
1 teaspoon paprika
8 ounces pancetta
3 cups water

Directions

Press the "Sauté" button to preheat your Instant Pot; now, cook the pancetta until browned and reserve.

Add the black eyed peas, cream of celery soup, water, salt, pepper, and paprika to the inner pot.

Secure the lid. Choose the "Bean/Chili" mode and cook for 30 minutes at High pressure. Once cooking is complete, use a natural pressure release for 15 minutes; carefully remove the lid.

Ladle into serving bowls and garnish with fresh parsley and the reserved pancetta. Bon appétit!

Per serving: 308 Calories; 3.7g Fat; 46.3g Carbs; 24.1g Protein; 6.1g Sugars

90. Borlotti Beans with Tomato and Herbs

(Ready in about 35 minutes | Servings 5)

Ingredients

1 ½ pounds dry Borlotti beans
2 bell peppers, seeded and chopped
Salt and freshly ground black pepper, to taste
2 garlic cloves, minced
4 cups roasted vegetable broth
2 ripe tomatoes, puréed
1/2 teaspoon oregano
1 purple onion, chopped

1 heaping tablespoon fresh parsley leaves, chopped
1 serrano pepper, seeded and minced
1/2 green plantain, cut into slices
2 bay leaves
1 tablespoon olive oil
1/2 teaspoon cumin
1/2 teaspoon dried basil

Directions

Press the "Sauté" button to preheat your Instant Pot. Now, heat the oil until sizzling; sauté the onion for 2 minutes or until tender.

Then, add the peppers, garlic, and plantain; continue to sauté an additional minute or until they are fragrant; reserve.

Add the remaining ingredients to your Instant Pot; stir to combine.

Secure the lid. Choose the "Bean/Chili" mode and High pressure; cook for 25 minutes. Once cooking is complete, use a natural pressure release; carefully remove the lid.

Add the reserved onion/pepper mixture. Seal the lid and let it sit for 5 minutes more or until everything is thoroughly warmed.

Discard bay leaves. Taste for salt and serve warm.

Per serving: 553 Calories; 5.2g Fat; 93.3g Carbs; 37.2g Protein; 8.5g Sugars

91. Traditional Japanese Kuromame

(Ready in about 30 minutes | Servings 4)

Ingredients

3-inch square of kombu
1 cup sugar
A pinch of kosher salt

1/2 pound black soybeans, rinsed
4 cups water
1 tablespoon soy sauce

Directions

Add all ingredients to the inner pot of your Instant Pot.

Secure the lid. Choose the "Manual" mode and cook for 15 minutes at High pressure. Once cooking is complete, use a natural pressure release for 10 minutes; carefully remove the lid.

Let the beans soak in the sauce for 24 hours. The black soybeans should be soft and glossy. Cover and refrigerate. Enjoy!

Per serving: 302 Calories; 1.5g Fat; 61.2g Carbs; 12.5g Protein; 26.4g Sugars

92. Kidney Beans with Carrot and Peppers

(Ready in about 40 minutes | Servings 4)

Ingredients

3/4 pound white kidney beans
2 bay leaves
4 garlic cloves, minced
1 bell pepper, thinly sliced
6 cups water
1 heaping teaspoon cayenne pepper

2 medium-sized carrots, thinly sliced
1 tablespoon olive oil
1 cup onions, chopped
Seasoned salt and ground black pepper, to taste

Directions

Press the "Sauté" button to preheat your Instant Pot. Heat the oil and sauté the onions and garlic for 2 minutes or until tender and fragrant.

Add the remaining ingredients. Stir to combine well.

Secure the lid. Choose the "Bean/Chili" mode and High pressure; cook for 30 minutes. Once cooking is complete, use a natural pressure release; carefully remove the lid.

Ladle into individual bowls and garnish with dried chili peppers if desired. Bon appétit!

Per serving: 238 Calories; 6.7g Fat; 40.1g Carbs; 4.6g Protein; 2.2g Sugars

93. Greek-Style Bean Salad

(Ready in about 35 minutes | Servings 4)

Ingredients

1/2 cup Kalamata olives, pitted and halved
1/2 cup Halloumi cheese, crumbled
1 teaspoon garlic, minced
1 pepperoncini, seeded and diced
6 basil leaves, roughly chopped
1/4 cup extra virgin olive oil
1 cucumber, sliced

1 onion, thinly sliced
3 tablespoons balsamic vinegar, or more to taste
2 sweet peppers, seeded and diced
Sea salt and freshly cracked black pepper, to taste
1 cup fresh tomatoes, sliced
1 pound cannellini beans, rinsed

Directions

Add the cannellini beans to the inner pot of your Instant Pot. Pour in 8 cups of water.

Secure the lid. Choose the "Bean/Chili" mode and cook for 30 minutes at High pressure. Once cooking is complete, use a quick pressure release; carefully remove the lid.

Transfer your beans to a salad bowl. Add the remaining ingredients and toss to combine well.

Serve well chilled.

Per serving: 572 Calories; 19.8g Fat; 70.8g Carbs; 30.9g Protein; 4.7g Sugars

94. Spicy Yellow Lentils with Green Onions

(Ready in about 15 minutes | Servings 5)

Ingredients

1 1/3 cups yellow lentils, rinsed

2 cups vegetable broth

1 tablespoon fresh ginger, minced

1 bell pepper, chopped

Salt and ground black pepper, to taste

1/2 teaspoon red pepper flakes

1 habanero pepper, chopped

1 medium-sized carrot, chopped

1/2 teaspoon fennel seeds

1/2 cup green onions, chopped

1 tablespoon sesame oil

1 teaspoon turmeric powder

2 garlic cloves, minced

Directions

Press the "Sauté" button to preheat your Instant Pot. Now, heat the oil and cook the green onions, garlic, ginger, peppers, and carrot until they are softened.

Secure the lid. Choose the "Manual" mode and High pressure; cook for 2 minutes. Once cooking is complete, use a natural pressure release; carefully remove the lid.

You can thicken the cooking liquid on "Sauté" function if desired. Bon appétit!

Per serving: 243 Calories; 4.8g Fat; 37.3g Carbs; 14.3g Protein; 2.3g Sugars

95. Perfect Mong Daal Khichri

(Ready in about 30 minutes | Servings 3)

Ingredients

1 cup moong dal lentils

1 cup basmati rice

1 teaspoon cumin seeds

1/2 teaspoon ground turmeric

Sea salt and ground black pepper, to taste

2 bay leaves

1 shallot, sliced

2 tablespoons butter

Directions

Press the "Sauté" button and melt the butter. Once hot, sauté the cumin seeds and bay leaf until they are fragrant.

Now, add the shallot and continue to sauté an additional 3 minute or until it is just tender.

Add the remaining ingredients; stir to combine.

Secure the lid. Choose the "Manual" mode and cook for 4 minutes at High pressure. Once cooking is complete, use a natural pressure release for 15 minutes; carefully remove the lid. Serve warm.

Per serving: 530 Calories; 8.8g Fat; 92.3g Carbs; 20.2g Protein; 1.3g Sugars

96. Famous Vegan Lentil Tacos

(Ready in about 30 minutes | Servings 6)

Ingredients

1 ¼ cups green lentils, dried

12 corn tortillas

1 (1.25-ounce) package taco seasoning

2 overripe Roma tomatoes, chopped

2 garlic cloves, minced

Sea salt and ground pepper, to taste

1/2 teaspoon ground cumin

1 cup vegetable broth

1 cup water

1/2 cup leeks, chopped

1 tablespoon yellow mustard

1 cup baby spinach

2 tablespoons olive oil

Directions

Press the "Sauté" button to preheat the Instant Pot. Once hot, add the olive oil; now, sauté the leeks and garlic until they are tender and fragrant.

Add the seasonings, broth, water, tomatoes, and lentils.

Secure the lid. Choose the "Soup" mode and High pressure; cook for 20 minutes. Once cooking is complete, use a natural pressure release; carefully remove the lid.

Spoon the lentil mixture on tortillas. Serve with mustard and baby spinach. Enjoy!

Per serving: 520 Calories; 42.1g Fat; 29.9g Carbs; 10.8g Protein; 0.7g Sugars

97. Easiest Lebanese Mujadara Ever

(Ready in about 35 minutes | Servings 4)

Ingredients

1 cup brown lentils, sorted and rinsed

2 tablespoons fresh lemon juice

4 cups mustard greens

3 cloves garlic, rough chopped

1 teaspoon cumin

1 cinnamon stick

1/2 teaspoon ground ginger

1/2 cup red cooking wine

1 large onion, thinly sliced

3 cups water

2 tablespoons fresh parsley

1 teaspoon turmeric powder

1 cup basmati rice, rinsed

2 tablespoons grapeseed oil

Kosher salt and red pepper, to season

Directions

Press the "Sauté" button and heat the oil until sizzling. Once hot, cook the onion and garlic until just tender and fragrant.

Stir in the remaining ingredients, except for the mustard greens. Give it a good stir.

Secure the lid. Choose the "Manual" mode and cook for 10 minutes at High pressure. Once cooking is complete, use a natural pressure release for 10 minutes; carefully remove the lid.

Add the mustard greens to the inner pot. Seal the lid and let it sit in the residual heat for 10 minutes. Serve warm.

Per serving: 403 Calories; 17.8g Fat; 26.7g Carbs; 36.7g Protein; 13g Sugars

98. Black-Eyed Peas with Bacon

(Ready in about 15 minutes | Servings 3)

Ingredients

1/2 pound dried black-eyed peas, well-rinsed
1 yellow onion, chopped
4 cups vegetable broth
Salt and ground black pepper, to taste
2 garlic cloves, minced
4 slices bacon

Directions

Press the "Sauté" button to preheat your Instant Pot. Once hot, cook the bacon until crisp; set aside to drain on paper towels.

Add the onion and garlic and continue to sauté in pan drippings. Cook until they are tender and aromatic.

Add the black-eyed peas, broth, salt, and black pepper to your Instant Pot.

Secure the lid. Choose the "Manual" mode and High pressure; cook for 10 minutes. Once cooking is complete, use a natural pressure release; carefully remove the lid.

Serve topped with reserved bacon. Bon appétit!

Per serving: 266 Calories; 18.8g Fat; 10.2g Carbs; 13.3g Protein; 4.9g Sugars

99. Herbed Pea Spread

(Ready in about 45 minutes | Servings 8)

Ingredients

1/2 teaspoon hot sauce
2 cups water
1 tablespoon fresh cilantro, chopped
1 fresh lemon, zested and juiced
1 teaspoon cayenne pepper
1/4 cup basil leaves, roughly chopped
2 tablespoons fresh parsley, chopped
Kosher salt and freshly ground black pepper, to taste
14 ounces frozen peas
2 tablespoons fresh chives, chopped

Directions

Add the frozen peas and water to the inner pot of your Instant Pot.

Secure the lid. Choose the "Manual" mode and cook for 10 minutes at High pressure. Once cooking is complete, use a natural pressure release for 15 minutes; carefully remove the lid.

Transfer the boiled green peas to a bowl of your food processor; add the remaining ingredients and process until creamy and smooth, gradually adding the cooking liquid.

Serve with pita bread, tortilla chips or bread sticks if desired. Bon appétit!

Per serving: 42 Calories; 0.1g Fat; 7.8g Carbs; 2.7g Protein; 2.9g Sugars

100. Japanese-Style Chickpeas

(Ready in about 35 minutes | Servings 4)

Ingredients

1 (19-ounce) can chickpeas, drained
1/2 teaspoon cayenne pepper
2 cups water
1 cup dashi stock
Sea salt and ground black pepper, to taste
3 tablespoons shallots, chopped
1 ½ cups brown rice
1/2 teaspoon garlic powder

Directions

Place the brown rice, water, dashi stock, garlic powder, salt, black pepper, and cayenne pepper in the Instant Pot; stir to combine well.

Secure the lid. Choose the "Manual" mode and High pressure; cook for 30 minutes. Once cooking is complete, use a natural pressure release; carefully remove the lid.

Add the canned chickpeas and stir to combine; seal the lid and let it sit until thoroughly warmed.

Serve topped with fresh shallots. Enjoy!

Per serving: 366 Calories; 4.3g Fat; 70.5g Carbs; 11.7g Protein; 4.3g Sugars

101. Farmhouse Split Pea Soup with Ham

(Ready in about 35 minutes | Servings 3)

Ingredients

1 ½ cups split peas, rinsed
4 ounces ham, diced
3 cups chicken stock, veggie stock, water, or a mixture
1 leek, diced
1 turnip, diced
1/2 teaspoon dried thyme
1/2 teaspoon garlic powder
2 tablespoons butter
Kosher salt and ground black pepper, to taste
1 celery stalk, diced
1 carrot, diced
1 jalapeno pepper, seeded and minced

Directions

Press the "Sauté" button and melt the butter. Once hot, sauté the leek, celery, carrot, turnip, and jalapeno until they have softened.

Add the remaining ingredients to the inner pot.

Secure the lid. Choose the "Manual" mode and cook for 15 minutes at High pressure. Once cooking is complete, use a natural pressure release for 15 minutes; carefully remove the lid.

Taste and adjust seasonings. Serve warm.

Per serving: 403 Calories; 17.8g Fat; 26.7g Carbs; 36.7g Protein; 13g Sugars

102. Egyptian Ful Mudammas

(Ready in about 20 minutes | Servings 4)

Ingredients

1 pound dried fava beans, soaked overnight
2 garlic cloves, minced
1 red bell pepper, chopped
2 cups vegetable broth
2 bay leaves
1/2 cup shallots, chopped
1 green bell pepper, chopped
Seasoned salt and freshly ground black pepper, to taste
1 tablespoon canola oil
1 cup water
1/2 teaspoon ground cumin

Directions

Press the "Sauté" button to preheat your Instant Pot. Now, heat the oil and cook the shallots, garlic, and peppers until they are softened; reserve.

Add the remaining ingredients; stir to combine.

Secure the lid. Choose the "Manual" mode and High pressure; cook for 12 minutes. Once cooking is complete, use a natural pressure release; carefully remove the lid.

Divide the cooked fava beans between four serving bowl; top with the sautéed shallot/pepper mixture. Serve immediately.

Per serving: 210 Calories; 5.4g Fat; 34.4g Carbs; 14.1g Protein; 17.8g Sugars

103. Indian Sorakkai Sambar

(Ready in about 35 minutes | Servings 3)

Ingredients

1 cup tomato sauce
1 teaspoon Urad Dal
2 teaspoons sesame oil
1 yellow onion, chopped
1 tablespoon tamarind
1 tablespoon sambar powder
Sea salt and ground black pepper, to taste
1 teaspoon cayenne pepper
1 cup Pigeon pea lentils
1 Indian ghost jolokia chili pepper, chopped
6 curry leaves
1 teaspoon turmeric powder

Directions

Add the lentils and 4 cups of water to the inner pot.

Secure the lid. Choose the "Manual" mode and cook for 10 minutes at High pressure. Once cooking is complete, use a natural pressure release for 10 minutes; carefully remove the lid.

Meanwhile, heat a saucepan over medium-high heat. Cook the onion for about 3 minutes or until translucent. Now, add the curry leaves and chili pepper to the skillet. Let it cook for a further minute or until they are aromatic.

Add the other ingredients, cover, and reduce the heat to medium-low; let it simmer for about 13 minutes or until everything is thoroughly cooked.

Transfer the onion/tomato mixture to the inner pot of your Instant Pot. Stir to combine and serve immediately. Bon appétit!

Per serving: 248 Calories; 7.9g Fat; 36.8g Carbs; 6.9g Protein; 13.4g Sugars

104. Adzuki Bean Purée

(Ready in about 30 minutes | Servings 4)

Ingredients

1 ½ cups Adzuki beans
1/2 cup scallions, chopped
2 cups water
3 cups beef bone broth
Sea salt and freshly ground black pepper, to taste
1 teaspoon paprika
4 cloves garlic, smashed
1 tablespoon canola oil

Directions

Press the "Sauté" button to preheat your Instant Pot. Then, heat the oil and cook the scallions and garlic until tender; reserve.

Wipe down the Instant Pot with a damp cloth. Add the Adzuki beans, water, broth, salt, pepper, and paprika.

Secure the lid. Choose the "Bean/Chili" mode and High pressure; cook for 20 minutes. Once cooking is complete, use a natural pressure release; carefully remove the lid.

Transfer to your food processor and add the reserved scallion/garlic mixture. Then, process the mixture, working in batches. Process until smooth and uniform. Serve warm and enjoy!

Per serving: 95 Calories; 4.9g Fat; 7.7g Carbs; 6.4g Protein; 0.4g Sugars

105. Rajma with Adzuki Beans

(Ready in about 35 minutes | Servings 3)

Ingredients

1 cup dried adzuki beans
1 ghost jolokia chili pepper, chopped
1 tablespoon butter, at room temperature
1 bay leaf
1-inch cinnamon stick
1 teaspoon cumin seeds
1 teaspoon red pepper flakes, crushed
1 teaspoon garam masala
4 cups vegetable broth, preferably homemade
1 green cardamom
1 onion, chopped
Kosher salt and ground black pepper, to taste
1 teaspoon coriander
2 ripe tomatoes, pureed
2 cloves garlic, pressed

Directions

Press the "Sauté" button and melt the butter. Once hot, cook the cumin seeds for 30 seconds to 1 minute or until the seeds begin to sizzle.

Now, stir in the onion, garlic, and chili pepper; continue to sauté an additional 3 minutes or until they have softened.

Stir in the remaining ingredients.

Secure the lid. Choose the "Bean/Chili" mode and cook for 25 minutes at High pressure. Once cooking is complete, use a quick pressure release; carefully remove the lid.

Serve with hot steamed rice if desired. Enjoy!

Per serving: 304 Calories; 5.6g Fat; 50.1g Carbs; 16.5g Protein; 4.6g Sugars

106. Baked Beans with Italian sausage

(Ready in about 20 minutes | Servings 4)

Ingredients

1 pound smoked Italian sausage, sliced
2 tablespoons brown sugar
1 carrot, sliced
1 parsnip, sliced
1 Pepperoncini, seeded and minced
1 bay leaf
2 tomatoes, puréed
1/2 teaspoon cayenne pepper
Sea salt, to taste
1 yellow onion, chopped
2 cloves garlic, minced
2 bell peppers, seeded and chopped
1/2 cup sour cream
1 pound pinto beans, soaked overnight
1 teaspoon dried marjoram
1/2 teaspoon freshly ground black pepper
1/2 teaspoon dried rosemary

Directions

Add the pinto beans to your Instant Pot; now, pour in enough water to cover the beans completely.

Next, stir in the sugar, bay leaf, tomatoes, rosemary, marjoram, black pepper, cayenne pepper, and salt; stir to combine well.

Secure the lid. Choose the "Bean/Chili" mode and High pressure; cook for 10 minutes. Once cooking is complete, use a natural pressure release; carefully remove the lid.

In the meantime, cook the sausage with the onion, garlic, carrot, parsnip, and peppers for 3 to 4 minutes; transfer the sausage mixture to the Instant Pot.

Top with well-chilled sour cream and serve. Bon appétit!

Per serving: 449 Calories; 26.8g Fat; 35.1g Carbs; 25g Protein; 10.2g Sugars

107. Kidney Bean Soup with Bacon

(Ready in about 25 minutes | Servings 4)

Ingredients

2 cups dried red kidney beans, soaked and rinsed
1 carrot, coarsely chopped
1 leek, chopped
2 garlic cloves, sliced
2 canned chipotle chilis in adobo, chopped
1 teaspoon basil
4 cups chicken broth
A small handful cilantro leaves, roughly chopped
6 ounces bacon, cut into small pieces
Sea salt and freshly cracked black pepper, to taste
1/2 teaspoon rosemary
1 parsnip, coarsely chopped

Directions

Press the "Sauté" button to preheat your Instant Pot. Now, cook the bacon until crisp; reserve.

Add the leek and garlic; continue to sauté an additional 3 minute or until they are fragrant.

Stir in the other ingredients, except for the fresh cilantro.

Secure the lid. Choose the "Manual" mode and cook for 8 minutes at High pressure. Once cooking is complete, use a natural pressure release for 10 minutes; carefully remove the lid.

Afterwards, purée your soup using a food processor or an immersion blender. Serve garnished with fresh cilantro and the reserved bacon. Bon appétit!

Per serving: 534 Calories; 15.2g Fat; 72.5g Carbs; 31.4g Protein; 5.9g Sugars

108. French Lentil Salad

(Ready in about 25 minutes | Servings 4)

Ingredients

1 ½ cups dried French green lentils, rinsed
A bunch of spring onions, roughly chopped
1 teaspoon mixed peppercorns, freshly cracked
1 green bell pepper, thinly sliced
1 red bell pepper, thinly sliced
2 tablespoons balsamic vinegar
1/4 cup fresh basil, snipped
Sea salt, to taste
3 cups water
2 bay leaves
2 carrots, shredded
1/2 cup radishes, thinly sliced
1 cucumber, thinly sliced
2 garlic cloves, minced
1/4 cup extra-virgin olive oil

Directions

Place the water, lentils, and bay leaves in your Instant Pot. Secure the lid.

Choose "Soup" function and cook for 20 minutes under High pressure. Once cooking is complete, use a quick release; carefully remove the lid.

Drain the green lentils and discard bay leaves; transfer to a large salad bowl.

Add the spring onions, garlic, carrots, bell peppers, radishes, cucumber, olive oil, vinegar, and basil. Season with crushed peppercorns and sea salt.

Toss to combine and place in your refrigerator until ready to serve. Bon appétit!

Per serving: 183 Calories; 13.8g Fat; 13.7g Carbs; 3.5g Protein; 4g Sugars

109. Colorful Lentil and Pepper Salad

(Ready in about 30 minutes | Servings 4)

Ingredients

1 cucumber, sliced
4 cups water
1/4 cup extra-virgin olive oil
Sea salt and ground white pepper, to taste
1 red bell pepper, seeded and sliced
1 green bell pepper, seeded and sliced
1 carrot, julienned
1 cup grape tomatoes, halved
1 fresh lemon, juiced
1/2 cup scallions, chopped
1/2 teaspoon red pepper flakes
2 cups green lentils, rinsed

Directions

Add the lentils and water to the inner pot.

Secure the lid. Choose the "Manual" mode and cook for 8 minutes at High pressure. Once cooking is complete, use a natural pressure release for 15 minutes; carefully remove the lid.

In a salad bowl, combine the lentils with the remaining ingredients. Toss to combine well. Serve well chilled. Bon appétit!

Per serving: 492 Calories; 14.9g Fat; 68.6g Carbs; 25.6g Protein; 6.1g Sugars

110. Seafood with Green Lentils

(Ready in about 15 minutes | Servings 5)

Ingredients

5 ounces crabmeat
1 ½ pounds shrimp, cleaned and deveined
1 cup French green lentils
1/2 (14-ounce) can diced tomatoes
2 tablespoons butter, at room temperature
2 garlic cloves, minced
1 ½ tablespoons apple cider vinegar
Sea salt and ground black pepper, to taste
1 cup vegetable broth
1/3 cup Sauvignon Blanc

Directions

Press the "Sauté" button to preheat your Instant Pot. Melt the butter. Then, sauté the garlic until aromatic about 40 seconds.

Now, add the canned tomatoes, Sauvignon Blanc, broth, vinegar, salt, black pepper, and lentils to your Instant Pot.

Secure the lid and choose the "Manual" setting. Cook for 6 minutes at High pressure. Once cooking is complete, use a quick release; carefully remove the lid.

Press the "Sauté" button again. Stir in the shrimp and crabmeat; simmer until they become pink. Ladle into soup bowls. Bon appétit!

Per serving: 277 Calories; 9.2g Fat; 8.3g Carbs; 36.7g Protein; 3.1g Sugars

111. Country-Style Beans with Sausage

(Ready in about 45 minutes | Servings 4)

Ingredients

1 ½ cups dry pinto beans
2 cloves garlic, minced
4 cups chicken broth
1 tomato, crushed
2 tablespoons canola oil
1 onion, chopped
1 bell pepper, sliced
1 teaspoon dried sage
1 teaspoon cayenne pepper
6 ounces turkey sausage sliced
2 bay leaves
Sea salt and ground black pepper, to taste

Directions

Press the "Sauté" button and heat the oil. Sauté the sausage until it becomes slightly crispy.

Now, add the onion, garlic, and pepper; continue to cook until they are tender. Add the remaining ingredients to the inner pot.

Secure the lid. Choose the "Bean/Chili" mode and cook for 30 minutes at High pressure. Once cooking is complete, use a natural pressure release for 10 minutes; carefully remove the lid.

Press the "Sauté" button and let it simmer until the cooking liquid has thickened. Serve with your favorite toppings. Bon appétit!

Per serving: 469 Calories; 13.6g Fat; 57.6g Carbs; 28.8g Protein; 4.9g Sugars

112. Portuguese Baked Beans

(Ready in about 40 minutes | Servings 4)

Ingredients

1 pound dry Cannellini beans
2 cups tomatoes, puréed
1/2 cup Madeira wine
2 bay leaves
1 teaspoon whole grain mustard
1 lime, cut into wedges
2 red onions, thinly sliced
2 garlic cloves, smashed
2 canned chipotle chilies
2 tablespoons tomato ketchup

Directions

Add the red onions, garlic, beans, tomatoes, ketchup, mustard, bay leaves, and chilies to the Instant Pot.

Secure the lid. Choose the "Bean/Chili" mode and High pressure; cook for 30 minutes. Once cooking is complete, use a natural pressure release; carefully remove the lid.

Ladle into individual bowls; squeeze the lime wedges into each serving; add the Madeira wine and stir to blend well. Serve warm.

Per serving: 226 Calories; 4.5g Fat; 29.3g Carbs; 12.9g Protein; 10.2g Sugars

113. Refried Beans with Cheese

(Ready in about 1 hour 5 minutes | Servings 4)

Ingredients

1 ½ cups white kidney beans, rinsed
1 cup Colby cheese, shredded
Kosher salt and ground black pepper, to taste
1 tablespoon olive oil
1 chili pepper, seeded and chopped
6 cups roasted vegetable broth
1 onion, chopped
2 cloves garlic, pressed
1 teaspoon ground cumin
2 bay leaves

Directions

Press the "Sauté" button and heat the olive oil until sizzling. Then, sauté the onion for about 3 minutes or until tender.

Now, stir in the garlic and chili pepper; continue to cook for 1 minute more or until fragrant. Add a splash of broth to deglaze the pan.

Add the remaining broth, beans, bay leaves, salt, black pepper, and cumin to the inner pot of your Instant Pot.

Secure the lid. Choose the "Bean/Chili" mode and cook for 40 minutes at High pressure. Once cooking is complete, use a natural pressure release for 20 minutes; carefully remove the lid. Reserve 1 cup of the cooking liquid.

Then, puree the beans with an immersion blender until they reach your desired consistency. Sprinkle with the shredded Colby cheese and serve warm.

Per serving: 472 Calories; 16.6g Fat; 49.1g Carbs; 32.3g Protein; 4.4g Sugars

114. Classic Bean Soup with Herbs

(Ready in about 40 minutes | Servings 5)

Ingredients

1 pound dried red beans, soaked and rinsed
1 red bell pepper, seeded and chopped
1 cup red onions, chopped
Kosher salt and freshly ground black pepper, to taste
2 bay leaves
1 carrot, chopped
3 garlic cloves, minced
2 tablespoons canola oil
1 teaspoon dried oregano
1 teaspoon dried sage
1 parsnip, chopped
1 teaspoon dried rosemary
5 cups beef bone broth

Directions

Press the "Sauté" button to preheat your Instant Pot. Now, heat the oil and sweat the onions until they are translucent.

Then, add the parsnip, bell pepper, carrot, and garlic; cook an additional 3 minutes or until the vegetables are softened.

Stir in the remaining ingredients.

Secure the lid. Choose the "Bean/Chili" mode and High pressure; cook for 25 minutes. Once cooking is complete, use a natural pressure release for 10 minutes; carefully remove the lid.

Discard the bay leaves. You can purée the soup in your blender if desired; serve in individual bowls. Bon appétit!

Per serving: 188 Calories; 9.6g Fat; 16.2g Carbs; 11.9g Protein; 4g Sugars

115. Authentic Spicy Hummus

(Ready in about 1 hour | Servings 6)

Ingredients

2 tablespoons tahini (sesame butter)
4 dashes hot pepper sauce
1 ½ teaspoons sea salt
1 teaspoon baking soda
1/4 cup olive oil
1 teaspoon cayenne pepper
2 garlic cloves
1 ½ cups dry chickpeas, rinsed
2 tablespoons fresh lemon juice

Directions

Add the dry chickpeas to the inner pot; pour in 6 cups of water. Add the sea salt and baking soda.

Secure the lid. Choose the "Manual" mode and cook for 35 minutes at High pressure. Once cooking is complete, use a natural pressure release for 20 minutes; carefully remove the lid. Reserve the cooking liquid.

Transfer the warm, drained chickpeas to your food processor; add the remaining ingredients. While the food processor is running, pour in the cooking liquid to achieve the desired consistency.

To serve, drizzle olive oil on top of the hummus if desired. Bon appétit!

Per serving: 266 Calories; 12.2g Fat; 29.5g Carbs; 11.8g Protein; 1.2g Sugars

116. Pinto Beans with Rice and Herbs

(Ready in about 30 minutes | Servings 6)

Ingredients

1 cup dry pinto beans
1 cup dry brown rice
2 tablespoons fresh chives, roughly chopped
3 cups water
1 tablespoon fresh rosemary, chopped
1 tablespoon fresh mint, chopped
3 bouillon cubes
1 tablespoon fresh parsley, chopped
1 ancho chili pepper, chopped
2 tomatoes, puréed
2 tablespoons olive oil

Directions

Add all ingredients, except for the chives, to your Instant Pot.

Secure the lid. Choose the "Bean/Chili" mode and High pressure; cook for 25 minutes. Once cooking is complete, use a natural pressure release; carefully remove the lid.

Garnish with the chopped chives and enjoy!

Per serving: 277 Calories; 5.9g Fat; 46.3g Carbs; 9.9g Protein; 2.4g Sugars

117. French Du Lentilles du Puy

(Ready in about 35 minutes | Servings 8)

Ingredients

1 ½ cups du Puy lentils
1 teaspoon garlic, chopped
1 teaspoon cayenne pepper
1 teaspoon fennel seeds
2 cups cream of celery soup
1 cup shallots, chopped
1 ½ cups brown rice, rinsed
1 bay leaf
1 tablespoon balsamic vinegar
Kosher salt and black pepper, to season
1 cup water

Directions

Place all ingredient, except for the vinegar, in the inner pot of your Instant Pot.

Secure the lid. Choose the "Manual" mode and cook for 15 minutes at High pressure. Once cooking is complete, use a natural pressure release for 15 minutes; carefully remove the lid.

Afterward, stir in the vinegar and serve immediately. Enjoy!

Per serving: 285 Calories; 2.9g Fat; 53.5g Carbs; 12.2g Protein; 1.9g Sugars

118. Black Beans with Tomato and Cilantro

(Ready in about 30 minutes | Servings 5)

Ingredients

1 ¼ pounds dry black beans, rinsed and drained
1 bell pepper, chopped
2 bay leaves
2 cups tomatoes, puréed
2 cups vegetable broth
1 teaspoon cayenne pepper
1/2 teaspoon ancho chili pepper, minced

2 tablespoons olive oil
2 red onions, diced
3 cloves garlic, smashed
2 tablespoons fresh cilantro leaves, roughly chopped
Morton kosher salt and ground black pepper, to taste

Directions

Press the "Sauté" button to preheat your Instant Pot. Now, heat the oil and sauté the onions until tender and aromatic.

Then, add the garlic and peppers; cook an additional 1 minute 30 seconds or until fragrant. After that, stir the puréed tomatoes, black beans, broth, salt, black pepper, cayenne pepper, and bay leaves into your Instant Pot.

Secure the lid. Choose the "Bean/Chili" mode and High pressure; cook for 25 minutes. Once cooking is complete, use a natural pressure release; carefully remove the lid.

Garnish with fresh cilantro leaves and serve.

Per serving: 276 Calories; 6.7g Fat; 43.1g Carbs; 13.3g Protein; 9.8g Sugars

119. Classic Lentil Curry

(Ready in about 30 minutes | Servings 3)

Ingredients

1 cups brown lentils, rinsed
1 onion, chopped
1 teaspoon cayenne pepper
2 tablespoons freshly squeezed lime juice
1 tablespoon fresh ginger, peeled and grated
2 garlic cloves, minced

1 teaspoon coconut sugar
12 ounces canned coconut milk
Sea salt and white pepper, to taste
1/2 teaspoon ground turmeric
4 curry leaves
1 tablespoon sesame oil

Directions

Press the "Sauté" button and heat the sesame oil. Once hot, cook the onion until tender and translucent.

Now, add the ginger and garlic and continue to sauté an additional minute or so.

Stir in the coconut sugar, salt, white pepper, ground turmeric, curry leaves, brown lentils, and cayenne pepper. Pour in 2 cups of water.

Secure the lid. Choose the "Manual" mode and cook for 14 minutes at High pressure. Once cooking is complete, use a natural pressure release for 10 minutes; carefully remove the lid.

Now, pour in the coconut milk and press the "Sauté" button. Let it simmer on the lowest setting until thoroughly warmed.

Taste and adjust the seasoning. Serve with a few drizzles of lime juice. Enjoy!

Per serving: 319 Calories; 5.6g Fat; 52.1g Carbs; 7.5g Protein; 6.1g Sugars

120. Rancher's Texas Chili

(Ready in about 35 minutes | Servings 8)

Ingredients

2 pounds red kidney beans, soaked overnight
1 cup onion, chopped
1 cup water
1 teaspoon cayenne pepper
1 teaspoon red chili powder
1 teaspoon Mexican oregano
1 cup chicken stock
3 garlic cloves, smashed
1/2 pound ground pork
1/2 pound ground beef

3 garlic cloves, smashed
2 bell peppers, deveined and chopped
Sea salt and freshly ground black pepper, to taste
1 bay leaf
1 cup Pepper-Jack cheese, grated
1 tablespoon lard
2 cups tomato, puréed
1 cup onion, chopped

Directions

Press the "Sauté" button to preheat your Instant Pot. Now, melt the lard and cook the onion until tender and translucent.

Add the garlic and ground meat; continue to cook until the meat is delicately browned.

Now, stir in the beans, tomato, onion, garlic, peppers, water, stock, salt, black pepper, cayenne pepper, chili powder, oregano and bay leaf.

Secure the lid. Choose the "Bean/Chili" mode and High pressure; cook for 30 minutes. Once cooking is complete, use a natural pressure release; carefully remove the lid.

Ladle into individual bowls; serve topped with grated cheese and enjoy!

Per serving: 300 Calories; 19.1g Fat; 9.7g Carbs; 22g Protein; 2.9g Sugars

121. Italian-Style Heirloom Beans

(Ready in about 45 minutes | Servings 3)

Ingredients

1 pound heirloom beans
1 bell pepper, seeded and chopped
1 tablespoon Italian Seasoning blend

1 jalapeño pepper, seeded and chopped
1 teaspoon granulated garlic
1 teaspoon liquid smoke
1 teaspoon onion powder
4 cups water

Directions

Add all ingredients to the inner pot of your Instant Pot.

Secure the lid. Choose the "Bean/Chili" mode and cook for 30 minutes at High pressure. Once cooking is complete, use a natural pressure release for 10 minutes; carefully remove the lid.

Ladle into serving bowls and garnish with fresh scallions if desired. Bon appétit!

Per serving: 525 Calories; 1.3g Fat; 95.2g Carbs; 36.3g Protein; 5.2g Sugars

122. Warm Red Lentil Salad

(Ready in about 20 minutes | Servings 4)

Ingredients

2 cups red lentils
1 handful fresh cilantro leaves, chopped
1 teaspoon garlic, minced
1 teaspoon sweet paprika
1/2 cup scallions, finely chopped

1 (15-ounce) can tomatoes, crushed
1 bay leaf
1 tablespoon olive oil
1 teaspoon turmeric powder
Sea salt and ground black pepper, to taste

Directions

Add the olive oil, lentils, scallions, garlic, turmeric, salt, black pepper, paprika, tomatoes, and bay leaf to your Instant Pot.

Secure the lid. Choose the "Manual" mode and cook for 12 minutes under High pressure. Once cooking is complete, use a natural release; carefully remove the lid.

Discard the bay leaf and spoon lentil into serving bowls. Serve topped with fresh cilantro. Enjoy!

Per serving: 405 Calories; 5.9g Fat; 67.5g Carbs; 24.5g Protein; 3.8g Sugars

123. Tarragon Green Peas

(Ready in about 20 minutes | Servings 4)

Ingredients

1 (10-oz) bag frozen green peas
2 garlic cloves, minced
1/2 teaspoon dried tarragon
1/2 teaspoon dried dill
1 cups cream of mushroom soup

1 cup tomato sauce
2 teaspoons avocado oil
1 shallot, chopped
2 cup water
Kosher salt and freshly ground black pepper, to taste

Directions

Press the "Sauté" button and heat the oil. Once hot, cook the shallot until tender and translucent; add the garlic to the inner pot and continue sautéing an additional 30 seconds.

Now, stir in the remaining ingredients.

Secure the lid. Choose the "Manual" mode and cook for 12 minutes at High pressure. Once cooking is complete, use a quick pressure release; carefully remove the lid.

Ladle into soup bowls. Bon appétit!

Per serving: 178 Calories; 6g Fat; 24.6g Carbs; 4.9g Protein; 9.7g Sugars

124. Split Pea Sauce

(Ready in about 15 minutes | Servings 8)

Ingredients

1 tablespoon fresh parsley, chopped
1/2 teaspoon paprika
1 tablespoon fresh lemon juice
4 tablespoons extra-virgin olive oil
6 cups vegetable stock

1 teaspoon fresh mint, chopped
1 pound dried split peas, rinsed
Sea salt and freshly ground black pepper, to taste

Directions

Add the split peas and vegetable stock to your Instant Pot.

Secure the lid. Choose the "Manual" mode and cook for 5 minutes under High pressure. Once cooking is complete, use a natural release; carefully remove the lid.

Transfer split peas to your food processor; add the remaining ingredients. Process until everything is creamy and well combined. Serve well chilled. Bon appétit!

Per serving: 79 Calories; 4.5g Fat; 4.4g Carbs; 5.6g Protein; 2.3g Sugars

125. Authentic Tarka Dhal

(Ready in about 20 minutes | Servings 4)

Ingredients

Moong Dal:
4 cups water
1 teaspoon Garam masala
1 teaspoon curry paste
Kosher salt and red pepper, to taste
1 cup moong dal, soaked 2 hours and drained

Tarka:
1 bird eye chili, sliced
3 garlic cloves, pressed
1 white onion, chopped
2 tablespoons butter
1/2 teaspoon cumin seeds

Directions

Add the moong dal, water, curry paste, salt, pepper, and Garam masala to the inner pot.

Secure the lid. Choose the "Manual" mode and cook for 2 minutes at High pressure. Once cooking is complete, use a natural pressure release for 10 minutes; carefully remove the lid.

Melt the butter in a nonstick skillet over medium-high heat. Then, sauté the cumin seeds for 30 seconds or until fragrant.

After that, sauté the garlic, onion, and chili pepper for 4 to 5 minutes or until they have softened. Stir the contents of the skillet into the warm dal.

Bon appétit!

Per serving: 235 Calories; 6.3g Fat; 33.8g Carbs; 12.3g Protein; 2.2g Sugars

126. Classic Lentil Gumbo

(Ready in about 15 minutes | Servings 4)

Ingredients

2 tablespoons sesame oil
1 shallot, chopped
3 cloves garlic, minced
1 teaspoon jalapeño pepper, minced
1 celery stalk, chopped
1 carrot, chopped
1 parsnip, chopped
1/2 teaspoon dried basil
1 teaspoon dried parsley flakes

1 teaspoon red pepper flakes, crushed
1 1/3 cups lentils, regular
4 cups vegetable broth
1 ½ cups fresh or frozen chopped okra
2 ripe tomatoes, chopped
Salt, to taste
1/2 teaspoon ground black pepper
1 teaspoon light brown sugar

Directions

Press the "Sauté" button to preheat the Instant Pot. Heat the oil and now, sauté the shallot until tender and fragrant.

After that, stir in the garlic; cook an additional 30 seconds or until aromatic. Then, stir in the remaining ingredients.

Secure the lid. Choose the "Manual" mode and High pressure; cook for 12 minutes. Once cooking is complete, use a natural pressure release; carefully remove the lid.

Taste, adjust the seasonings and serve warm. Bon appétit!

Per serving: 196 Calories; 8.8g Fat; 22.7g Carbs; 9.6g Protein; 7.7g Sugars

RICE, PASTA & GRAINS

127. Brown Rice Risotto with Olives

(Ready in about 40 minutes | Servings 4)

Ingredients

1 cup brown rice, well-rinsed
1/2 cup black olives, pitted and sliced
1 teaspoon oregano
1 teaspoon basil
2 garlic cloves, smashed

1 bell pepper, seeded and chopped
1/2 cup water
1 teaspoon ancho chili powder
1 tablespoon olive oil
1 shallot, chopped
1 cup tomato, puréed

Directions

Press the "Sauté" button to preheat your Instant Pot. Heat the oil and sauté the onion, garlic, and pepper for 3 minutes.

Add the tomato purée, rice, water, oregano, basil, and chili powder.

Secure the lid. Choose the "Manual" mode and High pressure; cook for 22 minutes. Once cooking is complete, use a natural pressure release for 10 minutes; carefully remove the lid.

Serve topped with black olives. Bon appétit!

Per serving: 238 Calories; 6.7g Fat; 40.1g Carbs; 4.6g Protein; 2.2g Sugars

128. Cajun Rice Chowder

(Ready in about 35 minutes | Servings 4)

Ingredients

4 cups chicken bone broth
1 egg, whisked
1 tablespoon Cajun seasoning
Sea salt and cracked black pepper, to taste
1 onion, chopped
1 carrot, chopped
1 parsnip, chopped

2 bay leaves
1 cup wild rice
1 handful fresh cilantro, chopped
2 cloves garlic, pressed
2 tablespoons cornstarch
2 tablespoons olive oil

Directions

Add the wild rice, broth, vegetables, spices, and olive oil to the inner pot of your Instant Pot.

Secure the lid. Choose the "Soup/Broth" mode and cook for 30 minutes at High pressure. Once cooking is complete, use a quick pressure release; carefully remove the lid.

Mix the cornstarch with 4 tablespoons of water and the whisked egg. Stir the mixture into the cooking liquid.

Press the "Sauté" button and let it simmer for 3 to 4 minutes or until heated through.

Ladle into individual bowls. Top each serving with fresh cilantro and serve warm. Bon appétit!

Per serving: 320 Calories; 11.1g Fat; 41.6g Carbs; 13.8g Protein; 4.1g Sugars

129. Saucy and Peppery Millet

(Ready in about 20 minutes | Servings 4)

Ingredients

1 ½ cups millet
3 cups water
1/2 teaspoon granulated garlic
1 tablespoon olive oil
1 red onion, chopped
1 ancho chili pepper, deveined and chopped
1 teaspoon salt

1/4 teaspoon ground black pepper
1 red bell pepper, deveined and sliced
1 green bell pepper, deveined and sliced
1/4 teaspoon cayenne pepper

Directions

Press the "Sauté" button to preheat your Instant Pot. Then, heat the oil until sizzling; sauté the onions until they are caramelized.

Stir in the peppers and continue to sauté an additional 2 minutes or until they are tender and fragrant.

Add the granulated garlic, salt, black pepper, cayenne pepper, millet, and water.

Secure the lid. Choose the "Manual" mode and High pressure; cook for 5 minutes. Once cooking is complete, use a natural pressure release for 10 minutes; carefully remove the lid.

Lastly, fluff the millet with a fork. Spoon into individual bowls and serve immediately. Bon appétit!

Per serving: 339 Calories; 6.6g Fat; 60.6g Carbs; 9.2g Protein; 2.9g Sugars

130. Creamed Ziti with Mozzarella

(Ready in about 20 minutes | Servings 4)

Ingredients

9 ounces dry ziti pasta
1 cup Mozzarella cheese, shredded
2 garlic cloves, minced
1 ½ cups tomato sauce

1/2 cup double cream
2 cups vegetable broth
Sea salt and ground black pepper, to taste

Directions

Add the broth, double cream, garlic, salt, black pepper, ziti pasta, and tomato sauce to the inner pot.

Secure the lid. Choose the "Manual" mode and cook for 8 minutes at High pressure. Once cooking is complete, use a quick pressure release; carefully remove the lid.

Stir in the Mozzarella cheese and seal the lid; let it sit in the residual heat until the cheese melts. The sauce will thicken as it cools. Bon appétit!

Per serving: 459 Calories; 8.2g Fat; 74.9g Carbs; 19.8g Protein; 13g Sugars

131. Japanese-Style Okayu

(Ready in about 15 minutes | Servings 6)

Ingredients

2 cups white short-grain rice, rinsed
1 teaspoon gochujang
2 tablespoons Shoyu sauce
1 cup white onions, chopped
1 carrot, chopped
1 cup water
2 cups dashi stock
1 teaspoon garlic, minced
Sea salt and ground black pepper, to taste
1 tablespoon sesame oil
1 thumb-size ginger, julienned

Directions

Press the "Sauté" button to preheat your Instant Pot. Then, heat the oil and sauté the onions until translucent.

Add the garlic and ginger; continue to sauté for 30 seconds more. Add the carrot, rice, water, stock, salt, black pepper, and gochujang.

Secure the lid. Choose the "Manual" mode and High pressure; cook for 8 minutes. Once cooking is complete, use a quick pressure release; carefully remove the lid.

After that, add the Shoyu sauce and stir to combine; divide the okayu among 6 serving bowls and serve immediately.

Per serving: 288 Calories; 3.3g Fat; 56.8g Carbs; 6.6g Protein; 1.9g Sugars

132. Basic Breakfast Oatmeal

(Ready in about 25 minutes | Servings 4)

Ingredients

A pinch of grated nutmeg
4 ½ cups water
1 ½ cups steel cut oats
A pinch of kosher salt

Directions

Place all ingredients in the inner pot.

Secure the lid. Choose the "Manual" mode and cook for 3 minutes at High pressure. Once cooking is complete, use a natural pressure release for 20 minutes; carefully remove the lid.

Serve warm with a splash of milk and fruits of choice. Enjoy!

Per serving: 228 Calories; 4.1g Fat; 60.6g Carbs; 9.6g Protein; 0g Sugars

133. Cremini Mushroom Pilau

(Ready in about 15 minutes | Servings 5)

Ingredients

1/2 pound Cremini mushrooms, thinly sliced
2 cups water
2 tablespoons butter
2 cups jasmine rice
2 garlic cloves, minced
1/4 teaspoon kosher salt
1 onion, chopped

Directions

Rinse the rice under cold running water and transfer to the Instant Pot; add water and 1/4 teaspoon of salt.

Secure the lid and select the "Manual" mode. Cook at High pressure for 6 minutes. Once cooking is complete, use a natural release; remove the lid carefully.

Fluff the rice with the rice paddle or fork; reserve.

Press the "Sauté" button and melt the butter. Now, sauté the onion until tender and translucent. Add the garlic and cook an additional minute or until it is fragrant and lightly browned.

Add the Cremini mushrooms and continue to sauté until they are slightly browned. Add the reserved jasmine rice, stir and serve warm. Bon appétit!

Per serving: 335 Calories; 14.9g Fat; 60g Carbs; 11g Protein; 2.3g Sugars

134. Polenta with Feta Cheese

(Ready in about 15 minutes | Servings 4)

Ingredients

4 cups water
8 ounces Feta cheese, crumbled
1/2 teaspoon dried parsley flakes
1 cup polenta
1 teaspoon dried onion flakes
4 tablespoons butter
A pinch of sea salt
1/2 teaspoon red pepper flakes, crushed
1/2 teaspoon oregano

Directions

Add the polenta, water, and salt to the inner pot of your Instant Pot. Press the "Sauté" button and bring the mixture to a simmer. Press the "Cancel" button.

Add the spices to your polenta. Secure the lid. Choose the "Manual" mode and cook for 8 minutes at High pressure. Once cooking is complete, use a quick pressure release; carefully remove the lid.

Stir the butter into the polenta, whisking until it has melted. Add more salt, if needed.

Top with Feta cheese and serve warm.

Per serving: 309 Calories; 23.9g Fat; 14.7g Carbs; 9.4g Protein; 2.7g Sugars

135. Kamut with Sweet Onions

(Ready in about 15 minutes | Servings 4)

Ingredients

1 ½ cups kamut
4 ½ cups water
1/2 teaspoon ground cinnamon
1/2 teaspoon cardamom
Sea salt and ground white pepper, to taste
2 tablespoons olive oil
2 sweet onions, thinly sliced

Directions

Press the "Sauté" button and heat the olive oil. Add the sweet onions, together with the cinnamon and cardamom; sauté until sweet onions are caramelized.

Add the kamut, water, salt, and ground pepper. Now, secure the lid. Choose the "Manual" mode and cook at High pressure for 8 minutes.

Once cooking is complete, use a natural release; remove the lid carefully. Bon appétit!

Per serving: 349 Calories; 8.3g Fat; 62.1g Carbs; 11.5g Protein; 13.7g Sugars

136. Amaranth with Eggs and Cheddar Cheese

(Ready in about 15 minutes | Servings 2)

Ingredients

2 eggs
1/2 cup cheddar cheese, shredded
Sea salt and freshly cracked black pepper, to taste
1 tablespoon olive oil
1/2 cup milk
2 cups water
2 tablespoons fresh chives, roughly chopped
3/4 cup amaranth

Directions

Place the amaranth, water, and milk in the inner pot of your Instant Pot.

Secure the lid. Choose the "Manual" mode and cook for 4 minutes at High pressure. Once cooking is complete, use a quick pressure release; carefully remove the lid. Season with salt and black pepper.

Meanwhile, heat the oil in a skillet over medium-high heat. Then, fry the egg until crispy on the edges.

Divide the cooked amaranth between serving bowls; top with the fried eggs and cheese. Garnish with fresh chives. Bon appétit!

Per serving: 536 Calories; 28.6g Fat; 46.5g Carbs; 24.5g Protein; 8.8g Sugars

137. Mom's Barley with Vegetables

(Ready in about 45 minutes | Servings 4)

Ingredients

1 cup pot barley
1 ½ cups button mushrooms, thinly sliced
1/3 teaspoon freshly ground black pepper
1/2 teaspoon ground bay leaf
1 yellow onion, chopped
2 garlic cloves, minced
1/2 teaspoon salt
1/4 teaspoon paprika
1 tablespoon olive oil
1 carrot, chopped
4 cups stock, preferably homemade

Directions

Press the "Sauté" button and heat up your Instant Pot. Heat olive oil until sizzling. Once hot, sweat onion until tender.

Now, add the garlic, carrot, and mushrooms; cook until the mushrooms start to release their moisture and carrots are softened.

Rinse and drain barley; transfer to the Instant Pot. Add the remaining ingredients; stir to combine.

Select the "Manual" mode and cook for 30 minutes under High pressure. Once cooking is complete, use a natural release for 10 minutes; remove the lid carefully. Bon appétit!

Per serving: 286 Calories; 8.3g Fat; 43.3g Carbs; 11.4g Protein; 2.6g Sugars

138. Traditional Spanish Paella

(Ready in about 25 minutes | Servings 4)

Ingredients

1 cup basmati rice
1 pound tiger prawns, deveined
1 red bell pepper, cut in strips
1 bay leaf
1 tablespoon capers, drained
2 cups chicken broth
1 cup green peas, thawed
1 teaspoon paprika
1/4 teaspoon saffron threads
2 tablespoons ghee, at room temperature
2 cloves garlic, pressed
Sea salt and ground black pepper, to taste

Directions

Press the "Sauté" button and melt the ghee. Once hot, cook the garlic and pepper for about 2 minutes or until just tender and fragrant.

Add the basmati rice, tiger prawns, salt, black pepper, bay leaf, paprika, saffron, capers, and chicken broth to the inner pot.

Secure the lid. Choose the "Manual" mode and cook for 4 minutes at High pressure. Once cooking is complete, use a natural pressure release for 10 minutes; carefully remove the lid.

Add the green peas to the inner pot; press the "Sauté" button one more time and let it simmer until heated through. Enjoy!

Per serving: 389 Calories; 7.8g Fat; 48.1g Carbs; 31.2g Protein; 2.7g Sugars

139. Tangy Wild Rice Soup

(Ready in about 35 minutes | Servings 4)

Ingredients

1 cup wild rice
1 celery stalk, chopped
6 cups water, bone broth, or a combination
1/2 teaspoon granulated garlic
2 tablespoons olive oil
2 carrots, halved lengthwise and finely sliced
1 onion, chopped
1/4 cup freshly squeezed lime juice
2 tablespoons bouillon granules

Directions

Press the "Sauté" button to preheat the Instant Pot. Then, heat the oil; sauté the onions until tender and translucent.

Now, stir in the carrots and celery; continue to sauté until tender.

Add the rice, water, granulated garlic, and bouillon granules to the Instant Pot.

Secure the lid. Choose the "Soup" mode and High pressure; cook for 30 minutes. Once cooking is complete, use a natural pressure release; carefully remove the lid.

Ladle into soup bowls; drizzle each serving with fresh lime juice. Enjoy!

Per serving: 236 Calories; 7.7g Fat; 36.7g Carbs; 6.9g Protein; 3.2g Sugars

140. Pilaf with Petite Peas and Peanuts

(Ready in about 30 minutes | Servings 4)

Ingredients

2 tablespoons peanut oil
1 tomato, pureed
1 ½ cups vegetable broth
2 cloves garlic, minced
1 teaspoon cayenne pepper
1 bay leaf
1/2 cup frozen petite peas, thawed
1 cup white rice
1 Vidalia onion, chopped
1/2 cup peanuts, dry roasted and roughly chopped
Sea salt and ground black pepper, to taste

Directions

Add the white rice, peanut oil, Vidalia onion, garlic, cayenne pepper, salt, black pepper, tomato, vegetable broth, and bay leaf to the inner pot.

Secure the lid. Choose the "Manual" mode and cook for 5 minutes at High pressure. Once cooking is complete, use a natural pressure release for 20 minutes; carefully remove the lid.

Now, stir in the thawed petite peas and seal the lid. Let it sit in the residual heat until everything is heated through.

Serve with roasted peanuts and enjoy!

Per serving: 473 Calories; 19.5g Fat; 63g Carbs; 14.6g Protein; 8.9g Sugars

141. Spanish Rice with Chorizo Sausage

(Ready in about 20 minutes | Servings 4)

Ingredients

1 cup white long-grain rice
1/2 pound Chorizo sausage, sliced
1 yellow onion, chopped
1/4 cup lightly packed fresh coriander, roughly chopped
2 carrots, trimmed and chopped
1 cup black olives, pitted and sliced
2 tablespoons butter, melted
2 cups chicken stock
Sea salt and ground black pepper, to taste

Directions

Press the "Sauté" button to preheat your Instant Pot. Now, melt the butter and cook the onion until aromatic.

Then, add the carrot and Chorizo; cook an additional 2 minutes. Add the remaining ingredients and stir to combine well.

Secure the lid. Choose the "Manual" mode and High pressure; cook for 3 minutes. Once cooking is complete, use a natural pressure release for 10 minutes; carefully remove the lid.

Ladle into individual bowls and serve warm. Bon appétit!

Per serving: 576 Calories; 34.7g Fat; 44.8g Carbs; 20.5g Protein; 2.3g Sugars

142. Tangy Farro Salad

(Ready in about 15 minutes | Servings 4)

Ingredients

2 tablespoons fresh parsley leaves, chopped
1 Walla Walla onion, chopped
4 tablespoons extra-virgin olive oil
1 tablespoon fresh lime juice
1 ¼ cups farro, semi-pearled and rinsed
1 cup cherry tomatoes, halved
2 green garlic stalks, minced
Salt and ground black pepper, to taste
3 cups water

Directions

Add the rinsed farro and water to your Instant Pot.

Secure the lid. Choose the "Manual" mode and High pressure; cook for 10 minutes. Once cooking is complete, use a quick pressure release; carefully remove the lid.

Drain well; allow it to cool completely. Add the onion, tomatoes, garlic, salt, and pepper; toss to combine.

Toss with the olive oil, lime juice, and parsley leaves. Bon appétit!

Per serving: 329 Calories; 6.8g Fat; 61.3g Carbs; 7.6g Protein; 9.9g Sugars

143. Authentic Asian Congee

(Ready in about 35 minutes | Servings 3)

Ingredients

2 tablespoons chili oil
1 teaspoon fresh ginger, grated
2 tablespoons soy sauce
1 cup sushi rice, rinsed

1 cup pao cai
Kosher salt and ground black pepper, to taste
6 cups roasted vegetable broth

Directions

Place the rice, vegetable broth, ginger, and salt in the inner pot of the Instant Pot.

Secure the lid. Choose the "Multigrain" mode and cook for 20 minutes at High pressure. Once cooking is complete, use a natural pressure release for 10 minutes; carefully remove the lid.

Your congee will thicken as it cools. Stir in the black pepper, soy sauce, and chili oil. Serve garnished with pao cai and enjoy!

Per serving: 326 Calories; 22.5g Fat; 26.8g Carbs; 16.4g Protein; 4.1g Sugars

144. Pakistani Basmati Rice

(Ready in about 30 minutes | Servings 4)

Ingredients

1 ½ cups basmati rice, rinsed
2 black cardamoms
2 green cardamoms
2 garlic cloves, minced
Sea salt and white pepper, to taste
1 teaspoon coriander seeds

2 tez patta (bay leaf)
1 teaspoon turmeric powder
1 shallot, chopped
2 tablespoons ghee
1 cup sweet corn kernels, thawed
2 cups vegetable broth

Directions

Press the "Sauté" button and melt the ghee. Once hot, cook the shallot for 4 minutes or until just tender and fragrant. Stir in the garlic and cook an additional minute or until aromatic.

Now, add the basmati rice, broth, and spices.

Secure the lid. Choose the "Manual" mode and cook for 4 minutes at High pressure. Once cooking is complete, use a natural pressure release for 15 minutes; carefully remove the lid.

Add the sweet corn kernels and seal the lid again. Let it sit in the residual heat until thoroughly heated. Enjoy!

Per serving: 392 Calories; 7.3g Fat; 72.2g Carbs; 9.2g Protein; 0.9g Sugars

145. Sweet Couscous with Almonds and Pears

(Ready in about 15 minutes | Servings 4)

Ingredients

1/3 cup almonds, slivered
2 medium-sized pears, cored and diced
A pinch of salt
1/3 teaspoon ground cinnamon

1/2 teaspoon freshly grated nutmeg
1 teaspoon pure vanilla extract
1/3 cup honey
1/4 teaspoon ground cloves
3 cups water
1 ½ cups couscous, well rinsed

Directions

Place all of the above ingredients, except for the almonds, into your Instant Pot; stir to combine well.

Secure the lid. Choose the "Manual" mode and High pressure; cook for 8 minutes. Once cooking is complete, use a quick pressure release; carefully remove the lid.

Serve topped with the slivered almonds. Bon appétit!

Per serving: 207 Calories; 0.3g Fat; 50g Carbs; 2.6g Protein; 31.8g Sugars

146. Greek Rizogalo with Cinnamon

(Ready in about 30 minutes | Servings 4)

Ingredients

1 ½ cups white rice
1 teaspoon ground cinnamon
2 ounces sugar
1 teaspoon vanilla extract

2 tablespoons butter
4 tablespoons honey
4 cups milk
1 (3-inch strip) of lemon rind

Directions

Place the butter, rice, milk, sugar, lemon rind, and vanilla extract in the inner pot.

Secure the lid. Choose the "Rice" mode and cook for 10 minutes at Low pressure. Once cooking is complete, use a natural pressure release for 15 minutes; carefully remove the lid.

Ladle your rizogalo into four serving bowls; top with cinnamon and honey and serve at room temperature.

Per serving: 550 Calories; 14.7g Fat; 91.6g Carbs; 12.6g Protein; 31.5g Sugars

147. Sweet Brioche Bread Pudding

(Ready in about 40 minutes | Servings 6)

Ingredients

1 large brioche loaf, torn into pieces
1/4 cup sultanas, soaked in rum
1/4 cup white chocolate chips
1/2 teaspoon ground cinnamon
1/4 teaspoon grated nutmeg
2 tablespoons coconut oil, melted
1/4 cup Turbinado sugar
1 cup water
2 eggs, whisked
1/3 cup buttermilk
1 teaspoon vanilla paste

Directions

In a mixing dish, thoroughly combine the eggs, buttermilk, cinnamon, nutmeg, vanilla, and melted coconut oil.

Add the brioche and let it soak for 20 minutes; press the bread lightly with the back of a large spoon.

Stir in the chocolate chips, Turbinado sugar, and sultanas; stir gently to combine. Then, lightly grease a baking pan with a nonstick cooking spray.

Pour water into the base of your Instant Pot; add a metal trivet. Lower the baking pan onto the trivet. Secure the lid.

Choose the "Manual" mode, High pressure, and 15 minutes. Once cooking is complete, use a quick release; remove the lid carefully. Bon appétit!

Per serving: 337 Calories; 13g Fat; 42.4g Carbs; 12.1g Protein; 10.8g Sugars

148. Rice and Chicken Bake

(Ready in about 50 minutes | Servings 4)

Ingredients

1 cup wild rice
2 cups chicken breasts, cut into chunks
1 cup sour cream
1 onion, chopped
1 teaspoon garlic, minced
1 cup tomato sauce
Sea salt and ground black pepper, to taste
2 cup goat cheese, crumbled
2 tablespoons butter
2 celery ribs, chopped
1 cup cream of celery soup

Directions

Press the "Sauté" button and melt the butter. Once hot, cook the chicken until it is no longer pink; reserve.

Now, sauté the onion in the pan drippings until tender. Then, add the celery and garlic; continue to sauté an additional minute or so.

Add the wild rice, cream of celery soup, tomato sauce, salt, and black pepper to the inner pot. Stir in the reserved chicken.

Secure the lid. Choose the "Manual" mode and cook for 30 minutes at High pressure. Once cooking is complete, use a natural pressure release for 15 minutes; carefully remove the lid.

Mix the sour cream with the goat cheese; place the cheese mixture over your casserole. Let it sit, covered, for 10 minutes before serving. Bon appétit!

Per serving: 489 Calories; 20.1g Fat; 42.5g Carbs; 36.3g Protein; 5.2g Sugars

149. Greek-Style Oats

(Ready in about 15 minutes | Servings 3)

Ingredients

1/2 cup feta cheese, crumbled
Ground black pepper, to your liking
2 3/4 cups water
1/2 cup Kalamata olives, pitted and sliced
1/3 teaspoon cayenne pepper
1 rosemary sprig, leaves picked and chopped
1 ½ cups oats, quick cooking
2 tablespoons flax seeds
1/2 teaspoon sea salt

Directions

Add the quick cooking oats and water to your Instant Pot. Add the flax seeds, cayenne pepper, rosemary, salt, and black pepper. Secure the lid.

Choose the "Manual" button and cook for 6 minutes at High pressure. Once cooking is complete, use a natural release; remove the lid carefully.

Ladle the prepared oatmeal into individual bowls. Top with crumbled feta cheese and sliced olives and serve. Enjoy!

Per serving: 244 Calories; 14g Fat; 35.3g Carbs; 13.1g Protein; 1.8g Sugars

150. Basic Japanese Sushi Rice

(Ready in about 30 minutes | Servings 4)

Ingredients

1 tablespoon brown sugar
2 tablespoons soy sauce
1 ½ cups water
1/4 cup rice vinegar
1/2 teaspoon salt
1 ½ cups sushi rice, rinsed

Directions

Place the sushi rice and water in the inner pot of your Instant Pot.

Secure the lid. Choose the "Rice" mode and cook for 10 minutes at Low pressure. Once cooking is complete, use a natural pressure release for 15 minutes; carefully remove the lid.

Meanwhile, whisk the rice vinegar, sugar, salt and soy sauce in a mixing dish; microwave the sauce for 1 minute.

Pour the sauce over the sushi rice; stir to combine. Assemble your sushi rolls and enjoy!

Per serving: 291 Calories; 1.9g Fat; 60.7g Carbs; 5.1g Protein; 3.5g Sugars

151. Sweet Kamut with Cherries

(Ready in about 45 minutes | Servings 4)

Ingredients

1/3 cup honey
1 cup sour cream
1 cup dried cherries
1/4 teaspoon grated nutmeg
4 ½ cups water

A pinch of salt
2 tablespoons butter
1/2 teaspoon ground cinnamon
1 ½ cups kamut, well-rinsed

Directions

Add the kamut, water, and salt to your Instant Pot.

Secure the lid. Choose the "Multigrain" mode and High pressure; cook for 40 minutes. Once cooking is complete, use a natural pressure release; carefully remove the lid.

Now, add the butter, nutmeg, cinnamon and cherries to the Instant Pot; stir to combine and divide the porridge between four serving bowls.

Top each serving with sour cream; drizzle honey over the top and serve. Enjoy!

Per serving: 473 Calories; 13.4g Fat; 82.1g Carbs; 12.7g Protein; 33.2g Sugars

152. Spelt Risotto with Mushrooms and Spinach

(Ready in about 35 minutes | Servings 3)

Ingredients

1 cup spelt grains
1 cup cremini mushrooms, sliced
1 leek, chopped
1 teaspoon garlic, minced

Sea salt and white pepper, to taste
1 tablespoon oyster sauce
1 cup spinach leaves
2 tablespoons olive oil
2 cups water

Directions

Press the "Sauté" button and heat the oil until sizzling. Then, sauté the leek for 3 to 4 minutes or until tender.

Add the garlic and mushrooms and cook an additional 2 minutes or until they are fragrant. Reserve the sautéed mixture.

Add the spelt grains, water, salt, pepper, and oyster sauce to the inner pot.

Secure the lid. Choose the "Porridge" mode and cook for 30 minutes at High pressure. Once cooking is complete, use a quick pressure release; carefully remove the lid.

Afterwards, stir in the spinach leaves and seal the lid; let it sit until the leaves wilt. Serve topped with the sautéed mushroom mixture. Bon appétit!

Per serving: 307 Calories; 10.5g Fat; 47.7g Carbs; 9.6g Protein; 5.9g Sugars

153. Barley and Chickpea Salad with Cheese

(Ready in about 15 minutes | Servings 4)

Ingredients

1/2 cup canned chickpea, rinsed
4 ounces feta cheese, crumbled
1 cup pickles, diced
3 cups water
1 leek, thinly sliced
2 cloves garlic, crushed

1/2 cup fresh parsley, chopped
2 tablespoons lime juice, freshly squeezed
1 ½ cups pearl barley
4 tablespoons extra-virgin olive oil
Sea salt and ground black pepper, to taste

Directions

Add the barley and water to the Instant Pot.

Secure the lid. Choose the "Manual" mode and High pressure; cook for 9 minutes. Once cooking is complete, use a natural pressure release; carefully remove the lid.

Allow the barley to cool completely; then, transfer it to a salad bowl. Add the remaining ingredients and toss to combine well. Place in your refrigerator until ready to serve. Enjoy!

Per serving: 582 Calories; 22.1g Fat; 81g Carbs; 17.6g Protein; 6.4g Sugars

154. Creamed Corn with Cottage Cheese

(Ready in about 15 minutes | Servings 3)

Ingredients

1/2 cup double cream
6 ounces Cottage cheese, at room temperature
Kosher salt and ground black pepper, to taste
1/2 teaspoon red pepper flakes

2 tablespoons cold butter, cut into pieces
1/2 teaspoon dried parsley flakes
2 cups corn kernels
1 cup water

Directions

Put all ingredients into the inner pot of your Instant Pot; stir to combine.

Secure the lid. Choose the "Manual" mode and cook for 4 minutes at High pressure. Once cooking is complete, use a quick pressure release; carefully remove the lid.

Ladle into serving bowls and enjoy!

Per serving: 279 Calories; 19.3g Fat; 19.8g Carbs; 10g Protein; 5.6g Sugars

155. Aromatic Amaranth Porridge with Almonds

(Ready in about 15 minutes | Servings 4)

Ingredients

1/2 cup almonds, slivered
1 cup soy milk
1/3 teaspoon cinnamon, ground

2 cups water
1/2 teaspoon ground cloves
1 ¼ cups amaranth
1/3 cup honey

Directions

Place the amaranth, water, milk, cinnamon, cloves and honey in your Instant Pot.

Secure the lid. Choose the "Manual" mode and High pressure; cook for 8 minutes. Once cooking is complete, use a natural pressure release; carefully remove the lid.

Ladle into individual bowls; top with the slivered almonds and serve warm. Bon appétit!

Per serving: 347 Calories; 6.3g Fat; 65.5g Carbs; 10.2g Protein; 27.1g Sugars

156. Festive Mac 'n' Cheese

(Ready in about 20 minutes | Servings 4)

Ingredients

2 cups dried elbow pasta
1 tablespoon flaxseed meal
1 shallot, chopped
2 garlic cloves, minced
1 cup cream cheese
Kosher salt and ground black pepper, to taste
1 teaspoon cayenne pepper

1 pound chicken drumsticks, boneless and cut into small cubes
2 cups chicken bone broth, preferably homemade
2 tablespoons olive oil
1 bell pepper, seeded and chopped
1 habanero pepper, seeded and chopped

Directions

Press the "Sauté" button and heat the olive oil. Once hot, brown the chicken drumsticks for 3 to 4 minutes, stirring frequently to ensure even cooking.

Add the shallot, garlic, and peppers; continue to cook an additional 3 minute or until they have softened.

Add the salt, black pepper, cayenne pepper, broth, and pasta to the inner pot.

Secure the lid. Choose the "Manual" mode and cook for 6 minutes at High pressure. Once cooking is complete, use a quick pressure release; carefully remove the lid.

Add the cream cheese and flaxseed meal; stir to combine and press the "Sauté" button; let it cook for a few minutes longer or until your sauce has reduced slightly and the flavors have concentrated. Bon appétit!

Per serving: 608 Calories; 39.1g Fat; 32.3g Carbs; 31.2g Protein; 3.9g Sugars

157. Spicy and Saucy Bulgur Wheat

(Ready in about 25 minutes | Servings 4)

Ingredients

1 ¼ cups bulgur wheat
1 yellow onion, chopped
1/2 cup Pico de gallo
2 garlic cloves, minced

Sea salt and white pepper, to taste
1 teaspoon smoked paprika
2 tablespoons vegetable oil
3 cups roasted vegetable broth

Directions

Press the "Sauté" button to preheat your Instant Pot. Now, sauté the onions with garlic for 1 minute or so.

Then, stir the bulgur wheat, broth, salt, pepper, and paprika into your Instant Pot.

Secure the lid. Choose the "Manual" mode and High pressure; cook for 12 minutes. Once cooking is complete, use a natural pressure release for 10 minutes; carefully remove the lid.

Serve topped with chilled Pico de gallo. Bon appétit!

Per serving: 184 Calories; 10.4g Fat; 17.8g Carbs; 6g Protein; 3.8g Sugars

158. Risotto Salad with Fruits

(Ready in about 30 minutes | Servings 4)

Ingredients

1/4 cup dried cranberries
1 3/4 cups water
1/2 cup pecans
2 tablespoons pomegranate arils
1 tablespoon orange zest
1/4 cup orange juice, freshly squeezed

1 cup grapes, cut in half
1/2 teaspoon table salt
4 tablespoons extra-virgin olive oil
1 ½ cups long-grain white rice, rinsed

Directions

Place the rice, water, and salt in the inner pot of your Instant Pot; stir to combine.

Secure the lid. Choose the "Rice" mode and cook for 10 minutes. Once cooking is complete, use a natural pressure release for 15 minutes; carefully remove the lid.

Fluff the rice with a fork and allow it to cool to room temperature.

Add the remaining ingredients to a nice salad bowl; add the chilled rice. Toss to combine and serve chilled or at room temperature. Bon appétit!

Per serving: 544 Calories; 23.6g Fat; 77.9g Carbs; 6.5g Protein; 14.1g Sugars

159. Barley, Chicken and Vegetable Soup

(Ready in about 40 minutes | Servings 6)

Ingredients

1 1/3 cups barley, pearled
1 ½ pounds chicken drumettes
1 onion, chopped
1/2 cup white wine
1/2 teaspoon sea salt
1/3 teaspoon freshly ground black pepper
2 parsnips, trimmed and sliced
2 carrots, trimmed and sliced
6 cups chicken broth, preferably homemade
2 bay leaves
1 celery stalk, chopped
2 cloves garlic, minced
1 tablespoon butter, melted

Directions

Press the "Sauté" button to heat up the Instant Pot. Now, melt the butter. Once hot, sear the chicken drumettes on all sides for 3 to 4 minutes. Discard the bones and reserve.

Then, sweat the onion until it is translucent.

Add the parsnips, carrots, and celery; cook an additional 3 minute or until the vegetables have softened. After that, stir in garlic and cook an additional 30 seconds.

Add the remaining ingredients and secure the lid. Choose "Soup" setting and cook at High pressure for 30 minutes.

Once cooking is complete, use a natural release; remove the lid carefully. Add the reserved chicken and stir to combine. Ladle into individual bowls and serve hot.

Per serving: 379 Calories; 5.9g Fat; 48.8g Carbs; 33.2g Protein; 5.3g Sugars

160. Italian Mushrooms Risotto with Cheese

(Ready in about 30 minutes | Servings 4)

Ingredients

1 cup Arborio rice
1/2 cup Romano cheese, grated
2 cups Cremini mushrooms, chopped
1 teaspoon garlic, minced
1/3 cup Sauvignon Blanc
1/2 teaspoon basil
1 teaspoon thyme
Sea salt and ground black pepper, to taste
4 cups vegetable broth
2 tablespoons olive oil
1 onion, chopped

Directions

Press the "Sauté" button and heat the olive oil until sizzling. Then, cook the onion until tender and translucent.

Now, stir in the garlic and mushrooms; cook until they are just tender or about 3 minutes.

Add the basil, thyme, salt, black pepper, Sauvignon Blanc, rice, and vegetable broth.

Secure the lid. Choose the "Manual" mode and cook for 4 minutes at High pressure. Once cooking is complete, use a natural pressure release for 15 minutes; carefully remove the lid.

Divide between individual bowls and serve garnished with Romano cheese. Bon appétit!

Per serving: 296 Calories; 19.5g Fat; 21.6g Carbs; 14.9g Protein; 3.3g Sugars

161. Buckwheat Breakfast Bowl

(Ready in about 20 minutes | Servings 5)

Ingredients

1 ½ cups buckwheat
2/3 cup sultanas
1 ½ cups water
1/2 teaspoon coconut extract
1 ½ cups coconut milk
1/2 teaspoon ground cinnamon
3/4 cup agave syrup
2 teaspoons coconut butter
A pinch of salt
A pinch of grated nutmeg

Directions

Press the "Sauté" button to preheat your Instant Pot. Now, melt the butter and toast the buckwheat, stirring frequently, until it is aromatic or about 3 minutes.

Add the remaining ingredients and stir to combine well.

Secure the lid. Choose the "Manual" mode and High pressure; cook for 3 minutes. Once cooking is complete, use a natural pressure release for 10 minutes; carefully remove the lid. Serve right away.

Per serving: 371 Calories; 19.1g Fat; 53.6g Carbs; 3.3g Protein; 42.1g Sugars

162. Shrimp Risotto with Herbs

(Ready in about 50 minutes | Servings 4)

Ingredients

1 pound shrimp, deveined
2 tablespoons fresh chives
1 cup wild rice
1 cup chicken broth
1 rosemary sprig
1 thyme sprig
1/2 teaspoon ground black pepper
1 teaspoon garlic, minced
2 bell peppers, chopped
1/2 teaspoon cayenne pepper
2 tablespoons olive oil
1 leek, chopped
1 teaspoon kosher salt

Directions

Press the "Sauté" button and heat the olive oil. Once hot, sauté the leek until just tender or about 3 minutes.

Then, stir in the garlic and peppers. Continue to cook for 3 minutes more or until they are tender and fragrant.

Add the wild rice, broth, and seasonings to the inner pot.

Secure the lid. Choose the "Manual" mode and cook for 30 minutes at High pressure. Once cooking is complete, use a natural pressure release for 10 minutes; carefully remove the lid.

Add the shrimp to the inner pot.

Choose the "Manual" mode and cook for 3 minutes at High pressure. Once cooking is complete, use a quick pressure release; carefully remove the lid.

Serve garnished with fresh chives and enjoy!

Per serving: 334 Calories; 8.5g Fat; 36.1g Carbs; 30.9g Protein; 3.1g Sugars

163. Classic Nutty Oatmeal with Banana

(Ready in about 25 minutes | Servings 4)

Ingredients

5 ½ cups water
1/2 cup walnuts, chopped
1/4 teaspoon grated nutmeg
2 bananas
2 cups steel cut oats
1/2 teaspoon ground cinnamon
1/4 teaspoon cardamom

Directions

Add the steel cut oats to your Instant Pot. Pour in the water. Add the cinnamon, cardamom, and nutmeg.

Secure the lid. Choose the "Manual" mode and cook for 10 minutes under High pressure.

Once cooking is complete, use a natural release for 10 minutes; remove the lid carefully. Ladle into serving bowls.

Top with bananas and walnuts. Bon appétit!

Per serving: 244 Calories; 10.1g Fat; 48.4g Carbs; 10.4g Protein; 9.2g Sugars

164. Smoked Salmon and Green Bean Pilau

(Ready in about 20 minutes | Servings 4)

Ingredients

1 cup white rice
1 pound smoked salmon steak
4 ounces green beans
1 cup vegetable broth
1 onion, chopped
2 cloves garlic, minced
1/2 cup milk
Sea salt and ground black pepper, to season
1 tablespoon butter

Directions

Press the "Sauté" button and melt the butter. When the butter starts to sizzle, add the onion; sauté the onion until just tender and fragrant.

Now, stir in the garlic and continue to sauté an additional minute or until fragrant.

Add the rice, broth, milk, salmon, and green beans; season with salt and black pepper.

Secure the lid. Choose the "Manual" mode and cook for 4 minutes at High pressure. Once cooking is complete, use a natural pressure release for 10 minutes; carefully remove the lid. Bon appétit!

Per serving: 340 Calories; 18.6g Fat; 20.6g Carbs; 30.2g Protein; 3.3g Sugars

165. Cheesy Polenta with Mushrooms and Olives

(Ready in about 15 minutes | Servings 3)

Ingredients

1 cup polenta
2 garlic cloves, smashed
1 pound Crimini mushrooms, thinly sliced
1 cup Kalamata olives, pitted and sliced
6 ounces feta cheese, crumbled
1/2 teaspoon dried oregano
1 teaspoon cayenne pepper
2 cups water
2 cups vegetable broth
1/2 teaspoon dried basil
1/2 teaspoon dried dill weed
2 tablespoons butter, at room temperature
1 cup scallions, chopped
Sea salt and freshly ground black pepper, to taste

Directions

Press the "Sauté" button to preheat your Instant Pot. Now, melt the butter and cook the scallions until tender.

Stir in the garlic and mushrooms; cook an additional 40 seconds or until aromatic.

Then, add the herbs, salt, black pepper, and cayenne pepper. Add a splash of water to deglaze the pot; reserve the mushroom mixture. Press the "Cancel" button.

Add the water and broth. Press the "Sauté" button again. Slowly and gradually, pour the polenta into the liquid; make sure to whisk continuously.

Secure the lid. Choose the "Manual" mode and High pressure; cook for 5 minutes. Once cooking is complete, use a quick pressure release; carefully remove the lid.

Top the warm polenta with the mushroom mixture, olives, and feta cheese. Serve immediately.

Per serving: 420 Calories; 26.2g Fat; 32.1g Carbs; 17.8g Protein; 6.3g Sugars

166. Italian Chicken and Rice Casserole

(Ready in about 30 minutes | Servings 4)

Ingredients

1 chicken breast, skinless
1 cup white rice
1 teaspoon Italian seasoning blend
1 shallot, sliced
1 teaspoon garlic, minced
1 teaspoon paprika
3 tablespoons butter, melted
1 pound broccoli florets
1 cup tomato puree
5 ounces cheddar cheese, shredded
Kosher salt and freshly ground pepper, to taste
2 cups chicken broth

Directions

Press the "Sauté" button and melt 1 tablespoon of butter. Once hot, cook the chicken breast until it is golden brown on both sides.

Shred the chicken with two forks. Add it back to the inner pot. Add the shallots, garlic, broccoli, rice, tomato puree, and chicken broth; stir in the remaining butter.

Season with the paprika, Italian seasonings, salt, and black pepper.

Secure the lid. Choose the "Rice" mode and cook for 10 minutes at Low pressure. Once cooking is complete, use a natural pressure release for 10 minutes; carefully remove the lid.

Top with cheese. Seal the lid again and let it sit in the residual heat until the cheese melts. Serve immediately.

Per serving: 563 Calories; 21.2g Fat; 56.5g Carbs; 36.5g Protein; 6.7g Sugars

167. Old-Fashioned Oatmeal with Figs

(Ready in about 25 minutes | Servings 3)

Ingredients

3 fresh or dried figs, chopped
1 cup water
1/2 cup walnuts, chopped or ground
1/2 cup coconut milk
1/2 teaspoon star anise
2 tablespoons honey
1 cup steel cut oats
2 tablespoons coconut flakes

Directions

Add the steel cut oats, water, milk, coconut flakes, anise, and honey to your Instant Pot.

Secure the lid. Choose the "Manual" mode and High pressure; cook for 10 minutes. Once cooking is complete, use a natural pressure release for 12 minutes; carefully remove the lid.

Divide the oatmeal among 3 serving bowls; top each serving with chopped figs and walnuts. Bon appétit!

Per serving: 270 Calories; 13.3g Fat; 43g Carbs; 9.2g Protein; 19.6g Sugars

168. Pilaf with Vegetables and Cheese

(Ready in about 25 minutes | Servings 4)

Ingredients

1 onion, chopped
1/2 cup Swiss cheese, shredded
1/2 cup Manchego cheese, shredded
1 cup carrots, chopped
1/2 teaspoon dried dill weed
2 cups roasted vegetable broth
1 cup celery ribs, chopped
1 cup white rice, rinsed
Sea salt and ground black pepper, to taste

Directions

Add the rice, onion, carrots, celery, salt, black pepper, dill, and vegetable broth to the inner pot.

Secure the lid. Choose the "Manual" mode and cook for 5 minutes at High pressure. Once cooking is complete, use a natural pressure release for 15 minutes; carefully remove the lid.

After that, stir in the cheese; stir well to combine and seal the lid. Let it sit in the residual heat until the cheese melts. Bon appétit!

Per serving: 444 Calories; 14.3g Fat; 48.7g Carbs; 27.2g Protein; 4.3g Sugars

169. Warm Winter Chocolate Oatmeal

(Ready in about 15 minutes | Servings 4)

Ingredients

2 tablespoons almond butter
1/2 cup chocolate chips
2 cups water
1 teaspoon cinnamon, ground
1 ½ cups regular oats
2 cups almond milk

Directions

Simply throw the oats, water, milk, and cinnamon into the Instant Pot.

Secure the lid. Choose the "Manual" mode and High pressure; cook for 10 minutes. Once cooking is complete, use a quick pressure release; carefully remove the lid.

Divide the oatmeal between serving bowls; top with almond butter and chocolate chips. Enjoy!

Per serving: 347 Calories; 12.1g Fat; 51.3g Carbs; 8.7g Protein; 25.1g Sugars

170. Arroz Estilo Mexicano

(Ready in about 35 minutes | Servings 4)

Ingredients

1 cup long grain rice, rinsed
1 cup Mexican blend cheese, shredded
1 cup sweet corn, frozen and thawed
1 cup vegetable broth
1/2 teaspoon cumin powder
1/3 teaspoon Mexican oregano
1 habanero pepper, seeded and minced
1 cup pinto beans, boiled
1 cup enchilada sauce
A small handful of cilantro, roughly chopped
1 tablespoon canola oil
2 garlic cloves, minced
1 sweet pepper, seeded and chopped
1 onion, chopped
Sea salt and ground black pepper, to taste

Directions

Press the "Sauté" button to preheat your Instant Pot and add the oil. Once hot, cook the onion, garlic, and peppers until they are just tender and fragrant.

Next, add the vegetable broth followed by rice, beans, corn, cumin powder, oregano, salt, black pepper, and enchilada sauce; do not stir.

Secure the lid. Choose the "Manual" mode and cook for 5 minutes at High pressure. Once cooking is complete, use a natural pressure release for 15 minutes; carefully remove the lid.

After that, stir in the Mexican blend cheese and seal the lid again. Let it sit in the residual heat for 5 to 10 minutes until the cheese melts.

Serve with fresh cilantro and enjoy!

Per serving: 559 Calories; 15.3g Fat; 83.4g Carbs; 24.1g Protein; 6.5g Sugars

171. Cheese Cilantro Cornbread

(Ready in about 35 minutes | Servings 8)

Ingredients

1 ½ cups cornmeal
3/4 cup fresh corn kernels
2 eggs
1 cup milk
1 teaspoon baking soda
2 tablespoons pure maple syrup
1 teaspoon baking powder
1/2 teaspoon kosher salt
1/2 teaspoon dried basil
1/4 teaspoon dried oregano
1/2 teaspoon ground allspice

1 cup Pepper-Jack cheese, grated
1/4 teaspoon cayenne pepper
2 tablespoons cilantro, roughly chopped
1/2 teaspoon lime juice
1/2 stick butter, melted
1/2 cup all-purpose flour
1 cup water
1/4 teaspoon black pepper, or more to taste

Directions

Add water and a metal trivet to the base of your Instant Pot. Lightly grease a baking pan that fits in your Instant Pot.

In a mixing bowl, thoroughly combine the cornmeal, flour, baking soda, baking powder, salt, black pepper, cayenne pepper, basil, oregano, and allspice.

Stir in the Pepper-Jack cheese, corn kernels, and cilantro. Mix to combine well.

In another mixing bowl, whisk the remaining ingredients; add this wet mixture to the dry mixture.

Pour the batter into the prepared baking pan. Cover with a paper towel; then, top with foil.

Lower the pan onto the trivet and secure the lid. Choose the "Manual" mode, High pressure, and 23 minutes. Once cooking is complete, use a natural release; remove the lid carefully.

Serve immediately and enjoy!

Per serving: 318 Calories; 14.3g Fat; 37.2g Carbs; 9.9g Protein; 5.6g Sugars

172. Hearty Beef Stew with Rice

(Ready in about 30 minutes | Servings 4)

Ingredients

1 cup brown rice
1 pound beef stew meat, cut into bite-sized chunks
1 bay leaf
1 teaspoon dried oregano
1 teaspoon dried rosemary
2 tablespoons cornstarch, dissolved in 1/4 cup cold water
2 garlic cloves, minced

2 sweet peppers, deveined and chopped
1 teaspoon dried basil
Sea salt and ground black pepper, to taste
2 tablespoons lard, at room temperature
4 cups beef bone broth
1 onion, chopped
1 red chili pepper, chopped

Directions

Press the "Sauté" button and melt the lard. When the lard starts to sizzle, add the beef stew meat and cook until browned on all sides; reserve.

Add a splash of beef broth to the inner pot; use a spoon to scrape the brown bits from the bottom of the pan.

Then, sauté the onion, garlic, and peppers for about 3 minutes or until they are just tender.

Add the other ingredients and stir to combine.

Secure the lid. Choose the "Soup/Broth" mode and cook for 20 minutes at High pressure. Once cooking is complete, use a quick pressure release; carefully remove the lid.

Mix the cornstarch with cold water in a small bowl; stir the slurry into the stew and cook on the "Sauté" function until the cooking liquid has thickened.

Serve warm and enjoy!

Per serving: 291 Calories; 1.9g Fat; 60.7g Carbs; 5.1g Protein; 3.5g Sugars

173. Rustic Pecorino Romano Risotto

(Ready in about 10 minutes | Servings 5)

Ingredients

1 cup Pecorino-Romano cheese, freshly grated
1 ½ cups Romano rice
1/2 cup tomatoes, puréed
1 tablespoon toasted sesame oil
2 tablespoons tomato ketchup

3 cups water
1 yellow onion, chopped
2 cloves garlic, pressed
1 teaspoon sweet paprika
2 ounces sun-dried tomatoes
Sea salt and ground black pepper, to taste

Directions

Press the "Sauté" button to preheat your Instant Pot. Then, heat the oil and sauté the onions until translucent.

Add the garlic and cook for a further 30 seconds. Add the Romano rice, salt, pepper, tomatoes, ketchup, water, and paprika.

Secure the lid. Choose the "Poultry" mode and High pressure; cook for 5 minutes. Once cooking is complete, use a natural pressure release; carefully remove the lid.

Ladle into individual bowls; garnish with sun-dried tomatoes and Pecorino-Romano cheese. Bon appétit!

Per serving: 354 Calories; 10.4g Fat; 52.7g Carbs; 11.1g Protein; 2.3g Sugars

174. Breakfast Millet Porridge

(Ready in about 25 minutes | Servings 5)

Ingredients

1/4 cup almonds, roughly chopped
1/2 cup golden raisins
1 tablespoon orange juice

A pinch of sea salt
3 cups water
1 ½ cups millet

Directions

Place all ingredients in the inner pot of your Instant Pot and close the lid.

Secure the lid. Choose the "Manual" mode and cook for 12 minutes at High pressure. Once cooking is complete, use a natural pressure release for 10 minutes; carefully remove the lid.

Taste and adjust the seasonings. Bon appétit!

Per serving: 372 Calories; 10.1g Fat; 60.6g Carbs; 10.6g Protein; 10.7g Sugars

175. Buttery Quinoa Porridge with Scallions

(Ready in about 10 minutes | Servings 4)

Ingredients

1 cup quinoa
2 tablespoons butter, melted
1/2 teaspoon dried rosemary
2 bell peppers, chopped
1/2 teaspoon turmeric powder
1/2 teaspoon paprika
1 ½ cups water
1 teaspoon garlic, minced
1 carrot, chopped
Salt and ground black pepper, to taste
2 tablespoons scallions, chopped

Directions

Press the "Sauté" button to preheat your Instant Pot. Melt the butter. Sauté the scallions, garlic, peppers, and carrot until tender.

Add the salt, black pepper, turmeric, paprika, and rosemary; cook an additional minute or until they are aromatic.

Wipe down the Instant Pot with a damp cloth. Then, stir in the water and quinoa.

Secure the lid. Choose the "Manual" mode and High pressure; cook for 1 minute. Once cooking is complete, use a natural pressure release; carefully remove the lid.

Ladle the prepared quinoa into individual bowls; top with scallion mixture and serve immediately.

Per serving: 225 Calories; 8.4g Fat; 31.3g Carbs; 6.7g Protein; 1.9g Sugars

176. Old-Fashioned Grits with Cream Cheese

(Ready in about 25 minutes | Servings 3)

Ingredients

1/2 cup milk
1/4 teaspoon porcini powder
1 cup stone ground grits
1/2 teaspoon sea salt
1/2 teaspoon paprika
1/2 teaspoon garlic powder
1 cup cream cheese, room temperature
2 cups of water

Directions

Place the water, grits, and salt in the inner pot of your Instant Pot.

Secure the lid. Choose the "Manual" mode and cook for 10 minutes at High pressure. Once cooking is complete, use a natural pressure release for 10 minutes; carefully remove the lid.

Now, stir the cheese, paprika, porcini powder, garlic powder and milk into warm grits; stir to combine well and serve immediately.

Per serving: 412 Calories; 25.7g Fat; 36.7g Carbs; 10.4g Protein; 5.1g Sugars

177. Rich Barley and Corn Soup

(Ready in about 55 minutes | Servings 5)

Ingredients

1 cup barley, whole
5 ounces sweet corn kernels, frozen and thawed
5 cups beef bone broth
2 carrots, chopped
1 parsnip, chopped
1 pound beef stew meat
1 shallot, chopped
Sea salt, to taste
2 celery stalks, chopped
1 teaspoon ginger-garlic paste
1/2 cup port wine
1 tablespoon butter, softened
1/4 teaspoon freshly ground black pepper, or more to taste

Directions

Press the "Sauté" button to preheat the Instant Pot. Then, melt the butter; cook the meat and shallot until the meat is no longer pink.

Add the salt, pepper, carrots, parsnip, celery, ginger-garlic paste, wine, broth and barley.

Secure the lid. Choose the "Soup" mode and High pressure; cook for 40 minutes. Once cooking is complete, use a natural pressure release for 10 minutes; carefully remove the lid.

Add the corn and seal the lid. Allow it to seat until heated through. Ladle into individual bowls and serve right away!

Per serving: 366 Calories; 8.4g Fat; 44.1g Carbs; 30.2g Protein; 3.9g Sugars

178. Three-Grain Porridge with Pepper

(Ready in about 30 minutes | Servings 5)

Ingredients

1/2 cup sorghum
1/2 cup congee
1 sweet pepper, deveined and sliced
1 medium-sized leek, chopped
2 garlic cloves, pressed
5 cups chicken bone broth
Sea salt and freshly ground black pepper, to taste
1/2 cup pearl barley
1 tablespoon olive oil

Directions

Press the "Sauté" button and heat the oil until sizzling. Once hot, sauté the leeks, garlic and peppers for 3 to 4 minutes or until just tender and fragrant.

Add a splash of broth to deglaze the pot. Next, stir in the remaining ingredients.

Secure the lid. Choose the "Multigrain" mode and cook for 20 minutes at High pressure. Once cooking is complete, use a quick pressure release; carefully remove the lid.

Ladle into individual bowls and serve immediately.

Per serving: 380 Calories; 8.6g Fat; 62.6g Carbs; 15.1g Protein; 2.2g Sugars

179. Vanilla Buckwheat Porridge with Fruits

(Ready in about 25 minutes | Servings 3)

Ingredients

1 teaspoon vanilla paste
1/2 cup hazelnuts, chopped
1 tablespoon orange rind strips, for garnish
1 cup water
1/4 teaspoon cardamom
1/2 teaspoon ground cinnamon
1/2 teaspoon anise seed powder
2 cups milk
1/3 cup dried cranberries
1/2 teaspoon hazelnut extract
3/4 cup raw buckwheat, rinsed

Directions

Add the buckwheat to the Instant Pot. Now, pour in water and milk.

Stir in the dried cranberries, cardamom, cinnamon, anise seed powder, vanilla, and hazelnut extract. Secure the lid.

Choose the "Manual" button and cook for 7 minutes at High pressure. Once cooking is complete, use a natural release for 15 minutes; remove the lid carefully.

Divide the hot porridge among 3 serving bowls and top with hazelnuts; garnish with orange rind strips and serve right now. Bon appétit!

Per serving: 301 Calories; 19.3g Fat; 24.4g Carbs; 10g Protein; 13g Sugars

180. Cheesy Farro Pilaf with Mushrooms

(Ready in about 35 minutes | Servings 3)

Ingredients

1 cup farro
1 cup mushrooms, sliced
2 garlic cloves, minced
1/2 cup white wine
2 ½ cups vegetable broth
2 sweet peppers, chopped
1/2 cup Swiss cheese, grated
1 heaping tablespoon fresh parsley, chopped
2 tablespoons olive oil
1 onion, chopped
Sea salt and ground black pepper, to taste

Directions

Press the "Sauté" button and heat the oil; now, cook the onion until tender or 3 to 4 minutes. Stir in the mushrooms and peppers and cook an additional 3 minutes.

Stir in the garlic and continue to sauté for a minute or so.

Add the white wine to deglaze the pan. Now, add the farro, vegetable broth, salt, and black pepper to the inner pot.

Secure the lid. Choose the "Manual" mode and cook for 11 minutes at High pressure. Once cooking is complete, use a natural pressure release for 10 minutes; carefully remove the lid.

Top each serving with cheese and fresh parsley. Bon appétit!

Per serving: 442 Calories; 16.7g Fat; 61.3g Carbs; 17.3g Protein; 9.6g Sugars

181. Oatmeal Soup with Onions

(Ready in about 30 minutes | Servings 4)

Ingredients

2/3 cup oat groat
1/2 teaspoon turmeric powder
2 cups spinach leaves, roughly chopped
2 garlic cloves, minced
2 cups water
1/2 teaspoon cayenne pepper
2 tablespoons ghee
1 purple onion, chopped
1 cup milk
Sea salt and ground black pepper, to taste
1 cup vegetable broth

Directions

Press the "Sauté" button to preheat your Instant Pot. Then, melt the ghee and cook the onion and garlic until tender and fragrant.

Add the oat groat, water, milk, broth, salt, black pepper, cayenne pepper, and turmeric powder; stir to combine.

Secure the lid. Choose the "Manual" mode and High pressure; cook for 22 minutes. Once cooking is complete, use a natural pressure release; carefully remove the lid.

Add the spinach and seal the lid; let it sit until the spinach is wilted. Serve warm and enjoy!

Per serving: 160 Calories; 9.3g Fat; 18.6g Carbs; 7g Protein; 5.2g Sugars

182. Movie Night Popcorn

(Ready in about 15 minutes | Servings 4)

Ingredients

1/4 cup parmesan cheese, grated
1 cup popcorn kernels
1 tablespoon truffle oil
1 stick butter
Sea salt, to taste

Directions

Press the "Sauté" button and melt the butter. Stir until it begins to simmer.

Stir in the popcorn kernels and cover. When the popping slows down, press the "Cancel" button.

Now, add the truffle oil, parmesan, and sea salt. Toss to combine and serve immediately.

Per serving: 365 Calories; 30.4g Fat; 18.8g Carbs; 5.1g Protein; 0.2g Sugars

183. Herb Buttermilk Cornbread

(Ready in about 30 minutes | Servings 8)

Ingredients

2 tablespoons honey
1/2 cup buttermilk
2/3 cup Cottage cheese, crumbled
1/2 teaspoon sea salt
1/3 cup olive oil
3 eggs
1/2 teaspoon garlic powder
1/2 teaspoon onion powder

1/2 teaspoon basil
1 teaspoon thyme
1 ½ cups polenta
1 teaspoon rosemary
1 cup all-purpose flour
1/2 teaspoon oregano
1 tablespoon baking powder
1/2 teaspoon baking soda

Directions

Begin by adding 1 cup of water and a metal trivet to the bottom of your Instant Pot. Spritz the bottom and sides of a baking pan with a nonstick cooking pan.

Thoroughly combine dry ingredients in a mixing bowl. In a separate mixing bowl, mix the wet ingredients.

Then, combine the wet mixture with the dry mixture; scrape the batter into the prepared baking pan. Place the baking pan on the trivet.

Secure the lid. Choose the "Porridge" mode and High pressure; cook for 20 minutes. Once cooking is complete, use a natural pressure release; carefully remove the lid.

Afterwards, transfer the cornbread to a cooling rack; allow it to sit for 5 to 6 minutes before slicing and serving. Enjoy!

Per serving: 266 Calories; 13.7g Fat; 27g Carbs; 8.2g Protein; 5.9g Sugars

184. Couscous, Chicken, and Vegetable Soup

(Ready in about 20 minutes | Servings 4)

Ingredients

1 cup couscous
1/2 pound chicken breasts, cubed
Sea salt and ground black pepper, to taste
1 tablespoon fresh parsley, chopped
1/2 teaspoon turmeric powder
1 tablespoon lemongrass, minced
1 teaspoon garlic paste

1/4 teaspoon mustard powder
4 cups chicken bone broth
1 onion, chopped
1 carrot, sliced
1 tablespoon fresh chives, chopped
1 celery rib, sliced
1 parsnip, sliced
1 tablespoon chicken schmaltz

Directions

Press the "Sauté" button and melt the chicken schmaltz. Once hot, sauté the chicken until golden brown; reserve.

Cook the onion, carrot, celery, and parsnip in pan drippings until just tender and aromatic.

Add the reserved chicken, lemongrass, garlic paste, turmeric, mustard powder, and broth.

Secure the lid. Choose the "Manual" mode and cook for 11 minutes at High pressure. Once cooking is complete, use a quick pressure release; carefully remove the lid.

Now, stir in the couscous; season with salt and pepper.

Secure the lid. Choose the "Manual" mode and cook for 2 minutes at High pressure. Once cooking is complete, use a quick pressure release; carefully remove the lid.

Serve garnished with fresh parsley and chives. Bon appétit!

Per serving: 343 Calories; 7.2g Fat; 44.7g Carbs; 23.3g Protein; 3.6g Sugars

185. Mediterranean-Style Kamut Pilaf

(Ready in about 25 minutes | Servings 4)

Per serving: 285 Calories; 5g Fat; 53.6g Carbs; 10.8g Protein; 7.4g Sugars

Ingredients

1 ½ cups kamut, soaked overnight
1/2 cup green olives, pitted and sliced
1 carrot, chopped
Salt and black pepper, to taste
1/2 teaspoon dried rosemary

1/4 cup fresh chives, chopped
2 shallots, chopped
2 cloves garlic minced
1/4 cup fresh parsley, chopped
1 tablespoon olive oil
1 celery stalk, chopped
3 cups water

Directions

Press the "Sauté" button to preheat your Instant Pot. Now, heat the oil until sizzling; sauté the shallots for 2 minutes or until tender.

Next, stir in the garlic, carrots and celery; continue to sauté until they are tender. Add kamut, water, salt, black pepper, and rosemary to the Instant Pot.

Secure the lid. Choose the "Porridge" mode and High pressure; cook for 20 minutes. Once cooking is complete, use a natural pressure release; carefully remove the lid.

Transfer to a serving bowl; garnish with chives, parsley and olives and serve. Enjoy!

PORK

186. Country-Style Pork Stew

(Ready in about 50 minutes | Servings 6)

Ingredients

1 ½ pounds pork stew meat, cubed

1/4 cup dry red wine

1/4 cup fresh parsley leaves, roughly chopped

1 cup leeks, chopped

1 teaspoon mustard seeds

1 teaspoon fennel seeds

2 tablespoons soy sauce

Hickory smoked salt and ground black pepper, to taste

2 garlic cloves, minced

1 (1-inch) piece fresh ginger root, grated

5 cups beef bone broth

1 ½ tablespoons lard, at room temperature

Directions

Press the "Sauté" button and melt the lard. Now, brown the pork stew meat for 4 to 6 minutes, stirring occasionally.

Season the pork with salt and black pepper to taste and set it aside. In the pan drippings, cook the leeks along with garlic and ginger until tender and aromatic.

Add the pork back to the Instant Pot; add the remaining ingredients and gently stir to combine. Secure the lid.

Choose "Meat/Stew" mode and cook at High pressure for 40 minutes. Once cooking is complete, use a quick release; remove the lid carefully.

Ladle into individual bowls and serve garnished with fresh parsley leaves. Bon appétit!

Per serving: 307 Calories; 17.2g Fat; 4.8g Carbs; 31.1g Protein; 2.5g Sugars

187. Melt-in-Your-Mouth Pork

(Ready in about 30 minutes | Servings 4)

Ingredients

2 pounds pork medallions

1 teaspoon garlic powder

1 lemon, juice and zest

1 cup vegetable broth

2 sprigs fresh rosemary

1 tablespoon butter, melted

Kosher salt and freshly ground black pepper, to taste

1 teaspoon shallot powder

Directions

Press the "Sauté" button and melt the butter. Sear the pork medallions until no longer pink.

Add the salt, black pepper, garlic powder, shallot powder, and vegetable broth.

Secure the lid. Choose the "Manual" mode and cook for 20 minutes at High pressure. Once cooking is complete, use a quick pressure release; carefully remove the lid.

Remove the pork medallions to a serving platter. Now, add the fresh rosemary, lemon juice and zest to the cooking liquid. Let it simmer for 2 to 3 minutes.

Spoon the sauce over the pork medallions and serve immediately. Enjoy!

Per serving: 340 Calories; 12.5g Fat; 1.7g Carbs; 52.2g Protein; 0.4g Sugars

188. Sticky Pulled Pork

(Ready in about 35 minutes | Servings 8)

Ingredients

1 cooking apple, cored and diced

1/2 cup barbecue sauce

1 tablespoon maple syrup

1 red chili pepper, minced

2 ½ pounds pork butt, cut into bite-sized cubes

1/2 teaspoon dried basil

1 lemon, sliced

1/2 cup vegetable broth

1 teaspoon dried oregano

Sea salt and ground black pepper

Directions

Add the pork, broth, barbecue sauce, salt, black pepper, oregano, basil, maple syrup, chili pepper, and apple to your Instant Pot.

Secure the lid. Choose the "Soup" setting and cook at High pressure for 30 minutes. Once cooking is complete, use a natural pressure release; carefully remove the lid.

Shred the pork with two forks. Return it back to the Instant Pot. Serve with lemon slices. Bon appétit!

Per serving: 434 Calories; 25.2g Fat; 13.6g Carbs; 36.1g Protein; 10.5g Sugars

189. Decadent Pork Chops with Pineapple

(Ready in about 35 minutes | Servings 4)

Ingredients

1 pound pork tenderloin, slice into 4 pieces

4 pineapple rings

1/2 cup unsweetened pineapple juice

1 teaspoon ground ginger

1 thyme sprig

1/2 cup vegetable broth

1 shallot, chopped

1 tablespoon canola oil

2 garlic cloves, chopped

1 rosemary sprig

Kosher salt and freshly ground black pepper, to taste

Directions

Press the "Sauté" button to preheat your Instant Pot. Heat the canola oil.

Season the pork tenderloin on both sides with salt and black pepper. Cook the pork chops with shallot and garlic for 3 minutes or until the pork chops are no longer pink.

Add the ginger, thyme, rosemary, pineapple juice, and vegetable broth.

Secure the lid. Choose the "Manual" mode and cook for 10 minutes at High pressure. Once cooking is complete, use a natural pressure release for 10 minutes; carefully remove the lid.

Preheat the broiler. Place the pork chops on a broil pan. Brush with the pan juices and place one pineapple ring on top of each pork piece. Broil for 5 minutes. Serve warm.

Per serving: 480 Calories; 34.3g Fat; 13.6g Carbs; 30.1g Protein; 11.5g Sugars

190. Spicy Pork-Bacon Meatballs

(Ready in about 15 minutes | Servings 6)

Ingredients

1/2 cup Romano cheese, freshly grated

2 slices bacon, chopped

2 chipotle chile in adobo

1/3 cup tortilla chips, crushed

1 egg

Sea salt and ground black pepper, to taste

1 teaspoon dried marjoram

2 cups tomato sauce

1 pound ground pork

2 tablespoons fresh cilantro

1 white onion, minced

1 cup ketchup

1 teaspoon garlic, minced

Directions

Thoroughly combine the ground pork, bacon, onion, garlic, tortilla chips, Romano cheese, egg, salt, black pepper, and marjoram. Shape the mixture into balls.

Now, add the ketchup, tomato sauce, and chipotle chile in adobo to the Instant Pot. Place the meatballs in your Instant Pot.

Secure the lid. Choose the "Manual" setting and cook at High pressure for 6 minutes. Once cooking is complete, use a quick pressure release; carefully remove the lid.

Serve warm garnished with fresh cilantro. Enjoy!

Per serving: 476 Calories; 24.5g Fat; 33.2g Carbs; 27.9g Protein; 19.5g Sugars

191. Sticky St. Louis-Style Ribs

(Ready in about 45 minutes | Servings 6)

Ingredients

2 cloves garlic, minced

1 cup tomato sauce

1 tablespoon soy sauce

1 tablespoon paprika

1/2 cup water

1 tablespoon brown sugar

1 tablespoon oyster sauce

1 (3-pounds) rack St. Louis-style pork ribs

Pink salt and ground black pepper, to taste

Directions

Place all ingredients in the inner pot.

Choose the "Meat/Stew" mode and cook for 35 minutes at High pressure. Once cooking is complete, use a quick pressure release; carefully remove the lid.

Turn your broiler to low. Coat the ribs with the pan juices and cook under the broiler for about 2 minutes.

Turn them over, coat with another layer of sauce and cook for 2 to 3 minutes more. Taste, adjust the seasonings and serve. Enjoy!

Per serving: 381 Calories; 13.4g Fat; 11.6g Carbs; 48.5g Protein; 6.6g Sugars

192. Macaroni with Pork Sausage and Cheese

(Ready in about 15 minutes | Servings 6)

Ingredients

1 pound macaroni

1 pound pork sausage, casing removed, coarsely chopped

4 ounces Colby cheese, shredded

1 cup water

1 teaspoon stone-ground mustard

1 cup tomato purée

2 cloves garlic, minced

1/2 teaspoon ground black pepper

1/2 teaspoon red pepper flakes, crushed

1 teaspoon dried basil

1 teaspoon dried oregano

1 tablespoon olive oil

1 yellow onion, finely chopped

Salt, to taste

Directions

Press the "Sauté" button to preheat your Instant Pot. Then, heat the oil; now, cook the onion until translucent.

Now, add the garlic and sausage; continue to cook for 4 minutes more. Stir in the seasonings, mustard, water, tomato purée, and macaroni

Secure the lid. Choose the "Manual" setting and cook at High pressure for 6 minutes. Once cooking is complete, use a quick pressure release; carefully remove the lid.

Top with the Colby cheese; seal the lid and let it sit in the residual heat until the cheese is melted. Bon appétit!

Per serving: 495 Calories; 15.2g Fat; 60g Carbs; 27.8g Protein; 4.5g Sugars

193. Pork Loin, Sausage with Polenta

(Ready in about 30 minutes | Servings 4)

Ingredients

1 pound boneless pork top loin roast, cut into cubes

1/2 teaspoon paprika

1 jalapeno pepper, sliced

2 garlic cloves, chopped

1 cup chicken bone broth

1 cup polenta

4 cups water

1 teaspoon salt

2 spicy pork sausages, sliced

1 tablespoon olive oil

1 bell pepper, sliced

Salt and ground black pepper, to taste

Directions

Press the "Sauté" button and heat the oil. Once hot, cook the pork until no longer pink; add the sausage and cook for 2 to 3 minutes more.

Add the peppers, garlic, broth, salt, and black pepper.

Secure the lid. Choose the "Manual" mode and cook for 15 minutes at High pressure. Once cooking is complete, use a quick pressure release; carefully remove the lid.

Clean the inner pot. Add the polenta, water and 1 teaspoon of salt and mix to combine.

Secure the lid. Choose the "Manual" mode and cook for 9 minutes at High pressure. Once cooking is complete, use a quick pressure release; carefully remove the lid.

Divide your polenta between serving bowls; top with the pork mélange and paprika. Serve warm.

Per serving: 474 Calories; 22.4g Fat; 16.8g Carbs; 45.9g Protein; 1.5g Sugars

194. Pulled Pork Taquitos

(Ready in about 1 hour | Servings 8)

Ingredients

2 pounds pork shoulder
1/2 cup Manchego cheese, shredded
1/2 cup dry red wine
1 teaspoon mixed peppercorns
1 tablespoon granulated sugar
1 teaspoon shallot powder
16 corn tortillas, warmed

1 cup tomato paste
1 tablespoon lard, melted
2 bay leaves
1 teaspoon chipotle powder
1 teaspoon granulated garlic
1 teaspoon ground cumin
1 cup ketchup
Salt and black pepper, to taste

Directions

Press the "Sauté" button to preheat your Instant Pot. Then, melt the lard. Sear the pork shoulder until it is delicately browned on all sides.

Add the sugar, shallot powder, garlic, salt, black pepper, cumin, ketchup, tomato paste, wine, peppercorns, bay leaves, and chipotle powder.

Secure the lid. Choose the "Meat/Stew" setting and cook at High pressure for 45 minutes. Once cooking is complete, use a natural pressure release; carefully remove the lid.

Shred the meat with two forks. Divide the shredded pork among tortillas. Top with the cheese. Roll each tortilla and brush it lightly with oil.

Arrange the tortillas on a cookie sheet. Bake approximately 13 minutes and serve. Enjoy!

Per serving: 417 Calories; 24.4g Fat; 16.6g Carbs; 32.3g Protein; 11.8g Sugars

195. Herbed Pork with Winter Vegetables

(Ready in about 30 minutes | Servings 5)

Ingredients

2 large celery stalks, cut into 1.5-inch chunks
1 parsnip, cut into 1.5-inch chunks
1/2 cup port
1 teaspoon garlic powder
1 teaspoon shallot powder
1 teaspoon mustard powder
1 teaspoon smoked paprika
2 tablespoons olive oil

2 mild green chilies, roasted, seeded and diced
1/2 cup roasted vegetable broth
1 teaspoon dried marjoram
1 tablespoon arrowroot powder
1 ½ pounds Boston butt, cut into small chunks
Sea salt and ground black pepper
2 large carrots, cut into 1.5-inch chunks

Directions

In a resealable bag, mix the garlic powder, shallot powder, salt, black pepper, marjoram, mustard powder, and paprika.

Add the pork cubes and shake to coat well. Press the "Sauté" button and heat the oil until sizzling.

Cook the Boston butt for 2 to 4 minutes, stirring periodically to ensure even cooking. Add the remaining ingredients, except for the arrowroot powder.

Secure the lid. Choose the "Meat/Stew" mode and cook for 20 minutes at High pressure. Once cooking is complete, use a quick pressure release; carefully remove the lid.

Stir in the arrowroot powder and let it simmer until the sauce thickens. Serve in individual bowls and enjoy!

Per serving: 511 Calories; 38.9g Fat; 11.6g Carbs; 29.7g Protein; 3.6g Sugars

196. Indian Pork Curry

(Ready in about 15 minutes + marinating time | Servings 6)

Ingredients

2 pounds pork rib chops
2 tablespoons honey
1 teaspoon garlic, minced
1 tablespoon lard, melted
4 dried Kashmiri chili peppers, stemmed and chopped
1/4 cup dry red wine

1 cinnamon stick
1 cup water
2 tablespoons white vinegar
Salt and ground black pepper, to taste
1 bay leaf

Directions

Place the water, wine, vinegar, salt, black pepper, garlic, honey and bay leaf in a ceramic dish. Add the rib chops and let them marinate for 2 hours in the refrigerator.

Press the "Sauté" button to preheat your Instant Pot. Melt the lard and sear the pork until it is delicately browned.

Then, transfer the pork along with the marinade to the Instant Pot. Add Kashmiri chili peppers and cinnamon stick.

Secure the lid. Now, select the "Manual" mode, High pressure and 8 minutes. Once cooking is complete, use a quick release; carefully remove the lid. Serve warm.

Per serving: 340 Calories; 14.8g Fat; 9.5g Carbs; 39.8g Protein; 7.7g Sugars

197. Pork Sausage and Peppers Casserole

(Ready in about 20 minutes | Servings 4)

Ingredients

1 pound pork sausages, sliced
1 bell pepper, sliced
1 red chili pepper, sliced
1 cup white wine
Sea salt and freshly ground black pepper, to taste
4 garlic cloves, minced
1 teaspoon dried basil

2 tomatoes, pureed
1 cup chicken stock
4 ounces streaky bacon
2 tablespoons canola oil
1 onion, sliced
1 teaspoon brown sugar
1 teaspoon dried rosemary

Directions

Press the "Sauté" button and heat the oil. Sear the pork sausage until no longer pink. Add the bacon and cook until it is crisp.

Add a layer of onions and garlic; then, add the peppers. Sprinkle with sugar, rosemary, basil, salt and black pepper.

Add the tomatoes, chicken stock, and wine to the inner pot.

Secure the lid. Choose the "Manual" mode and cook for 10 minutes at High pressure. Once cooking is complete, use a natural pressure release; carefully remove the lid. Bon appétit!

Per serving: 484 Calories; 41.8g Fat; 6.3g Carbs; 21.6g Protein; 4.1g Sugars

198. Braised Ribs with Tomatillos and Beer

(Ready in about 40 minutes | Servings 8)

Ingredients

1/2 cup chicken stock
1 (12-ounce) bottle dark beer
2 ripe tomatillos, chopped
2 garlic cloves, minced
1 bell pepper, deveined and chopped
1 jalapeno pepper, deveined and chopped
2 ½ pounds baby back ribs
Salt and ground black pepper, to taste
1/2 teaspoon ground allspice
1 teaspoon fennel seeds
Lime wedges, for serving

Directions

Simply throw all of the above ingredients, except for the lime wedges, into your Instant Pot. Secure the lid.

Choose the "Manual" setting and cook for 35 minutes at High pressure.

Once cooking is complete, use a natural release; remove the lid carefully. Serve garnished with lime wedges. Bon appétit!

Per serving: 405 Calories; 24.1g Fat; 3.2g Carbs; 40.5g Protein; 0.7g Sugars

199. Bourbon-Orange Glazed Ham

(Ready in about 20 minutes | Servings 6)

Ingredients

2 tablespoons bourbon
1/2 cup orange juice
4 tablespoons maple syrup
Sea salt and ground black pepper, to taste
3 pounds spiral sliced ham

Directions

Place 1 cup of water and a metal trivet in the inner pot.

Then, thoroughly combine the orange juice, bourbon, maple syrup, salt and pepper.

Place the ham on foil. Fold up the sides of the foil to make a bowl-like shape. Pour the orange glaze all over the ham; wrap the foil around the ham. Lower the ham onto the trivet.

Secure the lid. Choose the "Manual" mode and cook for 10 minutes at High pressure. Once cooking is complete, use a quick pressure release; carefully remove the lid.

Transfer to a cooling rack before serving. Bon appétit!

Per serving: 415 Calories; 19.5g Fat; 20g Carbs; 37.8g Protein; 9.7g Sugars

200. Chinese-Style Spicy Braised Pork

(Ready in about 2 hours 50 minutes | Servings 8)

Ingredients

3 pounds pork leg
2 garlic cloves, minced
A bunch of green onions, chopped
2 tablespoons tamari sauce
2 star anise
1/4 cup Shaoxing rice wine
1/2 cup water
2 tablespoons olive oil
1/4 cup tomato paste
1 ½ tablespoons honey
Sea salt and ground black pepper, to taste
1 teaspoon Aleppo red pepper

Directions

Add all ingredients, except for the olive oil and green onions, to a ceramic dish. Cover the dish and place in your refrigerator for 2 hours.

Then, press the "Sauté" button to preheat your Instant Pot. Heat the oil until sizzling. Now, cook the pork until delicately browned on all sides, about 10 minutes. Then, add the marinade.

Secure the lid. Choose the "Meat/Stew" setting and cook at High pressure for 35 minutes. Once cooking is complete, use a natural pressure release; carefully remove the lid.

Add the green onions to the Instant Pot; seal the lid and let it sit approximately 5 minutes. Serve warm.

Per serving: 287 Calories; 10g Fat; 10.8g Carbs; 38.2g Protein; 6.8g Sugars

201. Ground Pork Goulash with Cheese

(Ready in about 25 minutes | Servings 4)

Ingredients

1 onion, chopped
1/2 cup rice wine
2 ripe tomatoes, pureed
2 cloves garlic, minced
1 bay leaf
1 thyme sprig
1/2 pound ground turkey
1 cup beef bone broth
1 cup sweet corn kernels
1 cup green peas
1/2 cup Colby cheese, shredded
1 tablespoon olive oil
Sea salt and ground black pepper, to taste
1 rosemary sprig
1 teaspoon paprika
1 pound ground pork

Directions

Press the "Sauté" button to preheat your Instant Pot. Heat the oil and sear the meat until no longer pink, stirring continuously with a spatula.

Use a splash of wine to deglaze the pan.

Add the onion and garlic to the meat mixture and cook an additional 3 minutes or until tender and fragrant.

Next, stir in the spices, broth, wine, and tomatoes.

Secure the lid. Choose the "Manual" mode and cook for 10 minutes at High pressure. Once cooking is complete, use a quick pressure release; carefully remove the lid.

Press the "Sauté" button and add the corn and green peas. Cook an additional 3 minutes or until everything is heated through.

Top with the cheese and allow it to stand until the cheese has melted. Bon appétit!

Per serving: 570 Calories; 37.4g Fat; 22.2g Carbs; 38.2g Protein; 5.1g Sugars

202. Hawaiian Pork Sandwiches

(Ready in about 1 hour 10 minutes + marinating time | Servings 6)

Ingredients

1 ½ tablespoons olive oil
6 dinner rolls
1 head fresh Iceberg lettuce, leaves separated
2 tablespoons fresh scallions, chopped
1/2 cup pineapple juice
1 teaspoon cayenne pepper

1/4 teaspoon cumin
2 tablespoons Dijon mustard
4 cloves garlic, smashed
2 pounds pork loin roast, cut into cubes
Salt and black pepper, to taste
1/4 teaspoon mustard seeds

Directions

Place the pork, garlic, scallions, pineapple, juice, salt, black pepper, cayenne pepper, mustard seeds, and cumin in a mixing bowl; wrap with a foil and transfer to your refrigerator for 2 hours.

Press the "Sauté" button and heat olive oil. Now, cook the pork, working in batches, until it is well browned.

Secure the lid. Now, select the "Manual" mode, High pressure and 60 minutes. Once cooking is complete, use a natural release; carefully remove the lid.

Serve over dinner rolls, garnished with fresh lettuce and Dijon mustard. Bon appétit!

Per serving: 433 Calories; 18.8g Fat; 20.9g Carbs; 43.9g Protein; 6g Sugars

203. Authentic Tacos de Carnitas

(Ready in about 50 minutes | Servings 4)

Ingredients

1 cup Mexican coke
4 warm tortillas
1 teaspoon garlic powder
Sea salt and ground black pepper, to taste
1/2 cup tomato ketchup
2 tablespoons balsamic vinegar
1 jalapeno, deveined and chopped

1 teaspoon shallot powder
1/2 teaspoon Mexican oregano
1/2 teaspoon cumin powder
1 cup beef bone broth
2 pounds pork butt roast
1/4 cup honey
1 teaspoon liquid smoke

Directions

Place all ingredients, except for the tortillas, in the inner pot.

Secure the lid. Choose the "Meat/Stew" mode and cook for 35 minutes at High pressure. Once cooking is complete, use a quick pressure release; carefully remove the lid.

Remove the pork from the inner pot and shred with two forks.

Transfer the pork to a baking sheet lightly greased with cooking spray. Pour 1 ladle of the cooking liquid over the pork. Broil for 7 to 10 minutes until the meat becomes crispy on the edges.

Spoon the pulled pork into the warm tortillas and serve with your favorite toppings. Bon appétit!

Per serving: 555 Calories; 12.4g Fat; 54.3g Carbs; 55.2g Protein; 29.5g Sugars

204. Korean Momofuku Bo Ssam

(Ready in about 1 hour 5 minutes | Servings 10)

Ingredients

1 stick butter
3 pounds pork shoulder
1/4 cup doenjang (korean soybean paste)
1/2 teaspoon Gochugaru
1/2 cup chicken bone broth
1 tablespoon tamari sauce
Sea salt and ground black pepper, to taste

1 tablespoon castor sugar
2 tablespoons walnuts, ground
1/2 cup yellow onions, chopped
2 garlic cloves, minced
1 heaping tablespoon lard, at room temperature
1/2 cup orange juice
2 bay leaves

Directions

Press the "Sauté" button to preheat your Instant Pot. Melt the lard and brown the pork shoulder for 5 minutes, turning once or twice.

Add the onions, garlic, broth, orange juice, tamari sauce, salt, black pepper, teaspoon Gochugaru, and sugar.

Secure the lid. Choose the "Manual" setting and cook at High pressure for 50 minutes. Once cooking is complete, use a natural pressure release; carefully remove the lid.

Transfer the pork shoulder to a cutting board; allow it to cool; then, cut into slices.

Then, press the "Sauté" button again. Add the remaining ingredients and let it simmer for 5 to 6 minutes or until the sauce is thoroughly heated and reduced by half.

Spoon the sauce over the pork and serve. Bon appétit!

Per serving: 512 Calories; 37.2g Fat; 4.2g Carbs; 38.2g Protein; 2.3g Sugars

205. Christmas Pork with Mustard Gravy

(Ready in about 20 minutes | Servings 4)

Ingredients

1 pound Boston-style butt, sliced into four pieces
2 tablespoons plain flour, mixed with 2 tablespoons of cold water
1 tablespoon stone ground mustard
1 teaspoon basil
1 shallot, sliced
2 cloves garlic, sliced

1 stalk celery, chopped
1/2 cup chicken broth
1 teaspoon thyme
2 tablespoons olive oil
1 bell pepper, deveined and sliced
1/2 cup apple juice
Coarse sea salt and freshly ground black pepper, to taste

Directions

Press the "Sauté" button and heat the oil. Then, sear the Boston butt until it is golden brown on all sides.

Add the salt, pepper, shallot, garlic, celery, bell pepper, apple juice, chicken broth, mustard, basil, and thyme to the inner pot.

Secure the lid. Choose the "Manual" mode and cook for 15 minutes at High pressure. Once cooking is complete, use a quick pressure release; carefully remove the lid. Remove the meat from the cooking liquid.

Add the slurry and press the "Sauté" button one more time. Let it simmer until your sauce has thickened. Spoon the gravy over the pork and serve. Bon appétit!

Per serving: 388 Calories; 22.1g Fat; 6.8g Carbs; 36.7g Protein; 3.7g Sugars

206. Rustic Pork Pâté

(Ready in about 55 minutes + chilling time | Servings 10)

Ingredients

1 ½ pounds boneless pork shoulder, cubed
Sea salt and ground black pepper, to taste
1/2 cup heavy cream
2 tablespoons brandy
1/2 teaspoon ground ginger
1 red onion, chopped
2 cloves garlic, minced
1 teaspoon mustard powder
1 teaspoon ground nutmeg
1 teaspoon dried basil
1 teaspoon ground coriander
4 ounces pork liver
1 tablespoon olive oil

Directions

Press the "Sauté" button to preheat your Instant Pot. Heat the olive oil; once hot, sear the pork shoulder and pork liver until they are delicately browned; reserve.

Add the onion and garlic and continue to sauté them in pan drippings. Return the meat and pork liver back to the Instant Pot.

Add the remaining ingredients, except for heavy cream.

Secure the lid. Choose the "Manual" setting and cook at High pressure for 50 minutes. Once cooking is complete, use a natural pressure release; carefully remove the lid.

Fold in the heavy cream. Give it a good stir and seal the lid. Let it sit in the residual heat until thoroughly warmed. Refrigerate until it is completely chilled.

Per serving: 147 Calories; 6.4g Fat; 2.5g Carbs; 18.2g Protein; 0.9g Sugars

207. Perfect Pork Loin Chops

(Ready in about 25 minutes | Servings 4)

Ingredients

1 tablespoon canola oil
1/2 cup mayonnaise
1/2 teaspoon celery seeds
1 cup beef bone broth
2 cloves garlic, crushed
Kosher salt and ground black pepper, to taste
1 teaspoon paprika
1/2 teaspoon mustard powder
1 ½ pounds center-cut loin chops

Directions

Press the "Sauté" button and heat the oil. Sear the pork until it is golden brown on both sides.

Add the salt, black pepper, mustard powder, celery seeds oil, and broth.

Secure the lid. Choose the "Manual" mode and cook for 10 minutes at High pressure. Once cooking is complete, use a natural pressure release for 10 minutes; carefully remove the lid.

Meanwhile, whisk the mayonnaise with the garlic; serve the warm loin chops with the garlic mayo on the side. Bon appétit!

Per serving: 444 Calories; 30.5g Fat; 2.1g Carbs; 38.1g Protein; 0.8g Sugars

208. Pork Sausages with Black Beans

(Ready in about 15 minutes | Servings 4)

Ingredients

25 ounces canned black beans, rinsed and drained
1/2 cup Cubanelle peppers, chopped
2 shallots, chopped
2 garlic cloves, minced
1/2 teaspoon paprika
1/2 tablespoon shortening
1 bay leaf
4 spicy pork sausages, without casing
Sat, to taste
1/3 cup water

Directions

Press the "Sauté" button to preheat your Instant Pot. Once hot, warm the shortening. Now, cook the sausage, crumbling them with a spatula; reserve.

Next, cook the shallots and garlic in the pan drippings until tender and fragrant. Add the other ingredients, along with reserved pork sausages.

Secure the lid. Choose the "Manual" mode, High heat, and 6 minutes.

Once cooking is complete, use a natural release; remove the lid carefully. Discard bay leaf and serve over hot cooked rice. Bon appétit!

Per serving: 322 Calories; 24.4g Fat; 12.4g Carbs; 14.2g Protein; 2g Sugars

209. Marsala Pork and Vegetable Casserole

(Ready in about 25 minutes | Servings 4)

Ingredients

1 ½ pounds ground pork
1/4 cup Marsala wine
Kosher salt and ground black pepper, to taste
1 stalk celery, sliced
2 fresh tomatoes, pureed
2 sweet peppers, sliced
1 onion, sliced
4 cloves garlic, sliced
1 cup whole kernel corn, frozen
2 carrots, sliced
1 parsnip, sliced
1/2 cup water
1 teaspoon olive oil

Directions

Press the "Sauté" button and heat the oil. Once hot, cook the ground pork for 2 to 3 minutes, stirring frequently.

Add a splash of wine to deglaze the pot. Add the remaining ingredients.

Secure the lid. Choose the "Manual" mode and cook for 18 minutes at High pressure. Once cooking is complete, use a quick pressure release; carefully remove the lid.

Taste and adjust the seasonings. Bon appétit!

Per serving: 462 Calories; 29.9g Fat; 19.1g Carbs; 33.2g Protein; 5.7g Sugars

210. Pork and Mushroom Paprikash

(Ready in about 30 minutes | Servings 8)

Ingredients

2 pounds pork stew meat, cubed

1 cup button mushrooms, sliced

1 cup red onions, chopped

1 teaspoon Hungarian paprika

1 cup sour cream

2 garlic cloves, minced

1 chili pepper, deveined and minced

2 carrots, peeled and cut into large pieces

1 can tomatoes, crushed

6 cups chicken broth

Salt and ground black pepper, to taste

2 bell pepper, deveined and thinly sliced

1 bay leaf

2 tablespoons olive oil

Directions

Press the "Sauté" button to preheat your Instant Pot. Now, heat the oil until sizzling. Then, sauté the onion until tender and translucent.

Stir in the garlic and mushrooms; continue to sauté an additional 2 minute or until they are fragrant. Reserve.

Cook the meat for 2 to 3 minutes, stirring frequently; add the reserved onion/mushroom mixture to your Instant Pot.

Add the pepper, carrots, tomatoes, chicken broth, salt, pepper, paprika, and bay leaf.

Secure the lid. Choose the "Soup" setting and cook at High pressure for 20 minutes. Once cooking is complete, use a quick pressure release; carefully remove the lid.

Garnish each serving with a dollop of sour cream and serve.

Per serving: 549 Calories; 22.6g Fat; 9.6g Carbs; 72.9g Protein; 3.1g Sugars

211. Perfect Mexican Chile Verde

(Ready in about 40 minutes | Servings 4)

Ingredients

1/4 cup all-purpose flour

1 pound fresh tomatillos, husked and sliced into 1/2-inch wedges

1 tablespoon canola oil

3 fresh chili pepper, seeded and sliced

1 onion, chopped

2 cloves garlic, sliced

1/2 teaspoon turmeric powder

1 cup beef broth

1 sweet pepper, seeded and sliced

1/2 teaspoon coriander seeds

2 pounds pork shoulder, cut into bite-sized pieces

1/4 cup fresh cilantro leaves, roughly chopped

1 teaspoon Mexican oregano

1 teaspoon ground cumin

Kosher salt and ground black pepper, to your liking

Directions

Toss the pork pieces with the flour until everything is well coated. Generously season the pork with salt and pepper.

Press the "Sauté" button and heat the oil. Once hot, sear the pork, stirring periodically to ensure even cooking.

Now, add the remaining ingredients, except for the cilantro leaves.

Secure the lid. Choose the "Meat/Stew" mode and cook for 35 minutes at High pressure. Once cooking is complete, use a quick pressure release; carefully remove the lid.

Serve in individual bowls, garnished with fresh cilantro. Enjoy!

Per serving: 444 Calories; 18.1g Fat; 23.6g Carbs; 46.4g Protein; 8g Sugars

212. Pork and Corn Chowder

(Ready in about 15 minutes | Servings 4)

Ingredients

1 pound pork stew meat, cubed

1 cup corn, torn into pieces

1/2 cup onion, chopped

1 teaspoon celery seeds

1/4 teaspoon bay leaf, ground

1/2 teaspoon dried basil

1 tablespoon olive oil

4 cups water

Directions

Press the "Sauté" button to preheat your Instant Pot. Heat the olive oil; cook the onion until tender and translucent.

Add the pork and continue to cook until it is delicately browned. Add the water, ground bay leaf, basil, and celery seeds to the Instant Pot.

Secure the lid. Choose the "Manual" setting and cook at High pressure for 8 minutes. Once cooking is complete, use a quick pressure release; carefully remove the lid.

Stir in the corn kernels; seal the lid and allow it to sit in the residual heat until the corn is warmed through. Serve in individual bowls and enjoy!

Per serving: 358 Calories; 9.1g Fat; 32.4g Carbs; 36.1g Protein; 0.8g Sugars

213. Pork in Creamed Sauce

(Ready in about 30 minutes | Servings 3)

Ingredients

3 pork chops

1/2 cup double cream

Sea salt and ground black pepper, to taste

1 teaspoon garlic powder

1 tablespoon paprika

1/2 teaspoon onion powder

1/2 teaspoon xanthan gum

1 cup beef broth

1 tablespoon ghee, at room temperature

Directions

Press the "Sauté" button and melt the ghee. Once hot, sear the pork chops until golden browned, about 4 minutes per side.

Add the beef broth, garlic powder, onion powder, paprika, salt, and black pepper to the inner pot.

Secure the lid. Choose the "Manual" mode and cook for 10 minutes at High pressure. Once cooking is complete, use a natural pressure release; carefully remove the lid.

Transfer just the pork chops to a serving plate and cover to keep them warm. Press the "Sauté" button again.

Whisk in the cream and xanthan gum. Let it simmer approximately 4 minutes or until the sauce has thickened. Spoon the sauce over the pork chops and enjoy!

Per serving: 472 Calories; 28.8g Fat; 11.1g Carbs; 42.7g Protein; 6.6g Sugars

214. Mexican Pork Soup

(Ready in about 25 minutes | Servings 6)

Ingredients

1 cup Queso fresco cheese, crumbled

1 teaspoon fresh ginger, grated

1 teaspoon dried basil

Sea salt, to taste

1/2 cup yellow onion, chopped

5 cups water

2 bouillon cubes

2 garlic cloves, smashed

1 teaspoon dried oregano

1 fresh poblano chile, minced

1/4 teaspoon freshly ground pepper, or more to taste

1 cup tomato paste

2 pounds pork stew meat, cubed

Directions

Place all of the above ingredients, except for the Queso fresco cheese, in your Instant Pot.

Secure the lid. Choose the "Soup" setting and cook at High pressure for 20 minutes. Once cooking is complete, use a quick pressure release; carefully remove the lid.

Divide the warm soup among serving bowls; top each serving with the crumbled cheese and serve immediately.

Per serving: 334 Calories; 10.6g Fat; 10g Carbs; 48.4g Protein; 6.1g Sugars

215. Ground Pork Stuffed Peppers with Cheese

(Ready in about 30 minutes | Servings 4)

Ingredients

3/4 pound ground pork

1/2 pound brown mushrooms, sliced

2 cloves garlic, minced

2 ounces Colby cheese, shredded

1/2 teaspoon ground cumin

1 teaspoon cayenne pepper

1/2 teaspoon celery seeds

1 1/2 cups cooked rice

4 bell peppers, deveined and halved

1 (15-ounce) can tomatoes, crushed

1 tablespoon olive oil

1 onion, chopped

Sea salt and white pepper, to taste

Directions

Press the "Sauté" button and heat the oil. Cook the onion, garlic, and pork until the onion is translucent and the pork is no longer pink. Add the mushrooms and sauté until fragrant or about 2 minutes.

Add the rice, salt, white pepper, cayenne pepper, celery seeds, and ground cumin.

Add 1 cup of water and a metal trivet to the bottom. Fill the pepper halves with the meat/mushroom mixture. Place the peppers in a casserole dish; stir in the canned tomatoes.

Lower the casserole dish onto the trivet in the Instant Pot.

Secure the lid. Choose the "Manual" mode and cook for 9 minutes at High pressure. Once cooking is complete, use a natural pressure release for 5 minutes; carefully remove the lid.

Top with the cheese and secure the lid again; let it sit in the residual heat until the cheese melts approximately 10 minutes. Serve and enjoy!

Per serving: 499 Calories; 26.4g Fat; 35.6g Carbs; 30.8g Protein; 8.1g Sugars

216. Orange-Glazed Picnic Shoulder

(Ready in about 50 minutes | Servings 4)

Ingredients

1/2 cup fresh orange juice

1 teaspoon garlic powder

1/4 teaspoon cinnamon, ground

1 teaspoon oregano, dried

Sea salt and ground black pepper, to taste

1 ½ pounds pork picnic shoulder

1 cup beef bone broth

1/2 teaspoon cumin powder

1 teaspoon celery seeds

Directions

Place all of the above ingredients in the Instant Pot.

Secure the lid. Choose the "Meat/Stew" setting and cook at High pressure for 45 minutes. Once cooking is complete, use a natural pressure release; carefully remove the lid.

Test for doneness and thinly slice the pork; transfer to a serving platter. Serve warm and enjoy!

Per serving: 288 Calories; 12.7g Fat; 6.1g Carbs; 35.2g Protein; 3.2g Sugars

217. Pork Fajita Wraps

(Ready in about 35 minutes | Servings 4)

Ingredients

2 pounds Boston butt, cut into bite-sized pieces

4 warm corn tortillas

2 tablespoons salsa

1/2 teaspoon ground black pepper

1 cup tomato paste

1 teaspoon onion powder

1 tablespoon olive oil

1 teaspoon paprika

1/2 cup roasted vegetable broth

1 tablespoon fish sauce

4 eggs

1 tablespoon dark brown sugar

1 tablespoon coarse sea salt

1 teaspoon garlic powder

1 teaspoon ancho chili powder

Directions

In a resealable bag, mix the all spices and sugar. Add the pork chunks and shake to coat well.

Press the "Sauté" button and heat the oil until sizzling. Now, sear and brown the Boston butt on all sides until you have a crispy crust.

Add the tomato paste, broth, and fish sauce.

Secure the lid. Choose the "Manual" mode and cook for 30 minutes at High pressure. Once cooking is complete, use a quick pressure release; carefully remove the lid.

Meanwhile, crack the eggs into a lightly greased pan; fry your eggs until the whites are set.

Stack the tortilla, pork mixture, and corn salsa on a plate. Place the fried egg onto the stack using a spatula. Make four servings and enjoy!

Per serving: 533 Calories; 18.3g Fat; 29.5g Carbs; 62.2g Protein; 8.8g Sugars

218. Authentic Tacos with Morita Salsa

(Ready in about 45 minutes | Servings 6)

Ingredients

6 large tortillas, warmed
1 teaspoon dried marjoram
1 teaspoon mustard powder
1/2 teaspoon dried sage, crushed
1 cup stock
1 bay leaf
4 cloves garlic, halved
Seasoned salt and freshly ground black pepper, to taste

2 pounds meaty pork belly, skin-on
For the Sauce:
2 morita chiles, finely chopped
1/4 cup fresh lime juice
1 red onion, finely chopped
Salt, to your liking
1 cup tomatillos, finely chopped

Directions

Rub the pork belly with garlic halves. Sprinkle the pork belly with salt, black pepper, mustard powder, sage, and marjoram.

Brush the bottom of the Instant Pot with a nonstick cooking oil.

Press the "Sauté" button; add the pork belly, skin side down. Cook until it is browned on all sides.

Add the stock and bay leaf; secure the lid. Now, select the "Manual" mode, High pressure and 35 minutes.

Once cooking is complete, use a quick release; remove the lid carefully.

Meanwhile, make the sauce by mixing all the sauce ingredients.

Allow the pork belly to cool slightly. Place the pork belly, skin side up, on a cutting board. Slice across the grain.

Divide the sliced pork among warm tortillas, add the sauce and serve warm.

Per serving: 477 Calories; 20g Fat; 27.7g Carbs; 43.8g Protein; 3.2g Sugars

219. Roasted Pork with Red Wine

(Ready in about 1 hour 10 minutes | Servings 6)

Ingredients

2 ½ pounds pork butt
1 large leek, sliced into long pieces
2 teaspoons stone-ground mustard
1 teaspoon freshly grated lemon zest
1 tablespoon lard, at room temperature

1 carrot, halved lengthwise
2 garlic cloves, minced
1/2 cup red wine
Sea salt and ground black pepper, to taste

Directions

Combine the garlic, mustard, salt, pepper and lemon zest in a mixing bowl. Using your hands, spread the rub evenly onto the pork butt.

Press the "Sauté" button to preheat your Instant Pot. Melt the lard and sear the meat for 3 minutes per side.

Pour a splash of wine into the inner pot, scraping any bits from the bottom with a wooden spoon.

Place a trivet and 1 cup of water in the bottom of the inner pot. Lower the pork butt onto the trivet; scatter the leeks and carrots around.

Secure the lid. Choose the "Manual" mode and cook for 50 minutes at High pressure. Once cooking is complete, use a natural pressure release for 10 minutes; carefully remove the lid.

Transfer the pork butt to a cutting board and let it sit for 5 minutes before carving and serving. Enjoy!

Per serving: 545 Calories; 35.4g Fat; 4.2g Carbs; 48.2g Protein; 1.5g Sugars

220. Cajun Sticky Ribs

(Ready in about 30 minutes | Servings 6)

Ingredients

1 teaspoon Cajun seasoning
2 tablespoons soy sauce
1 tablespoon brown sugar
Sat, to taste
2 slices fresh ginger

1/2 cup dry wine
2 cloves garlic, sliced
1 cup beef bone broth
2 pounds baby back ribs

Directions

Add all of the above ingredients to your Instant Pot.

Secure the lid. Choose the "Meat/Stew" setting and cook at High pressure for 20 minutes. Once cooking is complete, use a natural pressure release; carefully remove the lid.

Serve warm and enjoy!

Per serving: 365 Calories; 25g Fat; 3.7g Carbs; 3.1g Protein; 2.6g Sugars

221. Parmesan Meatballs with Marinara Sauce

(Ready in about 20 minutes | Servings 4)

Ingredients

2 tablespoons vegetable oil
Meatballs:
1/2 cup Parmesan, grated
2 bread slices, soaked in 4 tablespoons of milk
Kosher salt and ground black pepper, to your liking
1 teaspoon chili flakes
1 teaspoon mustard powder
1 egg

1 ½ pounds ground pork
Marinara Sauce:
1 onion, chopped
1 cup water
2 large ripe tomatoes, crushed
1 tablespoon cayenne pepper
1 teaspoon maple syrup
1 teaspoon dried parsley flakes
3 cloves garlic, minced
2 tablespoons olive oil

Directions

Mix all ingredients for the meatballs until everything is well incorporated. Shape the mixture into small meatballs.

Press the "Sauté" button and heat 2 tablespoons of vegetable oil. Sear your meatballs until golden brown on all sides. Work in batches as needed. Reserve.

Press the "Sauté" button one more time; heat 2 tablespoons of olive oil. Cook the onion and garlic until tender and fragrant.

Now, add the remaining ingredients for the marinara sauce. Gently fold in the meatballs and secure the lid.

Choose the "Poultry" mode and cook for 5 minutes at High pressure. Once cooking is complete, use a quick pressure release; carefully remove the lid. Serve warm.

Per serving: 468 Calories; 24g Fat; 19.7g Carbs; 44.8g Protein; 6.2g Sugars

222. Italian Pasta Bolognese with a Twist

(Ready in about 30 minutes | Servings 4)

Ingredients

2 pounds penne rigate
1 jalapeno, finely chopped
1/4 cup heavy cream
2 garlic cloves, minced
1 celery stick, diced small
1 sweet pepper, finely chopped
1 ½ cups broth, preferably homemade
1 (28-ounce) can Italian tomatoes, finely chopped
1 cup leeks, chopped
1 ½ tablespoons olive oil
1 pound ground pork
1/2 pound ground beef

Directions

Press the "Sauté" button. Preheat your Instant Pot and add the oil. Once hot, sweat the leeks for 3 to 4 minutes, stirring frequently.

Add the garlic and cook for 30 seconds more. Add the ground meat and cook for 3 minutes more or until it is just browned.

Add the celery, peppers, broth, tomatoes, and penne rigate. Secure the lid. Choose the "Manual" setting and cook for 15 minutes at High pressure.

Once cooking is complete, use a quick release; remove the lid carefully. Press the "Sauté" button and fold in the heavy cream; stir until heated through.

Divide among individual bowls and eat warm. Bon appétit!

Per serving: 677 Calories; 39.5g Fat; 37.9g Carbs; 43.3g Protein; 2.5g Sugars

223. Italian Pork Chops with Cheese

(Ready in about 20 minutes | Servings 4)

Ingredients

4 pork chops, bone-in
4 ounces parmesan cheese, preferably freshly grated
1/4 cup tomato puree
1 cup chicken bone broth
1 tablespoon lard, at room temperature
Sea salt and freshly ground black pepper, to taste

Directions

Press the "Sauté" button and melt the lard. Sear the pork chops for 3 to 4 minutes per side. Season with salt and pepper.

Place the tomato puree and chicken broth in the inner pot.

Secure the lid. Choose the "Manual" mode and cook for 10 minutes at High pressure. Once cooking is complete, use a natural pressure release; carefully remove the lid.

Top with parmesan cheese and serve warm. Bon appétit!

Per serving: 475 Calories; 21.7g Fat; 5.8g Carbs; 60.4g Protein; 0.7g Sugars

224. Neapolitan Pork Ragù

(Ready in about 30 minutes | Servings 6)

Ingredients

1 ½ pounds pork stew meat, cubed
1 teaspoon Italian seasoning
2 cups roasted vegetable stock
2 carrots, sliced
1 celery with leaves, chopped
Salt and ground black pepper, to taste
1 onion, chopped
2 garlic cloves, chopped
1/4 cup red wine
1/2 (15-ounce) can tomato sauce
2 tablespoons olive oil

Directions

Press the "Sauté" button to preheat your Instant Pot. Heat the oil and sauté the pork and onions until the meat is delicately browned.

Add the remaining ingredients.

Secure the lid. Choose the "Soup" setting and cook at High pressure for 20 minutes. Once cooking is complete, use a quick pressure release; carefully remove the lid.

Serve topped with shredded cheese if desired. Bon appétit!

Per serving: 385 Calories; 25.4g Fat; 6.7g Carbs; 31.2g Protein; 3.7g Sugars

225. Pork Sliders with Cholula Sauce

(Ready in about 40 minutes | Servings 4)

Ingredients

2 pounds pork shoulder roast
1/2 cup tomato paste
4 hamburger buns
1/2 cup beef bone broth
1/4 cup balsamic vinegar
1 tablespoon mustard
1 teaspoon Cholula hot sauce
2 cloves garlic, minced
1/4 cup brown sugar
1 teaspoon dried marjoram
1 tablespoon olive oil

Directions

Add all ingredients, except for the hamburger buns, to the inner pot.

Secure the lid. Choose the "Meat/Stew" mode and cook for 35 minutes at High pressure. Once cooking is complete, use a quick pressure release; carefully remove the lid.

Remove the pork from the inner pot and shred with two forks. Spoon the pulled pork into the hamburger buns and serve with your favorite toppings. Bon appétit!

Per serving: 516 Calories; 14.4g Fat; 37.1g Carbs; 56.7g Protein; 15.2g Sugars

226. Thai Green Curry with Pork

(Ready in about 15 minutes | Servings 4)

Ingredients

2 tablespoons Thai green curry paste
1/2 teaspoon cumin seeds
1 cup beef bone broth
1 jalapeño pepper, seeded and minced
Zest and juice of 1 lime
1 bay leaf
2 cloves garlic, minced
1 tablespoon apple cider vinegar
1 ½ tablespoons fish sauce
1/2 teaspoon cayenne pepper
1 pound pork medallions
2 teaspoons coconut oil
Salt and ground black pepper, to taste

Directions

Press the "Sauté" button to preheat the Instant Pot. Heat the coconut oil. Once hot, sear the pork medallions for 2 to 3 minutes.

Add the remaining ingredients, including roasted seasonings.

Secure the lid. Choose the "Manual" setting and cook at High pressure for 8 minutes. Once cooking is complete, use a quick pressure release; carefully remove the lid.

Serve with basmati rice and enjoy!

Per serving: 286 Calories; 15.3g Fat; 5.8g Carbs; 30.5g Protein; 1.7g Sugars

227. Authentic Venezuelan Pork Arepas

(Ready in about 40 minutes | Servings 6)

Ingredients

2 pounds boneless pork butt roast
6 Venezuelan-style arepas (corn cakes)
2 tablespoons Worcestershire sauce
4 cloves garlic, finely chopped
1 teaspoon cayenne pepper
1/4 teaspoon ground cumin
1 teaspoon garlic powder
1 teaspoon onion powder
1 cup cream of mushroom soup
Sea salt and ground black pepper, to taste
1 tablespoon butter

Directions

Place all ingredients, except for the arepas, in the inner pot.

Secure the lid. Choose the "Meat/Stew" mode and cook for 35 minutes at High pressure. Once cooking is complete, use a quick pressure release; carefully remove the lid.

Remove the pork from the inner pot and shred with two forks.

Fill each arepa with the pork mixture and serve with your favorite toppings. Enjoy!

Per serving: 386 Calories; 17.2g Fat; 21.2g Carbs; 34.7g Protein; 5.4g Sugars

228. Mexican Pork and Hominy Stew (Posole Rojo)

(Ready in about 35 minutes | Servings 8)

Ingredients

2 pounds pork butt, cut into 2-inch pieces
1 (15-ounce) can white hominy, drained and rinsed
2 dried ancho chiles, chopped
2 cloves garlic, sliced
2 sprigs thyme, leaves chopped
Sea salt and ground black pepper, to taste
4 cups chicken bone broth
1 cup shallots, chopped
2 bay leaves
1 celery with leaves, chopped
1 red bell pepper, thinly sliced
1 teaspoon Mexican oregano
1 heaping tablespoon lard, melted
1/2 teaspoon cumin
1/2 cup fresh ripe tomato, puréed

Directions

Press the "Sauté" button to preheat your Instant Pot. Now, melt the lard. Once hot, sauté the shallots and garlic until they are tender and fragrant.

Add the pork and cook an additional 3 minutes or until it is delicately browned. Add the remaining ingredients and gently stir to combine.

Secure the lid. Choose the "Poultry" setting and cook at High pressure for 30 minutes. Once cooking is complete, use a natural pressure release; carefully remove the lid.

Divide between individual bowls and serve warm. Enjoy!

Per serving: 503 Calories; 30.4g Fat; 11.6g Carbs; 42.6g Protein; 2.9g Sugars

229. Tangy Braised Pork Loin Roast

(Ready in about 45 minutes | Servings 6)

Ingredients

2 ½ pounds pork loin roast, boneless
1 cup milk
1 cup vegetable broth
1 teaspoon dried basil
1 teaspoon dried oregano
1/2 lemon, juiced and zested
2 tablespoons sesame oil
1/2 teaspoon paprika
Sea salt and freshly ground black pepper, to taste

Directions

Press the "Sauté" button and heat the oil until sizzling; once hot, sear the pork for 4 to 5 minutes or until browned on all sides. Work in batches.

Add the remaining ingredients.

Secure the lid. Choose the "Meat/Stew" mode and cook for 35 minutes at High pressure. Once cooking is complete, use a quick pressure release; carefully remove the lid.

Turn on your broiler. Roast the pork under the broiler for about 3 minutes or until the skin is crisp.

To carve the pork, remove the cracklings and cut the crisp pork skin into strips. Carve the pork roast across the grain into thin slices and serve.

Per serving: 436 Calories; 22.8g Fat; 2.6g Carbs; 52.2g Protein; 2.2g Sugars

230. Authentic Pork Cassoulet

(Ready in about 40 minutes | Servings 6)

Ingredients

1 pound pork shoulder, cut into cubes
1 pound dry cannellini beans
1 ½ cups sour cream
1 cloves garlic, finely minced
1/2 teaspoon mustard seeds
1/2 teaspoon cumin powder
1 cup water
1 tablespoon beef bouillon granules

1 yellow onion, sliced
1 parsnip, sliced
1 carrots, sliced
1 teaspoon celery seeds
1/2 pound pork sausage, sliced
Sea salt and ground black pepper, to taste
1 tablespoon olive oil

Directions

Press the "Sauté" button to preheat your Instant Pot. Heat the olive oil until sizzling.

Then, brown the meat and sausage for 3 to 4 minutes, stirring periodically.

Add the water, beef bouillon granules, cannellini beans, garlic, onion, parsnip, carrot, and seasonings.

Secure the lid. Choose the "Bean/Chili" setting and cook at High pressure for 30 minutes. Once cooking is complete, use a natural pressure release; carefully remove the lid.

Serve topped with sour cream. Enjoy!

Per serving: 491 Calories; 27g Fat; 25.5g Carbs; 36.1g Protein; 7.1g Sugars

231. Ground Pork Omelet

(Ready in about 25 minutes | Servings 2)

Ingredients

1 tablespoon canola oil
4 eggs, whisked
1 teaspoon oyster sauce
Kosher salt and ground black pepper, to taste
1/2 teaspoon paprika

1 yellow onion, thinly sliced
1/2 teaspoon garlic powder
1/3 teaspoon cumin powder
1/2 pound ground pork
1 red chili pepper, minced

Directions

Press the "Sauté" button and heat the oil until sizzling; once hot, cook the ground pork until no longer pink, crumbling with a spatula.

Add the onion and pepper; cook an additional 2 minutes. Whisk the eggs with the remaining ingredients. Pour the egg mixture over the meat mixture in the inner pot.

Secure the lid. Choose the "Manual" mode and cook for 8 minutes at High pressure. Once cooking is complete, use a natural pressure release for 10 minutes; carefully remove the lid. Bon appétit!

Per serving: 449 Calories; 33.6g Fat; 4.3g Carbs; 32.2g Protein; 1.6g Sugars

232. Mustard Pork Belly with Herbs

(Ready in about 50 minutes | Servings 8)

Ingredients

1/2 teaspoon dried marjoram
1/2 teaspoon red pepper flakes, crushed
1/2 dry white wine
1 teaspoon stone-ground mustard
1 ½ pounds pork belly, scored and patted dry

3 tablespoons maple syrup
1/2 teaspoon ground allspice
1 teaspoon garlic paste
Sea salt and ground black pepper, to taste
1/2 cup water

Directions

Spread the garlic paste over the pork belly; sprinkle with salt, black pepper, dried marjoram and red pepper flakes.

Press the "Sauté" button to preheat your Instant Pot. Then, sear the pork belly for 3 minutes per side.

In a mixing bowl, thoroughly combine water, wine, maple syrup, mustard, and allspice. Pour this mixture over the pork belly in the Instant Pot.

Secure the lid. Choose the "Meat/Stew" setting and cook at High pressure for 40 minutes. Once cooking is complete, use a natural pressure release; carefully remove the lid.

Cut the prepared pork belly into pieces; serve with some extra mustard, if desired. Bon appétit!

Per serving: 475 Calories; 45.1g Fat; 6.1g Carbs; 8.1g Protein; 4.9g Sugars

233. Cajun Pork and Pepper Casserole

(Ready in about 40 minutes | Servings 4)

Ingredients

2 pounds pork steaks, cut into large pieces
1 cup goat cheese, crumbled
1 tablespoon Cajun seasonings
4 sage leaves
2 cloves garlic, sliced
1 serrano pepper, deveined and chopped
1 teaspoon mustard

4 mixed colored peppers, deveined and chopped
2 tablespoons red wine
1 onion, thinly
1 cup chicken broth
1 tablespoon lard, melted
Sea salt and ground black pepper, to taste

Directions

Press the "Sauté" button and melt the lard; once hot, sear the pork in batches until golden brown all over.

Add the onions, garlic, and peppers. Season with salt, black pepper, and Cajun seasonings. Add the sage leaves, mustard, wine, and broth.

Secure the lid. Choose the "Manual" mode and cook for 30 minutes at High pressure. Once cooking is complete, use a quick pressure release; carefully remove the lid.

Add the goat cheese on top, seal the lid again, and let it sit in the residual heat until the cheese melts.

Let it rest for 5 to 10 minutes before slicing and serving. Bon appétit!

Per serving: 501 Calories; 26.8g Fat; 10g Carbs; 53.5g Protein; 4.7g Sugars

234. Macaroni and Cheese with Pork Sausage

(Ready in about 15 minutes | Servings 6)

Ingredients

1 pound pork sausage, casing removed, coarsely chopped
1 pound macaroni
2 cloves garlic, minced
Salt, to taste
1 teaspoon dried basil
1 teaspoon dried oregano
1 yellow onion, finely chopped
1 cup water

1/2 teaspoon red pepper flakes, crushed
4 ounces Colby cheese, shredded
1 teaspoon stone-ground mustard
1 tablespoon olive oil
1 cup tomato purée
1/2 teaspoon ground black pepper

Directions

Press the "Sauté" button to preheat your Instant Pot. Then, heat the oil; now, cook the onion until translucent.

Now, add the garlic and sausage; continue to cook for 4 minutes more. Stir in the seasonings, mustard, water, tomato purée, and macaroni.

Secure the lid. Choose the "Manual" setting and cook at High pressure for 6 minutes. Once cooking is complete, use a quick pressure release; carefully remove the lid.

Top with the Colby cheese; seal the lid and let it sit in the residual heat until the cheese has melted. Bon appétit!

Per serving: 495 Calories; 15.2g Fat; 60g Carbs; 27.8g Protein; 4.5g Sugars

235. German Pork with Sauerkraut

(Ready in about 40 minutes | Servings 4)

Ingredients

14 ounces sauerkraut, drained
1 ½ pounds pork shoulder, cubed
2 garlic cloves, minced
4 ounces pork sausage, sliced
1/2 teaspoon black peppercorns

1 cup beef broth
1 onion, sliced
1 tablespoon oil
2 bay leaves
1 dried chili pepper, minced
1/2 teaspoon smoked paprika
Sea salt and, to taste

Directions

Press the "Sauté" button and heat the oil. Once hot, cook the pork and sausage until they are no longer pink.

Add the remaining ingredients; gently stir to combine.

Secure the lid. Choose the "Meat/Stew" mode and cook for 35 minutes at High pressure. Once cooking is complete, use a quick pressure release; carefully remove the lid. Enjoy!

Per serving: 435 Calories; 27.7g Fat; 6.5g Carbs; 38.2g Protein; 2.5g Sugars

236. Smothered Pork Chops with Mustard

(Ready in about 15 minutes | Servings 4)

Ingredients

4 pork loin chops
1 tablespoon Dijon mustard
1 cup sour cream
1 teaspoon smoked paprika
1/2 cup cream of celery soup

2 tablespoons canola oil
1/2 cup chicken broth
Salt and ground black pepper, to taste

Directions

Press the "Sauté" button to preheat your Instant Pot. Then, heat the oil and sear the pork chops for 2 minutes per side.

Then, stir in the salt, black pepper, paprika, cream of celery soup, and chicken broth.

Secure the lid. Choose the "Manual" setting and cook at High pressure for 9 minutes. Once cooking is complete, use a quick pressure release; carefully remove the lid.

Remove the pork chops from the Instant Pot.

Fold in the sour cream and Dijon mustard. Press the "Sauté" button again and let it simmer until the sauce is reduced and heated through. Bon appétit!

Per serving: 433 Calories; 22.7g Fat; 7g Carbs; 48.3g Protein; 0.8g Sugars

237. Goan Pork Masala

(Ready in about 30 minutes | Servings 3)

Ingredients

1 cup yogurt
1 tablespoon garam masala
1 teaspoon curry powder
1/2 teaspoon Fenugreek seeds
2 dried chiles de árbol, chopped
2 green cardamoms
2 onions, sliced
2 cloves garlic, sliced

1/2 teaspoon ground allspice
1 tablespoon cider vinegar
1 tablespoon ghee
Salt and black pepper, to taste
1 teaspoon coriander seeds
1 (1-inch) piece ginger
1/3 cup all-purpose flour
1 pound pork stew meat, cubed

Directions

Toss the pork stew meat with the flour until well coated.

Press the "Sauté" button and melt the ghee. Once hot, cook the pork for 3 to 4 minutes, stirring frequently to ensure even cooking.

Add the remaining ingredients, except for the yogurt.

Secure the lid. Choose the "Manual" mode and cook for 15 minutes at High pressure. Once cooking is complete, use a natural pressure release for 10 minutes; carefully remove the lid.

Add the yogurt and press the "Sauté" button; let it cook for a few minutes more or until everything is thoroughly heated. Bon appétit!

Per serving: 436 Calories; 19.8g Fat; 18.3g Carbs; 43.7g Protein; 5.2g Sugars

238. Perfect Pulled Pork Sliders

(Ready in about 50 minutes | Servings 6)

Ingredients

2 pounds pork shoulder roast, rind removed, boneless
12 soft lunch rolls, warmed
2 garlic cloves, chopped
1 cup pickles, sliced
1 tablespoon maple syrup 1/3 teaspoon ground black pepper
1/4 cup dry red wine
1 cup water
1/2 tablespoon Worcestershire sauce

1 (1-inch) piece fresh ginger, peeled and grated
2 sprig thyme
2 whole star anise
1 tablespoon arrowroot powder
2 teaspoons lard, at room temperature
Sea salt, to taste

Directions

Press the "Sauté" button to preheat your Instant Pot. Now, melt the lard. Once hot, sear the pork shoulder roast for 3 minutes per side.

Add the garlic, ginger, maple syrup, wine, water, Worcestershire sauce, and seasonings to the Instant Pot.

Secure the lid. Choose the "Meat/Stew" setting and cook at High pressure for 45 minutes. Once cooking is complete, use a natural pressure release; carefully remove the lid.

Transfer the pork shoulder to a chopping board. Shred the meat and return it back to the Instant Pot.

Whisk the arrowroot powder with 2 tablespoons of water; press the "Sauté" button again and add the slurry. Let it simmer until thickened.

Assemble the sandwiches with the pork and pickles. Bon appétit!

Per serving: 480 Calories; 18.4g Fat; 30.1g Carbs; 45.1g Protein; 3.3g Sugars

239. Pork Romano Meatloaf

(Ready in about 35 minutes | Servings 4)

Ingredients

1 pound ground pork
1/4 cup Romano cheese, grated
1/2 cup tomato sauce
1 tablespoon mustard
1 egg, beaten
1 tablespoon fish sauce
1/2 cup breadcrumbs

1 teaspoon dried basil
1 teaspoon dried oregano
1 onion, chopped
4 cloves garlic, minced
1/2 teaspoon chili flakes
1 teaspoon dried sage
4 ounces bacon, chopped

Directions

Place a steamer rack inside the inner pot; add 1/2 cup of water. Cut 1 sheet of heavy-duty foil and brush with cooking spray.

In mixing dish, thoroughly combine all ingredients.

Shape the meat mixture into a loaf; place the meatloaf in the center of the foil. Wrap your meatloaf in foil and lower onto the steamer rack.

Secure the lid. Choose the "Meat/Stew" mode and cook for 20 minutes at High pressure. Once cooking is complete, use a quick pressure release; carefully remove the lid. Let it stand for 10 minutes before cutting and serving. Bon appétit!

Per serving: 520 Calories; 36.6g Fat; 18.7g Carbs; 28.4g Protein; 5.7g Sugars

240. Pork Steak in Red Wine Sauce

(Ready in about 15 minutes | Servings 6)

Ingredients

1 ½ pounds pork steaks
1/2 cup red wine
1 tablespoon lard, melted
2 bay leaves

1 teaspoon dried oregano
1 cup demi-glace
Sea salt and ground black pepper, to taste

Directions

Press the "Sauté" button to preheat your Instant Pot. Melt the lard. Now, sear the pork steaks approximately 3 minutes per side.

Add the remaining ingredients to the Instant Pot.

Secure the lid. Choose the "Manual" setting and cook at High pressure for 8 minutes. Once cooking is complete, use a quick pressure release; carefully remove the lid.

Press the "Sauté" button one more time and continue simmering until the cooking liquid has reduced by three-fourths. Bon appétit!

Per serving: 330 Calories; 22.2g Fat; 1.7g Carbs; 28.7g Protein; 0.6g Sugars

241. Pork Fajitas with Pico de Gallo

(Ready in about 50 minutes | Servings 4)

Ingredients

2 pounds pork tenderloins, halved crosswise
1 cup Pico de Gallo
16 small flour tortillas
1/4 cup balsamic vinegar
1 tablespoon grapeseed oil
1 cup sour cream
1 teaspoon paprika

1 teaspoon dried sage
1/2 teaspoon ground cumin
1/4 cup tomato puree
1/2 cup beef broth
A bunch of scallions, chopped
1 tablespoon brown sugar
Coarse sea salt and freshly ground pepper, to taste

Directions

Mix the paprika, sugar, sage, cumin, salt, and black pepper. Rub the spice mixture all over the pork tenderloins.

Press the "Sauté" button to preheat your Instant Pot. Heat the oil and sear the pork until browned, about 4 minutes per side.

Add the balsamic vinegar, tomato puree, and beef broth.

Secure the lid. Choose the "Manual" mode and cook for 40 minutes at High pressure. Once cooking is complete, use a quick pressure release; carefully remove the lid.

Warm the tortillas until soft; serve with the pork mixture, scallions, sour cream, and Pico de Gallo. Enjoy!

Per serving: 618 Calories; 18.8g Fat; 53.8g Carbs; 55.7g Protein; 11.7g Sugars

242. Perfect Saucissons Provençal

(Ready in about 15 minutes | Servings 4)

Ingredients

1 pound pork sausages, sliced
1 tablespoon Herbs de Provence
2 ripe tomatoes, chopped
1 (15-ounce) can black beans
1/4 teaspoon freshly ground black pepper
2 tablespoons white wine
1 tablespoon oyster sauce
1 teaspoon cayenne pepper
1/2 teaspoon ground bay leaf
1 leek, thinly sliced
2 garlic cloves, crushed
1 cup vegetable broth
Sea salt, to taste

Directions

Press the "Sauté" button to preheat your Instant Pot. Then, heat the oil until sizzling. Brown the sausage for 2 to 3 minutes.

Add the remaining ingredients and gently stir to combine.

Secure the lid. Choose the "Manual" setting and cook at High pressure for 8 minutes. Once cooking is complete, use a quick pressure release; carefully remove the lid.

Divide among individual bowls and serve warm. Bon appétit!

Per serving: 376 Calories; 29.6g Fat; 12.9g Carbs; 15g Protein; 3.1g Sugars

243. Glazed Picnic Ham

(Ready in about 30 minutes + marinating time | Servings 5)

Ingredients

2 pounds picnic ham
2 tablespoons olive oil
1/3 cup red wine
2 sweet peppers, julienned
2 cloves garlic, minced
1 tablespoon mustard
2 tablespoons parsley, chopped
2/3 cup fresh orange juice
1 shallot, sliced
1/2 teaspoon cayenne pepper

Directions

Mix the olive oil, cayenne pepper, red wine, orange juice, garlic, and mustard in a glass bowl. Add the pork and let it marinate for 2 hours.

Transfer the pork along with its marinade to the inner pot. Add the parsley, shallot, and peppers.

Secure the lid. Choose the "Meat/Stew" mode and cook for 20 minutes at High pressure. Once cooking is complete, use a quick pressure release; carefully remove the lid.

Spoon over hot steamed rice. Bon appétit!

Per serving: 427 Calories; 28.1g Fat; 9.5g Carbs; 32.9g Protein; 3.1g Sugars

244. Mexican Meatloaf with Salsa

(Ready in about 35 minutes | Servings 6)

Ingredients

1 egg
1 teaspoon smoked paprika
1 cup bottled chipotle salsa
2 garlic cloves, minced
2 tablespoons ketchup
1/2 cup scallions, minced
1 pound ground pork
1 teaspoon fresh lime juice
1/2 cup Cotija cheese, crumbled
1/2 cup whole grain tortilla chips, finely crushed
Sea salt and ground black pepper, to taste

Directions

Prepare your Instant Pot by adding 1 cup of water and a metal rack to its bottom.

Thoroughly combine the ground pork, egg, scallions, garlic, crushed tortilla chips, Cotija cheese, salt, black pepper, paprika, and 1/2 cup of salsa in a mixing bowl.

Now, shape the mixture into a meatloaf. Transfer the meatloaf to a lightly greased baking pan. Lower the baking pan onto the rack.

In a bowl, mix the remaining 1/2 cup of salsa with ketchup and lime juice. Brush the salsa mixture over top of the meatloaf.

Secure the lid. Choose the "Bean/Chili" setting and cook at High pressure for 30 minutes. Once cooking is complete, use a quick pressure release; carefully remove the lid. Bon appétit!

Per serving: 352 Calories; 22.1g Fat; 13.2g Carbs; 24.8g Protein; 3.7g Sugars

245. Spicy Pork Frittata

(Ready in about 50 minutes | Servings 3)

Ingredients

6 eggs, beaten
1 pound pork shoulder
1/2 cup cream cheese
1 cup chicken broth
Sea salt and ground black pepper, to taste
2 tablespoons butter, at room temperature
1 shallot, thinly sliced
1/2 teaspoon paprika
1/2 teaspoon hot sauce
2 cloves garlic, minced

Directions

Press the "Sauté" button to preheat your Instant Pot. Melt the butter and brown the pork for 4 minutes per side.

Add the chicken broth, salt, and black pepper.

Secure the lid. Choose the "Manual" mode and cook for 15 minutes at High pressure. Once cooking is complete, use a natural pressure release for 5 minutes; carefully remove the lid.

Shred the meat with two forks.; add the remaining ingredients and stir to combine well.

Lightly spritz a baking pan with cooking oil. Spoon the meat/egg mixture into the baking pan.

Cover with foil. Add 1 cup of water and a metal trivet to the Instant Pot. Lower the baking pan onto the trivet.

Secure the lid. Choose the "Manual" mode and cook for 15 minutes at High pressure. Once cooking is complete, use a natural pressure release for 10 minutes; carefully remove the lid. Bon appétit!

Per serving: 533 Calories; 36.6g Fat; 4.4g Carbs; 44.3g Protein; 2.6g Sugars

246. Spicy Pork Spare Ribs

(Ready in about 45 minutes | Servings 4)

Ingredients

1 cup tomato ketchup
1/4 cup dark soy sauce
1 tablespoon sea salt
1 teaspoon shallot powder
1 teaspoon garlic powder
1 teaspoon fennel seeds
1 tablespoon sugar

1/2 teaspoon black pepper
1/2 teaspoon chili flakes
1 cup chicken stock
1 teaspoon cayenne pepper
2 pounds pork spare ribs, cut into 4 equal portions

Directions

Generously sprinkle the pork spare ribs with all spices and sugar. Add the chicken stock and secure the lid.

Choose the "Meat/Stew" mode and cook for 35 minutes at High pressure. Once cooking is complete, use a quick pressure release; carefully remove the lid.

Transfer the pork ribs to a baking pan. Mix the tomato ketchup and soy sauce; pour the mixture over the pork ribs and roast in the preheated oven at 425 degrees F for 6 to 8 minutes. Bon appétit!

Per serving: 500 Calories; 28.6g Fat; 8.9g Carbs; 49.2g Protein; 6.1g Sugars

247. Balsamic Boston Butt

(Ready in about 1 hour 5 minutes | Servings 8)

Ingredients

3 pounds Bost1 teaspoon celery seeds
1 teaspoon fennel seeds on butt
1/2 teaspoon whole black peppercorns
1 bay leaf
1 teaspoon salt
For the Sauce:

1/4 cup balsamic vinegar
4 tablespoons brown sugar
1 teaspoon shallot powder
1 teaspoon chipotle powder
1 tablespoon Worcestershire sauce
1 cup water
1 ½ cups ketchup

Directions

Season the Boston butt with salt and add it to the Instant Pot that is previously greased with a nonstick cooking spray.

Add enough water to cover the meat. Stir in the black peppercorns, bay leaf, celery seeds, and fennel seeds.

Secure the lid and select the "Manual" mode. Cook for 55 minutes at High pressure.

In the meantime, in a saucepan, place the remaining ingredients for the sauce. Bring this mixture to a boil, and then, immediately, reduce the heat to medium-low.

Cook until it is thickened and heated through, stirring continuously.

Once cooking is complete, use a quick pressure release; remove the lid; reserve about 1 cup of cooking liquid. Shred the pork with two forks, add cooking liquid and stir to combine well.

Serve with the prepared sauce.

Per serving: 333 Calories; 8.6g Fat; 55.5g Carbs; 10.8g Protein; 27.1g Sugars

248. Asian-Style Pork with Mushrooms

(Ready in about 30 minutes | Servings 3)

Ingredients

1 ½ pounds pork medallions
6 ounces mushrooms, chopped
1 tablespoon Sriracha sauce
1/2 teaspoon salt
1 tablespoon maple syrup
2 cloves garlic, minced
1/2 cup tamari sauce

1/2 cup chicken stock
1 tablespoon sesame oil
1 tablespoon arrowroot powder, dissolved in 2 tablespoons of water
1/4 cup rice vinegar
1/2 teaspoon cayenne pepper

Directions

Press the "Sauté" button and heat the oil; once hot, cook the pork medallions for 3 minutes per side.

Add the tamari sauce, chicken stock, vinegar, cayenne pepper, salt, maple syrup, Sriracha, garlic, and mushrooms to the inner pot.

Secure the lid. Choose the "Meat/Stew" mode and cook for 20 minutes at High pressure. Once cooking is complete, use a quick pressure release; carefully remove the lid. Remove the pork from the inner pot.

Add the thickener to the cooking liquid. Press the "Sauté" button again and let it boil until the sauce has reduced slightly and the flavors have concentrated.

Serve over hot steamed rice if desired. Enjoy!

Per serving: 355 Calories; 10.1g Fat; 13g Carbs; 51g Protein; 7.2g Sugars

249. Old-Fashioned Pork Steaks

(Ready in about 15 minutes | Servings 6)

Ingredients

1 ½ pounds pork steaks
1/2 teaspoon mixed peppercorns
2 sprigs rosemary
1 tablespoon fresh parsley

1 sprig thyme
Salt, to taste
1 cup roasted vegetable broth
2 teaspoons lard

Directions

Press the "Sauté" button to preheat your Instant Pot; melt the lard. Once hot, sear the pork until delicately browned.

Stir in the remaining ingredients.

Secure the lid. Choose the "Manual" setting and cook at High pressure for 8 minutes. Once cooking is complete, use a quick pressure release; carefully remove the lid.

Press the "Sauté" button to thicken the sauce. Serve warm and enjoy!

Per serving: 476 Calories; 44.2g Fat; 0.1g Carbs; 21.2g Protein; 0.1g Sugars

250. Home-Style Pork Cheeseburgers

(Ready in about 20 minutes | Servings 3)

Ingredients

1 large sweet pepper, minced
3 (1-ounce) slices Swiss cheese, sliced
1/2 teaspoon red pepper flakes, crushed
3 burger buns

1 chipotle pepper, minced
2 cloves garlic, minced
1 pound ground pork
Sea salt and ground black pepper, to taste

Directions

Mix the ground pork, peppers, garlic, salt, black pepper, and red pepper flakes until well combined.

Form the meat mixture into 3 patties. Place your patties on squares of aluminum foil and wrap them loosely.

Add 1 cup water and a metal trivet to the Instant Pot; lower the foil packs onto the top of the metal trivet.

Secure the lid. Choose the "Meat/Stew" mode and cook for 10 minutes at High pressure. Once cooking is complete, use a natural pressure release; carefully remove the lid.

Place your patties on a baking sheet and broil for 5 to 6 minutes. Serve on buns topped with Swiss cheese. Enjoy!

Per serving: 428 Calories; 15.4g Fat; 28.4g Carbs; 44.2g Protein; 6.5g Sugars

251. Easy BBQ Pork

(Ready in about 30 minutes | Servings 6)

Ingredients

1 teaspoon ground mustard
1/4 cup champagne vinegar
1 teaspoon garlic powder
1 cup ketchup
3 tablespoons brown sugar

1/2 teaspoon sea salt
1/2 tablespoon fresh ground black pepper.
3 pounds pork butt roast
1/2 cup water

Directions

Add all of the above ingredients to your Instant Pot.

Secure the lid and select the "Meat/Stew" mode. Cook for 20 minutes under High pressure. Once cooking is complete, use a natural pressure release; carefully remove the lid.

Shred the meat and return it back to the Instant Pot. Serve the pork loin with the sauce and enjoy!

Per serving: 435 Calories; 18.9g Fat; 15.1g Carbs; 48.8g Protein; 12.4g Sugars

252. Country-Style Pork Ribs

(Ready in about 45 minutes | Servings 4)

Ingredients

1 cup BBQ sauce
1/2 cup Marsala wine
1/2 cup chicken broth
1 rack country style pork ribs

1 teaspoon red pepper flakes
Coarse sea salt and freshly ground black pepper, to taste

Directions

Place the pork ribs, salt, black pepper, red pepper, wine, and chicken broth in the inner pot.

Choose the "Meat/Stew" mode and cook for 35 minutes at High pressure. Once cooking is complete, use a quick pressure release; carefully remove the lid.

Transfer the pork ribs to a baking pan. Pour the BBQ sauce over the pork ribs and roast in the preheated oven at 425 degrees F for 6 to 8 minutes. Bon appétit!

Per serving: 386 Calories; 14.9g Fat; 4.9g Carbs; 54.7g Protein; 2.9g Sugars

253. Pork with Riesling Sauce

(Ready in about 30 minutes | Servings 6)

Ingredients

2 pounds pork shoulder, cut into four pieces
1/2 cup Riesling
2 garlic cloves, chopped
2 sprigs rosemary
1 sprig thyme
2 tablespoons honey

1 tablespoon Worcestershire sauce
Kosher salt and ground black pepper, to taste
2 tablespoons lard, melted
1/2 cup water

Directions

Press the "Sauté" button to preheat your Instant Pot. Melt the lard. Then, sear the meat for 2 to 3 minutes, stirring frequently.

Add the remaining ingredients and gently stir to combine.

Secure the lid. Choose the "Meat/Stew" setting and cook at High pressure for 20 minutes. Once cooking is complete, use a quick pressure release; carefully remove the lid. Bon appétit!

Per serving: 483 Calories; 31g Fat; 7.3g Carbs; 38g Protein; 6.1g Sugars

254. Pork Liver Mousse with Brandy

(Ready in about 20 minutes | Servings 6)

Ingredients

1 pound pork livers
1/4 cup brandy
1 cup water
2 sprigs rosemary
2 sprigs thyme
1 onion, chopped

2 cloves garlic, minced
2 tablespoons butter
1/2 cup heavy cream
Himalayan pink salt and
ground black pepper, to taste

Directions

Press the "Sauté" button and melt the butter. Then, sauté the onion and garlic until just tender and aromatic.

Add the pork livers and cook for 3 minutes on both sides or until the juices run clear. Deglaze the pan with a splash of brandy.

Add the water, thyme, rosemary, salt, and ground black pepper.

Secure the lid. Choose the "Manual" mode and cook for 5 minutes at High pressure. Once cooking is complete, use a quick pressure release; carefully remove the lid.

Add the brandy and heavy cream. Press the "Sauté" button and cook for 2 to 3 minutes more.

Transfer to your food processor and blend the mixture to a fine mousse. Bon appétit!

Per serving: 177 Calories; 11.7g Fat; 3.1g Carbs; 14.4g Protein; 1.5g Sugars

255. Ale-Braised Pork Ham Hock with Herbs

(Ready in about 55 minutes | Servings 6)

Ingredients

2 pounds pork ham hocks
1/2 cup ale beer
1/2 teaspoon dried sage,
crushed
1/2 teaspoon marjoram
A bunch of scallions, chopped
2 bay leaves

2 garlic cloves, minced
1 cup water
Sea salt and ground black
pepper, to taste
1/2 teaspoon cayenne pepper,
or more to taste

Directions

Place all of the above ingredients in the Instant Pot.

Secure the lid. Choose the "Meat/Stew" setting and cook at High pressure for 45 minutes. Once cooking is complete, use a natural pressure release; carefully remove the lid.

Remove the ham hocks from the Instant Pot; allow them to cool enough to be handled. Remove the meat from the ham hocks and return it to the cooking liquid.

Serve on individual plates and enjoy!

Per serving: 304 Calories; 19.1g Fat; 2.6g Carbs; 30.5g Protein; 0.6g Sugars

256. Japanese Buta Niku No Mushimono

(Ready in about 15 minutes | Servings 4)

Ingredients

1 pound ground pork
2 tablespoons sake
4 fresh shiitake, sliced
2 cloves garlic, minced
1 cup chicken broth

1 teaspoon fresh ginger, grated
1 teaspoon sesame oil
2 tablespoons tamari sauce
Sea salt and ground black
pepper, to taste

Directions

Press the "Sauté" button and heat the oil. Once hot, cook the ground pork until no longer pink.

Add the fresh shiitake, chicken broth, tamari sauce, garlic, sake, ginger, salt, and black pepper.

Secure the lid. Choose the "Poultry" mode and High pressure; cook for 5 minutes. Once cooking is complete, use a quick release.

Spoon into individual bowls. Enjoy!

Per serving: 460 Calories; 28.9g Fat; 2.7g Carbs; 42.7g Protein; 0.8g Sugars

257. Sticky Pulled Pork with Apples

(Ready in about 35 minutes | Servings 8)

Ingredients

2 ½ pounds pork butt, cut into
bite-sized cubes
1 red chili pepper, minced
1 cooking apple, cored and
diced
1 lemon, sliced

Sea salt and ground black
pepper
1 teaspoon dried oregano
1/2 teaspoon dried basil
1 tablespoon maple syrup
1/2 cup vegetable broth
1/2 cup barbecue sauce

Directions

Add the pork, broth, barbecue sauce, salt, black pepper, oregano, basil, maple syrup, chili pepper, and apple to your Instant Pot.

Secure the lid. Choose the "Soup" setting and cook at High pressure for 30 minutes. Once cooking is complete, use a natural pressure release; carefully remove the lid.

Shred the pork with two forks. Return it back to the Instant Pot. Serve with lemon slices. Bon appétit!

Per serving: 434 Calories; 25.2g Fat; 13.6g Carbs; 36.1g Protein; 10.5g Sugars

258. Dad's Pork Chops and Potatoes

(Ready in about 20 minutes | Servings 4)

Ingredients

4 pork chops
1 pound potatoes, quartered
1 cup chicken broth
1 onion, sliced

Sea salt and ground black pepper, to taste
2 tablespoons lard, at room temperature

Directions

Press the "Sauté" button and melt the lard. Once hot, brown the pork chops for 3 minutes per side.

Add the remaining ingredients.

Secure the lid. Choose the "Manual" mode and cook for 10 minutes at High pressure. Once cooking is complete, use a natural pressure release; carefully remove the lid.

Serve warm.

Per serving: 484 Calories; 24.3g Fat; 20.2g Carbs; 43.7g Protein; 1.1g Sugars

259. Pork Loin with Salsa Sause

(Ready in about 35 minutes | Servings 6)

Ingredients

1 tablespoon chipotle paste
1 cup broth
1 ½ pounds pork loin, boneless and well-trimmed
2 tablespoons brown sugar
1 teaspoon grainy mustard
1/3 teaspoon ground allspice
1/2 teaspoon ground bay leaf
1 (1-inch) piece fresh ginger root, grated
Kosher salt and ground black pepper, to your liking

For the Salsa Sauce:
1 ½ tablespoons lime juice
Salt, to your liking
2 ripe tomatoes, peeled, seeds removed, chopped
1 clove garlic, minced
1 mild chile pepper
2 tablespoons onion, finely chopped
2 tablespoons cilantro, chopped

Directions

Sprinkle the pork loin with all seasonings. Spritz the Instant Pot with a nonstick cooking spray.

Press the "Sauté" button to heat up your Instant Pot. Sear pork loin on both sides until just browned.

Add the brown sugar, chipotle paste, and broth. Secure the lid. Choose the "Manual" setting and cook for 25 minutes at High Pressure.

Once cooking is complete, use a natural release; remove the lid carefully.

Meanwhile, make the salsa by mixing all ingredients. Serve the pork loin with fresh salsa on the side. Bon appétit!

Per serving: 398 Calories; 19.4g Fat; 8.1g Carbs; 45.5g Protein; 5.9g Sugars

260. Loin Roast with Cream Cheese Sauce

(Ready in about 30 minutes | Servings 4)

Ingredients

1 pound pork loin roast, cut into three pieces
1 tablespoon lard, at room temperature
Sauce:
1 cup cream cheese
1 tablespoons flaxseed meal

2 garlic cloves, chopped
1/4 cup rice vinegar
1/4 cup dry white wine
2 tablespoons tamari sauce
1/2 cup water
2 tablespoons maple syrup

Directions

Press the "Sauté" button and melt the lard. Once hot, cook the pork loin until no longer pink.

Add the garlic, maple syrup, vinegar, water, wine and tamari sauce.

Secure the lid. Choose the "Manual" mode and cook for 10 minutes at High pressure. Once cooking is complete, use a natural pressure release for 10 minutes; carefully remove the lid. Reserve the meat.

Meanwhile, make the slurry by whisking the flaxseed meal with 2 tablespoons of cold water.

Stir in the slurry and press the "Sauté" button again. Cook the sauce until it has thickened; fold in the cheese and stir until heated through. Bon appétit!

Per serving: 491 Calories; 32.9g Fat; 10.9g Carbs; 36.4g Protein; 8.6g Sugars

261. Pork and Vegetable Medley

(Ready in about 40 minutes | Servings 4)

Ingredients

1 pound pork shanks, trimmed of skin
1 cup beef bone broth
2 bay leaves
1 carrot, sliced
1 serrano pepper, deveined and sliced
Sea salt and ground black pepper, to taste
1 celery stalk, chopped

1 parsnip, sliced
1 teaspoon red pepper flakes, crushed
1 teaspoon turmeric powder
2 tablespoons vermouth
1 teaspoon garlic powder
1 bell pepper, deveined and sliced
2 teaspoons olive oil

Directions

Press the "Sauté" button to preheat your Instant Pot; heat the olive oil. Once hot, cook the pork shanks until they are delicately browned.

Stir in the remaining ingredients.

Secure the lid. Choose the "Meat/Stew" setting and cook at High pressure for 35 minutes. Once cooking is complete, use a natural pressure release; carefully remove the lid.

Serve warm over mashed potatoes and enjoy!

Per serving: 348 Calories; 25.1g Fat; 12.1g Carbs; 17.3g Protein; 4.5g Sugars

262. Creamy Italian-Style Pork with Mushrooms

(Ready in about 30 minutes | Servings 6)

Ingredients

6 pork chops
1 tablespoon Italian seasoning blend
1 pound white mushrooms, sliced
1/2 cup cream of onion soup
2 cloves garlic crushed
1/2 cup double cream
2 tablespoons butter
1/2 teaspoon coarse sea salt
1/2 teaspoon cracked black pepper
1 tablespoon fresh coriander, chopped
1 teaspoon dill weed, minced

Directions

Press the "Sauté" button and melt the butter. Once hot, sear the pork chops until golden browned, about 4 minutes per side.

Add the remaining ingredients and gently stir to combine.

Secure the lid. Choose the "Meat/Stew" mode and cook for 20 minutes at High pressure. Once cooking is complete, use a quick pressure release; carefully remove the lid.

Serve over mashed potatoes. Bon appétit!

Per serving: 438 Calories; 25.8g Fat; 7.2g Carbs; 42.8g Protein; 2.7g Sugars

263. Beer-Braised Paprika Ribs

(Ready in about 30 minutes | Servings 8)

Ingredients

1 (12-ounce) bottle light beer
2 pounds pork ribs
Sea salt, to taste
1 tablespoon ground cumin
1 teaspoon garlic powder
1 cup tomato paste
1 tablespoon honey
1/2 teaspoon shallot powder
1 teaspoon paprika
1/2 cup beef bone broth
1/2 teaspoon ground black pepper

Directions

Add all ingredients to your Instant Pot.

Secure the lid. Choose the "Meat/Stew" setting and cook at High pressure for 20 minutes. Once cooking is complete, use a natural pressure release; carefully remove the lid.

Serve over roasted potatoes and enjoy!

Per serving: 268 Calories; 8.9g Fat; 19.7g Carbs; 26.7g Protein; 15.1g Sugars

264. Pork Cutlets with Ricotta Cheese

(Ready in about 30 minutes | Servings 3)

Ingredients

3 pork cutlets
6 ounces Ricotta cheese
1 cup water
1 onion, thinly sliced
2 chicken bouillon cubes
2 tablespoons olive oil
Sea salt and freshly ground black pepper, to taste

Directions

Press the "Sauté" button and heat the oil until sizzling. Sear the pork cutlets for 3 minutes per side.

Add the salt, black pepper, onion, chicken bouillon cubes, water to the Instant Pot.

Secure the lid. Choose the "Manual" mode and cook for 10 minutes at High pressure. Once cooking is complete, use a natural pressure release for 10 minutes; carefully remove the lid.

Top with the Ricotta cheese; seal the lid and let it stand for 5 to 10 minutes or until thoroughly heated. Bon appétit!

Per serving: 447 Calories; 30.3g Fat; 3.6g Carbs; 38.1g Protein; 0.6g Sugars

265. Spare Ribs with Hoisin Sauce

(Ready in about 30 minutes + marinating time | Servings 6)

Ingredients

6 country-style spare rib rashes
2 tablespoons hoisin sauce
1 teaspoon smoked paprika
Salt and black pepper, to your liking
1 teaspoon fresh ginger, finely grated
2 teaspoons sesame oil
1 teaspoon chili powder
1/2 teaspoon ground allspice
1/4 cup tomato sauce
2 garlic cloves, smashed
1 teaspoon whole grain mustard
1/4 cup honey
1/4 cup soy sauce

Directions

Thoroughly combine the honey, soy sauce, hoisin sauce, tomato sauce, garlic, ginger, and sesame oil in a bowl.

Place the spare rib rashes in a large ceramic dish and pour over the honey/sauce. Cover with a plastic wrap and transfer to your refrigerator; let it sit at least 4 hours to develop the flavors.

Add spare rib rashes to the Instant Pot; add the remaining ingredients, along with the reserved marinade.

Secure the lid. Select the "Manual" button and cook for 23 minutes at High pressure.

Once cooking is complete, use a natural release; remove the lid carefully. Now, press the "Sauté" button and continue to cook, uncovered, until the liquid is concentrated. Serve warm and enjoy!

Per serving: 388 Calories; 14.7g Fat; 19.2g Carbs; 42.2g Protein; 16.3g Sugars

266. Chunky Pork Soup with Peppers

(Ready in about 30 minutes | Servings 4)

Ingredients

2 ripe tomatoes, pureed
4 cups chicken stock
1 teaspoon garlic powder
Sea salt and ground black pepper, to taste

1 jalapeno pepper, seeded and minced
2 sweet peppers, seeded and sliced
1 pound ground pork
1 teaspoon Italian seasoning

Directions

Press the "Sauté" button to preheat your Instant Pot. Then, brown the ground pork until no longer pink or about 3 minutes.

Add the remaining ingredients to the inner pot and stir.

Secure the lid. Choose the "Manual" mode and cook for 10 minutes at High pressure. Once cooking is complete, use a natural pressure release for 10; carefully remove the lid.

Serve warm. Bon appétit!

Per serving: 382 Calories; 26.2g Fat; 10.5g Carbs; 26.3g Protein; 2.4g Sugars

267. Decadent Pork with Port and Raisins

(Ready in about 35 minutes | Servings 6)

Ingredients

2 pounds pork loin roast, boneless
1/2 cup port wine
4 ounces raisins
2 cloves garlic, crushed
1 cup pomegranate juice
1 teaspoon paprika
1/2 teaspoon mustard powder

1 teaspoon dried marjoram
1/2 teaspoon fresh ginger, grated
Kosher salt, to taste
1/2 teaspoon ground black pepper
1 tablespoon canola oil

Directions

Press the "Sauté" button to preheat your Instant Pot. Now, heat the oil; sear the pork loin for 3 minutes on each side.

Then, add the remaining ingredients to your Instant Pot.

Secure the lid. Choose the "Poultry" setting and cook at High pressure for 15 minutes. Once cooking is complete, use a natural pressure release; carefully remove the lid.

Serve the pork topped with the raisin-port sauce. Bon appétit!

Per serving: 395 Calories; 15.9g Fat; 21.4g Carbs; 40.9g Protein; 16.7g Sugars

268. Traditional Bosanski Lonac

(Ready in about 45 minutes | Servings 5)

Ingredients

2 pounds pork loin roast, cut into cubes
1/2 pound green beans, cut into 1-inch pieces
2 tablespoons fresh parsley leaves, roughly chopped
2 carrots, cut into chunks
1 teaspoon paprika
2 celery ribs, cut into chunks

1 pound potatoes, cut into chunks
Se salt and ground black pepper, to taste
2 tomatoes, pureed
2 garlic cloves, chopped
1 onion, chopped
2 cups chicken bone broth
2 tablespoons safflower oil

Directions

Press the "Sauté" button and heat the oil until sizzling. Once hot, cook the pork until it is no longer pink on all sides.

Add the garlic and onion and cook for a minute or so, stirring frequently.

Stir in the carrots, celery, potatoes, salt, black pepper, paprika, tomatoes, and chicken bone broth.

Secure the lid. Choose the "Meat/Stew" mode and cook for 35 minutes at High pressure. Once cooking is complete, use a quick pressure release; carefully remove the lid.

Add the green beans to the inner pot. Press the "Sauté" button again and let it simmer for a few minutes more. Serve in individual bowls garnished with fresh parsley.

Per serving: 406 Calories; 13.8g Fat; 23.5g Carbs; 45.7g Protein; 3.3g Sugars

269. Pork with Herb-Wine Sauce

(Ready in about 15 minutes + marinating time | Servings 6)

Ingredients

6 pork chops
1 teaspoon mustard powder
1/2 teaspoon ground cumin
1/2 cup beef bone broth
2 tablespoons fresh parsley, chopped
1 teaspoon rosemary, minced
2 tablespoons olive oil

1/2 cup dry white wine
2 tablespoons fresh lemon juice
2 garlic cloves, smashed
1 teaspoon thyme, minced
Sea salt and ground black pepper, to taste

Directions

Place the lemon juice, garlic, mustard powder, ground cumin, rosemary, thyme, salt, black pepper, 1 tablespoon of olive oil, and pork chops in a ceramic dish. Allow the pork to marinate at least 2 hours.

Press the "Sauté" button to preheat the Instant Pot. Heat the remaining tablespoon of olive oil. Then, brown the pork for 3 minutes per side.

Deglaze the bottom of the inner pot with the white wine. Pour in the broth.

Secure the lid. Choose the "Manual" setting and cook at High pressure for 8 minutes. Once cooking is complete, use a quick pressure release; carefully remove the lid. Serve garnished with fresh parsley. Bon appétit!

Per serving: 405 Calories; 24g Fat; 1.9g Carbs; 42.9g Protein; 0.6g Sugars

270. Summer Ribs with Spicy Sauce

(Ready in about 45 minutes | Servings 4)

Per serving: 500 Calories; 28.6g Fat; 8.9g Carbs; 49.2g Protein; 6.1g Sugars

Ingredients

1 cup tomato ketchup
1/4 cup dark soy sauce
1/2 teaspoon chili flakes
1 tablespoon sea salt
1 teaspoon garlic powder
1 teaspoon fennel seeds
1/2 teaspoon black pepper

1 teaspoon cayenne pepper
1 teaspoon shallot powder
1 tablespoon sugar
1 cup chicken stock
2 pounds pork spare ribs, cut into 4 equal portions

Directions

Generously sprinkle the pork spare ribs with all spices and sugar. Add the chicken stock and secure the lid.

Choose the "Meat/Stew" mode and cook for 35 minutes at High pressure. Once cooking is complete, use a quick pressure release; carefully remove the lid.

Transfer the pork ribs to a baking pan. Mix the tomato ketchup and soy sauce; pour the mixture over the pork ribs and roast in the preheated oven at 425 degrees F for 6 to 8 minutes. Bon appétit!

POULTRY

271. Cheesy Loaded Meatloaf

(Ready in about 35 minutes | Servings 8)

Ingredients

1 cup Romano cheese, grated
1 cup breadcrumbs
2 tablespoons tomato ketchup
1 tablespoon Worcestershire sauce
1 egg, chopped
2 garlic cloves, minced
Salt and ground black pepper, to taste

1/2 cup scallions, chopped
6 ounces tomatoes, puréed
1/2 cup water
1 teaspoon Old Sub Sailor seasoning
1 ½ pounds ground turkey
1 pound ground pork

Directions

Prepare your Instant Pot by adding a metal rack and 1 ½ cups of water to the bottom.

In a large mixing bowl, thoroughly combine the ground turkey, pork, breadcrumbs, Romano cheese, Worcestershire sauce, egg, salt, black pepper, scallions, and garlic.

Shape this mixture into a meatloaf; place the meatloaf in a baking dish and lower the dish onto the rack.

Then, in a mixing bowl, thoroughly combine the puréed tomatoes, ketchup, water, and Old Sub Sailor seasoning. Spread this mixture over the top of your meatloaf.

Secure the lid. Choose the "Meat/Stew" setting and cook for 20 minutes at High pressure. Once cooking is complete, use a natural pressure release; carefully remove the lid.

You can place the meatloaf under the preheated broiler for 4 to 6 minutes if desired. Bon appétit!

Per serving: 387 Calories; 24g Fat; 5g Carbs; 36.9g Protein; 1.7g Sugars

272. Chicken with Millet and Green Beans

(Ready in about 25 minutes | Servings 4)

Ingredients

1 cup millet
1 cup green beans
1 bay leaf
1/2 cup shallots, chopped
1/2 teaspoon red pepper flakes, crushed
1/2 teaspoon dried basil
1/2 teaspoon dried oregano
1 ½ tablespoons olive oil
2 garlic cloves, finely chopped

1 bell pepper, deseeded and chopped
1 cup vegetable broth
1/2 teaspoon ground cumin
1 cup tomato puree
Sea salt and ground black pepper, to taste
4 chicken drumsticks, skinless and boneless

Directions

Season the chicken drumsticks with salt, black pepper, red pepper, basil, oregano, and cumin.

Press the "Sauté" button and heat the olive oil. Sear the chicken drumsticks for 5 minutes, turning them to ensure even cooking.

Add the shallots, garlic, pepper, millet, broth, tomato puree, and bay leaf to the Instant Pot.

Secure the lid and choose the "Poultry" mode. Cook for 15 minutes at High pressure. Once cooking is complete, use a quick pressure release; carefully remove the lid.

Add the green beans and secure the lid again; let it sit in the residual heat until wilts. Enjoy!

Per serving: 440 Calories; 12.8g Fat; 47.1g Carbs; 34g Protein; 4.6g Sugars

273. Farmhouse Beer Turkey Chili

(Ready in about 25 minutes | Servings 4)

Ingredients

1 pound ground turkey
1 (14-ounce) can kidney beans, drained and rinsed
6 ounces beer
1 tablespoon apple butter
1 bell pepper, chopped
1 cup chicken bone broth
1/2 cup shallots, finely chopped

1 carrot, sliced
1 jalapeño pepper, chopped
1 tablespoon cacao powder
1 teaspoon dried basil
1 (14-ounce) can tomatoes
2 garlic cloves, finely minced
1 tablespoon olive oil

Directions

Press the "Sauté" button to heat up your Instant Pot. Then, heat the oil; cook the garlic, shallot, carrot, and bell peppers for about 5 minutes.

Stir in the ground turkey and cook for 3 minutes more, crumbling with a fork.

Secure the lid. Choose the "Poultry" setting and cook for 5 minutes under High pressure. Once cooking is complete, use a quick pressure release; carefully remove the lid. Serve hot and enjoy!

Per serving: 484 Calories; 29.3g Fat; 14.1g Carbs; 41.5g Protein; 4.4g Sugars

274. Chinese-Style Glazed Duck

(Ready in about 25 minutes | Servings 4)

Ingredients

1 cup chicken broth
2 pounds duck breasts
1 teaspoon ground star anise
1 teaspoon red pepper flakes
1 tablespoon paprika
1 teaspoon ground ginger
Kosher salt and ground black pepper, to taste
1 teaspoon dry mustard
1 teaspoon sesame oil

Sea salt and freshly ground black pepper, to taste
Ginger Glaze:
1/4 cup honey
1 tablespoon Sriracha sauce
1-inch piece ginger, finely chopped
3 cloves garlic, finely chopped
1/4 cup low-sodium soy sauce
1 tablespoon peanut oil

Directions

Press the "Sauté" button to preheat your Instant Pot.

Heat the sesame seed oil and sear the duck breasts for 5 minutes, stirring periodically. Sprinkle your spices all over the duck breasts. Add the chicken broth.

Secure the lid and choose the "Poultry" mode. Cook for 15 minutes. Afterwards, use a quick release and carefully remove the lid. Remove the duck breasts from the inner pot.

After that, stir in the other ingredients for the ginger glaze; stir well to combine.

Press the "Sauté" button to preheat your Instant Pot. Cook until thoroughly heated. Place the duck breasts in the serving plates and brush with the ginger glaze. Serve warm and enjoy!

Per serving: 411 Calories; 14.5g Fat; 22.1g Carbs; 47.6g Protein; 18.5g Sugars

275. Country-Style Chicken Thigh Soup

(Ready in about 40 minutes | Servings 6)

Ingredients

6 cups chicken stock, preferably homemade
Freshly ground black pepper, to taste
2 garlic cloves, minced
1 tablespoon fresh coriander leaves, chopped
1 celery with leaves, chopped
1 leek, chopped
2 parsnips, chopped
1 teaspoon dried basil
1/2 teaspoon sea salt
2 carrots, trimmed and chopped
1 pound chicken thighs

Directions

Simply throw all of the above ingredients into your Instant Pot.

Secure the lid. Choose the "Meat/Stew" mode and High pressure; cook for 35 minutes. Once cooking is complete, use a quick pressure release; carefully remove the lid.

Serve in individual bowls garnished with garlic croutons. Enjoy!

Per serving: 245 Calories; 14.6g Fat; 9.8g Carbs; 18.5g Protein; 2.7g Sugars

276. Beer-Braised Turkey Drumsticks

(Ready in about 30 minutes | Servings 5)

Ingredients

1 (12-ounce) bottle beer
2 sprigs rosemary, chopped
2 bay leaves
2 pounds turkey drumsticks, boneless
2 garlic cloves, sliced
1/2 teaspoon ground allspice
Sea salt and freshly ground black pepper, to taste
2 carrots, sliced
1 medium-sized leek, sliced

Directions

Add all ingredients to the inner pot.

Secure the lid. Choose the "Manual" mode and cook for 20 minutes at High pressure. Once cooking is complete, use a natural pressure release; carefully remove the lid.

You can thicken the pan juices if desired. Enjoy!

Per serving: 394 Calories; 17.3g Fat; 3.7g Carbs; 50.1g Protein; 0.7g Sugars

277. Creamed Taco Chicken Salad

(Ready in about 15 minutes | Servings 5)

Ingredients

1 bell pepper, sliced
1/2 cup radishes, sliced
1 cucumber, chopped
1/2 teaspoon taco seasoning
1 teaspoon Dijon mustard
1 cup frozen corn, thawed
1 sprig thyme
1 sprig sage
2 garlic cloves, pressed
1 cup green onions, sliced
1 carrot, shredded
2 chicken breasts, boneless and skinless
2 tablespoons cilantro, chopped
1 sprig rosemary
1/2 cup sour cream
1/2 cup mayonnaise
Seasoned salt and ground black pepper, to taste

Directions

Add 1 ½ cups of water and a metal trivet to your Instant Pot.

Then, season the chicken breast with salt, black pepper and taco seasoning. Place the seasoned chicken breast onto the trivet. Top with thyme, rosemary, sage, and garlic.

Now, secure the lid. Choose the "Poultry" setting and cook for 5 minutes under High pressure. Once cooking is complete, use a natural pressure release; carefully remove the lid.

Allow the chicken to cool and cut it into strips. Stir in the remaining ingredients; gently stir to combine well. Serve well-chilled.

Per serving: 441 Calories; 30.2g Fat; 14.1g Carbs; 27.1g Protein; 3.7g Sugars

278. Sticky Duck in Cherry Sauce

(Ready in about 30 minutes | Servings 5)

Ingredients

6 ounces canned red tart cherries
2 pounds whole duck
1 cup vegetable broth
2 garlic cloves, minced
2 tablespoons dry white wine
1/2 teaspoon curry paste
1 onion, finely chopped
2 tablespoons balsamic vinegar
1 tablespoon lemon rind, grated
Salt and ground black pepper, to taste

Directions

Place all ingredients in the inner pot.

Secure the lid. Choose the "Manual" mode and cook for 20 minutes at High pressure. Once cooking is complete, use a quick pressure release; carefully remove the lid.

Remove the duck from the inner pot.

Press the "Sauté" button and cook the cooking liquid until it is reduced by about half. Bon appétit!

Per serving: 454 Calories; 28.2g Fat; 14.6g Carbs; 34.1g Protein; 7.5g Sugars

279. Turkey Fillets with Cremini Mushrooms

(Ready in about 30 minutes | Servings 6)

Ingredients

2 cups Crimini mushrooms, halved or quartered
1/2 teaspoon turmeric powder
1 cup water
1 ½ pounds turkey fillets
A bunch of scallions, chopped
1 tablespoon olive oil
2 cloves garlic, peeled and crushed
1 cup coconut cream
1 teaspoon fresh coriander, minced
Sea salt and freshly ground black pepper, to taste
1/2 teaspoon brown yellow mustard

Directions

Press the "Sauté" button to preheat your Instant Pot. Heat the oil and sear the turkey fillets for 2 to 3 minutes per side.

Stir in the scallion, mushrooms and garlic; sauté them for 2 minutes more or until they are tender and fragrant.

Next, add the salt, black pepper, mustard, turmeric powder, and water to the Instant Pot.

Secure the lid. Choose the "Meat/Stew" setting and cook for 20 minutes under High pressure. Once cooking is complete, use a quick pressure release; carefully remove the lid.

Then, fold in the coconut cream and seal the lid. Let it sit in the residual heat until everything is thoroughly warmed. Garnish with coriander. Bon appétit!

Per serving: 289 Calories; 18.3g Fat; 4.7g Carbs; 28g Protein; 0.6g Sugars

280. Chicken, Cheese and Pasta Bake

(Ready in about 20 minutes | Servings 5)

Ingredients

4 cups elbow pasta
7 ounces Ricotta cheese, crumbled, at room temperature
1 cup water
2 garlic cloves, minced
1 ½ pounds chicken legs, boneless skinless, cubed
2 tablespoons olive oil
1 onion, sliced
2 sweet peppers, seeded and thinly sliced
1 cup chicken broth
2 strips bacon, diced
2 ounces vermouth

Directions

Press the "Sauté" button to preheat your Instant Pot.

Once hot, heat the olive oil. Now, cook the garlic and bacon until they are fragrant.

Stir in the cubed chicken and cook for 3 minutes more or until it is no longer pink. Use vermouth to scrape the remaining bits of meat off the bottom of the inner pot.

Add the softened Ricotta cheese and water. Secure the lid. Choose the "Poultry" mode and High pressure; cook for 5 minutes. Once cooking is complete, use a quick release.

Add the elbow pasta, onion, and peppers. Pour in the chicken broth; gently stir to combine.

Secure the lid and choose the "Manual" mode. Cook for 4 minutes longer. Afterwards, use a quick release and carefully remove the lid. Bon appétit!

Per serving: 544 Calories; 21.8g Fat; 39.7g Carbs; 44.9g Protein; 1.1g Sugars

281. Stuffed Turkey with Chèvre Cheese

(Ready in about 35 minutes | Servings 4)

Ingredients

2 pounds turkey breast tenderloins
4 ounces chèvre cheese
1/3 teaspoon turmeric powder
2 shallots, chopped
2 tablespoons fresh coriander, chopped
Sea salt and freshly ground black pepper, to your liking
1 teaspoon paprika
2 garlic cloves, smashed
1 carrot, chopped
1/2 teaspoon cumin powder
1 parsnip, chopped
2 ½ cups turkey stock, preferably homemade
3 tablespoons olive oil
1 cup dried bread flakes
1/2 teaspoon garlic powder

Directions

Press the "Sauté" button to preheat your Instant Pot. Now, heat 1 tablespoon of olive oil and sauté the shallots, garlic, carrot, and parsnip until they have softened.

Add the coriander, salt, black pepper, paprika, dried bread flakes, garlic powder, cumin, and turmeric powder; stir to combine well.

Now, slowly and gradually pour in 1/2 cup of turkey stock. Add chèvre and mix to combine well.

Place the turkey breast on a work surface and spread the stuffing mixture over it. Tie a cotton kitchen string around each tenderloin.

Press the "Sauté' button on High heat.

Once hot, add the remaining 2 tablespoons of olive oil. Sear the turkey about 4 minutes on each side. Add the remaining turkey stock and secure the lid.

Choose "Manual", High pressure and 25 minutes cooking time. Use a natural pressure release; carefully remove the lid. Transfer the stuffed turkey tenderloins to a serving platter.

Press the "Sauté" button again and thicken the cooking liquid. Serve with stuffed turkey tenderloins and enjoy!

Per serving: 475 Calories; 25.4g Fat; 8.2g Carbs; 50g Protein; 2.9g Sugars

282. Chicken Breast and Salsa Casserole

(Ready in about 20 minutes | Servings 4)

Ingredients

1 pound chicken breast, boneless, cut into chunks
2 cups spiral pasta
1 cup fresh breadcrumbs
1 cup queso fresco, crumbled
1 ½ cups spiral pasta
1 cup salsa
2 tablespoons olive oil
1 cup Cotija cheese, crumbled
2 cups cream of celery soup

Directions

Press the "Sauté" button and heat the olive oil. Now, brown the chicken breasts for 3 to 4 minutes.

Add the remaining ingredients in the order listed above.

Secure the lid. Choose "Manual" mode and cook for 6 minutes at High pressure. Once cooking is complete, use a natural pressure release; carefully remove the lid. Serve warm.

Per serving: 756 Calories; 34.9g Fat; 66g Carbs; 45.2g Protein; 4.7g Sugars

283. Mexican Chicken Carnitas

(Ready in about 25 minutes | Servings 6)

Ingredients

1/3 cup apple juice
2/3 cup vegetable stock
1/2 teaspoon paprika
2 cloves garlic, pressed
2 tablespoons olive oil
2 tablespoons fresh coriander, chopped

1 teaspoon dried Mexican oregano
1 teaspoon chili powder
2 pounds chicken stew meat, cut into pieces
Sea salt and ground black pepper, to taste

Directions

Simply throw all of the above ingredients, except for the coriander, in the Instant Pot.

Secure the lid. Choose the "Poultry" setting and cook for 15 minutes. Once cooking is complete, use a quick pressure release; carefully remove the lid.

Shred the chicken with two forks. Spread the chicken on a sheet pan and broil for 7 minutes until crispy.

Add the fresh coriander leaves. Serve in taco shells and enjoy!

Per serving: 227 Calories; 9g Fat; 3.1g Carbs; 31.9g Protein; 1.7g Sugars

284. Japanese Teriyaki Chicken

(Ready in about 30 minutes | Servings 4)

Ingredients

1 pound chicken drumettes, skinless, boneless, cut into bite-sized chunks
3 tablespoons Mirin
1 teaspoon ground ginger
2 tablespoons rice wine
2 garlic cloves, minced

1/4 cup brown sugar
1 pound broccoli florets
1 teaspoon arrowroot powder
1/4 cup soy sauce
1/2 cup rice vinegar
2 tablespoons sesame oil
1/2 cup water

Directions

Press the "Sauté" button to preheat your Instant Pot. Heat the sesame oil and cook the chicken drumettes for 3 to 4 minutes.

Then, add the garlic and cook for 30 seconds more or until fragrant. Add the soy sauce, water, vinegar, sugar, ginger, rice wine, and Mirin. Secure the lid.

Choose the "Manual" mode and cook for 10 minutes at High pressure. Once cooking is complete, use a quick pressure release; carefully remove the lid.

Add the broccoli florets and secure the lid. Choose the "Manual" mode and cook for 2 minutes at High pressure. Once cooking is complete, use a quick pressure release; carefully remove the lid.

Transfer the chicken and broccoli to a nice serving platter.

Press the "Sauté" button to preheat your Instant Pot again. Add the arrowroot powder and stir until it is completely dissolved. Cook for 5 to 6 minutes or until the sauce thickens slightly. Spoon over the chicken and serve.

Per serving: 294 Calories; 13.3g Fat; 15.1g Carbs; 27g Protein; 9.8g Sugars

285. Chicken with Cheese Parsley Dip

(Ready in about 1 hour 15 minutes | Servings 6)

Ingredients

6 chicken drumsticks
1 red chili pepper
1/4 cup sesame oil
2 garlic cloves, minced
Sea salt and ground black pepper, to taste
1 cup dry white wine
Cheese Parsley Dip:

1/3 cup cream cheese
1/2 teaspoon cayenne pepper
1 tablespoon fresh lime juice
1/3 cup mayonnaise
1 garlic clove, minced
1/2 cup fresh parsley leaves, chopped

Directions

Place the garlic, whine, chili pepper, salt, black pepper, and sesame oil in a ceramic container. Add chicken drumsticks; let them marinate for 1 hour in your refrigerator.

Add the chicken drumsticks, along with the marinade, to the Instant Pot.

Secure the lid. Choose the "Poultry" setting and cook for 10 minutes. Once cooking is complete, use a quick pressure release; carefully remove the lid.

In a mixing bowl, thoroughly combine parsley, cream cheese mayonnaise, garlic, cayenne pepper, and lime juice.

Serve the chicken drumsticks with the parsley sauce on the side. Bon appétit!

Per serving: 468 Calories; 37.8g Fat; 2.1g Carbs; 28.7g Protein; 0.7g Sugars

286. Ground Turkey Casserole

(Ready in about 20 minutes | Servings 4)

Ingredients

1 ½ pounds ground turkey
Salt and ground black pepper, to taste
2 ripe tomatoes, pureed
1 red chili pepper, minced
3 garlic cloves, smashed
2 tablespoons fresh parsley, roughly chopped

1 bay leaf
1 yellow onion, chopped
1 (1 ½-pound) head of cabbage, shredded
1 tablespoon lard
1 sweet pepper, sliced

Directions

Press the "Sauté" button and melt the lard. Now, brown the ground turkey until no longer pink, about 3 minutes.

Add the remaining ingredients and secure the lid.

Secure the lid. Choose the "Manual" mode and cook for 10 minutes at High pressure. Once cooking is complete, use a natural pressure release; carefully remove the lid.

Divide between individual bowls and serve warm. Enjoy!

Per serving: 385 Calories; 19.1g Fat; 19g Carbs; 37.1g Protein; 8.6g Sugars

287. Grandma's Chicken Soup

(Ready in about 25 minutes | Servings 4)

Ingredients

1 pound chicken wings, halved
1 cup leeks, thinly sliced
1 tablespoon chicken granulated bouillon
1/2 cup garlic croutons, to garnish
2 carrots, chopped
2 garlic cloves, finely minced
3 cups water
1 tablespoon flaxseed meal
1 celery with leaves, chopped
1 tablespoon champagne vinegar
1 ½ tablespoons butter, softened
Sea salt and freshly ground black pepper, to taste

Directions

Press the "Sauté" button to preheat your Instant Pot. Now, melt the butter; sauté the leeks until just tender and fragrant.

Now, add the salt, pepper, chicken, carrots, celery, and garlic. Continue to sauté until the chicken is no longer pink and the vegetables are softened.

Add a splash of water to prevent burning and sticking. Press the "Cancel" button. Add the water and chicken granulated bouillon. Secure the lid.

Choose the "Poultry" setting, High pressure. Cook for 20 minutes. Once cooking is complete, use a natural release.

Then, press the "Sauté" button again. Make the slurry by whisking flaxseed meal with a few tablespoons of the cooking liquid. Return the slurry to the instant Pot and stir to combine.

Add the champagne vinegar and cook for 1 to 2 minutes more. Serve in individual bowls with garlic croutons. Bon appétit!

Per serving: 263 Calories; 9.9g Fat; 15.2g Carbs; 27.7g Protein; 3.3g Sugars

288. Duck with Harvest Vegetables

(Ready in about 30 minutes | Servings 4)

Ingredients

1 cup chicken stock
1 green bell pepper, deseeded and sliced
2 tablespoons balsamic vinegar
4 cloves garlic, sliced
2 carrots, sliced
1 teaspoon smoked paprika
2 rosemary sprigs
1 thyme sprig
1 red bell pepper, deseeded and sliced
1 celery stalk, sliced
2 tablespoons Worcestershire sauce
2 pounds whole duck
1 bay leaf
1 tablespoon butter, melted
1 onion, quartered
Kosher salt and ground black pepper, to taste

Directions

Press the "Sauté" button to preheat your Instant Pot. Now, place the duck skin-side down in the inner pot and sear until the skin is crisp and brown. Turn and cook the other side for 4 to 5 minutes.

Add the chicken stock, salt, black pepper, smoked paprika, and bay leaf to the inner pot.

Secure the lid and choose the "Manual" mode. Cook for 20 minutes at High pressure. Afterwards, use a quick release and carefully remove the lid.

Add the remaining ingredients in the order listed above.

Secure the lid. Choose the "Manual" mode and cook for 3 minutes at High pressure. Once cooking is complete, use a quick pressure release; carefully remove the lid. Serve immediately.

Per serving: 554 Calories; 38g Fat; 9.3g Carbs; 41.9g Protein; 5.2g Sugars

289. Greek-Style Chicken-Stuffed Peppers

(Ready in about 20 minutes | Servings 6)

Ingredients

1 cup Greek-Style yogurt
1 ½ pounds ground chicken
6 bell peppers, tops, membrane and seeds removed
1/4 teaspoon ground cumin
1 teaspoon cayenne pepper
5 ounces Colby cheese, grated
1 teaspoon garlic, minced
1 red onion, chopped
2 teaspoons olive oil
Sea salt and ground black pepper, to taste

Directions

Press the "Sauté" button to heat up the Instant Pot. Then, heat the oil until sizzling.

Cook the chicken with onion and garlic for 3 minutes, stirring periodically. Add the salt, black pepper, cayenne pepper, and cumin; stir to combine.

Fold in the Colby cheese, stir, and reserve.

Wipe down the Instant Pot with a damp cloth. Add 1 ½ cups of water and a metal rack to the Instant Pot.

Fill the peppers with the meat/cheese mixture; don't pack the peppers too tightly.

Place the peppers on the rack and secure the lid. Choose the "Poultry" mode and High pressure; cook for 15 minutes.

Once cooking is complete, use a natural pressure release; carefully remove the lid. Serve with Greek-style yogurt and enjoy!

Per serving: 321 Calories; 19.7g Fat; 8.8g Carbs; 27.9g Protein; 5.1g Sugars

290. Fettuccine with Duck Ragout

(Ready in about 30 minutes | Servings 4)

Ingredients

1 pound duck legs
2 sweet peppers, deseeded and finely chopped
2 cloves garlic, crushed
2 tablespoons dry cooking wine
1 onion, chopped
1/2 cup tomato purée
1 red chili pepper, minced
1/2 cup chicken bone broth
1 pound fettuccine
Sea salt and freshly ground black pepper, to taste

Directions

Bring a pot of salted water to a boil. Cook the fettuccine, stirring occasionally, until al dente. Drain, reserving 1 cup of the pasta water; set aside.

Add the reserved pasta water along with the duck legs to the Instant Pot.

Secure the lid. Choose the "Manual" mode and cook for 20 minutes at High pressure. Once cooking is complete, use a quick pressure release; carefully remove the lid.

Shred the meat with two forks. Add the meat back to the Instant Pot. Add the remaining ingredients and press the "Sauté" button.

Let it cook for 5 to 7 minutes more or until everything is heated through. Serve with the reserved pasta and enjoy!

Per serving: 496 Calories; 23.2g Fat; 26.1g Carbs; 45.5g Protein; 7.8g Sugars

291. Chicken and Bean Medley

(Ready in about 20 minutes | Servings 4)

Ingredients

4 chicken drumsticks
1 (15-ounce) can red kidney beans, rinsed and drained
1/2 cup shallots, chopped
2 carrots, trimmed and chopped
1/2 teaspoon salt
1 celery stalk, chopped
2 ripe tomatoes, chopped
1 cup chicken broth

2 garlic cloves, minced
1/2 cup water
1/4 teaspoon ground black pepper
1/2 cup dry white wine
1 tablespoon olive oil
1/2 pound potatoes, peeled and quartered
1 teaspoon cayenne pepper

Directions

Press the "Sauté" button to preheat your Instant Pot.

Then, heat the oil and cook the shallots, carrots, and celery until they are tender.

Stir in the garlic; cook for another minute. Add the remaining ingredients.

Secure the lid. Choose the "Poultry" mode and High pressure; cook for 15 minutes. Once cooking is complete, use a natural pressure release; carefully remove the lid.

Then, pull the meat off the bones; return the chicken to the Instant Pot. Serve warm and enjoy!

Per serving: 463 Calories; 23.6g Fat; 19.8g Carbs; 41.1g Protein; 3.6g Sugars

292. Chicken Breasts with Vegetables and Herbs

(Ready in about 20 minutes | Servings 4)

Ingredients

1 pound chicken breasts, sliced into serving-size pieces
1 eggplant, diced
1 teaspoon dried marjoram
1/2 head cabbage, diced
2 cups butternut squash, diced
1/2 teaspoon dried sage
Sea salt, to taste

1/2 cup leeks, sliced
2 garlic cloves, sliced
1 cup chicken bone broth
1/2 teaspoon ground black pepper
1/4 cup fresh chives, chopped
2 tablespoons lard, at room temperature

Directions

Press the "Sauté" button and melt the lard until sizzling.

Then, sear the chicken breasts until it is lightly browned or about 5 minutes. Add the spices and stir to combine.

Add the leeks and garlic. Pour in the chicken bone broth. Afterwards, add the vegetables and secure the lid.

Choose the "Manual" mode. Cook for 8 minutes at High pressure. Once cooking is complete, use a quick pressure release; carefully remove the lid.

Using a slotted spoon, remove the chicken and vegetables to a serving platter.

Press the "Sauté" button and simmer the cooking liquid for about 3 minutes until slightly thickened. Serve garnished with fresh chives. Bon appétit!

Per serving: 447 Calories; 21.5g Fat; 24.5g Carbs; 40.1g Protein; 9.5g Sugars

293. Classic Chicken Salad with Herbs

(Ready in about 15 minutes + chilling time | Servings 6)

Ingredients

1 fresh or dried rosemary sprig
2 bay leaves
1 fresh or dried thyme sprig
1 cup mayonnaise
2 garlic cloves
2 tablespoons sour cream
1 yellow onion, thinly sliced
1 carrot, grated

1 cup water
1 teaspoon yellow mustard
2 stalks celery, chopped
1 ½ pounds chicken breasts
1/2 teaspoon seasoned salt
1/3 teaspoon black pepper, ground

Directions

Place the chicken, water, rosemary, thyme, garlic, salt, black pepper, and bay leaves in the Instant Pot.

Secure the lid. Choose the "Poultry" setting and cook for 10 minutes under High pressure. Once cooking is complete, use a natural pressure release; carefully remove the lid.

Remove the chicken breasts from the Instant Pot and allow them to cool.

Slice the chicken breasts into strips; place the chicken in a salad bowl. Add the remaining ingredients; stir to combine well. Serve well-chilled.

Per serving: 337 Calories; 23.7g Fat; 3.1g Carbs; 26.4g Protein; 0.9g Sugars

294. Italian-Style Turkey with Vegetables

(Ready in about 30 minutes | Servings 6)

Ingredients

1 cup cream of celery soup
1 tablespoon Italian spice blend
1 celery stalk, cut into bite-sized chunks
1 tablespoon arrowroot powder

2 bell pepper, cut into bite-sized chunks
4 cloves garlic, halved
1/4 cup tomato paste
2 medium carrots, cut into bite-sized chunks
3 pounds whole turkey breasts
1 onion, quartered

Directions

Place the turkey breasts and cream of celery soup in the inner pot.

Secure the lid. Choose the "Manual" mode and cook for 20 minutes at High pressure. Once cooking is complete, use a natural pressure release; carefully remove the lid.

Add the vegetables and tomato paste; sprinkle with the Italian spice blend.

Secure the lid. Choose the "Manual" mode and cook for 3 minutes at High pressure. Once cooking is complete, use a quick pressure release; carefully remove the lid.

Transfer the turkey and vegetables to a serving bowl.

Press the "Sauté" button; add the arrowroot powder and cook until the cooking liquid is reduced by about half. Bon appétit!

Per serving: 391 Calories; 5.9g Fat; 11.2g Carbs; 69.9g Protein; 3.9g Sugars

295. Rich Meatball Soup

(Ready in about 20 minutes | Servings 6)

Ingredients

2 teaspoons sesame oil
1 pound cavatappi pasta
1 cup tomato puree
2 tablespoons fresh coriander, chopped
1 celery with leaves, chopped
1/2 white onion, finely chopped
2 garlic cloves, minced
1 tablespoon oyster sauce

Sea salt and ground black pepper, to your liking
1 pound ground turkey
1/2 pound ground pork
1 teaspoon dill weed
1 carrot, thinly sliced
6 cups chicken stock
1 teaspoon cayenne pepper
1 whole egg

Directions

Thoroughly combine the ground meat, coriander, onion, garlic, oyster sauce, salt, black pepper, and cayenne pepper. Shape the mixture into meatballs; set aside.

Press the "Sauté" button to heat up the Instant Pot. Heat the oil and sear the meatballs until they are browned on all sides.

Now, stir in the remaining ingredients.

Secure the lid. Choose the "Manual" setting and cook for 12 minutes under High pressure. Once cooking is complete, use a quick pressure release; carefully remove the lid. Bon appétit!

Per serving: 408 Calories; 18.4g Fat; 27.4g Carbs; 33.8g Protein; 2.8g Sugars

296. Asian-Style Saucy Duck

(Ready in about 40 minutes | Servings 6)

Ingredients

1 cup roasted vegetable broth
1 bay leaf
1/2 cup Hoisin sauce
2 carrots, chopped
1 small bunch of fresh coriander stalks, roughly chopped
2 cloves garlic, sliced

Salt and ground black pepper, to your liking
1 head broccoli, chopped into florets
1 leek, white part only, chopped
1 lemon, cut into wedges
3 pounds whole duck

Directions

Press the "Sauté" button to preheat your Instant Pot.

Now, cook the duck for 4 to 5 minutes or until the skin turns golden brown. Pour in the roasted vegetable broth.

Secure the lid and choose the "Manual" mode. Cook for 25 minutes at High pressure. Afterwards, use a quick release and carefully remove the lid.

Add the vegetables, coriander, garlic, and bay leaf.

Secure the lid. Choose the "Manual" mode and cook for 3 minutes at High pressure. Once cooking is complete, use a quick pressure release; carefully remove the lid.

Remove the duck to a chopping board and rest for 5 minutes before cutting and serving.

Lastly, slice the duck and serve with the braised vegetables, Hoisin sauce, and lemon wedges. Bon appétit!

Per serving: 385 Calories; 14.6g Fat; 17.5g Carbs; 43.8g Protein; 8.1g Sugars

297. Chicken Thigh and Green Bean Soup

(Ready in about 20 minutes | Servings 6)

Ingredients

2 tablespoons ghee
1 cup green beans
6 cups water
1 ½ tablespoons chicken bouillon granules
2 shallots, chopped
2 carrots, thinly sliced
1 turnip, chopped
1/2 teaspoon dried rosemary
1 (1-inch) piece ginger root, finely chopped

2 cups tomato puree
2 bay leaves
1/3 cup crumbled crackers, for garnish
1/2 teaspoon dried oregano
1 teaspoon cayenne pepper
Kosher salt and ground black pepper, to taste
4 cloves garlic minced
4 chicken thighs

Directions

Season the chicken thighs with salt and black pepper to your liking. Press the "Sauté" button to preheat your Instant Pot.

Once hot, melt the ghee and sear the chicken thighs for 3 minutes per side.

Add the shallots, garlic, chopped ginger, carrot, and turnip; continue to sauté until just tender, about 4 minutes.

Now, add the oregano, cayenne pepper, and rosemary. Stir for 30 seconds more.

Add the tomato puree, green beans, water, chicken bouillon granules, and bay leaves. Secure the lid.

Choose the "Manual", High pressure and 10 minutes. Once cooking is complete, use a natural release and carefully remove the lid. Discard bay leaves.

Ladle into individual bowls and serve garnished with crumbled crackers.

Per serving: 354 Calories; 10.8g Fat; 11.4g Carbs; 51.3g Protein; 5.3g Sugars

298. Dijon Herbed Turkey Meatloaf

(Ready in about 40 minutes | Servings 5)

Ingredients

1/2 cup Romano cheese, grated
1 teaspoon Dijon mustard
1 tablespoon garlic and herb seasoning blend
1 ½ pounds ground turkey
1 teaspoon molasses
1/3 cup fine breadcrumbs

1 shallot, minced
1 egg, whisked
1/2 cup ketchup
1 tablespoon soy sauce
1 tablespoon olive oil
Sea salt and ground black pepper, to taste

Directions

Press the "Sauté" button to preheat your Instant Pot. Heat the oil and sauté the shallot until tender and aromatic.

Add the ground turkey, cheese, breadcrumbs, egg, salt, pepper, and herb seasoning blend. Shape the mixture into a meatloaf and wrap it into a piece of foil.

Mix the ketchup, molasses, mustard and soy sauce in a small bowl. Pour the mixture on top of the meatloaf, spreading it into an even layer.

Place a steamer rack and 1/2 cup of water inside the inner pot. Lower your meatloaf onto the steamer rack.

Secure the lid. Choose the "Poultry" mode and cook for 30 minutes at High pressure. Once cooking is complete, use a quick pressure release; carefully remove the lid.

Let your meatloaf stand for 10 minutes before cutting and serving. Bon appétit!

Per serving: 365 Calories; 19.8g Fat; 14.6g Carbs; 33.3g Protein; 9.1g Sugars

299. Chicken Lasagna with Pepper-Jack Cheese

(Ready in about 20 minutes | Servings 6)

Ingredients

8 ounces lasagna noodles
1 cup Pepper-Jack cheese, grated
1 (28-ounce) can tomatoes, crushed
2 slices bacon, chopped
1 onion, chopped
2 garlic cloves, minced
1 pound ground chicken
1 serrano pepper, seeded and chopped
1 bell pepper, seeded and chopped
Sea salt and ground black pepper, to taste
1 cup chicken stock
1 tablespoon olive oil

Directions

Press the "Sauté" button to heat up your Instant Pot. Heat the oil until sizzling. Then, sauté the onion, peppers, and garlic about 5 minutes or until they are fragrant and tender.

Stir in the ground chicken; continue to cook an additional 3 minutes.

Stir in the bacon, salt, pepper, tomatoes, stock, and noodles.

Secure the lid. Choose the "Poultry" setting and cook for 10 minutes under High pressure. Once cooking is complete, use a quick pressure release; carefully remove the lid.

Top with Pepper-Jack cheese and seal the lid. Let it sit in the residual heat until it is melted. Bon appétit!

Per serving: 335 Calories; 19.4g Fat; 17.6g Carbs; 23.8g Protein; 5.1g Sugars

300. Mediterranean Turkey Salad with Feta Cheese

(Ready in about 25 minutes + chilling time | Servings 4)

Ingredients

1 cup chicken bone broth
1 cup feta cheese, cubed
1 red onion
1/2 teaspoon dried dill
1/2 teaspoon dried oregano
1/2 cup Kalamata olives, pitted and sliced
1 tablespoon mustard
1 tablespoon champagne vinegar
1/4 cup extra-virgin olive oil
2 sweet peppers, deseeded and thinly sliced
1 serrano pepper, deseeded and thinly sliced
Sea salt and ground black pepper, to taste
1 pound turkey breast, skinless and boneless, slice into bite-sized pieces
1 tablespoon fresh lime juice

Directions

Place the turkey breasts in the inner pot; pour in the chicken bone broth.

Secure the lid. Choose the "Manual" mode and cook for 12 minutes at High pressure. Once cooking is complete, use a quick pressure release; carefully remove the lid. Transfer to a big tray and allow it to cool.

Place the chilled turkey breast in a serving bowl. Add the red onion and peppers. In a small dish, whisk the mustard, lime juice, vinegar, olive oil, dill, oregano, salt, and black pepper.

Dress the salad and serve topped with feta cheese and Kalamata olives. Serve well chilled and enjoy!

Per serving: 473 Calories; 32.2g Fat; 13.2g Carbs; 33.1g Protein; 3.5g Sugars

301. Perfect Chicken Cutlets with Sherry

(Ready in about 20 minutes | Servings 4)

Ingredients

3 teaspoons butter, softened
1 ½ tablespoons dry sherry
1 pound chicken cutlets, pounded to 1/4-inch thickness
Ground black pepper and cayenne pepper, to taste
2 tablespoons fresh lime juice
1 teaspoon dried thyme
2 teaspoons sesame oil
1 chicken bouillon cube
1 teaspoon dried marjoram
1 teaspoon mustard powder
2 garlic cloves, peeled and halved
1/3 teaspoon salt
3/4 cup water

Directions

Rub the chicken with garlic halves; then, season with salt, black pepper, and cayenne pepper. Press the "Sauté" button.

Once hot, heat the sesame oil and sauté chicken cutlets for 5 minutes, turning once during cooking. Add the water and dry sherry and stir; scrape the bottom of the pan to deglaze.

Secure the lid. Choose the "Manual" mode and High pressure; cook for 4 minutes. Once cooking is complete, use a quick pressure release; carefully remove the lid. Reserve the chicken cutlets, keeping them warm.

Stir the bouillon cube, lime juice, thyme, marjoram, and mustard powder into the cooking liquid.

Press the "Sauté" button and simmer for 6 minutes or until the cooking liquid has reduced and concentrated.

Add the butter to the sauce, stir to combine, and adjust the seasonings. Pour the prepared sauce over the reserved chicken cutlets and serve warm. Bon appétit!

Per serving: 190 Calories; 8.4g Fat; 4.3g Carbs; 23.6g Protein; 2g Sugars

302. Thanksgiving Turkey Breasts

(Ready in about 35 minutes | Servings 6)

Ingredients

1/4 cup dry white wine
1 cup turkey stock
2 bell peppers, deseeded and chopped
1 teaspoon dried sage
1/2 teaspoon dried dill
1 serrano pepper, deseeded and chopped
2 garlic cloves, minced
3 tablespoons olive oil
2 thyme sprigs
2 tablespoons butter
1 tablespoon flour
2 ½ pounds turkey breasts
Sea salt and ground black pepper, to taste

Directions

Add the turkey, peppers, garlic, turkey stock, olive oil, thyme, sage, dried dill, salt, and black pepper to the inner pot.

Secure the lid. Choose the "Manual" mode and cook for 25 minutes at High pressure. Once cooking is complete, use a natural pressure release; carefully remove the lid.

Press the "Sauté" button again and melt the butter. Now, add the flour, wine, salt, and pepper; let it cook until the sauce has thickened.

Spoon the gravy over the turkey breasts and serve warm. Bon appétit!

Per serving: 458 Calories; 26.1g Fat; 4.1g Carbs; 49g Protein; 1.3g Sugars

303. 4-Cheese Chicken Alfredo

(Ready in about 15 minutes | Servings 4)

Ingredients

1/2 cup 4-Cheese Italian, shredded
4 chicken fillets, boneless and skinless
Water
2 ripe tomatoes, chopped
1/2 teaspoon cumin, ground
1 teaspoon paprika
1/2 teaspoon curry powder
2 rosemary sprigs, leaves picked
2 tablespoons butter, softened
1/4 cup fresh chives, chopped
3 garlic cloves, minced
Salt and ground black pepper, to taste

Directions

Press the "Sauté" button to heat up your Instant Pot. Now, melt the butter.

Add the garlic and rosemary, and sauté until they are fragrant.

Now, stir in the chopped tomatoes, ground cumin, paprika, curry powder, salt, and black pepper. Top with chicken fillets and pour in water to cover the chicken.

Secure the lid and select the "Poultry" mode. Cook for 6 minutes. Once cooking is complete, use a natural release and carefully remove the lid.

Press the "Sauté" button. Add the shredded cheese and cook 2 to 3 minutes more or until the cheese has melted. Serve right away garnished with fresh chopped chives. Bon appétit!

Per serving: 193 Calories; 12.5g Fat; 5g Carbs; 15.8g Protein; 2.3g Sugars

304. Skinny Turkey Salad

(Ready in about 20 minutes + chilling time | Servings 4)

Ingredients

1 apple, cored and diced
1/2 cup spring onions, chopped
1 head butterhead lettuce, shredded
1 cup water
2 celery stalks, diced
1 tablespoon fresh lemon juice
1 teaspoon sage
1 cup mayonnaise
1 ½ pounds turkey breasts, boneless and skinless
1/2 cup cream cheese
Kosher salt and white pepper, to taste

Directions

Place the turkey breasts and water in the inner pot.

Secure the lid. Choose the "Manual" mode and cook for 9 minutes at High pressure. Once cooking is complete, use a natural pressure release; carefully remove the lid.

Add the remaining ingredients; gently stir to combine. Serve well chilled and enjoy!

Per serving: 391 Calories; 5.9g Fat; 11.2g Carbs; 69.9g Protein; 3.9g Sugars

305. Turkey Thighs with Dill-Wine Sauce

(Ready in about 30 minutes | Servings 6)

Ingredients

1 ½ pounds turkey thighs
1/2 cup dry white wine
1 teaspoon dried dill weed
1/2 teaspoon paprika
1 cup turkey bone broth
1 shallot, chopped
1 tablespoon maple syrup
2 tablespoons lard, melted
Sea salt, to taste
1/2 teaspoon ground black pepper

Directions

Press the "Sauté" button to preheat the Instant Pot; melt the lard. Now, brown the turkey thighs for 4 to 5 minutes on each side.

Add the remaining ingredients.

Secure the lid. Choose the "Meat/Stew" setting and cook for 20 minutes. Once cooking is complete, use a natural pressure release; carefully remove the lid.

Press the "Sauté" button again to thicken the cooking liquid. Spoon the sauce over turkey thighs and serve warm.

Per serving: 257 Calories; 13.3g Fat; 5.6g Carbs; 27.2g Protein; 3.8g Sugars

306. Mexican Taco Meat

(Ready in about 35 minutes | Servings 6)

Ingredients

1 Old El Paso Taco spice mix
A small handful of coriander, roughly chopped
1 fresh jalapeño chili, seeded and finely chopped
Kosher salt and ground black pepper, to taste
Fresh juice of 1 orange
2 pounds whole chicken, meat and skin
1 cup chicken broth
1 tablespoon canola oil

Directions

Toss the chicken in the Taco spice mix to coat. Press the "Sauté" button to preheat your Instant Pot.

Heat the canola oil and sear the chicken, stirring periodically, for 3 to 4 minutes or until golden brown.

Add the jalapeño chili, salt, black pepper, fresh orange juice, and chicken broth; stir to combine. Secure the lid.

Choose the "Poultry" mode and High pressure; cook for 30 minutes. Once cooking is complete, use a quick release.

Shred the chicken and garnish with fresh coriander leaves. Enjoy!

Per serving: 412 Calories; 27.8g Fat; 1.1g Carbs; 36.9g Protein; 0.4g Sugars

307. Harvest Vegetable and Chicken Soup

(Ready in about 25 minutes | Servings 5)

Ingredients

1 carrot, thinly sliced
1 parsnip, thinly sliced
1 green bell pepper, seeded and sliced
1 orange bell pepper, seeded and sliced
1 pound chicken drumettes
1 yellow onion, chopped
2 cloves garlic, minced
1 red bell peppers, seeded and sliced

1/2 teaspoon dried dill
1/2 teaspoon dried oregano
2 tablespoons olive oil
1 tablespoon granulated chicken bouillon
4 cups water
Sea salt and ground black pepper, to your liking
1/4 cup Rose wine

Directions

Press the "Sauté" button to heat up your Instant Pot; now, heat the oil until sizzling. Then, sauté the onion and garlic until tender and fragrant.

Add the peppers, carrots and parsnip; cook an additional 3 minutes or until the vegetables are softened. Add a splash of rose wine to deglaze the bottom of your Instant Pot.

Then, stir in the remaining ingredients; stir to combine well.

Secure the lid. Choose the "Soup" mode and High pressure; cook for 20 minutes. Once cooking is complete, use a quick pressure release. Carefully remove the lid.

Remove the chicken wings from the cooking liquid; discard the bones and chop the meat.

Add the chicken meat back to the Instant Pot, stir, and serve hot. Bon appétit!

Per serving: 238 Calories; 17g Fat; 5.4g Carbs; 16.4g Protein; 2.6g Sugars

308. Fontina Cheese-Stuffed Meatballs

(Ready in about 15 minutes | Servings 4)

Ingredients

4 ounces Fontina cheese, cut into 16 pieces
1 teaspoon dried basil
1 teaspoon dried rosemary
1 pound ground turkey
1/2 pound ground beef
1 shallot, finely minced
1 bell pepper, deseeded and finely minced

2 garlic cloves, minced
2 slices bacon, chopped
1 teaspoon dried parsley flakes
1/2 cup buttermilk
1 teaspoon mustard
1 cup marinara sauce
1 cup crushed saltines
Sea salt and freshly cracked black pepper, to taste

Directions

Press the "Sauté" button to preheat your Instant Pot. Cook the chopped bacon until crisp; reserve. Cook the ground turkey, beef, shallot, pepper, and garlic until the meat is no longer pink.

Add the crushed saltines, salt, black pepper, basil, rosemary, parsley, and buttermilk. Stir in the reserved bacon. Shape the meat mixture into 16 meatballs. Insert 1 cube of Fontina cheese into the center of each meatball.

Add the mustard and marinara sauce to the inner pot; stir to combine and fold in the meatballs.

Secure the lid. Choose the "Poultry" mode and cook for 5 minutes at High pressure. Once cooking is complete, use a quick pressure release; carefully remove the lid. Serve warm.

Per serving: 485 Calories; 23.3g Fat; 14.7g Carbs; 54.1g Protein; 6.4g Sugars

309. Chicken Sausage and Cauliflower Chowder

(Ready in about 15 minutes | Servings 8)

Ingredients

8 ounces chicken sausage, cooked and thinly sliced
1 cup spinach, torn into pieces
1 teaspoon ginger garlic paste
1 pound cauliflower, chopped into florets
1 pinch red pepper flakes

Kosher salt, to taste
1/2 teaspoon freshly ground black pepper, to taste
1/2 cup scallions, chopped
4 cups vegetable broth
1 tablespoon lard, melted

Directions

Add all ingredients, except for the spinach, to your Instant Pot.

Secure the lid. Choose the "Manual" setting and cook for 9 minutes under High pressure. Once cooking is complete, use a quick pressure release; carefully remove the lid.

Puree the mixture in your food processor.

Afterwards, add the spinach and seal the lid. Let it stand until the spinach is wilted. Serve in individual bowls. Enjoy!

Per serving: 360 Calories; 28.1g Fat; 7.8g Carbs; 19.1g Protein; 2.7g Sugars

310. Chinese-Glazed Chicken Drumsticks

(Ready in about 25 minutes | Servings 4)

Ingredients

4 chicken drumsticks
1/4 teaspoon fresh ground pepper, or more to taste
1/2 cup water
1 tablespoon fresh cilantro, chopped
Small bunch scallions, chopped
Sea salt, to taste
6 tablespoons honey

3 cloves garlic, minced
1/3 cup low-sodium soy sauce
1/3 cup no salt ketchup
1 tablespoon Chinese rice vinegar
2 tablespoons sesame seed oil
2 tablespoons sweet chili sauce

Directions

Press the "Sauté" button to preheat your Instant Pot.

Heat the sesame seed oil and sear the chicken for 5 minutes, stirring periodically. Season with black pepper and salt.

After that, stir in the vinegar, honey, chili sauce, garlic, soy sauce, ketchup, water, and cilantro; stir well to combine.

Secure the lid and choose the "Poultry" mode. Cook for 15 minutes. Afterwards, use a natural release and carefully remove the lid.

Garnish with chopped scallions. Bon appétit!

Per serving: 394 Calories; 18.9g Fat; 30.6g Carbs; 26g Protein; 27.2g Sugars

311. Spicy Chicken Drumettes

(Ready in about 15 minutes | Servings 3)

Ingredients

1/2 teaspoon red pepper flakes, crushed
1/2 teaspoon Mexican oregano
1 tablespoon fresh coriander, minced
1 tablespoon fresh lime juice
2 ripe tomatoes, chopped
1 Cascabel chili pepper, minced
1/2 cup scallions, chopped
Seasoned salt and ground black pepper, to taste
2 garlic cloves, minced
1 teaspoon fresh ginger, grated
6 chicken drumettes, skinless and boneless

Directions

Press the "Sauté" button to heat up your Instant Pot. Sear the chicken drumettes for 3 minutes on each side or until they are browned.

In a bowl, mix the remaining ingredients. Spoon the mixture over the browned chicken.

Secure the lid. Choose the "Manual" mode and High pressure; cook for 10 minutes. Once cooking is complete, use a natural pressure release; carefully remove the lid. Bon appétit!

Per serving: 199 Calories; 4.3g Fat; 7.1g Carbs; 32.2g Protein; 3.4g Sugars

312. Indian Duck Masala

(Ready in about 35 minutes | Servings 6)

Ingredients

3 pounds duck thighs
1 tablespoon Garam masala
1/4 teaspoon crushed black peppercorns, or more to taste
2 garlic cloves, sliced
1/2 cup tomato paste
1 tablespoon rosemary
1 tablespoon sage
1/2 cup bone broth
2 tablespoons butter, melted at room temperature
1 small bunch of fresh coriander, roughly chopped
1 teaspoon ginger powder
1/2 teaspoon chili powder
1/2 teaspoon allspice berries, lightly crushed
Sea salt, to taste

Directions

Press the "Sauté" button and melt the butter. Now, cook the duck thighs until golden brown on both sides. Add all seasonings.

Next, stir in the garlic, tomato paste, broth, and Garam masala.

Secure the lid. Choose the "Manual" mode and cook for 25 minutes at High pressure. Once cooking is complete, use a quick pressure release; carefully remove the lid.

Serve with fresh coriander. Enjoy!

Per serving: 539 Calories; 38.2g Fat; 5.2g Carbs; 45.1g Protein; 2.7g Sugars

313. Turkey and Zucchini Casserole

(Ready in about 15 minutes | Servings 4)

Ingredients

1 pound ground turkey
2 zucchinis, thinly sliced
1/2 teaspoon dried thyme
1 teaspoon dried basil
1/4 cup breadcrumbs
Salt and ground black pepper, to taste
5 ounces Swiss cheese, freshly grated
1 teaspoon serrano pepper, minced
1 teaspoon garlic, smashed
2 red bell pepper, sliced lengthwise into strips
1 cup tomato paste
1 teaspoon brown sugar
1 tablespoon sesame oil
1/2 cup Romano cheese, grated

Directions

Press the "Sauté" button to heat up the Instant Pot. Now, heat the oil until sizzling.

Then, sauté the ground turkey until it is delicately browned, crumbling it with a spoon. Now, stir in the cheese, crumbs, salt, black pepper, serrano pepper, garlic, thyme, and basil.

Cook for 1 to 2 minutes more; reserve.

Wipe down the Instant Pot with a damp cloth; brush the inner pot with a nonstick cooking spray. Arrange 1/2 of zucchini slices on the bottom.

Spread 1/3 of meat mixture over zucchini. Place the layer of bell peppers; add ground meat mixture. Repeat the layering until you run out of ingredients.

Next, thoroughly combine the tomato paste and sugar. Pour this tomato mixture over the layers.

Secure the lid. Choose the "Manual" mode and High pressure; cook for 10 minutes. Once cooking is complete, use a quick pressure release; carefully remove the lid.

Afterwards, top your casserole with grated Swiss cheese; allow the Swiss cheese to melt in the residual heat. Bon appétit!

Per serving: 464 Calories; 24.4g Fat; 11.2g Carbs; 43.2g Protein; 1.8g Sugars

314. Roasted Turkey with Mayo and Herbs

(Ready in about 35 minutes | Servings 8)

Ingredients

1 cup mayonnaise
2 thyme sprigs
1 lemon, sliced
2 rosemary sprigs
1 teaspoon mixed peppercorns, crushed
2 tablespoons ghee, softened
3 pounds turkey breasts
4 garlic cloves, smashed
2 teaspoons coarse salt

Directions

Pat the turkey dry. In a mixing dish, thoroughly combine the garlic, thyme, rosemary, mayonnaise, salt, peppercorns, and ghee.

Rub the mayonnaise mixture all over the turkey breasts.

Add a steamer rack and 1/2 cup of water to the bottom of your Instant Pot. Throw in the lemon slices.

Secure the lid. Choose the "Manual" mode and cook for 20 minutes at High pressure. Once cooking is complete, use a natural pressure release; carefully remove the lid.

Let your turkey stand for 5 to 10 minutes before slicing and serving. Bon appétit!

Per serving: 393 Calories; 25g Fat; 1.9g Carbs; 39.2g Protein; 0.4g Sugars

315. Mediterranean-Style Chicken Drumsticks

(Ready in about 1 hour 15 minutes | Servings 4)

Ingredients

2 teaspoons olive oil
3/4 cup mayonnaise
2 tablespoons lemon juice
1/2 teaspoon freshly ground black pepper
1 tablespoon oyster sauce

1 tablespoon chicken bouillon granules
1/2 cup dry white wine
4 chicken drumsticks, bone-in, skin-on
3 cloves garlic, minced
1 cup water

Directions

Place the chicken, olive oil, oyster sauce, water, chicken bouillon granules, black pepper and wine in a ceramic bowl.

Allow it to marinate for 1 hour in your refrigerator. Add the chicken and marinade to the Instant Pot.

Secure the lid. Now, press the "Manual" button. Cook for 12 minutes under High pressure.

Once cooking is complete, use a natural pressure release; carefully remove the lid.

In the meantime, mix the mayonnaise with the garlic and lemon juice until well combined. Serve chicken drumsticks with the aioli on the side. Bon appétit!

Per serving: 441 Calories; 34.8g Fat; 3.4g Carbs; 27.1g Protein; 0.5g Sugars

316. Smothered Chicken Cutlets with Pasta

(Ready in about 25 minutes | Servings 6)

Ingredients

6 cups pasta, cooked
1/2 cup double cream
1 teaspoon dried oregano
1 teaspoon dried basil
Kosher salt and ground black pepper, to taste
1/4 cup dry white wine

2 cups vegetable broth
2 garlic cloves, minced
2 tablespoons cornstarch
1 teaspoon dried rosemary
1 teaspoon dried parsley flakes
2 pounds chicken cutlets

Directions

Season the chicken cutlets with salt, black pepper, oregano, basil, rosemary, and parsley. Press the "Sauté" button to preheat your Instant Pot.

Once hot, cook the seasoned chicken cutlets for 5 minutes, turning once during cooking. Add the white wine and scrape the bottom of the pan to deglaze.

Pour in the vegetable broth. Add the garlic and secure the lid.

Choose the "Manual" mode and High pressure; cook for 8 minutes. Once cooking is complete, use a quick release and remove the lid. Reserve the chicken cutlets, keeping them warm.

Stir the double cream and cornstarch into the cooking liquid.

Press the "Sauté" button and simmer for 6 minutes or until the cooking liquid has reduced by half. Serve with warm pasta. Bon appétit!

Per serving: 422 Calories; 8.5g Fat; 41.5g Carbs; 45.6g Protein; 2g Sugars

317. Old-Fashioned Turkey and Tomato Soup

(Ready in about 25 minutes | Servings 5)

Ingredients

1 pound turkey thighs
1 medium-sized leek, chopped
1 celery stalk, chopped
1/2 teaspoon dried rosemary
2 bay leaves
1/2 teaspoon cayenne pepper
5 cups turkey bone broth
2 tablespoons fresh coriander, roughly chopped

1/2 teaspoon ginger-garlic paste
1 carrot, chopped
1 (28-ounce) can diced tomatoes
1 tablespoon peanut oil
Sea salt and ground black pepper

Directions

Press the "Sauté" button to preheat your Instant Pot. Heat the peanut oil until sizzling. Cook the leek until tender.

Add the ginger-garlic paste, tomatoes, celery, carrot, rosemary, bay leaves, salt, black pepper, cayenne pepper, turkey thighs, and broth.

Secure the lid. Choose the "Soup" setting and cook for 20 minutes at High pressure. Once cooking is complete, use a quick pressure release; carefully remove the lid.

Remove the turkey thighs from the soup, shred the meat and discard the bones. After that, return the meat to the Instant Pot.

Divide among five soup bowls. Top each bowl with fresh coriander and serve immediately.

Per serving: 194 Calories; 7.9g Fat; 12.7g Carbs; 18.8g Protein; 7.4g Sugars

318. Asian-Style Chicken Drumsticks with Rice

(Ready in about 20 minutes | Servings 6)

Ingredients

6 chicken drumsticks
1 cup rice
2 tablespoons Worcestershire sauce
2 tablespoons champagne vinegar
2 cups water

Salt and ground black pepper, to taste
1 teaspoon Wuxiang powder
3 tablespoons sesame oil
2 cups vegetable broth
2 tablespoons flaxseed meal
4 garlic cloves, minced
1/4 cup honey

Directions

Press the "Sauté" button and heat 2 tablespoons of the sesame oil. Sear the chicken drumsticks until slightly brown on all sides. Add the garlic and cook for 1 minute or so, until aromatic.

Add the remaining ingredients, except for the flaxseed meal.

Secure the lid. Choose "Poultry" mode. Cook for 15 minutes at High pressure. Once cooking is complete, use a quick pressure release; carefully remove the lid.

Afterwards, stir in the flaxseed meal; stir until everything is well combined. Press the "Sauté" button and cook until the cooking liquid is reduced by about half. Bon appétit!

Per serving: 471 Calories; 20.8g Fat; 41.1g Carbs; 28.2g Protein; 12.7g Sugars

319. Turkey Stew with Root Vegetables

(Ready in about 20 minutes | Servings 4)

Ingredients

1 pound turkey legs
1/2 teaspoon Hungarian paprika
2 tablespoons fresh cilantro leaves, chopped
1 red bell pepper, chopped
1 parsnip, chopped
1 cup turnip, chopped
1/2 pound carrots, chopped

1/2 cup leeks, chopped
2 garlic cloves, minced
1 green bell pepper, chopped
1 Serrano pepper, chopped
Sea salt and ground black pepper, to taste
2 tablespoons butter, at room temperature
2 cups turkey stock

Directions

Press the "Sauté" button to preheat your Instant Pot and melt the butter. Now, sear the turkey, skin side down, 3 minutes on each side.

Sprinkle the turkey legs with salt and black pepper as you cook them.

Stir the remaining ingredients into the Instant Pot. Secure the lid and select the "Manual" mode. Cook for 15 minutes at High pressure.

Once cooking is complete, use a natural pressure release. Transfer the turkey legs to a bowl and let them cool. Then, strip the meat off the bones, cut it into small pieces and return to the Instant Pot.

Serve hot and enjoy!

Per serving: 403 Calories; 18.5g Fat; 17.1g Carbs; 40.9g Protein; 6g Sugars

320. Cheesy Chicken Tenders

(Ready in about 25 minutes | Servings 4)

Ingredients

1 ½ pounds chicken tenders
1 cup Cottage cheese, crumbled
1 teaspoon shallot powder
Sea salt and freshly ground black pepper, to taste

2 tablespoons butter, softened
2 heaping tablespoons fresh chives, roughly chopped
1 teaspoon garlic powder
1/2 teaspoon smoked paprika
1 cup vegetable broth

Directions

Press the "Sauté" button and melt the butter. Sear the chicken tenders for 2 to 3 minutes.

Add the vegetable broth, shallot powder, garlic powder, paprika, salt, and black pepper.

Secure the lid. Choose "Manual" mode and cook for 8 minutes at High pressure. Once cooking is complete, use a natural pressure release; carefully remove the lid.

Stir in the cheese; cover with the lid and let it sit in the residual heat for 5 minutes. Garnish with fresh chives and serve immediately.

Per serving: 305 Calories; 13.1g Fat; 2.8g Carbs; 41.9g Protein; 1.7g Sugars

321. Pinot Grigio Chicken

(Ready in about 15 minutes | Servings 6)

Ingredients

1/2 cup Pinot Grigio
2 pounds chicken wings, skin-on
1 cup cream cheese
1/2 lemon, cut into slices
1 teaspoon mustard powder
1 teaspoon smoked paprika

1 cup tomato puree
1/2 cup water
2 garlic cloves, sliced
1 tablespoon butter, melted
Sea salt and ground black pepper, to taste

Directions

Press the "Sauté" button to preheat the Instant Pot. Melt the butter and brown the chicken wings for 1 to 2 minutes on each side.

Stir in the garlic, mustard powder, paprika, salt, black pepper, Pinot Grigio, tomato puree, and water.

Secure the lid. Choose the "Manual" mode and High pressure; cook for 10 minutes. Once cooking is complete, use a natural pressure release; carefully remove the lid.

Serve with cream cheese and lemon slices. Bon appétit!

Per serving: 273 Calories; 14.1g Fat; 5.3g Carbs; 27.8g Protein; 2.9g Sugars

322. Traditional Locrio de Pollo

(Ready in about 20 minutes | Servings 5)

Ingredients

5 ounces chorizo sausage, casings removed and crumbled
1 cup short-grain white rice
1/2 cup brown onion, chopped
2 tablespoons fresh parsley, roughly chopped
1 ½ cups chicken broth
1 cup tomato puree
1 teaspoon dried oregano

1 pound chicken breasts, trimmed and cut into bite-sized pieces
1/2 teaspoon saffron threads
5 ounces seafood mix
2 tablespoons Rueda
1 lemon, juiced and zested
1 tablespoon olive oil
Sea salt and ground black pepper, to taste

Directions

Press the "Sauté" button and heat the olive oil.

Now, cook the brown onion and chicken until the onion is translucent and the chicken is no longer pink or about 4 minutes. Deglaze the pot with the Rueda wine.

Stir in the rice, broth, tomato puree, oregano, salt, black pepper, and saffron.

Secure the lid and choose the "Manual" mode. Cook for 5 minutes at High pressure. Afterwards, use a quick release and carefully remove the lid.

Add the seafood mix and sausage. Secure the lid and choose the "Manual" mode. Cook for 4 to 5 minutes at High pressure; use a quick release and carefully remove the lid.

Add the lemon and parsley and serve immediately. Bon appétit!

Per serving: 537 Calories; 23.1g Fat; 44.4g Carbs; 36.9g Protein; 6.1g Sugars

323. Thai Chicken Curry

(Ready in about 20 minutes | Servings 6)

Ingredients

1 ½ pounds chicken breast, cubed
1 cup vegetable broth
1 tablespoon red Thai curry paste
1 stalk lemongrass
1/2 teaspoon cayenne pepper
2 garlic cloves, minced
1 tablespoon fish sauce
1 cup coconut cream
1 tablespoon peanut oil
1 ½ cups button mushrooms, sliced
1 tablespoon fresh coriander
Salt and freshly ground black pepper, to taste

Directions

Press the "Sauté" button to heat up the Instant Pot; heat the oil. Once hot, cook the chicken for 5 minutes, stirring periodically.

Add the lemongrass, cayenne pepper, salt, black pepper, Thai curry paste, mushrooms, and garlic. Continue to sauté for 3 minutes more or until the mushrooms are fragrant.

Now, stir in the vegetable broth and fish sauce.

Secure the lid. Choose the "Manual" setting and cook for 10 minutes at High pressure. Once cooking is complete, use a quick pressure release; carefully remove the lid.

Afterwards, fold in the coconut cream; press the "Sauté" button and stir until the sauce is reduced and thickened. Serve garnished with fresh coriander. Bon appétit!

Per serving: 296 Calories; 19.6g Fat; 4.9g Carbs; 26.3g Protein; 0.2g Sugars

324. Asian-Style Duck Breast

(Ready in about 20 minutes + marinating time | Servings 4)

Ingredients

1 cup Chinese cabbage, shredded
2 tablespoons Mirin
1/4 cup loosely packed fresh parsley leaves, roughly chopped
2 tablespoons tamari
2 tablespoons sesame seeds, toasted
1 tablespoon sesame oil
1 cup vegetable broth
4 eggs
Sea salt and freshly ground pepper, to taste
1 shallot, chopped
1 fresh lemon, juiced
2 tablespoons extra-virgin oil
1 red chili, finely chopped
2 garlic cloves, grated
1 teaspoon honey
2 cups cooked rice
1 tablespoon olive oil
2 tablespoons orange juice
2 pounds duck breasts, skinless and boneless

Directions

Place the duck breasts, orange juice, Mirin, and tamari sauce in a ceramic dish. Let it marinate for 1 hour in your refrigerator.

Press the "Sauté" button and heat the oil until sizzling. Cook the duck for about 5 minutes or until it is no longer pink.

Add the vegetable broth and secure the lid.

Choose the "Manual" mode and cook for 10 minutes at High pressure. Once cooking is complete, use a quick pressure release; carefully remove the lid.

Slice the duck and transfer to a nice serving bowl. Add the garlic, honey, salt, black pepper, shallot, fresh parsley, lemon, oil, cabbage, sesame seeds, chili pepper, and cooked rice.

Heat the olive oil in a skillet over medium-high flame. Fry the eggs until the whites are completely set. Place the fried eggs on the top and serve immediately.

Per serving: 631 Calories; 31.2g Fat; 28.8g Carbs; 56.6g Protein; 3.6g Sugars

325. Decadent Turkey Breasts in Sweet Apricot Sauce

(Ready in about 20 minutes | Servings 8)

Ingredients

2 pounds turkey breasts, cubed
1/3 cup Port wine
1/2 teaspoon dried sage
1 teaspoon red pepper flakes, crushed
1 teaspoon dried rosemary
1/3 cup chicken stock, preferably homemade
2 teaspoons sesame oil
Sea salt and freshly ground black pepper, to taste
For the Sauce:
3 teaspoons honey
1 teaspoon fresh ginger root, minced
1/2 teaspoon chili powder
1/2 teaspoon soy sauce
1/3 cup all-natural apricot jam
1 ½ tablespoons rice vinegar

Directions

Press the "Sauté" button and preheat your Instant Pot. Now, heat the oil; sear the turkey breasts, stirring occasionally, for 3 to 4 minutes.

Season the turkey breasts with salt, black pepper, red pepper flakes, rosemary, and sage.

Add the Port wine and chicken stock to the Instant Pot and deglaze the bottom.

Return turkey to the Instant Pot and secure the lid. Choose the "Manual" setting and High pressure. Cook for 10 minutes.

Once cooking is complete, use a natural release and carefully remove the lid. Transfer the turkey breasts to a platter.

Add the sauce ingredients to the Instant Pot. Cook until the sauce reaches preferred consistency. Pour over the turkey and serve immediately. Bon appétit!

Per serving: 256 Calories; 10.2g Fat; 5.9g Carbs; 33.1g Protein; 5.2g Sugars

326. Duck with Wild Mushrooms and Port Wine

(Ready in about 30 minutes | Servings 4)

Ingredients

1 mushroom soup cube
1 pound wild mushrooms, sliced
1 cup water
1/2 teaspoon sea salt
1/2 teaspoon mustard powder
1/4 cup Port wine
1/2 teaspoon red chili pepper
1 teaspoon cayenne pepper
2 medium-sized shallots, sliced
2 garlic cloves, minced
1/2 teaspoon freshly ground black pepper
1 tablespoon tallow, melted
1 (1-inch) piece fresh ginger, peeled and grated
1 pound duck breast, sliced

Directions

Season the duck breast with chili pepper, cayenne pepper, salt, mustard powder, and black pepper.

Press the "Sauté" button to heat up your Instant Pot. Then, melt the tallow. Sear the seasoned duck for 4 to 6 minutes, turning periodically; set it aside.

Pour in the Port wine to scrape up any brown bits from the bottom of the Instant Pot. Stir in the remaining ingredients.

Secure the lid. Choose the "Poultry" mode and High pressure; cook for 20 minutes. Once cooking is complete, use a quick pressure release; carefully remove the lid. Serve immediately.

Per serving: 203 Calories; 8.5g Fat; 5.5g Carbs; 26.5g Protein; 2.7g Sugars

327. The Best Chicken Tacos Ever

(Ready in about 20 minutes | Servings 6)

Ingredients

1 head butter lettuce
6 (approx. 6-inch diameter) tortillas
Salt, to taste
2 cloves garlic, minced
1 onion, chopped
1 cup canned black beans, drained
1 tablespoon Dijon mustard
1 cup water
1 tablespoon tamari sauce
1/2 teaspoon freshly ground black pepper

1 teaspoon Mexican oregano
1 pound ground chicken
1 pound ground turkey
1 cup sweet corn kernels, cooked
1 teaspoon jalapeno pepper, minced
2 sweet peppers, deseeded and chopped
1 serrano pepper, deseeded and chopped
2 tomatoes, sliced
1/3 cup hoisin sauce
1 tablespoon olive oil

Directions

Press the "Sauté" button. Once hot, heat the olive oil until sizzling. Now, brown the ground meat for 2 to 3 minutes, stirring continuously.

Add the garlic, onion, peppers, hoisin sauce, water, tamari sauce, salt, black pepper, and Mexican oregano.

Secure the lid. Choose the "Manual" mode and High pressure; cook for 6 minutes. Once cooking is complete, use a quick pressure release; carefully remove the lid.

Assemble the tortillas with the ground chicken filling, corn, beans, mustard, jalapeno pepper, tomatoes, and lettuce. Enjoy!

Per serving: 502 Calories; 22.5g Fat; 39.4g Carbs; 36.3g Protein; 6.9g Sugars

328. French Coq au Vin

(Ready in about 25 minutes | Servings 4)

Ingredients

2 chicken drumettes
2 teaspoons all-purpose flour
1/4 cup tomato puree
2 sprigs fresh thyme, leaves picked
1 chicken breast
2 cloves garlic, crushed
1 cup vegetable stock
1/3 cup red wine

1/2 teaspoon red pepper flakes
2 shallots, chopped
1/4 teaspoon curry powder
2 teaspoons peanut oil
1/2 pound chestnut mushrooms, halved
Sea salt and ground black pepper, to your liking

Directions

Press the "Sauté" button and heat peanut oil. Add the chicken, skin-side down, and cook for 7 minutes or until browned; reserve.

Now, add the shallots and sauté until they're tender and fragrant. Now, stir in the garlic and mushrooms, and cook until aromatic.

Add 1/2 cup of vegetable stock and red wine, and scrape the bottom of your Instant Pot to loosen any stuck-on bits.

Add the salt, black pepper, red pepper flakes, and curry powder; continue to cook, stirring constantly.

Now, add the reserved chicken, tomato puree and the remaining 1/2 cup of vegetable stock. Sprinkle with all-purpose flour and fresh thyme leaves.

Secure the lid. Choose the "Manual" and cook at High pressure for 11 minutes. Once cooking is complete, use a quick pressure release; carefully remove the lid. Bon appétit!

Per serving: 255 Calories; 12.1g Fat; 6.9g Carbs; 29.2g Protein; 2.7g Sugars

329. BBQ Meatloaf with Parmesan Cheese

(Ready in about 45 minutes | Servings 5)

Ingredients

1 egg, beaten
1 tablespoon Worcestershire sauce
1 chili pepper, deseeded and finely chopped
1 onion, finely chopped
1 pound ground chicken
1/2 pound ground beef
Smoked salt flakes and freshly ground black pepper, to taste

1 medium carrot, grated
2 sweet peppers, deseeded and chopped
2 garlic cloves, minced
1/2 cup crackers, crushed
1/4 cup Parmesan cheese, grated
2 tablespoons olive oil
1/2 cup BBQ sauce

Directions

Place a steamer rack inside the inner pot; add 1/2 cup water. Cut 1 sheet of heavy-duty foil and brush with cooking spray.

In large mixing dish, thoroughly combine all ingredients until mixed well.

Shape the meat mixture into a loaf; place the meatloaf in the center of the foil. Wrap your meatloaf in the foil and lower onto the steamer rack.

Secure the lid. Choose the "Poultry" mode and cook for 30 minutes at High pressure. Once cooking is complete, use a quick pressure release; carefully remove the lid.

Then, transfer your meatloaf to a cutting board. Let it stand for 10 minutes before cutting and serving. To serve, brush with some extra BBQ sauce, if desired. Bon appétit!

Per serving: 450 Calories; 27.8g Fat; 15.6g Carbs; 34.2g Protein; 5.9g Sugars

330. Chicken Fillets with Cheese and Peppers

(Ready in about 15 minutes | Servings 4)

Ingredients

1 pound chicken fillets
1/2 cup Cheddar cheese, grated
1/2 cup cream cheese
1/2 teaspoon dried oregano
1 teaspoon dried sage
1 green bell pepper, seeded and sliced
1 orange bell pepper, seeded and sliced
1/2 teaspoon dried basil
1 cup heavy cream

1 teaspoon cayenne pepper
2 cloves garlic, smashed
1 jalapeño pepper, seeded and chopped
1 cup roasted vegetable broth
1 white onion, chopped
1 red bell pepper, seeded and sliced
1 tablespoon olive oil
Kosher salt and ground black pepper, to taste

Directions

Press the "Sauté" button to preheat your Instant Pot. Now, heat the oil and cook the chicken for 2 to 3 minutes per side.

Stir in the garlic, jalapeño pepper, onion, and peppers.

Add the seasonings and gently stir to combine. Pour in the roasted vegetable broth.

Secure the lid. Choose the "Poultry" setting and cook for 5 minutes at High pressure. Once cooking is complete, use a natural pressure release; carefully remove the lid.

Now, add the heavy cream, cream cheese and Cheddar cheese; press the "Sauté" button again and cook until cheesy is melted and everything is thoroughly heated. Serve immediately and enjoy!

Per serving: 463 Calories; 32.3g Fat; 11.1g Carbs; 32.6g Protein; 6.1g Sugars

331. Mexican-Style Chicken Sliders

(Ready in about 25 minutes | Servings 4)

Ingredients

8 slider buns
1 pound chicken breasts, boneless and skinless
8 ounces canner red enchilada sauce
1 cup chicken broth
1 cup spring onions, sliced
Kosher salt and freshly ground black pepper, to taste

Directions

Place the chicken breasts in the inner pot. Season with salt and pepper; pour in the chicken broth and enchilada sauce.

Secure the lid. Choose the "Manual" mode and cook for 9 minutes at High pressure. Once cooking is complete, use a quick pressure release; carefully remove the lid.

Place the bottom half of the slider buns on a baking sheet. Top with layers of the chicken mixture and spring onions. Put on the top buns and spritz with cooking spray.

Bake about 10 minutes in the preheated oven until buns are golden. Enjoy!

Per serving: 504 Calories; 17.2g Fat; 49.1g Carbs; 36.3g Protein; 6.7g Sugars

332. Ranch Chicken with Onions

(Ready in about 25 minutes | Servings 6)

Ingredients

1 packet dry ranch salad dressing mix
1/2 cup onion, sliced
1 teaspoon celery salt
1/4 cup tamari sauce
3 tablespoons brown sugar
2 tablespoons champagne vinegar
4 cloves garlic, smashed
1 ½ pounds chicken drumettes
1 ½ tablespoons butter, melted
1/4 teaspoon freshly ground black pepper, or more to taste

Directions

Season the chicken drumettes with celery salt and black pepper. Press the "Sauté" button and warm the butter.

Now, sear the chicken pieces for 6 minutes or until browned on all sides.

Add the remaining ingredients in the order listed above. Secure the lid.

Choose the "Manual" setting and cook for 10 minutes at High pressure. Once cooking is complete, use a natural release and carefully remove the lid.

You can thicken the sauce on the "Sauté" mode. Serve over hot cooked pasta and enjoy!

Per serving: 189 Calories; 7.2g Fat; 6.3g Carbs; 23.5g Protein; 4.8g Sugars

333. Sticky Turkey Thighs

(Ready in about 25 minutes | Servings 4)

Ingredients

1 teaspoon red pepper flakes
4 tablespoons honey
2 tablespoons all-purpose flour
1 teaspoon dried parsley flakes
1 orange, sliced
1/2 cup turkey stock
4 tablespoons olive oil
2 pounds turkey thighs
Sea salt and freshly ground black pepper, to taste
1/2 cup water

Directions

Rub the salt, black pepper, red pepper, and parsley flakes all over the turkey thighs.

Press the "Sauté" button and heat the olive oil. Sear the turkey thighs for 3 minutes per side. Then, add the orange, water, stock, and honey.

Secure the lid. Choose the "Manual" mode and cook for 15 minutes at High pressure. Once cooking is complete, use a quick pressure release; carefully remove the lid.

Then, add the flour to thicken the cooking liquid. Spoon the sauce over the turkey thighs and serve warm. Bon appétit!

Per serving: 479 Calories; 25g Fat; 20.5g Carbs; 41.7g Protein; 17.2g Sugars

334. Mexican-Style Turkey Tacos

(Ready in about 15 minutes | Servings 6)

Ingredients

2 pounds turkey breasts
1 cup Pico de Gallo
1/2 cup crushed red pepper flakes
1/4 cup fresh cilantro leaves, chopped
1/2 teaspoon seasoned salt
1/4 teaspoon ground black pepper
6 corn tortillas, warmed
2 garlic cloves, smashed
1/2 cup turkey stock

Directions

Put the turkey breast into your Instant Pot. Now, pour in the stock.

Add the garlic, salt, black pepper, red pepper flakes, and cilantro leaves. Secure the lid. Choose the "Manual" setting and cook for 10 minutes at High pressure.

Once cooking is complete, use a natural release and carefully remove the lid. Shred the turkey breasts.

Serve the shredded turkey breasts over corn tortillas garnished with Pico de Gallo. Bon appétit!

Per serving: 323 Calories; 12g Fat; 15.2g Carbs; 37.1g Protein; 2.8g Sugars

335. Traditional Szechuan Duck

(Ready in about 35 minutes | Servings 6)

Per serving: 525 Calories; 37.2g Fat; 4.5g Carbs; 40.5g Protein; 2.9g Sugars

Ingredients

2 tablespoons salt
1 tablespoon dark brown sugar
1/4 cup Shaoxing rice wine
1 cup water
3 pounds whole duck
1/4 cup soy sauce
4 cloves garlic, sliced
2 star anise
1 red chili pepper, chopped
2 tablespoons Szechuan peppercorns
1 teaspoon Chinese 5-spice powder

Directions

Press the "Sauté" button to preheat your Instant Pot. Then, add the Szechuan peppercorn to the inner pot and roast until really fragrant. Remove it to a spice grinder and ground into a powder.

Add the Chinese 5-spice powder and salt. Rub the duck with the spice mixture. Leave it to marinate overnight.

Press the "Sauté" button to preheat your Instant Pot. Now, place the duck skin-side down in the inner pot and sear until the skin is crisp and brown. Turn and cook the other side for 4 to 5 minutes.

Stir in the other ingredients.

Secure the lid and choose the "Manual" mode. Cook for 25 minutes at High pressure. Afterwards, use a quick release and carefully remove the lid. Serve warm.

336. Italian-Style Turkey and Rice

(Ready in about 25 minutes | Servings 4)

Per serving: 498 Calories; 21.2g Fat; 25.4g Carbs; 59g Protein; 7.1g Sugars

Ingredients

1 cup Arborio rice
Sea salt and ground black pepper, to taste
1/2 teaspoon dried rosemary
2 slices bacon, chopped
1/2 cup dry white wine
1 onion, chopped
1 serrano pepper, chopped
2 cloves garlic, finely minced
1 teaspoon dried oregano
1 tablespoon butter, melted
2 chicken breasts, cut into slices
1 (28-ounce) can diced tomatoes
1 ½ cups water

Directions

Press the "Sauté" button to preheat your Instant Pot. Melt the butter. Then, sear the chicken breasts for 5 minutes. Set them aside.

Stir in the bacon, onion, serrano pepper, and garlic; cook until the vegetables are tender.

Stir in the remaining ingredients. Return the reserved chicken to the Instant Pot.

Secure the lid. Choose the "Poultry" setting and cook for 15 minutes under High pressure. Once cooking is complete, use a quick pressure release; carefully remove the lid. Bon appétit!

337. Turkey Sandwich with Cheese and Lettuce

(Ready in about 35 minutes | Servings 4)

Ingredients

8 slices walnut bread
4 (1-ounce) slices white cheddar cheese
2 tablespoons Dijon mustard
1 teaspoon thyme
1 teaspoon marjoram
1 teaspoon basil
2 tablespoons butter, at room temperature
Salt and ground black pepper, to taste
8 lettuce leaves
1 ½ pounds turkey breast
1 clove garlic
1 cup vegetable broth

Directions

Place the turkey breasts, garlic, salt, black pepper, thyme, marjoram, basil, and butter in the inner pot; pour in the vegetable broth.

Secure the lid. Choose the "Manual" mode and cook for 25 minutes at High pressure. Once cooking is complete, use a natural pressure release; carefully remove the lid.

Spread the mustard on 4 slices of bread. Layer the slices of bread with the turkey, lettuce, and cheese.

Place the remaining 4 slices of bread on top of the sandwiches and serve immediately.

Per serving: 560 Calories; 29.1g Fat; 22.5g Carbs; 49g Protein; 3.1g Sugars

338. Mexican-Style Turkey and Sausage Meatloaf

(Ready in about 25 minutes | Servings 6)

Ingredients

1/2 cup tortilla chips, crushed
2 eggs
1 onion, chopped
1 cup tomato puree
3 teaspoons brown sugar
1/2 cup dried bread flakes
Salt and ground black pepper, to taste
1 teaspoon cayenne pepper
3/4 pound ground turkey
1/2 pound cooked beef sausage, crumbled
1 tablespoon oyster sauce
2 garlic cloves, chopped

Directions

In a mixing bowl, thoroughly combine the ground turkey, beef sausage, tortilla chips, dried bread flakes, oyster sauce, eggs, onion, and garlic.

Season with salt, black pepper, and cayenne pepper; stir until everything is well incorporated.

Add 1 ½ cups of water to the bottom of your Instant Pot. Shape the meat mixture into a log that will fit into the steamer rack.

Place an aluminum foil sling on the rack and carefully lower the meatloaf onto the foil. Mix the tomato puree with 3 teaspoons of brown sugar. Spread this mixture over the top of your meatloaf.

Secure the lid and choose the "Manual" mode. Cook at High pressure for 20 minutes or to an internal temperature of 160 degrees F.

Once cooking is complete, use a natural release and carefully remove the lid. Bon appétit!

Per serving: 273 Calories; 14.8g Fat; 14.5g Carbs; 22.6g Protein; 4.5g Sugars

339. Duck Salad with Peanut Butter

(Ready in about 25 minutes | Servings 6)

Ingredients

2 tomatoes, diced
2 red onions, sliced diagonally
1 cup water
2 tablespoons tamari sauce
2 tablespoons peanut butter
Salt and black pepper, to taste

2 tablespoons balsamic vinegar
1 garlic clove, minced
1 teaspoon fresh ginger, grated
3 pounds duck breasts
2 heads romaine lettuce, torn
into small pieces

Directions

Put the duck breasts and water into the inner pot.

Secure the lid and choose the "Poultry" mode. Cook for 15 minutes at High pressure. Afterwards, use a quick release and carefully remove the lid.

Now, slice the meat into strips and place in a salad bowl. Season with salt and pepper. Add the romaine lettuce, tomatoes, and onion.

In a small mixing dish, whisk the balsamic vinegar, garlic, ginger, tamari sauce, and peanut butter. Dress the salad and serve well chilled. Bon appétit!

Per serving: 349 Calories; 11.3g Fat; 12.3g Carbs; 48.6g Protein; 6.3g Sugars

340. Chicken Breasts with Mayo-Cheese Sauce

(Ready in about 15 minutes | Servings 4)

Ingredients

1 tablespoon olive oil
1 teaspoon dried marjoram
1 cup water
1/2 teaspoon dried basil
Salt, to taste
4 chicken breasts halves
1/4 teaspoon ground black
pepper, or more to taste
1/4 teaspoon ground bay leaf

Mayo-Cheese Sauce:
1/2 teaspoon porcini powder
1/2 cup Cottage cheese, at
room temperature
1 teaspoon garlic powder
2 tablespoons mayonnaise
1/2 cup Gruyère cheese,
grated

Directions

Press the "Sauté" button to heat up your Instant Pot; heat the oil. Once hot, sear the chicken breasts for 2 minutes per side.

Add the black pepper, ground bay leaf, dried basil, salt, and marjoram; pour in the water.

Secure the lid. Choose the "Poultry" setting and cook for 5 minutes at High pressure. Once cooking is complete, use a natural pressure release; carefully remove the lid.

Clean the Instant Pot and press the "Sauté" button again. Add the sauce ingredients and stir until everything is heated through.

Top the chicken with the sauce and serve immediately. Bon appétit!

Per serving: 268 Calories; 14.9g Fat; 1.5g Carbs; 30.5g Protein; 0.8g Sugars

341. Lebanese Tabouli Salad

(Ready in about 20 minutes | Servings 4)

Ingredients

1 cup pearl barley
1 tablespoon harissa paste
2 limes, freshly squeezed
4 tablespoons extra-virgin
olive oil
1 bay leaf
1 bunch spring onions, thinly
sliced
1 medium cucumber, sliced
2 carrots, trimmed and thinly
sliced

2 ½ cups vegetable broth
1/4 teaspoon freshly ground
black pepper
1 pound turkey breast fillet,
slice into bite-sized pieces
Pink salt, to taste
2 medium vine-ripened
tomatoes, sliced
1 garlic clove, crushed

Directions

Add the turkey breast fillets, barley, bay leaf, carrots, and vegetable broth to the inner pot.

Secure the lid. Choose the "Manual" mode and cook for 9 minutes at High pressure. Once cooking is complete, use a quick pressure release; carefully remove the lid.

Drain, chill and transfer to a serving bowl. Add the spring onions, cucumber, tomatoes, and garlic to the bowl.

In a small mixing dish, thoroughly combine the remaining ingredients. Drizzle this dressing over your salad and serve immediately. Bon appétit!

Per serving: 426 Calories; 14.5g Fat; 43.6g Carbs; 30.1g Protein; 2.4g Sugars

342. Dijon Chicken Meatballs

(Ready in about 15 minutes | Servings 6)

Ingredients

4 slices bacon, chopped
1 tablespoon Worcestershire
sauce
2 tablespoons ruby port
2 tablespoons olive oil
2 cups tomato purée
3 garlic cloves, minced
1/2 teaspoon paprika
2 tablespoons Dijon mustard

1 ¼ pounds ground chicken
1 cup seasoned breadcrumbs
1 onion, finely chopped
1/4 cup chicken broth
1/2 tablespoon fresh rosemary,
finely chopped
2 eggs, beaten
Salt and ground black pepper,
to taste

Directions

Thoroughly combine the ground chicken, bacon, breadcrumbs, onion, garlic, rosemary, eggs, salt, black pepper, and paprika.

Shape the mixture into meatballs and reserve.

Press the "Sauté" button on High heat to preheat your Instant Pot. Heat the olive oil and sear the meatballs until they are browned on all sides; work in batches.

Add the other ingredients. Choose the "Manual" setting and cook at High pressure for 7 minutes. Use a quick pressure release and carefully remove the lid. Bon appétit!

Per serving: 412 Calories; 23.1g Fat; 21.2g Carbs; 26g Protein; 7.2g Sugars

343. Thai-Style Duck Breasts

(Ready in about 50 minutes | Servings 4)

Ingredients

2 pounds duck breast
1 tablespoon Thai red curry paste
2 thyme sprigs, chopped
2 rosemary sprigs, chopped
1 cup light coconut milk
1/2 cup chicken broth, preferably homemade
1 teaspoon cayenne pepper
1 teaspoon sea salt
4 garlic cloves, minced
1/4 small pack coriander, roughly chopped
Zest and juice of 1 fresh lime
1 tablespoon olive oil
1/2 teaspoon black peppercorns, crushed

Directions

Combine the red curry paste with the lime zest and juice; rub the mixture all over the duck breast and leave it to marinate for 30 minutes.

Press the "Sauté" button and heat the oil until sizzling. Cook the duck breast until slightly brown on both sides.

Then, season the duck breasts with the peppercorns, cayenne pepper, and salt. Add the garlic, thyme, rosemary, coconut milk, and chicken broth.

Secure the lid. Choose the "Poultry" mode and cook for 15 minutes at High pressure. Once cooking is complete, use a quick pressure release; carefully remove the lid.

Garnish with chopped coriander and serve warm. Bon appétit!

Per serving: 467 Calories; 27.8g Fat; 6.8g Carbs; 47.6g Protein; 2.5g Sugars

344. Swiss Spicy Turkey Meatballs

(Ready in about 15 minutes | Servings 6)

Ingredients

8 ounces Swiss cheese, cubed
1/2 teaspoon dried basil
1/2 teaspoon dried oregano
1 tablespoon olive oil
1 yellow onion, chopped
2 garlic cloves, minced
Kosher salt, to taste
1/4 teaspoon freshly ground black pepper
1/2 cup water
1 cup tortilla chips, crumbled
1/2 teaspoon paprika
1 tablespoon sugar
1/2 teaspoon chili powder
1 ½ pounds ground turkey
1/2 cup tomato, pureed
2 eggs

Directions

Thoroughly combine the ground turkey, eggs, onion, garlic, crumbled tortilla chips, paprika, salt, pepper, basil, and oregano.

Roll the mixture into meatballs. Press 1 cheese cube into center of each meatball, sealing it inside.

Press the "Sauté" button to heat up your Instant Pot; now, heat the olive oil. Brown the meatballs for a couple of minutes, turning them periodically. Add the tomato sauce, water, sugar, and chili powder.

Secure the lid. Choose the "Manual" setting and cook for 9 minutes under High pressure. Once cooking is complete, use a quick pressure release; carefully remove the lid. Bon appétit!

Per serving: 404 Calories; 24.9g Fat; 9.6g Carbs; 35.3g Protein; 3.1g Sugars

345. Blood Orange Duck Breast

(Ready in about 35 minutes | Servings 4)

Ingredients

1 ½ pounds duck breast
1/2 cup dry white wine
2 tablespoons apricot jam
2 blood oranges, juiced
1 tablespoon olive oil
1 teaspoon dried dill weed
1 cup chicken bone broth
Sea salt and ground black pepper, to taste
1/2 teaspoon cayenne pepper
2 tablespoons potato starch

Directions

Press the "Sauté" button and heat the oil until sizzling. Then, cook the duck breasts for 4 minutes per side.

Add the oranges, salt, black pepper, cayenne pepper, dill, and broth.

Secure the lid. Choose the "Poultry" mode and cook for 15 minutes at High pressure. Once cooking is complete, use a quick pressure release; carefully remove the lid.

Remove the duck from the cooking liquid using a slotted spoon. Add the remaining ingredients to the cooking liquid and press the "Sauté" button again.

Let it simmer for 5 to 7 minutes or until slightly thickened. Spoon the sauce onto the duck and serve immediately. Bon appétit!

Per serving: 472 Calories; 14.2g Fat; 42.8g Carbs; 42.4g Protein; 9.7g Sugars

346. Chicken with Port Wine Sauce

(Ready in about 25 minutes | Servings 4)

Ingredients

1 cup tomato puree
1 teaspoon fresh ginger, grated
2 cloves garlic, chopped
1 teaspoon dried oregano
1 teaspoon dried rosemary
2 shallots, cut into wedges
Salt and freshly ground black pepper, to taste
1 cup vegetable broth
1 pound chicken legs, bone-in
1/4 cup Port wine

Directions

Place the chicken legs in the Instant Pot. Pour in the tomato puree, vegetable broth, and Port wine.

Secure the lid. Choose the "Poultry" setting and cook for 15 minutes under High pressure. Once cooking is complete, use a quick pressure release; carefully remove the lid.

Stir in the remaining ingredients. Secure the lid. Choose the "Manual" setting and cook for 3 minutes under High pressure.

Once cooking is complete, use a quick pressure release; carefully remove the lid. Serve warm and enjoy!

Per serving: 308 Calories; 17.6g Fat; 12.9g Carbs; 24.4g Protein; 6.2g Sugars

347. Meatball and Mozzarella Sliders with Tomato Sauce

(Ready in about 15 minutes | Servings 4)

Ingredients

Meatballs:
1/2 cup seasoned breadcrumbs
Sea salt, to taste
1/2 teaspoon freshly cracked black pepper
2 tablespoons fresh cilantro, chopped
1 egg, whisked
2 cloves garlic, minced
1 pound ground turkey

Sauce:
1 cup tomatoes puree
1 teaspoon hot sauce
1 tablespoon butter, at room temperature
1/4 cup fresh basil, chopped
Salt, to taste
2 cloves garlic, minced
1 onion, minced
Meatball Sliders:
8 honey wheat slider buns, toasted
1/2 cup mozzarella, shredded

Directions

Mix all ingredients for the meatballs until everything is well incorporated; form the mixture into small balls.

Spritz the sides and bottom of the inner pot with cooking spray. Press the "Sauté" button and cook your meatball until they are golden brown on all sides.

Add all ingredients for the sauce to the inner pot. Fold in the meatballs.

Secure the lid. Choose the "Poultry" mode and cook for 5 minutes at High pressure. Once cooking is complete, use a quick pressure release; carefully remove the lid. Serve warm.

Preheat your oven to broil.

To assemble the slider, place 1 meatball and a spoonful of sauce on the bottom of each bun. Top with mozzarella. Place under the broiler and bake until the cheese has melted about 2 minutes.

Top with another bun half and serve immediately. Bon appétit!

Per serving: 502 Calories; 15.8g Fat; 52.9g Carbs; 37.3g Protein; 5.5g Sugars

348. Turkey, Herb and Green Bean Chowder

(Ready in about 25 minutes | Servings 4)

Ingredients

12 ounces green beans, cut into halves
1 pound turkey breasts, boneless, skinless and diced
Salt and ground black pepper, to taste
1 (28-ounce) can diced tomatoes
1 teaspoon dried oregano
1/2 teaspoon dried marjoram

2 cloves garlic, minced
2 carrots, diced
1/2 teaspoon dried thyme
2 tablespoons apple cider vinegar
1/2 teaspoon ground cumin
2 cups water
2 cups chicken stock
1 yellow onion, chopped

Directions

Place all of the above ingredients, except for the green beans, into the Instant Pot.

Secure the lid. Choose the "Poultry" mode and High pressure; cook for 15 minutes. Once cooking is complete, use a quick pressure release; carefully remove the lid.

Then, stir in the green beans. Seal the lid again; let it sit for 5 minutes to blanch the green beans. Bon appétit!

Per serving: 295 Calories; 12.2g Fat; 16.4g Carbs; 30.6g Protein; 8.4g Sugars

349. Chicken Siciliano with Marsala Wine

(Ready in about 25 minutes | Servings 4)

Ingredients

4 chicken drumsticks, boneless
1 teaspoon Italian seasoning mix
1/4 cup Marsala wine
2 bell peppers, deseeded and sliced
4 cloves garlic, smashed
1 cup scallions, chopped

1 cup chicken broth
2 tablespoons butter, room temperature
1/4 cup all-purpose flour
1/4 cup cream cheese
Sea salt and ground black pepper, to taste

Directions

Press the "Sauté" button to preheat your Instant Pot. Melt 1 tablespoon of the butter.

Dredge your chicken in the flour; season with spices and cook until slightly brown; reserve.

Melt the remaining tablespoon of butter and sauté the peppers, scallions, and garlic. Pour in the wine, scraping up any browned bits from the bottom of the pan. Add the chicken broth and secure the lid.

Choose the "Manual" mode and cook for 10 minutes at High pressure. Once cooking is complete, use a natural pressure release; carefully remove the lid.

Press the "Sauté" button to preheat your Instant Pot one more time. Add the cream cheese and cook for a further 4 to 5 minutes or until everything is thoroughly heated.

To serve, spoon the sauce over the chicken drumsticks. Bon appétit!

350. Chicken Sloppy Joes

(Ready in about 15 minutes | Servings 6)

Ingredients

1 pound ground chicken
1/2 pound ground pork
1 cup chicken broth
2 tomatoes, chopped
1/2 teaspoon paprika
1/2 teaspoon porcini powder
1/2 teaspoon fennel seeds

2 garlic cloves, minced
1 yellow onion, chopped
2 bay leaves
1 tablespoon olive oil
Sea salt and ground black pepper, to taste

Directions

Press the "Sauté" button to heat up your Instant Pot; heat the oil. Now, cook the ground meat until it is delicately browned; reserve.

Sauté the garlic and onion in pan drippings for 2 to 3 minutes. Stir in the remaining ingredients.

Now, secure the lid. Choose the "Poultry" setting and cook for 5 minutes under High pressure.

Once cooking is complete, use a natural pressure release; carefully remove the lid.

Spoon the mixture on toasted slider buns and serve.

Per serving: 329 Calories; 23.3g Fat; 3.2g Carbs; 25.1g Protein; 1.7g Sugars

BEEF

351. Japanese Beef Stew

(Ready in about 40 minutes + marinating time | Servings 4)

Ingredients

1 cup steamed rice
1/4 cup Shoyu sauce
1/4 cup brown sugar
2 eggs, whisked
2 bay leaves
1 rosemary sprig
1 tablespoon cider vinegar
2 tablespoons cornstarch
1 tablespoon olive oil
1 teaspoon onion powder

Salt and black pepper, to taste
2 tablespoons sake
2 tablespoons pickled red ginger
1 cup beef broth
2 cloves garlic, minced
2 pounds beef stew meat, cut into 1-inch cubes
1 teaspoon hot sauce

Directions

In a ceramic bowl, place the meat, Shoyu sauce, brown sugar, garlic, cider vinegar, sake, ginger, and hot sauce. Let it marinate for 2 hours.

Discard the marinade and toss the beef cubes with the cornstarch.

Press the "Sauté" button and heat the oil until sizzling. Brown the beef cubes for 3 to 4 minutes, stirring periodically.

Add the onion powder, bay leaves, rosemary sprig, salt, black pepper, and beef broth.

Secure the lid. Choose the "Meat/Stew" mode and cook for 35 minutes at High pressure. Once cooking is complete, use a quick pressure release; carefully remove the lid.

Slowly stir in the whisked eggs and press the "Sauté" button. Continue to cook until the eggs are done.

Serve over steamed rice.

Per serving: 598 Calories; 15.2g Fat; 54.5g Carbs; 57.6g Protein; 7.9g Sugars

352. Chinese Beef Rump Roast

(Ready in about 40 minutes | Servings 8)

Ingredients

2 garlic cloves, halved
4 carrots, peeled
1 ½ cups vegetable stock
2 parsnips, chopped
1 teaspoon dried rosemary
1 tablespoon olive oil

Salt and pepper, to your liking
1/3 cup Shaoxing wine
1 teaspoon dried thyme
2 pounds beef rump roast
1 cup leeks, chopped

Directions

Rub the beef rump roast with the garlic halves. Now, cut it into cubes. Season with salt, pepper, rosemary, and thyme.

Then, press the "Sauté" button and heat the olive oil. Sauté the leeks together with the carrot and parsnips.

Add a splash of Shaoxing wine to deglaze the pan. Place the beef pieces in a single layer on top of sautéed vegetables.

Pour in the vegetable stock and the remaining Shaoxing wine. Secure the lid. Select the "Manual" mode and cook for 35 minutes.

Once cooking is complete, use a quick release. Serve warm. Bon appétit!

Per serving: 269 Calories; 11.5g Fat; 10g Carbs; 31.7g Protein; 3.7g Sugars

353. Classic Sloppy Joes

(Ready in about 20 minutes | Servings 4)

Ingredients

1 pound ground beef
4 soft hamburger buns
1 teaspoon fresh garlic, minced
1/2 cup tomato puree
1/2 teaspoon red pepper flakes
1 teaspoon celery seeds
1/2 teaspoon dried rosemary
1 cup beef stock
1 sweet pepper, chopped

2 tablespoons ketchup
1 onion, chopped
1 teaspoon brown sugar
1 teaspoon lard
1 tablespoon stone ground mustard
1 serrano pepper, chopped
Salt and ground black pepper, to taste

Directions

Press the "Sauté" button and melt the lard. Once hot, cook the ground beef until it is brown.

Add the onion, garlic, and peppers; continue to cook for 1 to 2 minutes more.

Add the salt, black pepper, red pepper flakes, mustard, celery seeds, rosemary, stock, tomato puree, ketchup, and brown sugar. Mix to combine.

Secure the lid. Choose the "Manual" mode and cook for 5 minutes at High pressure. Once cooking is complete, use a natural pressure release for 10 minutes; carefully remove the lid.

Serve on hamburger buns and enjoy!

Per serving: 475 Calories; 16.6g Fat; 43g Carbs; 37.6g Protein; 9.2g Sugars

354. Spicy Thai Beef Salad

(Ready in about 45 minutes | Servings 6)

Ingredients

1 bunch fresh Thai basil, leaves picked
1 tablespoon Dijon mustard
1 tablespoon black peppercorns
1/4 cup lemon juice, freshly squeezed
1/4 cup sesame oil
Sea salt flakes, to taste
1 large-sized cucumber, sliced

2 long fresh red chilies, chopped
2 cups arugula
1/2 cup vegetable broth
3 kaffir lime leaves, shredded
2 pounds beef rump steak
2 bay leaves
1 tablespoon tamari sauce
1 cup red onions, thinly sliced
1 fresh tomato, diced
1/2 cup water

Directions

Add the beef, vegetable broth, water, black peppercorns, and bay leaves to your Instant Pot.

Secure the lid. Choose the "Meat/Stew" mode and High pressure; cook for 35 minutes. Once cooking is complete, use a natural pressure release; carefully remove the lid.

Thinly slice the beef across the grain and add to the salad bowl. In a small mixing bowl, make the dressing by whisking tamari sauce, lemon juice, sesame oil, and salt.

Add the remaining ingredients to the salad bowl; dress the salad. Serve at room temperature.

Per serving: 318 Calories; 17.7g Fat; 5.1g Carbs; 33.4g Protein; 1.9g Sugars

355. Saucy Delmonico Steak with Cheese

(Ready in about 20 minutes | Servings 4)

Ingredients

1 ½ pounds Delmonico steak, cubed

1/2 cup gorgonzola cheese, shredded

Sea salt and ground black pepper, to taste

1 cup beef broth

1/4 cup sour cream

1 teaspoon cayenne pepper

2 cloves garlic, minced

2 tablespoons butter

1 cup double cream

Directions

Press the "Sauté" button to preheat your Instant Pot. Melt the butter and brown the beef cubes in batches for about 4 minutes per batch.

Add the garlic, broth, double cream, and sour cream to the inner pot; season with cayenne pepper, salt, and black pepper.

Secure the lid. Choose the "Manual" mode and cook for 10 minutes at High pressure. Once cooking is complete, use a quick pressure release; carefully remove the lid.

Top with gorgonzola cheese and serve. Bon appétit!

Per serving: 572 Calories; 36.9g Fat; 5.8g Carbs; 55.3g Protein; 3.4g Sugars

356. Beef Goulash Soup

(Ready in about 40 minutes | Servings 4)

Ingredients

1 ½ pounds boneless beef chuck, cut into cubes

1 teaspoon garlic powder

1 teaspoon Hungarian paprika

2 tablespoons sesame oil

4 cups water

2 shallots, chopped

1 celery with leaves, chopped

2 carrots, sliced

1 red bell pepper, sliced

1/3 cup all-purpose flour

4 bullion cubes

Sea salt and freshly ground pepper, to taste

1/4 cup rose wine

1 bay leaf

Directions

In a mixing bowl, thoroughly combine the flour, salt, black pepper, and garlic powder. Now add the beef cubes to the flour mixture; toss to coat well.

Press the "Sauté" button. Heat the oil and sear the meat for 4 to 6 minutes.

Add the remaining ingredients and stir to combine.

Secure the lid. Choose the "Soup" mode and High pressure; cook for 30 minutes. Once cooking is complete, use a natural pressure release; carefully remove the lid.

Serve in individual bowls and enjoy!

Per serving: 336 Calories; 16.6g Fat; 10.5g Carbs; 36.5g Protein; 1.2g Sugars

357. French-Style Beef Tenderloin

(Ready in about 25 minutes | Servings 2)

Ingredients

1 tablespoon fresh tarragon

1 cup cream of onion soup

1 shallot, sliced

Kosher salt and ground black pepper, to taste

1 pound center-cut beef tenderloin

1 tablespoon butter

2 cloves garlic, finely minced

1/2 cup red wine

Directions

Add the beef and cream of onion soup to a lightly greased inner pot.

Secure the lid. Choose the "Manual" mode and cook for 13 minutes at High pressure. Once cooking is complete, use a quick pressure release; carefully remove the lid.

Press the "Sauté" button to preheat your Instant Pot. Melt the butter and cook the shallots until tender or about 3 minutes.

Then, stir in the garlic; cook an additional 30 seconds or so.

Pour the wine into the inner pot, scraping up all the browned bits on the bottom of the pan. Add the salt, pepper, and tarragon.

Continue boiling the sauce until it reduces by half. Serve the sliced chateaubriand with the wine sauce and enjoy!

Per serving: 559 Calories; 33.3g Fat; 19.6g Carbs; 47.1g Protein; 5.3g Sugars

358. Spicy Beef Chuck

(Ready in about 50 minutes | Servings 6)

Ingredients

2 pounds beef chuck, cut into bite-sized pieces

1 jalapeño pepper, finely minced

1/2 cup tomato paste

1/2 teaspoon dried basil

2 cloves garlic, minced

1 teaspoon dried rosemary, crushed

Sea salt, to taste

1/2 cup water

1/4 cup balsamic vinegar

2 tablespoons sesame oil

1 onion, chopped

1 tablespoon cilantro, finely chopped

1/2 teaspoon cayenne pepper

1/2 teaspoon ground black pepper

Directions

Press the "Sauté" button to preheat your Instant Pot. Heat the sesame oil until sizzling.

Once hot, cook the beef for 2 to 3 minutes. Add the remaining ingredients.

Secure the lid. Choose the "Meat/Stew" mode and High pressure; cook for 45 minutes. Once cooking is complete, use a natural pressure release; carefully remove the lid.

Afterwards, thicken the sauce on the "Sauté" function. Serve over hot macaroni and enjoy!

Per serving: 282 Calories; 13.3g Fat; 9.1g Carbs; 32.5g Protein; 5.4g Sugars

359. Steak Salad with Feta Cheese

(Ready in about 40 minutes | Servings 4)

Ingredients

1/2 cup feta cheese, crumbled
1/2 cup black olives, pitted and sliced
1 cup water
1/4 cup extra-virgin olive oil
2 tablespoons wine vinegar
1 red onion, thinly sliced
2 sweet peppers, cut into strips

1/2 cup red wine
Sea salt and ground black pepper, to taste
1/2 teaspoon red pepper flakes
1 butterhead lettuce, separate into leaves
1 ½ pounds steak

Directions

Add the steak, red wine, salt, black pepper, red pepper, and water to the inner pot.

Secure the lid. Choose the "Manual" mode and cook for 25 minutes at High pressure. Once cooking is complete, use a natural pressure release for 10 minutes; carefully remove the lid.

Thinly slice the steak against the grain and transfer to a salad bowl. Toss with the olive oil and vinegar.

Add the red onion, peppers, and lettuce; toss to combine well. Top with cheese and olives and serve. Bon appétit!

Per serving: 474 Calories; 28.8g Fat; 3.6g Carbs; 50.6g Protein; 1.7g Sugars

360. Classic Beef Brisket with Cheese

(Ready in about 1 hour 5 minutes | Servings 6)

Ingredients

2 pounds beef brisket
1 cup Monterey Jack cheese, freshly grated
1/2 teaspoon cayenne pepper
1 teaspoon mustard seeds
2 garlic cloves, chopped
Sea salt, to taste

1/2 teaspoon ground black pepper
1 leek, chopped
1 cup beef bone broth
1/2 teaspoon ground bay leaf
1/2 teaspoon celery seeds
2 tablespoons lard, at room temperature

Directions

Press the "Sauté" button to preheat your Instant Pot. Then, melt the lard.

Once hot, sear the brisket for 2 to 3 minutes on each side. Then, add the seasonings, garlic, leek, and beef bone broth.

Secure the lid. Choose the "Manual" mode and High pressure; cook for 60 minutes. Once cooking is complete, use a natural pressure release; carefully remove the lid.

Slice the beef into strips and top with cheese.

Press the "Sauté" button once again and allow it to simmer until cheese is melted. Serve warm.

Per serving: 434 Calories; 33.7g Fat; 3.2g Carbs; 28g Protein; 0.7g Sugars

361. Cheeseburger and Tomato Soufflé

(Ready in about 45 minutes | Servings 4)

Ingredients

1 cup cheddar cheese, shredded
2 ounces cream cheese, at room temperature
1 pound ground beef
1 tomato, sliced
1 onion, chopped
1/2 teaspoon oregano

1/2 teaspoon basil
1/2 teaspoon thyme
4 eggs
1/2 cup milk
2 cloves garlic, minced
Sea salt and ground black pepper, to taste
1 tablespoon olive oil

Directions

Press the "Sauté" button and heat the olive oil until sizzling. Now, cook the ground beef until no longer pink.

Transfer the browned beef to a lightly greased soufflé dish. Add the onion, garlic, and seasonings.

In a mixing dish, whisk the eggs, milk, and cream cheese. Top with the cheddar cheese. Cover with a foil.

Place the rack and 1 ½ cups of water inside the Instant Pot. Lower the soufflé dish onto the rack.

Secure the lid. Choose the "Manual" mode and cook for 30 minutes at High pressure. Once cooking is complete, use a quick pressure release; carefully remove the lid.

Let it rest for 10 minutes before slicing and serving. Garnish with tomatoes and serve. Enjoy!

Per serving: 465 Calories; 28.2g Fat; 9.4g Carbs; 41.5g Protein; 5.7g Sugars

362. Beef with Vegetables and Port Wine

(Ready in about 45 minutes + marinating time | Servings 6)

Ingredients

1 tablespoon olive oil
1/2 cup leeks, chopped
1 ½ cups port wine
1 1/3 cups vegetable stock
Salt and black pepper, to taste
1 teaspoon celery seeds

12 teaspoon dried thyme
2 garlic cloves, crushed
2 potatoes, diced
2 carrots, chopped
1 ½ pounds beef shanks, cut into pieces

Directions

Add the beef shanks to a bowl; now, add port, red wine, garlic, celery seeds, and dried thyme. Let it marinate overnight.

On an actual day, preheat your Instant Pot on "Sauté" function. Add olive oil; once hot, brown marinated shanks on all sides; reserve.

Now, cook the leeks, potatoes and carrots in the pan drippings until they have softened. Add the vegetable stock, salt, and pepper to taste.

Pour in the reserved marinade and secure the lid.

Select the "Meat/Stew" and cook for 35 minutes at High pressure. Once cooking is complete, use a quick release; remove the lid.

Now, press the "Sauté" button to thicken the cooking liquid for 5 to 6 minutes. Taste, adjust the seasonings and serve right away!

Per serving: 329 Calories; 10.5g Fat; 25.8g Carbs; 32g Protein; 2.7g Sugars

363. Syrah-Braised Beef

(Ready in about 40 minutes | Servings 4)

Ingredients

1/4 cup Syrah wine
1/2 cup dark brown sugar
1 bay leaf
1 cup beef bone broth
2 pounds beef stew meat, cubed
1/4 cup soy sauce

1 teaspoon red pepper flakes
2 tablespoons arrowroot powder
6 cloves garlic, sliced
1/4 cup scallions, roughly chopped
2 tablespoons olive oil

Directions

Press the "Sauté" button and heat the oil until sizzling. Then, brown the beef in batches.

Add a splash of red wine to deglaze the pot. Add the remaining wine, sugar, garlic, broth, soy sauce, red pepper, and bay leaf.

Secure the lid. Choose the "Meat/Stew" mode and cook for 35 minutes at High pressure. Once cooking is complete, use a quick pressure release; carefully remove the lid.

Press the "Sauté" button again and add the arrowroot powder. Let it cook until the sauce has reduced slightly and the flavors have concentrated. Serve garnished with fresh scallions and enjoy!

Per serving: 460 Calories; 18.7g Fat; 22.5g Carbs; 51.3g Protein; 15.7g Sugars

364. Best-Ever Homemade Tacos

(Ready in about 15 minutes | Servings 8)

Ingredients

2 pounds ground sirloin
2 cloves garlic, pressed
1 cup sour cream
12 whole-wheat flour tortillas, warmed
1/2 teaspoon ground cumin
Sea salt, to taste
1 can (16-ounces) diced tomatoes, undrained
2 canned chipotle chili in adobo sauce, drained

1/2 cup roasted vegetable broth
1/2 cup ketchup
1/2 teaspoon fresh ground pepper
1 teaspoon paprika
1 head romaine lettuce
1 tablespoon olive oil
1/2 cup shallots, chopped

Directions

Press the "Sauté" button and preheat the Instant Pot. Heat the oil and cook the shallots and garlic until aromatic.

Now, add the ground sirloin and cook an additional 2 minutes or until it is no longer pink.

Add the ground cumin, broth, ketchup, salt, black pepper, paprika, tomatoes, and chili in adobo sauce to your Instant Pot.

Secure the lid. Choose the "Poultry" mode and High pressure; cook for 5 minutes. Once cooking is complete, use a natural pressure release; carefully remove the lid.

Divide the beef mixture between tortillas. Garnish with lettuce and sour cream and serve.

Per serving: 566 Calories; 33.4g Fat; 38.6g Carbs; 30.7g Protein; 6.5g Sugars

365. Rustic Beef Brisket with Vegetables

(Ready in about 1 hour 25 minutes | Servings 6)

Ingredients

2 sprigs thyme
1 sprig rosemary
1/2 pound rutabaga, peeled and cut into 1-inch chunks
1/2 pound turnips, peeled and cut into 1-inch chunks
2 tablespoons olive oil
1 cup chicken broth

1 medium leek, sliced
2 parsnips, cut into 1-inch chunks
2 cloves peeled garlic
2 bell peppers, halved
2 ½ pounds corned beef brisket
1/4 cup tomato puree

Directions

Place the beef brisket, garlic, thyme, rosemary, olive oil, chicken broth, and tomato puree in the inner pot.

Secure the lid. Choose the "Manual" mode and cook for 80 minutes at High pressure. Once cooking is complete, use a quick pressure release; carefully remove the lid.

Add the other ingredients. Gently stir to combine.

Secure the lid. Choose the "Manual" mode and cook for 4 minutes at High pressure. Once cooking is complete, use a quick pressure release; carefully remove the lid. Bon appétit!

Per serving: 563 Calories; 35.8g Fat; 19.5g Carbs; 39.3g Protein; 6.5g Sugars

366. Beef with Wontons and Cream Cheese

(Ready in about 30 minutes | Servings 6)

Ingredients

1 ½ pounds beef brisket, cut into 2-inch cubes
6 ounces wonton noodles
3/4 cup cream cheese
2 tablespoons toasted sesame seeds
2 sprigs dried rosemary, leaves picked
1 teaspoon red pepper flakes, crushed
2 garlic cloves, minced

2 sprigs dried thyme, leaves picked
1 ½ tablespoons flaxseed meal
1/2 cup chicken stock
1 shallot, diced
1 tablespoon lard, at room temperature
1 teaspoon caraway seeds
Sea salt and freshly ground pepper, to taste

Directions

Press the "Sauté" button to preheat your Instant Pot. Now, melt the lard; once hot, sweat the shallot for 2 to 3 minutes.

Toss the beef brisket with salt, ground pepper, and red pepper flakes. Add the beef to the Instant pot; continue cooking for 3 minutes more or until it is no longer pink.

After that, stir in the garlic, rosemary, thyme, and caraway seeds; cook an additional minute, stirring continuously.

Add the flaxseed meal, chicken stock, and wonton noodles. Stir to combine well and seal the lid. Choose the "Meat/Stew" setting and cook at High pressure for 20 minutes.

Once cooking is complete, use a quick release; remove the lid. Divide the beef mixture among 6 serving bowls.

To serve, stir in the cream cheese and garnish with toasted sesame seeds. Bon appétit!

Per serving: 485 Calories; 30.9g Fat; 12.8g Carbs; 37.1g Protein; 2.4g Sugars

367. Creamed New York Strip

(Ready in about 30 minutes | Servings 4)

Ingredients

2 pounds New York strip, sliced into thin strips
1/2 cup heavy cream
2 carrots, sliced
1 cup cream of mushroom soup
1 small leek, sliced
2 cloves garlic, sliced
1 tablespoon tamari sauce
1/2 cup dry red wine
2 tablespoons sesame oil
Kosher salt and ground black pepper, to taste

Directions

Press the "Sauté" button to preheat your Instant Pot. Heat the sesame oil until sizzling. Once hot, brown the beef strips in batches.

Add wine to deglaze the pan. Stir in the remaining ingredients, except for the heavy cream.

Secure the lid. Choose the "Manual" mode and cook for 20 minutes at High pressure. Once cooking is complete, use a quick pressure release; carefully remove the lid.

Remove the beef from the cooking liquid. Mash the vegetables using a potato masher.

Press the "Sauté" button one more time. Now, bring the liquid to a boil. Heat off and stir in the heavy cream.

Spoon the sauce over the New York strip and serve immediately. Enjoy!

Per serving: 439 Calories; 21.9g Fat; 9.8g Carbs; 50g Protein; 2.3g Sugars

368. Harvest Beef Stew

(Ready in about 30 minutes | Servings 6)

Ingredients

1 cup sweet corn kernels, frozen
1/2 cup Pinot Noir
1/2 teaspoon mustard powder
1/2 pound carrots, chopped
1 teaspoon celery seeds
1 yellow onion, chopped
2 bell peppers, chopped
1 red chili pepper, chopped
Sea salt and ground black pepper, to taste
4 cups bone broth
2 pounds beef stewing meat, cut into cubes

Directions

Add all ingredients, except for the sweet corn, to the Instant Pot.

Secure the lid. Choose the "Soup" mode and High pressure; cook for 20 minutes. Once cooking is complete, use a quick pressure release; carefully remove the lid.

Stir in the sweet corn kernels and press the "Sauté" button. Let it simmer until thoroughly heated. Taste, adjust the seasonings and serve. Bon appétit!

Per serving: 223 Calories; 5.6g Fat; 14.4g Carbs; 28.1g Protein; 3.4g Sugars

369. Classic Beef Stroganoff

(Ready in about 50 minutes | Servings 5)

Ingredients

1 ½ pounds button mushrooms, quartered
2 pounds beef sirloin, cut into bite-sized chunks
1/2 teaspoon cayenne pepper
2 tablespoons tomato paste
1 teaspoon smoked paprika
2 cloves garlic, peeled and halved
2 cups beef broth
1 red onion, quartered
1 teaspoon dried basil
1/2 teaspoon dried marjoram
1 tablespoon lard, melted
1/2 cup double cream
Coarse sea salt, to taste
1/2 teaspoon ground black pepper
2 tablespoons cornstarch

Directions

In a shallow dish, combine the cornstarch with the salt, black pepper, cayenne pepper, and smoked paprika.

Dredge the beef pieces in the seasoned mixture to coat on all sides.

Press the "Sauté" button to preheat your Instant Pot. Melt the lard and brown the beef until no longer pink.

Add the basil, marjoram, garlic, and beef broth.

Secure the lid. Choose the "Meat/Stew" mode and cook for 35 minutes at High pressure. Once cooking is complete, use a quick pressure release; carefully remove the lid.

Add the button mushrooms, onions and tomato paste.

Secure the lid. Choose the "Manual" mode and cook for 3 minutes at High pressure. Once cooking is complete, use a quick pressure release; carefully remove the lid.

Stir in the double cream; seal the lid and let it sit in the residual heat for 5 to 7 minutes. Serve warm.

Per serving: 474 Calories; 28.1g Fat; 12.5g Carbs; 43.1g Protein; 5.4g Sugars

370. Chunky Hamburger Soup

(Ready in about 25 minutes | Servings 4)

Ingredients

1 pound ground beef
1/2 cup tomato purée
Sea salt and ground black pepper, to taste
2 carrots, thinly sliced
1 onion, peeled and finely chopped
4 cups beef bone broth
2 garlic cloves, minced
1 tablespoon olive oil
1 parsnip, thinly sliced
1 teaspoon cayenne pepper

Directions

Press the "Sauté" button to preheat your Instant Pot. Heat the olive oil and brown the ground beef and onions until the meat is no longer pink.

Add the remaining ingredients to your Instant Pot

Secure the lid. Choose the "Soup" mode and High pressure; cook for 20 minutes. Once cooking is complete, use a quick pressure release; carefully remove the lid.

Ladle into individual bowls and serve hot. Bon appétit!

Per serving: 340 Calories; 16.3g Fat; 15.7g Carbs; 31.9g Protein; 7.2g Sugars

371. Ground Beef, Cheese and Bean Bowl

(Ready in about 20 minutes | Servings 4)

Ingredients

1 ½ pounds lean ground chuck
1 ½ cups Monterey-Jack cheese, shredded
1 (15-ounce) can black beans, drained and rinsed
1 cup vegetable broth
1 onion, chopped
2 garlic cloves, minced
1 cup tomato puree
1 tablespoon chipotle paste

1 (1-ounce) packet taco seasoning mix
2 tablespoons fresh cilantro leaves, chopped
1 teaspoon olive oil
1 red bell pepper, deseeded and sliced
1 green bell pepper, deseeded and sliced

Directions

Press the "Sauté" button to preheat your Instant Pot. Heat the oil and cook the ground chuck for 2 to 3 minutes or until mostly brown.

Next, add the taco seasoning mix, broth, onion, garlic, and peppers.

Secure the lid. Choose the "Manual" mode and cook for 10 minutes at High pressure. Once cooking is complete, use a natural pressure release; carefully remove the lid.

Divide the meat mixture between four serving bowls. Add the tomato puree, chipotle paste, and black beans; gently stir to combine.

Top with the cheese and serve garnished with fresh cilantro leaves. Enjoy!

Per serving: 535 Calories; 31.2g Fat; 16.9g Carbs; 48.1g Protein; 6.7g Sugars

372. Authentic Hungarian Pörkölt

(Ready in about 30 minutes | Servings 4)

Ingredients

1 ½ pounds beef stewing meat, cut into bite-sized chunks
2 tablespoons sweet Hungarian paprika
Kosher salt, to taste
1 cup sour cream
1/4 teaspoon freshly ground black pepper, or more to taste
4 cups beef bone broth
1 cup tomato purée

2 sprigs thyme
2 bay leaves
1 cup scallions, chopped
2 cloves garlic, minced
2 carrots, sliced
1 jalapeño pepper, minced
1 tablespoon sesame oil
1 teaspoon dried sage, crushed
1/2 teaspoon mustard seeds

Directions

Press the "Sauté" button to preheat your Instant Pot. Then, heat the sesame oil. Sear the beef for 3 to 4 minutes or until it is delicately browned; reserve.

Cook the scallions and garlic in the pan drippings until tender and fragrant. Now, add the remaining ingredients, except for sour cream.

Secure the lid. Choose the "Soup" mode and High pressure; cook for 20 minutes. Once cooking is complete, use a quick pressure release; carefully remove the lid.

Divide your stew among four soup bowls; serve with a dollop of sour cream and enjoy!

Per serving: 487 Calories; 19g Fat; 11.3g Carbs; 65g Protein; 2.7g Sugars

373. Ground Beef and Tomato Frittata

(Ready in about 25 minutes | Servings 2)

Ingredients

1/2 pound ground chuck
1 small tomato, chopped
1/2 teaspoon garlic powder
Sea salt and freshly ground black pepper, to your liking

1/2 teaspoon paprika
4 eggs, whisked
1 tablespoon olive oil
A small bunch of green onions, chopped

Directions

Press the "Sauté" button to preheat your Instant Pot. Heat the oil and brown the beef for 2 to 3 minutes, stirring continuously.

Lightly spritz a baking pan with cooking oil. Add all ingredients, including the browned beef to the baking pan.

Cover with foil. Add 1 cup of water and a metal trivet to the Instant Pot. Lower the baking pan onto the trivet.

Secure the lid. Choose the "Manual" mode and cook for 6 minutes at High pressure. Once cooking is complete, use a natural pressure release for 10 minutes; carefully remove the lid.

Slice in half and serve. Bon appétit!

Per serving: 368 Calories; 24.1g Fat; 3.7g Carbs; 33.9g Protein; 2.4g Sugars

374. Classic Beef Sandwich

(Ready in about 45 minutes | Servings 6)

Ingredients

2 pounds sirloin
6 sandwich buns, split
1/2 cup water
1/4 cup dry vermouth
1 tablespoon Dijon mustard
1/2 cup vegetable broth

1 tablespoon tamari sauce
2 cloves garlic, minced
1 red chili pepper
1 tablespoon olive oil
Salt and black pepper, to taste
1/2 teaspoon cayenne pepper

Directions

Press the "Sauté" button to preheat your Instant Pot. Then, heat the oil until sizzling. Sear the beef until browned on all sides.

Add the broth, water, vermouth, mustard, tamari sauce, salt, black pepper, cayenne pepper, garlic, and red chili pepper.

Secure the lid. Choose the "Soup" mode and High pressure; cook for 40 minutes. Once cooking is complete, use a natural pressure release; carefully remove the lid.

Then, pull the cooked beef apart into chunks. Return it back to the Instant Pot and stir well to combine. Assemble the sandwiches with buns and serve. Enjoy!

Per serving: 503 Calories; 23.7g Fat; 36.2g Carbs; 34.3g Protein; 19.8g Sugars

375. Boozy and Spicy Short Ribs

(Ready in about 40 minutes + marinating time | Servings 8)

Ingredients

1 cup apple cider
2 tablespoons honey
1 teaspoon marjoram
1 tablespoon Sriracha sauce
2 tablespoons tomato paste
Kosher salt and cracked black pepper, to taste
1 teaspoon shallot powder
1/2 teaspoon paprika
1 tablespoon stone ground mustard
1 teaspoon garlic powder
1 cup beef bone broth
2 racks chuck short ribs
2 shots tequila

Directions

Place all ingredients, except for the beef broth, in a ceramic dish. Cover with a foil and let it marinate for 3 hours in your refrigerator.

Place the beef along with its marinade in the inner pot. Pour in the beef bone broth.

Secure the lid. Choose the "Meat/Stew" mode and cook for 35 minutes at High pressure. Once cooking is complete, use a natural pressure release; carefully remove the lid.

Bon appétit!

Per serving: 399 Calories; 29.2g Fat; 13.3g Carbs; 20.7g Protein; 5g Sugars

376. Beef Stew with Muffin Top

(Ready in about 45 minutes | Servings 6)

Ingredients

1 ½ pounds beef steak, thinly sliced
1 bay leaf
4 cups water
4 bouillon cubes
2 garlic cloves, crushed
1 cup parsnip, chopped
2 bell peppers, chopped
1 cup celery with leaves
1 cup carrots, chopped
1 (14-ounce) can tomatoes, diced
1 large-sized leek, chopped
1 heaping tablespoon lard, at room temperature
Topping:
1 cup Swiss cheese, grated
1 teaspoon baking powder
1/2 cup full-fat milk
1 cup plain flour

Directions

Press the "Sauté" button to preheat your Instant Pot. Melt the lard and brown the beef for 3 to 4 minutes, stirring occasionally.

Then, add the leeks and cook an additional 2 minutes or until it has softened. Add the garlic, celery, carrot, parsnip, peppers, tomatoes, water, bouillon cubes, and bay leaf.

Secure the lid. Choose the "Meat/Stew" mode and High pressure; cook for 20 minutes. Once cooking is complete, use a quick pressure release; carefully remove the lid.

In a mixing bowl, thoroughly combine all of the topping ingredients. Spread the topping over the top of your stew. Seal the lid and press the "Sauté" button.

Let it simmer for 15 minutes longer or until golden. Serve immediately.

Per serving: 404 Calories; 15.5g Fat; 31.1g Carbs; 34.4g Protein; 7g Sugars

377. Saucy and Spicy Rump Steak

(Ready in about 1 hour | Servings 6)

Ingredients

3 pounds rump steak, trimmed and sliced into small pieces
1/2 teaspoon marjoram
1/2 teaspoon hot sauce
1/2 teaspoon ginger powder
1/4 cup flour
2 carrots, sliced
1 cup vegetable broth
2 ripe tomatoes, pureed
Sea salt, to taste
2 tablespoons olive oil
3 garlic cloves, halved
1 teaspoon mixed peppercorns, crushed

Directions

In a shallow dish, combine the salt, black peppercorns, marjoram, ginger powder, and flour. Dredge the beef pieces in the seasoned mixture to coat on all sides.

Press the "Sauté" button to preheat your Instant Pot. Heat the oil and brown the beef until no longer pink.

Add the remaining ingredients.

Secure the lid. Choose the "Manual" mode and cook for 60 minutes at High pressure. Once cooking is complete, use a quick pressure release; carefully remove the lid. Bon appétit!

Per serving: 355 Calories; 14.2g Fat; 6.5g Carbs; 50.9g Protein; 1.3g Sugars

378. Wine Braised-Beef with Cabbage Slaw

(Ready in about 1 hour 10 minutes | Servings 6)

Ingredients

1/2 cup dry red wine
1/2 teaspoon cayenne pepper
1/4 cup tomato purée
2 garlic cloves, pressed
1 carrot, chopped
1/2 cup water
2 sprigs rosemary
1 ½ pounds beef brisket
4 bacon slices, chopped
1/2 teaspoon mixed peppercorns, whole
1/2 teaspoon sea salt
1/2 teaspoon ground black pepper
2 teaspoons olive oil
Cole Slaw:
4 tablespoons sour cream
4 tablespoons mayonnaise
1 head cabbage
1 yellow onion, thinly sliced
1 carrot, grated
Salt, to taste

Directions

Press the "Sauté" button to preheat your Instant Pot. Then, heat the oil until sizzling. Sear the beef for 3 to 4 minutes or until it is delicately browned; reserve.

Add the bacon to the Instant Pot; sear the bacon approximately 3 minutes; reserve. Then, cook the garlic for 1 minute or until fragrant.

Add the carrot, wine, water, rosemary, mixed peppercorns, tomato purée, salt, black pepper, and cayenne pepper. Return the beef brisket and bacon back to the Instant Pot.

Secure the lid. Choose the "Manual" mode and High pressure; cook for 60 minutes. Once cooking is complete, use a quick pressure release; carefully remove the lid.

Meanwhile, make the cabbage slaw by mixing the remaining ingredients. Serve and enjoy!

Per serving: 397 Calories; 29.4g Fat; 10.9g Carbs; 21.4g Protein; 5.1g Sugars

379. Spanish-Style Pot Roast

(Ready in about 55 minutes | Servings 4)

Ingredients

1 teaspoon smoked Spanish paprika
1/4 cup all-purpose flour
2 carrots, cut into bite-sized chunks
2 celery ribs, cut into bite-sized chunks
1 ½ cups water
1 habanero pepper, minced
2 garlic cloves, chopped
1 teaspoon achiote seasoning
1 tablespoon bouillon granules
1 tablespoon butter, melted
1/2 cup shallots, chopped
Sea salt and ground black pepper, to taste
2 pounds pot roast, cut into bite-sized chunks

Directions

Toss the beef with flour.

Press the "Sauté" button to preheat your Instant Pot. Melt the butter and cook the beef chunks for 4 to 5 minutes, stirring frequently.

Add the habanero pepper, garlic, Spanish paprika, achiote seasoning, bouillon granules, and water.

Secure the lid. Choose the "Meat/Stew" mode and cook for 35 minutes at High pressure. Once cooking is complete, use a natural pressure release; carefully remove the lid.

Add the vegetables, salt, and black pepper.

Secure the lid. Choose the "Manual" mode and cook for 7 minutes at High pressure. Once cooking is complete, use a quick pressure release; carefully remove the lid. Serve the beef and vegetables in individual bowls and enjoy!

Per serving: 393 Calories; 17g Fat; 11.6g Carbs; 48.5g Protein; 1.9g Sugars

380. Turkish Doner Kebab

(Ready in about 30 minutes | Servings 4)

Ingredients

1 ½ pounds lean steak beef, cubed
4 Bazlama flatbread
1/3 cup mayonnaise
Salt and ground black pepper, to taste
1 teaspoon Aleppo chili flakes
1 tablespoon champagne vinegar
1/2 teaspoon sumac
1/2 teaspoon turmeric powder
1/3 cup chicken stock
1/2 cup onion, sliced
2 cloves garlic, minced
2 tablespoons fresh cilantro, chopped
4 tablespoons pickled slaw
2 tablespoons olive oil

Directions

Press the "Sauté" button to heat up the Instant Pot. Now, heat olive oil and brown beef cubes, stirring frequently.

Add the onion, garlic, and seasonings to the Instant Pot. Cook an additional 4 minutes or until onion is translucent.

Pour the chicken stock and champagne vinegar over the meat. Seal the lid.

Choose the "Meat/Stew" setting and cook for 20 minutes at High pressure. Once cooking is complete, use a quick release; remove the lid.

Assemble the sandwiches with the meat mixture, mayonnaise, pickled slaw, and Bazlama bread. Bon appétit!

Per serving: 590 Calories; 29g Fat; 22.5g Carbs; 58g Protein; 1.8g Sugars

381. Basic Korean Bulgogi

(Ready in about 50 minutes + marinating time | Servings 4)

Ingredients

2 pounds rib-eye steak, cut into strips
2 tablespoons Korean rice wine
1/2 Asian pear, cored and sliced
1 onion, sliced
2 cloves garlic, minced
2 tablespoons sesame seeds, toasted
2 tablespoons agave syrup
2 tablespoons sesame oil
1 tablespoon pickled red ginger
1/4 cup tamari sauce
Salt and black pepper, to taste

Directions

Mix the tamari sauce, rice, wine, agave syrup, salt, and black pepper in a ceramic bowl; add the beef, cover, and let it marinate for 1 hour.

Press the "Sauté" button and heat the sesame oil. Once hot, brown the beef strips in batches. Add the onion, garlic, pickled ginger, and Asian pear.

Secure the lid. Choose the "Meat/Stew" mode and cook for 35 minutes at High pressure. Once cooking is complete, use a natural pressure release for 10 minutes; carefully remove the lid.

Serve garnished with toasted sesame seeds. Enjoy!

Per serving: 530 Calories; 29.5g Fat; 19g Carbs; 50.6g Protein; 13.6g Sugars

382. Perfect Ossobuco Milanese

(Ready in about 30 minutes | Servings 8)

Ingredients

1 ½ pounds Osso buco
1 onion, chopped
Sea salt and ground black pepper, to taste
1 sprig dried rosemary
1 teaspoon dried sage, crushed
1 celery with leaves, diced
1 cup beef bone broth
2 carrots, sliced
2 bay leaves
1/2 cup rose wine
2 garlic cloves, chopped
1/2 teaspoon tarragon
2 tablespoons olive oil

Directions

Press the "Sauté" button to preheat your Instant Pot. Now, heat the olive oil. Sear the beef on all sides.

Add the remaining ingredients.

Secure the lid. Choose the "Meat/Stew" mode and High pressure; cook for 25 minutes. Once cooking is complete, use a natural pressure release; carefully remove the lid. Bon appétit!

Per serving: 302 Calories; 7.2g Fat; 21.7g Carbs; 34.3g Protein; 3g Sugars

383. Winter Short Ribs with Leeks

(Ready in about 1 hour 45 minutes | Servings 6)

Ingredients

2 tablespoons olive oil
1 sprig rosemary
1/2 teaspoon celery seeds
2 cloves garlic, sliced
1 cup water
1 packet of onion soup mix
1 sprig thyme
1 medium leek, sliced
4 pounds beef short ribs, bone-in
Sea salt and ground black pepper, to taste

Directions

Place all ingredients in the inner pot.

Secure the lid. Choose the "Manual" mode and cook for 90 minutes at High pressure. Once cooking is complete, use a natural pressure release; carefully remove the lid.

Afterwards, place the short ribs under the broiler until the outside is crisp or about 10 minutes.

Transfer the ribs to a serving platter and enjoy!

Per serving: 655 Calories; 50.8g Fat; 3.3g Carbs; 43.7g Protein; 0.6g Sugars

384. Traditional Lavaş with Beef

(Ready in about 20 minutes | Servings 4)

Ingredients

1 ¼ pounds ground beef
1/2 cup baba ghanoush
1/2 teaspoon caraway seeds
1/4 teaspoon chipotle powder
1/3 cup chicken stock
1 cup tomato puree
Salt and pepper, to taste
1 teaspoon coriander
1/4 teaspoon cloves, ground
1 small Habanero pepper, deveined and minced
2 garlic cloves, chopped
1/2 cup scallions, chopped
4 lavash, warmed
1 ½ tablespoons olive oil

Directions

Press the "Sauté" button to heat up your Instant Pot; heat the oil.

Once hot, sauté the ground beef along with garlic, scallions, and Habanero pepper; cook until ground beef is no longer pink.

Add the tomato puree and continue to cook 3 minutes longer. Add seasonings and chicken stock.

Secure the lid. Choose the "Manual" mode; cook for 6 minutes at High pressure. Once cooking is complete, use a natural release and carefully remove the lid.

Spread the meat mixture evenly across the lavash. Top with the baba ghanoush. Now, gently wrap the lavash and serve. Bon appétit!

Per serving: 521 Calories; 22.6g Fat; 35.4g Carbs; 44.8g Protein; 6.2g Sugars

385. Breakfast Cheeseburger Cups

(Ready in about 30 minutes | Servings 6)

Ingredients

1 cup Cheddar cheese, shredded
1 ½ pounds ground beef
1 teaspoon onion powder
1 tablespoon maple syrup
1/2 teaspoon garlic powder
1 teaspoon Dijon mustard
1 tablespoon Italian seasoning blend
1/2 cup tomato paste
Sea salt and ground black pepper, to taste

Directions

Spritz a silicone muffin pan with non-stick cooking oil.

In a large bowl, thoroughly combine the ground beef, salt, black pepper, onion powder, garlic powder, Italian seasoning blend, tomato paste, and Dijon mustard with your hands.

Scrape the beef mixture into the silicone muffin pan.

Place a steamer rack inside the inner pot; add 1/2 cup of water. Lower the muffin pan onto the rack.

Secure the lid. Choose the "Manual" mode and cook for 20 minutes at High pressure. Once cooking is complete, use a quick pressure release; carefully remove the lid.

Top with cheese; allow the cheese to melt and serve warm.

Per serving: 390 Calories; 24.8g Fat; 6g Carbs; 33.8g Protein; 3.9g Sugars

386. Pakistani Beef Biryani

(Ready in about 25 minutes | Servings 6)

Ingredients

2 garlic cloves, peeled and chopped
1 (28-ounce) can tomatoes, crushed
4 hard-boiled eggs, peeled and sliced
2 ounces almonds, flaked
1 cup shallot, chopped
1 teaspoon coriander seeds
1/2 teaspoon ground cumin
8 ounces natural yoghurt
Kosher salt and ground black pepper, to taste
1 heaping teaspoon caster sugar
1 tablespoon Garam Masala
1 teaspoon saffron strands
1 ½ pounds braising steak, cut into bite-sized cubes

Directions

Add the beef steak, canned tomatoes, shallot, garlic, coriander seeds, cumin, Garam Masala, saffron strands, salt, black pepper, and sugar to the Instant Pot.

Secure the lid. Choose the "Meat/Stew" setting and cook at High pressure for 20 minutes. Once cooking is complete, use a natural pressure release; carefully remove the lid.

Add the yogurt and seal the lid. Let it sit in the residual heat until everything is heated through. Serve garnished with eggs and flaked almonds. Enjoy!

Per serving: 370 Calories; 16g Fat; 9.4g Carbs; 49g Protein; 5.5g Sugars

387. Homemade Philly Cheesesteak Sandwich

(Ready in about 35 minutes | Servings 8)

Ingredients

1 tablespoon Dijon mustard
8 ounces yellow American cheese, sliced
2 ½ pounds top sirloin steak, sliced into thin strips
8 Hoagie rolls
1 red chili pepper, minced
2 onions, sliced
2 sweet peppers, deseeded and sliced
1 teaspoon paprika
1/2 cup dry red wine
1 cup beef broth
8 ounces mild Provolone cheese, sliced
Kosher salt and freshly ground pepper, to taste
1 tablespoon lard, melted

Directions

Press the "Sauté" button to preheat your Instant Pot. Melt the lard and cook your steak for about 4 minutes.

Add the onions, peppers, salt, black pepper, paprika, wine, and broth.

Secure the lid. Choose the "Manual" mode and cook for 25 minutes at High pressure. Once cooking is complete, use a quick pressure release; carefully remove the lid.

Serve the meat mixture in rolls topped with mustard and cheese. Bon appétit!

Per serving: 579 Calories; 30.6g Fat; 27.1g Carbs; 45.9g Protein; 6.1g Sugars

388. Kheema Pav (Bombay Sloppy Joes)

(Ready in about 10 minutes | Servings 6)

Ingredients

2 pounds beef, ground
1 cup water
1/2 cup light plain yogurt
2 tablespoons fresh green onions, chopped
1 ripe tomato, diced
1 red chili pepper
Salt and ground black pepper, to taste
1/2 teaspoon ground cumin
1 teaspoon curry powder
1 tablespoon olive oil
1/2 cup onion, chopped
2 cloves garlic, smashed
1/2 teaspoon mustard seeds
1 teaspoon chili paste

Directions

Press the "Sauté" button to preheat your Instant Pot. Heat the olive oil and cook the ground beef for 2 to 3 minutes.

Then, process the onion, garlic, tomato and chili pepper in your blender. Add this mixture to the Instant Pot.

Next, add the salt, black pepper, cumin, mustard seeds, chili paste, curry powder, and water.

Secure the lid. Choose the "Manual" mode and High pressure; cook for 5 minutes. Once cooking is complete, use a natural pressure release; carefully remove the lid.

After that, fold in the yogurt and seal the lid. Let it sit in the residual heat until thoroughly heated. Serve garnished with fresh green onions. Bon appétit!

Per serving: 265 Calories; 12.5g Fat; 6g Carbs; 3.7g Protein; 4.4g Sugars

389. Winter Chili with Ground Chuck

(Ready in about 25 minutes | Servings 4)

Ingredients

1 pound ground chuck
2 (15-ounces) cans black beans, drained and rinsed
Kosher salt and ground black pepper, to taste
1 cup beef stock
2 cloves garlic, minced
1 teaspoon dried oregano
1/2 teaspoon cumin powder
1 teaspoon ancho chili powder
1 red chili pepper, minced
1/2 cup leeks, chopped
1 (14-ounce) can tomatoes, diced
4 tablespoon tomato ketchup
1 teaspoon dried basil
1 tablespoon olive oil

Directions

Press the "Sauté" button and heat the oil. Once hot, cook the ground chuck, leeks, and garlic until the meat is no longer pink.

Add the remaining ingredients; gently stir to combine.

Secure the lid. Choose the "Manual" mode and cook for 15 minutes at High pressure. Once cooking is complete, use a quick pressure release; carefully remove the lid.

Serve in individual bowls garnished with green onions if desired. Bon appétit!

Per serving: 393 Calories; 17.4g Fat; 23.6g Carbs; 37.4g Protein; 6.9g Sugars

390. Risotto with Ground Beef

(Ready in about 15 minutes | Servings 4)

Ingredients

2 cups Arborio rice
1 ½ pounds ground chuck
1 teaspoon garlic, minced
1 jalapeño pepper, minced
1 (1-inch) piece ginger root, peeled and grated
1/2 cup leeks, chopped
Sea salt, to taste
1/3 teaspoon ground black pepper, or more to taste
1 teaspoon red pepper flakes
1 cup tomato purée
1 ½ cups roasted vegetable broth
1 tablespoon sesame oil

Directions

Press the "Sauté" button to preheat your Instant Pot. Now, heat the sesame oil and sauté the leeks until tender.

Then, add the garlic, jalapeño and ginger; cook for 1 minute more or until aromatic.

Add the remaining ingredients; stir well to combine.

Secure the lid. Choose the "Manual" mode and High pressure; cook for 7 minutes. Once cooking is complete, use a quick pressure release; carefully remove the lid. Serve immediately.

Per serving: 493 Calories; 28.8g Fat; 34.9g Carbs; 42.1g Protein; 3.3g Sugars

391. Filet Mignon with Mushroom Sauce

Ready in about 30 minutes | Servings 4)

Ingredients

2 cups wild mushrooms, sliced
1/2 teaspoon ground black pepper
2 garlic cloves, sliced
2 tablespoons butter
1 onion, thinly sliced
1 cup chicken broth

1/2 teaspoon sea salt
1/2 teaspoon red pepper flakes, crushed
1/4 cup all-purpose flour
1 ½ pounds filet mignon, about 1 ½-inch thick

Directions

Toss the filet mignon with salt, red pepper, black pepper, and flour.

Press the "Sauté" button and melt the butter. Once hot, sear the filet mignon for 2 minutes. Turn it over and cook for 2 minutes more on the other side.

Add the remaining ingredients and secure the lid.

Choose the "Meat/Stew" mode and cook for 20 minutes at High pressure. Once cooking is complete, use a quick pressure release; carefully remove the lid.

You can thicken the sauce on the "Sauté" mode if desired. Serve warm.

Per serving: 332 Calories; 14.6g Fat; 8.8g Carbs; 41.8g Protein; 1.3g Sugars

392. Vietnamese Pho Bo

(Ready in about 15 minutes | Servings 4)

Ingredients

1 pound round steak, sliced paper thin
1 bunch of cilantro, roughly chopped
2 stalks scallions, diced
1 celery stalk, trimmed and diced
1 cinnamon stick
3 star of anise

1/2 (14-ounce) package rice noodles
1 tablespoon sesame oil
4 cups roasted vegetable broth
Kosher salt and ground black pepper, to taste
2 carrots, trimmed and diced
1 tablespoon brown sugar

Directions

Press the "Sauté" button and preheat the Instant Pot. Heat the oil and sear the round steak for 1 to 2 minutes.

Add the broth, sugar, salt, black pepper, carrots, celery, cinnamon stick, and star anise. Top with rice noodles so they should be on top of the other ingredients.

Secure the lid. Choose the "Manual" mode and High pressure; cook for 3 minutes. Once cooking is complete, use a quick pressure release; carefully remove the lid.

Serve in individual bowls, topped with cilantro and scallions. Enjoy!

Per serving: 417 Calories; 14g Fat; 27.5g Carbs; 43.1g Protein; 3.6g Sugars

393. Rich Taco Meatloaf

(Ready in about 35 minutes | Servings 4)

Ingredients

1 pound ground beef
1/2 pound ground pork
1 package taco seasoning
1 cup tortilla chips, crushed
1 small-sized onion, finely chopped
1 sweet pepper, finely chopped
1 cup tomato puree
1 teaspoon mustard

2 cloves garlic, minced
Sea salt and ground black pepper, to taste
1/2 teaspoon rosemary
2 tablespoons brown sugar
1/2 cup milk
1 tablespoon tamari sauce
1 egg, beaten

Directions

Place a steamer rack inside the inner pot; add 1/2 cup of water. Cut 1 sheet of heavy-duty foil and brush with cooking spray.

In mixing dish, combine the egg, milk, tortilla chips, onion, sweet pepper, garlic, salt, black pepper, rosemary, and ground meat.

Shape the meat mixture into a loaf; place the meatloaf in the center of foil. Wrap your meatloaf in foil and lower onto the steamer rack.

Secure the lid. Choose the "Meat/Stew" mode and cook for 20 minutes at High pressure. Once cooking is complete, use a quick pressure release; carefully remove the lid.

Then, transfer your meatloaf to a cutting board. Let it stand for 10 minutes before cutting and serving. Bon appétit!

Per serving: 564 Calories; 28.7g Fat; 23.8g Carbs; 51.1g Protein; 10.5g Sugars

394. Classic Steak Pepperonata with Red Wine

(Ready in about 1 hour 10 minutes | Servings 6)

Ingredients

2 pounds top round steak, cut into bite-sized chunks
1/2 cup dry red wine
1 pound mixed bell peppers, deveined and thinly sliced
2 cloves garlic, minced
1 tablespoon Italian seasoning blend

1 red onion, chopped
1 tablespoon salt-packed capers, rinsed and drained
2 teaspoons lard, at room temperature
Sea salt and ground black pepper, to taste
1 cup water

Directions

Press the "Sauté" button to preheat your Instant Pot. Then, melt the lard. Cook the round steak approximately 5 minutes, stirring periodically; reserve.

Then, sauté the onion for 2 minutes or until translucent.

Stir in the remaining ingredients, including the reserved beef.

Secure the lid. Choose the "Manual" mode and High pressure; cook for 60 minutes. Once cooking is complete, use a natural pressure release; carefully remove the lid. Bon appétit!

Per serving: 309 Calories; 7.4g Fat; 10.8g Carbs; 46.9g Protein; 5.1g Sugars

395. Bulgarian Palneni Chushki

(Ready in about 25 minutes | Servings 3)

Per serving: 331 Calories; 13.5g Fat; 36.9g Carbs; 24.1g Protein; 15.2g Sugars

Ingredients

3 large bell peppers, deseeded, cored and halved
1 cup cheddar cheese, grated
2 tablespoons ketchup
1 onion, chopped
2 garlic cloves, minced
1 carrot, grated
1 teaspoon basil
1/2 teaspoon celery seeds
1/2 teaspoon mustard seeds
1 cup tomato puree
1/2 cup parboiled rice
1 pound ground beef
Sea salt and ground black pepper, to taste
1 teaspoon cayenne pepper

Directions

In a mixing bowl, thoroughly combine the rice, ground beef, onion, garlic, carrot, salt, black pepper, cayenne pepper, celery seeds, mustard seeds, and basil.

Add 1 cup of water and a metal trivet to the bottom. Fill the pepper halves with the rice/meat mixture. Place the peppers in a casserole dish; add the tomato puree and ketchup.

Lower the casserole dish onto the trivet in the Instant Pot.

Secure the lid. Choose the "Manual" mode and cook for 9 minutes at High pressure. Once cooking is complete, use a natural pressure release for 5 minutes; carefully remove the lid.

Afterwards, broil your peppers until the cheese melts approximately 5 minutes. Serve and enjoy!

396. Chianti Beef Mélange

(Ready in about 55 minutes | Servings 6)

Ingredients

2 pounds beef roast
2 carrots, sliced
1 parsnip, sliced
1/2 cup Chianti
1 cup shallots, chopped
2 cloves garlic, pressed
2 bay leaves
2 tablespoons olive oil
Sea salt and ground black pepper, to taste
1 teaspoon red pepper flakes, crushed
1 cup vegetable broth

Directions

Add the olive oil, beef, broth, Chianti, salt, black pepper, red pepper, shallots, garlic, and bay leaves to the Instant Pot.

Secure the lid. Choose the "Meat/Stew" mode and High pressure; cook for 45 minutes. Once cooking is complete, use a quick pressure release; carefully remove the lid.

Then, add the carrots and parsnip to the Instant Pot.

Secure the lid. Choose the "Manual" mode and High pressure; cook for 5 minutes. Once cooking is complete, use a quick pressure release; carefully remove the lid.

You can thicken the cooking liquid on "Sauté" function if desired. Bon appétit!

Per serving: 363 Calories; 17.6g Fat; 6.1g Carbs; 41.6g Protein; 1.8g Sugars

397. Roast Beef with Gravy

(Ready in about 1 hour 15 minutes | Servings 6)

Ingredients

1 teaspoon paprika
2 cloves garlic, smashed
1 bell pepper, deseeded and sliced
1 ½ pounds fingerling potatoes
1 onion, thinly sliced
3 cups beef bone broth
3 pounds top round roast
1 ½ tablespoons potato starch
1 teaspoon dried rosemary
1 tablespoon lard, melted
Sea salt and ground black pepper, to taste

Directions

Toss the beef with the salt, black pepper, paprika, and rosemary until well coated on all sides.

Press the "Sauté" button to preheat your Instant Pot and melt the lard. Sear the beef for about 4 minutes per side until it is browned.

Scatter the potatoes, onion, garlic, peppers around the top round roast. Add the beef bone broth.

Secure the lid. Choose the "Manual" mode and cook for 60 minutes at High pressure. Once cooking is complete, use a natural pressure release for 10 minutes; carefully remove the lid.

Transfer the roast and vegetables to a serving platter; shred the roast with 2 forks.

Mix the potato starch with 4 tablespoons of water. Press the "Sauté" button to preheat your Instant Pot again. Once the liquid is boiling, add the slurry and let it cook until the gravy thickens.

Taste and adjust the seasonings. Serve warm.

Per serving: 470 Calories; 8.8g Fat; 38.5g Carbs; 60.5g Protein; 2.6g Sugars

398. Chinese Sirloin Steak

(Ready in about 1 hour | Servings 8)

Ingredients

2 pounds boneless sirloin steak, thinly sliced
2 sweet peppers, deveined and sliced
1/2 cup beef bone broth
1/2 cup hoisin sauce
1 teaspoon chili powder
2 tablespoons fresh parsley, chopped
1/2 cup red onion, sliced
1 tablespoon lard, at room temperature
2 garlic cloves, minced
Sea salt and ground black pepper, to your liking

Directions

Press the "Sauté" button and preheat the Instant Pot; melt the lard. Once hot, brown the sirloin steak for 6 minutes, flipping halfway through cooking time.

Season with salt and pepper; add chili powder, parsley, onion, garlic, and peppers. Pour in beef bone broth and secure the lid.

Select "Manual" setting, High pressure and 50 minutes. Once cooking is complete, use a natural release and carefully remove the lid.

Shred the beef and return it to the Instant Pot; stir to combine. Afterwards, pour the hoisin sauce over shredded beef and vegetables and serve immediately. Bon appétit!

Per serving: 283 Calories; 14.9g Fat; 10.9g Carbs; 24.8g Protein; 4.6g Sugars

399. Perfect Beef Bourguignon

(Ready in about 55 minutes | Servings 6)

Ingredients

1/2 cup Burgundy wine
8 ounces mushrooms, sliced
1 teaspoon red pepper flakes
2 tablespoons olive oil
2 cloves garlic, sliced
2 tablespoons cornstarch

2 pounds boneless beef steak,
cut into bite-sized pieces
1 shallot, chopped
1 cup beef bone broth
Coarse sea salt and ground
black pepper, to taste

Directions

Toss the beef steak with the cornstarch, salt, black pepper, and red pepper flakes.

Press the "Sauté" button to preheat your Instant Pot. Heat the oil until sizzling. Now, cook the beef until well browned.

Add the remaining ingredients; gently stir to combine.

Secure the lid. Choose the "Manual" mode and cook for 40 minutes at High pressure. Once cooking is complete, use a natural pressure release for 10 minutes; carefully remove the lid.

Divide between individual bowls and serve warm with garlic croutons if desired. Enjoy!

Per serving: 418 Calories; 23.5g Fat; 5.3g Carbs; 44.1g Protein; 1.5g Sugars

400. Beef Sirloin Soup with Potatoes

(Ready in about 45 minutes | Servings 4)

Ingredients

1/2 pound beef sirloin, ground
2 Yukon Gold potatoes, chopped
1/2 cup tomato puree
1/2 teaspoon salt
1/2 teaspoon dried basil
1 teaspoon dried marjoram
1/2 teaspoon ground black pepper

4 cups bone broth
2 teaspoons dark soy sauce
2 carrots, chopped
2 bay leaves
1 teaspoon celery seeds
1/2 cup shallots, chopped
1 teaspoon garlic, minced
1 tablespoon olive oil

Directions

Press the "Sauté" button to heat up your Instant Pot. Heat the olive oil and brown the ground beef sirloin, crumbling with a fork. Season with salt and black pepper.

Add the bone broth to deglaze the pot. Stir in the remaining ingredients.

Secure the lid and choose the "Soup" button.

Cook for 30 minutes at High pressure. Once cooking is complete, use a natural release for 10 minutes; carefully remove the lid. Bon appétit!

Per serving: 276 Calories; 11.8g Fat; 22.6g Carbs; 19.3g Protein; 4.4g Sugars

401. Homemade Beef Tacos

(Ready in about 30 minutes | Servings 4)

Ingredients

1 ½ pounds ground beef
1/2 cup sour cream
1/2 cup chunky salsa
Kosher salt and ground black pepper, to taste
1 teaspoon cumin powder
1 chili pepper, minced
1 teaspoon marjoram
1 teaspoon Mexican oregano

1/2 teaspoon red pepper flakes
1 teaspoon mustard seeds
1 onion, chopped
2 sweet peppers, deseeded and sliced
12 small taco shells
4 garlic cloves, minced
1 head lettuce
1 tablespoon canola oil

Directions

Press the "Sauté" button to preheat your Instant Pot. Heat the oil and sear the ground chuck for 2 to 3 minutes or until mostly brown.

Add the onion, peppers, garlic, and spices to the inner pot.

Secure the lid. Choose the "Manual" mode and cook for 10 minutes at High pressure. Once cooking is complete, use a natural pressure release; carefully remove the lid.

Press the "Sauté" button and cook, stirring continuously, until the liquid has almost evaporated or about 10 minutes.

To assemble your tacos, layer the beef mixture and lettuce in each taco shell. Serve with the salsa and sour cream. Enjoy!

Per serving: 618 Calories; 37.8g Fat; 21g Carbs; 47.1g Protein; 4.4g Sugars

402. Nana's Steak Soup with Root Vegetables

(Ready in about 25 minutes | Servings 4)

Ingredients

1 cup water
Sea salt and ground black pepper, to taste
1 bay leaf
1 cup roasted vegetable broth
1 parsnip, chopped
2 (8-ounce) cans tomato sauce
1 turnip, chopped

2 bell peppers, deveined and chopped
2 cloves garlic, minced
1 shallot, diced
2 carrots, chopped
1 pound beef steak, cut into cubes

Directions

Simply throw all of the above ingredients in your Instant Pot that is previously greased with a nonstick cooking spray.

Secure the lid. Choose the "Soup" mode and High pressure; cook for 20 minutes. Once cooking is complete, use a quick pressure release; carefully remove the lid.

Divide the soup among four serving bowls and serve warm.

Per serving: 278 Calories; 7.6g Fat; 22.3g Carbs; 30.4g Protein; 9.7g Sugars

403. Rustic Beef Short Ribs

(Ready in about 1 hour 45 minutes | Servings 6)

Ingredients

1 packet of onion soup mix
1 medium leek, sliced
1 cup water
1 sprig thyme
2 tablespoons olive oil
1 sprig rosemary

2 cloves garlic, sliced
1/2 teaspoon celery seeds
Sea salt and ground black pepper, to taste
4 pounds beef short ribs, bone-in

Directions

Place all ingredients in the inner pot.

Secure the lid. Choose the "Manual" mode and cook for 90 minutes at High pressure. Once cooking is complete, use a natural pressure release; carefully remove the lid.

Afterwards, place the short ribs under the broiler until the outside is crisp or about 10 minutes.

Transfer the ribs to a serving platter and enjoy!

Per serving: 655 Calories; 50.8g Fat; 3.3g Carbs; 43.7g Protein; 0.6g Sugars

404. Easy Shoulder Roast with Russet Potatoes

(Ready in about 45 minutes | Servings 8)

Ingredients

3 pounds shoulder roast
2 pounds russet potatoes, peeled and quartered
1 ½ cups vegetable broth
1 packet ranch dressing mix

1 tablespoon tallow, at room temperature
4 pepperoncini peppers
1 teaspoon ginger garlic paste
Sea salt and ground black pepper, to taste

Directions

Press the "Sauté" button to preheat your Instant Pot. Now, melt the tallow. Sear the roast until it is delicately browned on all sides.

Then, add the ginger garlic paste, salt, black pepper, ranch dressing mix, and vegetable broth. Top with the pepperoncini peppers.

Secure the lid. Choose the "Meat/Stew" mode and High pressure; cook for 35 minutes. Once cooking is complete, use a natural pressure release; carefully remove the lid. Shred the meat with two forks.

Add the potatoes and secure the lid. Choose "Manual" mode and High pressure; cook for 5 minutes. Once cooking is complete, use a quick pressure release; carefully remove the lid.

Serve the pulled beef with potatoes and enjoy!

Per serving: 313 Calories; 8.1g Fat; 24.8g Carbs; 34.6g Protein; 3.1g Sugars

405. Festive Glazed Chuck Roast

(Ready in about 1 hour | Servings 6)

Ingredients

1 cup beef broth
1/2 teaspoon red pepper flakes
2 cloves garlic, sliced
1/4 cup champagne vinegar
Sea salt and ground black pepper, to taste
1/4 cup soy sauce

2 pounds chuck roast
Margarita Glaze:
2 tablespoons dark brown sugar
1/4 cup orange juice
1/4 lime juice
1/2 cup tequila

Directions

Add the chuck roast, beef broth, soy sauce, champagne vinegar, salt, black pepper, red pepper flakes, and garlic to the inner pot.

Secure the lid. Choose the "Manual" mode and cook for 40 minutes at High pressure. Once cooking is complete, use a natural pressure release for 10 minutes; carefully remove the lid.

Meanwhile, whisk all ingredients for the margarita glaze. Now, glaze the ribs and place under the broiler for 5 minutes; then, turn them over and glaze on the other side. Broil an additional 5 minutes.

Cut the chuck roast into slices and serve the remaining glaze on the side as a sauce. Bon appétit!

Per serving: 348 Calories; 14.9g Fat; 10.3g Carbs; 42.7g Protein; 7.7g Sugars

406. Corned Beef Brisket

(Ready in about 1 hour 25 minutes | Servings 6)

Ingredients

2 cloves peeled garlic
1/4 cup tomato puree
1 medium leek, sliced
2 parsnips, cut into 1-inch chunks
2 bell peppers, halved
2 tablespoons olive oil
1 cup chicken broth

1/2 pound rutabaga, peeled and cut into 1-inch chunks
1/2 pound turnips, peeled and cut into 1-inch chunks
2 ½ pounds corned beef brisket
2 sprigs thyme
1 sprig rosemary

Directions

Place the beef brisket, garlic, thyme, rosemary, olive oil, chicken broth, and tomato puree in the inner pot.

Secure the lid. Choose the "Manual" mode and cook for 80 minutes at High pressure. Once cooking is complete, use a quick pressure release; carefully remove the lid.

Add the other ingredients. Gently stir to combine.

Secure the lid. Choose the "Manual" mode and cook for 4 minutes at High pressure. Once cooking is complete, use a quick pressure release; carefully remove the lid. Bon appétit!

Per serving: 563 Calories; 35.8g Fat; 19.5g Carbs; 39.3g Protein; 6.5g Sugars

407. Spicy Shredded Beef

(Ready in about 50 minutes | Servings 8)

Ingredients

2 pounds chuck roast, cut into pieces
1 cup salsa, to serve
1 teaspoon ancho chili powder
1 teaspoon mustard powder
2 cups tomato purée
1 red onion, chopped
2 garlic cloves, minced
1 cup water
1/2 teaspoon coriander seeds
1/2 teaspoon fennel seeds
2 beef bouillon cubes
1 tablespoon corn oil
Sea salt and ground black pepper, to taste
1 teaspoon Mexican oregano

Directions

Press the "Sauté" button to preheat your Instant Pot. Then, heat the oil. Brown the chuck roast for 3 minutes.

Add the onion and garlic and cook an additional 2 minutes, stirring continuously. Stir in the remaining ingredients, except for the salsa.

Secure the lid. Choose the "Soup" mode and High pressure; cook for 40 minutes. Once cooking is complete, use a natural pressure release; carefully remove the lid.

Remove the beef from the Instant Pot and let it cool slightly. After that, shred the meat using two forks.

Meanwhile, press the "Sauté" button again and simmer the cooking liquid until the sauce has reduced and thickened. Adjust the seasonings and return the shredded meat back to the Instant Pot.

Serve with salsa. Enjoy!

Per serving: 250 Calories; 11.6g Fat; 6.1g Carbs; 31.4g Protein; 3.1g Sugars

408. Beef Brisket with Riesling Sauce

(Ready in about 1 hour 5 minutes | Servings 6)

Ingredients

1 ½ pounds beef brisket
1/3 cup dried apricots, chopped
1 tablespoon Worcestershire sauce
1 tablespoon honey
1 celery, diced
1 onion, cut into wedges
1 cup vegetable broth
3 cloves garlic, minced or pressed
1 carrot, diced
1/4 cup late-harvest Riesling
2 tablespoons olive oil

Directions

Press the "Sauté" button to preheat your Instant Pot. Heat the olive oil. Once hot, cook the beef brisket until it is delicately browned on all sides.

Add the remaining ingredients, except for the dried apricots, to the Instant Pot.

Secure the lid. Choose the "Manual" setting and cook at High pressure for 60 minutes. Once cooking is complete, use a natural pressure release; carefully remove the lid.

Garnish with dried apricots and serve immediately. Bon appétit!

Per serving: 338 Calories; 21.7g Fat; 15.5g Carbs; 18.4g Protein; 10.4g Sugars

409. Authentic Beef Gulyás

(Ready in about 30 minutes | Servings 5)

Ingredients

1/4 cup Hungarian red wine
1 tablespoon Hungarian paprika
2 pounds beef chuck, cut into bite-sized pieces
2 garlic cloves, crushed
2 onions, sliced
1 beef stock cube
2 ripe tomatoes, puréed
2 bay leaves
2 tablespoons olive oil
1 red chili pepper, minced
Sea salt and freshly ground black pepper, to taste
2 cups water

Directions

Press the "Sauté" button and heat the oil. Once hot, cook the beef until no longer pink. Add the red wine and stir with a wooden spoon, scraping up the browned bits on the bottom of the inner pot.

Stir in the remaining ingredients

Secure the lid. Choose the "Meat/Stew" mode. Cook for 20 minutes at High pressure. Once cooking is complete, use a quick pressure release; carefully remove the lid.

Serve in individual bowls and enjoy!

Per serving: 311 Calories; 16g Fat; 4.3g Carbs; 38.1g Protein; 2.1g Sugars

410. Romano and Bacon Meatballs

(Ready in about 10 minutes | Servings 6)

Ingredients

1/2 cup Romano cheese, grated
1 cup seasoned breadcrumbs
1/2 cup scallions, chopped
1 tablespoon canola oil
1 (10 ¼-ounce) can condensed mushroom soup
2 garlic cloves, crushed
1 cup tomato paste
1 pound ground beef
2 slices bacon, chopped
2 large eggs, beaten
1/3 cup milk

Directions

Thoroughly combine the ground beef, bacon, cheese, breadcrumbs, scallions, garlic, eggs, and milk. Roll the mixture into meatballs.

Press the "Sauté" button to preheat the Instant Pot. Heat the oil and sear the meatballs until they are browned on all sides.

Add the canned mushroom soup and tomato paste to the Instant Pot.

Secure the lid. Choose the "Manual" mode and High pressure; cook for 6 minutes. Once cooking is complete, use a quick pressure release; carefully remove the lid.

Serve warm, garnished with mashed potatoes. Bon appétit!

Per serving: 450 Calories; 24g Fat; 26.7g Carbs; 27.8g Protein; 9.9g Sugars

411. Winter Stew with Beef and Macaroni

(Ready in about 20 minutes | Servings 4)

Ingredients

1/2 (16-ounce) package macaroni
1/2 pound ground beef
1/2 pound pork sausage, crumbled
1 leek, chopped
1 ½ cups tomato puree
1 ½ cups chicken broth
2 garlic cloves, minced
2 carrots, chopped
1 (14.5-ounce) can stewed tomatoes
1 tablespoon canola oil
2 cups green beans, cut into thirds
Seasoned salt and black pepper, to taste

Directions

Press the "Sauté" button and heat the oil. Now, sauté the leek, garlic and carrot until they have softened.

Then, add the macaroni, ground beef, sausage, tomato puree, chicken broth, salt, and black pepper to the inner pot.

Secure the lid. Choose the "Manual" mode. Cook for 10 minutes at High pressure. Once cooking is complete, use a quick pressure release; carefully remove the lid.

After that, add the canned tomatoes and green beans; let it simmer on the "Sauté" function for 2 to 3 minutes more or until everything is heated through. Bon appétit!

Per serving: 536 Calories; 15.1g Fat; 66.8g Carbs; 39g Protein; 11.9g Sugars

412. Peppery Strip Steak with Pine Nuts

(Ready in about 25 minutes | Servings 4)

Ingredients

1 sweet red bell pepper, chopped
1 sweet green bell pepper, chopped
2 tablespoons toasted pine nuts, for garnish
2 tablespoons Worcestershire sauce
1 tablespoon oyster sauce
2 tablespoons flaxseed meal
1 teaspoon paprika
1 tablespoon lard, melted
2 sweet onions, chopped
2 cloves garlic, smashed
1/2 cup beef broth
1/2 cup tomato sauce
1 pound New York strip, cut into pieces
Salt and ground black pepper, to taste

Directions

Toss the beef with salt, black pepper, and paprika. Press the "Sauté" button on your Instant Pot. Once hot, melt the lard.

Brown the beef for 4 to 5 minutes, stirring periodically; add a splash of beef broth, if necessary; reserve.

Then, cook the sweet onions, garlic, and bell peppers until they are softened.

Add the beef broth, tomato sauce, Worcestershire, and oyster sauce to the Instant Pot. Return the browned beef to the Instant Pot.

Choose "Manual" setting, High pressure, and 15 minutes. Once cooking is complete, use a quick release.

Press the "Sauté" button, stir in flaxseed meal, and cook until the sauce is concentrated. Serve garnished with toasted pine nuts. Bon appétit!

Per serving: 322 Calories; 12.7g Fat; 25.5g Carbs; 27g Protein; 14.3g Sugars

413. Beef Curry Stew

(Ready in about 50 minutes | Servings 5)

Ingredients

2 pounds beef chuck, cubed
1/2 (13.5-ounce) can full-fat coconut milk
2 cups cauliflower florets
1/4 cup Thai red curry paste
1 (2-inch) galangal piece, peeled and sliced
1 Bird's eye chili pepper, seeded and minced
1/2 cup tomato paste
1/2 teaspoon ground cloves
2 onions, thinly sliced
2 cloves garlic, pressed
1/2 teaspoon cardamom
1/2 teaspoon cumin
1 cinnamon quill
Sea salt and ground white pepper, to taste
2 tablespoons fresh cilantro, roughly chopped
4 cups chicken bone broth
1 tablespoon soy sauce
2 tablespoons sesame oil

Directions

Press the "Sauté" button and heat the sesame oil. When the oil starts to sizzle, cook the meat until browned on all sides.

Add a splash of broth and use a spoon to scrape the brown bits from the bottom of the pot.

Next, stir in the onion, garlic, galangal, chili pepper, tomato paste, broth, curry paste, soy sauce, and spices.

Secure the lid. Choose the "Soup/Broth" mode and cook for 40 minutes at High pressure. Once cooking is complete, use a quick pressure release; carefully remove the lid.

After that, add the coconut milk and cauliflower to the inner pot.

Secure the lid. Choose the "Manual" mode and cook for 4 minutes at High pressure. Once cooking is complete, use a quick pressure release; carefully remove the lid.

Serve garnished with fresh cilantro. Enjoy!

Per serving: 487 Calories; 28.6g Fat; 16.7g Carbs; 45.5g Protein; 7.4g Sugars

414. Sticky Quinoa Meatballs

(Ready in about 20 minutes | Servings 5)

Ingredients

1 cup quinoa, cooked
16 dinner rolls
1/2 pound ground pork
1 pound lean beef, ground
2 garlic cloves, chopped
1/2 teaspoon chili powder
1 cup breadcrumbs
2 tablespoons olive oil
2 ½ cups tomato sauce
1 egg, beaten
1/4 cup milk
1/2 teaspoon dried rosemary, chopped
1/4 cup brown sugar
2 tablespoons vinegar
1 dash allspice
4 tablespoons scallions, chopped
Salt and black pepper, to taste
1/2 teaspoon crushed red pepper flakes
1 tablespoon fresh cilantro, chopped

Directions

In a mixing bowl, combine the ground beef, pork, quinoa, garlic, scallions, cilantro, breadcrumbs egg, and milk; now, season with salt, black pepper, red pepper, and rosemary.

Shape the meat mixture into 16 meatballs. Press the "Sauté" button to preheat your Instant Pot. Now, heat the oil until sizzling. Once hot, brown your meatballs on all sides.

Add the tomato sauce, sugar, vinegar, allspice and chili powder.

Select the "Manual" mode and cook for 12 minutes. Once cooking is complete, use a quick release.

Place one meatball on top of the bottom half of a dinner roll. Spoon the sauce on top of your meatball. Top with the other half of the dinner roll.

Repeat until you run out of ingredients. Bon appétit!

Per serving: 577 Calories; 26.2g Fat; 44.9g Carbs; 40g Protein; 8.4g Sugars

415. Simple Perfect Enchiladas

(Ready in about 15 minutes | Servings 4)

Ingredients

1 pound ground chuck
1 pound elbow macaroni
1/2 cup Cotija cheese, crumbled
1 bay leaf
1 teaspoon paprika
1 tablespoon olive oil
1 cup beef bone broth
1 cup water
8 ounces canned enchilada sauce
Sea salt and ground black pepper, to taste

Directions

Press the "Sauté" button to preheat your Instant Pot. Heat the oil and brown the ground chuck for 2 to 3 minutes.

Add the other ingredients, except for the cheese, to the Instant Pot.

Secure the lid. Choose the "Manual" mode and cook for 5 minutes at High pressure. Once cooking is complete, use a natural pressure release; carefully remove the lid.

Serve in individual bowls topped with the crumbled cheese. Enjoy!

Per serving: 693 Calories; 18.1g Fat; 90.1g Carbs; 40.1g Protein; 6.1g Sugars

416. Steak with Spicy Rum Sauce

(Ready in about 25 minutes | Servings 6)

Ingredients

1 ½ pounds beef flank steak
1/4 cup white rum
1 shallot, halved and sliced
1 cup sour cream
1 teaspoon cayenne pepper
1/2 teaspoon dried basil
1 cup water
2 bell peppers, deveined and chopped
1 teaspoon dried marjoram
1/2 teaspoon dried thyme
1 Chile de Arbol, deveined and minced
2 tablespoons olive oil
Sea salt and freshly ground black pepper, to taste

Directions

Press the "Sauté" button to preheat your Instant Pot. Then, heat the oil until sizzling. Once hot, cook the beef until browned on all sides.

Add the seasonings. Deglaze the inner pot with white rum and add the water, peppers, and shallot.

Secure the lid. Choose the "Poultry" setting and cook at High pressure for 15 minutes. Once cooking is complete, use a quick pressure release; carefully remove the lid.

Transfer the meat to a cutting board; slice the beef against the grain.

Now, fold in the sour cream and press the "Sauté" button; let it simmer until the cooking liquid is thoroughly warmed and reduced. Serve warm.

Per serving: 293 Calories; 15.6g Fat; 4.3g Carbs; 27.3g Protein; 0.9g Sugars

417. Traditional Beef Peperonata

(Ready in about 30 minutes + marinating time | Servings 4)

Ingredients

1 pound blade roast, sliced into 1/2-inch pieces
1 tablespoon canola oil
Salt and ground black pepper, to taste
1 onion, thinly sliced
4 sweet peppers, cut Julienne
2 tablespoons soy sauce
2 tablespoons tomato paste
3 cloves garlic, minced
1 teaspoon cayenne pepper
2 tablespoons capers with juices
1/4 cup rice vinegar
1 tablespoon brown sugar
1 ½ cups broth
1 serrano pepper, minced

Directions

In a ceramic or glass dish, mix the soy sauce, tomato paste, vinegar, sugar, and garlic. Place the blade roast in the dish, cover with plastic wrap and let it marinate at least 3 hours in the refrigerator.

Press the "Sauté" button to preheat your Instant Pot. Heat the oil and brown the beef for 4 to 5 minutes, brushing occasionally with the marinade.

Add the other ingredients. Secure the lid. Choose the "Meat/Stew" mode and cook for 20 minutes at High pressure.

Once cooking is complete, use a quick pressure release; carefully remove the lid. Serve warm.

Per serving: 432 Calories; 28g Fat; 21.1g Carbs; 24.5g Protein; 6.3g Sugars

418. Beef Stroganoff with Cream Cheese

(Ready in about 25 minutes | Servings 6)

Ingredients

9 ounces fresh button mushrooms, sliced
1/2 cup ketchup
6 ounces cream cheese
1 teaspoon minced garlic
1 bell pepper, seeded and chopped
1 ½ pounds stewing meat, cubed
1/2 cup rose wine
1 cup tomato paste
1 can (10 ¾-ounce) condensed golden mushroom soup
1/4 cup fresh chives, coarsely chopped
2 tablespoons sesame oil
1/2 cup shallots, chopped
1 celery with leaves, chopped
1 parsnip, chopped

Directions

Press the "Sauté" button to preheat your Instant Pot. Heat the oil and sauté the shallots until they have softened.

Stir in the garlic and pepper; continue to sauté until tender and fragrant.

Add the meat, celery, parsnip, wine, tomato paste, ketchup, mushroom soup, and mushrooms.

Secure the lid. Choose the "Meat/Stew" mode and High pressure; cook for 20 minutes. Once cooking is complete, use a quick pressure release; carefully remove the lid.

Stir the cream cheese into the beef mixture; seal the lid and let it sit until melted. Serve garnished with fresh chives. Enjoy!

Per serving: 536 Calories; 19.6g Fat; 45g Carbs; 50g Protein; 8.5g Sugars

419. Boozy Chuck Roast

(Ready in about 1 hour | Servings 6)

Ingredients

1 cup beef broth
1/2 teaspoon red pepper flakes
2 cloves garlic, sliced
1/4 cup soy sauce
Sea salt and ground black pepper, to taste
2 pounds chuck roast
1/4 cup champagne vinegar
Margarita Glaze:
1/4 cup orange juice
2 tablespoons dark brown sugar
1/4 lime juice
1/2 cup tequila

Directions

Add the chuck roast, beef broth, soy sauce, champagne vinegar, salt, black pepper, red pepper flakes, and garlic to the inner pot.

Secure the lid. Choose the "Manual" mode and cook for 40 minutes at High pressure. Once cooking is complete, use a natural pressure release for 10 minutes; carefully remove the lid.

Meanwhile, whisk all ingredients for the margarita glaze. Now, glaze the ribs and place under the broiler for 5 minutes; then, turn them over and glaze on the other side. Broil an additional 5 minutes.

Cut the chuck roast into slices and serve the remaining glaze on the side as a sauce. Bon appétit!

Per serving: 348 Calories; 14.9g Fat; 10.3g Carbs; 42.7g Protein; 7.7g Sugars

420. BBQ Pot Roast

(Ready in about 45 minutes | Servings 6)

Ingredients

2 pounds chuck roast
1 ½ tablespoons fresh parsley leaves, roughly chopped
1 cup barbeque sauce
1 teaspoon garlic, minced
3 teaspoons fresh ginger root, thinly sliced
4 carrots, sliced
1/2 cup leek, sliced
1/2 cup teriyaki sauce
2 tablespoons lard, at room temperature
Salt and pepper, to taste

Directions

Press the "Sauté" button on your Instant Pot. Now, melt the lard until hot.

Sear the chuck roast until browned, about 6 minutes per side. Add the other ingredients.

Choose "Manual" setting and cook for 35 minutes at High pressure or until the internal temperature of the chuck roast is at least 145 degrees F.

Once cooking is complete, use a quick release; remove the lid.

Serve with crusty bread and fresh salad of choice. Bon appétit!

Per serving: 252 Calories; 9.9g Fat; 9g Carbs; 30.1g Protein; 5.9g Sugars

421. Sticky Spicy Asian Ribs

(Ready in about 1 hour | Servings 8)

Ingredients

1 cup Asian BBQ sauce
Sea salt and ground black pepper, to taste
2 teaspoons toasted sesame seeds
1 red Fresno chili, sliced
10 ounces beer
2-inch piece fresh ginger, minced
4 tablespoons tamari sauce
2 tablespoons agave nectar
1 onion, chopped
2 garlic cloves, minced
2 racks back ribs

Directions

Place the back ribs, beers, BBQ sauce, onion, garlic, Fresno chili, and ginger in the inner pot.

Secure the lid. Choose the "Manual" mode and cook for 40 minutes at High pressure. Once cooking is complete, use a natural pressure release for 10 minutes; carefully remove the lid.

Add the tamari sauce, agave, salt and pepper and place the beef ribs under the broiler. Broil the ribs for 10 minutes or until they are evenly browned. Serve garnished with sesame seeds. Bon appétit!

Per serving: 480 Calories; 14.5g Fat; 10.3g Carbs; 70g Protein; 4.1g Sugars

422. Sage Merlot Roast Beef

(Ready in about 50 minutes | Servings 6)

Ingredients

1 ½ pounds beef roast
1 tablespoon fresh sage
1/2 cups Merlot
1 celery stalk, diced
1 cup water
Sea salt, to taste
1 carrot, chopped
1 tablespoon soy sauce
1 teaspoon butter
1/4 cup fresh chives, chopped
1 red onion, chopped
2 garlic cloves, smashed
2 teaspoons lard, at room temperature
1/2 teaspoon ground black pepper
1 teaspoon paprika
2 bay leaves

Directions

Press the "Sauté" button to preheat the Instant Pot. Melt the lard and sear the beef until it is browned on all sides.

Add the onion, garlic, carrot, celery, water, merlot, salt, black pepper, paprika, bay leaves, sage, and soy sauce.

Secure the lid. Choose the "Meat/Stew" mode and High pressure; cook for 40 minutes. Once cooking is complete, use a natural pressure release; carefully remove the lid.

Transfer the roast to a cutting board; allow it to cool slightly before slicing.

Press the "Sauté" button and let it simmer until the sauce is reduced. Stir in the butter and press the "Cancel" button.

Spoon the sauce over the sliced beef. Serve garnished with fresh chives and enjoy!

Per serving: 283 Calories; 12.2g Fat; 5.4g Carbs; 30.9g Protein; 2.1g Sugars

423. Serbian-Style Moussaka with Cheese

(Ready in about 40 minutes | Servings 4)

Ingredients

1 pound Russet potatoes, peeled and thinly sliced
1 ½ pounds ground beef
1/2 cup Colby cheese, shredded
1 shallot, thinly sliced
1 cup cream of celery soup
1/2 cup half-and-half
2 garlic cloves, sliced
Kosher salt and ground pepper, to taste
1 tablespoon olive oil
1 egg

Directions

Press the "Sauté" button to preheat your Instant Pot. Heat the olive oil and cook the ground beef until no longer pink.

Now, add the layer of potatoes; top with the layer of shallots and garlic. Pour in the soup.

Whisk the egg with half-and-half until well combined; season with salt and pepper. Pour the egg mixture on top of the meat and vegetable layers.

Smooth the sauce on top with a spatula.

Secure the lid. Choose the "Meat/Stew" mode and cook for 35 minutes at High pressure. Once cooking is complete, use a quick pressure release; carefully remove the lid.

Add the shredded cheese and seal the lid again. Let it sit in the residual heat until the cheese melts. Bon appétit!

Per serving: 592 Calories; 33.3g Fat; 31.6g Carbs; 42.8g Protein; 4.9g Sugars

424. Beef Sausage and Kidney Bean Casserole

(Ready in about 25 minutes | Servings 6)

Ingredients

1 ½ pounds lean beef chipolata sausages
3/4 cup Colby cheese, grated
1 (20-ounce) can red kidney beans
1 teaspoon cocoa powder
1 cup tomato purée
1 teaspoon red pepper flakes
1/2 cup beef bone broth
2 tablespoons ketchup
1 tablespoon tamari sauce
1/3 teaspoon freshly ground black pepper
1 leek, thinly sliced
2 garlic cloves, minced
1 teaspoon dried saffron
1 tablespoon olive oil
Salt, to taste
2 bay laurels

Directions

Press the "Sauté" button to preheat your Instant Pot. Now, heat the oil until sizzling. Brown the sausage for 2 minutes; reserve.

Then, sauté the leeks and garlic in pan drippings for 2 more minutes; return the sausage back to the Instant Pot.

Add the tomato purée, broth, ketchup, tamari sauce, cocoa powder, bay leaves, beans, red pepper flakes, salt, black pepper, and saffron to the Instant Pot.

Secure the lid. Choose the "Poultry" mode and High pressure; cook for 15 minutes. Once cooking is complete, use a quick pressure release; carefully remove the lid.

Top with the grated cheese and seal the lid again. Let it sit until cheese is melted. Serve warm.

Per serving: 498 Calories; 40.5g Fat; 11.2g Carbs; 21.8g Protein; 2.6g Sugars

425. Parmesan Dijon Meatballs

(Ready in about 40 minutes | Servings 4)

Ingredients

1/4 cup parmesan cheese
1 teaspoon Dijon mustard
1 tablespoon canola oil
1 egg, beaten
1 cup tomato puree
1/2 teaspoon cayenne pepper
1 shallot, minced
2 cloves garlic, smashed
1 cup chicken bone broth
2/3 pound ground beef
2 slices bread (soaked in 4 tablespoons of milk)
1/3 pound beef sausage, crumbled
Kosher salt and ground black pepper, to taste

Directions

In a mixing dish, thoroughly combine the beef, sausage, shallot, garlic, egg, soaked bread, parmesan, salt, black pepper, and cayenne pepper

Mix to combine well and shape the mixture into 12 meatballs. Set aside.

Press the "Sauté" button and heat the oil. Once hot, brown the meatballs for 7 to 8 minutes, rolling them around so that they will brown evenly all around.

Mix the tomato puree, broth and mustard in the inner pot. Gently fold in the meatballs.

Secure the lid. Choose the "Meat/Stew" mode and cook for 20 minutes at High pressure. Once cooking is complete, use a natural pressure release for 10 minutes; carefully remove the lid. Bon appétit!

Per serving: 509 Calories; 30.2g Fat; 14.6g Carbs; 43.1g Protein; 4.3g Sugars

426. Steak with Celery and Marinara

(Ready in about 55 minutes | Servings 8)

Ingredients

1/4 cup marinara sauce
1 celery with leaves, chopped
3 tablespoons chickpea flour
2 cloves garlic, minced
1 cup red wine
1/3 cup bone broth
1/4 cup olive oil
1/2 teaspoon ground bay leaf
2 shallots, chopped
2 ½ pounds round steak, cut into 1-inch pieces
Kosher salt and freshly ground black pepper, to taste

Directions

Press the "Sauté" button to preheat your Instant Pot. Toss the round steak with salt, pepper, ground bay leaf, and chickpea flour.

Once hot, heat the olive oil and cook the beef for 6 minutes, stirring periodically; reserve.

Stir in the shallots and garlic and cook until they are tender and aromatic. Pour in the wine to deglaze the bottom of the pan. Continue to cook until the liquid has reduced by half.

Add the other ingredients, stir, and seal the lid. Choose the "Meat/Stew" setting and cook at High pressure for 45 minutes.

Once cooking is complete, use a natural release; remove the lid. Taste, adjust the seasonings and serve warm.

Per serving: 363 Calories; 17.9g Fat; 3.1g Carbs; 44.5g Protein; 1.1g Sugars

427. Chinese Wine-Braised Beef

(Ready in about 45 minutes | Servings 4)

Ingredients

1 teaspoon Chinese five spice powder
1/2 cup rice wine
1 ½ pounds beef shank
1 dried red chili, sliced
1 cup water
2 cloves star anise
2 tablespoons soy sauce
1 cup instant dashi granules
1 teaspoon garlic, minced
1 tablespoon sesame oil

Directions

Add all ingredients to the inner pot.

Secure the lid. Choose the "Manual" mode and cook for 30 minutes at High pressure. Once cooking is complete, use a natural pressure release for 10 minutes; carefully remove the lid.

Slice across the grain and serve over hot cooked rice if desired. Enjoy!

Per serving: 316 Calories; 11.4g Fat; 11.6g Carbs; 39.2g Protein; 1.8g Sugars

428. Sausage and Bean Hotpot

(Ready in about 35 minutes | Servings 6)

Ingredients

1/2 pound beef chipolata sausages, sliced
1 (15-ounce) can white beans, drained and rinsed
1 ½ pounds beef shoulder, cut into bite-sized chunks
1 cup beef stock
1 tablespoon fresh thyme leaves
1/2 cup tomato purée
1/2 tablespoon ancho chili powder
1 onion, chopped
2 garlic cloves, minced
1 cup sour cream
1 tablespoon olive oil
Sea salt and ground black pepper, to taste

Directions

Press the "Sauté" button and preheat the Instant Pot. Heat the oil and sear the meat and sausage until they are delicately browned; reserve.

Then, sauté the onion in pan drippings for 3 to 4 minutes.

Stir in the garlic, stock, tomato purée, ancho chili powder, salt, black pepper, thyme leaves and beans.

Secure the lid. Choose the "Bean/Chili" mode and High pressure; cook for 25 minutes. Once cooking is complete, use a quick pressure release; carefully remove the lid.

Garnish each serving with sour cream and serve. Bon appétit!

Per serving: 376 Calories; 19.3g Fat; 18.1g Carbs; 36.3g Protein; 1.6g Sugars

429. Roast Beef with Small Potatoes

(Ready in about 50 minutes | Servings 6)

Ingredients

1/4 cup tomato puree
2 tablespoons olive oil, divided
2 pounds whole small potatoes
2 pounds beef round roast, cut into bite-sized pieces
1 white onion, chopped
1 garlic clove, sliced
1/4 cup dry red wine
1 cup beef broth
1 bell pepper, sliced

Directions '

Press the "Sauté" button to preheat your Instant Pot. Heat the oil and brown the beef round roast for 3 to 4 minutes, working in batches.

Add the white onion, garlic, pepper, tomato puree, red wine, and broth.

Secure the lid. Choose the "Meat/Stew" mode and cook for 35 minutes at High pressure. Once cooking is complete, use a quick pressure release; carefully remove the lid.

Add the potatoes. Secure the lid. Choose the "Manual" mode and cook for 10 minutes at High pressure. Once cooking is complete, use a quick pressure release; carefully remove the lid.

Serve in individual bowls and enjoy!

Per serving: 426 Calories; 11.4g Fat; 29.9g Carbs; 48.7g Protein; 2.8g Sugars

430. Beef and Pinto Bean Wraps

(Ready in about 25 minutes | Servings 6)

Ingredients

2 cans (16-ounce) pinto beans, drained
3/4 teaspoon cocoa powder, unsweetened
1 pound ground chuck
2 tablespoons fresh cilantro leaves, chopped
1 teaspoon cumin, ground
1/2 teaspoon mustard seeds
2 onions, diced
6 medium store-bought taco shells
1/2 cup sour cream
3 garlic cloves, smashed
1 envelope (1-ounce) taco seasoning mix
1 tablespoon chipotle powder
1 teaspoon dried marjoram
1/2 teaspoon dried basil
Salt and pepper, to taste
2 tablespoons tamari sauce
2 teaspoons lard
2 ripe tomatoes, pureed
1 cup beef bone broth

Directions

Press the "Sauté" button to heat up your Instant Pot and melt the lard. Once hot, cook the ground chuck, crumbling with a fork. Set aside.

Cook the onions and garlic in pan drippings, stirring occasionally; add a splash of bone broth, if necessary, to prevent sticking.

Now, stir in the tomatoes, beef bone broth, and taco seasoning mix; cook, stirring continuously, an additional minute or until warmed through.

Next, stir in the canned beans, chipotle powder, cumin, mustard seeds, marjoram, basil, salt, pepper, tamari sauce, and cocoa powder. Secure the lid.

Select the "Manual" mode and cook at High Pressure for 12 minutes. Once cooking is complete, use a natural release and carefully remove the lid.

To assemble, divide the beef/bean mixture among taco shells; top each with sour cream and fresh chopped cilantro. Bon appétit!

Per serving: 361 Calories; 14.6g Fat; 34.5g Carbs; 24.1g Protein; 3.8g Sugars

LOW CARB

431. Ham Bone Soup with Harvest Vegetables

(Ready in about 30 minutes | Servings 5)

Ingredients

1 ham bone
5 cups chicken stock
1 parsnip, diced
2 carrots, diced
1 rib celery, diced
2 tablespoons olive oil
1/2 cup onion, chopped
Sea salt and ground black pepper, to taste

Directions

Press the "Sauté" button and heat the olive oil until sizzling. Then, sauté the onion, carrot, celery, and parsnip until tender.

Add the ham bone, chicken stock, salt, and black pepper to the inner pot.

Secure the lid. Choose the "Manual" mode and cook for 15 minutes at High pressure. Once cooking is complete, use a natural pressure release for 10 minutes; carefully remove the lid.

Remove the ham bone from the inner pot. Chop the meat from the bone; add back into the soup.

Serve in individual bowls and enjoy!

Per serving: 197 Calories; 10.2g Fat; 9.3g Carbs; 17.7g Protein; 3.7g Sugars

432. Home-Style Blueberry Yogurt

(Ready in about 24 hours + chilling time | Servings 12)

Ingredients

1 cup blueberries, fresh or frozen (and thawed)
15 grams probiotic yogurt starter
1 teaspoon stevia powder
3 quarts raw milk

Directions

Add the milk to the Instant Pot.

Secure the lid. Choose "Yogurt" mode; now, press the "Adjust" button until you see the word "Boil". Turn off the Instant Pot.

Use a food thermometer to read temperature; 115 degrees is fine; stir in the starter.

Press the "Yogurt" button again and then, press the "Adjust" button to reach 24 hours.

Place in your refrigerator for a few hours to set up. Add the stevia and blueberries; serve well chilled. Bon appétit!

Per serving: 92 Calories; 0.6g Fat; 6.6g Carbs; 14.7g Protein; 5.4g Sugars

433. Deviled Eggs with Cottage Cheese

(Ready in about 10 minutes | Servings 6)

Ingredients

1/4 cup Cottage cheese, crumbled
Sea salt and ground black pepper, to taste
2 tablespoons fresh parsley, minced
1 teaspoon paprika
1 tablespoon butter, softened
6 eggs

Directions

Place 1 cup of water and a steamer rack in the inner pot. Arrange the eggs on the rack.

Secure the lid. Choose the "Manual" mode and cook for 5 minutes at High pressure. Once cooking is complete, use a quick pressure release; carefully remove the lid.

Peel the eggs and slice them into halves.

In a mixing bowl, thoroughly combine the Cottage cheese, butter, parsley, paprika, sea salt, and black pepper. Stir in the egg yolks. Stir to combine well.

Use a piping bag to fill the egg white halves. Place on a nice serving platter and enjoy!

Per serving: 93 Calories; 6.5g Fat; 1.6g Carbs; 6.7g Protein; 0.8g Sugars

434. Mini Frittatas with Bacon and Cheese

(Ready in about 15 minutes | Servings 6)

Ingredients

3 egg, beaten
1/2 teaspoon dried dill weed
1/2 teaspoon cayenne pepper
2 tablespoons cream cheese, room temperature
1 red bell pepper, chopped
1 green bell pepper, chopped
1 teaspoon shallot powder
Salt and black pepper, to taste
6 thin meaty bacon slices
4 teaspoons butter, melted
1 large-sized zucchini, grated
1/2 cup Colby cheese, shredded

Directions

Start by adding 1 ½ cups of water and a metal trivet to the bottom of your Instant Pot.

Place the bacon slices in 6 silicone cupcake liners. Add the zucchini and bell peppers.

Now, mix the butter, Colby cheese, eggs, cream cheese, shallot powder, dried dill weed, cayenne pepper, salt, and black pepper. Spoon this mixture into the liners.

Put the liners into an oven-safe bowl. Cover with a piece of foil. Lower the bowl onto the trivet.

Secure the lid. Choose "Manual" mode and High pressure; cook for 10 minutes. Once cooking is complete, use a natural pressure release; carefully remove the lid. Bon appétit!

Per serving: 226 Calories; 20.1g Fat; 2.3g Carbs; 9.3g Protein; 1.3g Sugars

435. Fake-Out Mac n' Cheese

(Ready in about 15 minutes | Servings 4)

Ingredients

1 ½ cups Cheddar cheese, shredded
1/4 cup Parmesan cheese
4 ounces Ricotta cheese
1 cup heavy cream
1/2 teaspoon celery seeds
1/2 teaspoon garlic powder

1/2 teaspoon shallot powder
1/2 teaspoon red pepper flakes
1 pound cauliflower florets
Sea salt and ground white pepper, to taste

Directions

Place 1 cup of water and a steamer basket in the inner pot of your Instant Pot. Throw the cauliflower florets into the steamer basket.

Secure the lid. Choose the "Manual" mode and cook for 2 minutes at High pressure. Once cooking is complete, use a quick pressure release; carefully remove the lid. Drain and reserve.

Press the "Sauté" button and use the lowest setting. Now, cook the heavy cream, Ricotta cheese, Cheddar cheese, and spices; let it simmer until the cheeses has melted.

Add in the cauliflower and gently stir to combine. Scatter the Parmesan cheese over the cauliflower and cheese and serve warm. Bon appétit!

Per serving: 387 Calories; 31.2g Fat; 10.2g Carbs; 18.2g Protein; 3.8g Sugars

436. Skinny Spinach Muffins

(Ready in about 15 minutes | Servings 6)

Ingredients

1 ½ cups spinach, chopped
1/2 cup cheddar cheese, grated
1/3 cup double cream
1/2 teaspoon cayenne pepper
1/4 cup green onions, chopped

1/4 cup cream cheese
Sea salt and freshly ground black pepper, to taste
1 ripe tomato, chopped
6 eggs

Directions

Start by adding 1 cup of water and a metal rack to the Instant Pot. Now, spritz a muffin tin with a nonstick cooking spray.

In a mixing dish, thoroughly combine the eggs, double cream, cream cheese, salt, black pepper, and cayenne pepper.

Then, divide the spinach, green onions, tomato, and scallions among the cups. Pour the egg mixture over the vegetables. Top with cheddar cheese.

Lower the cups onto the rack.

Secure the lid. Choose "Manual" mode and High pressure; cook for 10 minutes. Once cooking is complete, use a natural pressure release; carefully remove the lid. Serve immediately.

Per serving: 236 Calories; 18.8g Fat; 3.3g Carbs; 13.2g Protein; 2.2g Sugars

437. Eggs with Chanterelles and Mexican Cheese

(Ready in about 30 minutes | Servings 4)

Ingredients

5 eggs
1 cup chanterelle mushrooms, chopped
1 cup Mexican cheese blend, crumbled
1 Poblano pepper, seeded and minced

2 cloves garlic, minced
1 bell pepper, sliced
4 ounces cream cheese
Sea salt and ground black pepper, to taste
1 tablespoon olive oil
1 medium onion, chopped

Directions

Add 1 cup of water and a metal rack to the inner pot of your Instant Pot. Spray a souffle dish and set aside.

Mix all ingredients until well combined. Scrape the mixture into the prepared dish. Lower the souffle dish onto the rack.

Secure the lid. Choose the "Manual" mode and cook for 11 minutes at High pressure. Once cooking is complete, use a natural pressure release for 15 minutes; carefully remove the lid.

Serve with salsa if desired. Enjoy!

Per serving: 333 Calories; 26.6g Fat; 8.6g Carbs; 16.2g Protein; 3.9g Sugars

438. Asian Saucy Duck Breast

(Ready in about 2 hours 15 minutes | Servings 4)

Ingredients

2 tablespoons peanut oil
1/2 cup dry red wine
1/4 teaspoon Sichuan peppercorn powder
1 tablespoon sake
1/2 teaspoon coarse sea salt

1/2 cup chicken broth
1 pound duck breast, boneless, skinless and cut into 4 pieces
1/2 teaspoon cayenne pepper
2 garlic cloves, minced

Directions

Place all ingredients, except for the broth, in the ceramic dish; place the dish in your refrigerator and let it marinate for 1 to 2 hours.

Then, transfer the meat along with its marinade to the Instant Pot. Pour in the chicken broth.

Secure the lid. Choose "Manual" mode and High pressure; cook for 10 minutes. Once cooking is complete, use a quick pressure release; carefully remove the lid.

Serve warm and enjoy!

Per serving: 256 Calories; 13.7g Fat; 1g Carbs; 29.1g Protein; 0g Sugars

439. Ground Chuck and Tomato Frittata

(Ready in about 25 minutes | Servings 2)

Ingredients

1/2 pound ground chuck
1 small tomato, chopped
1/2 teaspoon paprika
4 eggs, whisked
A small bunch of green onions, chopped

1/2 teaspoon garlic powder
1 tablespoon olive oil
Sea salt and freshly ground black pepper, to your liking

Directions

Press the "Sauté" button to preheat your Instant Pot. Heat the oil and brown the beef for 2 to 3 minutes, stirring continuously.

Lightly spritz a baking pan with cooking oil. Add all ingredients, including the browned beef to the baking pan.

Cover with foil. Add 1 cup of water and a metal trivet to the Instant Pot. Lower the baking pan onto the trivet.

Secure the lid. Choose the "Manual" mode and cook for 6 minutes at High pressure. Once cooking is complete, use a natural pressure release for 10 minutes; carefully remove the lid.

Slice in half and serve. Bon appétit!

Per serving: 368 Calories; 24.1g Fat; 3.7g Carbs; 33.9g Protein; 2.4g Sugars

440. Chicken Liver Pate with Wine

(Ready in about 10 minutes | Servings 8)

Ingredients

1/2 cup white wine
1/2 teaspoon dried basil
1/2 teaspoon dried oregano
1 tablespoon olive oil
1 sprig rosemary
1/4 teaspoon ground black pepper

A pinch of salt
1 Spanish onion, chopped
1/2 cup chicken stock
A pinch of ground cloves
1 cup heavy cream
1 pound chicken livers

Directions

Simply mix all ingredients in your Instant Pot

Secure the lid. Choose "Manual" mode and High pressure; cook for 3 minutes. Once cooking is complete, use a quick pressure release; carefully remove the lid.

Afterwards, purée the mixture with an immersion blender until smooth and uniform. Serve with veggie sticks. Bon appétit!

Per serving: 143 Calories; 10.1g Fat; 2.2g Carbs; 10.4g Protein; 1.2g Sugars

441. Mustard Beer Braised Chuck Roast

(Ready in about 45 minutes | Servings 5)

Ingredients

2 pounds chuck roast, slice into pieces
1 tablespoon mustard
1/2 (12-ounce) bottle beer
2 tablespoons sesame seeds, toasted
1 teaspoon ginger powder
1 teaspoon onion powder

1 teaspoon garlic powder
1/4 teaspoon ground allspice
1/2 cup beef bone broth
1 tablespoon granulated sugar
2 tablespoons sesame oil
Kosher salt and freshly ground black pepper, to taste

Directions

Press the "Sauté" button to preheat your Instant Pot. Heat the oil and brown the beef in batches; cook for about 3 minutes per batch.

Add the broth, beer, mustard, sugar, salt, black pepper, onion powder, garlic powder, ginger, and ground allspice.

Secure the lid. Choose the "Manual" mode and cook for 40 minutes at High pressure. Once cooking is complete, use a quick pressure release; carefully remove the lid.

Serve garnished with toasted sesame seeds. Enjoy!

Per serving: 322 Calories; 17.8g Fat; 3.1g Carbs; 38.1g Protein; 1.6g Sugars

442. Aromatic Zucchini Bread

(Ready in about 35 minutes | Servings 8)

Ingredients

1 cup zucchini, grated
1 teaspoon baking powder
1/3 cup olive oil
1 cup almond flour
A pinch of salt

A pinch of grated nutmeg
2 tablespoons coconut flour
1 teaspoon stevia, liquid
1 teaspoon ground cardamom
4 eggs

Directions

Prepare the Instant Pot by adding 1 ½ cups of water and a metal rack to its bottom. Lightly grease a baking pan with a nonstick cooking spray.

In a mixing dish, thoroughly combine the dry ingredients. Then, in another bowl, thoroughly combine the wet ingredients.

Add the wet mixture to the dry mixture; continue to mix until uniform, creamy and smooth. Pour the batter into the prepared pan.

Lower the pan onto the trivet.

Secure the lid. Choose "Bean/Chili" mode and High pressure; cook for 25 minutes. Once cooking is complete, use a natural pressure release; carefully remove the lid.

Allow the zucchini bread to cool completely before cutting and serving. Bon appétit!

Per serving: 205 Calories; 19.1g Fat; 4.3g Carbs; 6.1g Protein; 0.9g Sugars

443. Italian Pork with Dill-Mushroom Sauce

(Ready in about 30 minutes | Servings 6)

Ingredients

1 tablespoon Italian seasoning blend
6 pork chops
1/2 cup cream of onion soup
1 pound white mushrooms, sliced
2 cloves garlic crushed
1/2 cup double cream

1/2 teaspoon coarse sea salt
1/2 teaspoon cracked black pepper
1 tablespoon fresh coriander, chopped
1 teaspoon dill weed, minced
2 tablespoons butter

Directions

Press the "Sauté" button and melt the butter. Once hot, sear the pork chops until golden browned, about 4 minutes per side.

Add the remaining ingredients and gently stir to combine.

Secure the lid. Choose the "Meat/Stew" mode and cook for 20 minutes at High pressure. Once cooking is complete, use a quick pressure release; carefully remove the lid.

Serve over mashed potatoes. Bon appétit!

Per serving: 438 Calories; 25.8g Fat; 7.2g Carbs; 42.8g Protein; 2.7g Sugars

444. Cheese, Zucchini and Bacon Quiche

(Ready in about 25 minutes | Servings 8)

Ingredients

1 cup Colby cheese, shredded
1 cup Cottage cheese, room temperature
1/2 cup Greek yogurt, room temperature
1 clove garlic, minced
1/4 teaspoon dried rosemary
1 teaspoon dried parsley flakes

6 slices bacon, chopped
8 eggs, beaten
Sea salt and ground black pepper, to taste
1/4 teaspoon dried marjoram
1/2 pound zucchini, grated and squeezed dry
1 white onion, chopped

Directions

Start by adding 1 cup of water and a metal trivet to the bottom of your Instant Pot.

Mix the ingredients until everything is well incorporated. Spoon the mixture into a lightly greased casserole dish.

Lower the casserole dish onto the trivet.

Secure the lid. Choose "Manual" mode and High pressure; cook for 20 minutes. Once cooking is complete, use a quick pressure release; carefully remove the lid. Bon appétit!

Per serving: 320 Calories; 24.3g Fat; 5.3g Carbs; 19.7g Protein; 2.9g Sugars

445. Holiday Pork Butt with Leeks

(Ready in about 1 hour 10 minutes | Servings 6)

Ingredients

2 ½ pounds pork butt
1 large leek, sliced into long pieces
1 carrot, halved lengthwise
2 garlic cloves, minced
1 teaspoon freshly grated lemon zest

1 tablespoon lard, at room temperature
1/2 cup red wine
2 teaspoons stone-ground mustard
Sea salt and ground black pepper, to taste

Directions

Combine the garlic, mustard, salt, pepper and lemon zest in a mixing bowl. Using your hands, spread the rub evenly onto the pork butt.

Press the "Sauté" button to preheat your Instant Pot. Melt the lard and sear the meat for 3 minutes per side.

Pour a splash of wine into the inner pot, scraping any bits from the bottom with a wooden spoon.

Place a trivet and 1 cup of water in the bottom of the inner pot. Lower the pork butt onto the trivet; scatter the leeks and carrots around.

Secure the lid. Choose the "Manual" mode and cook for 50 minutes at High pressure. Once cooking is complete, use a natural pressure release for 10 minutes; carefully remove the lid.

Transfer the pork butt to a cutting board and let it sit for 5 minutes before carving and serving. Enjoy!

Per serving: 545 Calories; 35.4g Fat; 4.2g Carbs; 48.2g Protein; 1.5g Sugars

446. Deviled Eggs with Avocado and Tomatoes

(Ready in about 25 minutes | Servings 5)

Ingredients

1 avocado, pitted, peeled and mashed
1 ripe tomato, chopped
3 tablespoons spring onions, roughly chopped
1/2 teaspoon cayenne pepper

1/2 teaspoon chili powder
1 tablespoon fresh lemon juice
5 eggs
Kosher salt and white pepper, to taste

Directions

Pour 1 cup of water into the Instant Pot; add a steamer basket to the bottom.

Arrange the eggs in a steamer basket.

Secure the lid. Choose "Manual" mode and High pressure; cook for 5 minutes. Once cooking is complete, use a natural pressure release; carefully remove the lid.

Allow the eggs to cool for 15 minutes. Peel the eggs, slice them into halves, and separate egg whites from yolks.

To make a filling, mix the avocado, lemon juice, tomato, cayenne pepper, salt, white pepper, and chili powder; stir in the reserved egg yolks. Now, stuff the egg whites with this mixture.

Garnish with green onions. Arrange on a nice serving platter and serve.

Per serving: 138 Calories; 10.2g Fat; 6.2g Carbs; 6.8g Protein; 1.7g Sugars

447. Dijon Mustard-Herb Chicken

(Ready in about 20 minutes | Servings 4)

Ingredients

1 tablespoon Dijon mustard
1 pound chicken breasts, boneless
1 teaspoon garlic powder
1/2 teaspoon dried sage
1/2 cup heavy cream
1 teaspoon paprika
1 cup chicken bone broth
1 teaspoon dried basil
1/2 teaspoon dried oregano
2 tablespoons olive oil, divided
Sea salt and ground black pepper, to taste

Directions

Press the "Sauté" button and heat the olive oil. Sear the chicken breasts until they are no longer pink.

Add the seasonings, mustard, and chicken bone broth.

Secure the lid. Choose "Manual" mode and cook for 8 minutes at High pressure. Once cooking is complete, use a natural pressure release; carefully remove the lid.

Lastly, add the heavy cream, cover with the lid, and let it sit in the residual heat for 6 to 8 minutes. Serve in individual bowls. Enjoy!

Per serving: 413 Calories; 27.2g Fat; 3.3g Carbs; 37.5g Protein; 1.2g Sugars

448. Loaded Barbecue Meatloaf Cups

(Ready in about 40 minutes | Servings 8)

Ingredients

1/4 cup barbecue sauce, sugar-free
1/4 cup pork rinds, crushed
1/3 cup Romano cheese, grated
1/2 cup onion, chopped
2 garlic cloves, minced
4 eggs, whisked
2 ripe tomatoes, puréed
1 pound ground pork
1 pound ground beef
Salt and ground black pepper, to taste

Directions

Start by adding 1 cup of water and a metal trivet to the bottom of your Instant Pot.

In a mixing bowl, thoroughly combine ground meat, onion, garlic, salt, black pepper, cheese, pork rinds, and eggs.

Mix until everything is well incorporated. Divide the mixture among muffin cups.

In a small mixing bowl, whisk puréed tomatoes with barbecue sauce. Lastly, top your muffins with the tomato sauce.

Secure the lid. Choose "Manual" mode and High pressure; cook for 25 minutes. Once cooking is complete, use a quick pressure release; carefully remove the lid.

Allow them to cool for 10 minutes before removing from the muffin tin. Bon appétit!

Per serving: 375 Calories; 22.2g Fat; 6.5g Carbs; 35.4g Protein; 4.5g Sugars

449. Rustic Chicken Fingers

(Ready in about 25 minutes | Servings 4)

Ingredients

1 ½ pounds chicken tenders
1 cup Cottage cheese, crumbled
1/2 teaspoon smoked paprika
1 cup vegetable broth
1 teaspoon shallot powder
2 heaping tablespoons fresh chives, roughly chopped
1 teaspoon garlic powder
2 tablespoons butter, softened
Sea salt and freshly ground black pepper, to taste

Directions

Press the "Sauté" button and melt the butter. Sear the chicken tenders for 2 to 3 minutes.

Add the vegetable broth, shallot powder, garlic powder, paprika, salt, and black pepper.

Secure the lid. Choose "Manual" mode and cook for 8 minutes at High pressure. Once cooking is complete, use a natural pressure release; carefully remove the lid.

Stir in the cheese; cover with the lid and let it sit in the residual heat for 5 minutes. Garnish with fresh chives and serve immediately.

Per serving: 305 Calories; 13.1g Fat; 2.8g Carbs; 41.9g Protein; 1.7g Sugars

450. Easy Mini Pizzas

(Ready in about 20 minutes | Servings 6)

Ingredients

1 cup pizza sauce
1 teaspoon dried oregano
2 cups mozzarella cheese
1/2 cup Kalamata olives, pitted and sliced
1 teaspoon dried basil
12 turkey bacon slices

Directions

Start by adding 1 cups of water and a metal rack to the bottom of the Instant Pot.

Place two slices of bacon crisscrossed in each muffin cup. Divide the remaining ingredients among cups.

Lower the muffin pan onto the rack.

Secure the lid. Choose "Manual" mode and High pressure; cook for 10 minutes. Once cooking is complete, use a quick pressure release; carefully remove the lid.

Allow these pizza cups to stand for 5 minutes before removing from the muffin pan. Bon appétit!

Per serving: 301 Calories; 22.1g Fat; 6.2g Carbs; 19.5g Protein; 2.5g Sugars

451. Pork Loin with Milk and Herbs

(Ready in about 45 minutes | Servings 6)

Ingredients

2 ½ pounds pork loin roast, boneless
1 cup milk
1/2 teaspoon paprika
1/2 lemon, juiced and zested
1 cup vegetable broth
1 teaspoon dried basil
1 teaspoon dried oregano
2 tablespoons sesame oil
Sea salt and freshly ground black pepper, to taste

Directions

Press the "Sauté" button and heat the oil until sizzling; once hot, sear the pork for 4 to 5 minutes or until browned on all sides. Work in batches.

Add the remaining ingredients.

Secure the lid. Choose the "Meat/Stew" mode and cook for 35 minutes at High pressure. Once cooking is complete, use a quick pressure release; carefully remove the lid.

Turn on your broiler. Roast the pork under the broiler for about 3 minutes or until the skin is crisp.

To carve the pork, remove the cracklings and cut the crisp pork skin into strips. Carve the pork roast across the grain into thin slices and serve.

Per serving: 436 Calories; 22.8g Fat; 2.6g Carbs; 52.2g Protein; 2.2g Sugars

452. Swiss Chard and Cheese Bake

(Ready in about 35 minutes | Servings 6)

Ingredients

1/2 cup Pepper-Jack cheese, freshly grated
1 habanero pepper, seeded and chopped
1 tomato, chopped
2 cups Swiss chard, roughly chopped
1/2 cup red onion, thinly sliced
10 large eggs
1/2 cup double cream
1 teaspoon cayenne pepper
Seasoned salt and ground black pepper, to taste

Directions

Start by adding 1 ½ cups of water and a metal trivet to the bottom of your Instant Pot. Now, lightly grease a baking dish with a nonstick cooking spray.

In a mixing bowl, thoroughly combine the eggs with double cream, salt, black pepper, and cayenne pepper.

Now, stir in the chard, habanero pepper, tomato, and onion. Spoon the mixture into the prepared baking dish.

Cover with a piece of aluminum foil, making a foil sling.

Secure the lid. Choose "Manual" mode and High pressure; cook for 20 minutes. Once cooking is complete, use a quick pressure release; carefully remove the lid.

Top with the cheese and cover with the lid; allow it to sit in the residual heat for 10 minutes.

Serve immediately and enjoy!

Per serving: 183 Calories; 14.4g Fat; 5.6g Carbs; 8.1g Protein; 2.8g Sugars

453. Spicy Ground Pork Omelet

(Ready in about 25 minutes | Servings 2)

Ingredients

4 eggs, whisked
1/2 pound ground pork
1 teaspoon oyster sauce
1/2 teaspoon garlic powder
1/2 teaspoon paprika
1/3 teaspoon cumin powder
Kosher salt and ground black pepper, to taste
1 yellow onion, thinly sliced
1 red chili pepper, minced
1 tablespoon canola oil

Directions

Press the "Sauté" button and heat the oil until sizzling; once hot, cook the ground pork until no longer pink, crumbling with a spatula.

Add the onion and pepper; cook an additional 2 minutes. Whisk the eggs with the remaining ingredients. Pour the egg mixture over the meat mixture in the inner pot.

Secure the lid. Choose the "Manual" mode and cook for 8 minutes at High pressure. Once cooking is complete, use a natural pressure release for 10 minutes; carefully remove the lid. Bon appétit!

Per serving: 449 Calories; 33.6g Fat; 4.3g Carbs; 32.2g Protein; 1.6g Sugars

454. Easy Keto Granola

(Ready in about 1 hour 35 minutes | Servings 4)

Ingredients

1 small apple, sliced
1 teaspoon apple pie spice mix
1 ½ tablespoons pumpkin seeds
1 ½ tablespoons sunflower seeds
A pinch of salt
1 cup coconut, shredded
1/4 cup walnuts, chopped
1 teaspoon stevia powder
3 tablespoons coconut oil

Directions

Place the coconut oil, stevia powder, coconut, walnuts, sunflower seeds, pumpkin seeds, apple pie spice mix, and salt in your Instant Pot.

Secure the lid. Choose "Slow Cook" mode and High pressure; cook for 1 hours 30 minutes. Once cooking is complete, use a quick pressure release; carefully remove the lid.

Spoon into individual bowls, garnish with apples and serve warm. Bon appétit!

Per serving: 234 Calories; 22.2g Fat; 5.5g Carbs; 2.5g Protein; 5.3g Sugars

455. Cholula Chicken Wings

(Ready in about 40 minutes | Servings 4)

Ingredients

1/2 cup Cholula hot sauce
1/2 teaspoon cayenne pepper flakes
1/2 cup roasted vegetable broth
1 teaspoon barbecue sauce
1 tablespoon brown sugar
2 garlic cloves, halved

1 teaspoon sea salt
1/2 teaspoon ground black pepper
1 teaspoon corn starch, dissolved in 1 tablespoon of water
2 pounds chicken wings
4 tablespoons butter, melted

Directions

Rub the chicken legs with the garlic halves; then, season with salt, black pepper, and cayenne pepper. Press the "Sauté" button.

Once hot, melt 2 tablespoons of the melted butter and sear the chicken wings approximately 4 minutes, turning them once during the cooking time. Add a splash of vegetable broth to deglaze the bottom of the pan.

Now, add the remaining broth and secure the lid. Choose the "Manual" mode and High pressure; cook for 12 minutes. Once the cooking is complete, use a quick pressure release; carefully remove the lid.

Remove the chicken wings from the Instant Pot, reserving the cooking liquid. Place the chicken wings on a lightly greased baking sheet.

Turn your oven on to High Broil. Broil the chicken wings approximately 15 minutes until it is crisp and golden brown; make sure to turn them over halfway through the cooking time.

Press the "Sauté" button and add the remaining 2 tablespoons of butter. Once hot, add the hot sauce, sugar, and barbecue sauce; pour in the reserved cooking liquid.

Let it simmer for 4 minutes; add the corn starch slurry and continue to simmer until the cooking liquid has reduced and concentrated.

Pour the prepared sauce over the reserved chicken and serve warm. Bon appétit!

Per serving: 408 Calories; 22.1g Fat; 8.8g Carbs; 41.6g Protein; 2.8g Sugars

456. The Best Shirred Eggs Ever

(Ready in about 10 minutes | Servings 4)

Ingredients

4 eggs
4 tablespoons butter, melted
4 tablespoons double cream
1/4 teaspoon freshly ground pepper
1/2 teaspoon granulated garlic

1/4 teaspoon dill weed
4 scallions, chopped
2 red peppers, seeded and chopped
1/4 teaspoon sea salt

Directions

Start by adding 1 cup of water and a metal rack to the Instant Pot.

Grease the bottom and sides of each ramekin with melted butter. Divide the ingredients among the prepared four ramekins.

Lower the ramekins onto the metal rack.

Secure the lid. Choose "Manual" mode and High pressure; cook for 5 minutes. Once cooking is complete, use a natural pressure release; carefully remove the lid. Bon appétit!

Per serving: 208 Calories; 18.7g Fat; 3.9g Carbs; 6.7g Protein; 2.3g Sugars

457. Mediterranean-Style Chicken Fillets

(Ready in about 20 minutes | Servings 6)

Ingredients

1/2 cup Kalamata olives, pitted and halved
1/2 cup tamari sauce
1/2 cup chicken broth
1 tablespoon molasses
2 garlic cloves, halved
1 ½ tablespoons olive oil

1/2 teaspoon red pepper flakes
1 bay leaf
1 rosemary sprig
1/2 cup tomato puree
2 pounds chicken fillets
Sea salt and freshly ground black pepper, to taste

Directions

Rub the chicken fillets with the garlic halves on all sides. Press the "Sauté" button to preheat your Instant Pot.

Heat the olive oil and sear the chicken fillets for 2 minutes per side.

Add the tamari sauce, tomato puree, broth, molasses, salt, black pepper, red pepper, bay leaf and rosemary sprig.

Secure the lid. Choose the "Manual" mode and High pressure; cook for 9 minutes. Once cooking is complete, use a quick release; remove the lid.

Serve garnished with Kalamata olives. Enjoy!

Per serving: 268 Calories; 10.1g Fat; 7g Carbs; 35.9g Protein; 4.4g Sugars

458. Keto Cucumber Canapés

(Ready in about 10 minutes | Servings 8)

Ingredients

2 cucumbers, sliced
1/2 teaspoon sea salt
1/4 teaspoon ground black pepper, or more to taste
1 pound tuna fillets

1/4 cup mayonnaise, preferably homemade
1/2 teaspoon dried dill

Directions

Prepare your Instant Pot by adding 1 ½ cups of water and steamer basket to the inner pot.

Place the tuna fillets in your steamer basket.

Secure the lid. Choose "Manual" mode and High pressure; cook for 4 minutes. Once cooking is complete, use a quick pressure release; carefully remove the lid. Flake the fish with a fork.

Add the mayonnaise, dill, salt, and black pepper. Divide the mixture among cucumber slices and place on a serving platter. Enjoy!

Per serving: 112 Calories; 5.8g Fat; 1.2g Carbs; 12.8g Protein; 0.7g Sugars

459. French-Style Dijon Chicken

(Ready in about 20 minutes | Servings 4)

Ingredients

1 tablespoon Dijon mustard
1/2 teaspoon dried sage
1 teaspoon paprika
1 teaspoon garlic powder
1 teaspoon dried basil
1/2 cup heavy cream
1/2 teaspoon dried oregano

Sea salt and ground black pepper, to taste
1 cup chicken bone broth
2 tablespoons olive oil, divided
1 pound chicken breasts, boneless

Directions

Press the "Sauté" button and heat the olive oil. Sear the chicken breasts until they are no longer pink.

Add the seasonings, mustard, and chicken bone broth.

Secure the lid. Choose "Manual" mode and cook for 8 minutes at High pressure. Once cooking is complete, use a natural pressure release; carefully remove the lid.

Lastly, add the heavy cream, cover with the lid, and let it sit in the residual heat for 6 to 8 minutes. Serve in individual bowls. Enjoy!

Per serving: 413 Calories; 27.2g Fat; 3.3g Carbs; 37.5g Protein; 1.2g Sugars

460. Mini Lasagna Cups

(Ready in about 20 minutes | Servings 6)

Ingredients

1/2 cup pasta sauce
2 eggs, beaten
1/2 teaspoon dried dill weed
10 ounces mozzarella cheese, grated

1 teaspoon cayenne pepper
1 zucchini, thinly sliced
4 ounces cream cheese

Directions

Add 1 ½ cups of water and a metal rack to the bottom of your Instant Pot. Spritz six cupcake molds with a nonstick cooking spray.

Line each cupcake mold with a zucchini slice.

In a mixing bowl, thoroughly combine eggs, cheese, dill, and cayenne pepper. Add 1/3 of this mixture to the cupcake molds; top with pasta sauce.

Repeat layers of zucchini, cheese mixture, and sauce, creating 3 layers in all, ending with pasta sauce.

Lower the cupcake molds onto the rack.

Secure the lid. Choose "Manual" mode and High pressure; cook for 15 minutes. Once cooking is complete, use a quick pressure release; carefully remove the lid. Bon appétit!

Per serving: 173 Calories; 8.7g Fat; 4.3g Carbs; 19.7g Protein; 2.5g Sugars

461. Festive Herb Chicken

(Ready in about 35 minutes | Servings 4)

Ingredients

1 (3 ½ pounds) whole chicken
Salt and ground black pepper, to taste
1 tablespoon paprika
4 tablespoons butter, softened

1 head of garlic, crushed
2 quarts water
2 rosemary sprigs, crushed
2 thyme sprigs, crushed

Directions

In a small mixing dish, thoroughly combine the butter, garlic, salt, black pepper, paprika, rosemary, and thyme.

Pour the water into the inner pot.

Pat the chicken dry. Then, rub the butter mixture all over the chicken to season well. Place the chicken in the inner pot.

Secure the lid. Choose "Manual" mode. Cook for 20 minutes at High pressure. Once cooking is complete, use a natural pressure release; carefully remove the lid.

Afterwards, place the chicken under the broiler for 10 minutes until the skin is lightly crisped. Bon appétit!

Per serving: 376 Calories; 18.2g Fat; 2g Carbs; 49.1g Protein; 0.7g Sugars

462. Savory Cauliflower Crepes

(Ready in about 35 minutes | Servings 4)

Ingredients

2 tablespoons butter, melted
1 teaspoon garlic powder
Sea salt and white pepper, to taste

4 eggs, beaten
1/2 teaspoon onion powder
3/4 pound cauliflower, riced
1/2 cup goat cheese, crumbled

Directions

Simply combine all ingredients in a mixing bowl.

Now, spritz the bottom and sides of your Instant Pot with a nonstick cooking spray. Pour the batter into the Instant Pot.

Secure the lid. Choose "Bean/Chili" mode and Low pressure; cook for 30 minutes. Once cooking is complete, use a natural pressure release; carefully remove the lid.

Serve with some extra butter or cream cheese if desired. Bon appétit!

Per serving: 198 Calories; 15.2g Fat; 4.9g Carbs; 11.2g Protein; 1.9g Sugars

463. Thanksgiving Roast Turkey

(Ready in about 45 minutes | Servings 5)

Ingredients

2 pounds turkey breasts, boneless
1 teaspoon basil, chopped
1 cup chicken bone broth
1 tablespoon cornstarch, dissolved in 1 tablespoon of water
1 tablespoon mustard

1 teaspoon rosemary, chopped
1 teaspoon paprika
1 splash dry white wine
2 tablespoons half-and-half
3 tablespoons olive oil
1 teaspoon sage, chopped
Sea salt and freshly cracked black pepper, to taste

Directions

Mix the olive oil with the spices; brush the mixture all over the turkey breasts. Press the "Sauté" button to preheat your Instant Pot.

Add the turkey breasts, skin side down and cook until slightly brown on all sides. Add a splash of wine to deglaze the pot.

Pour the chicken bone broth into the inner pot. Add the mustard and half-and-half.

Secure the lid. Choose the "Poultry" mode and cook for 30 minutes at High pressure. Once cooking is complete, use a natural pressure release; carefully remove the lid.

Afterwards, place the turkey breast under the broiler until the outside is crisp.

Meanwhile, press the "Sauté" button to preheat your Instant Pot again; add the cornstarch slurry and whisk to combine well. Let it cook until the sauce is slightly thickened. Slice the turkey breasts and serve with the pan juices. Enjoy!

Per serving: 449 Calories; 24.4g Fat; 3.7g Carbs; 50.6g Protein; 0.8g Sugars

464. Traditional Hungarian Sausage Stew

(Ready in about 15 minutes | Servings 4)

Ingredients

9 ounces Hungarian smoked sausage, casing removed and sliced
1 carrot, cut into thick slices
1 bay leaf
1/4 cup fresh cilantro leaves, roughly chopped
1 celery stalk, diced

1/2 cup shallot, peeled and diced
2 bell peppers, cut into wedges
2 cups roasted vegetable broth
1/2 tablespoon hot pepper flakes
1 tablespoon grapeseed oil
Sea salt and ground black pepper, to taste

Directions

Press the "Sauté" button to heat up the Instant Pot. Now, heat the oil and brown the sausage for 2 to 3 minutes.

Stir in the other ingredients.

Secure the lid. Choose "Manual" mode and High pressure; cook for 10 minutes. Once cooking is complete, use a natural pressure release; carefully remove the lid. Bon appétit!

Per serving: 292 Calories; 21.6g Fat; 6.4g Carbs; 15.7g Protein; 3.5g Sugars

465. Easy Homemade Cheeseburger

(Ready in about 45 minutes | Servings 6)

Ingredients

6 ounces Monterey-Jack cheese, sliced
1 tablespoon tomato puree
2 garlic cloves, minced
1/2 teaspoon cayenne pepper

1/2 onion, finely chopped
2 pounds ground chuck
Sea salt and freshly ground black pepper, to taste

Directions

Mix the ground chuck, tomato puree, salt, black pepper, cayenne pepper, onion, and garlic until well combined.

Form the meat mixture into patties. Place your patties on squares of aluminum foil and wrap them loosely.

Add 1 cup water and a metal trivet to the Instant Pot; lower the foil packs onto the top of the metal trivet.

Secure the lid. Choose the "Meat/Stew" mode and cook for 35 minutes at High pressure. Once cooking is complete, use a natural pressure release; carefully remove the lid.

Place your patties on a baking sheet and broil for 5 to 6 minutes. Serve on buns topped with cheese. Enjoy!

Per serving: 441 Calories; 25.4g Fat; 2.9g Carbs; 47.5g Protein; 1.7g Sugars

466. Cheese, Kale and Egg Quiche

(Ready in about 30 minutes | Servings 6)

Ingredients

1 cup Colby cheese, shredded
2 cups cream cheese, shredded
2 garlic cloves, minced
2 cups kale leaves, torn into pieces

7 eggs, whisked
1/4 teaspoon paprika
1/2 cup leeks, chopped
2 tablespoons olive oil
Sea salt and ground black pepper, to taste

Directions

Start by adding 1 cup of water and a metal trivet to the Instant Pot. Grease a baking pan with a nonstick cooking spray.

Simply mix all of the above ingredients until everything is well combined.

Spoon the batter into the prepared baking pan. Now, lower the baking pan onto the trivet.

Secure the lid. Choose "Meat/Stew" mode and High pressure; cook for 25 minutes. Once cooking is complete, use a quick pressure release; carefully remove the lid. Serve warm.

Per serving: 473 Calories; 43g Fat; 5.9g Carbs; 16.6g Protein; 3.2g Sugars

467. Cod Fish, Herb and Tomato Chowder

(Ready in about 12 minutes | Servings 4)

Ingredients

1 onion, chopped
1/4 teaspoon hot sauce
1/2 teaspoon paprika
2 garlic cloves, minced
1/2 teaspoon dried dill weed
1/4 cup cooking wine
1 pound cod fish, cut into bite-sized pieces
1/2 teaspoon basil

2 ripe tomatoes, pureed
2 tablespoons tomato paste
1/4 teaspoon dried oregano
1/2 stick butter, at room temperature
1 cup shellfish stock
Sea salt and freshly ground black pepper, to taste

Directions

Press the "Sauté" button and melt the butter; once hot, cook the onion and garlic for about 2 minutes or until they are just tender.

Add the remaining ingredients.

Secure the lid. Choose the "Manual" mode and cook for 5 minutes at High pressure. Once cooking is complete, use a quick pressure release; carefully remove the lid.

Ladle into serving bowls and serve immediately.

Per serving: 232 Calories; 12.4g Fat; 7.3g Carbs; 20.1g Protein; 3.9g Sugars

468. Sloppy Joe Zucchini Boats

(Ready in about 10 minutes | Servings 2)

Ingredients

1 medium-sized zucchini, cut into 4 slices lengthwise
1/2 pound ground beef
2 teaspoons mustard

Salt and ground black pepper, to taste
1 tomato, sliced
4 lettuce leaves
1 tablespoon olive oil

Directions

Add the olive oil, ground beef, salt, and black pepper to your Instant Pot.

Secure the lid. Choose "Manual" mode and High pressure; cook for 5 minutes. Once cooking is complete, use a natural pressure release; carefully remove the lid.

Divide the ground meat mixture between 2 zucchini slices. Add the tomato slices, lettuce, and mustard. Top with the second slice of zucchini. Bon appétit!

Per serving: 159 Calories; 9.8g Fat; 1.5g Carbs; 15.5g Protein; 0.7g Sugars

469. Basic Hamburger Soup

(Ready in about 30 minutes | Servings 5)

Ingredients

1 pound ground beef
2 bay leaves
1/4 teaspoon paprika
1 leek, diced
1 teaspoon fish sauce
2 cloves garlic, sliced
1 can condensed tomato soup

1 teaspoon basil
1/2 teaspoon oregano
1 tablespoon olive oil
2 tablespoons cooking sherry
4 cups beef broth
Sea salt and ground black pepper, to taste

Directions

Press the "Sauté" button and heat the oil. Once hot, brown the ground beef for 2 to 3 minutes, stirring and crumbling with a wooden spoon.

Stir in the leeks and garlic; continue to sauté an additional 2 minutes, stirring continuously.

Add a splash of cooking sherry to deglaze the pot. Add the other ingredients to the inner pot.

Secure the lid. Choose the "Manual" mode and cook for 10 minutes at High pressure. Once cooking is complete, use a natural pressure release for 10 minutes; carefully remove the lid.

Serve warm with crusty bread, if desired. Bon appétit!

Per serving: 283 Calories; 14.4g Fat; 6g Carbs; 29.4g Protein; 1.9g Sugars

470. Cheese Mushroom Pâté

(Ready in about 10 minutes | Servings 8)

Ingredients

1 cup cream cheese, at room temperature
1 pound brown mushrooms, chopped
2 tablespoons cognac
1/3 teaspoon black pepper

1/2 yellow onion, chopped
2 garlic cloves, minced
1/2 teaspoon cayenne pepper
3 tablespoons olive oil
Sea salt, to taste

Directions

Press the "Sauté" button to heat up the Instant Pot. Now, heat the oil and cook the mushrooms with the onions until softened and fragrant.

Stir in the garlic, cognac, salt, black pepper, and cayenne pepper.

Secure the lid. Choose "Manual" mode and High pressure; cook for 5 minutes. Once cooking is complete, use a quick pressure release; carefully remove the lid.

Transfer the mixture to a food processor. Add the cream cheese and continue to mix until everything is well incorporated. Serve with veggie sticks. Bon appétit!

Per serving: 162 Calories; 14.4g Fat; 3.6g Carbs; 3.9g Protein; 2.4g Sugars

471. French-Style Beef Bourguignon

(Ready in about 30 minutes | Servings 6)

Ingredients

2 pounds beef round roast, cut into 1-inch cubes
1 cup red Burgundy wine
2 thyme sprigs
2 bay leaves
2 tablespoons bouquet garni, chopped
2 celery stalks, diced
4 cloves garlic, minced
2 tablespoons tomato paste
2 cups beef broth
2 onions, thinly sliced
2 carrots, diced
4 thick slices bacon, diced
Sea salt and ground black pepper, to taste

Directions

Press the "Sauté" button to preheat your Instant Pot. Cook the bacon until it is golden-brown; reserve.

Add the beef to the inner pot; sear the beef until browned or about 3 minutes per side.

Stir in the other ingredients; stir to combine well.

Secure the lid. Choose the "Meat/Stew" mode. Cook for 20 minutes at High pressure. Once cooking is complete, use a quick pressure release; carefully remove the lid.

Serve in individual bowls topped with the reserved bacon. Bon appétit!

Per serving: 364 Calories; 14.5g Fat; 5.3g Carbs; 49.4g Protein; 2.4g Sugars

472. Keto Cereals with Berries

(Ready in about 15 minutes | Servings 4)

Ingredients

1 tablespoon flaxseed meal
1/4 teaspoon kosher salt
2 ounces raspberries
1 ounce blueberries
1/4 coconut flour
4 tablespoons Swerve, granulated
2 tablespoons double cream
1/4 stick butter
1/4 cup almond flour
1/2 cup milk
1/2 cup water
2 eggs, beaten

Directions

Add all ingredients to the Instant Pot.

Secure the lid. Choose "Manual" mode and High pressure; cook for 5 minutes. Once cooking is complete, use a quick pressure release; carefully remove the lid.

Serve garnished with some extra berries if desired. Enjoy!

Per serving: 185 Calories; 14.4g Fat; 6.2g Carbs; 5.9g Protein; 6.8g Sugars

473. Traditional Beef Ragù with Italian Wine

(Ready in about 20 minutes | Servings 5)

Ingredients

1 pound ground chuck
1/2 cup Italian red wine
1/2 teaspoon kosher salt
1/2 teaspoon black pepper
1 stalk celery, diced
5 ounces bacon, diced
1/4 cup tomato puree
2 cups chicken stock
1 medium leek, diced
1 tablespoon Italian seasoning blend
2 carrots, diced
2 tablespoons butter, melted

Directions

Press the "Sauté" button and melt the butter. Sauté the leek, carrot, celery and garlic for 2 to 3 minutes.

Add the bacon and ground beef to the inner pot; continue to cook an additional 3 minutes, stirring frequently. Add the remaining ingredients to the inner pot.

Secure the lid. Choose the "Manual" mode and cook for 5 minutes at High pressure. Once cooking is complete, use a quick pressure release; carefully remove the lid.

Serve with hot pasta if desired. Bon appétit!

Per serving: 475 Calories; 40.6g Fat; 6.1g Carbs; 20.7g Protein; 2.5g Sugars

474. Summer Berry Cupcakes

(Ready in about 30 minutes | Servings 6)

Ingredients

1/2 cup fresh mixed berries
1/4 cup coconut flour
1/4 cup almond flour
3 ounces cream cheese, softened
1/4 cup double cream
1/4 teaspoon cardamom powder
1/2 teaspoon star anise, ground
A pinch of salt
1/3 cup Swerve, granulated
1 teaspoon baking powder
4 eggs
1/4 cup coconut oil, softened

Directions

Start by adding 1 ½ cups of water and a metal rack to your Instant Pot.

Mix the coconut oil, cream cheese, and double cream in a bowl. Fold in the eggs, one at a time, and continue to mix until everything is well incorporated.

In another bowl, thoroughly combine the flour, salt, Swerve, baking powder, cardamom, and anise.

Add the cream/egg mixture to this dry mixture. Afterwards, fold in fresh berries and gently stir to combine.

Divide the batter between silicone cupcake liners. Cover with a piece of foil. Place the cupcakes on the rack.

Secure the lid. Choose "Manual" mode and High pressure; cook for 25 minutes. Once cooking is complete, use a natural pressure release; carefully remove the lid. Enjoy!

Per serving: 238 Calories; 21.6g Fat; 4.1g Carbs; 7.5g Protein; 2.2g Sugars

475. Classic Chicken Veggie Stock

(Ready in about 1 hour 10 minutes | Servings 9)

Ingredients

1 celery rib, cut into 2-inch pieces
9 cups cold water
1 bay leaf
1 bunch parsley

1 large onion, quartered
Sea salt, to taste
1 teaspoon mixed peppercorns
1 chicken carcass
2 carrots, cut into 2-inch pieces

Directions

Place all ingredients in the inner pot.

Secure the lid. Choose the "Soup/Broth" mode and cook for 40 minutes at High pressure. Once cooking is complete, use a natural pressure release for 20 minutes; carefully remove the lid.

Remove the bones and vegetables with a slotted spoon. Use immediately or store for later use.

Bon appétit!

Per serving: 79 Calories; 2.9g Fat; 2.6g Carbs; 21.9g Protein; 1.2g Sugars

476. Italian Keto Balls with Marinara Sauce

(Ready in about 15 minutes | Servings 6)

Ingredients

1 ½ cups Romano cheese, grated
Sea salt and ground black pepper, to your liking
2 cloves garlic, finely chopped
2 tablespoons fresh parsley, chopped

1 tablespoon olive oil
8 eggs, whisked
1 cup pork rinds, crushed
1 ½ cups low-carb marinara sauce

Directions

Press the "Sauté" button to heat up the Instant Pot. Add the marinara sauce and bring it to a boil.

Now, in a mixing bowl, thoroughly combine the remaining ingredients. Form the mixture into balls.

Then, drop the balls into the hot marinara sauce.

Secure the lid. Choose "Manual" mode and High pressure; cook for 8 minutes. Once cooking is complete, use a quick pressure release; carefully remove the lid. Bon appétit!

Per serving: 395 Calories; 26.2g Fat; 5.6g Carbs; 29.4g Protein; 5.1g Sugars

477. Meat Sauce with Malvasia and Herbs

(Ready in about 55 minutes | Servings 10)

Ingredients

2 ½ pounds pork butt, ground
1/4 cup Malvasia wine, or other Sicilian wine
2 fresh tomatoes, pureed
1/2 teaspoon salt
1 teaspoon dried rosemary
1/2 teaspoon cayenne pepper
1 cup chicken broth
2 tablespoons fresh cilantro, chopped

1 teaspoon dried basil
1/2 teaspoon black pepper, freshly cracked
2 tablespoons olive oil
5 ounces tomato paste
2 bay leaves
1 onion, chopped
4 garlic cloves, pressed

Directions

Press the "Sauté" button and heat the oil. When the oil starts to sizzle, cook the pork until no longer pink.

Add the onion and garlic and continue to cook for a few minutes more or until they are tender and fragrant. Add a splash of wine to deglaze the pot.

Stir in the other ingredients.

Secure the lid. Choose the "Meat/Stew" mode and cook for 35 minutes at High pressure. Once cooking is complete, use a natural pressure release for 15 minutes; carefully remove the lid.

Next, remove the meat from the inner pot; shred the meat, discarding the bones. Return the meat to your sauce and serve over pasta if desired.

Per serving: 378 Calories; 24.5g Fat; 3.2g Carbs; 34.2g Protein; 1.1g Sugars

478. Two-Cheese Cauliflower Muffins

(Ready in about 15 minutes | Servings 6)

Ingredients

1/2 cup Cotija cheese, grated
1 cup Romano cheese, preferably freshly grated
1/4 teaspoon dried oregano
2 garlic cloves, minced
1/2 cup scallions, chopped
1/2 teaspoon dried dill weed
1/2 teaspoon dried basil

Salt and ground black pepper, to taste
7 eggs, beaten
1/2 pound cauliflower, riced
Sea salt and ground black pepper, to taste
1/2 teaspoon cayenne pepper
2 tablespoons olive oil

Directions

Start by adding 1 ½ cups of water and a metal rack to the bottom of the Instant Pot. Spritz each muffin cup with a nonstick cooking spray.

Mix the ingredients until everything is well incorporated.

Now, spoon the mixture into lightly greased muffin cups. Lower the cups onto the rack in the Instant Pot.

Secure the lid. Choose "Manual" mode and High pressure; cook for 10 minutes. Once cooking is complete, use a natural pressure release; carefully remove the lid. Bon appétit!

Per serving: 335 Calories; 25.9g Fat; 5.8g Carbs; 19.8g Protein; 2.6g Sugars

479. Basic Marinara Sauce

(Ready in about 25 minutes | Servings 8)

Ingredients

4 tablespoons tomato paste
1 (28-ounce) can crushed tomatoes with juice
1 cup water
1 tablespoon fresh parsley, minced
Sea salt to taste
2 tablespoons fresh basil, minced
4 tablespoons olive oil
4 garlic cloves, minced

Directions

Press the "Sauté" button and heat olive oil. Once hot, cook the garlic for a minute or so or until it is fragrant but not browned.

Now, stir in the remaining ingredients.

Secure the lid. Choose the "Soup/Broth" mode and cook for 40 minutes at High pressure. Once cooking is complete, use a quick pressure release; carefully remove the lid. Bon appétit!

Per serving: 86 Calories; 7g Fat; 5.4g Carbs; 1.3g Protein; 3.6g Sugars

480. Ricotta and Chorizo Dipping Sauce

(Ready in about 15 minutes | Servings 12)

Ingredients

15 ounces Ricotta cheese
3/4 pound Chorizo, casings removed and crumbled
1 onion, peeled and chopped
2 tablespoons fresh chives, chopped
1/2 teaspoon ground black pepper
2 tablespoons fresh parsley
1 tablespoon olive oil

Directions

Press the "Sauté" button to heat up the Instant Pot. Now, heat the oil and brown Chorizo sausage for 2 to 3 minutes.

Add the onion, cheese and black pepper to the Instant Pot.

Secure the lid. Choose "Manual" mode and High pressure; cook for 10 minutes. Once cooking is complete, use a quick pressure release; carefully remove the lid.

Garnish with fresh parsley and chives. Bon appétit!s

Per serving: 210 Calories; 16.6g Fat; 3.8g Carbs; 11g Protein; 1.5g Sugars

481. Classic Bolognese Sauce

(Ready in about 20 minutes | Servings 4)

Ingredients

1 pound ground beef
2 tablespoons tomato ketchup
1/2 teaspoon dried sage
1/2 teaspoon cayenne pepper, or to taste
2 ripe tomatoes, pureed
1 onion, chopped
2 cups beef broth
1 teaspoon brown sugar
1 teaspoon fresh garlic, minced
2 tablespoons olive oil
1 teaspoon dried oregano
1 teaspoon dried basil
Sea salt and ground black pepper, to taste

Directions

Press the "Sauté" button and heat the oil. When the oil starts to sizzle, cook the ground beef until no longer pink; crumble it with a wooden spatula.

Add the onion and garlic and continue to cook for a few minutes more or until they are tender and fragrant. Add a splash of beef broth to deglaze the pot.

Stir in the remaining ingredients; stir to combine well.

Secure the lid. Choose the "Manual" mode and cook for 6 minutes at High pressure. Once cooking is complete, use a natural pressure release for 5 minutes; carefully remove the lid.

Serve over pasta if desired. Bon appétit!

Per serving: 358 Calories; 20.3g Fat; 8.7g Carbs; 34.1g Protein; 4.7g Sugars

482. Old Bay Dipping Sauce

(Ready in about 20 minutes | Servings 10)

Ingredients

1 teaspoon Old Bay seasoning
30 ounces frozen lobster
1 onion, chopped
1 cup chicken broth
2 cups cream cheese
1 cup Cheddar cheese, shredded
2 tomatoes, puréed
Salt and ground black pepper, to taste
1/2 teaspoon paprika
2 tablespoons butter
1 celery, chopped
2 garlic cloves, minced

Directions

Press the "Sauté" button to heat up the Instant Pot. Now, melt the butter and sauté the onion and celery until softened.

Then, add the garlic and continue to cook an additional minute or until aromatic.

Add the tomatoes, chicken broth, spices, lobster and cream cheese.

Secure the lid. Choose "Manual" mode and Low pressure; cook for 12 minutes. Once cooking is complete, use a quick pressure release; carefully remove the lid.

Using an immersion blender, puree the mixture to your desired consistency. Return the mixture to the Instant Pot.

Press the "Sauté" button and add the Cheddar cheese. Let it simmer until everything is melted and incorporated. Bon appétit!

Per serving: 291 Calories; 20.7g Fat; 4.9g Carbs; 21.2g Protein; 3.2g Sugars

483. Two-Cheese and Bacon Dip

(Ready in about 15 minutes | Servings 10)

Ingredients

10 ounces Cottage cheese, at room temperature
1 cup Pepper Jack cheese, grated
4 ounces bacon, diced
1/2 teaspoon ground cumin
1/2 teaspoon turmeric powder
2 cloves garlic, pressed

1 cup vegetable broth
1 onion, chopped
1 red chili pepper, seeded and minced
2 ripe tomatoes, chopped
Kosher salt and ground black pepper, to taste

Directions

Press the "Sauté" button to preheat your Instant Pot. Then, cook the bacon for 2 to 3 minutes. Reserve.

Add the onion and pepper to the inner pot and continue to cook until they are fragrant. Stir in the garlic and continue to sauté for 30 seconds more.

Now, add the tomatoes, spices, and broth.

Secure the lid. Choose the "Manual" mode and cook for 5 minutes at High pressure. Once cooking is complete, use a quick pressure release; carefully remove the lid.

Lastly, stir in the cheese. Seal the lid again and let it sit in the residual heat until the cheese melts.

Ladle into a nice serving bowl, top with the reserved bacon, and serve.

Per serving: 135 Calories; 9.5g Fat; 4.5g Carbs; 8.3g Protein; 2.5g Sugars

484. Ground Meat and Cheese-Stuffed Peppers

(Ready in about 25 minutes | Servings 4)

Ingredients

1 cup Cotija cheese, grated
4 eggs, whisked
1 (1-ounce) package taco seasoning mix
4 bell peppers, remove seeds and cut the tops off
8 ounces canned tomato sauce

2 garlic cloves, minced
1/2 cup onion, chopped
1/2 pound ground beef
1/4 pound ground pork
Salt and ground black pepper, to taste

Directions

Start by adding 1 cup of water and a metal rack to the bottom of the Instant Pot. Spritz a casserole dish with a nonstick cooking spray.

In a mixing bowl, thoroughly combine the ground meat, eggs, garlic, onion, salt, pepper, taco seasoning mix, and Cotija cheese.

Fill the peppers with the cheese/meat mixture. Place the peppers on the rack in the Instant Pot. Pour the tomato sauce over the peppers.

Secure the lid. Choose "Manual" mode and High pressure; cook for 20 minutes. Once cooking is complete, use a natural pressure release; carefully remove the lid. Bon appétit!

Per serving: 407 Calories; 27g Fat; 6.3g Carbs; 32.4g Protein; 3.7g Sugars

485. Hot Pepper Sauce

(Ready in about 40 minutes | Servings 10)

Ingredients

5 jalapeño peppers, seeded and chopped
5 serrano peppers, seeded and chopped
2 tablespoons white sugar
2 tomatoes, chopped
1 teaspoon garlic, minced

1 cup white vinegar
1 cup water
1 tablespoon butter, melted
1 banana shallot, chopped
Sea salt and ground black pepper, to taste

Directions

Press the "Sauté" button and melt the butter. Once hot, cook the shallot for 3 to 4 minute or until it is tender and fragrant.

Now, add the garlic and continue to cook an additional 30 seconds or until aromatic.

Add the remaining ingredients.

Secure the lid. Choose the "Manual" mode and cook for 25 minutes at High pressure. Once cooking is complete, use a natural pressure release for 10 minutes; carefully remove the lid.

Let it cool. Serve your sauce hot or at room temperature. Bon appétit!

Per serving: 39 Calories; 1.2g Fat; 5.8g Carbs; 0.8g Protein; 3.9g Sugars

486. Mashed Cauliflower with French Gravy

(Ready in about 20 minutes | Servings 4)

Ingredients

Mashed Cauliflower:
4 tablespoons Romano cheese, grated
1/4 cup double cream
1 teaspoon dried dill weed
3 cloves garlic minced
1 head of fresh cauliflower, broken into florets

2 tablespoons butter
Kosher salt and ground black pepper, to taste
French Gravy:
3 tablespoons butter
1/2 cup double cream
1 ½ cups beef stock

Directions

Add 1 cup of water and a steamer basket to the bottom of your Instant Pot.

Then, arrange the cauliflower in the steamer basket.

Secure the lid. Choose "Manual" mode and Low pressure; cook for 3 minutes. Once cooking is complete, use a quick pressure release; carefully remove the lid.

Now, puree the cauliflower with a potato masher. Add the remaining ingredients for the purée and stir well.

Press the "Sauté" button to heat up the Instant Pot. Now, combine the ingredients for the gravy and let it simmer for 10 minutes.

Stir until the gravy thickens down to a consistency of your liking. Serve cauliflower purée with the gravy on the side. Bon appétit!

Per serving: 291 Calories; 26.6g Fat; 7.1g Carbs; 7.1g Protein; 4.5g Sugars

487. Dip de Queso Crema

(Ready in about 10 minutes | Servings 10)

Ingredients

8 ounces Monterey Jack, shredded
1/2 teaspoon hot sauce
3 tablespoons all-purpose flour
3 tablespoons butter
Kosher salt, to taste
1 cup whole milk

Directions

Press the "Sauté" button and melt the butter. Now, add the flour and stir to combine well.

Gradually pour in the milk, stirring continuously to avoid clumps. Bring to a boil and press the "Cancel" button.

Add in the Monterey Jack cheese and stir until cheese has melted; add the salt and hot sauce. Serve warm with tortilla chips if desired. Bon appétit!

Per serving: 146 Calories; 11.2g Fat; 5.1g Carbs; 6.6g Protein; 3.3g Sugars

488. Cheese, Zucchini and Herb Quiche

(Ready in about 35 minutes | Servings 6)

Ingredients

1/2 cup Cheddar cheese, shredded
10 ounces cream cheese
1 ½ cups zucchini, grated
1/4 teaspoon dried rosemary
1/4 teaspoon dried basil
1 clove garlic, pressed
1 cup almond flour
1 teaspoon baking powder
Coarse sea salt and ground black pepper, to taste
1/2 stick butter, melted
1 tablespoon flaxseed meal
4 eggs, whisked

Directions

Begin by adding 1 cup of water and a metal rack to your Instant Pot. Then, spritz a heatproof bowl with a nonstick cooking spray and set aside.

In a mixing dish, thoroughly combine the cream and eggs. Gradually stir in the flour. Add the remaining ingredients, except for the Cheddar cheese.

Spoon the mixture into the prepared heatproof bowl; cover with a piece of aluminum foil, making a foil sling.

Secure the lid. Choose "Manual" mode and High pressure; cook for 25 minutes. Once cooking is complete, use a quick pressure release; carefully remove the lid.

Add the Cheddar cheese to the top of your tart and cover with the lid. Let it sit in a residual heat an additional 7 to 10 minutes. Bon appétit!

Per serving: 353 Calories; 32.1g Fat; 4g Carbs; 12.6g Protein; 2.5g Sugars

489. Greek-Style Deviled Eggs

(Ready in about 10 minutes | Servings 5)

Ingredients

2 tablespoons Greek-style yogurt
10 eggs
4 tablespoons mayonnaise
1 teaspoon fresh dill, chopped
1/2 teaspoon turmeric powder
2 teaspoons balsamic vinegar
1/2 teaspoon coarse sea salt
1/4 teaspoon black pepper, to taste

Directions

Place 1 cup of water and a steamer rack in the inner pot. Arrange the eggs on the rack.

Secure the lid. Choose the "Manual" mode and cook for 5 minutes at High pressure. Once cooking is complete, use a quick pressure release; carefully remove the lid.

Peel the eggs and slice them into halves.

In a mixing bowl, thoroughly combine the sea salt, black pepper, turmeric powder, vinegar, yogurt, and mayonnaise. Stir in the egg yolks.

Use a piping bag to fill the egg white halves. Garnish with fresh dill. Bon appétit!

Per serving: 209 Calories; 16.6g Fat; 1.6g Carbs; 12g Protein; 0.9g Sugars

490. Beef Keto Tacos

(Ready in about 15 minutes | Servings 4)

Ingredients

1 pound ground chuck
1 cup beef stock
1 bell pepper, seeded and sliced
1 teaspoon taco seasoning
1 tablespoon olive oil
1/2 red onion, chopped
Salt and ground black pepper, to taste

Directions

Press the "Sauté" button to heat up the Instant Pot. Now, heat the oil and sauté the onion until tender and translucent.

Then, add the ground chuck and cook an additional 2 minutes or until no longer pink.

Then, add the bell pepper, taco seasoning, stock, salt, and black pepper.

Secure the lid. Choose "Manual" mode and High pressure; cook for 5 minutes. Once cooking is complete, use a natural pressure release; carefully remove the lid.

To assemble the taco wraps, place a few lettuce leaves on each serving plate. Divide the meat mixture between lettuce leaves. Add toppings of choice and serve. Bon appétit!

Per serving: 219 Calories; 12.5g Fat; 2.7g Carbs; 24.1g Protein; 1.2g Sugars

491. Dilled Swiss Cheese Sauce

(Ready in about 15 minutes | Servings 10)

Ingredients

1 ½ cups Swiss cheese, grated
1/4 teaspoon dried dill weed
2 tablespoons tapioca starch
1 ½ cups whole milk
1/2 teaspoon onion powder
1/2 teaspoon garlic powder
1/2 stick butter
Sea salt and ground black pepper, to taste

Directions

Press the "Sauté" button and melt the butter. Now, add the onion powder, garlic powder, dill, salt, and black pepper. Stir in the tapioca starch and stir to combine well.

Gradually pour in the milk, stirring continuously to avoid clumps. Bring to a boil and press the "Cancel" button.

Add in the Swiss cheese and stir until the cheese has melted. Serve warm with breadsticks or veggie sticks. Bon appétit!

Per serving: 148 Calories; 11.3g Fat; 5.2g Carbs; 6.7g Protein; 2.4g Sugars

492. Pepper and Cheese Cups

(Ready in about 10 minutes | Servings 6)

Ingredients

1 ½ cups bell peppers, chopped
1 jalapeño pepper, seeded and minced
1/2 teaspoon salt
A pinch of ground allspice
1 tomato, chopped
1/2 cup Cotija cheese, crumbled
6 eggs
1/2 teaspoon Mexican oregano
1/4 cup green onions, chopped
1/4 cup almond milk, unsweetened

Directions

Prepare your Instant Pot by adding 1 ½ cups of water to the inner pot.

Spritz six ovenproof custard cups with a nonstick cooking spray.

In a mixing dish, thoroughly combine the eggs, milk, salt, allspice, and Mexican oregano; mix to combine well.

Add the green onions, tomato, bell peppers, and jalapeño pepper to the custard cups. Pour the egg mixture over them. Top with the cheese.

Lower 3 custard cups onto a metal trivet; then, place the second trivet on top. Lower the remaining 3 cups onto it.

Secure the lid. Choose "Manual" mode and High pressure; cook for 7 minutes. Once cooking is complete, use a quick pressure release; carefully remove the lid. Serve at room temperature.

Per serving: 189 Calories; 13.4g Fat; 4.3g Carbs; 12.5g Protein; 2.8g Sugars

493. Hard-Boiled Eggs with Chives

(Ready in about 15 minutes | Servings 3)

Ingredients

1/4 teaspoon red pepper flakes, crushed
2 tablespoons fresh chives, chopped
5 eggs
1/2 teaspoon salt

Directions

Place 1 cup of water and a steamer rack in the inner pot. Arrange the eggs on the rack.

Secure the lid. Choose the "Manual" mode and cook for 5 minutes at High pressure. Once cooking is complete, use a quick pressure release; carefully remove the lid.

Transfer the eggs to icy-cold water. Now, let them sit in the water bath a few minutes until cool.

Peel your eggs and season with salt and red pepper. Serve garnished with freshly chopped chives. Enjoy!

Per serving: 106 Calories; 6.9g Fat; 0.6g Carbs; 9.2g Protein; 0.3g Sugars

494. Cheesy Salmon Keto Fat Bombs

(Ready in about 15 minutes | Servings 6)

Ingredients

4 ounces Ricotta cheese, room temperature
2 tablespoons butter, softened
1 garlic clove, finely chopped
2 teaspoons fresh parsley, finely chopped
1/4 teaspoon smoked paprika
1/4 teaspoon hot paprika
1/4 cup green onions, chopped
1/2 pound salmon fillets
Salt and ground black pepper, to taste

Directions

Start by adding 1 ½ cups of water and a metal rack to the bottom of your Instant Pot.

Place the salmon on the metal rack.

Secure the lid. Choose "Manual" mode and Low pressure; cook for 8 minutes. Once cooking is complete, use a quick pressure release; carefully remove the lid.

Chop the salmon. Add the salt, pepper, paprika, butter, cheese, onions, and garlic. Shape the mixture into balls and roll them in chopped parsley.

Arrange the fat bombs on a serving platter and enjoy!

Per serving: 130 Calories; 9.1g Fat; 1.7g Carbs; 10.2g Protein; 0.5g Sugars

495. Ham and Swiss Cheese Muffins

(Ready in about 15 minutes | Servings 4)

Ingredients

1/2 cup Swiss cheese, shredded

1 teaspoon paprika

2 tablespoons cilantro, chopped

2 tablespoons scallions, chopped

Sea salt, to taste

8 ounces ham, chopped

2 tablespoons parsley, chopped

1 cup green peppers, seeded and chopped

8 eggs

1/2 cup sour cream

1/4 teaspoon ground black pepper, or more to taste

Directions

Mix all ingredients until everything is well combined.

Add 1 cup of water and a metal rack to the inner pot of your Instant Pot.

Spoon the prepared mixture into silicone molds. Lower the molds onto the prepared trivet.

Secure the lid. Choose the "Manual" mode and cook for 6 minutes at High pressure. Once cooking is complete, use a quick pressure release; carefully remove the lid. Bon appétit!

Per serving: 369 Calories; 23.7g Fat; 6.5g Carbs; 31.3g Protein; 1.5g Sugars

SNACKS & APPETIZERS

496. BBQ Appetizer Meatballs

(Ready in about 15 minutes | Servings 12)

Ingredients

For the Meatballs:
1/2 cup Romano cheese, preferably freshly grated
2/3 cup tortilla chips, crushed
1 onion, chopped
2 garlic cloves, minced
1 egg, well-beaten
Seasoned salt and ground black pepper, to taste
1 pound ground chuck
1/2 pound ground pork
For the Sauce:
1 teaspoon ground mustard
1/4 cup apple cider vinegar
1/2 teaspoon onion powder
1 cup water
1 cup ketchup
6 tablespoons light brown sugar

Directions

Mix all ingredients for the meatballs. Spritz a sauté pan with a nonstick cooking spray.

Heat the sauté pan over a medium-high heat. Then, brown the meatballs until they are delicately browned on all sides.

In another mixing dish, thoroughly combine all ingredients for the sauce. Add the sauce to the Instant Pot.

Drop the meatballs into the sauce.

Secure the lid and choose the "Poultry" function; cook for 5 minutes at High pressure. Once cooking is complete, use a natural release; carefully remove the lid.

Serve on a nice platter with toothpicks. Enjoy!

Per serving: 178 Calories; 9.4g Fat; 8.3g Carbs; 15g Protein; 5.1g Sugars

497. Hot Pizza Dip

(Ready in about 25 minutes | Servings 10)

Ingredients

1/2 cup Romano cheese, shredded
1/2 cup mozzarella cheese, shredded
1/2 cup green olives, pitted and sliced
1/2 teaspoon oregano
1/2 teaspoon garlic salt
10 ounces cream cheese
1 cup tomato sauce
1/2 teaspoon basil

Directions

Add 1 ½ cups of water and metal trivet to the inner pot. Spritz a souffle dish with cooking spray.

Place the cream cheese on the bottom of the souffle dish. Add the tomato sauce and mozzarella cheese. Scatter sliced olives over the top.

Add the oregano, basil, and garlic salt. Top with the Romano cheese. Lower the dish onto the prepared trivet.

Secure the lid. Choose the "Manual" mode and cook for 18 minutes at High pressure. Once cooking is complete, use a quick pressure release; carefully remove the lid.

Serve with chips or breadsticks if desired. Enjoy!

Per serving: 158 Calories; 11.8g Fat; 6.9g Carbs; 5.7g Protein; 3.9g Sugars

498. Aromatic Fingerling Potatoes with Herbs

(Ready in about 25 minutes | Servings 6)

Ingredients

1 ½ pounds fingerling potatoes
2 sprigs thyme
2 sprigs rosemary
1/2 teaspoon shallot powder
1/2 teaspoon porcini powder
4 tablespoons butter, melted
1/2 teaspoon ground black pepper
1/2 teaspoon cayenne pepper
1 teaspoon garlic paste
3/4 cup vegetable broth
Sea salt, to taste

Directions

Press the "Sauté" button to preheat your Instant Pot; now, melt the butter.

Sauté the potatoes, rolling them around for about 9 minutes. Now, pierce the middle of each potato with a knife.

Secure the lid. Choose the "Manual" mode and High pressure; cook for 10 minutes. Once cooking is complete, use a quick pressure release; carefully remove the lid.

Serve with toothpicks and enjoy!

Per serving: 391 Calories; 35.1g Fat; 19.9g Carbs; 2.4g Protein; 0.8g Sugars

499. Polenta with Cream Cheese and Herbs

(Ready in about 20 minutes | Servings 8)

Ingredients

1 cup milk
1 teaspoon kosher salt
1 teaspoon basil
1/2 cup bread crumbs
2 tablespoons cilantro, finely chopped
1 tablespoon thyme
1 teaspoon rosemary
2 tablespoons olive oil
1 tablespoon butter
1/2 cup cream cheese
1 cup cornmeal
3 cups water
2 tablespoons chives, finely chopped

Per serving: 181 Calories; 8.2g Fat; 22.6g Carbs; 4.1g Protein; 2.7g Sugars

Directions

Add the polenta, water, milk. and salt to the inner pot of your Instant Pot. Press the "Sauté" button and bring the mixture to a simmer. Press the "Cancel" button.

Secure the lid. Choose the "Manual" mode and cook for 8 minutes at High pressure. Once cooking is complete, use a quick pressure release; carefully remove the lid.

Grease a baking pan with butter. Add the cream cheese and herbs to your polenta.

Scoop the hot polenta into the prepared baking pan and refrigerate until firm. Cut into small squares. Spread the breadcrumbs on a large plate; coat each side of the polenta squares with breadcrumbs.

Heat the olive oil in a nonstick pan over medium heat; cook the polenta squares approximately 3 minutes per side or until golden brown. Bon appétit!

500. Pork Taco Meat with Coleslaw

(Ready in about 1 hour | Servings 10)

Ingredients

2 pounds pork shoulder
2 cups coleslaw, for serving
1 cup beer
1/2 cup ketchup
2 tablespoons honey
1/4 teaspoon freshly ground
black pepper

1 teaspoon cayenne pepper
1/3 cup rice wine
1 tablespoon rice vinegar
1/2 teaspoon celery seeds
1 teaspoon ground cumin
2 tablespoons olive oil
Kosher salt, to taste

Directions

Press the "Sauté" button to preheat your Instant Pot. Then, heat the oil until sizzling.

Once hot, cook the pork until well browned on all sides. Add the honey, salt, black pepper, cayenne pepper, celery seeds, cumin, wine, vinegar, and beer to your Instant Pot.

Secure the lid. Choose the "Manual" mode and High pressure; cook for 50 minutes. Once cooking is complete, use a natural pressure release; carefully remove the lid.

Then, shred the meat with two forks. Return it to the Instant Pot. Add ketchup and seal the lid one more time.

Press the "Sauté" button and let it simmer for 2 to 3 minutes more or until heated through. Serve in 6-inch corn tortillas, garnished with coleslaw.

Per serving: 388 Calories; 25.9g Fat; 13.1g Carbs; 25.1g Protein; 9.4g Sugars

501. Nacho Cheese Sauce

(Ready in about 35 minutes | Servings 10)

Ingredients

2 cloves garlic, minced
1 ounce package taco
seasoning mix
1 cup Cheddar cheese,
shredded
1 cup queso fresco cheese,
crumbled
1 red chili pepper, finely
chopped
1 cup pinto beans, rinsed

1 teaspoon ground cumin
Kosher salt and ground black
pepper, to taste
1 tablespoon olive oil
1 onion, chopped
2 tablespoons fresh cilantro,
chopped
1/2 cup chunky salsa
2 cups vegetable broth

Directions

Press the "Sauté" button and heat the olive oil until sizzling. Once hot, cook the onion for 3 to 4 minutes or until tender and fragrant.

After that, stir in the garlic and chili pepper; continue sautéing an additional 30 to 40 seconds.

Stir in the beans, salsa, broth, cumin, salt, black pepper, and taco seasoning mix.

Secure the lid. Choose the "Bean/Chili" mode and cook for 25 minutes at High pressure. Once cooking is complete, use a quick pressure release; carefully remove the lid.

Then, mash your beans with a potato masher or use your blender. Return to the Instant Pot and press the "Sauté" button; stir in the cheese and let it melt on the lowest setting. Serve garnished with cilantro and enjoy!

Per serving: 146 Calories; 4.8g Fat; 17.3g Carbs; 8.1g Protein; 2.5g Sugars

502. Basic Hummus Dip

(Ready in about 45 minutes | Servings 8)

Ingredients

1 ½ cups dried chickpeas
4 cups water
1 yellow onion, chopped
2 garlic cloves, minced

3 tablespoons tahini paste
1 tablespoon olive oil
2 tablespoons fresh lemon
juice

Directions

Press the "Sauté" button to preheat your Instant Pot. Once hot, heat the olive oil until sizzling. Then, cook the onion and garlic until tender and fragrant; reserve.

Wipe down the Instant Pot with a damp cloth. Then, add the chickpeas and water to the Instant Pot.

Secure the lid and choose the "Bean/Chili" function; cook for 40 minutes at High pressure. Once cooking is complete, use a natural release; carefully remove the lid.

Drain the chickpeas, reserving cooking liquid. Now, transfer the chickpeas to your blender. Add the tahini, lemon juice, and reserved onion/garlic mixture.

Process until everything is creamy, uniform, and smooth, adding a splash of cooking liquid. Serve with pita bread and vegetable sticks.

Per serving: 206 Calories; 8.1g Fat; 26.1g Carbs; 8.8g Protein; 4.6g Sugars

503. Two-Cheese Artichoke Dip

(Ready in about 15 minutes | Servings 8)

Ingredients

1 cup Ricotta cheese
1 ¼ cups Romano cheese,
grated
12 ounces canned artichoke
hearts, chopped
1 teaspoon garlic powder
1/2 teaspoon shallot powder

1 teaspoon gourmet mustard
Salt and ground black pepper,
to taste
1/2 teaspoon cumin powder
2 cups kale, chopped
1/2 cup mayonnaise

Directions

Lightly grease a baking pan that fits inside your Instant Pot. Add all of the above ingredients and stir to combine well.

Add a metal rack to the Instant Pot.

Then, create a foil sling and place it on a rack; lower the baking pan onto the foil strip.

Secure the lid and choose "Manual" function; cook for 9 minutes at High pressure. Once cooking is complete, use a quick release; remove the lid carefully.

Serve with breadsticks on the side. Bon appétit!

Per serving: 190 Calories; 13.2g Fat; 8.3g Carbs; 10.3g Protein; 1g Sugars

504. Buttery Button Mushrooms with Herbs

(Ready in about 10 minutes | Servings 5)

Ingredients

2 tablespoons butter
20 ounces button mushrooms, brushed clean
1 teaspoon smoked paprika
Coarse sea salt and ground black pepper, to taste
1 teaspoon dried basil
1 cup vegetable broth
2 tablespoons tomato paste
2 cloves garlic, minced
1/2 teaspoon dried oregano
1/2 teaspoon dried rosemary
1 teaspoon onion powder

Directions

Place the mushrooms, garlic, spices, and broth in the inner pot.

Secure the lid. Choose the "Manual" mode and cook for 4 minutes at High pressure. Once cooking is complete, use a quick pressure release; carefully remove the lid.

Now, stir in the butter and tomato paste. Serve with cocktail sticks or toothpicks. Enjoy!

Per serving: 88 Calories; 5.5g Fat; 7.6g Carbs; 5.2g Protein; 3.6g Sugars

505. Corn on the Cob with Chips

(Ready in about 10 minutes | Servings 4)

Ingredients

1/3 cup barbecue sauce
4 ears corn on the cob, husks removed
1/2 cup potato chips, crushed

Directions

Add water and metal trivet to the base of your Instant Pot. Place ears corn on the cob on a metal trivet.

Secure the lid. Choose the "Steam" mode and cook for 2 minutes under High pressure. Once cooking is complete, use a quick release; carefully remove the lid.

Brush each corn on the cob with barbecue sauce; sprinkle with crushed chips. Bon appétit!

Per serving: 260 Calories; 5.2g Fat; 52.5g Carbs; 5.7g Protein; 7.8g Sugars

506. Buffalo Cheese and Chicken Dip

(Ready in about 25 minutes | Servings 12)

Ingredients

1 cup cream cheese, softened
2 cups cheddar cheese, shredded
10 ounces hot sauce
4 tablespoons butter
2 tablespoons fresh parsley, chopped
1 pound chicken breasts, chopped
2 tablespoons fresh chives, chopped
Salt to taste

Directions

Add the chicken breasts to the inner pot of your Instant Pot; add in the hot sauce and butter.

Secure the lid. Choose the "Manual" mode and cook for 8 minutes at High pressure. Once cooking is complete, use a quick pressure release; carefully remove the lid.

Stir in the cream cheese and salt. Spoon the chicken dip into a baking dish; top with the cheddar cheese and bake at 395 degrees F for about 8 minutes or until cheese is bubbling.

Scatter fresh parsley and chives over the top and serve warm.

Per serving: 219 Calories; 17g Fat; 2.6g Carbs; 14g Protein; 1.7g Sugars

507. 4-Ingredient Little Smokies

(Ready in about 10 minutes | Servings 12)

Ingredients

1 cup grape jelly
1 pound bacon slices
1 (12-ounce) bottle chili sauce
2 pounds Little Smokies sausage

Directions

Wrap each sausage in a piece of bacon; secure with toothpicks; place in your Instant Pot.

Add the chili sauce and grape jelly.

Secure the lid. Choose the "Manual" mode and High pressure; cook for 5 minutes. Once cooking is complete, use a quick pressure release; carefully remove the lid. Bon appétit!

Per serving: 317 Calories; 21.5g Fat; 12.8g Carbs; 17.1g Protein; 8.2g Sugars

508. Steamed Artichokes with Greek Dip

(Ready in about 20 minutes | Servings 4)

Ingredients

2 tablespoons Greek yogurt
1 tablespoon Dijon mustard
4 artichokes
4 tablespoons mayonnaise
1/2 teaspoon tzatziki spice mix

Directions

Place 1 cup of water and a steamer basket in the inner pot of your Instant Pot.

Place the artichokes in the steamer basket.

Secure the lid. Choose the "Manual" mode and cook for 11 minutes at High pressure. Once cooking is complete, use a quick pressure release; carefully remove the lid.

Meanwhile, whisk the remaining ingredients to prepare the sauce. Serve the artichokes with the Greek sauce on the side. Bon appétit!

Per serving: 177 Calories; 10.9g Fat; 17.6g Carbs; 5.8g Protein; 2.1g Sugars

509. Herb Ricotta Hummus

(Ready in about 45 minutes | Servings 10)

Ingredients

1/3 cup ricotta cheese
2 tablespoons light tahini
2 tablespoons fresh lemon juice
1/2 teaspoon cumin powder
1 teaspoon spicy brown mustard
1 teaspoon garlic, minced
1/2 teaspoon dried dill weed
1/2 teaspoon dried oregano
1/4 cup extra-virgin olive oil
1 teaspoon kosher salt
1 ½ cups dried garbanzo beans, soaked overnight
1/2 teaspoon red chili pepper
4 cups water
1 teaspoon onion powder

Directions

Add the soaked garbanzo beans with 4 cups of water to your Instant Pot.

Secure the lid and choose the "Bean/Chili" function; cook for 40 minutes at High pressure. Once cooking is complete, use a natural release; carefully remove the lid.

Drain the garbanzo beans, reserving cooking liquid. Transfer the chickpeas to your food processor. Add the olive oil, tahini, lemon juice, garlic, onion powder, dill weed, oregano, cumin powder, mustard, and salt.

Add the ricotta cheese and about 1 cup of cooking liquid; process until everything is creamy and smooth. Sprinkle red chili pepper over the top. Bon appétit!

Per serving: 153 Calories; 5.7g Fat; 19.8g Carbs; 6.7g Protein; 3.3g Sugars

510. Mini Stuffed Peppers

(Ready in about 20 minutes | Servings 5)

Ingredients

10 mini sweet bell peppers, seeds and membranes removed
1 small onion, chopped
1 garlic clove, minced
1 teaspoon Taco seasoning mix
2 tablespoons fresh cilantro, finely chopped
4 ounces bacon, chopped
6 ounces Mexican cheese blend, crumbled
1 teaspoon Worcestershire sauce

Directions

Press the "Sauté" button to preheat your Instant Pot. Now, cook the bacon until it is crisp; crumble with a spatula and reserve.

Now, cook the onion and garlic in pan drippings until just tender and fragrant. Add the cheese, Worcestershire sauce, and Taco seasoning mix. Stir in the reserved bacon.

Evenly divide the bacon/cheese mixture among the peppers.

Place a metal trivet and 1 cup of water in your Instant Pot. Arrange the stuffed peppers onto the trivet.

Secure the lid. Choose the "Manual" mode and cook for 5 minutes at High pressure. Once cooking is complete, use a natural pressure release for 5 minutes; carefully remove the lid.

Serve on a platter garnished with fresh cilantro. Enjoy!

Per serving: 234 Calories; 15.7g Fat; 11.9g Carbs; 13.3g Protein; 5.7g Sugars

511. Harvest Vegetable and Tahini Dip

(Ready in about 10 minutes | Servings 8)

Ingredients

1 head cauliflower, cut into florets
1/2 teaspoon cayenne pepper
1/2 teaspoon cumin powder
1 cup broccoli, cut into florets
2 bell pepper, chopped
2 garlic cloves, chopped
2 tomatoes, pureed
1 serrano pepper, chopped
1 celery, sliced
1 carrot, sliced
1/3 cup tahini
1 teaspoon onion powder
1 ½ cups water
Salt and ground black pepper, to taste

Directions

Add the water, cauliflower, broccoli, celery, and carrot to your Instant Pot.

Choose the "Manual" function and cook at High pressure for 3 minutes. Once cooking is complete, use a quick release; carefully remove the lid.

Then, drain the excess water out of vegetables. Transfer to a food processor and add the other ingredients. Blend until everything is well incorporated. Serve with pita bread and enjoy!

Per serving: 77 Calories; 5.5g Fat; 5.9g Carbs; 2.9g Protein; 1.7g Sugars

512. Garlicky Buttery Shrimp

(Ready in about 10 minutes | Servings 8)

Ingredients

1 ½ pounds shrimp, deveined
2 tablespoons fresh scallions, chopped
2 garlic cloves, minced
1/4 cup soy sauce
Sea salt and ground black pepper, to taste
1/2 stick butter

Directions

Throw all ingredients, except for the scallions, into the inner pot of your Instant Pot.

Secure the lid. Choose the "Manual" mode and cook for 4 minutes at High pressure. Once cooking is complete, use a quick pressure release; carefully remove the lid.

Transfer your shrimp to a nice serving bowl. The sauce will thicken as it cools. Garnish with fresh scallions and serve with toothpicks.

Per serving: 142 Calories; 6.2g Fat; 4.5g Carbs; 17.4g Protein; 3.3g Sugars

513. Turnip Greens with Sesame Seeds

(Ready in about 10 minutes | Servings 6)

Ingredients

1 pound turnip greens, leaves separated
2 tablespoons sesame seeds, toasted
1 shallot, chopped
2 garlic cloves, minced
2 teaspoons Worcestershire sauce
1 cup vegetable broth
Sea salt, to taste
1 tablespoon sesame oil
1/2 teaspoon ground black pepper
1 teaspoon red pepper flakes

Directions

Place the "Sauté" button to preheat your Instant Pot. Once hot, heat the sesame oil.

Then, cook the shallot and garlic until they are fragrant and tender. Add the turnip greens, broth, salt, black pepper, red pepper flakes, and Worcestershire sauce.

Secure the lid. Choose the "Manual" mode and High pressure; cook for 3 minutes. Once cooking is complete, use a quick pressure release; carefully remove the lid.

Sprinkle sesame seeds over the top and serve right away!

Per serving: 73 Calories; 4.3g Fat; 7.1g Carbs; 2.6g Protein; 1.2g Sugars

514. Sicilian-Style Chicken Wings

(Ready in about 25 minutes | Servings 4)

Ingredients

1 pound chicken wings, boneless
1 teaspoon Italian seasoning mix
1/4 cup Marsala wine
4 cloves garlic, smashed
1 cup chicken broth
2 bell peppers, deseeded and sliced
1 cup scallions, chopped
1/4 cup cream cheese
2 tablespoons butter, room temperature
1/4 cup all-purpose flour
Sea salt and ground black pepper, to taste

Directions

Press the "Sauté" button to preheat your Instant Pot. Melt 1 tablespoon of the butter.

Dredge your chicken in the flour; season with the spices and cook until slightly brown; reserve.

Melt the remaining tablespoon of butter and sauté the peppers, scallions, and garlic. Pour in the wine, scraping up any browned bits from the bottom of the pan. Add the chicken broth and secure the lid.

Choose the "Manual" mode and cook for 10 minutes at High pressure. Once cooking is complete, use a natural pressure release; carefully remove the lid.

Press the "Sauté" button to preheat your Instant Pot one more time. Add the cream cheese and cook for a further 4 to 5 minutes or until everything is thoroughly heated.

To serve, spoon the sauce over the chicken drumsticks. Bon appétit!

Per serving: 457 Calories; 26.3g Fat; 13.7g Carbs; 39.8g Protein; 3.1g Sugars

515. Spicy BBQ Cocktail Wieners

(Ready in about 10 minutes | Servings 12)

Ingredients

2 jalapenos, sliced
1 teaspoon garlic powder
1 teaspoon cumin powder
1/2 teaspoon mustard powder
1/2 (18-ounce) bottle barbeque sauce
1/2 cup ketchup
3 tablespoons honey
1/2 yellow onion, chopped
2 (16-ounce) packages little wieners

Directions

Add the little wieners, barbecue sauce, ketchup, honey, onion, jalapenos, garlic powder, cumin, and mustard powder to the Instant Pot. Stir to combine well.

Choose "Manual" setting and cook at Low pressure for 2 minutes.

Once cooking is complete, use a natural release; carefully remove the lid. You can thicken the sauce to your desired thickness on the "Sauté" function.

Serve warm with toothpicks. Bon appétit!

Per serving: 333 Calories; 23.4g Fat; 19.6g Carbs; 10g Protein; 13.2g Sugars

516. Mexican-Style Boozy Ribs

(Ready in about 40 minutes + marinating time | Servings 8)

Ingredients

1 tablespoon stone ground mustard
1 cup beef bone broth
1/2 teaspoon paprika
1 cup apple cider
2 tablespoons honey
1 teaspoon marjoram
1 tablespoon Sriracha sauce

2 tablespoons tomato paste
2 racks chuck short ribs
1 teaspoon garlic powder
1 teaspoon shallot powder
2 shots tequila
Kosher salt and cracked black pepper, to taste

Directions

Place all ingredients, except for the beef broth, in a ceramic dish. Cover with a foil and let it marinate for 3 hours in your refrigerator.

Place the beef along with its marinade in the inner pot. Pour in the beef bone broth.

Secure the lid. Choose the "Meat/Stew" mode and cook for 35 minutes at High pressure. Once cooking is complete, use a natural pressure release; carefully remove the lid.

Bon appétit!

Per serving: 399 Calories; 29.2g Fat; 13.3g Carbs; 20.7g Protein; 5g Sugars

517. Aromatic Baby Potato Bites

(Ready in about 15 minutes | Servings 6)

Ingredients

2 pounds baby potatoes
1/4 cup fresh Italian parsley, chopped
1 sprig rosemary, leaves only
1/2 teaspoon cayenne pepper
1 sprig thyme, leaves only

1 tablespoon olive oil
1 cup vegetable broth
1 tablespoon butter, melted
3 garlic cloves, with outer skin
Sea salt and ground black pepper, to taste

Directions

Press the "Sauté" button to preheat your Instant Pot. Once hot, warm the butter; now, cook potatoes with garlic for 5 to 6 minutes.

Add the salt, black pepper, cayenne pepper, thyme, rosemary, olive oil, and broth.

Secure the lid. Choose the "Manual" mode and High pressure; cook for 5 minutes. Once cooking is complete, use a quick pressure release; carefully remove the lid.

Scatter chopped parsley over potatoes and serve warm.

Per serving: 166 Calories; 4.6g Fat; 28.1g Carbs; 4.2g Protein; 1.6g Sugars

518. Glazed Little Smokies

(Ready in about 10 minutes | Servings 12)

Ingredients

1 jalapeno, minced
1/2 cup roasted vegetable broth
1/3 cup chili sauce
14 ounces grape jelly

2 tablespoons white vinegar
1/3 brown sugar
1/2 cup light beer
16 ounces little smokies

Directions

Place all ingredients in the inner pot of your Instant Pot.

Secure the lid. Choose the "Manual" mode and cook for 2 minutes at High pressure. Once cooking is complete, use a quick pressure release; carefully remove the lid.

Serve hot or keep on warm in your Instant Pot until ready to serve.

Per serving: 209 Calories; 16.1g Fat; 11.5g Carbs; 7g Protein; 6.2g Sugars

519. Mexican Queso Dip

(Ready in about 15 minutes | Servings 10)

Ingredients

2 cans green chiles, chopped
1 pound block processed cheese
2 cloves garlic, minced
2 cups tomatoes, pureed

2 shallots, chopped
1 pound hot breakfast sausage, ground
1 cup broth

Directions

Press the "Sauté" button to heat up your Instant Pot. Now, cook the ground sausage with shallots.

Stir in garlic and cook 30 seconds more, stirring frequently. Add the tomatoes, green chiles, and broth.

Secure the lid and choose "Manual" function; cook for 6 minutes at Low pressure. Once cooking is complete, use a quick release; remove the lid carefully.

Add the block of processed cheese and stir until it has melted. Bon appétit!

Per serving: 295 Calories; 24.2g Fat; 10.1g Carbs; 13g Protein; 2.4g Sugars

520. Tangy Chicken Wings

(Ready in about 30 minutes | Servings 4)

Ingredients

1 lime, freshly squeezed
8 chicken wings
3 cloves garlic, minced
1/2 cup chicken broth
1 teaspoon cayenne pepper
1/2 teaspoon smoked paprika
2 teaspoons butter
1/4 cup fresh cilantro, chopped
Sea salt and ground black pepper, to taste

Directions

Press the "Sauté" button and heat the olive oil until sizzling. Once hot, brown the chicken wings for 2 to 3 minutes per side.

Add in the remaining ingredients and toss to coat well.

Secure the lid. Choose the "Manual" mode and cook for 10 minutes at High pressure. Once cooking is complete, use a natural pressure release for 10 minutes; carefully remove the lid.

Broil the chicken wings for about 5 minutes or until they are golden brown. Bon appétit!

Per serving: 108 Calories; 4.3g Fat; 3.3g Carbs; 13.9g Protein; 0.9g Sugars

521. Swiss Cheese and Cauliflower Bites

(Ready in about 25 minutes | Servings 6)

Ingredients

1 cup Swiss cheese, shredded
1/2 cup Parmesan cheese, grated
2 eggs, beaten
1 pound cauliflower, broken into small florets
1 teaspoon cayenne pepper
2 tablespoons butter
2 cloves garlic, minced
Sea salt and ground black pepper, to taste
2 tablespoons fresh parsley, minced

Directions

Prepare your Instant Pot by adding 1 cup of water and a steamer basket to its bottom.

Place the cauliflower florets in the steamer basket.

Secure the lid. Choose the "Steam" mode and High pressure; cook for 3 minutes. Once cooking is complete, use a quick pressure release; carefully remove the lid.

Transfer the cauliflower florets to your blender. Add the remaining ingredients; process until everything is well incorporated.

Roll the cauliflower mixture into bite-sized balls. Bake in the preheated oven at 400 degrees F for 16 minutes. Bon appétit!

Per serving: 194 Calories; 13.8g Fat; 6.5g Carbs; 11.6g Protein; 1.8g Sugars

522. Jelly Glazed Meatballs

(Ready in about 20 minutes | Servings 8)

Ingredients

16 ounces grape jelly
1 egg
1 onion, finely chopped
2 garlic cloves, minced
1 tablespoon olive oil
1/2 pound ground chicken
1/2 pound ground turkey
1 cup tortilla chips, crumbled
1/2 teaspoon basil
Sea salt and ground black pepper, to taste

Directions

In a mixing bowl, thoroughly combine all ingredients, except for the olive oil and grape jelly. Shape the mixture into 24 meatballs.

Press the "Sauté" button and heat the olive oil. Once hot, brown meatballs for 3 to 4 minutes.

Add the grape jelly to the inner pot.

Secure the lid. Choose the "Manual" mode and cook for 6 minutes at High pressure. Once cooking is complete, use a natural pressure release for 5 minutes; carefully remove the lid.

Serve with cocktail sticks and enjoy!

Per serving: 199 Calories; 9.1g Fat; 17.2g Carbs; 12.9g Protein; 11.4g Sugars

523. Bean, Tomato and Sour Cream Dip

(Ready in about 30 minutes | Servings 12)

Ingredients

2 cups dried pinto beans, soaked overnight
2 (14.5-ounce) cans tomatoes
1 teaspoon sweet paprika
1 teaspoon mustard powder
1 red chili pepper, minced
1 cup beef bone broth
1 teaspoon marjoram, dried
2 cloves garlic, minced
1/2 cup shallots, chopped
2 heaping tablespoons fresh chives, roughly chopped
1/4 teaspoon ground bay leaves
1 cup sour cream
Sea salt and ground black pepper, to taste

Directions

Add the beans, garlic, shallots, chili pepper, tomatoes, broth, salt, black pepper, paprika, mustard powder, marjoram, and ground bay leaves to your Instant Pot.

Secure the lid. Choose "Bean/Chili" mode and High pressure; cook for 25 minutes. Once cooking is complete, use a natural pressure release; carefully remove the lid.

Transfer the bean mixture to your food processor; mix until everything is creamy and smooth. Serve topped with sour cream and fresh chives. Enjoy!

Per serving: 154 Calories; 2.6g Fat; 25.1g Carbs; 8.3g Protein; 3.1g Sugars

524. Chicken Lettuce Wraps

(Ready in about 20 minutes | Servings 4)

Ingredients

1 small head butter lettuce, leaves separated
1/2 pound chicken breasts
2 garlic cloves, minced
2 tablespoons soy sauce
2 teaspoons sesame oil
1 teaspoon ginger, minced
2 tablespoons hoisin sauce
1 small onion, finely diced
2 tablespoons rice vinegar
Kosher salt and ground black pepper, to taste

Directions

Add the chicken breasts and 1 cup of water to the inner pot of your Instant Pot.

Secure the lid. Choose the "Manual" mode and cook for 8 minutes at High pressure. Once cooking is complete, use a quick pressure release; carefully remove the lid. Shred your chicken with two forks.

Press the "Sauté" button and heat the oil. Once hot, cook the onion and garlic for 3 to 4 minutes or until they are softened.

Now, add the chicken and cook for 2 to 3 minutes more. Add the ginger, salt, black pepper, hoisin sauce, soy sauce, and rice vinegar; let it cook for a few minutes more.

Spoon the chicken mixture into the lettuce leaves, wrap them and serve immediately. Bon appétit!

Per serving: 179 Calories; 9.3g Fat; 9.7g Carbs; 13.7g Protein; 5.4g Sugars

525. Shrimp and Salad Skewers

(Ready in about 10 minutes | Servings 6)

Ingredients

1/2 cup black olives, pitted
1 ½ cups cherry tomatoes
1 red onion, cut into wedges
1 red bell pepper, sliced
1 tablespoon lime juice
1 cup water
1 teaspoon paprika
2 tablespoon apple cider vinegar
1 teaspoon oregano
2 tablespoons olive oil
1 green bell pepper, sliced
1 orange bell pepper, sliced
1/2 cup ground black pepper
1 ½ pounds shrimp, peeled and deveined
Sea salt, to taste

Directions

Place the shrimp, vinegar, lime juice, and water in your Instant Pot.

Secure the lid. Choose the "Manual" mode and High pressure; cook for 1 minute. Once cooking is complete, use a quick pressure release; carefully remove the lid.

Thread the cooked shrimp, onion, peppers, olives and cherry tomatoes onto cocktail sticks.

Drizzle olive oil over them; sprinkle with black pepper, salt, paprika, and oregano. Bon appétit!

Per serving: 185 Calories; 7.3g Fat; 5.1g Carbs; 23.9g Protein; 2.3g Sugars

526. Maple Glazed Nuts

(Ready in about 25 minutes | Servings 12)

Ingredients

1 cup almonds
1 cup pecans halves
1/2 cup maple syrup
1/4 teaspoon kosher salt
1 cup Sultanas
2 tablespoons sunflower seeds
2 tablespoons pumpkin seeds
1/4 teaspoon grated nutmeg
1 cup canned chickpeas
1/4 teaspoon ground ginger
2 tablespoons butter

Directions

Place all ingredients, except for the Sultanas, in the inner pot of your Instant Pot. Stir to combine well.

Press the "Sauté" button and cook until the butter has melted and the nuts are well coated.

Secure the lid. Choose the "Manual" mode and cook for 10 minutes at High pressure. Once cooking is complete, use a quick pressure release; carefully remove the lid.

Bake on a roasting pan at 370 degrees F for about 8 minutes. Add the Sultanas and stir to combine. Bon appétit!

Per serving: 149 Calories; 9.5g Fat; 14.6g Carbs; 2.8g Protein; 9.1g Sugars

527. Glazed and Dilled Baby Carrots

(Ready in about 15 minutes | Servings 6)

Ingredients

2 tablespoons coconut oil
1/4 cup honey
1 teaspoon dill
2 ½ pounds baby carrots, trimmed
1 teaspoon thyme
Salt and white pepper, to taste
1 ½ cups water

Directions

Add 1 ½ cups of water to the base of your Instant Pot.

Now, arrange the baby carrots in the steaming basket. Transfer the steaming basket to the Instant Pot.

Secure the lid and choose the "Manual" function; cook for 3 minutes at High pressure. Once cooking is complete, use a quick release; carefully remove the lid.

Strain the baby carrots and reserve.

Then, add the other ingredients to the Instant Pot. Press the "Sauté" button and cook until everything is heated through.

Add the reserved baby carrots and gently stir. Bon appétit!

Per serving: 151 Calories; 4.8g Fat; 28g Carbs; 1.3g Protein; 21.1g Sugars

528. Short Ribs with Herbs and Molasses

(Ready in about 1 hour 45 minutes | Servings 8)

Ingredients

3 pounds short ribs
1 tablespoon lard
4 cloves of garlic
1 teaspoon cayenne pepper
2 tablespoons rice vinegar
2 tablespoons molasses

2 rosemary sprigs
2 thyme sprigs
1 cup beef bone broth
1/2 cup port wine
Sea salt and ground black pepper, to season

Directions

Press the "Sauté" button and melt the lard. Once hot, cook the short ribs for 4 to 5 minutes, turning them periodically to ensure even cooking.

Add the other ingredients.

Secure the lid. Choose the "Manual" mode and cook for 90 minutes at High pressure. Once cooking is complete, use a natural pressure release; carefully remove the lid.

Afterwards, place the short ribs under the broiler until the outside is crisp or about 10 minutes. Transfer the ribs to a platter and serve immediately.

Per serving: 372 Calories; 27.6g Fat; 4.9g Carbs; 25.7g Protein; 3.4g Sugars

529. Popcorn with A Twist

(Ready in about 10 minutes | Servings 4)

Ingredients

1/2 tablespoon ground cinnamon
1/2 cup popcorn kernels

1/4 cup icing sugar
2 tablespoons coconut oil

Directions

Press the "Sauté" button and melt the coconut oil. Stir until it begins to simmer.

Stir in the popcorn kernels and cover. When the popping slows down, press the "Cancel" button.

Toss the freshly popped corn with icing sugar and cinnamon. Toss to evenly coat the popcorn and serve immediately.

Per serving: 295 Calories; 11.5g Fat; 42.2g Carbs; 6.3g Protein; 6.6g Sugars

530. BBQ Glazed Ribs

(Ready in about 25 minutes | Servings 6)

Ingredients

1/2 teaspoon ancho chili powder
1/2 cup whiskey
1/2 teaspoon mustard seeds
1 ½ pounds baby back ribs
1 teaspoon celery seeds
1/4 cup rice vinegar
1 teaspoon fish sauce
1 teaspoon Worcestershire sauce

1 teaspoon salt
1/2 teaspoon ground black pepper
1 teaspoon smoked paprika
1 cup ketchup
1/3 cup dark brown sugar
1/2 teaspoon granulated garlic
1 teaspoon shallot powder

Directions

Season the ribs with salt, black pepper, paprika, chili powder, garlic, shallot powder, mustard seeds, and celery seeds.

Add the seasoned ribs to the Instant Pot.

In a mixing bowl, thoroughly combine the whiskey, ketchup, sugar, vinegar, fish sauce, and Worcestershire sauce.

Then, pour the sauce into the Instant Pot.

Secure the lid and choose the "Meat/Stew" function; cook for 20 minutes at High pressure. Once cooking is complete, use a natural release; carefully remove the lid. Reserve the ribs.

Press the "Sauté" button to preheat your Instant Pot. Simmer the sauce until it has reduced to your desired thickness. Pour the glaze over the ribs and serve. Bon appétit!

Per serving: 359 Calories; 17.9g Fat; 28g Carbs; 22.8g Protein; 25.1g Sugars

531. Minty Fava Bean Dip

(Ready in about 50 minutes | Servings 10)

Ingredients

1 pound fava beans, rinsed
1 teaspoon garlic, minced
Sea salt and ground black pepper, to taste
1 tablespoon fresh mint leaves, roughly chopped

1 teaspoon basil
1/2 cup Kalamata olives, pitted
1 tablespoon olive oil
1 red onion, finely chopped
1 teaspoon oregano
Juice of 1/2 lemon

Directions

Press the "Sauté" button and heat the oil. Once hot, cook the onion until tender and translucent.

Now, stir in the garlic and let it cook for 30 seconds more, stirring frequently. Then, add the salt, pepper, fava beans, basil, and oregano. Add enough water to fully submerge the beans.

Secure the lid. Choose the "Bean/Chili" mode and cook for 40 minutes at High pressure. Once cooking is complete, use a natural pressure release for 5 minutes; carefully remove the lid.

Add the lemon juice and puree the mixture with an immersion blender, Transfer to a nice serving bowl and serve garnished with Kalamata olives and mint leaves. Enjoy!

Per serving: 178 Calories; 2.5g Fat; 29.4g Carbs; 11g Protein; 1.7g Sugars

532. Paprika Mushroom Bites

(Ready in about 10 minutes | Servings 5)

Ingredients

1/3 cup water
2 garlic cloves, minced
1 teaspoon paprika
1 tablespoon peanut butter
1 tablespoon molasses
2 tablespoons olive oil
1 tablespoon apple cider vinegar

3 tablespoons soy sauce
1/2 teaspoon hot sauce
Sea salt and ground black pepper, to taste
20 ounces fresh white mushrooms

Directions

Add all ingredients to your Instant Pot.

Secure the lid. Choose the "Manual" mode and High pressure; cook for 5 minutes. Once cooking is complete, use a quick pressure release; carefully remove the lid; remove the mushrooms from the cooking liquid.

Then, press the "Sauté" button and continue to simmer until the sauce has reduced and thickened.

Place the reserved mushrooms in a serving bowl, add the sauce and serve.

Per serving: 124 Calories; 8.1g Fat; 10.2g Carbs; 4.4g Protein; 7.7g Sugars

533. Baby Carrots with Sesame Seeds and Raisins

(Ready in about 10 minutes | Servings 6)

Ingredients

2 tablespoons sesame seeds, toasted
1/2 cup water
2 tablespoons soy sauce
1 teaspoon mustard powder
1/4 teaspoon cumin seeds
1 teaspoon garlic powder
1/2 teaspoon shallot powder

2 tablespoons raisins
2 teaspoons butter, at room temperature
2 pounds baby carrots, trimmed and scrubbed
1/2 cup orange juice
2 tablespoons Shaoxing wine

Directions

Place all ingredients, except for the sesame seeds, in the inner pot of your Instant Pot.

Secure the lid. Choose the "Manual" mode and cook for 2 minutes at High pressure. Once cooking is complete, use a quick pressure release; carefully remove the lid.

Serve in a nice bowl, sprinkle the sesame seeds over the top and enjoy!

Per serving: 110 Calories; 4.5g Fat; 17.2g Carbs; 2.3g Protein; 8.1g Sugars

534. Dijon-Glazed Sausages

(Ready in about 15 minutes | Servings 8)

Ingredients

1 teaspoon Dijon mustard
1/2 teaspoon Szechuan pepper
1 teaspoon cayenne pepper
2 tablespoons tamari sauce
1 tablespoon rice vinegar
1 teaspoon chili powder
10 hot dogs, chopped into thirds

1/2 teaspoon fresh ginger, peeled and grated
2 teaspoons toasted sesame oil
1/2 cup ketchup
1/3 cup chicken stock
Salt, to taste

Directions

Add all of the above ingredients to the Instant Pot.

Secure the lid. Choose "Manual" mode and High pressure; cook for 5 minutes. Once cooking is complete, use a quick pressure release; carefully remove the lid.

Serve with cocktail sticks; garnish with sesame seeds if desired. Enjoy!

Per serving: 270 Calories; 20g Fat; 5.4g Carbs; 16.4g Protein; 3.5g Sugars

535. Butter Mushrooms with Herbs

(Ready in about 20 minutes | Servings 3)

Ingredients

1 pound white mushrooms
2 garlic cloves, minced
3 tablespoons butter
1 teaspoon cayenne pepper

1 thyme sprig, chopped
1 rosemary sprig, chopped
Sea salt and ground black pepper, to taste

Directions

Press the "Sauté" button and melt the butter. Once hot, cook your mushrooms for about 4 minutes, stirring occasionally to ensure even cooking.

Add the garlic and spices; toss to coat.

Secure the lid. Choose the "Manual" mode and cook for 12 minutes at High pressure. Once cooking is complete, use a natural pressure release for 5 minutes; carefully remove the lid. Serve warm.

Per serving: 147 Calories; 12.2g Fat; 8.7g Carbs; 3.5g Protein; 3.6g Sugars

536. Calamari Bites with Herbs and Wine

(Ready in about 15 minutes | Servings 6)

Ingredients

1 pound squid, cleaned and sliced into rings
1 cup dry white wine
4 garlic cloves, whole
2 teaspoons olive oil
1 heaping tablespoon fresh cilantro leaves, chopped
1 cup tomatoes, puréed
1 cup chicken stock
1 fresh lemon, cut into wedges
1 teaspoon dried basil
1 teaspoon dried marjoram
Sea salt and ground black pepper, to taste
1/2 teaspoon red pepper flakes
1 teaspoon dried rosemary

Directions

Press the "Sauté" button to preheat your Instant Pot. Once hot, heat the olive oil. Then, sauté the squid with garlic for 3 to 4 minutes or so.

Add a splash of wine to deglaze the bottom of the Instant Pot.

Now, add the basil, rosemary, marjoram, puréed tomatoes, chicken stock, salt, black pepper, and red pepper flakes.

Secure the lid. Choose the "Manual" mode and cook for 4 minutes under High pressure. Once cooking is complete, use a natural release; carefully remove the lid.

Serve garnished with fresh cilantro leaves and lemon wedges. Enjoy!

Per serving: 155 Calories; 6.9g Fat; 5.7g Carbs; 17.1g Protein; 1.3g Sugars

537. Easy Asparagus Bites

(Ready in about 10 minutes | Servings 2)

Ingredients

1 teaspoon garlic powder
1 tablespoon sesame oil
2 tablespoons sesame seeds, toasted
Kosher salt and red pepper, to taste
1 pound fresh asparagus, trimmed

Directions

Add 1 cup of water and a steamer basket to the inner pot. Place the asparagus in the steamer basket.

Secure the lid. Choose the "Steam" mode and cook for 3 minutes at High pressure. Once cooking is complete, use a quick pressure release; carefully remove the lid.

Toss the warm asparagus with the other ingredients. Enjoy!

Per serving: 156 Calories; 11.9g Fat; 9.7g Carbs; 6.6g Protein; 4.3g Sugars

538. Sweet Potato Bites

(Ready in about 1 hour 5 minutes | Servings 10)

Ingredients

1 onion, chopped
1 cup blue cheese, crumbled
2 eggs, whisked
2/3 cup breadcrumbs
1 garlic clove, minced
1/2 teaspoon ground allspice
1 teaspoon dried marjoram
1 teaspoon basil
2 pounds sweet potatoes, peeled and diced
1/2 stick butter, softened
Sea salt and ground black pepper, to taste

Directions

Prepare your Instant Pot by adding 1 ½ cups of water and a metal trivet to its bottom. Lower the sweet potatoes onto the trivet.

Secure the lid. Choose the "Manual" mode and cook for 15 minutes under High pressure. Once cooking is complete, use a natural release; carefully remove the lid.

Peel and mash the prepared sweet potatoes with the onion, garlic, and all of the seasonings. Now, stir in the softened butter, cheese, and eggs.

Place this mixture in your refrigerator for 30 minutes; then, shape into bite-sized balls.

Coat each ball with breadcrumbs. Now, sprits the balls with a nonstick cooking spray. Bake the balls in the preheated oven at 425 degrees F approximately 15 minutes. Bon appétit!

Per serving: 200 Calories; 10.6g Fat; 19.7g Carbs; 7.1g Protein; 1.8g Sugars

539. Italian-Style Broccoli with Mayonnaise

(Ready in about 10 minutes | Servings 4)

Ingredients

3 garlic cloves, smashed
1 tablespoon Italian seasoning mix
1/2 cup mayonnaise
1 pound broccoli florets
Kosher salt and ground black pepper, to taste

Directions

Add 1 cup of water and steamer basket to the inner pot. Place the broccoli florets in the steamer basket.

Secure the lid. Choose the "Manual" mode and cook for 1 minute at High pressure. Once cooking is complete, use a quick pressure release; carefully remove the lid.

Sprinkle the garlic, salt, and black pepper over the cooked broccoli florets.

Mix the mayonnaise with the Italian seasoning mix; serve your broccoli with the Italian mayo on the side. Bon appétit!

Per serving: 227 Calories; 21.2g Fat; 6.4g Carbs; 4.5g Protein; 1.4g Sugars

540. Borani or Kashkeh Bademjoon

(Ready in about 10 minutes | Servings 10)

Ingredients

1/4 cup tahini, plus more as needed
1/3 teaspoon cayenne pepper
1/4 cup brine-cured black olives, brine-cured
1/2 cup yellow onion, chopped
1 teaspoon fresh oregano, chopped
1/4 teaspoon ground black pepper, or more to taste
1 cup water
1 garlic cloves, roasted and 1 raw, crushed
Sea salt, to taste
3 tablespoons olive oil
1 tablespoon fresh lime juice
3/4 pound eggplant

Directions

Add water to the base of your Instant Pot. Now, choose the "Manual" and cook eggplant in the steaming basket for 4 minutes at High Pressure.

Once cooking is complete, use a quick release; remove the lid carefully.

Drain the excess water out of the eggplant. Then, peel and slice the eggplant.

Press the "Sauté" button and add the oil. Once hot, cook the eggplant with onions and garlic until they have softened.

Season with salt, oregano, cayenne pepper, and ground black pepper. Transfer the mixture to your blender or food processor.

Add the lime juice, tahini, and olives. Blend until everything is well incorporated. Serve well chilled and enjoy!

Per serving: 209 Calories; 18.9g Fat; 8.5g Carbs; 4.6g Protein; 1.5g Sugars

541. German-Style Krautsalat

(Ready in about 10 minutes | Servings 4)

Ingredients

1 pound purple cabbage, shredded
Kosher salt and ground black pepper, to taste
1/2 cup green onions, sliced
2 tablespoons soy sauce
2 tablespoons olive oil
3 cloves garlic, minced
2 carrots, cut into sticks

Directions

Press the "Sauté" button and add the oil. Once hot, cook the garlic and green onions until softened.

Add the cabbage, carrots, salt, and black pepper.

Secure the lid. Choose the "Manual" mode and cook for 4 minutes at High pressure. Once cooking is complete, use a quick pressure release.

Lastly, add the soy sauce to the cabbage mixture and stir to combine well. Place in a serving bowl and serve immediately.

Per serving: 136 Calories; 8.4g Fat; 14.5g Carbs; 2.8g Protein; 7.6g Sugars

542. Chicken Nacho Sauce

(Ready in about 15 minutes | Servings 16)

Ingredients

1 cup Mexican cheese blend, grated
1 tablespoon jalapeño, seeded and minced
10 ounces tortilla chips, baked
2 bell peppers, chopped
1 cup beef stock
20 ounces tomato, puréed
1/2 cup avocado, chopped
1 pound chicken breasts, boneless and skinless

Directions

Place the chicken, tomato, peppers, and stock in your Instant Pot.

Secure the lid. Choose the "Manual" mode and High pressure; cook for 7 minutes. Once cooking is complete, use a natural pressure release; carefully remove the lid.

Add the Mexican cheese blend to the Instant Pot. Seal the lid and let it sit until warmed through.

Shred the chicken with two forks; top with the chopped avocado and serve with tortilla chips. Enjoy!

Per serving: 145 Calories; 6.5g Fat; 11.6g Carbs; 9.8g Protein; 1.9g Sugars

543. Ranch Potato Bites

(Ready in about 20 minutes | Servings 4)

Ingredients

1 teaspoon fresh parsley, chopped
1/2 cup sour cream
1 teaspoon fresh chives, chopped
4 tablespoons reduced-fat mayonnaise
1 garlic clove, minced
4 large Yukon gold potatoes
Sea salt and ground black pepper, to taste

Directions

Add 1 ½ cups of water and a steamer basket to the inner pot. Now, place the potatoes in the steamer basket.

Secure the lid. Choose the "Steam" mode and cook for 10 minutes at High pressure. Once cooking is complete, use a quick pressure release; carefully remove the lid.

Meanwhile, in a mixing bowl, whisk together the sour cream and mayonnaise. Stir in the fresh herbs, garlic, salt, and black pepper.

Drain your potatoes, peel and slice them; toss your potatoes with ranch dressing. Bon appétit!

Per serving: 379 Calories; 9.4g Fat; 66.7g Carbs; 8.5g Protein; 2.9g Sugars

544. Ricotta and Chicken Dipping Sauce

(Ready in about 10 minutes | Servings 12)

Ingredients

1 cup barbecue sauce
3 ounces blue cheese dressing
1 parsnip, chopped
1/2 teaspoon dried rosemary
6 ounces Ricotta cheese
Sea salt, to taste

1/2 teaspoon cayenne pepper
1 pound chicken white meat, boneless
1/4 teaspoon ground black pepper, or more to taste
1/3 cup water

Directions

Place all of the above ingredients in your Instant Pot.

Secure the lid. Choose the "Manual" mode and High pressure; cook for 6 minutes. Once cooking is complete, use a natural pressure release; carefully remove the lid.

Transfer to a nice serving bowl and serve warm or at room temperature. Bon appétit!

Per serving: 179 Calories; 7.5g Fat; 14.3g Carbs; 12.9g Protein; 10.3g Sugars

545. Zingy Cauliflower Bites with Tahini Sauce

(Ready in about 15 minutes | Servings 4)

Ingredients

1/3 cup tahini
Kosher salt and freshly ground black pepper, to taste
2 tablespoons fresh parsley, chopped
2 cloves garlic, grated

1 tablespoon olive oil
1 teaspoon agave syrup
1 pound cauliflower florets
2 tablespoons freshly squeezed lemon juice

Directions

Place 1 cup of water and a steamer basket in your Instant Pot. Place the cauliflower florets in the steamer basket.

Secure the lid. Choose the "Steam" mode and cook for 3 minutes at High pressure. Once cooking is complete, use a quick pressure release; carefully remove the lid.

Press the "Sauté" button and heat the oil. Roast the cauliflower florets for 2 to 3 minutes, stirring periodically to ensure even cooking.

Whisk the tahini, lemon juice, garlic agave syrup, salt, and black pepper until everything is well incorporated. Drizzle the tahini sauce over the roasted cauliflower and garnish with fresh parsley. Enjoy!

Per serving: 185 Calories; 14.2g Fat; 12.8g Carbs; 5.4g Protein; 3.7g Sugars

546. Broccoli Tots with Colby Cheese

(Ready in about 30 minutes | Servings 8)

Ingredients

1 cup Colby cheese, grated
1 head of broccoli, broken into florets
1 garlic clove, minced
2 eggs, beaten
1 tablespoon fresh coriander, chopped

Sea salt and ground black pepper, to taste
1 tablespoon fresh parsley, chopped
1 ½ cups water
1 white onion, minced

Directions

Add 1 cup of water and a steamer basket to the bottom of your Instant Pot. Place the broccoli florets in the steamer basket.

Secure the lid and choose the "Steam" mode; cook for 6 minutes under High pressure. Once cooking is complete, use a quick release; carefully remove the lid.

Allow the broccoli florets to cool completely; then, add the remaining ingredients.

Mash the mixture and shape into tots with oiled hands.

Place the broccoli tots on a lightly greased baking sheet. Bake in the preheated oven at 390 degrees F approximately 18 to 20 minutes, flipping them once. Bon appétit!

Per serving: 142 Calories; 8.1g Fat; 9.6g Carbs; 9.5g Protein; 2.7g Sugars

547. Sausage and Cheese-Stuffed Mushrooms

(Ready in about 15 minutes | Servings 5)

Ingredients

1/2 pound smoked pork sausage, crumbled
1/2 cup cheddar cheese, shredded
2 tablespoons fresh parsley leaves, roughly chopped
4 ounces cream cheese, softened

1/2 cup vegetable broth
1 shallot, finely chopped
2 cloves garlic, minced
20 button mushrooms, stems removed
1/2 cup seasoned breadcrumbs

Directions

Clean your mushrooms and set them aside.

Press the "Sauté" button to preheat your Instant Pot. Then, brown the sausage until it is fully cooked.

Stir in the shallot and garlic; cook for a further 4 minutes, or until they have softened. Scoop this mixture out of the inner pot into a mixing bowl. Stir in the cream cheese, breadcrumbs, and cheddar cheese.

Now, add a splash of the vegetable broth to deglaze the pan. Press the "Cancel" button.

Next, fill the mushroom caps with the stuffing mixture. Arrange the mushrooms in the bottom of the inner pot.

Secure the lid. Choose the "Manual" mode and cook for 5 minutes at High pressure. Once cooking is complete, use a quick pressure release; carefully remove the lid.

Sprinkle fresh parsley leaves on top before serving and enjoy!

Per serving: 254 Calories; 20.3g Fat; 7.2g Carbs; 11.5g Protein; 2.7g Sugars

548. Turkey Cocktail Meatballs

(Ready in about 15 minutes | Servings 8)

Ingredients

1 cup button mushrooms, chopped
2 pounds turkey, ground
3/4 cup broth, preferably homemade
2 garlic cloves, minced
1 teaspoon dried oregano
2 sprigs rosemary, leaves picked
1 parsnip, grated

2 carrots, grated
2 tablespoons olive oil
3 ripe tomatoes, pureed
2 sprigs thyme, leaves picked
2 shallots, peeled and finely chopped
Sea salt and ground black pepper, to taste
1/2 cup all-purpose flour

Directions

In a mixing bowl, combine the shallots, garlic, parsnip, carrots, mushrooms, flour, salt, pepper, and ground turkey.

Shape the mixture into small cocktail meatballs.

Press the "Sauté" button and heat the olive oil. Once hot, sear the meatballs on all sides until they are browned.

Thoroughly combine the pureed tomatoes, oregano, rosemary, and thyme. Pour in tomato mixture and broth. Secure the lid.

Now, choose the "Manual" function; cook for 9 minutes at High pressure. Once cooking is complete, use a natural release; remove the lid carefully.

Serve with cocktail sticks or toothpicks. Bon appétit!

Per serving: 319 Calories; 21.9g Fat; 12.6g Carbs; 17.5g Protein; 3g Sugars

549. Easy Buttery Sweet Potatoes

(Ready in about 30 minutes | Servings 5)

Ingredients

1/2 stick butter
5 medium sweet potatoes, scrubbed

1 cup water

Directions

Place 1 cup of water and a steamer basket in your Instant Pot. Place the sweet potatoes in the steamer basket.

Secure the lid. Choose the "Manual" mode and cook for 15 minutes at High pressure. Once cooking is complete, use a natural pressure release for 10 minutes; carefully remove the lid.

Garnish with butter and serve. Bon appétit!

Per serving: 196 Calories; 9.3g Fat; 26.7g Carbs; 2.1g Protein; 8.7g Sugars

550. Creole Boiled Peanuts

(Ready in about 1 hour 25 minutes | Servings 8)

Ingredients

2 tablespoons Creole seasoning
Water
1 ½ pounds raw peanuts in the shell, rinsed an cleaned
1 teaspoon lemon pepper

2 tablespoons red pepper flakes
1 teaspoon garlic powder
1/2 cup salt
3 jalapenos, sliced

Directions

Place the peanuts and salt in your Instant Pot; cover with water. Add all seasonings and stir to combine.

Place a trivet on top to hold down the peanuts.

Secure the lid and choose the "Manual" mode. Cook for 1 hour 20 minutes at High pressure.

Once cooking is complete, use a natural release; remove the lid carefully. Enjoy!

Per serving: 340 Calories; 28.1g Fat; 13.6g Carbs; 14.1g Protein; 3.6g Sugars

551. Winter Vegetable Puree

(Ready in about 10 minutes | Servings 4)

Ingredients

1/2 pound pumpkin, cut into small pieces
1/2 teaspoon basil
2 cloves garlic, crushed
1/2 teaspoon thyme

1/2 pound carrots, quartered
1/2 pound parsnip, quartered
1/2 teaspoon rosemary
2 tablespoons butter

Directions

Add the carrots, parsnips, and pumpkin to the inner pot of your Instant Pot. Pour in 1 cup of water.

Secure the lid. Choose the "Manual" mode and cook for 6 minutes at High pressure. Once cooking is complete, use a quick pressure release; carefully remove the lid.

Drain your vegetables and mash them with a potato masher.

Press the "Sauté" button and melt the butter; the, sauté the aromatics for 1 minute or so. Add the vegetable mash and stir to combine well.

Transfer to a nice serving bowls and garnish with some extra herbs if desired. Bon appétit!

Per serving: 134 Calories; 6.3g Fat; 19.8g Carbs; 2g Protein; 6.9g Sugars

552. Dad's Barbecued Wings

(Ready in about 20 minutes | Servings 3)

Ingredients

6 chicken wings
1 cup water
For the Barbecue Sauce:
1 tablespoon olive oil
1/4 teaspoon freshly ground black pepper
1/4 teaspoon ground allspice
2 tablespoons brown sugar

2 tablespoons blackstrap molasses
1 tablespoon mustard
1 teaspoon chipotle powder
1 tablespoon cider vinegar
1 teaspoon garlic, minced
1/3 cup water
1/3 cup ketchup
1/4 teaspoon sea salt

Directions

Pour 1 cup of water into the base of your Instant Pot.

Now, arrange the wings in the steaming basket. Transfer the steaming basket to the Instant Pot.

Secure the lid and choose the "Poultry" function; cook for 15 minutes at High pressure. Once cooking is complete, use a natural release; carefully remove the lid.

In a pan, combine all of the ingredients for the sauce and bring to a boil. Remove from the heat and stir well. Add the chicken wings and serve. Bon appétit!

Per serving: 204 Calories; 6.7g Fat; 23.1g Carbs; 13.2g Protein; 20.1g Sugars

553. Mixed Vegetable Appetizer

(Ready in about 10 minutes | Servings 4)

Ingredients

1/2 pound acorn squash
2 cloves garlic, minced
2 cups roasted vegetable broth
1/2 pound broccoli florets
4 medium waxy potatoes, peeled and cubed

2 carrots, cut into 1-inch pieces
2 parsnips, cut into 1-inch pieces
2 tablespoons butter, at room temperature

Directions

Press the "Sauté" button and melt the butter. Once hot, sauté the garlic until aromatic but not browned.

Stir in the remaining ingredients.

Secure the lid. Choose the "Manual" mode and cook for 4 minutes at High pressure. Once cooking is complete, use a quick pressure release; carefully remove the lid.

Add some extra butter if desired and serve warm. Bon appétit!

Per serving: 329 Calories; 7.3g Fat; 60g Carbs; 9.8g Protein; 8.5g Sugars

554. Buttery Brussels Sprout Bites

(Ready in about 10 minutes | Servings 4)

Ingredients

1 ½ pounds Brussels sprouts, trimmed and halved
2 tablespoons butter
Salt, to taste
1/4 cup dry white wine

1 cup water
1/4 teaspoon ground black pepper, or more to taste
1/2 cup shallots, chopped

Directions

Press the "Sauté" button to preheat your Instant Pot. Once hot, melt the butter and sauté the shallots until tender.

Add a splash of wine to deglaze the bottom of the Instant Pot. Add the remaining ingredients to the Instant Pot.

Secure the lid. Choose the "Manual" mode and High pressure; cook for 4 minutes. Once cooking is complete, use a quick pressure release; carefully remove the lid. Bon appétit!

Per serving: 145 Calories; 7.7g Fat; 15.5g Carbs; 7.3g Protein; 3.8g Sugars

555. Italian-Style Cauliflower Salad

(Ready in about 10 minutes + chilling time | Servings 3)

Ingredients

1 red onion, thinly sliced
1 teaspoon hot mustard
4 ounces mozzarella cheese, crumbled
1/4 cup extra-virgin olive oil
2 tablespoons fresh lime juice
1/2 cup fresh flat-leaf parsley, coarsely chopped

1/4 cup green olives, pitted and coarsely chopped
Sea salt and ground black pepper, to taste
1 pound cauliflower florets
2 bell peppers, thinly sliced

Directions

Add 1 cup of water and steamer basket to the inner pot. Place the cauliflower in the steamer basket.

Secure the lid. Choose the "Steam" mode and cook for 2 minutes at High pressure. Once cooking is complete, use a quick pressure release; carefully remove the lid.

Toss the cooked cauliflower with peppers, onion, parsley, and olives. In a small bowl, prepare the salad dressing by mixing the olive oil, lime juice, mustard, salt, and black pepper.

Dress your salad and serve garnished with the crumbled mozzarella cheese. Bon appétit!

Per serving: 188 Calories; 8.4g Fat; 14.8g Carbs; 16.3g Protein; 6.2g Sugars

556. Gourmet Spicy Deviled Eggs

(Ready in about 20 minutes | Servings 8)

Ingredients

8 eggs
Crunchy sea salt, to taste
3 tablespoons fresh chives, thinly sliced
1 tablespoon sour cream
1 teaspoon gourmet mustard
1/2 teaspoon hot sauce
1/3 teaspoon ground black pepper
3 teaspoons mayonnaise
1 ½ cups water

Directions

Pour the water into the base of your Instant Pot.

Now, arrange the eggs in the steaming basket. Transfer the steaming basket to the Instant Pot.

Secure the lid and choose the "Manual" function; cook for 13 minutes at Low pressure. Once cooking is complete, use a quick release; remove the lid carefully.

Peel the eggs under running water. Remove the yolks and smash them with a fork; reserve.

Now, mix the mayonnaise, sour cream, gourmet mustard, hot sauce, black pepper, and salt; add reserved yolks and mash everything.

Fill the whites with this mixture, heaping it lightly. Garnish with fresh chives and place in the refrigerator until ready to serve. Bon appétit!

Per serving: 138 Calories; 10.4g Fat; 1.2g Carbs; 9.1g Protein; 0.7g Sugars

557. Artichokes with Garlic-Mayo Dip

(Ready in about 20 minutes | Servings 3)

Ingredients

1 bay leaf
1 teaspoon garlic, pressed
2 tablespoons fresh parsley, minced
Sea salt, to taste
1/2 cup mayonnaise
1 lemon wedge
3 medium artichokes, trimmed
1 cup water

Directions

Place water and bay leaf in the inner pot. Rub the lemon wedge all over the outside of the prepared artichokes. Season them with salt.

Place the artichokes in the steamer basket; lower the steamer basket into the inner pot.

Secure the lid. Choose the "Manual" mode and cook for 11 minutes at High pressure. Once cooking is complete, use a quick pressure release; carefully remove the lid.

Meanwhile, mix the mayonnaise with the garlic and parsley. Serve the artichokes with the mayo dip on the side. Bon appétit!

Per serving: 331 Calories; 27.7g Fat; 18.8g Carbs; 5.8g Protein; 2.3g Sugars

558. Party Chicken Bites

(Ready in about 30 minutes | Servings 6)

Ingredients

1/2 teaspoon mixed peppercorns, crushed
1/3 cup ketchup
1 teaspoon garlic powder
1/2 stick butter, melted
2 tablespoons hot sauce
1/2 teaspoon cayenne pepper
1 teaspoon shallot powder
1 tablespoon fish sauce
1 ½ pounds chicken wings
Kosher salt, to taste

Directions

Prepare your Instant Pot by adding 1 cup of water and metal trivet to its bottom. Place the chicken wings on the trivet.

Secure the lid. Choose the "Manual" mode and High pressure; cook for 6 minutes. Once cooking is complete, use a natural pressure release; carefully remove the lid.

Toss the chicken wings with the remaining ingredients.

Arrange chicken wings, top side down, on a broiler pan. Place rack on top. Broil for 10 minutes; flip over and broil for 10 minutes more.

Top with remaining sauce and serve immediately.

Per serving: 212 Calories; 10.7g Fat; 4.6g Carbs; 23.6g Protein; 3.2g Sugars

559. Decadent Broccoli Salad

(Ready in about 10 minutes | Servings 3)

Ingredients

1/2 cup scallions, chopped
1 tablespoon fresh lemon juice
1/2 cup mayonnaise
1/2 cup sour cream
1/4 cup sesame seeds, toasted
1 tablespoon balsamic vinegar
1/4 cup raisins
1/4 cup sunflower seeds, to toasted
1 pound broccoli florets
Sea salt and ground black pepper, to taste

Directions

Add 1 cup of water and steamer basket to the inner pot. Place the broccoli florets in the steamer basket.

Secure the lid. Choose the "Manual" mode and cook for 1 minute at High pressure. Once cooking is complete, use a quick pressure release; carefully remove the lid.

Transfer the chilled broccoli florets to a nice salad bowl. Add the salt, black pepper, scallions, raisins, and seeds to the salad bowl.

Next, stir in the balsamic vinegar, lemon juice, mayo, and sour cream. Bon appétit!

Per serving: 407 Calories; 33.8g Fat; 20.1g Carbs; 11.3g Protein; 5.2g Sugars

560. Cajun Meat Dipping Sauce

(Ready in about 20 minutes | Servings 10)

Ingredients

1/2 pound ground beef
2 ripe tomatoes, chopped
1 teaspoon harissa spice blend
1/2 teaspoon cayenne pepper
1 teaspoon sea salt
1/2 cup leeks, finely chopped
1 garlic clove, minced

1/2 teaspoon ground black pepper, to taste
1 ½ teaspoons Cajun seasonings
2 tablespoons canola oil
1 pound ground pork

Directions

Press the "Sauté" button and heat the oil. Once hot, cook the ground meat, stirring with a Silicone spatula so that it gets broken up as it cooks.

Stir in the leeks and garlic; cook until they are tender and fragrant. Stir in the Cajun seasonings, harissa spice blend, cayenne pepper, sea salt, and ground black pepper.

Add the pureed tomatoes and secure the lid. Now, choose the "Manual" mode and cook for 13 minutes at High pressure.

Once cooking is complete, use a natural release; remove the lid carefully. Serve with fresh veggie sticks. Bon appétit!

Per serving: 226 Calories; 15.4g Fat; 2.2g Carbs; 18.6g Protein; 0.8g Sugars

561. Traditional Sofrito Sauce

(Ready in about 20 minutes | Servings 6)

Ingredients

4 cloves garlic, minced
2 onions, chopped
1/2 bunch parsley leaves, roughly chopped
2 teaspoons paprika

2 sweet peppers, chopped
10 tomatoes, pureed
5 tablespoons extra-virgin olive oil

Directions

Press the "Sauté" button and heat 2 tablespoons of olive oil until sizzling. Now, sauté the onion until just tender and fragrant.

Add the garlic and peppers and continue to sauté an additional minute or until fragrant. Add the other ingredients.

Secure the lid. Choose the "Manual" mode and cook for 4 minutes at High pressure. Once cooking is complete, use a natural pressure release for 10 minutes; carefully remove the lid.

Let your sofrito cool completely and store in the refrigerator for a week. Enjoy!

Per serving: 178 Calories; 12.4g Fat; 16.7g Carbs; 3.4g Protein; 7.1g Sugars

562. Habanero BBQ Almond Popcorn

(Ready in about 10 minutes | Servings 4)

Ingredients

1/4 cup popcorn kernels
2 tablespoons Habanero BBQ almonds
Sea salt, to taste

A pinch of sugar
3 tablespoons butter, at room temperature

Directions

Press the "Sauté" button to heat up the Instant Pot. Melt the butter until sizzling.

Stir in the popcorn kernels; stir until they are covered with melted butter.

Once the popcorn starts popping, cover with the lid. Shake for a few seconds.

Now, turn off the Instant Pot when 2/3 of kernels have popped. Allow all kernels to pop.

Add salt and Habanero BBQ almonds; toss and serve immediately. Enjoy!

Per serving: 119 Calories; 9.5g Fat; 7.3g Carbs; 1.3g Protein; 0.1g Sugars

563. Yellow Bean and Tofu Bowl

(Ready in about 15 minutes | Servings 4)

Ingredients

1 ½ pounds yellow beans
1 cup smoked tofu cubes
2 sweet peppers, seeded and sliced
2 stalks green garlic, sliced
2 tablespoons fresh cilantro, roughly chopped
Coarse sea salt, to taste

1 red chili pepper, seeded and minced
1 cup scallions, chopped
2 tablespoons freshly squeezed lemon juice
1/2 cup coconut milk
2 tablespoons olive oil

Directions

Mix the olive oil, lemon juice, and coconut milk in your blender or food processor. Reserve.

Place 1 cup of water and a steamer basket in the inner pot of your Instant Pot. Place the yellow beans in the steamer basket.

Secure the lid. Choose the "Manual" mode and cook for 3 minutes at High pressure. Once cooking is complete, use a quick pressure release; carefully remove the lid.

Toss the chilled yellow beans with the other ingredients, including the reserved dressing; toss to combine well. Serve well chilled and enjoy!

Per serving: 232 Calories; 9g Fat; 33.3g Carbs; 8g Protein; 3.7g Sugars

564. Spicy Party Mix

(Ready in about 25 minutes | Servings 10)

Ingredients

1/2 teaspoon Tabasco sauce
1 cup raw walnuts, halved
2 cups raw almonds
1/3 cup raw pumpkin seeds
Salt and black pepper, to taste
2 tablespoons light brown sugar
1/2 teaspoon dried oregano
1/3 cup raw sunflower seeds
1 cup roasted peas
2 tablespoons butter
2 cups puffed-rice cereal
1/2 teaspoon cayenne pepper
1/2 teaspoon garlic powder

Directions

Press the "Sauté" button to heat up the Instant Pot. Now, melt the butter.

Add the other ingredients and stir until they are coated with butter; add water as needed. Secure the lid.

Select the "Manual" mode and cook for 11 minutes at High pressure. Once cooking is complete, use a natural release; carefully remove the lid.

Transfer the mixture to a parchment-lined cookie sheet.

Next, preheat your oven to 365 degrees F. Bake the party mix for 8 minutes, turning halfway through cooking time. Store in an airtight container. Bon appétit!

Per serving: 208 Calories; 16.8g Fat; 16.9g Carbs; 6.5g Protein; 3.1g Sugars

565. Candied Baby Carrots

(Ready in about 15 minutes | Servings 4)

Ingredients

3 tablespoons butter
1/4 teaspoon white pepper
1/2 teaspoon cayenne pepper
2 tablespoons molasses
1/2 teaspoon kosher salt
1 ½ pounds baby carrots

Directions

Add water and a steamer basket to the inner pot of your Instant Pot. Place the carrots in the steamer basket.

Secure the lid. Choose the "Steam" mode and cook for 3 minutes at High pressure. Once cooking is complete, use a quick pressure release; carefully remove the lid.

Discard the water and press the "Sauté" button. Once hot, melt the butter. Stir in the cooked carrots, molasses, salt, white pepper, and cayenne pepper. Sauté approximately 2 minutes, stirring frequently. Serve warm.

Per serving: 165 Calories; 8.8g Fat; 21.5g Carbs; 1.8g Protein; 15.5g Sugars

566. Perfect Cheeseburger Dip

(Ready in about 15 minutes | Servings 10)

Ingredients

10 ounces Colby cheese, shredded
1 tablespoon Worcestershire sauce
10 ounces Ricotta cheese, crumbled
1 pound ground turkey
2 cups ripe tomato purée
1/4 cup vegetable broth
1 tablespoon canola oil
1 onion, chopped
1 clove garlic, chopped

Directions

Press the "Sauté" button to preheat your Instant Pot. Once hot, heat the oil.

Then, cook the ground turkey, onion and garlic for 2 to 3 minutes or until the meat is no longer pink. Add the tomato purée, broth, and Worcestershire sauce.

Secure the lid. Choose the "Manual" mode and High pressure; cook for 5 minutes. Once cooking is complete, use a quick pressure release; carefully remove the lid.

Now, stir in the cheese. Stir until everything is well incorporated; serve immediately.

Per serving: 253 Calories; 17.7g Fat; 4.2g Carbs; 19.3g Protein; 1.6g Sugars

567. Traditional Dijon and Carrot Salad

(Ready in about 10 minutes + chilling time | Servings 4)

Ingredients

1 teaspoon honey
1 tablespoon Dijon mustard
1/4 teaspoon red pepper flakes
2 scallions, finely sliced
1 tablespoon lime juice
2 tablespoons olive oil
1/4 teaspoon ground white pepper, to taste
1 ½ pounds carrots, sliced to 2-inch chunks
1/2 teaspoon Himalayan salt

Directions

Add 1 cup of water and a steamer basket to the inner pot of your Instant Pot.

Place the carrots in the steamer basket.

Secure the lid. Choose the "Steam" mode and cook for 3 minutes at High pressure. Once cooking is complete, use a quick pressure release; carefully remove the lid.

Toss your carrots with the remaining ingredients and serve chilled. Enjoy!

Per serving: 141 Calories; 7.3g Fat; 18.9g Carbs; 1.4g Protein; 9.9g Sugars

568. Pizza-Style Dipping Sauce

(Ready in about 10 minutes | Servings 10)

Ingredients

8 ounces pancetta, chopped
2/3 cup beef bone broth
9 ounces Mozzarella cheese, crumbled
1 teaspoon dried oregano
1 teaspoon dried basil
1 teaspoon dried marjoram
1/2 cup green olives, pitted and halved

1 bell pepper, chopped
1 teaspoon garlic powder
1 teaspoon shallot powder
1 teaspoon porcini powder
2 ripe Roma tomatoes, puréed
6 ounces Parmigiano-Reggiano cheese, grated
8 ounces Asiago cheese, grated

Directions

Combine all ingredients, except for the Parmigiano-Reggiano cheese, in your Instant Pot.

Secure the lid. Choose the "Manual" mode and High pressure; cook for 5 minutes. Once cooking is complete, use a quick pressure release; carefully remove the lid.

Top with the Parmigiano-Reggiano cheese; cover and allow it to sit in the residual heat until the cheese has melted. Bon appétit!

Per serving: 209 Calories; 11.4g Fat; 5.3g Carbs; 21.1g Protein; 3.3g Sugars

569. Apple and Rutabaga Salad

(Ready in about 15 minutes | Servings 4)

Ingredients

1 Granny Smith apple, cored and diced
1 teaspoon Dijon mustard
1 tablespoon agave syrup
1/4 cup almonds, slivered

2 tablespoons fresh lemon juice
1 pound rutabaga, peeled and cut into 1/4-inch chunks
1/2 pound cabbage, shredded
1/4 cup olive oil

Directions

Add 1 cup of water and a steamer basket to the inner pot of your Instant Pot. Now, place the rutabaga in the steamer basket.

Secure the lid. Choose the "Manual" mode and cook for 6 minutes at High pressure. Once cooking is complete, use a quick pressure release; carefully remove the lid.

Toss the rutabaga chunks with the cabbage, apple, and almonds. Mix the remaining ingredients to prepare the salad dressing.

Dress your salad and serve chilled. Enjoy!

Per serving: 222 Calories; 13.9g Fat; 24.4g Carbs; 2.3g Protein; 15.6g Sugars

570. Smoked Sausage Cheese Dip

(Ready in about 20 minutes | Servings 12)

Ingredients

1 teaspoon yellow mustard
1 teaspoon basil
1/2 cup sour cream
1 pound turkey smoked sausage
2 red chili peppers, minced
1 teaspoon oregano

1 (28-ounce) can tomatoes, crushed
1/2 cup water
1 (8-oz) package cream cheese, at room temperature
1 tablespoon canola oil

Directions

Press the "Sauté" button to preheat your Instant Pot. Once hot, heat the oil. Then, cook the sausage until it is delicately browned, crumbling it with a fork.

Then, add the canned tomatoes, water, peppers, mustard, basil, and oregano.

Secure the lid. Choose the "Manual" mode and cook for 6 minutes under High pressure. Once cooking is complete, use a natural release; carefully remove the lid.

Add the cream cheese and sour cream; seal the lid. Allow it to sit for at least 5 minutes or until heated through. Serve with tortilla chips or pretzel bun bites. Enjoy!

Per serving: 157 Calories; 11.4g Fat; 6.3g Carbs; 8.1g Protein; 4.1g Sugars

FISH & SEAFOOD

571. Fish en Papillote

(Ready in about 15 minutes | Servings 4)

Ingredients

1 cup cherry tomatoes, halved
4 teaspoon olive oil
1 onion, sliced
2 garlic cloves, minced
1 red bell pepper, sliced
1 green bell pepper, sliced
1 teaspoon dried rosemary

1 teaspoon basil
1/2 teaspoon oregano
12 ounces halibut steaks, cut into four pieces
1/2 teaspoon paprika
Sea salt and ground black pepper, to taste

Directions

Place 1 cup of water and a metal trivet in the bottom of the inner pot.

Place 4 large sheets of heavy-duty foil on a flat surface. Divide the ingredients between sheets of foil. Add a splash of water.

Bring the ends of the foil together; fold in the sides to seal. Place the fish packets on the trivet.

Secure the lid. Choose the "Steam" mode and cook for 10 minutes at Low pressure. Once cooking is complete, use a quick pressure release; carefully remove the lid. Bon appétit!

Per serving: 238 Calories; 16.4g Fat; 9.5g Carbs; 13.5g Protein; 6.5g Sugars

572. Portuguese Seafood Stew

(Ready in about 15 minutes | Servings 4)

Ingredients

2 tablespoons peanut oil
1 ½ cups seafood stock
1 teaspoon Piri Piri
2 bay leaves
2 fresh tomatoes, puréed
1 tablespoon loosely packed saffron threads
1 yellow onion, chopped
1 celery with leaves, chopped
2 carrots, chopped
2 cloves garlic, minced

1 green bell pepper, thinly sliced
1/3 cup dry vermouth
Sea salt and ground black pepper, to taste
1/4 cup fresh cilantro, roughly chopped
1 pound fish, mixed pieces for fish soup, cut into bite-sized pieces
1/2 lemon, sliced

Directions

Simply throw all of the above ingredients, except for the cilantro and lemon, into your Instant Pot.

Secure the lid and choose the "Manual" setting. Cook for 8 minutes at Low pressure. Once cooking is complete, use a quick release; carefully remove the lid.

Ladle the medley into individual bowls; serve with fresh cilantro and lemon. Enjoy!

Per serving: 342 Calories; 20.8g Fat; 14.7g Carbs; 24.6g Protein; 9.2g Sugars

573. Wine-Braised Blue Crab

(Ready in about 15 minutes | Servings 4)

Ingredients

1/2 cup dry white wine
2 sprigs rosemary
2 sprigs thyme
1 lemon, cut into wedges

1/2 cup water
Sea salt and ground black pepper, to taste
2 pounds frozen blue crab

Directions

Add the frozen crab legs, water, wine, salt, black pepper, rosemary, and thyme to the inner pot.

Secure the lid. Choose the "Manual" mode and cook for 3 minutes at High pressure. Once cooking is complete, use a quick pressure release; carefully remove the lid.

Serve warm, garnished with fresh lemon wedges. Bon appétit!

Per serving: 145 Calories; 4.3g Fat; 2.1g Carbs; 23.7g Protein; 0.9g Sugars

574. Thai-Style Mussels with Beer

(Ready in about 15 minutes | Servings 4)

Ingredients

1 ½ pounds mussels, cleaned and debearded
1 (12-ounce) bottles lager beer
2 cloves garlic, minced
2 medium-sized ripe tomatoes, puréed
Sea salt and freshly ground black pepper, to taste

2 Thai chili peppers, stemmed and split
1 tablespoon olive oil
1/2 cup scallions, chopped
1 cup water
1 tablespoon fresh cilantro, chopped

Directions

Press the "Sauté" button to preheat your Instant Pot. Heat the oil and cook the scallions until tender and fragrant.

Then, stir in the garlic and cook an additional 30 seconds or until fragrant. Add the remaining ingredients.

Secure the lid and choose the "Manual" setting. Cook for 3 minutes at Low pressure. Once cooking is complete, use a quick release; carefully remove the lid.

Serve with garlic croutons. Bon appétit!

Per serving: 241 Calories; 7.3g Fat; 15.3g Carbs; 21.9g Protein; 3g Sugars

575. Seafood and Rice Hotpot

(Ready in about 25 minutes | Servings 4)

Ingredients

1 pound shrimp
2 sweet peppers, deveined and sliced
1 tablespoon olive oil
1/2 pound chicken breasts, cubed
Sea salt and ground black pepper, to taste
1 tablespoon cornstarch
1 habanero pepper, deveined and sliced
1 cup chicken bone broth

2 bay leaves
1 teaspoon oregano
1 teaspoon sage
1 teaspoon basil
1 onion, chopped
4 cloves garlic, minced
1 tablespoon fish sauce
1 cup jasmine rice
1 teaspoon paprika
1 tablespoon butter

Directions

Combine the rice, butter and 1 ½ cups of water in a pot and bring to a rapid boil. Cover and let it simmer on low for 15 minutes. Fluff with a fork and reserve.

Press the "Sauté" button and heat the oil. Once hot, cook the chicken breasts for 3 to 4 minutes, stirring periodically.

Add the remaining ingredients, except for the cornstarch.

Secure the lid. Choose the "Manual" mode and cook for 3 minutes at Low pressure. Once cooking is complete, use a quick pressure release; carefully remove the lid.

Mix the cornstarch with 2 tablespoons of cold water. Add the cornstarch slurry to the cooking liquid and stir on the "Sauté" mode until the sauce thickens.

Serve over hot jasmine rice. Bon appétit!

Per serving: 492 Calories; 13.1g Fat; 52.1g Carbs; 41.2g Protein; 2.6g Sugars

576. Spanish-Style Spicy Calamari

(Ready in about 1 hour | Servings 4)

Ingredients

1 ½ pounds frozen calamari, thawed and drained
1 teaspoon dried thyme, chopped
2 cloves garlic chopped
1/3 cup dry sherry
1/2 teaspoon red pepper flakes, crushed
1 ½ cups stock, preferably homemade

1 teaspoon dried rosemary, chopped
2 tablespoons fresh chives, chopped
2 tablespoons olive oil
1/2 cup leeks, chopped
3 Pimentos, stem and core removed
Seas salt and ground black pepper, to taste
2 tablespoons fish sauce

Directions

Split your Pimentos into halves and place them over the flame. Cook, turning a couple of times, until the skin is blistering and blackened.

Allow them to stand for 30 minutes; peel your Pimentos and coarsely chop them.

Press the "Sauté" button to heat up your Instant Pot; add olive oil. Once hot, cook the leeks until tender and fragrant, about 4 minutes.

Now, stir in the garlic and cook an additional 30 seconds or until just browned and aromatic.

Add the stock, fish sauce, dry sherry, salt, pepper, red pepper flakes, rosemary, and thyme. Add roasted Pimentos. Lastly, place calamari on top. Pour in 3 cups of water.

Secure the lid. Select the "Manual" mode. Cook for 20 minutes at High pressure. Once cooking is complete, use a quick release; remove the lid carefully.

Serve warm garnished with fresh chopped chives. Enjoy!

Per serving: 325 Calories; 10.7g Fat; 17.2g Carbs; 38.6g Protein; 6.5g Sugars

577. Traditional Spicy Gumbo

(Ready in about 15 minutes | Servings 4)

Ingredients

1 tablespoon Creole seasoning
1/4 cup ketchup
1 pound tuna, cut into 2-inch chunks
2 ripe tomatoes, pureed
1 jalapeno pepper, sliced
2 carrots, sliced
1 teaspoon filé powder
2 celery stalks, diced
1 cup beef broth

2 tablespoons Worcestershire sauce
1 pound raw shrimp, deveined
1 shallot, diced
1 sweet pepper, sliced
Sea salt and freshly ground black pepper, to taste
2 tablespoons butter, melted
1 bay leaf

Directions

Press the "Sauté" button and melt the butter. Once hot, cook the shallot and peppers for about 3 minutes until just tender and fragrant.

Add the remaining ingredients; gently stir to combine.

Secure the lid. Choose the "Manual" mode and cook for 5 minutes at High pressure. Once cooking is complete, use a quick pressure release; carefully remove the lid. Serve in individual bowls and enjoy!

Per serving: 339 Calories; 8.7g Fat; 18g Carbs; 47.3g Protein; 8.5g Sugars

578. Rich Tuna and Green Pea Soup

(Ready in about 15 minutes | Servings 5)

Ingredients

1 ½ cups frozen green peas
4 slices ham, chopped
1/2 teaspoon mustard powder
1 ½ cups double cream
2 carrots, chopped
1 ¼ pounds tuna steak, diced
5 cups seafood stock

1 teaspoon cayenne pepper
1/2 teaspoon ground bay leaf
1 cup shallots, chopped
2 cloves garlic, minced
2 tablespoons olive oil
Sea salt and ground black pepper, to taste

Directions

Press the "Sauté" button to preheat your Instant Pot. Heat the oil and fry the ham until crispy.

Then, add the shallot and garlic; continue to cook an additional 2 minutes or until tender and fragrant.

Add the carrot, stock, tuna, salt, black pepper, cayenne pepper, ground bay leaf, and mustard powder.

Secure the lid. Choose the "Manual" mode and High pressure; cook for 6 minutes. Once cooking is complete, use a natural pressure release; carefully remove the lid.

Add the double cream and frozen peas. Press the "Sauté" button again and cook for a couple of minutes more or until heated through. Bon appétit!

Per serving: 360 Calories; 11.2g Fat; 25.7g Carbs; 38.5g Protein; 9.6g Sugars

579. Mussels with Wine-Scallion Sauce

(Ready in about 10 minutes | Servings 4)

Ingredients

1 ½ pounds frozen mussels, cleaned and debearded
1 cup water
2 tablespoons butter
1 bunch scallion, chopped
1/2 cup cooking wine
2 garlic cloves, sliced

Directions

Add the water, wine, and garlic to the inner pot. Add a metal rack to the inner pot.

Put the mussels into the steamer basket; lower the steamer basket onto the rack.

Secure the lid. Choose the "Steam" mode and cook for 3 minutes at Low pressure. Once cooking is complete, use a quick pressure release; carefully remove the lid.

Press the "Sauté" button and add butter and scallions; let it cook until the sauce is thoroughly heated and slightly thickened. Press the "Cancel" button and add the mussels. Serve warm. Bon appétit!

Per serving: 225 Calories; 9.6g Fat; 7.8g Carbs; 20.4g Protein; 0.4g Sugars

580. Seafood with Halloumi Cheese and Olives

(Ready in about 10 minutes | Servings 4)

Ingredients

1 ½ pounds prawns, cleaned
6 ounces Halloumi cheese, sliced
1 teaspoon dried oregano
2 ripe tomatoes, chopped
1/2 cup Kalamata olives, pitted and sliced
2 garlic cloves, minced
Sea salt and ground black pepper, to taste
1/2 teaspoon cayenne pepper, or more taste
2 tablespoons fresh cilantro, chopped
1 tablespoon olive oil
1/2 cup scallions, chopped

Directions

Press the "Sauté" button to preheat your Instant Pot. Then, heat the oil; sauté the scallions and garlic until tender and fragrant.

Add the salt, black pepper, cayenne pepper, oregano, tomatoes, and prawns.

Secure the lid. Choose the "Manual" mode and Low pressure; cook for 3 minutes. Once cooking is complete, use a quick pressure release; carefully remove the lid.

Ladle into serving bowls; top each serving with cheese, olives and fresh cilantro. Bon appétit!

Per serving: 351 Calories; 16.6g Fat; 11.9g Carbs; 37.8g Protein; 5.6g Sugars

581. Tarragon Tuna Fillets

(Ready in about 10 minutes | Servings 2)

Ingredients

A few sprigs of tarragon
1 pound tuna filets
1 tablespoon butter, melted
1 large onion, sliced into rings
1 cup water
1 lemon, sliced
Sea salt and freshly ground black pepper, to taste

Directions

Put the water, herbs and lemon slices in the inner pot; now, place the steamer rack in the inner pot.

Lower the tuna fillets onto the rack. Add the butter, salt, and pepper; top with onion slices.

Secure the lid. Choose the "Steam" mode and cook for 3 minutes at Low pressure. Once cooking is complete, use a quick pressure release; carefully remove the lid. Serve immediately.

Per serving: 333 Calories; 7g Fat; 8.7g Carbs; 56.3g Protein; 3.7g Sugars

582. Spicy and Saucy Halibut

(Ready in about 15 minutes | Servings 4)

Ingredients

1 pound halibut steaks, rinsed and cubed
1 cup coconut milk, unsweetened
1 tablespoon olive oil
Salt and ground black pepper, to taste
1 teaspoon ginger garlic paste
1 tablespoon red curry paste
1/2 teaspoon ground cumin
1 cup scallions, chopped
1/2 cup beef bone broth
1 cup tomato purée
1 jalapeño pepper, seeded and minced

Directions

Press the "Sauté" button to preheat your Instant Pot. Now, heat the olive oil; cook the scallions until tender and fragrant.

Then, use the broth to deglaze the bottom of the inner pot. Stir in the remaining ingredients.

Secure the lid. Choose the "Manual" mode and Low pressure; cook for 7 minutes. Once cooking is complete, use a quick pressure release; carefully remove the lid.

Taste, adjust the seasonings and serve right now.

Per serving: 325 Calories; 10.7g Fat; 17.2g Carbs; 38.6g Protein; 6.5g Sugars

583. Cheesy Cod Fish

(Ready in about 10 minutes | Servings 4)

Ingredients

1 ½ pounds cod fish fillets
1 cup goat cheese, crumbled
1/2 teaspoon smoked paprika
2 tablespoons fresh Italian parsley, chopped
2 cloves garlic, minced

2 tablespoons coconut oil, at room temperature
Sea salt and freshly ground pepper, to taste
1 pound baby potatoes
1/2 teaspoon fresh ginger, grated

Directions

Place the potatoes in the bottom of the inner pot. Add 1 cup of water; then, add coconut oil, salt and pepper. Place the rack over the potatoes.

Place the cod fish fillets on the rack. Season the fillets with paprika and parsley.

Secure the lid. Choose the "Steam" mode and cook for 3 minutes at Low pressure. Once cooking is complete, use a quick pressure release; carefully remove the lid.

Remove the salmon and the rack from the inner pot. Continue to cook the potatoes until fork tender; add the ginger and garlic and cook for 2 minutes more.

Top with goat cheese and serve. Bon appétit!

Per serving: 390 Calories; 17.6g Fat; 20.8g Carbs; 36.5g Protein; 1.1g Sugars

584. Tilapia with Herb-Mushroom Sauce

(Ready in about 15 minutes | Servings 3)

Ingredients

1 cup Cremini mushrooms, thinly sliced
2 sprigs rosemary, leaves picked
2 tablespoons avocado oil
1 teaspoon cayenne pepper
1/2 cup yellow onions, sliced

2 cloves garlic, peeled and minced
2 sprigs thyme, leaves picked
3 tilapia fillets
1/2 teaspoon sea salt
Freshly ground black pepper, to taste

Directions

Season the tilapia fillets with salt, black pepper, and cayenne pepper on all sides. Place the tilapia fillets in the steaming basket fitted for your Instant Pot.

Place the sliced mushroom and yellow onions on top of the fillets. Add the garlic, thyme, and rosemary; drizzle avocado oil over everything.

Add 1 ½ cups of water to the base of your Instant Pot. Add the steaming basket to the Instant Pot and secure the lid.

Select the "Manual" mode. Cook for 8 minutes at Low pressure.

Once cooking is complete, use a quick release; remove the lid carefully. Serve immediately.

Per serving: 218 Calories; 12.9g Fat; 2.2g Carbs; 23.6g Protein; 0.7g Sugars

585. Italian-Style Sole with Vegetables

(Ready in about 20 minutes | Servings 4)

Ingredients

1 pound sole fillets
2 tablespoons fresh Italian parsley
1 cup beef stock
1 ripe tomato, puréed
1 pound fennel, quartered

1 small shallot, quartered
4 cloves garlic, sliced
1 lemon, cut into wedges
2 tablespoons coconut oil
Salt and ground black pepper, to taste

Directions

Press the "Sauté" button and melt the coconut oil. Once hot, sauté the shallot and garlic until tender and aromatic.

Add the beef stock, tomato, salt, pepper, and fennel.

Secure the lid. Choose the "Manual" mode and cook for 10 minutes at High pressure. Once cooking is complete, use a quick pressure release; carefully remove the lid.

Then, remove all the vegetables with a slotted spoon and reserve, keeping them warm.

Add the sole fillets to the inner pot. Secure the lid. Choose the "Steam" mode and cook for 3 minutes at Low pressure. Once cooking is complete, use a quick pressure release; carefully remove the lid.

Garnish the fish fillets with lemon and parsley; serve with the reserved vegetables. Enjoy!

Per serving: 218 Calories; 9.8g Fat; 16.6g Carbs; 18.2g Protein; 8.2g Sugars

586. Lemony Grouper Filets

(Ready in about 15 minutes | Servings 4)

Ingredients

2 tablespoons fresh lemon juice
4 grouper filets
2 garlic cloves, smashed
1/2 teaspoon dried basil

4 tablespoons butter
Sea salt and ground black pepper, to taste
1/2 teaspoon sweet paprika

Directions

Add 1 ½ cups of water and steamer basket to the Instant Pot. Then, place the fish fillets in the steamer basket.

Add the butter; drizzle with lemon juice; add the garlic, paprika, basil, salt, and black pepper.

Secure the lid. Choose the "Manual" mode and Low pressure; cook for 4 minutes. Once cooking is complete, use a quick pressure release; carefully remove the lid.

Serve immediately.

Per serving: 344 Calories; 14.1g Fat; 1.1g Carbs; 50.1g Protein; 0.2g Sugars

587. Japanese-Style Pollock Curry

(Ready in about 15 minutes | Servings 4)

Ingredients

1 onion, chopped
1 package Japanese curry roux
2 tablespoons Shoyu sauce
2 ripe tomatoes, pureed
1/2 pound shrimps, deveined
2 tablespoons sesame oil
1 (3-inch) kombu (dried kelp)
1 (1-inch) pieces fresh ginger, ground

1 red chili, deseeded and minced
2 tablespoons butter, softened
2 cloves garlic, minced
1 pound pollock, cut into large chunks
1 tablespoon garam masala
1 teaspoon curry paste

Directions

Press the "Sauté" button and melt the butter; cook the onion, garlic, ginger, and red chili until just tender and fragrant.

Add the pollack and shrimp and continue to sauté for a couple of minutes more. Add the remaining ingredients.

Secure the lid. Choose the "Manual" mode and cook for 5 minutes at Low pressure. Once cooking is complete, use a quick pressure release; carefully remove the lid.

Serve your curry over hot steamed rice. Enjoy!

Per serving: 390 Calories; 25.5g Fat; 7.1g Carbs; 34.4g Protein; 3.2g Sugars

588. Tuna with Tangy Butter Sauce

(Ready in about 15 minutes | Servings 3)

Ingredients

1 ½ tablespoons sesame oil, melted
1 cup water
1 tablespoon fresh cilantro, chopped
1/2 teaspoon salt
1/4 teaspoon black pepper, to taste

1/4 teaspoon smoked paprika
3 tuna steaks
For the Sauce:
1 tablespoon fresh lime juice
1 tablespoon butter, at room temperature
1 teaspoon Worcestershire sauce

Directions

Brush the tuna steaks with sesame oil. Season the tuna steaks with salt, black pepper, and smoked paprika.

Place the fish in the steaming basket; transfer it to the Instant Pot.

Pour 1 cup of water into the base of your Instant Pot. Secure the lid.

Choose "Manual" mode, Low pressure and 4 minutes. Once cooking is complete, use a quick release; carefully remove the lid.

Meanwhile, warm the butter over medium-low heat. Add the lime juice and Worcestershire sauce; remove from heat and stir until everything is well incorporated.

Spoon the sauce over the tuna steaks, sprinkle with fresh cilantro leaves and serve. Bon appétit!

Per serving: 316 Calories; 18g Fat; 1g Carbs; 35.4g Protein; 0.3g Sugars

589. Saucy Tilapia with Spinach

(Ready in about 15 minutes | Servings 4)

Ingredients

1 pound tilapia, cut into 4 pieces
1 tablespoon Worcestershire sauce
2 cloves garlic, sliced

2 tablepsoons butter, melted
2 cups fresh spinach
1 cup chicken broth
Salt and ground black pepper, to taste

Directions

Place the chicken broth and garlic in the inner pot. Place the trivet on top.

Place the tilapia fillets on a sheet of foil; add Worcestershire sauce, salt, pepper, and butter. Bring up all sides of the foil to create a packet around your fish.

Secure the lid. Choose the "Steam" mode and cook for 10 minutes at Low pressure. Once cooking is complete, use a quick pressure release; carefully remove the lid.

Add the spinach leaves to the cooking liquid. Press the "Sauté" function and let it simmer for 1 to 2 minutes or until wilted.

Place the fish fillets on top of the wilted spinach, adjust the seasonings, and serve immediately. Bon appétit!

Per serving: 265 Calories; 11.9g Fat; 2.7g Carbs; 36.5g Protein; 0.7g Sugars

590. Red Snapper in Tomatillo Sauce

(Ready in about 15 minutes | Servings 4)

Ingredients

1 pound red snapper, cut into bite-sized chunks
1 cup chicken stock, preferably homemade
2 shallots, peeled and chopped
2 tablespoons coriander
1 (11-ounce) can tomatillo, chopped

2 tablespoons tomato ketchup
Salt and freshly ground black pepper, to taste
1/2 stick butter, at room temperature
2 garlic cloves, minced
1 cup brown mushrooms, thinly sliced

Directions

Press the "Sauté" button to preheat your Instant Pot. Then, melt the butter. Once hot, cook the shallots with garlic until tender and aromatic.

Stir in the mushrooms; cook an additional 3 minutes or until they have softened.

Stir the remaining ingredients into your Instant Pot.

Secure the lid and choose the "Manual" setting. Cook for 6 minutes at High pressure. Once cooking is complete, use a quick release; carefully remove the lid.

Serve over hot basmati rice if desired. Enjoy!

Per serving: 242 Calories; 13.6g Fat; 3.7g Carbs; 25.7g Protein; 1.7g Sugars

591. Japanese Teriyaki Salmon

(Ready in about 15 minutes | Servings 4)

Ingredients

4 (6-ounce) salmon steaks
2 tablespoons brown sugar
2 teaspoons wine vinegar
2 cloves garlic, smashed
1/3 cup soy sauce

1 (1-inch) piece fresh ginger, peeled and grated
1 tablespoon cornstarch
2 tablespoons butter, melted
1/2 cup water

Directions

Press the "Sauté" button and melt the butter. Once hot, cook the salmon steaks for 2 minutes per side.

Add the garlic, ginger, soy sauce, water, sugar, and vinegar.

Secure the lid. Choose the "Manual" mode and cook for 5 minutes at Low pressure. Once cooking is complete, use a quick pressure release; carefully remove the lid. Reserve the fish steaks.

Mix the cornstarch with 2 tablespoons of cold water. Add the slurry to the cooking liquid. Let it simmer until the sauce thickens. Spoon the sauce over the fish steaks. Bon appétit!

Per serving: 325 Calories; 16.1g Fat; 11.5g Carbs; 31.8g Protein; 7.9g Sugars

592. Hungarian Parikash (Harcsapaprikás)

(Ready in about 15 minutes | Servings 4)

Ingredients

2 bell peppers, seeded and sliced
Sea salt and ground black pepper, to taste
2 tomatoes, puréed
2 garlic cloves, minced
2 tablespoons fresh cilantro, roughly chopped
1 teaspoon sweet paprika
1 teaspoon hot paprika

2 cups vegetable broth
2 sprigs thyme
1 sprig rosemary
2 cups water
1 ½ pounds cod fish, cut into bite-sized chunks
2 tablespoons butter, at room temperature
1 cup leeks, chopped
1 cup sour cream, well-chilled

Directions

Press the "Sauté" button to preheat your Instant Pot. Melt the butter and sauté the leeks until fragrant.

Then, stir in the peppers and garlic and continue to sauté an additional 40 seconds.

Add the thyme, rosemary, paprika, salt, black pepper, tomatoes, broth, water, and fish.

Secure the lid and choose the "Manual" setting. Cook for 6 minutes at High pressure. Once cooking is complete, use a quick release; carefully remove the lid.

Ladle into individual bowls and serve garnished with fresh cilantro and well-chilled sour cream. Bon appétit!

Per serving: 310 Calories; 13.7g Fat; 14.4g Carbs; 32.3g Protein; 4.5g Sugars

593. Peppery Tilapia Filets

(Ready in about 10 minutes | Servings 4)

Ingredients

4 (6-ounce) tilapia fillets, skin on
Sea salt and white pepper, to taste
1 lemon, sliced
1 red onion, sliced into rings
2 sweet peppers, julienned

1 tablespoon fresh parsley, chopped
1 tablespoon fresh tarragon, chopped
4 tablespoons dry white wine
4 teaspoons olive oil

Directions

Place the lemon slices, 1 cup of water and a metal trivet in the bottom of the inner pot.

Place 4 large sheets of heavy-duty foil on a flat surface. Divide the ingredients between the sheets of foil.

Bring the ends of the foil together; fold in the sides to seal. Place the fish packets on the trivet.

Secure the lid. Choose the "Steam" mode and cook for 3 minutes at Low pressure. Once cooking is complete, use a quick pressure release; carefully remove the lid. Bon appétit!

Per serving: 239 Calories; 7.6g Fat; 8.5g Carbs; 35.6g Protein; 1.3g Sugars

594. Creole Fish Stew

(Ready in about 15 minutes | Servings 4)

Ingredients

2 (6-ounce) cans crab, juice reserved
2 garlic cloves, smashed
1 tablespoon Creole seasoning
2 carrots, diced
1/2 pound cod, cut into bite-sized chunks
Sea salt, to taste

1/2 teaspoon freshly ground black pepper
1 cup double cream
1 tablespoon lemon juice
1 tablespoon olive oil
2 shallots, diced
2 bay leaves
2 cups water

Directions

Press the "Sauté" button to preheat your Instant Pot. Then, heat the oil and sauté the shallots until tender.

Stir in the garlic and carrots; cook an additional minute or so. Add the canned crab meat, cod, salt, black pepper, bay leaves, Creole seasoning, and water.

Secure the lid and choose the "Manual" setting. Cook for 6 minutes at High pressure. Once cooking is complete, use a quick release; carefully remove the lid.

Lastly, stir in the double cream and lemon juice. Press the "Sauté" button one more time; let it simmer until heated through. Enjoy!

Per serving: 254 Calories; 15.4g Fat; 15.5g Carbs; 13.9g Protein; 7.9g Sugars

595. Mix-and-Match Fish Packets

(Ready in about 10 minutes | Servings 4)

Ingredients

Sea salt and white pepper, to taste

1/2 pound sugar snap peas, trimmed

2 tablespoons olive oil

2 garlic cloves, minced

1 tablespoon fresh chives, chopped

1 tablespoon fresh parsley, chopped

2 tomatillos, sliced

4 (7-ounces) rainbow trout fillets

Directions

Place 1 cup of water and a metal rack in your Instant Pot.

Place all ingredients in a large sheet of foil. Fold up the sides of the foil to make a bowl-like shape. Lower the fish packet onto the rack.

Secure the lid. Choose the "Steam" mode and cook for 3 minutes at Low pressure. Once cooking is complete, use a quick pressure release; carefully remove the lid. Bon appétit!

Per serving: 285 Calories; 12.5g Fat; 6.9g Carbs; 34.6g Protein; 3.5g Sugars

596. Sole with Tartar Sauce

(Ready in about 10 minutes | Servings 4)

Ingredients

1 tablespoon pickle juice

1/2 cup mayonnaise

2 cloves garlic, smashed

1 ½ pounds sole fillets

1 teaspoon paprika

Sea salt and ground black pepper, to taste

Directions

Sprinkle the fillets with salt, black pepper, and paprika.

Add 1 ½ cups of water and a steamer basket to the Instant Pot. Place the fish in the steamer basket.

Secure the lid and choose "Manual" setting. Cook for 3 minutes at Low pressure. Once cooking is complete, use a quick release; carefully remove the lid.

Then, make the sauce by mixing the mayonnaise with the pickle juice and garlic. Serve the fish fillets with the well-chilled sauce on the side. Bon appétit!

Per serving: 211 Calories; 12.0g Fat; 3.9g Carbs; 22.3g Protein; 1.1g Sugars

597. Honey-Orange Sea Bass

(Ready in about 15 minutes | Servings 4)

Ingredients

1 tablespoon honey

1 orange, juiced

1 pound sea bass

2 cloves garlic, minced

1/2 teaspoon dried dill weed

1/4 teaspoon white pepper

Sea salt, to taste

2 tablespoons tamari sauce

1 tablespoon safflower oil

Directions

Press the "Sauté" button and heat the oil. Now, cook the sea bass for 1 to 2 minutes per side. Season your fish with salt and pepper.

Add 1 cup of water and a steamer rack to the bottom of your Instant Pot. Lower the fish onto the rack.

Secure the lid. Choose the "Steam" mode and cook for 10 minutes at Low pressure. Once cooking is complete, use a quick pressure release; carefully remove the lid. Reserve.

Add the remaining ingredients to the cooking liquid and stir to combine well. Press the "Sauté" button again and let it simmer until the sauce thickens.

Spoon the sauce over the reserved fish. Bon appétit!

Per serving: 217 Calories; 9.4g Fat; 7.8g Carbs; 26.4g Protein; 6.5g Sugars

598. Louisiana-Style Jambalaya

(Ready in about 15 minutes | Servings 4)

Ingredients

1 teaspoon Creole seasoning

1 ½ pounds shrimp, cleaned and deveined

1 yellow onion, chopped

2 ripe tomatoes, puréed

2 chicken bouillon cubes

1 teaspoon garlic, minced

1 red chili pepper, seeded and minced

2 carrots, thinly sliced

Sea salt and ground black pepper, to taste

1 teaspoon fresh ginger, grated

2 sweet peppers, seeded and sliced

2 ½ cups water

6 ounces Andouille sausage, sliced

Directions

Press the "Sauté" button to preheat your Instant Pot. Now, cook the sausage until delicately browned, about 3 minutes; add the onion, garlic, and ginger and continue to cook for a further 2 minutes, stirring periodically.

Throw the rest of the above ingredients into your Instant Pot.

Secure the lid. Choose the "Manual" mode and Low pressure; cook for 6 minutes. Once cooking is complete, use a quick pressure release; carefully remove the lid.

Ladle into individual bowls and serve garnished with fresh lemon slices if desired. Bon appétit!

Per serving: 366 Calories; 13g Fat; 18.3g Carbs; 45.1g Protein; 4.1g Sugars

599. Old Bay Crab

(Ready in about 15 minutes | Servings 5)

Ingredients

1 teaspoon Old Bay seasoning
1 ½ pounds crabs
2 cloves garlic, minced
1 lemon, sliced
1 stick butter

Directions

Place 1 cup water and a metal trivet in the bottom of your Instant Pot.

Lower the crabs onto the trivet.

Secure the lid. Choose the "Steam" mode and cook for 3 minutes at Low pressure. Once cooking is complete, use a quick pressure release; carefully remove the lid. Reserve.

Press the "Sauté" button and melt butter. Once hot, sauté the garlic and Old Bay seasoning for 2 to 3 minutes or until fragrant and thoroughly heated.

Add the cooked crabs and gently stir to combine. Serve with lemon slices. Bon appétit!

Per serving: 285 Calories; 19.8g Fat; 1.2g Carbs; 24.8g Protein; 0.6g Sugars

600. Herbed Carp Risotto

(Ready in about 15 minutes | Servings 4)

Ingredients

1 pound carp, chopped
Sea salt and ground black pepper, to taste
1 teaspoon dried rosemary, crushed
1/2 teaspoon dried marjoram leaves
1/2 teaspoon dried oregano leaves
1 cup chicken stock
1 cup tomato paste
1 cup Arborio rice
1 tablespoon olive oil
1 tablespoon dried parsley

Directions

Simply throw all of the above ingredients into your Instant Pot.

Secure the lid. Choose the "Manual" mode and High pressure; cook for 6 minutes. Once cooking is complete, use a quick pressure release; carefully remove the lid.

Serve in individual serving bowls, garnished with fresh lemon slices.

Per serving: 336 Calories; 16.7g Fat; 28.4g Carbs; 28.6g Protein; 8.8g Sugars

601. Creamed Crab Salad

(Ready in about 10 minutes | Servings 4)

Ingredients

1 teaspoon Old Bay seasoning
1/2 teaspoon hot sauce
1/2 cup celery stalk, chopped
8 mini slider rolls
2 cups Iceberg lettuce, torn into pieces
1/2 cup mayonnaise
2 garlic cloves, minced
1 tablespoon fresh lime juice
10 ounces crabmeat
4 heaping tablespoons fresh chives, chopped

Directions

Add 1 cup of water, metal trivet, and a steamer basket to your Instant Pot.

Place the crabmeat in the prepared steamer basket.

Secure the lid. Choose the "Steam" mode and cook for 3 minutes at Low pressure. Once cooking is complete, use a quick pressure release; carefully remove the lid.

Add the chives, garlic, mayo, hot sauce, Old Bay seasoning, celery, and lime juice; stir to combine well.

Divide the mixture between slider rolls and garnish with lettuce. Serve and enjoy!

Per serving: 413 Calories; 25g Fat; 28.5g Carbs; 18.5g Protein; 2.1g Sugars

602. Tuna with Lemon and Eschalot

(Ready in about 10 minutes | Servings 4)

Ingredients

1 pound tuna fillets
2 eschalots, thinly sliced
1 tablespoon dried parsley flakes
2 tablespoons butter, melted
2 lemons, 1 whole and 1 freshly squeezed
Sea salt and ground black pepper, to taste

Directions

Place 1 cup of water and lemon juice in the Instant Pot. Add a steamer basket too.

Place the tuna fillets in the steamer basket. Sprinkle the salt, pepper, and parsley over the fish; drizzle with butter and top with thinly sliced eschalots.

Secure the lid. Choose the "Steam" mode and Low pressure; cook for 3 minutes. Once cooking is complete, use a quick pressure release; carefully remove the lid.

Serve immediately with lemon. Bon appétit!

Per serving: 249 Calories; 9.1g Fat; 11.7g Carbs; 29.5g Protein; 5.6g Sugars

603. Croissants with Salmon Salad

(Ready in about 10 minutes + chilling time | Servings 6)

Ingredients

6 croissants, split
1/2 teaspoon dried rosemary, only leaves crushed
1 ½ pounds salmon fillets
2 cups Iceberg lettuce leaves, torn into pieces
1 red onion, thinly sliced
2 tablespoons sour cream
1 cup cherry tomatoes, halved
Salt and white pepper, to taste
1/2 teaspoon red pepper flakes, crushed
1/2 teaspoon dried oregano
1/4 cup prepared horseradish, drained
1/4 cup mayonnaise

Directions

Add 1 cup of water and metal trivet to your Instant Pot. Lower the salmon fillets onto the trivet.

Secure the lid. Choose the "Steam" mode and cook for 3 minutes at Low pressure. Once cooking is complete, use a quick pressure release; carefully remove the lid.

Add the remaining ingredients and stir to combine well. Place in your refrigerator until ready to serve.

Serve on croissants and enjoy!

Per serving: 412 Calories; 2.7g Fat; 26.8g Carbs; 28.8g Protein; 9.8g Sugars

604. Ocean Trout with Spring Onions

(Ready in about 15 minutes | Servings 4)

Ingredients

2 garlic cloves, minced
1 teaspoon mixed peppercorns
1 tablespoon fish sauce
Sea salt, to taste
2 tablespoons champagne vinegar
2 ½ cups broth, preferably homemade
1 teaspoon caraway seeds
1/2 teaspoon mustard seeds
1 pound ocean trout fillets
1/2 teaspoon paprika
1/2 cup spring onions, chopped

Directions

Place the steaming basket in your Instant Pot. Sprinkle the ocean trout fillets with salt, caraway seeds, mustard seeds, and paprika.

Place the ocean trout fillet in the steaming basket. Add the other ingredients.

Secure the lid and choose the "Manual" setting. Cook for 3 minutes at Low pressure. Once cooking is complete, use a quick release; carefully remove the lid.

You can thicken the sauce using the "Sauté" button. Bon appétit!

Per serving: 122 Calories; 2.2g Fat; 1.6g Carbs; 22.7g Protein; 0.5g Sugars

605. Classic Dijon Shrimp Salad

(Ready in about 15 minutes + chilling time | Servings 4)

Ingredients

1 tablespoon Dijon mustard 1 lime, juiced and zested
1 onion, thinly sliced
2 heaping tablespoons fresh parsley, chopped
1 head romaine lettuce, torn into pieces
4 tablespoons extra-virgin olive oil
1 sweet pepper, thinly sliced
1 jalapeno pepper, deseeded and minced
1 pound shrimp, deveined
Kosher salt and white pepper, to taste

Directions

Add a metal trivet and 1 cup of water to your Instant Pot.

Put the shrimp into the steamer basket. Lower the steamer basket onto the trivet.

Secure the lid. Choose the "Steam" mode and cook for 3 minutes at Low pressure. Once cooking is complete, use a quick pressure release; carefully remove the lid.

Transfer the steamed shrimp to a salad bowl; toss your shrimp with the remaining ingredients and serve well chilled. Bon appétit!

Per serving: 271 Calories; 15.4g Fat; 10.8g Carbs; 25.7g Protein; 2.9g Sugars

606. Haddock with Tomato and Beans

(Ready in about 10 minutes | Servings 2)

Ingredients

2 haddock fillets
1 can black beans, drained
Salt and ground black pepper, to taste
2 tablespoons fresh cilantro, roughly chopped
2 sprigs thyme, chopped
1/2 teaspoon paprika
4 tomato slices
2 teaspoons coconut butter, at room temperature
1/4 teaspoon caraway seeds
1/2 teaspoon tarragon
1 cup water

Directions

Add 1 cup of water to the bottom of your Instant Pot. Add a steamer insert.

Brush the haddock fillets with coconut butter. Now, season the haddock fillets with salt and pepper.

Place the haddock fillets on top of the steamer insert. Add the thyme, caraway seeds, tarragon, and paprika. Place 2 tomato slices on each fillet.

Secure the lid and choose "Manual" setting. Cook for 3 minutes at Low pressure. Once cooking is complete, use a natural release; remove the lid carefully.

Transfer the haddock fillets to serving plates. Scatter chopped cilantro over each fillet and serve garnished with black beans. Bon appétit!

Per serving: 183 Calories; 4.8g Fat; 1.3g Carbs; 31.8g Protein; 0.8g Sugars

607. Authentic Paella Valenciana

(Ready in about 15 minutes | Servings 5)

Ingredients

1 ½ pounds shrimp, deveined
2 sweet peppers, sliced
1/3 cup white wine
1 yellow onion, chopped
1 cup green peas, fresh or thawed
1 cup chicken broth
3 cloves garlic, minced
1 cup Arborio rice, rinsed
1/2 teaspoon curry paste
Sea salt and white pepper, to taste
2 tablespoons olive oil
1 Chiles de Árbol, minced
2 links (6-ounce) Spanish chorizo sausage, cut into slices
1/4 cup fresh parsley leaves, roughly chopped
1 cup water

Directions

Press the "Sauté" button and heat the oil until sizzling. Cook the sausage for 2 minutes, stirring continuously to ensure even cooking.

Stir in the onions and garlic; cook for about a minute longer, stirring frequently.

Add the peppers, rice, shrimp, broth, water, wine, curry paste, salt, and white pepper.

Secure the lid. Choose the "Manual" mode and cook for 3 minutes at High pressure. Once cooking is complete, use a quick pressure release; carefully remove the lid.

Add the green peas and seal the lid one more time; let it sit in the residual heat until warmed through.

Serve garnished with fresh parsley and enjoy!

Per serving: 435 Calories; 19.6g Fat; 24.8g Carbs; 46g Protein; 2.6g Sugars

608. Creamed Codfish with Basmati Rice

(Ready in about 15 minutes | Servings 4)

Ingredients

1 ¼ pounds cod, slice into small pieces
2 tablespoons lemon juice
1/2 cup heavy cream
1 teaspoon paprika
2 bay leaves
1 teaspoon coriander
1 teaspoon lemon thyme
1 cup Parmesan cheese, freshly grated
2 cups water
Salt and ground black pepper, to taste
2 cups basmati rice

Directions

Choose the "Manual" button and cook basmati rice with water for 4 minutes. Once cooking is complete, use a natural release; carefully remove the lid. Reserve.

Now, press the "Sauté" button on your Instant Pot. Add the remaining ingredients and cook until Parmesan has melted.

Serve the fish mixture over hot basmati rice and enjoy!

Per serving: 443 Calories; 25.4g Fat; 33.7g Carbs; 36.9g Protein; 1.1g Sugars

609. Old Bay Sausage, Prawn and Potato Boil

(Ready in about 15 minutes | Servings 4)

Ingredients

1 teaspoon Old Bay seasoning
1 pound prawns
1/4 cup butter
2 cloves garlic, minced
Sea salt and white pepper, to taste
1/4 teaspoon Tabasco sauce
1 fresh lemon, juiced
1 cup fume (fish stock)
1/2 pound beef sausage, sliced
4 baby potatoes

Directions

Place the sausage and potatoes in the inner pot; cover with the fish stock.

Secure the lid. Choose the "Manual" mode and cook for 5 minutes at High pressure. Once cooking is complete, use a quick pressure release; carefully remove the lid. Reserve. Clean the inner pot.

Press the "Sauté" button and melt the butter. Once hot, sauté the minced garlic until aromatic or about 1 minute. Stir in the Old Bay seasoning, Tabasco, salt, and white pepper. Lastly, stir in the prawns.

Continue to simmer for 1 to 2 minutes or until the shrimp turn pink. Press the "Cancel" button. Add the sausages and potatoes, drizzle lemon juice over the top and serve warm.

Per serving: 441 Calories; 28.6g Fat; 14.5g Carbs; 32.4g Protein; 1.6g Sugars

610. Easy Sea Bass Pilau

(Ready in about 10 minutes | Servings 4)

Ingredients

1 ½ pounds sea bass fillets, diced
2 cups basmati rice
2 cups vegetable broth
1/2 cup leeks, sliced
2 garlic cloves, minced
1/2 teaspoon ground black pepper
Salt, to taste
1 teaspoon fresh ginger, grated
2 tablespoons butter, melted
1 cup water

Directions

Press the "Sauté" button to preheat your Instant Pot. Then, melt the butter and sweat the leeks for 2 to 3 minutes.

Stir in the garlic; continue to sauté an additional 40 seconds. Add the remaining ingredients.

Secure the lid. Choose the "Manual" mode and Low pressure; cook for 4 minutes. Once cooking is complete, use a quick pressure release; carefully remove the lid.

Serve warm in individual bowls and enjoy!

Per serving: 432 Calories; 22.2g Fat; 32.2g Carbs; 42g Protein; 1.1g Sugars

611. Classic Fish Tacos

(Ready in about 13 minutes | Servings 4)

Ingredients

1 pound haddock fillets
4 (6-inch) flour tortillas
4 tablespoons mayonnaise
1 teaspoon dried basil
1 tablespoon ancho chili powder
4 tablespoons sour cream
2 tablespoons olive oil
2 tablespoons fresh cilantro, chopped
1 teaspoon garlic powder
1/2 teaspoon paprika
1/2 teaspoon ground cumin
1/2 teaspoon onion powder
1 lemon, sliced
Sea salt and freshly ground black pepper, to taste

Directions

Add 1/2 cup of water, 1/2 of lemon slices, and a steamer rack to the bottom of the inner pot.

Press the "Sauté" button and heat the olive oil until sizzling. Now, sauté the haddock fillets for 1 to 2 minutes per side.

Season the fish fillets with all the spices and lower them onto the rack.

Secure the lid. Choose the "Steam" mode and cook for 3 minutes at Low pressure. Once cooking is complete, use a quick pressure release; carefully remove the lid.

Break the fish fillets into large bite-sized pieces and divide them between the tortillas.

Add the mayonnaise, sour cream and cilantro to each tortilla. Garnish with the remaining lemon slices and enjoy!

Per serving: 475 Calories; 23.4g Fat; 40g Carbs; 25.2g Protein; 2.9g Sugars

612. Buttery Mackerel with Peppers

(Ready in about 15 minutes | Servings 5)

Ingredients

1 tablespoon butter, melted
5 mackerel fillets, skin on
1 green bell pepper, deveined and sliced
1 red bell pepper, deveined and sliced
1/2 teaspoon cayenne pepper
1/2 teaspoon dried rosemary
1 teaspoon marjoram
Sea salt, to taste
1/4 teaspoon ground black pepper, to taste

Directions

Prepare your Instant Pot by adding 1 ½ cups of water and steamer basket to its bottom.

Season the mackerel fillets with the salt, black pepper, cayenne pepper, rosemary, and marjoram.

Place the mackerel fillets in the steamer basket. Drizzle with melted butter. Top with sliced peppers.

Secure the lid and choose the "Manual" setting. Cook for 3 minutes at Low pressure. Once cooking is complete, use a quick release; carefully remove the lid. Serve immediately.

Per serving: 423 Calories; 7.9g Fat; 1.6g Carbs; 80g Protein; 0.9g Sugars

613. Greek-Style Seafood Bake

(Ready in about 20 minutes | Servings 4)

Ingredients

1/2 cup Greek-style yogurt
1/2 pound raw shrimp, chopped
1 teaspoon dried basil
Himalayan salt and ground black pepper, to taste
1 pound crab meat, chopped
1 teaspoon cayenne pepper
1 teaspoon dried oregano
1 cup Colby cheese, shredded
6 eggs
1/2 cup cream cheese

Directions

In a mixing bowl, whisk the eggs with the cream cheese and yogurt. Season with salt, black pepper, cayenne pepper, basil, and oregano.

Stir in the seafood; stir to combine and spoon the mixture into a lightly greased baking pan. Lastly, top with the shredded cheese.

Cover with a piece of aluminum foil.

Secure the lid. Choose the "Steam" mode and cook for 10 minutes at Low pressure. Once cooking is complete, use a quick pressure release; carefully remove the lid. Bon appétit!

Per serving: 468 Calories; 26.9g Fat; 4.5g Carbs; 50.4g Protein; 2.4g Sugars

614. Tandoori Fish Tikka

(Ready in about 15 minutes | Servings 4)

Ingredients

1 ½ pounds haddock fillets, cut into bite-sized chunks
1/3 teaspoon ground allspice
1 lime, cut into wedges
1 (14-ounce) can diced tomatoes
1 teaspoon hot paprika
1 cup vegetable broth
2 garlic cloves, minced
1 tablespoon brown sugar
1/4 cup tikka masala curry paste
1 cup natural yogurt
2 tablespoons olive oil
1/2 cup scallions, chopped

Directions

Press the "Sauté" button to preheat your Instant Pot; heat the oil. Then, sauté the scallions until tender and translucent.

Now, add the garlic; continue to sauté for a further 30 seconds.

Stir the curry paste, allspice, tomatoes, sugar, paprika, broth, and haddock into the Instant Pot.

Secure the lid and choose the "Manual" setting. Cook for 5 minutes at Low pressure. Once cooking is complete, use a quick release; carefully remove the lid.

Then, fold in the natural yogurt and stir to combine well; seal the lid again and allow it to sit in the residual heat until warmed through.

Serve in individual bowls, garnished with lime wedges. Enjoy!

Per serving: 273 Calories; 9.3g Fat; 13.5g Carbs; 34.9g Protein; 6.6g Sugars

615. Tunisian-Style Couscous

(Ready in about 10 minutes | Servings 4)

Ingredients

2 cups couscous
2 tablespoons almonds, slivered
1 teaspoon ancho chili powder
1 cup vegetable broth
1 cup coconut milk
1 teaspoon dried basil
2 bay leaves
4 cardamom pods
2 ripe tomatoes, pureed

1 ½ pounds halibut, cut into chunks
1 teaspoon coriander
1 teaspoon garam masala
1 yellow onion, chopped
2 cups water
2 tablespoons butter
Sea salt and ground black pepper, to taste
1 teaspoon cayenne pepper
1 teaspoon curry paste

Directions

Press the "Sauté" button and melt the butter. Once hot, cook the onions until tender and translucent.

Add the remaining ingredients, except for the slivered almonds, to the inner pot; stir to combine.

Secure the lid. Choose the "Manual" mode and cook for 4 minutes at High pressure. Once cooking is complete, use a quick pressure release; carefully remove the lid.

Serve garnished with almonds. Bon appétit!

Per serving: 505 Calories; 11.2g Fat; 61.1g Carbs; 37.7g Protein; 5.1g Sugars

616. Sea Scallops in Champagne Sauce

(Ready in about 10 minutes | Servings 3)

Ingredients

1/2 cup champagne
2 tablespoons butter
1 cup vegetable broth
1/2 teaspoon cayenne pepper
1 teaspoon ginger garlic paste

Sea salt and ground black pepper, to taste
1 pound scallops
1/4 teaspoon pink peppercorns, crushed

Directions

Add all of the above ingredients to the Instant Pot.

Secure the lid. Choose the "Manual" mode and Low pressure; cook for 3 minutes. Once cooking is complete, use a quick pressure release; carefully remove the lid.

Then, press the "Sauté" button and cook the sauce, whisking constantly, until it has reduced by half. Bon appétit!

Per serving: 165 Calories; 7.6g Fat; 5.7g Carbs; 17.6g Protein; 0.3g Sugars

617. Spicy Red Snapper Boil

(Ready in about 10 minutes | Servings 4)

Ingredients

3 (6-ounce) red snapper fillets
4 cloves garlic, minced
1 tablespoon capers
1 teaspoon Fish taco seasoning mix
1 red chili pepper, seeded and chopped
1 teaspoon basil
1/2 teaspoon oregano

2 medium ripe tomatoes, chopped
1 cup chicken broth
1/2 teaspoon rosemary
1 tablespoon ghee, at room temperature
1 medium-sized leek, chopped
1 lemon, cut into wedges
Coarse sea salt and ground black pepper, to taste

Directions

Press the "Sauté" button and melt the ghee. Once hot, sauté the leek and garlic until tender.

Add the remaining ingredients, except for the lemon wedges, to the inner pot.

Secure the lid. Choose the "Manual" mode and cook for 4 minutes at High pressure. Once cooking is complete, use a quick pressure release; carefully remove the lid.

Serve in individual bowls, garnished with lemon wedges. Enjoy!

Per serving: 289 Calories; 15.4g Fat; 13.8g Carbs; 24.5g Protein; 5.5g Sugars

618. Vegetable Salmon Skewers

(Ready in about 15 minutes | Servings 4)

Ingredients

1 pound salmon, skinned, deboned and cut into bite-sized chunks
1 red onion, cut into wedges
2 bell peppers, cut into strips
1 teaspoon red pepper flakes
8 sticks fresh rosemary, lower leaves removed

2 tablespoons toasted sesame oil
Sea salt and ground black pepper, to taste
1/2 pound yellow squash
zucchini, cubed

Directions

Prepare your Instant Pot by adding 1½ cups of water and metal rack to its bottom.

Thread the vegetables and fish alternately onto rosemary sticks.

Drizzle with the sesame oil; sprinkle with salt, black pepper, and red pepper flakes. Cover with a piece of foil.

Secure the lid. Choose "Manual" mode and Low pressure; cook for 6 minutes. Once cooking is complete, use a quick pressure release; carefully remove the lid. Serve immediately.

Per serving: 263 Calories; 15.1g Fat; 6.4g Carbs; 24.8g Protein; 3.7g Sugars

619. Codfish and Tomato Casserole

(Ready in about 10 minutes | Servings 4)

Ingredients

1 ½ pounds cod fillets
1/2 cup Greek olives, pitted and sliced
Sea salt and ground black pepper, to taste
2 sprigs rosemary, chopped
1 bay leaf
2 cloves garlic, smashed
1 pound tomatoes, chopped
2 tablespoons olive oil
2 sprigs thyme, chopped

Directions

Place 1 cup of water and a metal trivet in the bottom of the inner pot. Brush the sides and bottom of a casserole dish with olive oil.

Place the cod fillets in the greased casserole dish. Add the tomatoes, salt, pepper, rosemary, thyme, bay leaf, and garlic.

Lower the dish onto the trivet.

Secure the lid. Choose the "Steam" mode and cook for 3 minutes at Low pressure. Once cooking is complete, use a quick pressure release; carefully remove the lid.

Serve garnished with Greek olives and enjoy!

Per serving: 246 Calories; 9.9g Fat; 7.1g Carbs; 31.6g Protein; 2.5g Sugars

620. Halibut Steaks in Chardonnay Sauce

(Ready in about 15 minutes | Servings 4)

Ingredients

1 pound halibut steaks
1/4 cup Chardonnay
1 yellow onion, chopped
1 cup fish stock
2 garlic cloves, pressed
2 bell peppers, chopped
2 ripe tomatoes, puréed
1/2 teaspoon ground black pepper, to taste
1 dried red chili, coarsely chopped
1/2 teaspoon nigella seeds
2 bay leaves
Sea salt, to taste
2 tablespoons butter, melted

Directions

Press the "Sauté" button to preheat your Instant Pot. Then, melt the butter and sauté the onion until tender and translucent.

Then, stir in the garlic and bell peppers; continue to cook an additional 2 minutes or until the peppers have softened.

Add a splash of wine to deglaze the bottom of the inner pot. Add the remaining ingredients and stir to combine.

Secure the lid and choose the "Manual" setting. Cook for 5 minutes at Low pressure. Once cooking is complete, use a quick release; carefully remove the lid.

Taste, adjust the seasonings and serve warm. Bon appétit!

Per serving: 174 Calories; 6.5g Fat; 27.7g Carbs; 6.2g Protein; 13.9g Sugars

621. Spicy Haddock Curry

(Ready in about 10 minutes | Servings 4)

Ingredients

1 pound haddock
Sea salt and freshly ground black pepper
1 can reduced fat coconut milk
1 onion, chopped
2 garlic cloves, minced
1 teaspoon mustard seeds
1 teaspoon turmeric powder
1 teaspoon ground cumin
1 cup chicken stock
2 long red chilis, deseeded and minced
2 tablespoons tamarind paste
2 tablespoons peanut oil
1 (1-inch) piece fresh root ginger, peeled and grated

Directions

Press the "Sauté" button and heat the peanut oil; once hot, sauté the onion, garlic, ginger, and chilis until aromatic.

Add the remaining ingredients and gently stir to combine.

Secure the lid. Choose the "Manual" mode and cook for 4 minutes at Low pressure. Once cooking is complete, use a quick pressure release; carefully remove the lid.

Divide between serving bowls and serve warm. Enjoy!

Per serving: 315 Calories; 22.4g Fat; 8.4g Carbs; 21.9g Protein; 4.3g Sugars

622. Creamy Ham Hock and Seafood Soup

(Ready in about 45 minutes | Servings 6)

Ingredients

1 ham hock
3/4 pound shrimp, peeled and deveined
5 cups broth, preferably homemade
2 sprigs rosemary
2 tablespoons olive oil
1/2 cup double cream
1/2 cup leeks, chopped
2 tablespoons tomato paste
2 teaspoons chipotle in adobo sauce, chopped
1 teaspoon lemon thyme
1 parsnip, diced
2 tablespoons chickpea flour
Sea salt, to taste
1/2 teaspoon mixed peppercorns, freshly cracked
2 garlic cloves, minced
2 carrots, diced
1 cup water

Directions

Press the "Sauté" button and add the olive oil. Once hot, sauté the leeks together with the garlic, carrots, and parsnips; cook until the vegetables are just tender.

Add the chickpea flour and cook for a further 1 minute 30 seconds, stirring frequently.

Stir in the tomato paste, chipotle in adobo sauce, ham hock, water, and broth. Season with rosemary, lemon thyme, salt and mixed peppercorns. Secure the lid.

Choose the "Soup" function, High pressure and 35 minutes. Once cooking is complete, use a natural release; carefully remove the lid.

Place the ham hock on a cutting board; allow it to rest. Pull the meat from the ham hock bone and shred. Add it back to the Instant Pot.

Stir in the shrimp and double cream. Close the Instant Pot and cook your shrimp in the residual heat for 8 minutes. Bon appétit!

Per serving: 298 Calories; 13.5g Fat; 10.5g Carbs; 34.1g Protein; 3.7g Sugars

623. Buttery Lobster Tails

(Ready in about 10 minutes | Servings 4)

Ingredients

1/2 stick butter, at room temperature
1/2 teaspoon red pepper flakes
1 ½ pounds lobster tails, halved
Sea salt and freshly ground black pepper, to taste

Directions

Add a metal trivet, steamer basket, and 1 cup of water in your Instant Pot.

Place the lobster tails, shell side down, in the prepared steamer basket.

Secure the lid. Choose the "Steam" mode and cook for 3 minutes at Low pressure. Once cooking is complete, use a quick pressure release; carefully remove the lid.

Drizzle with butter. Season with salt, black pepper, and red pepper and serve immediately. Enjoy!

Per serving: 292 Calories; 14.1g Fat; 4.2g Carbs; 35.1g Protein; 0.1g Sugars

624. Clams with Bacon and Wine

(Ready in about 10 minutes | Servings 5)

Ingredients

3 (6.5-ounce) cans clams, chopped
1/2 cup clam juice
2 tablespoons fresh chives, roughly chopped
5 lime juice
A pinch of cayenne pepper
1 bay leaf
1 sprig thyme
1/3 cup tarty white wine
1/2 cup bacon, smoked and cubed
2 onions, chopped
3 garlic cloves, minced
1/3 cup water

Directions

Press the "Sauté" button to preheat your Instant Pot. Add the cubed bacon. Once your bacon releases its fat, add the onions, garlic, and thyme.

Cook for 3 minutes more or until the onion is transparent.

Add the clams, white wine, water, clam juice, cayenne pepper, and bay leaf. Secure the lid. Select "Manual" mode and cook at Low pressure for 4 minutes.

Once cooking is complete, use a natural release; remove the lid carefully

Ladle into individual bowls and serve garnished with lime slices and fresh chives. Bon appétit!

Per serving: 157 Calories; 4.6g Fat; 27.7g Carbs; 3.4g Protein; 8.3g Sugars

625. Parmesan Prawn Dip

(Ready in about 10 minutes | Servings 8)

Ingredients

1/2 cup Parmesan cheese, grated
2 or so dashes of Tabasco
1/2 cup fresh breadcrumbs
2 cloves garlic, smashed
1/2 cup cream cheese, softened
1/2 cup mayonnaise
1 ½ tablespoons cornichon, finely chopped
1 onion, chopped
1/4 cup tomato paste
2 cups crabmeat, flaked

Directions

Place all ingredients, except for the breadcrumbs, in a baking dish. Stir until everything is well incorporated.

Top with breadcrumbs.

Secure the lid. Choose the "Steam" mode and cook for 3 minutes at Low pressure. Once cooking is complete, use a quick pressure release; carefully remove the lid.

Serve with raw vegetable sticks if desired. Bon appétit!

Per serving: 205 Calories; 16.7g Fat; 4.6g Carbs; 9.2g Protein; 2.2g Sugars

626. Herb Tomato Shrimp

(Ready in about 15 minutes | Servings 4)

Ingredients

1 ½ pounds shrimp, peeled and deveined
2 ripe tomatoes, chopped
1 tablespoon tamari sauce
1 teaspoon garlic, minced
1 sprig thyme
1 tablespoon butter, at room temperature
1 cup green onion, chopped
1 sprig rosemary

Directions

Press the "Sauté" button to preheat your Instant Pot. Melt the butter and cook the green onions until they have softened.

Now, stir in the garlic and cook an additional 30 seconds or until it is aromatic. Add the rest of the above ingredients.

Secure the lid. Choose the "Manual" mode and Low pressure; cook for 3 minutes. Once cooking is complete, use a quick pressure release; carefully remove the lid.

Serve over hot jasmine rice and enjoy!

Per serving: 214 Calories; 5.4g Fat; 3.9g Carbs; 35.5g Protein; 2.5g Sugars

627. Cá Kho Tộ (Caramelized & Braised Fish)

(Ready in about 10 minutes | Servings 4)

Ingredients

4 (7-ounce) sea bass fillets
2 tablespoons fresh chives, chopped
Sea salt and white pepper, to taste
2 tablespoons soy sauce
1 (1-inch) ginger root, grated
Juice of 1/2 lime
1 cup chicken broth
1/4 cup brown sugar
2 tablespoons coconut oil, melted
2 tablespoons fish sauce

Directions

Press the "Sauté" button and heat the coconut oil. Once hot, cook the brown sugar, fish sauce, soy sauce, ginger, lime, salt, white pepper, and broth. Bring to a simmer and press the "Cancel" button.

Add the sea bass. Secure the lid. Choose the "Manual" mode and cook for 4 minutes at High pressure. Once cooking is complete, use a quick pressure release; carefully remove the lid.

Remove the sea bass fillets from the cooking liquid. Press the "Sauté" button one more time. Reduce the sauce until it is thick and syrupy.

Spoon the sauce over the reserved sea bass fillets. Garnish with fresh chives. Bon appétit!

Per serving: 335 Calories; 15g Fat; 10.5g Carbs; 38.5g Protein; 8.7g Sugars

628. Festive Salmon with Pesto Sauce

(Ready in about 15 minutes | Servings 4)

Ingredients

1/2 cup Kalamata olives
1 pound salmon steaks
1/2 teaspoon whole mixed peppercorns
Sea salt, to taste
1 shallot, peeled and sliced
2 sprigs rosemary
2 tablespoons olive oil
Kale Pesto Sauce:
2 tablespoons fresh lemon juice
2 tablespoons extra-virgin olive oil
1 teaspoon garlic, crushed
2 tablespoons fresh parsley
1 cup kale
1 avocado

Directions

Prepare your Instant Pot by adding 1 ½ cups of water and a steamer basket to its bottom.

Place the salmon steaks in the steamer basket; add the shallots, olives, rosemary, olive oil, peppercorns, and salt.

Secure the lid. Choose the "Steam" mode and High pressure; cook for 5 minutes. Once cooking is complete, use a quick pressure release; carefully remove the lid.

Add the avocado, garlic, parsley, kale, and lemon juice to your blender. Then, mix on high until a loose paste forms.

Add the olive oil a little at a time and continue to blend until the desired consistency is reached; add a tablespoon or two of water if needed.

Serve the fish fillets with the pesto on the side. Bon appétit!

Per serving: 366 Calories; 27.1g Fat; 6.6g Carbs; 24.8g Protein; 0.7g Sugars

629. Codfish with Butter and Scallions

(Ready in about 10 minutes | Servings 3)

Ingredients

3 fillets smoked codfish
3 teaspoons butter
1 lemon, sliced
1/2 cup water
Sea salt and ground black pepper, to taste
3 tablespoons scallions, chopped

Directions

Place the lemon and water in the bottom of the Instant Pot. Place the steamer rack on top.

Place the cod fish fillets on the steamer rack. Add the butter, scallions, salt, and black pepper.

Secure the lid. Choose the "Steam" mode and cook for 3 minutes at Low pressure. Once cooking is complete, use a quick pressure release; carefully remove the lid.

Serve warm and enjoy!

Per serving: 203 Calories; 4.8g Fat; 1.5g Carbs; 36.3g Protein; 0.5g Sugars

630. Prawn, Tomato, and Herb Risotto

(Ready in about 15 minutes | Servings 5)

Ingredients

1 pound prawns, peeled and deveined
1 (14-ounce) can tomatoes, diced
2 cups basmati rice
1 serrano pepper, seeded and thinly sliced
2 ½ cups vegetable stock, preferably homemade
2 tablespoons fresh mint, roughly chopped
1 tablespoon tamari sauce
1/2 teaspoon dried oregano
1/2 teaspoon sweet paprika
1 teaspoon dried rosemary
2 tablespoons olive oil
2 cloves garlic, pressed
2 bell peppers, seeded and thinly sliced
1 cup red onions, thinly sliced
Sea salt and ground black pepper, to taste

Directions

Press the "Sauté" button to preheat your Instant Pot. Then, heat the oil and sauté the onions until tender and translucent.

Stir in the garlic; continue to sauté until aromatic. Add the rest of the above ingredients, except for mint, to the Instant Pot.

Secure the lid and choose the "Manual" setting. Cook for 3 minutes at Low pressure. Once cooking is complete, use a natural release; carefully remove the lid.

Serve garnished with fresh mint leaves. Bon appétit!

Per serving: 331 Calories; 17.6g Fat; 31.9g Carbs; 26.2g Protein; 4.6g Sugars

631. Halibut with Cheese-Mayo Sauce

(Ready in about 1 hour | Servings 6)

Ingredients

1 ½ pounds halibut steaks
1 teaspoon stone-ground mustard
4 tablespoons cream cheese
2 cloves garlic, minced
1/2 teaspoon salt flakes
2 tablespoons olive oil

Sea salt and ground pepper, to your liking
1 cup wild rice, rinsed and drained
1 tablespoon butter
4 tablespoons mayonnaise
1/2 teaspoon red pepper flakes, crushed

Directions

In a saucepan, bring 3 cups of water and rice to a boil. Reduce the heat to simmer; cover and let it simmer for 45 to 55 minutes. Add the butter, salt, and red pepper; fluff with a fork. Cover and reserve, keeping your rice warm.

Cut 4 sheets of aluminum foil. Place the halibut steak in each sheet of foil. Add the olive oil, salt, and black pepper to the top of the fish; close each packet and seal the edges.

Add 1 cup of water and a steamer rack to the bottom of your Instant Pot. Lower the packets onto the rack.

Secure the lid. Choose the "Steam" mode and cook for 3 minutes at Low pressure. Once cooking is complete, use a natural pressure release; carefully remove the lid.

Meanwhile, mix the cream cheese, mayonnaise, stone-ground mustard, and garlic until well combined. Serve the steamed fish with the mayo sauce and wild rice on the side. Bon appétit!

Per serving: 431 Calories; 28.5g Fat; 21.7g Carbs; 21.8g Protein; 1.5g Sugars

632. Ocean Trout and Noodle Salad

(Ready in about 15 minutes | Servings 4)

Ingredients

2 pieces ocean trout fillets, deboned and skinless
8 ounces dry egg noodles
2 Lebanese cucumbers, chopped
2 ripe Roma tomatoes, diced
1/4 cup freshly squeezed lime juice
1 green chili, seeded and minced

1 cup water
1/2 cup dry vermouth
Sea salt and ground black pepper, to taste
1/2 teaspoon sweet paprika
1 yellow onion, chopped
2 garlic cloves, minced
1/2 bunch coriander, leaves picked, roughly chopped
2 tablespoons olive oil

Directions

Press the "Sauté" button to preheat your Instant Pot. Now, heat the olive oil and sauté the onion until translucent.

Stir in the garlic and chili; continue to sauté until they are fragrant.

Add the fish, water, vermouth, salt, black pepper, sweet paprika, tomatoes, and noodles.

Secure the lid. Choose the "Manual" mode and Low pressure; cook for 10 minutes. Once cooking is complete, use a quick pressure release; carefully remove the lid.

Flake the fish and allow the mixture to cool completely. Add the cucumbers and coriander. Drizzle fresh lime juice over the salad and serve. Bon appétit!

Per serving: 506 Calories; 13.6g Fat; 56g Carbs; 39.1g Protein; 12.1g Sugars

633. Italian-Style Stuffed Salmon

(Ready in about 10 minutes | Servings 3)

Ingredients

1/2 cup mozzarella, shredded
1 lemon, cut into wedges
1/2 teaspoon celery seed, crushed
1/2 teaspoon cayenne pepper
1 cup frozen spinach, defrosted
1/2 cup sour cream

2 cloves garlic, minced
1 tablespoon olive oil
Kosher salt and freshly ground black pepper, to taste
3 (6-ounce) salmon fillets
1/2 teaspoon dried basil
1/2 teaspoon dried marjoram

Directions

Add 1 cup of water and a steamer rack to the bottom of your Instant Pot.

Sprinkle your salmon with all the spices. In a mixing bowl, thoroughly combine the sour cream, mozzarella, spinach, and garlic.

Cut a pocket in each fillet to within 1/2-inch of the opposite side. Stuff the pockets with the spinach/cheese mixture. Drizzle with olive oil.

Wrap the salmon fillets in foil and lower onto the rack.

Secure the lid. Choose the "Manual" mode and cook for 4 minutes at Low pressure. Once cooking is complete, use a quick pressure release; carefully remove the lid.

Garnish with lemon wedges and serve warm.

Per serving: 374 Calories; 19.9g Fat; 7.7g Carbs; 40.7g Protein; 1.2g Sugars

634. Vermouth Tilapia Medley

(Ready in about 15 minutes | Servings 4)

Ingredients

1 pound tilapia fillets, boneless, skinless and diced
2 garlic cloves, minced
1/3 cup dry vermouth
1/4 teaspoon freshly ground black pepper, or more to taste
1 cup scallions, chopped
1/2 teaspoon dried oregano
1/2 teaspoon dried basil

2 cups water
1 teaspoon hot paprika
1 tablespoon fresh lime juice
1 teaspoon dried rosemary
2 tablespoons sesame oil
2 ripe plum tomatoes, crushed
Sea salt, to taste
1 cup shellfish stock

Directions

Press the "Sauté" button to preheat your Instant Pot. Heat the oil and sauté the scallions and garlic until fragrant.

Add a splash of vermouth to deglaze the bottom of the inner pot.

Secure the lid. Choose the "Manual" mode and High pressure; cook for 5 minutes. Once cooking is complete, use a quick pressure release; carefully remove the lid.

Serve with some extra lime slices if desired. Bon appétit!

Per serving: 221 Calories; 9.3g Fat; 4.9g Carbs; 25g Protein; 1.8g Sugars

635. Shrimp with Carrots and Wine

(Ready in about 10 minutes | Servings 4)

Ingredients

1 ½ pounds shrimp, deveined and rinsed
2 carrots, grated
1/2 cup dry white wine
1 bunch scallions, chopped
1 teaspoon dried rosemary
1/2 teaspoon dried oregano
1/2 cup cream of celery soup
Sea salt and freshly cracked black pepper, to taste
1 teaspoon cayenne pepper
1/2 teaspoon dried basil
1 tablespoon olive oil
2 garlic cloves, sliced

Directions

Press the "Sauté" button and heat the oil. Once hot, cook the garlic, scallions, and carrots for 2 to 3 minutes or until fragrant; add a splash of wine to deglaze the inner pot.

Add the remaining ingredients.

Secure the lid. Choose the "Manual" mode and cook for 3 minutes at Low pressure. Once cooking is complete, use a quick pressure release; carefully remove the lid.

Divide between serving bowls and enjoy!

Per serving: 267 Calories; 9.4g Fat; 5.1g Carbs; 38.3g Protein; 1.6g Sugars

636. Classic Parmesan Fish

(Ready in about 15 minutes | Servings 4)

Ingredients

4 mahi-mahi fillets
8 ounces Parmesan cheese, freshly grated
2 tablespoons butter, at room temperature
Sea salt and ground black pepper, to taste
1 teaspoon dried rosemary
1/2 teaspoon dried thyme
2 ripe tomatoes, sliced
1 teaspoon dried marjoram

Directions

Add 1 ½ cups of water and a rack to your Instant Pot.

Spritz a casserole dish with a nonstick cooking spray. Arrange the slices of tomatoes on the bottom of the dish. Add the herbs.

Place the mahi-mahi fillets on the top; drizzle the melted butter over the fish. Season it with salt and black pepper. Place the baking dish on the rack.

Secure the lid. Choose the "Manual" mode and Low pressure; cook for 9 minutes. Once cooking is complete, use a quick pressure release; carefully remove the lid.

Top with parmesan and seal the lid again; allow the cheese to melt and serve.

Per serving: 376 Calories; 22.1g Fat; 9.4g Carbs; 34.2g Protein; 0.8g Sugars

637. Tuna, Asparagus and Tomato Quiche

(Ready in about 15 minutes | Servings 4)

Ingredients

1 cup Cheddar cheese, grated
1 teaspoon paprika
1 pound asparagus, trimmed
A pinch of fresh thyme
2 ripe tomatoes, pureed
1 tablespoon dry white wine
1 pound tuna fillets
Sea salt and ground black pepper, to taste

Directions

Place the tuna fillets in a lightly greased baking dish. Add the asparagus, tomatoes, salt, black pepper, paprika, thyme, and wine.

Place a steamer rack inside the inner pot; add 1/2 cup water. Cut 1 sheet of heavy-duty foil and brush with cooking spray.

Top with the cheese. Cover with foil and lower the baking dish onto the rack.

Secure the lid. Choose the "Manual" mode and cook for 9 minutes at Low pressure. Once cooking is complete, use a quick pressure release; carefully remove the lid.

Place the baking dish on a cooling rack for a couple of minutes before slicing and serving. Bon appétit!

Per serving: 494 Calories; 30.3g Fat; 21.1g Carbs; 36.4g Protein; 5.3g Sugars

638. Mahi-Mahi Fish with a Twist

(Ready in about 30 minutes | Servings 4)

Ingredients

1/2 cup shallots, sliced
1/4 cup fresh coriander, chopped
1 teaspoon dried sage
4 mahi-mahi fillets
2 tablespoons olive oil
1/2 teaspoon red pepper flakes, crushed
2 tablespoons fresh lemon juice
1 teaspoon epazote
1 cup water
Sea salt and ground black pepper, to taste
For Cumin Guacamole:
Fresh juice of 1 lime
2 tablespoons salsa verde
Sea salt to taste
2 medium tomatoes, chopped
1 large avocado, peeled, pitted and mashed
1 clove garlic, minced

Directions

Pour 1 cup of water to the base of your Instant Pot.

Brush the mahi-mahi fillets with olive oil; then, sprinkle with salt, black pepper, and red pepper flakes.

Place the mahi-mahi fillets in the steaming basket; transfer it to the Instant Pot. Add the shallots on top; add lemon juice, epazote, coriander, and sage.

Secure the lid. Choose "Manual" mode, Low pressure and 3 minutes. Once cooking is complete, use a quick release; carefully remove the lid.

Next, mix all ingredients for the cumin guacamole; place in your refrigerator at least 20 minutes. Serve mahi-mahi fillets with fresh cumin guacamole on the side. Bon appétit!

Per serving: 324 Calories; 18g Fat; 13.1g Carbs; 29.1g Protein; 4.6g Sugars

639. Classic Haddock and Green Beans

(Ready in about 15 minutes | Servings 4)

Ingredients

4 haddock fillets
4 cups green beans
1 tablespoon fresh parsley
4 teaspoons ghee
1 rosemary sprig
2 thyme sprigs
2 cloves garlic, minced
1 lime, cut into wedges
1/2 cup water
Sea salt and ground black pepper, to taste

Directions

Place the lime wedges and water in the inner pot. Add a steamer rack.

Lower the haddock fillets onto the rack; place the rosemary, thyme, parsley, and ghee on the haddock fillets. Season with salt and pepper.

Secure the lid. Choose the "Steam" mode and cook for 3 minutes at Low pressure. Once cooking is complete, use a quick pressure release; carefully remove the lid. Reserve.

Then, add the garlic and green beans to the inner pot.

Secure the lid. Choose the "Steam" mode and cook for 3 minutes at Low pressure. Once cooking is complete, use a quick pressure release; carefully remove the lid.

Serve the haddock fillets with green beans on the side. Bon appétit!

Per serving: 288 Calories; 13.1g Fat; 9.1g Carbs; 33.7g Protein; 1.9g Sugars

640. Halibut with Tomatoes and Wine

(Ready in about 40 minutes | Servings 4)

Ingredients

4 halibut steaks
2 tomatoes, sliced
1/2 cup dry white wine
1 (1-inch) piece fresh ginger, grated
2 teaspoons olive oil
2 spring onions, sliced
2 tablespoons oyster sauce
2 garlic cloves, crushed
1 cup mixed salad greens, to serve
2 tablespoons Worcestershire sauce
1 tablespoon Dijon mustard

Directions

In a mixing bowl, whisk Worcestershire sauce, oyster sauce, white wine, mustard, and ginger. Add fish steaks and let them marinate for 30 minutes in your refrigerator.

Meanwhile, press the "Sauté" button on your Instant Pot. Now, heat olive oil and sauté the tomatoes with spring onions and garlic until they are tender.

Add 2 cups of water to the base of your Instant Pot. Add the metal steamer insert to the Instant Pot.

Now, place the halibut steaks on top of the steamer insert. Secure the lid. Select the "Manual" mode. Cook for 5 minutes at Low pressure.

Once cooking is complete, use a quick release; remove the lid carefully. Serve the warm halibut steaks with sautéed vegetables and mixed salad greens. Enjoy!

Per serving: 166 Calories; 3.8g Fat; 5g Carbs; 21.7g Protein; 1.5g Sugars

VEGAN

641. Traditional Kongunad Kurma

(Ready in about 30 minutes | Servings 4)

Ingredients

2 tablespoons grapeseed oil
2 cups water
1 dried red chili pepper, minced
1 teaspoon turmeric powder
1 onion, chopped
1 cup tomato puree
1 cup fresh coconut, shredded
1 teaspoon cumin seeds

1 teaspoon fennel seeds
2 cups cauliflower florets
Kosher salt and ground black pepper, to taste
Tempering:
4 curry leaves
1 tablespoon peanut oil
1 teaspoon cumin seeds

Directions

Add 1 cup of water and a steamer basket to the inner pot of your Instant Pot. Place the cauliflower florets in the steamer basket.

Secure the lid. Choose the "Steam" mode and cook for 3 minutes at High pressure. Once cooking is complete, use a quick pressure release; carefully remove the lid. Drain and reserve.

Press the "Sauté" button and heat the grapeseed oil until sizzling. Now, sauté the cumin seeds and fennel seeds for 30 seconds.

Stir in the chili pepper and onion and continue to sauté an additional 2 to 3 minutes. Add the tomato puree and let it cook on the lowest setting for 3 minutes longer.

Add the salt, black pepper, turmeric, coconut, and water.

Secure the lid. Choose the "Manual" mode and cook for 5 minutes at High pressure. Once cooking is complete, use a natural pressure release for 10 minutes; carefully remove the lid. Stir in the steamed cauliflower florets.

Meanwhile, heat the peanut oil in a cast-iron skillet over medium heat. Cook the cumin seeds and curry leaves until they are fragrant. Stir the tempering into the cauliflower mixture and serve warm.

Per serving: 216 Calories; 11.2g Fat; 28.1g Carbs; 6g Protein; 14.3g Sugars

642. Basic Vegan Rice

(Ready in about 15 minutes | Servings 2)

Ingredients

1 cup Arborio rice
1 teaspoon smoked paprika
1 cup water
1 cup vegetable stock
1/2 teaspoon dried oregano
1/2 teaspoon dried basil

2 garlic cloves, minced
1 white onion, finely chopped
Sea salt and ground black pepper, to taste
1 tablespoon olive oil

Directions

Press the "Sauté" button to preheat your Instant Pot. Heat the oil and sauté the garlic and onion until tender and fragrant or about 3 minutes.

Add the remaining ingredients; stir to combine well.

Secure the lid. Choose the "Manual" mode and cook for 5 minutes under High pressure. Once cooking is complete, use a quick release; carefully remove the lid.

Ladle into individual bowls and serve warm. Enjoy!

Per serving: 291 Calories; 20g Fat; 35.4g Carbs; 11.3g Protein; 2.8g Sugars

643. Classic Garlicky Kale

(Ready in about 10 minutes | Servings 4)

Ingredients

1 pound kale, cleaned and trimmed
3 cloves garlic, slivered
1/4 teaspoon cayenne pepper
Fresh juice squeezed from 1/2 a lemon

1 tablespoon olive oil
1 cup water
Kosher salt and ground black pepper, to taste

Directions

Press the "Sauté" button and heat the oil until sizzling. Now, cook the garlic until just tender and aromatic.

Add the chopped kale and water to the inner pot. Sprinkle with salt, black pepper, and cayenne pepper.

Secure the lid. Choose the "Manual" mode and cook for 4 minutes at High pressure. Once cooking is complete, use a quick pressure release.

Scoop the kale out of the inner pot with a slotted spoon, leaving as much cooking liquid behind as possible. Drizzle fresh lemon juice over the kale and serve. Bon appétit!

Per serving: 89 Calories; 4.4g Fat; 10.4g Carbs; 5g Protein; 2.5g Sugars

644. Pepper and Green Pea Stew

(Ready in about 25 minutes | Servings 6)

Ingredients

2 ½ cups green peas, whole
2 ripe Roma tomatoes, seeded and crushed
3 cups roasted vegetable stock
Sea salt and ground black pepper, to taste
1 teaspoon cayenne pepper
1/2 teaspoon dried dill
2 cloves garlic, minced

2 carrots, chopped
2 parsnips, chopped
1 red bell pepper, seeded and chopped
2 bay leaves
1 shallot, diced
2 tablespoons canola oil
1 teaspoon cumin seeds

Directions

Press the "Sauté" button to preheat the Instant Pot. Once hot, add the oil. Then, sauté the cumin seeds for 30 seconds.

Add the shallot, garlic, carrots, parsnip and pepper; continue to sauté for 3 to 4 minutes more or until vegetables are tender.

Now, stir in the remaining ingredients.

Secure the lid. Choose the "Manual" mode and cook for 18 minutes under High pressure. Once cooking is complete, use a natural release; carefully remove the lid.

Serve with cream cheese if desired. Bon appétit!

Per serving: 173 Calories; 6.6g Fat; 22.7g Carbs; 7.7g Protein; 7.9g Sugars

645. Brussels Sprouts with a Twist

(Ready in about 10 minutes | Servings 4)

Ingredients

1 ½ pounds Brussels sprouts, halved
Kosher salt and freshly ground black pepper, to taste
1/4 cup balsamic vinegar
1/4 teaspoon dried dill weed
2 tablespoons sesame oil
4 cloves garlic, sliced
1 cup vegetable broth
6 tablespoons dried cranberries

Directions

Press the "Sauté" button and heat the oil; then, sauté the garlic until just tender and fragrant.

Stir in the Brussels sprouts and continue to sauté an additional 2 to 3 minutes.

Add the remaining ingredients to the inner pot.

Secure the lid. Choose the "Manual" mode and cook for 2 minutes at High pressure. Once cooking is complete, use a quick pressure release; carefully remove the lid. Bon appétit!

Per serving: 174 Calories; 7.7g Fat; 22.3g Carbs; 7.2g Protein; 9.1g Sugars

646. Mom's Festive Green Beans

(Ready in about 25 minutes | Servings 4)

Ingredients

6 dried shiitake mushrooms
1 ½ pounds green beans, fresh or frozen (and thawed)
1/4 teaspoon ground black pepper
2 tablespoons sesame oil
1/2 cup scallions, chopped
1/2 teaspoon red pepper flakes, crushed
1 bay leaf
Sea salt, to taste
2 cups water
2 cloves garlic, minced

Directions

Press the "Sauté" button and bring the water to a rapid boil; remove from the heat; add the dried shiitake mushrooms.

Allow the mushrooms to sit for 15 minutes to rehydrate. Then cut the mushrooms into slices; reserve the mushroom stock.

Wipe down the Instant Pot with a kitchen cloth. Press the "Sauté" button to preheat your Instant Pot. Once hot, heat the sesame oil.

Then, sauté the garlic and scallions until tender and aromatic. Add the green beans, black pepper, red pepper, bay leaf, salt, reserved mushrooms and stock; stir to combine well.

Secure the lid. Choose the "Manual" mode and cook for 4 minutes under High pressure. Once cooking is complete, use a quick release; carefully remove the lid. Serve warm.

Per serving: 119 Calories; 7.6g Fat; 12.6g Carbs; 2.6g Protein; 2.6g Sugars

647. Traditional Milagu Rasam Soup

(Ready in about 15 minutes | Servings 4)

Ingredients

2 cloves garlic
4 cups water
1/2 teaspoon turmeric
1 small ball of tamarind
2 dry red chili pepper
2 tablespoons coconut oil
6 curry leaves
Himalayan salt, to taste
1/2 teaspoon mustard seeds
2 medium tomatoes, diced
1 tablespoon cumin seeds
1 tablespoon whole black pepper

Directions

Grind the cumin seeds, whole black pepper, garlic, and red chili pepper to a coarse paste.

Press the "Sauté" button and heat the oil until sizzling. Now, cook the mustard seeds for a minute or so. Once they splutter, add chopped tomatoes and curry leaves. Cook for 3 to 4 minutes more.

Add the ground paste, turmeric powder, and freshly squeezed tamarind juice; add salt and the water and stir to combine.

Secure the lid. Choose the "Manual" mode and cook for 4 minutes at High pressure. Once cooking is complete, use a quick pressure release; carefully remove the lid. Serve hot and enjoy!

Per serving: 92 Calories; 7.8g Fat; 6.7g Carbs; 1.4g Protein; 2.8g Sugars

648. Exotic Curried Cabbage

(Ready in about 20 minutes | Servings 4)

Ingredients

1 (14-ounce) can coconut milk
1 medium-sized leek, chopped
1 cup vegetable broth
1/2 tablespoon fresh lime juice
1 teaspoon ground coriander
1 cup tomatoes, puréed
2 stalks celery, chopped
1 turnip, chopped
1/2 teaspoon dried dill
1 teaspoon dried basil
1 teaspoon ground turmeric
2 cloves garlic, smashed
1 parsnip, chopped
2 carrots, chopped
1 ½ pounds white cabbage, shredded
1 bay leaf
Kosher salt and ground black pepper, to taste
2 tablespoons olive oil

Directions

Press the "Sauté" button to preheat your Instant Pot. Now, heat the oil and cook the leeks and garlic until tender and fragrant.

After that, add the remaining ingredients; stir to combine well.

Secure the lid. Choose the "Manual" mode and cook for 12 minutes under High pressure. Once cooking is complete, use a natural release; carefully remove the lid.

Ladle into soup bowls and serve immediately.

Per serving: 223 Calories; 8.2g Fat; 33.8g Carbs; 7.6g Protein; 15.1g Sugars

649. Punjabi Bhindi Masala

(Ready in about 15 minutes | Servings 3)

Ingredients

1 pound okra, cut into small pieces
Himalayan salt, to taste
1 teaspoon ginger garlic paste
1 teaspoon Sriracha sauce
1/2 teaspoon ground turmeric
1 teaspoon Gram masala
1 teaspoon amchur (mango powder)
2 tablespoons coconut oil, at room temperature
1 cup tomato puree
1/2 teaspoon jeera (cumin seeds)
1 yellow onion, sliced

Directions

Press the "Sauté" button and heat the oil until sizzling. Now, cook the onion until it is tender and translucent.

Stir in the ginger-garlic paste and continue to cook for 30 to 40 seconds. Stir the remaining ingredients into the inner pot.

Secure the lid. Choose the "Manual" mode and cook for 4 minutes at High pressure. Once cooking is complete, use a quick pressure release; carefully remove the lid.

Serve warm.

Per serving: 253 Calories; 16.8g Fat; 24.9g Carbs; 5.4g Protein; 9.5g Sugars

650. Nana's Chili with Tortilla Chips

(Ready in about 15 minutes | Servings 6)

Ingredients

2 (15-ounce) cans beans, drained and rinsed
1/2 cup tortilla chips
1 green bell pepper, diced
2 cups vegetable stock
1 red chili pepper, minced
1 teaspoon cayenne pepper
1/2 teaspoon ground cumin
2 ripe tomatoes, chopped
3 cloves garlic minced or pressed
1 red bell pepper, diced
1 handful fresh cilantro leaves, chopped
2 tablespoons olive oil
1 red onion, chopped
Sea salt and ground black pepper, to taste

Directions

Press the "Sauté" button to preheat your Instant Pot. Now, heat the oil until sizzling.

Sauté the onion tender and translucent. Add the garlic, peppers, salt, and pepper; continue to sauté until they are tender.

Now, stir in the cayenne pepper, cumin, stock, tomatoes, and beans.

Secure the lid. Choose the "Manual" mode and cook for 10 minutes under High pressure. Once cooking is complete, use a quick release; carefully remove the lid.

Divide the chili between six serving bowls; top with fresh cilantro and tortilla chips. Enjoy!

Per serving: 204 Calories; 6.5g Fat; 27.9g Carbs; 10.4g Protein; 6.9g Sugars

651. Chinese-Style Bok Choy

(Ready in about 15 minutes | Servings 4)

Ingredients

1 ½ pounds Bok choy
2 cloves garlic, pressed
2 tablespoons rice wine vinegar
2 teaspoons sesame oil
4 tablespoons soy sauce
1 cup water

Directions

Press the "Sauté" button and heat the oil. Now, cook the garlic for 1 minute or until it is fragrant but not browned.

Add the Bok choy and water to the inner pot.

Secure the lid. Choose the "Manual" mode and cook for 5 minutes at High pressure. Once cooking is complete, use a quick pressure release; carefully remove the lid.

Meanwhile, in a mixing bowl, whisk the rice vinegar and soy sauce. Drizzle this sauce over the Bok choy and serve immediately.

Per serving: 92 Calories; 5.4g Fat; 8.1g Carbs; 3.8g Protein; 5.1g Sugars

652. Spanish Salmorejo with Pepitas

(Ready in about 15 minutes | Servings 4)

Ingredients

1 pound ripe tomatoes, puréed
2 tablespoons pepitas
1/2 teaspoon dried marjoram
1 teaspoon sweet paprika
2 carrots, roughly chopped
1 red chili pepper, seeded and chopped
1 zucchini, chopped
1 teaspoon dried rosemary
2 cloves garlic, crushed
1/2 teaspoon dried basil
1 cup vegetable stock
2 tablespoons fresh chives, chopped
2 tablespoons olive oil
1/2 cup green onions, chopped
Sea salt and ground black pepper, to taste

Directions

Press the "Sauté" button to preheat your Instant Pot. Then, heat the oil until sizzling.

Now, cook the green onions and garlic until tender and fragrant. Add the carrots, chili pepper, tomatoes, zucchini, seasonings, and stock.

Secure the lid. Choose the "Manual" mode and cook for 6 minutes under High pressure. Once cooking is complete, use a quick release; carefully remove the lid.

Then, purée the mixture with an immersion blender until the desired thickness is reached.

Ladle into soup bowls; serve garnished with fresh chives and pepitas. Enjoy!

Per serving: 125 Calories; 9.4g Fat; 8.1g Carbs; 4.2g Protein; 1.8g Sugars

653. Colorful Indian Curry

(Ready in about 20 minutes | Servings 4)

Ingredients

4 medium-sized sweet potatoes, diced
4 cups kale, torn into pieces
2 tablespoons fresh cilantro, chopped
1 teaspoon ginger-garlic paste
1 teaspoon ground cumin
Sea salt and freshly ground black pepper, to taste
1 cinnamon stick
2 tablespoons tomato paste
1 cup vegetable broth
1 tablespoon ground coriander
1 teaspoon ground turmeric
1 cup tomatoes juice
1 cup coconut milk
1 tablespoon grapeseed oil
1 onion, chopped

Directions

Press the "Sauté" button and heat the oil until sizzling. Now, sauté the onion until just tender and fragrant.

Now, stir in the ginger-garlic paste, spices, tomato paste, vegetable broth, sweet potatoes, and tomato juice.

Secure the lid. Choose the "Manual" mode and cook for 6 minutes at High pressure. Once cooking is complete, use a quick pressure release; carefully remove the lid.

After that, add the coconut milk and kale. Press the "Sauté" button and let it simmer for 5 to 6 minutes or until thoroughly heated.

Ladle into soup bowls and serve garnished with fresh cilantro. Enjoy!

Per serving: 355 Calories; 16.7g Fat; 47.7g Carbs; 8.4g Protein; 5.8g Sugars

654. Classic Homemade Hummus

(Ready in about 35 minutes | Servings 8)

Ingredients

3/4 pound dried chickpeas, soaked
1/2 teaspoon cayenne pepper
1/2 teaspoon dried basil
1 teaspoon granulated garlic
Salt and black pepper, to taste
2 tablespoons tahini
1/2 lemon, juiced
1/3 teaspoon ground cumin
3 tablespoon olive oil
10 cups water

Directions

Add the water and chickpeas to the Instant Pot. Secure the lid.

Choose the "Manual" mode and cook for 25 minutes under High pressure. Once cooking is complete, use a natural release; carefully remove the lid.

Now, drain your chickpeas, reserving the liquid. Transfer chickpeas to a food processor. Add the tahini, lemon juice, and seasonings.

Puree until it is creamy; gradually pour in the reserved liquid and olive oil until the mixture is smooth and uniform. Serve with a few sprinkles of cayenne pepper. Bon appétit!

Per serving: 186 Calories; 7.7g Fat; 22.8g Carbs; 7.6g Protein; 4g Sugars

655. Authentic Spanish Pisto

(Ready in about 20 minutes | Servings 4)

Ingredients

1/4 cup Spanish wine
1 Guajillo chili pepper, minced
2 tablespoons olive oil
1 pound zucchini, cut into 1-inch cubes
1 can (14-ounce) tomatoes with juice
2 cups cream of mushroom soup
1 onion, diced
4 cloves garlic, sliced
2 bell pepper, diced
Se salt and cracked black pepper, or to taste

Directions

Press the "Sauté" button and heat the olive oil. Now, cook the onion until just tender and translucent.

Then, stir in the garlic; continue to cook until fragrant. Add a splash of wine to deglaze the pan.

Stir in the remaining ingredients; stir to combine well.

Secure the lid. Choose the "Manual" mode and cook for 10 minutes at High pressure. Once cooking is complete, use a quick pressure release; carefully remove the lid. Serve immediately.

Per serving: 178 Calories; 10.7g Fat; 18.2g Carbs; 5.9g Protein; 6g Sugars

656. Italian Tomato Risotto

(Ready in about 25 minutes | Servings 4)

Ingredients

1 cup tomatoes, pureed
1 cup white rice, soaked for 30 minutes
2 cloves garlic, minced
Sea salt and freshly ground black pepper, to taste
1 teaspoon curry powder
1 teaspoon citrus & ginger spice blend
1/2 teaspoon paprika
1 tablespoon sesame oil
1 yellow onion, peeled and chopped
1 carrot, chopped
1 tablespoon tomato powder
2 ½ cups water

Directions

Press the "Sauté" button to heat up the Instant Pot. Heat the sesame oil until sizzling.

Sweat the onion for 2 to 3 minutes. Add the garlic and cook an additional 30 to 40 seconds.

Add the tomatoes and carrot; cook for a further 10 minutes, stirring periodically. Add seasonings, rice, and water to the Instant Pot. Secure the lid.

Select the "Manual" mode and cook for 8 minutes at High pressure. Once cooking is complete, use a natural release; remove the lid carefully.

Taste, adjust the seasonings and serve warm. Bon appétit!

Per serving: 251 Calories; 6.2g Fat; 44.1g Carbs; 4.2g Protein; 3g Sugars

657. Mexican Posole Rojo

(Ready in about 1 hour | Servings 4)

Ingredients

2 bay leaves
1 cup radishes, sliced
1 teaspoon garlic, sliced
1/2 pound dried hominy,
soaked overnight and rinsed
4 cups water
2 Roma tomatoes, chopped

1 tablespoon bouillon granules
2 dried pasilla chili peppers,
seeded and minced
1 teaspoon cumin seeds
1 onion, chopped
Kosher salt and ground black
pepper, to taste

Directions

Put the chilis in a bowl with hot water; let them soak for 15 minutes until soft. Transfer the chilis to your food processor; add the cumin seeds, garlic, salt, and black pepper.

Add 1 cup of water to the food processor and puree the mixture until well blended. Transfer the mixture to your Instant Pot.

Add the onion, hominy, water, tomatoes, bouillon granules, and bay leaves to the inner pot.

Secure the lid. Choose the "Soup/Broth" mode and cook for 40 minutes at High pressure. Once cooking is complete, use a quick pressure release; carefully remove the lid.

Serve warm, garnished with fresh radishes. Bon appétit!

Per serving: 233 Calories; 3.3g Fat; 45.8g Carbs; 5.8g Protein; 8.7g Sugars

658. Classic Vegetable, Noodle and Corn Soup

(Ready in about 20 minutes | Servings 6)

Ingredients

6 cups vegetable stock,
preferably homemade
9 ounces vegan noodles
1 turnip, chopped
1 cup corn kernels
1 carrot, chopped
1 parsnip, chopped
3 garlic cloves, smashed

1/2 teaspoon dried thyme
Salt and freshly ground black
pepper, to taste
2 tablespoons olive oil
1 teaspoon cumin powder
1/2 teaspoon dried rosemary
2 shallots, peeled and chopped

Directions

Press the "Sauté" button to heat up your Instant Pot. Now, heat the oil and sauté the shallots with carrot, parsnip, and turnip until they have softened.

Stir in the garlic and cook an additional 40 seconds. Add the cumin powder, rosemary, thyme, stock, and noodles.

Now, secure the lid and choose the "Soup" setting.

Cook for 7 minutes at High pressure. Once cooking is complete, use a quick release; remove the lid carefully.

Add the corn kernels, cover with the lid, and cook in the residual heat for 5 to 6 minutes more. Season with salt and pepper. Taste adjust the seasoning and serve warm. Bon appétit!

Per serving: 194 Calories; 5.4g Fat; 29.9g Carbs; 8g Protein; 5.1g Sugars

659. Kerala-Style Beets

(Ready in about 20 minutes | Servings 2)

Ingredients

1/2 cup shallots, chopped
1 chili pepper, chopped
1/2 teaspoon turmeric powder
2 garlic cloves, minced
10 curry leaves

1 pound small beets
1 tablespoon olive oil
Sea salt and ground black
pepper, to taste

Directions

Add 1 cup of water and a steamer basket to the inner pot. Place the beets in the steamer basket.

Secure the lid. Choose the "Steam" mode and cook for 15 minutes at High pressure. Once cooking is complete, use a quick pressure release; carefully remove the lid.

Once your beets are cool enough to touch, transfer them to a cutting board; peel and chop them into small pieces.

Press the "Sauté" button and heat the olive oil until sizzling. Then, cook the shallots, garlic, chili pepper, and curry leaves for about 4 minutes, or until they have softened.

Add the turmeric, salt, and black pepper; add the cooked beets to the inner pot and press the "Cancel" button. Serve warm.

Per serving: 184 Calories; 7.2g Fat; 27.1g Carbs; 4.8g Protein; 17.8g Sugars

660. Spaghetti Squash with Basil-Walnut Pesto

(Ready in about 15 minutes | Servings 4)

Ingredients

1 pound spaghetti squash, cut
into halves
1 cup water
For the Pesto:
1 ½ cups fresh basil
1/2 cup raw walnut halves
1 tablespoon fresh lemon juice

1/4 teaspoon ground black
2 cloves garlic, minced
1/4 teaspoon cayenne pepper
3 tablespoons olive oil
1 ½ tablespoons nutritional
yeast
Salt, to taste

Directions

Grab your spaghetti squash and scoop out the seeds and most of the stringy parts with an ice cream.

Pour water into the base of your Instant Pot. Add the squash to your Instant Pot and secure the lid.

Select the "Manual" mode and cook for 7 minutes under High pressure. Once cooking is complete, use a quick release; remove the lid carefully.

Next, place the walnuts, nutritional yeast, salt, black pepper, and cayenne pepper in your food processor; pulse until it is the consistency of fine meal.

Add the remaining ingredients for the pesto and pulse again until evenly combined. Serve the spaghetti squash with the pesto sauce. Bon appétit!

Per serving: 218 Calories; 16.9g Fat; 15.6g Carbs; 4.4g Protein; 0.5g Sugars

661. Farmhouse Vegetable Soup

(Ready in about 15 minutes | Servings 4)

Ingredients

1 medium zucchini, chopped
2 cups cabbage, shredded
2 carrots, thinly sliced
1 (15-ounce) can tomatoes, diced with their juice
2 celery stalks, thinly sliced
1 teaspoon dried sage
1 teaspoon dried parsley flakes
1 shallot, chopped
2 tablespoons olive oil
3 cups vegetable broth
1 teaspoon cayenne pepper
Kosher salt and ground black pepper, to taste

Directions

Press the "Sauté" button and heat the oil. Now, sauté the shallot until tender and translucent.

Add the remaining ingredients; stir to combine well.

Secure the lid. Choose the "Manual" mode and cook for 10 minutes at High pressure. Once cooking is complete, use a quick pressure release; carefully remove the lid.

Ladle into soup bowls and serve with garlic croutons if desired. Bon appétit!

Per serving: 227 Calories; 11.9g Fat; 12.3g Carbs; 17.8g Protein; 6.2g Sugars

662. Potato and Chanterelle Mushroom Mélange

(Ready in about 25 minutes | Servings 4)

Ingredients

3/4 pound chanterelle mushrooms, sliced
1 tablespoon paprika
1 tablespoon flax seeds meal
1/3 cup port wine
1 parsnip, chopped
2 sprigs fresh rosemary
2 sprigs fresh thyme
2 cups vegetable stock
1 teaspoon red chili flakes
2 tablespoons fresh parsley, chopped
1 tablespoon olive oil
1 carrot, chopped
1 ripe Roma tomato, chopped
1 yellow onion, chopped
2 cloves garlic, peeled and minced
Sea salt and ground black pepper, to taste
1 pound russet potatoes, peeled and diced

Directions

Throw all ingredients, except for the flax seeds meal, in your Instant Pot.

Secure the lid. Choose the "Soup" mode and High pressure; cook for 20 minutes. Once cooking is complete, use a natural pressure release; carefully remove the lid.

Stir the flax seeds into your Instant Pot. Press the "Sauté" button and let it simmer until cooking liquid has thickened and reduced. Serve hot. Bon appétit!

Per serving: 456 Calories; 5.7g Fat; 99g Carbs; 15.4g Protein; 7.9g Sugars

663. Steamed Winter Vegetables

(Ready in about 10 minutes | Servings 3)

Ingredients

1 celery rib, sliced
1/2 pound cauliflower florets
Sea salt and freshly ground black pepper, to taste
1 tablespoon fresh cilantro, chopped
2 carrots, sliced
3 tablespoons olive oil
1/2 teaspoon cayenne pepper
2 cloves garlic, minced

Directions

Add 1 cup water and a steamer basket to the inner pot of your Instant Pot. Place the vegetables in the steamer basket.

Secure the lid. Choose the "Steam" mode and cook for 3 minutes at High pressure. Once cooking is complete, use a quick pressure release; carefully remove the lid; reserve the steamed vegetables.

Press the "Sauté" button and heat the oil. Now, sauté the garlic until tender. Add the steamed vegetables back to the inner pot.

Season generously with cayenne pepper, salt, and black pepper. Garnish with fresh cilantro and serve.

Per serving: 147 Calories; 13.7g Fat; 5.8g Carbs; 1.3g Protein; 2.1g Sugars

664. Cabbage with Tomato and Rice

(Ready in about 25 minutes | Servings 4)

Ingredients

1 head purple cabbage, cut into wedges
1 garlic clove, minced
2 ripe tomatoes, pureed
Salt and freshly ground black pepper, to taste
1/4 cup fresh chives, chopped
2 tablespoons tomato ketchup
1 bay leaf
1/4 teaspoon marjoram
1 cup basmati rice
1 ½ cups water
1/2 teaspoon cayenne pepper
2 tablespoons olive oil
2 shallots, diced

Directions

Press the "Sauté" button to preheat the Instant Pot. Heat the olive oil and sauté the shallots until they are just tender.

Now, stir in the minced garlic and cook until it is lightly browned and aromatic.

Stir in the cabbage, tomatoes, ketchup, rice, water, bay leaf, marjoram, cayenne pepper, salt, and black pepper.

Secure the lid. Select the "Manual" mode and cook for 6 minutes under High pressure. Once cooking is complete, use a natural release for 15 minutes; remove the lid carefully. Serve warm garnished with fresh chopped chives. Bon appétit!

Per serving: 242 Calories; 13.3g Fat; 35.2g Carbs; 7.8g Protein; 10g Sugars

665. Authentic Minestrone Soup

(Ready in about 35 minutes | Servings 4)

Ingredients

4 medium-sized potatoes, peeled and diced
1 cup dried Great Northern beans
1 teaspoon garlic, minced
2 carrots, sliced
2 cups Swiss chard, torn into pieces
6 cups water
2 tomatoes, pureed
1 tablespoon Italian seasoning blend
Sea salt and ground black pepper, to taste
2 celery stalks, diced
1 cup yellow squash, diced
2 tablespoons olive oil
1 onion, chopped

Directions

Press the "Sauté" button and heat the olive oil until sizzling. Then, sauté the onion and garlic until just tender and fragrant.

Now, add the remaining ingredients, except for the Swiss chard.

Secure the lid. Choose the "Bean/Chili" mode and cook for 30 minutes at High pressure. Once cooking is complete, use a quick pressure release; carefully remove the lid.

Stir in the Swiss chard. Seal the lid and let it sit in the residual heat until it wilts. Serve warm.

Per serving: 414 Calories; 7.6g Fat; 73.4g Carbs; 15.6g Protein; 5.7g Sugars

666. Thai-Style Rice

(Ready in about 20 minutes | Servings 3)

Ingredients

1 yellow onion, chopped
2 cups vegetable broth
Zest of 1/2 lemon
Sea salt and ground black pepper, to taste
1 tablespoon olive oil
1 cup jasmine rice
1 tablespoon vegan margarine
Fresh juice of 1/2 lemon
1/4 cup water
1 teaspoon curry powder

Directions

Place the water, 1 cup of vegetable broth, olive oil, and rice in your Instant Pot.

Secure the lid. Choose the "Manual" mode and High pressure; cook for 2 minutes. Once cooking is complete, use a natural pressure release for 10 minutes; carefully remove the lid.

Fluff the rice with a fork and reserve.

Wipe down the Instant Pot with a kitchen cloth. Press the "Sauté" button and melt margarine. Then, sauté the onion until tender and translucent.

Add the remaining cup of vegetable broth, curry powder, lemon, salt, and black pepper. Press the "Sauté" button and stir until everything is incorporated.

Spoon the sauce over hot rice. Bon appétit!

Per serving: 353 Calories; 9.6g Fat; 56.8g Carbs; 8g Protein; 1.7g Sugars

667. Creole Boiled Peanuts

(Ready in about 1 hour 5 minutes | Servings 10)

Ingredients

2 tablespoons Creole seasoning
2 pounds raw peanuts in the shell
1 tablespoon cayenne pepper
2 jalapenos, sliced
1/2 cup salt
1 tablespoon garlic powder

Directions

Add all ingredients to the inner pot of your Instant Pot. Pour in enough water to cover the peanuts.

Use a steamer to gently press down your peanuts.

Secure the lid. Choose the "Manual" mode and cook for 45 minutes at High pressure. Once cooking is complete, use a natural pressure release for 15 minutes; carefully remove the lid.

Place in a container with a bunch of the liquid; refrigerate for 3 hours. Bon appétit!

Per serving: 235 Calories; 18.8g Fat; 10.7g Carbs; 9.3g Protein; 2.7g Sugars

668. Red Kidney Beans with Roasted Peppers

(Ready in about 30 minutes | Servings 4)

Ingredients

2 roasted peppers, cut into strips
1 teaspoon ground cumin
2 cups roasted vegetable broth
2 cloves garlic, chopped
1/2 teaspoon mustard powder
1 teaspoon celery seeds
Sea salt and ground black pepper, to taste
1 pound dried red kidney beans
1/2 cup shallots, chopped

Directions

Add all of the above ingredients to your Instant Pot.

Secure the lid. Choose the "Bean/Chili" mode and cook for 25 minutes under High pressure. Once cooking is complete, use a natural release; carefully remove the lid.

You can thicken the cooking liquid on "Sauté" function if desired. Serve warm.

Per serving: 418 Calories; 2.1g Fat; 72.9g Carbs; 30.1g Protein; 4.5g Sugars

669. Lentil Stew with Green Beans

(Ready in about 20 minutes | Servings 3)

Ingredients

1 cup green lentils
1 cup green beans, trimmed
Sea salt and ground black pepper, to season
2 cloves garlic, minced
1/2 teaspoon red pepper flakes, crushed
1 celery rib, chopped
1 teaspoon oregano
1 teaspoon basil
3 cups vegetable broth
2 bell peppers, chopped
2 carrots, chopped
1 cup tomato sauce
2 tablespoons peanut oil
1 cup scallions, chopped onion

Directions

Press the "Sauté" button and heat the oil until sizzling; once hot, cook the scallions, garlic, bell peppers, carrots, and celery until they have softened.

Add the spices, lentils, broth, and tomato sauce; gently stir to combine.

Secure the lid. Choose the "Manual" mode and cook for 8 minutes at High pressure. Once cooking is complete, use a natural pressure release for 5 minutes; carefully remove the lid.

Afterwards, add the green beans, salt, and black pepper to the inner pot; gently stir to combine.

Secure the lid. Choose the "Manual" mode and cook for 3 minutes at High pressure. Once cooking is complete, use a quick pressure release; carefully remove the lid. Serve warm.

Per serving: 306 Calories; 11.5g Fat; 39.3g Carbs; 12.3g Protein; 15.7g Sugars

670. Mediterranean-Style Zucchini

(Ready in about 15 minutes | Servings 4)

Ingredients

1 pound zucchini, sliced
1/2 cup Kalamata olives, pitted and sliced
1 garlic clove, minced
1/2 cup vegetable broth
1/2 teaspoon dried oregano
Salt, to taste
1/2 teaspoon ground black pepper
1/2 cup scallions, chopped
1/2 cup tomato paste
1/2 teaspoon dried basil
1 teaspoon paprika
2 tablespoons garlic-infused olive oil

Directions

Press the "Sauté" button to preheat the Instant Pot. Now, heat the oil; sauté the garlic and scallions for 2 minutes or until they are tender and fragrant.

Add the zucchinis, tomato paste, broth, salt, black pepper, oregano, basil, and paprika.

Secure the lid. Choose the "Manual" mode and Low pressure; cook for 4 minutes. Once cooking is complete, use a quick pressure release; carefully remove the lid.

Serve garnished with Kalamata olives. Bon appétit!

Per serving: 143 Calories; 9.4g Fat; 12.7g Carbs; 5.6g Protein; 4.4g Sugars

SOUPS, STOCKS & STEWS

671. Provençal Chicken and Kamut Soup

(Ready in about 20 minutes | Servings 4)

Ingredients

1 tablespoon Herbes de Provence
1/2 cup chicken thighs, boneless
1/2 cup kamut
1 parsnip, chopped
Sea salt and freshly ground black pepper, to taste
1 onion, chopped
1 celery stalk, chopped
3 cups chicken broth
1 carrot, chopped
1 cup tomato puree
1 tablespoon olive oil

Directions

Press the "Sauté" button and heat the oil; now, cook the chicken thighs for 3 to 4 minutes.

Add the onion and continue to sauté until tender and translucent. Add the remaining ingredients and stir to combine.

Secure the lid. Choose the "Manual" mode and cook for 12 minutes at High pressure. Once cooking is complete, use a quick pressure release; carefully remove the lid.

Ladle your soup into individual bowls. Bon appétit!

Per serving: 233 Calories; 9.1g Fat; 26.2g Carbs; 6.9g Protein; 1.1g Sugars

672. Classic Russian Borscht (Beet Soup)

(Ready in about 15 minutes | Servings 4)

Ingredients

1/2 pound beets, peeled and coarsely shredded
1/2 pound potatoes, peeled and diced
1/4 cup fresh dill, roughly chopped
4 cups vegetable stock
2 tablespoons red-wine vinegar
2 carrots, chopped
1 tomato, chopped
2 garlic cloves, pressed
Kosher salt and ground black pepper, to taste
1/2 teaspoon caraway seeds
1 ½ tablespoons olive oil
1/2 cup onions, chopped

Directions

Press the "Sauté" button to preheat your Instant Pot. Heat the oil and cook the onions and garlic until tender and fragrant.

Add the remaining ingredients, except for fresh dill.

Secure the lid. Choose the "Manual" mode and cook for 10 minutes under High pressure. Once cooking is complete, use a natural release; carefully remove the lid.

Serve the soup with chopped fresh dill. Enjoy!

Per serving: 183 Calories; 7.3g Fat; 22.5g Carbs; 8.4g Protein; 7.7g Sugars

673. Aromatic Fisherman's Stock

(Ready in about 55 minutes | Servings 8)

Ingredients

2 tablespoons olive oil
2 lemongrass stalks, chopped
1 onion, quartered
2 sprigs rosemary
2 sprigs thyme
2 carrots, chopped
1 parsnip, chopped
2 pounds meaty bones and heads of halibut, washed

Directions

Place all ingredients in the inner pot. Add cold water until the pot is 2/3 full.

Secure the lid. Choose the "Soup/Broth" mode and cook for 40 minutes at High pressure. Once cooking is complete, use a natural pressure release for 10 minutes; carefully remove the lid.

Strain the vegetables and fish. Bon appétit!

Per serving: 63 Calories; 3.5g Fat; 2.7g Carbs; 4.9g Protein; 1.3g Sugars

674. Thai-Style Vegetable Soup

(Ready in about 25 minutes | Servings 5)

Ingredients

5 cups vegetable stock
1 celery, chopped
1 teaspoon garlic, minced
1/2 cup coconut cream
2 carrots, chopped
1 zucchini, diced
1 parsnip, chopped
1 head cauliflower, cut into small florets
1 tablespoon olive oil
1/2 cup white onions, chopped
2 tablespoons fresh cilantro, chopped
Sea salt and ground black pepper, to taste

Directions

Press the "Sauté" button to preheat your Instant Pot. Now, heat the oil until sizzling.

Sauté the onion and garlic until tender. Add the carrots, parsnip, celery, cauliflower, zucchini, stock, salt, and black pepper, and stir to combine.

Secure the lid. Choose the "Soup" mode and cook for 20 minutes under High pressure. Once cooking is complete, use a quick release; carefully remove the lid.

Add the coconut cream and seal the lid; let it sit until heated through. Ladle into soup bowls and serve garnished with fresh cilantro. Bon appétit!

Per serving: 176 Calories; 13.1g Fat; 9.3g Carbs; 7.9g Protein; 3.4g Sugars

675. Roasted Vegetable and Wine Broth

(Ready in about 1 hour 15 minutes | Servings 10)

Ingredients

10 cups water
1 cup dry white wine
4 medium celery ribs, cut into 2-inch pieces
2 sprigs fresh thyme
3 tablespoons olive oil
Kosher salt and black peppercorns, to taste
2 onions, peeled and quartered
2 sprigs fresh rosemary
4 carrots, cut into 2-inch pieces

Directions

Start by preheating your oven to 400 degrees F. Grease a large roasting pan with cooking spray

Place the carrots, celery, onions, and herbs in the prepared roasting pan. Roast, tossing halfway through the cooking time, until the vegetables are tender about 35 minutes.

Transfer the vegetables to the inner pot. Add the remaining ingredients. Secure the lid. Choose the "Soup/Broth" mode and cook for 30 minutes at High pressure. Once cooking is complete, use a natural pressure release for 10 minutes; carefully remove the lid.

Strain the broth through a fine-mesh sieve and discard the solids. Let it cool completely before storing.

Per serving: 56 Calories; 3.4g Fat; 3.2g Carbs; 0.3g Protein; 1.4g Sugars

676. Vegetable and Rice Noodle Soup

(Ready in about 25 minutes | Servings 6)

Ingredients

1 parsnip, chopped
1 red onion, chopped
1/2 teaspoon freshly ground black pepper
1/2 teaspoon dried basil
2 cups rice noodles
1/2 tablespoon miso paste
1 teaspoon dried oregano
2 carrots, thinly sliced
1 celery stalk, chopped
2 cloves garlic, minced
1 cup brown mushrooms, chopped
1/4 teaspoon red pepper flakes, crushed
Salt, to taste
6 cups vegan cream of mushroom soup
1 teaspoon dried parsley flakes
1 teaspoon fennel seeds

Directions

Place the cream of mushroom soup, basil, oregano, parsley, fennel seeds, carrots, celery, parsnip, onion, garlic, mushrooms in your Instant Pot.

Secure the lid. Choose the "Soup" mode and cook for 8 minutes under High pressure. Once cooking is complete, use a natural release; carefully remove the lid.

Add the rice noodles, miso paste, black pepper, red pepper, and salt to the Instant Pot.

Press the "Sauté" button and cook an additional 7 to 10 minutes. Ladle into individual bowls and serve right away!

Per serving: 292 Calories; 13.7g Fat; 37.7g Carbs; 5.5g Protein; 3.1g Sugars

677. Italian Wedding Soup

(Ready in about 30 minutes | Servings 4)

Ingredients

Meatballs:
1/4 cup Pecorino Romano cheese, grated
2 cloves garlic, crushed
2 tablespoons cilantro, chopped
1/2 cup panko crumbs
1 egg, beaten
Sea salt and ground black pepper, to taste
1/2 pound ground beef
1/2 pound ground turkey

Soup:
4 cups chicken broth
1 celery stalk, chopped
6 ounces noodles
2 cloves garlic, minced
2 tomatoes, crushed
2 bay leaves
1 tablespoon olive oil
1 onion, chopped

Directions

In a mixing bowl, thoroughly combine all ingredients for the meatballs.

Form the mixture into 20 meatballs. Press the "Sauté" button and heat the oil. Now, brown the meatballs in batches; reserve.

Heat the olive oil; sauté the onion, celery, and garlic for 3 to 4 minutes or until they are fragrant.

Add the tomatoes, broth, and bay leaves to the inner pot.

Secure the lid. Choose the "Manual" mode and cook for 12 minutes at High pressure. Once cooking is complete, use a quick pressure release; carefully remove the lid.

Next, sit in the noodles and secure the lid again.

Choose the "Manual" mode and cook for 5 minutes at High pressure. Once cooking is complete, use a quick pressure release; carefully remove the lid. Bon appétit!

Per serving: 487 Calories; 21.9g Fat; 30.1g Carbs; 40.8g Protein; 4.7g Sugars

678. Sichuan Pickle and Corn Soup

(Ready in about 35 minutes | Servings 4)

Ingredients

2 garlic cloves, minced
4 cups vegetable broth
1 teaspoon Five-spice powder
1 tablespoon soy sauce
1 cup sweet corn kernels, frozen and thawed
1 cup zha cai
1 teaspoon fresh ginger, peeled and grated
1 celery stalk, chopped
2 carrots, chopped
Sea salt, to taste
1/2 teaspoon ground black pepper, to taste
1 yellow onion, peeled and chopped
1 teaspoon dried parsley flakes
2 ripe tomatoes, finely chopped
1 jalapeño pepper, minced
1/2 teaspoon red pepper flakes
1 tablespoon toasted sesame oil

Directions

Press the "Sauté" button to preheat your Instant Pot. Once hot, add the oil. Sauté the onion, garlic, ginger and jalapeño pepper for 2 to 3 minutes, stirring occasionally.

Add the remaining ingredients, except for the corn and zha cai; stir to combine well.

Secure the lid. Choose the "Bean/Chili" mode and cook for 25 minutes under High pressure. Once cooking is complete, use a natural release; carefully remove the lid.

After that, add the corn and seal the lid again. Let it sit until heated through. Serve in individual bowls with zha cai on the side. Enjoy!

Per serving: 177 Calories; 8.8g Fat; 18.5g Carbs; 7.8g Protein; 7.1g Sugars

679. Vegetarian Autumn Soup

(Ready in about 20 minutes | Servings 4)

Ingredients

1 ½ pounds acorn squash, chopped
1 tablespoon butter, softened
1 sprig fresh thyme
Himalayan salt and black pepper, to taste
1 turnip, chopped
1 carrot, chopped
2 cups vegetable broth
2 cloves garlic, sliced
1 medium-sized leek, chopped
2 cups water
1/2 teaspoon ground allspice

Directions

Press the "Sauté" button and melt the butter. Once hot, cook the garlic and leek until just tender and fragrant.

Add the remaining ingredients to the inner pot.

Secure the lid. Choose the "Manual" mode and cook for 10 minutes at High pressure. Once cooking is complete, use a quick pressure release; carefully remove the lid.

Puree the soup in your blender until smooth and uniform. Serve warm and enjoy!

Per serving: 152 Calories; 3.9g Fat; 27.4g Carbs; 5.1g Protein; 6.6g Sugars

680. Wild Rice Vegetable Soup

(Ready in about 35 minutes | Servings 4)

Ingredients

3/4 cup wild rice
2 garlic cloves, minced
Salt, to taste
1/2 teaspoon ground black pepper
1 bell pepper, chopped
1 fennel, diced
1 teaspoon fresh or dried rosemary
1 cup tomato purée
2 cups water
2 cups vegetable broth
1 serrano pepper, chopped
2 carrots, chopped
2 tablespoons fresh coriander, chopped
2 tablespoons olive oil
1/2 cup leeks, roughly chopped

Directions

Press the "Sauté" button to preheat your Instant Pot. Once hot, heat the oil.

Then, sauté the leeks, garlic, and pepper for 2 to 4 minutes, stirring periodically; add a splash of broth if needed.

Stir the remaining ingredients into your Instant Pot; stir to combine well.

Secure the lid. Choose the "Soup" mode and High pressure; cook for 30 minutes. Once cooking is complete, use a natural pressure release; carefully remove the lid.

Taste and adjust the seasonings; ladle into soup bowls and serve hot. Enjoy!

Per serving: 235 Calories; 8.1g Fat; 34.2g Carbs; 8.6g Protein; 6.3g Sugars

681. Classic Stroganoff Soup

(Ready in about 1 hour | Servings 4)

Ingredients

1/2 teaspoon porcini powder
1 teaspoon garlic powder
Sea salt and ground black pepper, to taste
5 cups beef bone broth
1/2 teaspoon dried oregano
1/2 teaspoon dried rosemary
1/2 cup sour cream
2 tablespoons potato starch, mixed with 4 tablespoons of cold water
1/2 teaspoon dried basil
1 teaspoon dried sage
1 teaspoon shallot powder
7 ounces button mushrooms, sliced
1 pound beef stew meat, cubed

Directions

In the inner pot, place the stew meat, broth, and spices.

Secure the lid. Choose the "Manual" mode and cook for 50 minutes at High pressure. Once cooking is complete, use a quick pressure release; carefully remove the lid.

Add the mushrooms and sour cream to the inner pot.

Choose the "Soup/Broth" mode. Bring to a boil and add the potato starch slurry. Continue to simmer until the soup thickens.

Ladle into serving bowls and serve immediately. Bon appétit!

Per serving: 267 Calories; 9.6g Fat; 11.4g Carbs; 34.2g Protein; 2.2g Sugars

682. Creamy Vegan Soup

(Ready in about 15 minutes | Servings 4)

Ingredients

1/2 cup raw cashews, soaked for 3 hours
1 tablespoon soy sauce
1/2 cup leeks, chopped
1 garlic clove, minced
1 red bell pepper, thinly sliced
1 green bell pepper, thinly sliced
Salt and ground black pepper, to taste
1 celery with leaves, chopped
1 carrot, trimmed and chopped
1 serrano pepper, deveined and thinly sliced
4 ½ cups water
3 teaspoons sesame oil
1/2 cup almond milk, unsweetened

Directions

Press the "Sauté" button on your Instant Pot. Heat sesame oil and sauté the leeks until they are just tender.

Add the garlic, celery, carrot, and peppers; continue sautéing until they have softened, about 3 minutes.

Add the water, salt, and pepper. Choose the "Manual" mode and cook for 4 minutes at High pressure.

Once cooking is complete, use a quick release; remove the lid carefully.

Next, puree the soy sauce, raw cashews, and almond milk in your food processor or blender; process until creamy and uniform.

Stir this cream base into the soup; cook in the residual heat until everything is well incorporated.

Divide the warm chowder among individual serving bowls. Side with crackers and enjoy!

Per serving: 282 Calories; 22.2g Fat; 18.4g Carbs; 6.1g Protein; 7.9g Sugars

683. Lentil, Spinach and Carrot Soup

(Ready in about 10 minutes | Servings 5)

Ingredients

2 cups fresh spinach leaves, torn into small pieces
2 carrots, sliced
1 teaspoon cumin
1 teaspoon smoked paprika
1 onion, chopped
2 cloves garlic, minced
6 cups water
2 bay leaves
2 cups red lentils, rinsed
Sea salt and ground black pepper, to taste

Directions

Place all ingredients, except for the fresh spinach, in the inner pot.

Secure the lid. Choose the "Manual" mode and cook for 3 minutes at High pressure. Once cooking is complete, use a quick pressure release; carefully remove the lid.

Stir in the spinach and seal the lid again; let it sit until the spinach just starts to wilt.

Serve in individual bowls and enjoy!

Per serving: 295 Calories; 1.9g Fat; 52.7g Carbs; 19.2g Protein; 1.6g Sugars

684. Codfish Soup in a Bread Bowl

(Ready in about 15 minutes | Servings 4)

Ingredients

3 cod fillets
4 (8-ounce) round bread loaves
1 parsnip, chopped
1 celery with leaves, chopped
1 ½ cups double cream
1 ½ cups stock, preferably homemade
2 garlic cloves, minced
1/2 teaspoon Vietnamese cinnamon
Salt, to taste
2 teaspoons capers, liquid reserved
1 teaspoon sumac powder
1 teaspoon fennel seeds
2 shallots, chopped
1 green bell pepper, chopped
2 tablespoons fish sauce
2 sweet potatoes, peeled and diced
2 ½ cups water
1/3 teaspoon ground black pepper

Directions

Add the water, cod fillets, sweet potatoes, parsnip, celery, shallot, bell pepper, garlic, salt, black pepper, capers, sumac powder, fennel seeds, Vietnamese cinnamon, stock, and fish sauce to your Instant Pot.

Secure the lid and choose "Manual" mode. Cook for 8 minutes at Low pressure.

Once cooking is complete, use a natural release; remove the lid carefully.

Fold in the double cream, press the "Sauté" button and continue to cook until it is thoroughly cooked.

Now, cut a slice off the top of each bread loaf. Now, gently pull the inner bread from the round with a tablespoon, leaving a 1/4-inch thick shell.

Ladle the soup into bread loaves and serve hot.

Per serving: 419 Calories; 29.9g Fat; 17.6g Carbs; 21.2g Protein; 5.4g Sugars

685. Easy Polish Bigos

(Ready in about 20 minutes | Servings 5)

Ingredients

1 pound Kielbasa, sliced
2 ½ cups beef stock
1/2 cup tomato puree
4 garlic cloves, sliced
1 teaspoon mustard seeds
1 teaspoon caraway seeds, crushed
1 pound fresh cabbage, shredded
1 teaspoon dried thyme
1 teaspoon dried basil
2 carrots, trimmed and diced
1 pound sauerkraut, drained
2 bay leaves
1 tablespoon cayenne pepper
Sea salt, to taste
1/2 pound pork stew meat, cubed
1 onion, chopped
1/2 teaspoon black peppercorns
1/2 cup dry red wine
2 slices smoked bacon, diced

Directions

Press the "Sauté" button to preheat your Instant Pot. Now, cook the bacon, Kielbasa, and pork stew meat until the bacon is crisp; reserve.

Add the onion and garlic, and sauté them until they're softened and starting to brown. Add the remaining ingredients to the inner pot, including the reserved meat mixture.

Secure the lid. Choose the "Manual" mode and cook for 15 minutes at High pressure. Once cooking is complete, use a quick pressure release; carefully remove the lid.

Ladle into individual bowls and serve warm.

Per serving: 417 Calories; 22.4g Fat; 23.6g Carbs; 31.8g Protein; 8.7g Sugars

686. Vegan Beluga Lentil Stew

(Ready in about 15 minutes | Servings 4)

Ingredients

1 cup beluga lentils
1 ½ cups tomato purée
1/2 cup cashew cream
2 cloves garlic, pressed
1 teaspoon fresh ginger, grated
1 bell pepper, chopped
1 serrano pepper, chopped
1/2 teaspoon ground allspice
1 teaspoon dried parsley flakes
Sea salt and black pepper, to taste
2 cups vegetable stock
2 cups kale leaves, torn into pieces
1 teaspoon fresh lemon juice
2 teaspoons toasted sesame oil
1/2 teaspoon ground cumin
1/2 teaspoon dried basil
1 yellow onion, chopped

Directions

Press the "Sauté" button to preheat your Instant Pot. Now, heat the oil; sauté the onion until tender and translucent.

Then, add the garlic, ginger, and peppers; continue to sauté until they have softened.

Add the seasonings, tomato purée, stock and lentils.

Secure the lid. Choose the "Manual" mode and High pressure; cook for 8 minutes. Once cooking is complete, use a natural pressure release; carefully remove the lid.

Add the kale and lemon juice; seal the lid again and let it sit until thoroughly warmed. Serve dolloped with cashew cream. Enjoy!

Per serving: 311 Calories; 22.9g Fat; 21.8g Carbs; 9.9g Protein; 6.7g Sugars

687. Hearty Beef Potato Stew

(Ready in about 30 minutes | Servings 6)

Ingredients

2 pounds chuck roast, cut into 2-inch cubes
4 potatoes, diced
4 bell peppers, deveined and chopped
2 bay leaves
2 onions, chopped
2 cloves garlic, minced
1 chili pepper, chopped
1 cup tomato puree
4 cups beef broth
Seasoned salt and ground black pepper, to taste
1 tablespoon lard, melted
2 tablespoons Hungarian paprika

Directions

Press the "Sauté" button and melt the lard. Once hot, cook the beef until no longer pink. Add a splash of broth and stir with a wooden spoon, scraping up the browned bits on the bottom of the inner pot.

Add the onion to the inner pot; continue sautéing an additional 3 minutes. Now, stir in the garlic and cook for 30 seconds more.

Stir in the remaining ingredients

Secure the lid. Choose the "Meat/Stew" mode. Cook for 20 minutes at High pressure. Once cooking is complete, use a quick pressure release; carefully remove the lid.

Discard the bay leaves and serve in individual bowls. Bon appétit!

Per serving: 425 Calories; 11.7g Fat; 35.3g Carbs; 44g Protein; 7.5g Sugars

688. Pork and Sour Cream Stew

(Ready in about 15 minutes | Servings 5)

Ingredients

1 pound pork stew meat, cubed
1 cup sour cream, for garnish
Kosher salt and black pepper, to taste
1 teaspoon ground cumin
1 leek, chopped
1 habanero pepper, deveined and minced
1 teaspoon ginger-garlic paste
1 teaspoon paprika
2 tablespoons fresh parsley, chopped
1 cup tomato paste
2 tablespoons fresh cilantro, chopped
5 cups beef bone broth
2 teaspoons olive oil

Directions

Press the "Sauté" button to preheat your Instant Pot; heat the oil. Now, sear the meat until it is delicately browned.

Add the tomato paste, cilantro, parsley, leek, habanero pepper, ginger-garlic paste, cumin, paprika, salt, black pepper, and broth.

Secure the lid. Choose the "Manual" setting and cook at High pressure for 8 minutes. Once cooking is complete, use a quick pressure release; carefully remove the lid.

Divide your stew among serving bowls; top each serving with sour cream. Enjoy!

Per serving: 279 Calories; 10.1g Fat; 18.1g Carbs; 30g Protein; 8.2g Sugars

689. Traditional French Beef Stew (Pot-Au-Feu)

(Ready in about 1 hour 10 minutes | Servings 5)

Ingredients

2 pounds beef pot roast, cut into 2-inch pieces
1 cup chèvre cheese, crumbled
3 garlic cloves, pressed
1 shallot, sliced
1/2 teaspoon sage
1 pound cremini mushrooms, sliced
2 tomatoes, pureed
1 cup dry red wine
1/2 teaspoon marjoram
2 tablespoons olive oil
1 onion, chopped
3 cups beef broth
2 carrots, chopped
Sea salt and ground black pepper, to taste

Directions

Press the "Sauté" button and heat the olive oil. Cook the beef in batches and transfer to a bowl.

Then, cook the onion in pan drippings. Stir in the carrots and garlic and continue to cook an additional 3 minutes.

Add the tomatoes, wine, broth, marjoram, sage, salt, and black pepper. Add the browned beef.

Secure the lid. Choose the "Meat/Stew" mode. Cook for 45 minutes at High pressure. Once cooking is complete, use a quick pressure release; carefully remove the lid.

Now, add the shallot and mushrooms; continue to simmer on the "Sauté" function for about 10 minutes or until everything is thoroughly heated.

Transfer your stew to a lightly greased casserole dish; top with the cheese and place under a preheated broiler for 10 minutes or until the cheese melts. Serve warm.

Per serving: 473 Calories; 25.7g Fat; 12.3g Carbs; 48g Protein; 6.2g Sugars

690. Japanese Hayashi Raisu

(Ready in about 30 minutes | Servings 6)

Ingredients

1 ½ pounds ribeye steaks, cut into bite-sized pieces
1 tablespoon Tonkatsu sauce
1 cup brown rice
1/2 teaspoon sweet paprika
2 cups beef bone broth
1 carrot, chopped
1 celery stalk, chopped
1/4 cup tomato paste
1/3 cup rice wine
1 sprig dried thyme, crushed
1 sprig dried rosemary, crushed
1/2 cup shallots, chopped
4 cloves garlic, minced
Salt and black pepper, to taste
1 tablespoon lard, at room temperature

Directions

Press the "Sauté" button to preheat your Instant Pot. Now, heat the oil and cook the beef until it is delicately browned.

Add the remaining ingredients; stir to combine.

Secure the lid. Choose the "Bean/Chili" mode and High pressure; cook for 25 minutes. Once cooking is complete, use a natural pressure release; carefully remove the lid. Bon appétit!

Per serving: 368 Calories; 16.1g Fat; 30.9g Carbs; 25.5g Protein; 3g Sugars

691. Basic Brown Stock

(Ready in about 2 hours 10 minutes | Servings 10)

Ingredients

2 brown onions, quartered
2 carrots, chopped
1 tablespoon olive oil
1 celery stalk, chopped
3 pounds meaty pork bones

Directions

Add all ingredients to the inner pot of your Instant Pot.

Secure the lid. Choose the "Soup/Broth" mode and cook for 120 minutes at Low pressure. Once cooking is complete, use a natural pressure release for 10 minutes; carefully remove the lid.

Remove the bones and vegetables using a metal spoon with holes and discard. Pour the liquid through the sieve into the bowl.

Use immediately or store in your refrigerator. Bon appétit!

Per serving: 91 Calories; 4.1g Fat; 3.3g Carbs; 9.9g Protein; 1.5g Sugars

692. Old-Fashioned Beef Stew

(Ready in about 35 minutes | Servings 6)

Ingredients

2 pounds beef sirloin steak, cut into bite-sized chunks
1 egg, beaten
1 pound bell peppers, seeded and sliced
1 cup vegetable broth
Salt and ground black pepper, to taste
1 cup red onion, chopped
2 garlic cloves, minced
1 teaspoon paprika
1 tablespoon olive oil
4 Italian plum tomatoes, crushed

Directions

Press the "Sauté" button to preheat your Instant Pot. Now, heat the oil. Cook the beef until it is no longer pink.

Add the onion and cook an additional 2 minutes. Stir in the minced garlic, peppers, broth, tomatoes, salt, black pepper, and paprika.

Secure the lid. Choose the "Soup" mode and High pressure; cook for 20 minutes. Once cooking is complete, use a quick pressure release; carefully remove the lid.

Afterwards, fold in the egg and stir well; seal the lid and let it sit in the residual heat for 8 to 10 minutes.

Serve in individual bowls with mashed potatoes. Enjoy!

Per serving: 403 Calories; 21.3g Fat; 16.4g Carbs; 36.8g Protein; 8.7g Sugars

693. Paprika Root Vegetable Soup

(Ready in about 45 minutes | Servings 8)

Ingredients

1 teaspoon paprika
2 carrots, chopped
2 bay leaves
1 pound potatoes, cubed
1 onion, chopped
2 garlic cloves, minced
4 cups water, or as needed
1/2 teaspoon mustard seeds
2 stalks celery, chopped
2 parsnips, chopped
Salt, to taste
1/2 teaspoon ground black pepper
1/2 pound turnip, chopped
3 cups chicken stock
1/2 stick butter, at room temperature

Directions

Place the celery, parsnip, carrots, potatoes, turnip, onion and garlic in the Instant Pot; now, pour in the water and stock.

Secure the lid. Select the "Soup" setting; cook for 25 minutes at High pressure. Once cooking is complete, use a quick pressure release; carefully remove the lid.

Stir in the butter and seasonings; press the "Sauté" button and continue to cook the soup for 14 to 16 minutes more or until everything is heated through. Discard the bay leaves and serve hot.

Per serving: 150 Calories; 6.7g Fat; 18.9g Carbs; 4.7g Protein; 3.3g Sugars

694. Country-Style Pork Broth

(Ready in about 55 minutes | Servings 10)

Ingredients

10 cups water, divided in half
4 carrots, cut into large chunks
2 bay leaves
1 onion, quartered
4 celery stalks, cut into large chunks
Sea salt and black peppercorns, to taste
3 garlic cloves, smashed
2 pounds pork bones

Directions

Preheat your oven to 400 degrees F. Coat a roasting pan with a piece of aluminum foil; brush with a little oil.

Arrange the pork bones and vegetables on the prepared roasting pan. Roast in the preheated oven for 25 to 30 minutes.

Transfer the roasted pork bones and vegetables to the inner pot of your Instant Pot. Now, stir in the bay leaves, salt, black peppercorns, and water.

Secure the lid. Choose the "Manual" mode and cook for 25 minutes at High pressure. Once cooking is complete, use a quick pressure release; carefully remove the lid.

Strain the stock and discard the solids. Keep in your refrigerator or freezer if desired. Enjoy!

Per serving: 91 Calories; 4.1g Fat; 3.3g Carbs; 9.9g Protein; 1.5g Sugars

695. Potato, Cauliflower and Cheese Soup

(Ready in about 35 minutes | Servings 6)

Ingredients

1/2 pound yellow potatoes, diced
1 cup yellow Swiss cheese, shredded
1 carrot, sliced
2 garlic cloves, pressed
1 pound cauliflower, broken into florets
1/2 cup yellow onion, chopped
1/4 teaspoon ground black pepper
1/2 teaspoon sea salt
1 cup water
1/2 teaspoon turmeric powder
1 celery, chopped
1/2 teaspoon mustard seeds
4 cups vegetable broth

Directions

Throw all of the above ingredients, except for the Swiss cheese, into the Instant Pot.

Secure the lid. Select the "Soup" setting; cook for 30 minutes at High pressure. Once cooking is complete, use a quick pressure release; carefully remove the lid.

After that, puree the soup with an immersion blender. Divide the soup among six soup bowls; top each serving with shredded Swiss cheese. Bon appétit!

Per serving: 175 Calories; 8.2g Fat; 13.9g Carbs; 11.7g Protein; 2.7g Sugars

696. Sicilian-Style Fish and Potato Stew

(Ready in about 15 minutes | Servings 5)

Ingredients

2 pounds halibut, cut into bite-sized pieces
1 pound Yukon Gold potatoes, diced
1/2 cup Marsala wine
1 teaspoon smoked paprika
1 ½ cups shellfish stock
1 cup water
2 ripe tomatoes, pureed
1 onion, sliced
3 garlic cloves, sliced
2 bay leaves
1/2 teaspoon hot sauce
2 tablespoons fresh cilantro, chopped
2 tablespoons canola oil
Sea salt and ground black pepper, to taste

Directions

Press the "Sauté" button and heat the oil. Once hot, cook the onions until softened; stir in the garlic and continue to sauté an additional 30 seconds.

Add the wine to deglaze the bottom of the inner pot, scraping up any browned bits.

Add the shellfish stock, water, potatoes, tomatoes, salt, black pepper, bay leaves, paprika, hot sauce, and halibut to the inner pot.

Secure the lid. Choose the "Manual" mode. Cook for 5 minutes at High pressure. Once cooking is complete, use a quick pressure release; carefully remove the lid. Serve with fresh cilantro and enjoy!

Per serving: 487 Calories; 31.5g Fat; 19.9g Carbs; 30.4g Protein; 2.8g Sugars

697. Mom's Pork Vegetable Soup

(Ready in about 40 minutes | Servings 4)

Ingredients

1 pound pork stew meat, cubed
2 cups spinach
Sea salt and ground black pepper, to taste
1 celery, sliced
1 carrot, sliced
1 turnip, peeled and sliced
4 cups beef bone broth
1 cup scallion, chopped
1 tablespoon olive oil

Directions

Press the "Sauté" button to preheat your Instant Pot; heat the oil. Now, sear the meat until it is delicately browned.

Add the remaining ingredients, except for the spinach.

Secure the lid. Choose the "Soup" setting and cook at High pressure for 30 minutes. Once cooking is complete, use a quick pressure release; carefully remove the lid.

Add the spinach to the Instant Pot; seal the lid and allow it to sit in the residual heat until wilted.

Ladle the soup into individual bowls and serve right away. Bon appétit!

Per serving: 264 Calories; 8.6g Fat; 6.6g Carbs; 38.2g Protein; 2.5g Sugars

698. Hearty Irish Burgoo

(Ready in about 30 minutes | Servings 8)

Ingredients

2 bell peppers, chopped
2 chicken thighs, boneless
2 pounds pork butt roast, cut into 2-inch pieces
3 tablespoons Worcestershire sauce
1 cup beer
1 (28-ounce) can tomatoes, crushed
2 pounds beef stew meat, cut into 2-inch pieces
Sea salt and ground black pepper, to taste
2 carrots, chopped
4 garlic cloves, chopped
4 cups beef bone broth
1 pound frozen corn kernels
1 tablespoon lard, melted
1 red chili pepper, chopped
1 onion, chopped

Directions

Press the "Sauté" button and melt the lard. Once hot, brown the meat in batches. Remove the browned meats to a bowl.

Then, sauté the peppers, onion, carrots for about 3 minutes or until tender and fragrant. Add the garlic and continue to cook for 30 seconds more.

Add the meat back to the Instant Pot. Stir in the remaining ingredients, except for the corn kernels.

Secure the lid. Choose the "Meat/Stew" mode and cook for 20 minutes at High pressure. Once cooking is complete, use a quick pressure release; carefully remove the lid.

Lastly, stir in the corn and continue to cook for a few minutes more on the "Sauté" function. Serve immediately.

Per serving: 522 Calories; 20.4g Fat; 22.2g Carbs; 61.6g Protein; 9.3g Sugars

699. Tex-Mex Taco Stew

(Ready in about 15 minutes | Servings 4)

Ingredients

1 pound ground chuck
1 onion, chopped
1 (1.25-ounce) package taco seasoning
1 (15-ounce) can beans, drained and rinsed
1 red chili pepper, seeded and chopped
4 tortilla bowls, baked
2 fresh tomatoes, chopped
1 tablespoon peanut oil
1 cup beef bone broth
1 bell pepper, seeded and chopped

Directions

Press the "Sauté" button and preheat the Instant Pot. Heat the oil and cook the ground chuck until it is no longer pink.

Add the broth, bell pepper, chili pepper, onion, and taco seasoning.

Secure the lid. Choose the "Manual" mode and High pressure; cook for 5 minutes. Once cooking is complete, use a quick pressure release; carefully remove the lid.

Divide the mixture between tortilla bowls. Top with beans and tomatoes. Enjoy!

Per serving: 409 Calories; 15.7g Fat; 37.5g Carbs; 29.5g Protein; 6.6g Sugars

700. Chicken Stew with Olives and Wine

(Ready in about 35 minutes | Servings 4)

Ingredients

4 chicken legs, boneless skinless
1/2 cup Kalamata olives, pitted and sliced
Sea salt and ground black pepper, to taste
1/4 cup dry red wine
2 carrots, chopped
1 teaspoon garlic, minced
1/2 teaspoon dried basil
2 ripe tomatoes, pureed
2 cups chicken bone broth
2 bay leaves
1 onion, chopped
1 stalk celery, chopped
1 teaspoon dried oregano
2 tablespoons olive oil

Directions

Press the "Sauté" button and heat the oil. Now, sauté the onion, celery, and carrot for 4 to 5 minutes or until they are tender.

Add the other ingredients, except for the Kalamata olives, and stir to combine.

Secure the lid. Choose the "Manual" mode. Cook for 15 minutes at High pressure. Once cooking is complete, use a natural pressure release for 10 minutes; carefully remove the lid.

Serve warm garnished with Kalamata olives. Bon appétit!

Per serving: 400 Calories; 27.9g Fat; 11.3g Carbs; 24.6g Protein; 5.1g Sugars

DESSERTS

701. Autumn Pumpkin Cake

(Ready in about 25 minutes + chilling time | Servings 10)

Ingredients

Batter:
3/4 cup applesauce
1 teaspoon baking powder
1/2 teaspoon cinnamon, ground
1 teaspoon vanilla extract
1 cup granulated sugar
1/8 teaspoon grated nutmeg
1/4 teaspoon cardamom, ground
1 ½ cups all-purpose flour

1/2 teaspoon crystallized ginger
1/8 teaspoon salt
2 cups pumpkin purée
1 tablespoon molasses
Cream Cheese Frosting:
2 cups powdered sugar
7 ounces cream cheese, at room temperature
1 stick butter, at room temperature

Directions

In a mixing bowl, combine all the dry ingredients for the batter. Then, in a separate mixing bowl, thoroughly combine all the wet ingredients.

Then, add the wet mixture to the dry mixture; pour the batter into a cake pan that is previously greased with melted butter.

Add 1 ½ cups of water and metal trivet to the Instant Pot. Lower the cake pan onto the trivet.

Secure the lid. Choose the "Porridge" mode and cook for 20 minutes under High pressure. Once cooking is complete, use a natural pressure release; carefully remove the lid.

Meanwhile, make the frosting. Beat the cream cheese and butter with an electric mixer on high speed. Add powdered sugar.

Continue to beat until the frosting has thickened. Spread the frosting on the cooled cake. Refrigerate until ready to serve. Bon appétit!

Per serving: 357 Calories; 15.2g Fat; 52.6g Carbs; 4.1g Protein; 34.9g Sugars

702. Mom's Lemon Cake

(Ready in about 35 minutes | Servings 6)

Ingredients

1/2 cup lemon juice
2 egg yolks
1/2 cup heavy cream
1 (14-ounce) can sweetened condensed milk

3 tablespoons honey
1/4 cup sugar
3 tablespoons butter, melted
1 egg
1 cup butter cookies, crumbled

Directions

Place a metal trivet and 1 cup of water in your Instant Pot. Spritz a baking pan with nonstick cooking spray.

Next, mix the cookies and butter until well combined. Press the crust into the prepared baking pan.

Then, thoroughly combine the eggs, lemon juice, condensed milk, and honey with a hand mixer.

Pour this mixture on top of the prepared crust. Lower the baking pan onto the trivet and cover with a piece of foil.

Secure the lid. Choose the "Manual" mode and cook for 15 minutes at High pressure. Once cooking is complete, use a natural pressure release for 15 minutes; carefully remove the lid.

Afterwards, whip the heavy cream with the sugar until the cream becomes stiff. Frost your cake and serve well chilled. Bon appétit!

Per serving: 369 Calories; 21.1g Fat; 40g Carbs; 7.3g Protein; 28.9g Sugars

703. Blood Orange Butter Cake

(Ready in about 45 minutes | Servings 8)

Ingredients

3 blood oranges, peeled and cut into slices
2 tablespoons fresh orange juice
1 1/3 cups cake flour
3 teaspoons granulated sugar
1 ½ teaspoons baking powder
A pinch of table salt
1 egg plus 1 egg yolk, beaten

1 cup sugar
1/2 teaspoon ground cloves
1/4 teaspoon ground cardamom
1/4 teaspoon ginger flavoring
1 stick butter, at room temperature
1/3 cup plain 2% yogurt
Nonstick cooking spray

Directions

Spritz a baking pan with a nonstick cooking spray. Now, arrange the orange slices at the bottom your pan.

In a mixing bowl, whisk the eggs until they are frothy. Now, add the sugar and mix well. Stir in the butter and mix again.

After that, add the yogurt, cloves, cardamom, ginger flavoring, and fresh orange juice. In another mixing bowl, thoroughly combine the flour with baking powder and salt.

Slowly and gradually, stir the flour mixture into the wet egg mixture; pour the batter on top of the orange slices.

Add 1 cup of water and a metal trivet to the bottom of your Instant Pot. Lower the baking pan onto the trivet.

Secure the lid. Choose the "Soup" mode and cook for 40 minutes at High pressure. Once cooking is complete, use a quick release; remove the lid carefully.

Place a platter on the cake and invert the baking pan, lifting it to reveal the oranges on top. Bon appétit!

Per serving: 354 Calories; 13.1g Fat; 55.4g Carbs; 4.3g Protein; 37.1g Sugars

704. Rum Croissant Pudding

(Ready in about 40 minutes | Servings 6)

Ingredients

3 eggs, whisked
3 tablespoons rum
1 cup granulated sugar
1 cup heavy cream
4 tablespoons water

1 cup milk
1/4 teaspoon ground cinnamon
6 stale croissants, cut into chunks

Directions

Place 1 cup of water and a metal trivet in the inner pot of your Instant Pot. Place the croissants in the lightly greased casserole dish.

Press the "Sauté" button and use the lowest setting. Then, place the granulated sugar and water and let it cook until the mixture turns a deep amber color.

Now, add the milk and heavy cream, and cook until heated through. Stir in the rum, cinnamon, and eggs; stir to combine.

Secure the lid. Choose the "Manual" mode and cook for 25 minutes at High pressure. Once cooking is complete, use a natural pressure release for 10 minutes; carefully remove the lid. Bon appétit!

Per serving: 414 Calories; 22.3g Fat; 39.4g Carbs; 10.2g Protein; 24.1g Sugars

705. Red Wine Berry Compote

(Ready in about 10 minutes | Servings 4)

Ingredients

1 cup mixed berries, dried
1 vanilla bean, split in half
1 cinnamon stick
2 tablespoons fresh orange juice

1 teaspoon cloves
3/4 cup sugar
1/2 cup rose wine
1 pound mixed berries, fresh

Directions

Simply throw all of the above ingredients into your Instant Pot.

Secure the lid. Choose the "Manual" and cook at High pressure for 6 minutes. Once cooking is complete, use a natural release; carefully remove the lid.

Serve over vanilla ice cream if desired and enjoy!

Per serving: 236 Calories; 0.8g Fat; 61.3g Carbs; 1.1g Protein; 50.2g Sugars

706. Mini Lava Molten Cakes

(Ready in about 30 minutes | Servings 4)

Ingredients

1 cup sugar
4 ounces bittersweet chocolate
4 ounces semisweet chocolate
3 tablespoons coconut milk
1 teaspoon vanilla

2 tablespoons cocoa powder
2 eggs
1 tablespoon carob powder
1/2 stick butter
1 ½ cups self-rising flour

Directions

Place a metal trivet and 1 cup of water in your Instant Pot. Butter custard cups and set aside.

Then, beat the butter and sugar until creamy. Fold in the eggs, one at a time, and mix until everything is well combined.

Add the milk and vanilla and mix again. Then, stir in the flour, cocoa powder, and carob powder. Fold in the chocolate and stir to combine. Divide the mixture between the prepared custard cups.

Lower the cups onto the trivet.

Secure the lid. Choose the "Steam" mode and cook for 15 minutes at High pressure. Once cooking is complete, use a natural pressure release for 10 minutes; carefully remove the lid. Enjoy!

Per serving: 671 Calories; 27.4g Fat; 95g Carbs; 10.6g Protein; 53.5g Sugars

707. Vanilla Orange Flan

(Ready in about 25 minutes | Servings 4)

Ingredients

1/4 cup orange juice
1/2 teaspoon pure vanilla extract
3 tablespoons water

15 ounces condensed milk, sweetened
10 ounces evaporated milk
2/3 cup muscovado sugar
5 eggs, whisked

Directions

Place the sugar and water in a microwave-safe dish; microwave approximately 3 minutes.

Now, pour the caramel into four ramekins.

Then, whisk the eggs with the milk, orange juice, and vanilla. Pour the egg mixture into ramekins.

Add 1 ½ cups of water and a metal rack to the Instant Pot. Now, lover your ramekins onto the rack.

Secure the lid. Choose the "Manual" and cook at High pressure for 9 minutes. Once cooking is complete, use a natural pressure release for 10 minutes; carefully remove the lid.

Refrigerate overnight and enjoy!

Per serving: 343 Calories; 17.8g Fat; 28.2g Carbs; 16.9g Protein; 27.4g Sugars

708. Hungarian Golden Pull-Apart Cake

(Ready in about 35 minutes | Servings 8)

Ingredients

1 teaspoon vanilla extract
4 ounces walnuts, ground
1 tablespoon fresh lemon juice
2 tablespoons cream cheese, at room temperature
1 tablespoon grated lemon peel

4 tablespoons butter, at room temperature
1/2 cup powdered sugar
1 cup granulated sugar
16 ounces refrigerated buttermilk biscuits

Directions

Place 1 cup of water and a metal trivet in the inner pot of your Instant Pot. Lightly grease a loaf pan with shortening of choice.

In a shallow bowl mix the granulated sugar, walnuts, and lemon peel. Mix the melted butter and lemon juice in another shallow bowl.

Cut each biscuit in half. Dip your biscuits into the butter mixture; then, roll them in the walnut/sugar mixture.

Arrange them in the loaf pan.

Secure the lid. Choose the "Manual" mode and cook for 25 minutes at High pressure. Once cooking is complete, use a natural pressure release for 5 minutes; carefully remove the lid.

In the meantime, whip the cream cheese with the powdered sugar, and vanilla extract. Drizzle over the hot cake and serve.

Per serving: 485 Calories; 23.4g Fat; 64.9g Carbs; 6.8g Protein; 36.9g Sugars

709. Traditional Crème Brûlée

(Ready in about 15 minutes + chilling time | Servings 4)

Ingredients

4 egg yolks
1/8 teaspoon kosher salt
1/8 teaspoon grated nutmeg
1 teaspoon pure vanilla extract
8 tablespoons golden caster sugar
1/3 cup Irish cream liqueur
1 ½ cups double cream

Directions

Start by adding 1 cup of water and a metal rack to your Instant Pot.

Then, microwave the double cream until thoroughly warmed.

In a mixing bowl, whisk the egg yolks, Irish cream liqueur, vanilla extract, 4 tablespoons caster sugar, salt, and nutmeg.

Gradually add the warm cream, stirring continuously. Spoon the mixture into four ramekins; cover with foil; lower onto the rack.

Secure the lid. Choose the "Manual" mode and cook for 6 minutes under High pressure. Once cooking is complete, use a natural pressure release; carefully remove the lid.

Place in your refrigerator for 4 to 5 hours to set. To serve, top each cup with a tablespoon of sugar; use a kitchen torch to melt the sugar and form a caramelized topping. Serve right away.

Per serving: 334 Calories; 25.7g Fat; 20.7g Carbs; 5.6g Protein; 19.9g Sugars

710. Traditional Budin de Pan

(Ready in about 1 hour | Servings 8)

Ingredients

1/2 stick butter, melted
A pinch of salt
1/2 teaspoon ground cloves
2 tablespoons rum
1 teaspoon vanilla essence
1 cup brown sugar
4 cups coconut milk
1 cup water
1 teaspoon cinnamon powder
4 eggs, beaten
1 pound Puerto Rican sweet bread, torn into pieces

Directions

Place 1 cup of water and a metal trivet in the inner pot of your Instant Pot. Place the pieces of sweet bread in a lightly greased casserole dish.

Now, mix the remaining ingredients; stir to combine well and pour the mixture over the pieces of sweet bread. Let it stand for 20 minutes, pressing down with a wide spatula until the bread is covered.

Secure the lid. Choose the "Manual" mode and cook for 25 minutes at High pressure. Once cooking is complete, use a natural pressure release for 10 minutes; carefully remove the lid. Bon appétit!

Per serving: 377 Calories; 18.4g Fat; 41.7g Carbs; 10.1g Protein; 24.5g Sugars

711. Pineapple Almond Cake

(Ready in about 30 minutes | Servings 8)

Ingredients

1 tablespoon gelatin powder
1/2 cup margarine, melted
1 tablespoon orange juice
1 teaspoon baking powder
1/4 teaspoon salt
1/2 cup honey
1/2 cup cassava flour
1/2 cup almond flour
1/2 teaspoon vanilla extract
1/2 teaspoon coconut extract
1 pound pineapple, sliced
1/2 teaspoon baking soda

Directions

Add 1 ½ cups of water and a metal rack to the Instant Pot. Cover the bottom of your cake pan with a parchment paper.

Then, spread the pineapple slices evenly in the bottom of the cake pan; drizzle with orange juice.

In a mixing bowl, thoroughly combine the flour, baking powder, baking soda, and salt.

In another bowl, combine the margarine, honey, vanilla, and coconut extract; add gelatin powder and whisk until well mixed.

Add the honey mixture to the flour mixture; mix until you've formed a ball of dough. Flatten your dough; place on the pineapple layer.

Cover the pan with foil, creating a foil sling.

Secure the lid. Choose the "Bean/Chili" mode and cook for 25 minutes under High pressure. Once cooking is complete, use a natural pressure release; carefully remove the lid.

Lastly, turn the pan upside down and unmold it on a serving platter. Enjoy!

Per serving: 258 Calories; 14.4g Fat; 33.2g Carbs; 1.8g Protein; 26.5g Sugars

712. Classic Chocolate Brownie

(Ready in about 40 minutes | Servings 12)

Ingredients

1/2 cup dark chocolate, cut into chunks
1 cup coconut sugar
1 teaspoon vanilla extract
1/2 teaspoon cinnamon powder
A pinch of salt
A pinch of grated nutmeg
1/2 cardamom powder
1/2 cup cocoa powder
1/2 teaspoon baking soda
2 eggs
1/2 cup sunflower seed butter
1/2 cup walnut butter

Directions

Place a metal trivet and 1 cup of water in your Instant Pot. Spritz a baking pan with nonstick cooking spray.

In a mixing bowl, combine all ingredients, except for the chocolate; stir well to create a thick batter.

Spoon the batter into the prepared pan. Sprinkle the chocolate chunks over the top; gently press the chocolate chunks into the batter.

Lower the baking pan onto the trivet.

Secure the lid. Choose the "Manual" mode and cook for 20 minutes at High pressure. Once cooking is complete, use a natural pressure release for 10 minutes; carefully remove the lid.

Place your brownies on a cooling rack before slicing and serving. Bon appétit!

Per serving: 264 Calories; 18.1g Fat; 24.2g Carbs; 4.5g Protein; 19.3g Sugars

713. Banana and Peach Tapioca Pudding

(Ready in about 20 minutes | Servings 4)

Ingredients

4 peaches, diced
2 bananas, peeled and sliced
1/2 cup coconut sugar
4 cups coconut milk
1 teaspoon vanilla extract
1 teaspoon cardamom
1 cup small pearl tapioca, soaked and well-rinsed

Directions

Start by adding 1½ cups of water and a metal trivet to the base of your Instant Pot.

Mix the tapioca, cardamom, coconut milk, vanilla, and sugar in a baking dish. Lower the dish onto the trivet.

Secure the lid. Choose the "Multigrain" mode and cook for 10 minutes under High pressure. Once cooking is complete, use a quick pressure release; carefully remove the lid.

Add the banana and peaches; gently stir to combine and serve.

Per serving: 449 Calories; 8.5g Fat; 86.1g Carbs; 9.8g Protein; 45.7g Sugars

714. Chocolate Mini Muffins

(Ready in about 40 minutes | Servings 6)

Ingredients

1 cup chocolate syrup
1/4 teaspoon ground cinnamon
A pinch of salt
1/2 cup rice flour
1 cup milk
1/4 cup coconut oil
1 teaspoon vanilla paste
2 tablespoons granulated sugar
2 eggs, whisked
1 ½ teaspoons baking powder
1/2 cup all-purpose flour

Directions

Add 1 cup of water and a metal rack to the bottom of the inner pot. Lightly grease a mini muffin tin with shortening of choice.

Mix the flour, baking powder, vanilla, cinnamon, salt, sugar, eggs, milk, and coconut oil until thoroughly combined and smooth.

Pour the batter into the muffin tin and lower it onto the rack.

Secure the lid. Choose the "Manual" mode and cook for 25 minutes at High pressure. Once cooking is complete, use a natural pressure release for 10 minutes; carefully remove the lid.

Serve with chocolate syrup and enjoy!

Per serving: 364 Calories; 12.5g Fat; 56.5g Carbs; 6.1g Protein; 29.6g Sugars

715. Key Lime Butter Cakes

(Ready in about 35 minutes | Servings 6)

Ingredients

Cakes:
1/2 cup agave syrup
1/4 cup fresh key lime juice
3 eggs, beaten
3 tablespoons coconut milk
1 teaspoon baking powder
1 teaspoon vanilla extract
1/2 cup coconut flour
3 tablespoons butter, melted
Frosting:
3 tablespoons butter, softened
2 tablespoons agave syrup
3 ounces cream cheese

Directions

Spritz the bottom and sides of four ramekins with a nonstick cooking spray.

In a mixing bowl, whisk the eggs with the melted butter, coconut milk, vanilla, coconut flour, baking powder, agave syrup, and key lime juice.

Spoon the batter into greased ramekins and cover them loosely with foil.

Add 1 cup of water and a metal rack to the bottom of your Instant Pot. Now, lower the ramekins onto the rack.

Secure the lid. Choose the "Bean/Chili" mode and cook for 25 minutes under High pressure. Once cooking is complete, use a natural pressure release; carefully remove the lid.

Meanwhile, prepare the frosting by mixing the cream cheese and butter with an electric mixer. Add agave syrup and continue mixing until everything is well incorporated.

Transfer the mixture to a plastic bag for piping the frosting on your cupcakes. Bon appétit!

Per serving: 320 Calories; 20.7g Fat; 29.6g Carbs; 5.9g Protein; 29.2g Sugars

716. American-Style Cheesecake

(Ready in about 45 minutes | Servings 10)

Ingredients

2 tablespoons golden caster sugar
10 large graham crackers, crumbled
3 tablespoons almonds, ground
1/2 cup golden caster sugar
1 cup creme fraiche
1/3 teaspoon cinnamon
1 teaspoon vanilla extract
1 tablespoon lemon zest
1 tablespoon arrowroot powder
3 eggs
12 ounces Philadelphia cheese
4 tablespoons butter
4 tablespoons granulated sugar

Directions

Place a metal trivet and 1 cup of water in your Instant Pot. Spritz a baking pan with nonstick cooking spray.

Next, mix 4 tablespoons of granulated sugar, butter, crackers, almonds, and cinnamon into a sticky crust. Press the crust into the prepared baking pan.

In a mixing bowl, combine the Philadelphia cheese, vanilla extract, lemon zest, arrowroot powder, 1/2 cup of golden caster sugar, and eggs. Pour the filling mixture over the crust and cover it with a piece of foil.

Lower the baking pan onto the trivet.

Secure the lid. Choose the "Manual" mode and cook for 25 minutes at High pressure. Once cooking is complete, use a natural pressure release for 15 minutes; carefully remove the lid.

Lastly, beat the creme fraiche with 2 tablespoons of golden caster sugar. Spread this topping over the cheesecake right to the edges. Cover loosely with foil and refrigerate overnight. Bon appétit!

Per serving: 340 Calories; 20.1g Fat; 29.7g Carbs; 10.7g Protein; 18.1g Sugars

717. Lemon and Blueberry Mousse

(Ready in about 35 minutes | Servings 4)

Ingredients

1/2 cup fresh lemon juice
1 tablespoon lemon zest, finely grated
1 ¼ cups sugar
Mint leaves, for garnish
1 large egg yolks
A pinch of salt
2 teaspoons cornstarch
3 eggs
1/4 cup heavy whipping cream
6 tablespoons blueberries
1 stick butter, softened

Directions

Beat the butter and sugar with an electric mixer. Gradually, add the eggs and yolks; mix until pale and smooth.

Add the lemon juice and lemon zest; add salt and cornstarch; mix to combine well. Pour the mixture into four jars; cover your jars with the lids.

Add 1 cup of water and a trivet to the Instant Pot. Lower the jars onto the trivet; secure the lid. Select "Manual" mode, High pressure and 15 minutes.

Once cooking is complete, use a natural release for 15 minutes; carefully remove the lid. Serve well-chilled, garnished with heavy whipping cream, blueberries, and mint leaves. Bon appétit!

Per serving: 445 Calories; 30.1g Fat; 40.6g Carbs; 5.4g Protein; 36.7g Sugars

718. Grandma's Stuffed Apples

(Ready in about 25 minutes | Servings 4)

Ingredients

4 tablespoons currants
2 tablespoons coconut oil
1/3 cup granulated sugar
1/2 teaspoon cinnamon
1/3 cup walnuts, chopped
4 baking apples
1/2 teaspoon cardamom

Directions

Add 1 ½ cups of water and a metal rack to the bottom of the inner pot.

Core the apples and use a melon baller to scoop out a bit of the flesh. Mix the remaining ingredients. Divide the filling between your apples.

Secure the lid. Choose the "Steam" mode and cook for 15 minutes at High pressure. Once cooking is complete, use a quick pressure release; carefully remove the lid.

Serve with ice cream, if desired. Bon appétit!

Per serving: 266 Calories; 11.5g Fat; 43.9g Carbs; 1.6g Protein; 36g Sugars

719. Cinnamon Cherry Crumble

(Ready in about 20 minutes | Servings 6)

Ingredients

1 box yellow cake mix
1/4 teaspoon grated nutmeg
1/2 teaspoon ground cinnamon
1/2 teaspoon ground cardamom
1/2 cup coconut butter, melted
30 ounces cherry pie filling

Directions

Add 1 cup of water and metal rack to the Instant Pot. Place the cherry pie filling in a pan.

Mix the remaining ingredients; spread the batter over the cherry pie filling evenly.

Secure the lid. Choose the "Manual" mode and cook for 10 minutes under High pressure. Once cooking is complete, use a natural pressure release; carefully remove the lid.

Serve with whipped topping. Enjoy!

Per serving: 499 Calories; 16.2g Fat; 82g Carbs; 4.5g Protein; 24.3g Sugars

720. Cranberry Sweet Risotto

(Ready in about 20 minutes | Servings 4)

Ingredients

1/2 cup dried cranberries
A pinch of salt
A pinch of grated nutmeg
2 eggs, beaten
1 teaspoon vanilla extract
1/4 teaspoon cardamom
2 cups milk
1/3 cup maple syrup
1 cup white rice
1 ½ cups water

Directions

Place the rice, water, and salt in the inner pot of your Instant Pot.

Secure the lid. Choose the "Manual" mode and cook for 3 minutes at High pressure. Once cooking is complete, use a natural pressure release for 10 minutes; carefully remove the lid.

Add in the milk, maple syrup, eggs, vanilla extract, cardamom, and nutmeg; stir to combine well.

Press the "Sauté" button and cook, stirring frequently, until your pudding starts to boil. Press the "Cancel' button. Stir in the dried cranberries.

Pudding will thicken as it cools. Bon appétit!

Per serving: 403 Calories; 6.6g Fat; 75.6g Carbs; 9.8g Protein; 31.9g Sugars

721. Indian Kheer with Pistachios

(Ready in about 10 minutes | Servings 4)

Ingredients

3 cups coconut milk
1/2 cup jaggery
1/2 cup raisins
A pinch of coarse salt
1/4 teaspoon saffron, crushed

4 tablespoons unsalted pistachios, minced
1 ½ cups basmati rice
1 teaspoon rosewater

Directions

Add all of the above ingredients, except for the raisins, to your Instant Pot; stir to combine well.

Secure the lid. Choose the "Soup" mode and High pressure; cook for 3 minutes. Once cooking is complete, use a natural pressure release; carefully remove the lid.

Serve topped with raisins and enjoy!

Per serving: 408 Calories; 18.7g Fat; 62.4g Carbs; 13.8g Protein; 35.6g Sugars

722. French Chocolate Chip Custard

(Ready in about 25 minutes | Servings 6)

Ingredients

9 ounces chocolate chips
1 teaspoon instant coffee
4 egg yolks
1/3 cup sugar

A pinch of pink salt
1/2 cup whole milk
2 cups double cream

Directions

Place a metal trivet and 1 cup of water in your Instant Pot.

In a saucepan, bring the cream and milk to a simmer.

Then, thoroughly combine the egg yolks, sugar, instant coffee, and salt. Slowly and gradually whisk in the hot cream mixture.

Whisk in the chocolate chips and blend again. Pour the mixture into mason jars. Lower the jars onto the trivet.

Secure the lid. Choose the "Manual" mode and cook for 6 minutes at High pressure. Once cooking is complete, use a natural pressure release for 10 minutes; carefully remove the lid.

Serve well chilled and enjoy!

Per serving: 351 Calories; 19.3g Fat; 39.3g Carbs; 5.5g Protein; 32.1g Sugars

723. Coconut and Date Pudding

(Ready in about 15 minutes | Servings 4)

Ingredients

1/2 cup Medjool dates, finely chopped
1 ½ cups water
1/2 teaspoon ground cardamom

1 (14-ounce) can coconut milk
1/2 teaspoon ground cinnamon
1 ½ cups millet

Directions

Add all of the above ingredients to your Instant Pot; stir to combine well.

Secure the lid. Choose the "Manual" mode and cook for 1 minute at High pressure. Once cooking is complete, use a natural pressure release for 10 minutes; carefully remove the lid.

Serve warm or at room temperature.

Per serving: 320 Calories; 3.3g Fat; 63.1g Carbs; 9.3g Protein; 6.7g Sugars

724. Farmhouse Apple Cake

(Ready in about 1 hour 25 minutes | Servings 8)

Ingredients

1 1/3 cups flour
1/2 cup honey
1/2 teaspoon ground cloves
2 tablespoons orange juice
1/2 teaspoon vanilla paste
1/2 teaspoon ground cardamom

3 tablespoons sugar
1 teaspoon baking powder
A pinch of salt
1 stick butter, melted
1 teaspoon ground cinnamon
4 apples, peeled, cored and chopped

Directions

Grease and flour a cake pan and set it aside. Toss the apples with the ground cloves, cardamom. cinnamon and sugar.

In a mixing bowl, thoroughly combine the flour, baking powder and salt.

In another mixing bowl, mix the butter, honey, orange juice, and vanilla paste. Stir the wet ingredients into the dry ones; spoon 1/2 of the batter into the prepared cake pan.

Spread half of the apples on top of the batter. Pour in the remaining batter covering the apple chunks. Spread the remaining apples on top.

Cover the cake pan with a paper towel.

Add 1 cup of water and a metal rack to your Instant Pot. Lower the cake pan onto the rack.

Secure the lid. Choose the "Manual" mode and cook for 55 minutes at High pressure. Once cooking is complete, use a natural pressure release for 10 minutes; carefully remove the lid.

Transfer the cake to a cooling rack and allow it to sit for about 15 minutes before slicing and serving.

Per serving: 304 Calories; 11.8g Fat; 49.7g Carbs; 2.6g Protein; 30.2g Sugars

725. Rich Pudding Cake with Blackberries

(Ready in about 45 minutes | Servings 8)

Ingredients

2 cups blackberries
1/4 cup vanilla cookies, crumbled
1/3 cup brown sugar
2 eggs, whisked
3/4 cup all-purpose flour
4 dollops of vanilla ice cream, to serve
1 teaspoon baking powder
A pinch of grated nutmeg
A pinch of salt
1/2 cup almond milk
1 stick butter, cold
1/2 teaspoon baking soda
Nonstick cooking spray

Directions

Spritz a baking pan with a nonstick cooking spray.

In a mixing bowl, thoroughly combine the flour, baking soda, baking powder, nutmeg, and salt.

Cut in the butter using two knives; now, add crumbled cookies and sugar; mix until everything is combined well. Add the eggs and almond milk; fold in the blackberries.

Finally, scrape the mixture into the prepared baking pan. Cover with a sheet of foil; make sure that foil fits tightly around sides and under the bottom of your baking pan.

Add water and a metal trivet to the Instant Pot. Lower the baking pan onto the trivet and secure the lid.

Select the "Manual" mode. Bake for 30 minutes at High pressure.

Once cooking is complete, use a quick release; remove the lid carefully. Remove the baking pan from the Instant Pot using rack handles. Remove foil and allow the cake to cool approximately 10 minutes.

Serve on individual plates, garnished with a dollop of vanilla ice cream.

Per serving: 164 Calories; 0.3g Fat; 42.9g Carbs; 1.4g Protein; 16.9g Sugars

726. Double Chocolate Fudge

(Ready in about 15 minutes + chilling time | Servings 12)

Ingredients

8 ounces semisweet chocolate chips
8 ounces bittersweet chocolate chips
2 tablespoons peanut butter
1 teaspoon vanilla extract
1/2 teaspoon ground cardamom
1/2 teaspoon ground cinnamon
16 ounce canned condensed milk

Directions

Line the bottom of a baking sheet with a piece of foil.

Add the milk, peanut butter, cardamom, cinnamon, and vanilla to the inner pot of your Instant Pot; stir until everything is well incorporated.

Next, press the "Sauté" button and use the lowest setting to cook the mixture until thoroughly warmed. Now, fold in the chocolate chips and stir again to combine well.

Lastly, pour the mixture into the prepared baking sheet and transfer to your refrigerator; let it sit until solid.

Cut into squares and serve. Bon appétit!

Per serving: 223 Calories; 11g Fat; 27.7g Carbs; 3.2g Protein; 18.3g Sugars

727. Vanilla Stewed Fruit

(Ready in about 15 minutes | Servings 5)

Ingredients

1 large vanilla bean pod, split open lengthwise
1 teaspoon whole cloves
1 cup prunes, pitted
1 cinnamon stick
1/4 cup granulated sugar
1 tablespoon fresh apple juice
1/2 pound peaches, pitted and halved
1/2 teaspoon apple pie spice mix
1/2 pound pears, cored and quartered
1 tablespoon fresh lemon juice

Directions

Add all of the above ingredients to your Instant Pot. Secure the lid.

Choose the "Manual" mode and cook under High Pressure for 3 minutes. Once cooking is complete, use a natural release for 10 minutes; remove the lid carefully.

Serve warm or at room temperature. Enjoy!

Per serving: 164 Calories; 0.3g Fat; 42.9g Carbs; 1.4g Protein; 16.9g Sugars

728. Cinnamon Roll Pear Pie

(Ready in about 35 minutes | Servings 8)

Ingredients

5 pears, cored and sliced
1/3 cup pecans, chopped
2 tablespoons butter
1/4 cup packed brown sugar
1/2 teaspoon cinnamon
1/4 cup all-purpose flour
2 cans (12-ounce) refrigerated cinnamon rolls

Directions

Separate the dough into 8 rolls. Press and flatten the rolls into a lightly greased pie plate. Make sure there are no holes between the flattened rolls.

In a mixing bowl, mix the flour, brown sugar, cinnamon, butter, and pecans. Place the slices of pears on the prepared cinnamon roll crust. Spoon the streusel onto the pear slices.

Add 1 cup of water and a metal rack to the bottom of the inner pot. Lower the pie plate onto the rack.

Secure the lid. Choose the "Manual" mode and cook for 25 minutes at High pressure. Once cooking is complete, use a natural pressure release for 5 minutes; carefully remove the lid. Bon appétit!

Per serving: 497 Calories; 28.6g Fat; 56.5g Carbs; 4.9g Protein; 30.4g Sugars

729. Stewed Bramley Apples with Cranberries

(Ready in about 20 minutes | Servings 4)

Ingredients

1/3 cup cranberries, dried
1/2 cup granulated sugar
1/2 cup orange juice
1 teaspoon grated orange peel
1/3 teaspoon ground star anise
1 pound Bramley apples cored
1/2 cup red wine
1/3 teaspoon cinnamon

Directions

Place the cored apples in your Instant Pot. Now, add the remaining ingredients.

Secure the lid. Choose the "Manual" mode and cook for 3 minutes under High pressure. Once cooking is complete, use a natural pressure release for 10 minutes; carefully remove the lid.

Serve with whipped cream if desired. Bon appétit!

Per serving: 184 Calories; 0.2g Fat; 47.5g Carbs; 0.6g Protein; 42.2g Sugars

730. Vanilla Cupcakes with Cream Cheese Frosting

(Ready in about 40 minutes | Servings 4)

Ingredients

4 ounces cream cheese
A pinch of salt
1/4 teaspoon ground cinnamon
1 cup cake flour
1 ½ teaspoons baking powder
1 teaspoon vanilla extract
1 egg
1/3 cup powdered sugar
1 cup heavy cream, cold
1/2 cup honey
1/4 almond milk
1/4 teaspoon ground cardamom

Directions

In a mixing bowl, thoroughly combine the flour, baking powder, salt, cardamom, cinnamon, and vanilla.

Then, gradually add in the egg, honey, and milk. Mix to combine well. Now, spoon the batter into silicone cupcake liners and cover them with foil.

Place 1 cup of water and a metal trivet in your Instant Pot. Lower your cupcakes onto the trivet.

Secure the lid. Choose the "Manual" mode and cook for 25 minutes at High pressure. Once cooking is complete, use a natural pressure release for 10 minutes; carefully remove the lid.

While the cupcakes are cooking, prepare the frosting by mixing the remaining ingredients. Frost your cupcakes and enjoy!

Per serving: 497 Calories; 17.8g Fat; 77g Carbs; 9.8g Protein; 48.5g Sugars

731. Mason Jar Cake

(Ready in about 15 minutes | Servings 4)

Ingredients

2 ounces sour cream
2 eggs
4 tablespoons orange curd
1/3 cup coconut sugar
1/2 teaspoon coconut extract
1 teaspoon orange zest
1/2 teaspoon vanilla extract
1/2 cup coconut flakes
12 ounces cream cheese

Directions

Start by adding 1 ½ cups of water and a metal trivet to the bottom of the Instant Pot.

In a mixing bowl, combine the cream cheese, sour cream, coconut sugar, vanilla, coconut extract, and orange zest.

Now, add the coconut flakes and eggs; whisk until everything is well combined.

Divide the batter between four jars. Top with the orange curd. Lower the jars onto the trivet. Now, cover your jars with foil.

Secure the lid. Choose the "Manual" and cook at High pressure for 9 minutes. Once cooking is complete, use a natural pressure release; carefully remove the lid.

Garnish with fruits if desired. Bon appétit!

Per serving: 425 Calories; 33.6g Fat; 20.2g Carbs; 11.4g Protein; 16.7g Sugars

732. Chocolate Apricot Cake

(Ready in about 55 minutes | Servings 10)

Ingredients

1 ½ cups chocolate chips
1/2 cup dried apricots, chopped
1/2 cup peanut butter
3 cups milk
1 package vanilla cake mix
4 ounces instant pudding mix

Directions

In a mixing bowl, thoroughly combine the pudding mix and milk. Por the mixture into a lightly greased inner pot.

Prepare the cake mix according to the manufacturer's instructions, gradually adding in the peanut butter. Pour the batter over the pudding.

Secure the lid. Choose the "Manual" mode and cook for 30 minutes at High pressure. Once cooking is complete, use a natural pressure release for 10 minutes; carefully remove the lid.

Sprinkle the chocolate chips and dried apricots on top. Seal the lid and let it stand for 10 to 15 minutes until the chocolate melts. Enjoy!

Per serving: 408 Calories; 13.9g Fat; 64.2g Carbs; 8.2g Protein; 39.7g Sugars

733. Peanut Butter Penuche

(Ready in about 10 minutes + chilling time | Servings 8)

Ingredients

1/2 cup peanut butter
1/2 cup agave syrup
4 ounces coconut cream, at room temperature
1 teaspoon pure almond extract

1 teaspoon pure vanilla extract
1/2 cup coconut oil
1/2 cup cocoa butter
8 ounces cream cheese, at room temperature
2/3 cup almond flour

Directions

Press the "Sauté" button to preheat your Instant Pot. Add the cheese, sour cream, coconut oil, cocoa butter, and peanut butter to your Instant Pot.

Let it simmer until it is melted and warmed through.

Add the vanilla, almond extract, almond flour, and agave syrup; continue to stir until everything is well combined.

Then, spoon the mixture into a cookie sheet lined with a piece of foil. Place in your refrigerator; refrigerate at least for 2 hours.

Cut into squares and serve.

Per serving: 415 Calories; 36.3g Fat; 21.9g Carbs; 3.4g Protein; 20.8g Sugars

734. Autumn Squash and Coconut Mousse

(Ready in about 20 minutes | Servings 6)

Ingredients

1 cup coconut cream
2 pounds butternut squash, peeled, seeded, and diced
1 teaspoon pumpkin pie spice mix

6 tablespoons almond milk
A pinch of kosher salt
1/2 cup maple syrup

Directions

Add 1 cup of water and a metal rack to the bottom of the inner pot. Place your squash in a steamer basket; lower the basket onto the rack.

Secure the lid. Choose the "Steam" mode and cook for 10 minutes at High pressure. Once cooking is complete, use a quick pressure release; carefully remove the lid.

Stir the remaining ingredients into the cooked squash; combine all ingredients with a potato masher.

Let it cook on the "Sauté" function until everything is thoroughly heated or about 4 minutes. Serve immediately.

Per serving: 315 Calories; 8.8g Fat; 60.5g Carbs; 2.3g Protein; 42.1g Sugars

735. Golden Key Cake

(Ready in about 20 minutes | Servings 6)

Ingredients

3/4 cup canned dulce de leche
1 teaspoon vanilla extract
1/4 teaspoon ground cinnamon
1/2 teaspoon pure almond extract
1/4 teaspoon star anise, ground

1/3 cup powdered sugar
3 eggs, beaten
4 tablespoons all-purpose flour
1/4 cup butter, melted
1/8 teaspoon kosher salt
1 tablespoon granulated sugar
A nonstick cooking spray

Directions

Spritz a cake pan with a nonstick cooking spray. Then, sprinkle the bottom of your pan with granulated sugar.

Beat the butter with the eggs, vanilla, almond extract, star anise, and ground cinnamon. Add the powdered sugar, canned dulce de leche, flour, and salt. Mix until a thick batter is achieved.

Scrape the batter into the prepared cake pan.

Place 1 cup of water and metal trivet in the Instant Pot. Place the cake pan on the trivet.

Secure the lid. Choose the "Manual" mode and cook for 10 minutes under High pressure. Once cooking is complete, use a quick pressure release; carefully remove the lid. Serve hot with ice cream.

Per serving: 301 Calories; 15.4g Fat; 32.5g Carbs; 7.7g Protein; 26.1g Sugars

736. Granny's Monkey Bread with Hazelnuts

(Ready in about 35 minutes | Servings 8)

Ingredients

4 tablespoons hazelnuts, ground
1 teaspoon vanilla extract
1/4 cup powdered sugar
1 stick butter, melted

4 ounces cream cheese, at room temperature
2 tablespoons apple juice
10 refrigerated biscuits
1 cup granulated sugar

Directions

Place 1 cup of water and a metal trivet in the inner pot of your Instant Pot. Lightly grease 10-inch fluted tube pan with cooking spray.

In a shallow bowl, mix the 1 cup of granulated sugar and ground hazelnuts.

Cut each biscuit in half. Dip your biscuits into the melted butter; then, roll them in the hazelnut/sugar mixture.

Arrange them in the fluted tube pan.

Secure the lid. Choose the "Manual" mode and cook for 25 minutes at High pressure. Once cooking is complete, use a natural pressure release for 5 minutes; carefully remove the lid.

In the meantime, whip the cream cheese with the powdered sugar, apple juice, and vanilla extract. Drizzle over the hot cake and serve.

Per serving: 444 Calories; 28.9g Fat; 42.4g Carbs; 5.9g Protein; 18.3g Sugars

737. Rustic Chocolate and Raisin Cake

(Ready in about 45 minutes | Servings 8)

Ingredients

3 teaspoons coconut oil
1 teaspoon vanilla extract
1/3 cup raisins, soaked for 15 minutes
7 ounces sour cheese
1 cup granulated sugar
14 ounces chocolate cookies, crumbled

3 eggs
2 tablespoons cornstarch
10 ounces cream cheese
Topping:
1/2 cup coconut, shredded
4 ounces dark chocolate, melted
1 cup sweetened coconut milk

Directions

In a mixing bowl, thoroughly combine the cream cheese, sour cream, and sugar. Add the eggs and mix again; add the cornstarch and vanilla.

In another bowl, thoroughly combine the cookies, raisins, and coconut oil. Press the crust into the bottom of a cake pan.

Spread the cheesecake mixture over the crust.

Add 1 ½ cups of water and metal trivet to the Instant Pot. Lower the pan onto the trivet. Cover with a foil, making a foil sling.

Secure the lid. Choose "Multigrain" mode and cook for 40 minutes under High pressure. Once cooking is complete, use a quick pressure release; carefully remove the lid.

Meanwhile, make the topping by vigorously whisking all ingredients. Spread the topping over the cake.

Place in your refrigerator to cool completely. Enjoy!

Per serving: 575 Calories; 35.6g Fat; 54.1g Carbs; 11.1g Protein; 33.1g Sugars

738. Traditional Bismarck Pancake

(Ready in about 40 minutes | Servings 4)

Ingredients

5 eggs
1 cup canned blueberries with syrup
1 ¼ cups milk
1/2 teaspoon cinnamon powder

1 cup all-purpose flour
1/2 teaspoon vanilla extract
1/4 teaspoon kosher salt
4 tablespoons butter, melted

Directions

Place 1 cup of water and a metal trivet in your Instant Pot. Line the bottom of a springform pan with parchment paper; grease the bottom and sides of the pan with melted butter.

Mix the eggs, milk, flour, salt, cinnamon, and vanilla until everything is well combined. Now, spoon the batter into the prepared pan. Lower the pan onto the trivet.

Secure the lid. Choose the "Manual" mode and cook for 30 minutes at High pressure. Once cooking is complete, use a quick pressure release; carefully remove the lid.

Serve garnished with fresh blueberries and enjoy!

Per serving: 399 Calories; 19.8g Fat; 42.3g Carbs; 13.1g Protein; 17.5g Sugars

739. Stuffed Nectarines with Vanilla Yogurt

(Ready in about 15 minutes | Servings 4)

Ingredients

4 large-sized nectarines, halved and pitted
1/2 cup low-fat vanilla yogurt
1/2 teaspoon ground cardamom
5 tablespoons honey
1 teaspoon ground cinnamon
1/8 teaspoon salt
2 gingersnaps, crushed

3 tablespoons coconut oil
1/2 teaspoon pure vanilla extract
1/2 teaspoon pure coconut extract
1/4 cup tapioca starch
1/8 teaspoon nutmeg, preferably freshly grated

Directions

Start by adding 1 cup of water and a metal trivet to the bottom of your Instant Pot.

Mix the tapioca, honey, coconut oil, cinnamon, cardamom, nutmeg, salt, gingersnaps, vanilla, and coconut extract in a bowl.

Divide this mixture among nectarine halves. Place the nectarines on the metal trivet.

Secure the lid. Choose the "Manual" mode and cook for 4 minutes under High pressure. Once cooking is complete, use a natural pressure release; carefully remove the lid.

Serve topped with vanilla yogurt. Enjoy!

Per serving: 463 Calories; 12.8g Fat; 87.1g Carbs; 4.3g Protein; 40.6g Sugars

740. Authentic Greek Hosafi

(Ready in about 20 minutes | Servings 8)

Ingredients

2 tablespoons Greek honey
1/2 teaspoon whole cloves
1 cup prunes, pitted
1 cinnamon stick
1 cup sugar
1 vanilla bean

1/2 teaspoon whole star anise
1 cup dried apricots
1/2 cup sultana raisins
2 cups water
1/2 cup dried figs
1 cup almonds

Directions

Place all ingredients in the inner pot of your Instant Pot.

Secure the lid. Choose the "Manual" mode and cook for 2 minutes at High pressure. Once cooking is complete, use a natural pressure release for 10 minutes; carefully remove the lid.

Serve with Greek yogurt or ice cream, if desired.

Per serving: 215 Calories; 0.4g Fat; 55.4g Carbs; 1.8g Protein; 35.8g Sugars

741. Vanilla Rice Pudding Dates

(Ready in about 15 minutes | Servings 3)

Ingredients

1/8 teaspoon pumpkin pie spice
2 eggs, beaten
1 ½ cups water
10 dates, pitted, soaked and chopped
1 teaspoon pure vanilla extract
1 ½ cups jasmine rice, rinsed
2 teaspoons coconut oil, softened

Directions

Press the "Sauté" button to preheat your Instant Pot. Now, add the coconut oil and rice; stir until it is well coated.

Add the remaining ingredients and stir again.

Secure the lid. Choose the "Manual" mode and cook for 2 minutes under High pressure. Once cooking is complete, use a natural pressure release for 10 minutes; carefully remove the lid.

Divide between three dessert bowls and serve with double cream. Enjoy!

Per serving: 270 Calories; 12.5g Fat; 41.1g Carbs; 6g Protein; 14.2g Sugars

742. Coconut and Almond Mini Cheesecakes

(Ready in about 45 minutes | Servings 4)

Ingredients

16 ounces coconut milk
1/2 cup almonds
3/4 cup coconut yogurt
6 dates, chopped
1/2 cup sunflower kernels

Directions

Spritz four ramekins with nonstick cooking spray.

Process the almonds, sunflower kernels, and dates in your blender until it turns into a sticky mixture.

Press the crust mixture into the prepared ramekins.

Thoroughly combine the coconut milk and yogurt in a mixing bowl. Pour this mixture into the ramekins and cover them with a piece of foil.

Place a metal trivet and 1 cup of water in your Instant Pot. Lower the ramekins onto the trivet.

Secure the lid. Choose the "Manual" mode and cook for 25 minutes at High pressure. Once cooking is complete, use a natural pressure release for 15 minutes; carefully remove the lid. Bon appétit!

Per serving: 439 Calories; 39.2g Fat; 18.1g Carbs; 11.2g Protein; 8.5g Sugars

743. Rustic Sponge Cake

(Ready in about 25 minutes | Servings 6)

Ingredients

1/4 cup coconut milk
1/2 teaspoon pure coconut extract
1 stick butter, at room temperature
1/2 teaspoon pure vanilla extract
1 cup sugar
3 eggs, beaten
3 tablespoons crumbled butter cookies
1 ¼ cups cake flour
Nonstick cooking spray

Directions

Spritz the bottom and sides of a steam bowl with a nonstick cooking spray. Add the crumbled butter cookies to the bottom.

Then, beat the butter, sugar, vanilla, and coconut extract until very creamy; now, add the eggs, one at a time and continue to mix.

Stir in the flour and milk; mix to combine well. Scrape the batter into the prepared steam bowl.

Secure the lid. Choose the "Steam" mode and cook for 20 minutes under High pressure. Once cooking is complete, use a natural pressure release; carefully remove the lid. Bon appétit!

Per serving: 426 Calories; 26.4g Fat; 39.9g Carbs; 7.3g Protein; 17.3g Sugars

744. French Soufflé with a Twist

(Ready in about 1 hour | Servings 6)

Ingredients

3 eggs
1 stick butter, softened
1/3 cup cream cheese room temperature
1 teaspoon baking powder
1/2 teaspoon ground cinnamon
3 tablespoons flour
1 teaspoon vanilla paste
3/4 cup sugar
1 ½ pounds carrots, trimmed and cut into chunks
1/4 teaspoon ground cardamom

Directions

Place 1 cup of water and a steamer basket in the bottom of your Instant Pot. Place the carrots in the steamer basket.

Secure the lid. Choose the "Steam" mode and cook for 10 minutes at High pressure. Once cooking is complete, use a quick pressure release; carefully remove the lid.

Process the mashed carrots, sugar, baking powder, vanilla, cardamom, cinnamon, and flour in your food processor until creamy, uniform, and smooth.

Add the eggs one at a time and mix to combine well. Stir in the cream cheese and butter; mix to combine well.

Spritz a baking pan with cooking spray; spoon the carrot mixture into the baking dish.

Add 1 cup of water and metal trivet to the bottom of the inner pot; cover with a paper towel.

Secure the lid. Choose the "Manual" mode and cook for 35 minutes at High pressure. Once cooking is complete, use a natural pressure release for 10 minutes; carefully remove the lid. Bon appétit!

Per serving: 344 Calories; 24.1g Fat; 26.1g Carbs; 6.8g Protein; 17.1g Sugars

745. Orange Butterscotch Pudding

(Ready in about 20 minutes | Servings 4)

Ingredients

4 caramels
2 eggs, well-beaten
1/4 cup freshly squeezed
orange juice
1/3 cup sugar
1 cup cake flour
1/2 teaspoon baking powder

1/4 cup milk
1 stick butter, melted
1/2 teaspoon vanilla essence
Sauce:
1/2 cup golden syrup
2 teaspoons corn flour
1 cup boiling water

Directions

Melt the butter and milk in the microwave. Whisk in the eggs, vanilla, and sugar. After that, stir in the flour, baking powder, and orange juice.

Lastly, add the caramels and stir until everything is well combined and melted.

Divide between the four jars. Add 1 ½ cups of water and a metal trivet to the bottom of the Instant Pot. Lower the jars onto the trivet.

To make the sauce, whisk the boiling water, corn flour, and golden syrup until everything is well combined. Pour the sauce into each jar.

Secure the lid. Choose the "Steam" mode and cook for 15 minutes under High pressure. Once cooking is complete, use a natural pressure release; carefully remove the lid. Enjoy!

Per serving: 565 Calories; 25.9g Fat; 79.6g Carbs; 6.4g Protein; 51.5g Sugars

746. Mixed Berry and Orange Compote

(Ready in about 30 minutes | Servings 4)

Ingredients

1/2 pound strawberries
1 tablespoon orange juice
1/4 teaspoon ground cloves
1/2 cup brown sugar

1 vanilla bean
1 pound blueberries
1/2 pound blackberries

Directions

Place your berries in the inner pot. Add the sugar and let sit for 15 minutes. Add in the orange juice, ground cloves, and vanilla bean.

Secure the lid. Choose the "Manual" mode and cook for 2 minutes at High pressure. Once cooking is complete, use a natural pressure release for 10 minutes; carefully remove the lid.

As your compote cools, it will thicken. Bon appétit!

Per serving: 224 Calories; 0.8g Fat; 56.3g Carbs; 2.1g Protein; 46.5g Sugars

747. Old-Fashioned Pastry Cream

(Ready in about 15 minutes | Servings 4)

Ingredients

1/4 cup dark rum
1/4 cup raisins
3 eggs, beaten
2 tablespoons molasses

1/2 cup superfine sugar
1/2 teaspoon vanilla paste
2 cups milk

Directions

Add the milk to a sauté pan that is preheated over a moderate flame; bring to a boil.

Let it cool to room temperature.

In a mixing bowl, whisk the eggs, sugar, molasses, and vanilla paste until sugar dissolves.

Then, slowly and gradually pour the milk into the egg mixture, stirring continuously. Mix until smooth and uniform. Finally, add the rum and raisins.

Spoon the mixture into four ramekins. Cover with a foil.

Add 1 ½ cups of water and metal trivet to your Instant Pot. Then, lower the ramekins onto the trivet.

Secure the lid. Choose the "Manual" mode and cook for 9 minutes under High pressure. Once cooking is complete, use a quick pressure release; carefully remove the lid.

The custard will still wobble slightly but will firm up as it cools. Bon appétit!

Per serving: 324 Calories; 19.1g Fat; 21.9g Carbs; 9.7g Protein; 20.4g Sugars

748. Streuselkuchen with Peaches

(Ready in about 25 minutes | Servings 6)

Ingredients

1 cup rolled oats
1 teaspoon vanilla extract
1/3 cup orange juice
4 tablespoons raisins
2 tablespoons honey
4 tablespoons butter
4 tablespoons all-purpose flour

A pinch of grated nutmeg
1/2 teaspoon ground
cardamom
A pinch of salt
1 teaspoon ground cinnamon
6 peaches, pitted and chopped
1/3 cup brown sugar

Directions

Place the peaches on the bottom of the inner pot. Sprinkle with the cardamom, cinnamon and vanilla. Top with the orange juice, honey, and raisins.

In a mixing bowl, whisk together the butter, oats, flour, brown sugar, nutmeg, and salt. Drop by a spoonful on top of the peaches.

Secure the lid. Choose the "Manual" mode and cook for 8 minutes at High pressure. Once cooking is complete, use a natural pressure release for 10 minutes; carefully remove the lid. Bon appétit!

Per serving: 329 Calories; 10g Fat; 56g Carbs; 6.9g Protein; 31g Sugars

749. Fig and Homey Buckwheat Pudding

(Ready in about 15 minutes | Servings 4)

Ingredients

1/2 teaspoon ground cinnamon
1/2 cup dried figs, chopped
1/3 cup honey
1 teaspoon pure vanilla extract
3 ½ cups milk
1/2 teaspoon pure almond extract
1 ½ cups buckwheat

Directions

Add all of the above ingredients to your Instant Pot.

Secure the lid. Choose the "Multigrain" mode and cook for 10 minutes under High pressure. Once cooking is complete, use a natural pressure release; carefully remove the lid.

Serve topped with fresh fruits, nuts or whipped topping. Bon appétit!

Per serving: 320 Calories; 7.5g Fat; 57.7g Carbs; 9.5g Protein; 43.2g Sugars

750. Zingy Blueberry Sauce

(Ready in about 25 minutes | Servings 10)

Ingredients

1/4 cup fresh lemon juice
1 pound granulated sugar
1 tablespoon freshly grated lemon zest
1/2 teaspoon vanilla extract
2 pounds fresh blueberries

Directions

Place the blueberries, sugar, and vanilla in the inner pot of your Instant Pot.

Secure the lid. Choose the "Manual" mode and cook for 2 minutes at High pressure. Once cooking is complete, use a natural pressure release for 15 minutes; carefully remove the lid.

Stir in the lemon zest and juice. Puree in a food processor; then, strain and push the mixture through a sieve before storing. Enjoy!

Per serving: 230 Calories; 0.3g Fat; 59g Carbs; 0.7g Protein; 53.6g Sugars

751. Chocolate Almond Custard

(Ready in about 15 minutes | Servings 3)

Ingredients

3 chocolate cookies, chunks
A pinch of salt
1/4 teaspoon ground cardamom
3 tablespoons honey
1/4 teaspoon freshly grated nutmeg
2 tablespoons butter
3 tablespoons whole milk
1 cup almond flour
3 eggs
1 teaspoon pure vanilla extract

Directions

In a mixing bowl, beat the eggs with butter. Now, add the milk and continue mixing until well combined.

Add the remaining ingredients in the order listed above. Divide the batter among 3 ramekins.

Add 1 cup of water and a metal trivet to the Instant Pot. Cover ramekins with foil and lower them onto the trivet.

Secure the lid and select "Manual" mode. Cook at High pressure for 12 minutes. Once cooking is complete, use a quick release; carefully remove the lid.

Transfer the ramekins to a wire rack and allow them to cool slightly before serving. Enjoy!

Per serving: 304 Calories; 18.9g Fat; 23.8g Carbs; 10g Protein; 21.1g Sugars

752. Classic Berry Jam

(Ready in about 25 minutes | Servings 10)

Ingredients

2 tablespoons fresh lemon juice
3 tablespoons cornstarch
1 ¼ cups granulated sugar
2 ½ pounds fresh mixed berries

Directions

Add the fresh mixed berries, sugar, and lemon juice to the inner pot.

Secure the lid. Choose the "Manual" mode and cook for 2 minutes at High pressure. Once cooking is complete, use a natural pressure release for 15 minutes; carefully remove the lid.

Whisk the cornstarch with 3 tablespoons of water until well combined. Stir in the cornstarch slurry.

Press the "Sauté" button and bring the mixture to a rolling boil. Let it boil for about 5 minutes, stirring continuously, until your jam has thickened. Bon appétit!

Per serving: 143 Calories; 0.3g Fat; 36.1g Carbs; 0.7g Protein; 30.5g Sugars

753. Walnut and Cinnamon Butter Cake

(Ready in about 55 minutes | Servings 6)

Ingredients

1/4 cup walnuts, ground
1/2 stick butter, at room temperature
1 ¼ cups coconut flour
2 eggs plus 1 egg yolk, whisked
1 teaspoon orange zest, finely grated

1 ½ teaspoons baking powder
1/2 teaspoon grated nutmeg
1/4 teaspoon ground star anise
3/4 cup double cream
1 cup sugar
1 teaspoon ground cinnamon
1 ¼ cups coconut flour

Directions

Add 1 ½ cups of water and a steamer rack to your Instant Pot. Spritz the inside of a baking pan with a nonstick cooking spray.

Thoroughly combine dry ingredients. Then, mix the wet ingredients. Add the wet mixture to the dry flour mixture and mix until everything is well incorporated.

Scrape the batter mixture into the prepared baking pan. Now, cover the baking pan with a piece of foil, making a foil sling.

Place the baking pan on the steamer rack and secure the lid.

Select "Manual" mode. Bake for 35 minutes at High pressure. Once cooking is complete, use a natural release for 15 minutes; carefully remove the lid.

Just before serving, dust the top of the cake with icing sugar. Lastly cut the cake into wedges and serve. Bon appétit!

Per serving: 244 Calories; 17.3g Fat; 21.3g Carbs; 2.7g Protein; 18.8g Sugars

754. Honey Stewed Apples

(Ready in about 10 minutes | Servings 4)

Ingredients

2 tablespoons honey
1 teaspoon ground cinnamon

1/2 teaspoon ground cloves
4 apples

Directions

Add all ingredients to the inner pot. Now, pour in 1/3 cup of water.

Secure the lid. Choose the "Manual" mode and cook for 2 minutes at High pressure. Once cooking is complete, use a quick pressure release; carefully remove the lid.

Serve in individual bowls. Bon appétit!

Per serving: 128 Calories; 0.3g Fat; 34.3g Carbs; 0.5g Protein; 27.5g Sugars

755. Vanilla Almond Cheesecake

(Ready in about 45 minutes | Servings 8)

Ingredients

1/2 stick butter, melted
1 cup sour cream
1 ½ cups graham cracker crumbs
5 eggs
1/2 teaspoon pure almond extract

1/2 teaspoon pure vanilla extract
1/2 cup almonds, roughly chopped
1/4 cup flour
24 ounces Neufchâtel cheese

Directions

In a mixing bowl, beat the Neufchâtel cheese with the sour cream. Now, fold in the eggs, one at a time.

Stir in the flour, vanilla extract, and almond extract; mix to combine well.

In a separate mixing bowl, thoroughly combine the graham cracker crumbs, almonds, and butter. Press this crust mixture into a baking pan.

Pour the egg/cheese mixture into the pan. Cover with a sheet of foil; make sure that the foil fits tightly around the sides and under the bottom of your baking pan.

Add 1 cup of water and a metal trivet to your Instant Pot. Secure the lid. Choose the "Bean/Chili" mode and bake for 40 minutes at High pressure.

Once cooking is complete, use a quick release; carefully remove the lid. Allow your cheesecake to cool completely before serving. Bon appétit!

Per serving: 445 Calories; 33.2g Fat; 15.3g Carbs; 21.2g Protein; 7.4g Sugars

756. Greek-Style Compote with Yogurt

(Ready in about 20 minutes | Servings 4)

Ingredients

1 cup Greek yoghurt
1 cup pears
4 tablespoons honey
1 cup apples
1 vanilla bean

1 cinnamon stick
1/2 cup caster sugar
1 cup rhubarb
1 teaspoon ground ginger
1 cup plums

Directions

Place the fruits, ginger, vanilla, cinnamon, and caster sugar in the inner pot of your Instant Pot.

Secure the lid. Choose the "Manual" mode and cook for 2 minutes at High pressure. Once cooking is complete, use a natural pressure release for 10 minutes; carefully remove the lid.

Meanwhile, whisk the yogurt with the honey.

Serve your compote in individual bowls with a dollop of honeyed Greek yogurt. Enjoy!

Per serving: 304 Calories; 0.3g Fat; 75.4g Carbs; 5.1g Protein; 69.2g Sugars

757. Butterscotch Lava Cakes

(Ready in about 20 minutes | Servings 6)

Ingredients

7 tablespoons all-purpose flour
A pinch of coarse salt
6 ounces butterscotch morsels
3/4 cup powdered sugar
1/2 teaspoon vanilla extract
3 eggs, whisked
1 stick butter

Directions

Add 1 ½ cups of water and a metal rack to the Instant Pot. Line a standard-size muffin tin with muffin papers.

In a microwave-safe bowl, microwave butter and butterscotch morsels for about 40 seconds. Stir in the powdered sugar.

Add the remaining ingredients. Spoon the batter into the prepared muffin tin.

Secure the lid. Choose the "Manual" and cook at High pressure for 10 minutes. Once cooking is complete, use a quick release; carefully remove the lid.

To remove, let it cool for 5 to 6 minutes. Run a small knife around the sides of each cake and serve. Enjoy!

Per serving: 393 Calories; 21.1g Fat; 45.6g Carbs; 5.6g Protein; 35.4g Sugars

758. Cinnamon Coffee Cake

(Ready in about 40 minutes | Servings 10)

Ingredients

3/4 cup granulated sugar
1/2 cup firmly packed brown sugar
1 tablespoon ground cinnamon
3/4 cup butter, melted
1/2 cup raisins, if desired
1/4 teaspoon nutmeg, preferably freshly grated
2 (16.3-ounce) cans refrigerated biscuits

Directions

Place 1 cup of water and a metal trivet in the inner pot of your Instant Pot. Lightly grease 12-cup fluted tube pan with cooking spray.

In a food bag, mix the granulated sugar, cinnamon, and nutmeg.

Separate the dough into biscuits and cut each into quarters. Place them in the food bag and shake to coat on all sides. Place them in the prepared pan, adding raisins among the biscuit pieces.

In a small mixing bowl, whisk the melted butter with the brown sugar; pour the butter mixture over the biscuit pieces.

Secure the lid. Choose the "Manual" mode and cook for 25 minutes at High pressure. Bake until no longer doughy in the center.

Once cooking is complete, use a natural pressure release for 10 minutes; carefully remove the lid.

Turn upside down onto serving plate and serve warm. Bon appétit!

Per serving: 512 Calories; 24.1g Fat; 69.4g Carbs; 5.9g Protein; 21.3g Sugars

759. Bourbon Brioche Bread Pudding

(Ready in about 2 hours 45 minutes | Servings 8)

Ingredients

1/4 cup bourbon whiskey
4 eggs, beaten
1/4 cup coconut oil, melted
1 teaspoon vanilla extract
1/2 teaspoon coconut extract
4 tablespoons agave syrup
1 loaf Brioche bread, cubed
2 ½ cups milk

Directions

Place the bread in a baking dish that is previously greased with a nonstick cooking spray.

Then, in another bowl, thoroughly combine the milk, eggs, vanilla, coconut extract, coconut oil, agave syrup, and bourbon whiskey.

Pour the milk/bourbon mixture over the bread; press with a wide spatula to soak and place in the refrigerator for 1 to 2 hours.

Add 1 ½ cups of water and a metal trivet to your Instant Pot. Lower the baking dish onto the trivet.

Secure the lid. Choose the "Soup" mode and cook for 40 minutes at High pressure. Once cooking is complete, use a quick release; remove the lid carefully. Serve warm or at room temperature.

Per serving: 352 Calories; 13.2g Fat; 43.9g Carbs; 14.2g Protein; 10.1g Sugars

760. Mexican Pudding (Arroz Con Leche)

(Ready in about 25 minutes | Servings 4)

Ingredients

2 ¼ cups milk
Peel of 1/2 lemon
1 cup water
1 teaspoon vanilla extract
A pinch of salt
1/2 cup sugar
1/4 teaspoon grated nutmeg
1 teaspoon cinnamon
1 cup white pearl rice

Directions

Place the rice, water, and salt in the inner pot of your Instant Pot.

Secure the lid. Choose the "Rice" mode and cook for 10 minutes at Low pressure. Once cooking is complete, use a natural pressure release for 10 minutes; carefully remove the lid.

Add in the milk, sugar, nutmeg, vanilla, cinnamon, and lemon peel; stir to combine well.

Press the "Sauté" button and cook, stirring continuously, until your pudding starts to boil. Press the "Cancel' button. Enjoy!

Per serving: 370 Calories; 4.4g Fat; 72.4g Carbs; 7.6g Protein; 32.2g Sugars

761. Pumpkin Pudding Chocolate Ganache

(Ready in about 30 minutes + chilling time | Servings 4)

Ingredients

1 egg plus 1 egg yolk, beaten
1/2 teaspoon ground cinnamon
1 cup pumpkin puree
A pinch of table salt
1/3 cup Turbinado sugar
1/3 teaspoon crystallized ginger
1/4 teaspoon ground nutmeg
1/2 cup half-and-half
For the Chocolate:
1/4 cup double cream
1/2 cup chocolate chips

Directions

Prepare your Instant Pot by adding the water and a steam rack to the pot. Butter four ramekins and set them aside.

In a mixing bowl, thoroughly combine the half-and-half with pumpkin puree, and sugar; now, gently fold in the eggs and mix to combine well.

Then, scrape the mixture into the prepared ramekins, dividing evenly, and place side by side on the steam rack.

Secure the lid. Choose the "Manual" setting and cook at High pressure for 25 minutes. Once cooking is complete, use a quick release; carefully remove the lid.

Let the pudding cool about 2 hours before serving.

Meanwhile, make the chocolate ganache by melting the chocolate in the microwave for 30 seconds; stir and microwave for a further 15 seconds.

Add the double cream and stir to combine well.

Lastly, pour this chocolate ganache over the pumpkin puddings, letting it run over sides; spread gently with a table knife. Let them set in your refrigerator. Enjoy!

Per serving: 366 Calories; 19.3g Fat; 40.1g Carbs; 11.4g Protein; 29g Sugars

762. Rich Almond Cheesecake

(Ready in about 45 minutes | Servings 8)

Ingredients

1/2 cup almonds, slivered
2 eggs
1/3 cup sour cream
3 tablespoons coconut oil, melted
1/4 teaspoon grated nutmeg
1/2 teaspoon pure vanilla extract
18 ounces cream cheese
1 cup granulated sugar
1 cup cookies, crushed

Directions

Place a metal trivet and 1 cup of water in your Instant Pot. Spritz a baking pan with nonstick cooking spray.

Next, mix the cookies and coconut oil into a sticky crust. Press the crust into the prepared baking pan.

Thoroughly combine the cream cheese, sugar, eggs, sour cream, nutmeg, and vanilla extract in a mixing bowl. Pour this mixture over the crust and cover it with a piece of foil.

Lower the baking pan onto the trivet.

Secure the lid. Choose the "Manual" mode and cook for 25 minutes at High pressure. Once cooking is complete, use a natural pressure release for 15 minutes; carefully remove the lid.

Top with slivered almonds and serve well chilled. Bon appétit!

Per serving: 388 Calories; 28.8g Fat; 25.9g Carbs; 8.4g Protein; 19.9g Sugars

763. Vanilla Bread Pudding with Apricots

(Ready in about 20 minutes | Servings 6)

Ingredients

2 tablespoons coconut oil
1 1/3 cups heavy cream
4 eggs, whisked
1/2 cup dried apricots, soaked and chopped
1 teaspoon cinnamon, ground
1/2 teaspoon star anise, ground
A pinch of grated nutmeg
A pinch of salt
1/2 cup granulated sugar
2 tablespoons molasses
2 cups milk
4 cups Italian bread, cubed
1 teaspoon vanilla paste

Directions

Add 1 ½ cups of water and a metal rack to the Instant Pot.

Grease a baking dish with a nonstick cooking spray. Throw the bread cubes into the prepared baking dish.

In a mixing bowl, thoroughly combine the remaining ingredients. Pour the mixture over the bread cubes. Cover with a piece of foil, making a foil sling.

Secure the lid. Choose the "Porridge" mode and High pressure; cook for 15 minutes. Once cooking is complete, use a quick pressure release; carefully remove the lid. Enjoy!

Per serving: 410 Calories; 24.3g Fat; 37.4g Carbs; 11.5g Protein; 25.6g Sugars

764. Banana Bread with Coconut

(Ready in about 50 minutes | Servings 8)

Ingredients

2 bananas, mashed
1/2 cup coconut flaked
1 teaspoon baking soda
2 eggs
3/4 cup sugar
1 ½ cups all-purpose flour
1 stick butter, melted
1 teaspoon vanilla extract

Directions

Mix all ingredients in a bowl until everything is well incorporated.

Add 1 cup of water and metal trivet to the bottom of the inner pot. Spritz a baking pan with nonstick cooking oil.

Scrape the batter into the prepared pan. Lower the pan onto the trivet.

Secure the lid. Choose the "Manual" mode and cook for 45 minutes at High pressure. Once cooking is complete, use a quick pressure release; carefully remove the lid.

Allow the banana bread to cool slightly before slicing and serving. Enjoy!

Per serving: 320 Calories; 17.1g Fat; 37.1g Carbs; 5.4g Protein; 13.1g Sugars

765. Mediterranean-Style Carrot Pudding

(Ready in about 30 minutes | Servings 4)

Ingredients

1/3 cup almonds, ground
1/4 cup dried figs, chopped
2 large-sized carrots, shredded
1/2 cup water
1 ½ cups milk
1/2 teaspoon ground star anise
1/3 teaspoon ground cardamom

1/4 teaspoon kosher salt
1/3 cup granulated sugar
2 eggs, beaten
1/2 teaspoon pure almond extract
1/2 teaspoon vanilla extract
1 ½ cups jasmine rice

Directions

Place the jasmine rice, milk, water, carrots, and salt in your Instant Pot.

Stir to combine and secure the lid. Choose "Manual" and cook at High pressure for 10 minutes. Once cooking is complete, use a natural release for 15 minutes; carefully remove the lid.

Now, press the "Sauté" button and add the sugar, eggs, and almonds; stir to combine well. Bring to a boil; press the "Keep Warm/Cancel" button.

Add the remaining ingredients and stir; the pudding will thicken as it sits. Bon appétit!

Per serving: 331 Calories; 17.2g Fat; 44.5g Carbs; 13.9g Protein; 19.5g Sugars

766. Easy Dulce de Leche

(Ready in about 35 minutes | Servings 2)

Ingredients

1 can (14-ounce) sweetened condensed milk

Directions

Place a trivet and steamer basket in the inner pot. Place the can of milk in the steamer basket.

Add water until the can is covered.

Secure the lid. Choose the "Manual" mode and cook for 20 minutes at High pressure. Once cooking is complete, use a natural pressure release for 10 minutes; carefully remove the lid.

Don't open the can until it is completely cooled. Bon appétit!

Per serving: 360 Calories; 8.4g Fat; 66.1g Carbs; 7g Protein; 57g Sugars

767. Mango Mug Cake

(Ready in about 15 minutes | Servings 2)

Ingredients

1 medium-sized mango, peeled and diced
2 eggs
1 teaspoon vanilla

1/4 teaspoon grated nutmeg
1 tablespoon cocoa powder
2 tablespoons honey
1/2 cup coconut flour

Directions

Combine the coconut flour, eggs, honey, vanilla, nutmeg and cocoa powder in two lightly greased mugs.

Then, add 1 cup of water and a metal trivet to the Instant Pot. Lower the uncovered mugs onto the trivet.

Secure the lid. Choose the "Manual" mode and High pressure; cook for 10 minutes. Once cooking is complete, use a quick pressure release; carefully remove the lid.

Top with diced mango and serve chilled. Enjoy!

Per serving: 268 Calories; 10.5g Fat; 34.8g Carbs; 10.6g Protein; 31.1g Sugars

768. Chocolate Coffee Pots de Crème

(Ready in about 25 minutes | Servings 6)

Ingredients

1 teaspoon instant coffee
9 ounces chocolate chips
1/2 cup whole milk
1/3 cup sugar

A pinch of pink salt
4 egg yolks
2 cups double cream

Directions

Place a metal trivet and 1 cup of water in your Instant Pot.

In a saucepan, bring the cream and milk to a simmer.

Then, thoroughly combine the egg yolks, sugar, instant coffee, and salt. Slowly and gradually whisk in the hot cream mixture.

Whisk in the chocolate chips and blend again. Pour the mixture into mason jars. Lower the jars onto the trivet.

Secure the lid. Choose the "Manual" mode and cook for 6 minutes at High pressure. Once cooking is complete, use a natural pressure release for 10 minutes; carefully remove the lid.

Serve well chilled and enjoy!

Per serving: 351 Calories; 19.3g Fat; 39.3g Carbs; 5.5g Protein; 32.1g Sugars

769. Almond Cherry Crumble Cake

(Ready in about 15 minutes | Servings 4)

Ingredients

1/4 cup almonds, slivered
1/2 stick butter, at room temperature
1 teaspoon ground cinnamon
A pinch of grated nutmeg
1 cup rolled oats
1/3 teaspoon ground cardamom
1 teaspoon pure vanilla extract
1/3 cup honey
2 tablespoons all-purpose flour
A pinch of salt
1 pound sweet cherries, pitted
1/3 cup water

Directions

Arrange the cherries on the bottom of the Instant Pot. Sprinkle cinnamon, cardamom, and vanilla over the top. Add the water and honey.

In a separate mixing bowl, thoroughly combine the butter, oats, and flour. Spread topping mixture evenly over cherry mixture.

Secure the lid. Choose the "Manual" mode and High pressure; cook for 10 minutes. Once cooking is complete, use a natural pressure release; carefully remove the lid.

Serve at room temperature. Bon appétit!

Per serving: 335 Calories; 13.4g Fat; 60.5g Carbs; 5.9g Protein; 38.1g Sugars

770. Pull-Apart Dessert with Walnuts

(Ready in about 40 minutes | Servings 6)

Ingredients

1/4 cup walnuts, ground
1 tablespoon coconut milk
1/4 cup brown sugar
1/4 cup coconut oil, melted
1/3 cup powdered sugar
12 frozen egg dinner rolls, thawed
1 teaspoon ground cinnamon

Directions

Place 1 cup of water and a metal trivet in the inner pot of your Instant Pot. Spray a Bundt pan with cooking spray and set aside.

Cut each dinner roll in half.

In a mixing bowl, thoroughly combine the brown sugar, cinnamon, and walnuts. In another bowl, place the melted coconut oil. Dip the rolls halves in the coconut oil and roll them in the brown sugar mixture.

Arrange the rolls in the prepared Bundt pan. Cover the pan with a piece of aluminum foil; allow it to rise overnight at room temperature.

On the next day, lower the pan onto the trivet.

Secure the lid. Choose the "Manual" mode and cook for 25 minutes at High pressure. Once cooking is complete, use a natural pressure release for 10 minutes; carefully remove the lid.

After that, invert the bread onto a serving plate.

In a mixing bowl, whisk the powdered sugar and coconut milk until smooth. Drizzle the glaze over the top and sides of your cake. Bon appétit!

Per serving: 355 Calories; 15.8g Fat; 46.9g Carbs; 7.2g Protein; 12.7g Sugars

MORE INSTANT POT RECIPES

771. Swiss Cheese and Cauliflower Frittata

(Ready in about 30 minutes | Servings 4)

Ingredients

1 cup Swiss cheese, shredded
1 head cauliflower, cut into florets
2 tablespoons olive oil
Sea salt and ground black pepper, to your liking
1 teaspoon garlic, minced
1/2 teaspoon cayenne pepper
5 eggs, beaten
1/4 teaspoon dried dill weed
1/2 cup scallions, chopped
1 cup cream cheese, room temperature

Directions

Add 1 cup of water and the metal trivet to your Instant Pot Spritz a baking pan with a nonstick cooking spray.

Thoroughly combine the cream cheese with eggs and olive oil. Now, add the scallions, garlic, salt, black pepper, cayenne pepper, and dill; mix to combine well.

After that, stir in the Swiss cheese and cauliflower. Mix to combine and spoon the mixture into the prepared baking pan.

Lower the baking pan onto the trivet and secure the lid. Choose "Manual" function, High pressure and 10 minutes.

Once cooking is complete, use a natural release for 15 minutes; remove the lid carefully. Serve warm and enjoy!

Per serving: 489 Calories; 41.2g Fat; 10.2g Carbs; 21g Protein; 4.6g Sugars

772. Blueberry Butter Sauce

(Ready in about 25 minutes | Servings 10)

Ingredients

1/4 cup fresh lemon juice
1 pound granulated sugar
1 tablespoon freshly grated lemon zest
2 pounds fresh blueberries
1/2 teaspoon vanilla extract

Directions

Place the blueberries, sugar, and vanilla in the inner pot of your Instant Pot.
Secure the lid. Choose the "Manual" mode and cook for 2 minutes at High pressure. Once cooking is complete, use a natural pressure release for 15 minutes; carefully remove the lid.

Stir in the lemon zest and juice. Puree in a food processor; then, strain and push the mixture through a sieve before storing. Enjoy!

Per serving: 230 Calories; 0.3g Fat; 59g Carbs; 0.7g Protein; 53.6g Sugars

773. Breakfast Chocolate Chip Oatmeal

(Ready in about 15 minutes | Servings 4)

Ingredients

1 large banana, thinly sliced
2 cups chocolate milk
1/8 teaspoon salt
1/8 teaspoon grated nutmeg
2 cups water
1/2 teaspoon ground cinnamon
1/4 teaspoon crystallized ginger
1 ½ cups steel-cut oats
1/3 cup dark chocolate chips

Directions

Throw all of the above ingredients, except for the banana, in your Instant Pot.

Secure the lid. Choose the "Manual" mode and cook for 5 minutes under High pressure. Once cooking is complete, use a natural pressure release; carefully remove the lid.

Taste and adjust the sweetness. Serve in individual bowls topped with sliced banana. Bon appétit!

Per serving: 193 Calories; 6.6g Fat; 37.2g Carbs; 10.3g Protein; 10.8g Sugars

774. Spiced Rum Apple Cider

(Ready in about 55 minutes | Servings 6)

Ingredients

4 tablespoons rum
1 small naval orange
1 vanilla bean
1 teaspoon whole cloves
4 cups water
3/4 cup brown sugar
2 cinnamon sticks
6 apples, cored and diced

Directions

Place the ingredients in the inner pot of your Instant Pot.

Secure the lid. Choose the "Manual" mode and cook for 50 minutes at High pressure. Once cooking is complete, use a quick pressure release; carefully remove the lid.

Mash the apples with a fork or a potato masher. Pour the mixture over a mesh strainer and serve hot. Bon appétit!

Per serving: 173 Calories; 0.4g Fat; 39.5g Carbs; 0.6g Protein; 32.6g Sugars

775. Fancy Creamed Fruit Salad

(Ready in about 15 minutes | Servings 8)

Ingredients

2 cups water
1/3 cup dried figs, chopped
1/4 teaspoon ground nutmeg
20 ounces peaches, pitted and sliced
1/2 teaspoon ground cinnamon

10 ounces canned pineapple
1 stick butter, at room temperature
1/3 cup dried raisins, chopped
1/2 cup granulated sugar
1 cup pineapple juice

Directions

Add all of the above ingredients to your Instant Pot.

Secure the lid. Choose the "Manual" mode. Cook for 8 minutes at High pressure. Once cooking is complete, use a natural release; carefully remove the lid.

Ladle into individual bowls and serve with yogurt. Bon appétit!

Per serving: 276 Calories; 11.6g Fat; 45g Carbs; 1.2g Protein; 42.2g Sugars

776. Hibiscus Iced Tea

(Ready in about 20 minutes | Servings 4)

Ingredients

1/2 teaspoon fresh ginger, peeled and minced
1/2 cup dried hibiscus flowers

2 tablespoons lime juice
1/2 cup brown sugar
4 cups water

Directions

Combine all ingredients, except for the lime juice, in the inner pot of your Instant Pot.

Secure the lid. Choose the "Manual" mode and cook for 5 minutes at High pressure. Once cooking is complete, use a natural pressure release for 10 minutes; carefully remove the lid.

Stir in the lime juice and serve well chilled.

Per serving: 118 Calories; 0.2g Fat; 29.8g Carbs; 0.2g Protein; 28.5g Sugars

777. Eggs, Cheese and Toast

(Ready in about 15 minutes | Servings 6)

Ingredients

1/2 teaspoon paprika
6 eggs
Salt, to taste

6 slices toasted bread
6 tablespoons Feta cheese

Directions

Place 1 ½ cups of water and a steamer basket in the bottom of the Instant Pot. Add the eggs to the steamer basket.

Secure the lid. Choose the "Manual" mode. Cook for 7 minutes at High pressure. Once cooking is complete, use a quick release; carefully remove the lid.

Season your eggs with salt and paprika. Spread the feta cheese on toasted bread. Serve with the eggs and enjoy!

Per serving: 227 Calories; 13.5g Fat; 12.3g Carbs; 13.2g Protein; 2.9g Sugars

778. Authentic Mexican Horchata

(Ready in about 20 minutes | Servings 8)

Ingredients

5 tablespoons agave syrup
1 cinnamon stick
20 ounces rice milk, unsweetened

1 vanilla bean
8 ounces almond milk, unsweetened

Directions

Combine all ingredients in the inner pot of your Instant Pot.

Secure the lid. Choose the "Manual" mode and cook for 5 minutes at High pressure. Once cooking is complete, use a natural pressure release for 10 minutes; carefully remove the lid.

Serve garnished with a few sprinkles of ground cinnamon if desired. Enjoy!

Per serving: 107 Calories; 2.4g Fat; 17.5g Carbs; 4.6g Protein; 17.7g Sugars

779. Rum Banana Bread with Pecans

(Ready in about 1 hour 15 minutes | Servings 8)

Ingredients

1 teaspoon rum extract
2 tablespoons pecans, ground
1 pound ripe bananas, mashed
2 eggs plus 1 egg yolk, beaten
1/2 teaspoon baking powder
1/2 teaspoon ground cinnamon
1 tablespoon fresh lemon juice
1 stick butter, at room temperature

1/2 cup maple syrup
1/8 teaspoon kosher salt
1/2 teaspoon vanilla paste
1/4 teaspoon grated nutmeg
1 1/3 cups soy milk
2 ½ cups cake flour
1 teaspoon baking soda
1 cup sugar

Directions

Add water and a metal trivet to the Instant Pot. Spritz a bread loaf pan with a nonstick cooking spray.

In a mixing bowl, thoroughly combine the cake flour, baking soda, baking powder, salt, nutmeg, and cinnamon.

In another mixing bowl, mix the mashed bananas with fresh lemon juice; reserve.

Now, cream the butter with the sugar and maple syrup using an electric mixer. Fold in the eggs and mix again until smooth and uniform.

Stir in the vanilla, rum extract, soy milk, and ground pecans.

Then, stir in the dry flour mixture, and combine well. Afterwards, stir in the banana/lemon mixture and mix again.

Scrape the batter into the prepared pan. Lower the pan onto the trivet and secure the lid.

Choose the "Manual" mode; bake for 1 hour at High pressure. Once cooking is complete, use a natural release for 15 minutes; carefully remove the lid.

Transfer the pan to a wire rack to cool before serving and enjoy!

Per serving: 485 Calories; 13.3g Fat; 89.3g Carbs; 6.3g Protein; 42.7g Sugars

780. Tomato Sauce with Mediterranean Herb

(Ready in about 45 minutes | Servings 6)

Ingredients

1 teaspoon tamari sauce
2 tablespoons fresh parsley leaves, finely chopped
3 tablespoons olive oil
1 onion, quartered
1/2 teaspoon dried rosemary
1/2 teaspoon dried basil

1/2 tablespoon dried oregano
3 cloves garlic, minced
Kosher salt and freshly ground black pepper, to taste
2 (28-ounce) cans tomatoes, crushed

Directions

Reserve 1 cup of the crushed tomatoes.

Press the "Sauté" button and heat olive oil. Once hot, cook the garlic for a minute or so or until it is fragrant but not browned.

Now, stir in the rosemary, basil, and oregano; continue to sauté for 30 seconds more. Stir in the tomatoes, onion, salt, and pepper.

Secure the lid. Choose the "Soup/Broth" mode and cook for 40 minutes at High pressure. Once cooking is complete, use a quick pressure release; carefully remove the lid.

Add the reserved tomatoes, tamari sauce and parsley to your tomato sauce. Bon appétit!

Per serving: 115 Calories; 7.5g Fat; 12.1g Carbs; 2.6g Protein; 7.9g Sugars

781. Blackberry French Toast

(Ready in about 25 minutes | Servings 6)

Ingredients

3/4 cup fresh blackberries
1/2 cup milk
1/2 cup honey
3 eggs, beaten
1/4 teaspoon grated nutmeg
1/2 teaspoon ground cinnamon

1/2 cup applesauce
10 ounces Neufchâtel cheese, at room temperature
1 stick butter, cold
1 loaf Brioche bread, cubed

Directions

Start by adding 1 cup of water and a metal rack to the bottom of your Instant Pot. Now, spritz the bottom and sides of a baking pan with a nonstick cooking spray.

Add the bread to the prepared pan. Top with fresh blackberries.

In a mixing bowl, thoroughly combine the cheese, honey, eggs, cinnamon, nutmeg, milk, and applesauce.

Pour this mixture into the pan, pressing the bread down with a wide spatula. Cut in cold butter. Now, cover the pan with a few paper towels.

Secure the lid. Choose the "Manual" mode. Cook for 20 minutes at High pressure. Once cooking is complete, use a natural release; carefully remove the lid. Bon appétit!

Per serving: 435 Calories; 28.4g Fat; 35.6g Carbs; 12.2g Protein; 30.9g Sugars

782. Skinny Homemade Applesauce

(Ready in about 25 minutes | Servings 8)

Ingredients

10 dates, pitted and chopped
1 cup water
1 tablespoon fresh lemon juice
1/2 teaspoon cinnamon powder

6 Honeycrisp apples, peeled, cored and chopped
1/4 teaspoon ground cloves

Directions

Add all ingredients to the inner pot; stir to combine.

Secure the lid. Choose the "Manual" mode and cook for 10 minutes at High pressure. Once cooking is complete, use a natural pressure release for 10 minutes; carefully remove the lid.

Mash the apple mixture to the desired consistency. Serve warm or cold.

Per serving: 97 Calories; 0.3g Fat; 25.7g Carbs; 0.6g Protein; 19.8g Sugars

783. Breakfast Hash Browns

(Ready in about 30 minutes | Servings 5)

Ingredients

2 ½ cups hash browns, frozen
1 red bell pepper, seeded and chopped
Sea salt and ground black pepper, to taste
1/2 teaspoon dried oregano
3/4 cup cream cheese, at room temperature
1/2 teaspoon paprika

1 green bell pepper, seeded and chopped
5 eggs
1/3 cup milk
1/2 teaspoon dried basil
1 tablespoon olive oil
4 ounces Italian salami, chopped
1 Peperoncino, seeded and chopped

Directions

Press the "Sauté" button to preheat the Instant Pot. Now, heat the oil until sizzling. Cook the salami for 2 minutes or until crispy.

Add the peppers and hash browns; stir and continue to cook for a further 3 minutes.

Spritz the bottom and sides of a casserole dish with a nonstick cooking spray. Scrape the hash brown mixture into the dish.

In a mixing bowl, thoroughly combine the eggs, milk, cheese, salt, black pepper, basil, oregano, and paprika. Pour the mixture into the casserole dish.

Add 1 ½ cups of water and a metal rack to the Instant Pot. Lower the casserole dish onto the rack.

Secure the lid. Choose the "Meat/Stew" mode and cook for 20 minutes under High pressure. Once cooking is complete, use a quick pressure release; carefully remove the lid. Serve warm.

Per serving: 549 Calories; 39.9g Fat; 25.8g Carbs; 23.4g Protein; 3.5g Sugars

784. Red Wine Chicken Ragù

(Ready in about 20 minutes | Servings 4)

Ingredients

1/4 cup dry red wine
1 pound ground chicken
1 stalk celery, chopped
1 bell pepper, chopped
1 teaspoon fresh rosemary, chopped
1 teaspoon cayenne pepper
2 cups tomato sauce

1 cup chicken bone broth
1 teaspoon fresh basil, chopped
1 onion, chopped
2 cloves garlic, minced
2 tablespoons olive oil
Salt and fresh ground pepper to taste

Directions

Press the "Sauté" button and heat the oil. When the oil starts to sizzle, cook the ground chicken until no longer pink; crumble it with a wooden spatula.

Add the onion and garlic to the browned chicken; let it cook for a minute or so. Add a splash of wine to deglaze the pan.

Stir in the remaining ingredients.

Secure the lid. Choose the "Manual" mode and cook for 6 minutes at High pressure. Once cooking is complete, use a natural pressure release for 10 minutes; carefully remove the lid. Bon appétit!

Per serving: 431 Calories; 18g Fat; 33.7g Carbs; 29.1g Protein; 17.1g Sugars

785. Jammy Rice Pudding

(Ready in about 35 minutes | Servings 5)

Ingredients

1/2 cup berry jam
1 cup white long-grain rice, well-rinsed
1/2 teaspoon pure vanilla essence
1/3 cup honey
A pinch of salt
A pinch of grated nutmeg

1/2 teaspoon cardamom, ground
1/4 teaspoon star anise, ground
1/2 cup water
1/2 cup coconut cream
1 cup coconut milk

Directions

Add the rice, milk, water, coconut cream, honey, salt, nutmeg, vanilla, cardamom, and anise to the Instant Pot.

Secure the lid. Choose the "Porridge" mode. Cook for 20 minutes at High pressure. Once cooking is complete, use a natural release for 10 minutes; carefully remove the lid

Ladle into individual bowls; top with berry jam and serve immediately.

Per serving: 403 Calories; 10.2g Fat; 74.2g Carbs; 5.2g Protein; 36.4g Sugars

786. Spicy Chorizo Sauce

(Ready in about 20 minutes | Servings 4)

Ingredients

1 pound Chorizo sausage, sliced
1 (28-ounce) can diced tomatoes, with juice
1 cup chicken broth
1 habanero pepper, seeded and minced
1 teaspoon red pepper flakes
1 sweet pepper, seeded and finely chopped

1 teaspoon dried basil
1 teaspoon dried rosemary
1 onion, chopped
1 teaspoon garlic, minced
Sea salt and freshly ground black pepper, to taste
1 tablespoon olive oil
2 tablespoons sugar

Directions

Press the "Sauté" button and heat the oil. When the oil starts to sizzle, cook the Chorizo until no longer pink; crumble it with a wooden spatula.

Add the onion, garlic, and peppers and cook for a minute or so. Add a splash of chicken broth to deglaze the pan.

Stir in the remaining ingredients.

Secure the lid. Choose the "Manual" mode and cook for 6 minutes at High pressure. Once cooking is complete, use a natural pressure release for 10 minutes; carefully remove the lid. Bon appétit!

Per serving: 385 Calories; 24.9g Fat; 20.2g Carbs; 21.1g Protein; 11.1g Sugars

787. Balkan-Style Sponge Cake (Patispanj)

(Ready in about 55 minutes | Servings 4)

Ingredients

1 cup milk
1/2 cup golden syrup
1/2 cup strawberries, hulled and sliced
1 teaspoon grated lemon zest
1 teaspoon baking powder
1/2 teaspoon kosher salt
1 teaspoon brown sugar
1/2 cup water
1 ½ cups white flour
3 eggs

Directions

Whisk the eggs until frothy. Add the milk and water; whisk again.

Then, add the flour, baking powder, salt, brown sugar, and lemon zest. Mix until everything is well combined.

Spritz the bottom and sides of your Instant Pot with a nonstick cooking spray. Scrape the batter into the Instant Pot.

Secure the lid. Choose the "Multigrain" mode and cook for 50 minutes under High pressure. Once cooking is complete, use a quick pressure release; carefully remove the lid.

Serve topped with golden syrup and strawberries. Enjoy!

Per serving: 434 Calories; 9.8g Fat; 74.2g Carbs; 13.6g Protein; 37.9g Sugars

788. Kid-Friendly Pear Butter

(Ready in about 25 minutes | Servings 8)

Ingredients

1/2 cup sugar
1/2 teaspoon ground cardamom
1 teaspoon ground cinnamon
1 teaspoon vanilla essence
2 teaspoons freshly squeezed lemon juice
1 ½ pounds cup pears, cored, peeled and chopped

Directions

Add all ingredients to the inner pot; stir to combine.

Secure the lid. Choose the "Manual" mode and cook for 10 minutes at High pressure. Once cooking is complete, use a natural pressure release for 10 minutes; carefully remove the lid.

Mash the pear mixture to the desired consistency. Serve at room temperature or cold. Bon appétit!

Per serving: 73 Calories; 0.1g Fat; 19.2g Carbs; 0.3g Protein; 14.4g Sugars

789. Oatmeal with Coconut Milk and Seeds

(Ready in about 15 minutes | Servings 4)

Ingredients

1 ½ cups coconut milk
1 tablespoon sunflower seeds
1/4 teaspoon grated nutmeg
1/8 teaspoon kosher salt
1 tablespoon pumpkin seeds
1/2 teaspoon pure vanilla extract
1/2 teaspoon ground cinnamon
1/3 cup agave nectar
1 tablespoon flaxseeds
1 ½ cups rolled oats
2 cups water

Directions

Add all of the above ingredients to your Instant Pot.

Secure the lid. Choose the "Manual" mode. Cook for 10 minutes at High pressure. Once cooking is complete, use a natural release; carefully remove the lid.

Divide between four serving bowls and serve topped with some extra fresh or dried fruits, if desired. Bon appétit!

Per serving: 379 Calories; 23.7g Fat; 50.6g Carbs; 9.4g Protein; 23.6g Sugars

790. Beef Bone and Vegetable Broth

(Ready in about 3 hours 5 minutes | Servings 8)

Ingredients

1 teaspoon black pepper
2 bay leaves
8 cups water
3 pounds frozen beef bones
2 onions, halved
4 cloves garlic, whole
2 tablespoons apple cider vinegar
1 teaspoon sea salt
2 stalks celery, chopped
2 carrots, chopped

Directions

Start by preheating your oven to 390 degrees F. Line a baking pan with aluminum foil.

Place the beef bones, onions, celery, carrots, and garlic on the baking pan. Roast for 40 to 45 minutes.

Transfer the roasted beef bones and vegetables to the inner pot of your Instant Pot. Add the bay leaves, apple cider vinegar, sea salt, pepper, and boiling water to the inner pot.

Secure the lid. Choose the "Manual" mode and cook for 120 minutes at High pressure. Once cooking is complete, use a natural pressure release for 20 minutes; carefully remove the lid.

Remove the beef bones and vegetables and discard. Pour the broth through a strainer. Enjoy!

Per serving: 65 Calories; 2.4g Fat; 4.6g Carbs; 6.7g Protein; 1.9g Sugars

791. Double Chocolate Oatmeal

(Ready in about 15 minutes | Servings 4)

Ingredients

1/2 cup dark chocolate chips
2 cups almond milk
1/4 teaspoon star anise, ground
1/2 teaspoon pure vanilla extract

1 teaspoon carob powder
1/2 teaspoon cinnamon, ground
1 ½ cups rolled oats
2 cups water
3 teaspoons cocoa powder

Directions

Simply throw all of the above ingredients, except for the chocolate chips, into your Instant Pot; stir to combine well.

Secure the lid. Choose the "Manual" mode. Cook for 10 minutes at High pressure. Once cooking is complete, use a natural release; carefully remove the lid.

Divide between four serving bowls; serve garnished with the dark chocolate chips and enjoy!

Per serving: 247 Calories; 11.6g Fat; 39.8g Carbs; 10.9g Protein; 14.3g Sugars

792. Chili Bean Sauce

(Ready in about 35 minutes | Servings 8)

Ingredients

1/2 cup Pico de Gallo
1 jalapeño pepper, seeded and minced
1 ½ cups black beans, rinsed, drained
Sea salt and ground black pepper, to taste

1 teaspoon dried Mexican oregano
1/2 teaspoon ground cumin
1 ½ cups chicken broth
3 garlic cloves, chopped
1/4 cup fresh cilantro, chopped
2 tablespoons olive oil
1 brown onion, chopped

Directions

Press the "Sauté" button and heat the olive oil until sizzling. Once hot, cook the onion for 3 to 4 minutes or until tender and fragrant.

After that, stir in the garlic; continue sautéing an additional 30 to 40 seconds.

Add the jalapeño pepper, oregano, cumin, salt, black pepper, beans, and broth to the inner pot.

Secure the lid. Choose the "Bean/Chili" mode and cook for 25 minutes at High pressure. Once cooking is complete, use a quick pressure release; carefully remove the lid.

Then, mash your beans with a potato masher or use your blender. Serve garnished with cilantro and Pico de Gallo. Bon appétit!

Per serving: 181 Calories; 4.4g Fat; 27.3g Carbs; 9.5g Protein; 3.1g Sugars

793. Sparkling Cranberry Quencher

(Ready in about 25 minutes | Servings 8)

Ingredients

2 cups pulp-free orange juice
1 cup water

12 ounces fresh cranberries
1/2 cup granulated sugar

Directions

Place all ingredients in the inner pot.

Secure the lid. Choose the "Manual" mode and cook for 5 minutes at High pressure. Once cooking is complete, use a natural pressure release for 15 minutes; carefully remove the lid.

Divide between eight glasses and fill with club soda. Enjoy!

Per serving: 103 Calories; 0g Fat; 25.6g Carbs; 0.8g Protein; 24.7g Sugars

794. Mom's Festive Coulis

(Ready in about 20 minutes | Servings 6)

Ingredients

Zest from 1 organic orange, finely grated
1 cup brown sugar
1 tablespoon fresh ginger root, peeled and finely grated

1 cup water
1/2 cup fresh orange juice
1 (12-ounce) bag fresh or frozen raspberries

Directions

Add all the ingredients to the inner pot of your Instant Pot.

Secure the lid. Choose the "Manual" mode and cook for 3 minutes at High pressure. Once cooking is complete, use a natural pressure release for 10 minutes; carefully remove the lid.

Let it cool. Serve your sauce chilled or at room temperature. Bon appétit!

Per serving: 134 Calories; 0.2g Fat; 34g Carbs; 0.5g Protein; 30.3g Sugars

795. Cinnamon Roll Pear and Pecan Pie

(Ready in about 35 minutes | Servings 8)

Ingredients

5 pears, cored and sliced
1/4 cup all-purpose flour
1/4 cup packed brown sugar
2 tablespoons butter
1/3 cup pecans, chopped
1/2 teaspoon cinnamon
2 cans (12-ounce) refrigerated cinnamon rolls

Directions

Separate the dough into 8 rolls. Press and flatten the rolls into a lightly greased pie plate. Make sure there are no holes between the flattened rolls.

In a mixing bowl, mix the flour, brown sugar, cinnamon, butter, and pecans. Place the slices of pears on the prepared cinnamon roll crust. Spoon the streusel onto the pear slices.

Add 1 cup of water and a metal rack to the bottom of the inner pot. Lower the pie plate onto the rack.

Secure the lid. Choose the "Manual" mode and cook for 25 minutes at High pressure. Once cooking is complete, use a natural pressure release for 5 minutes; carefully remove the lid. Bon appétit!

Per serving: 497 Calories; 28.6g Fat; 56.5g Carbs; 4.9g Protein; 30.4g Sugars

796. Dad's Homemade Salsa

(Ready in about 40 minutes | Servings 8)

Ingredients

2 chili peppers, chopped
2 sweet peppers, chopped
2 tablespoons brown sugar
1/2 cup rice vinegar
2 ripe tomatoes, crushed
Sea salt and red pepper, to taste
2 garlic cloves, pressed
12 ounces canned tomato paste
1 teaspoon dried Mexican oregano
2 onions, chopped

Directions

Put all ingredients into the inner pot of your Instant Pot.

Secure the lid. Choose the "Manual" mode and cook for 25 minutes at High pressure. Once cooking is complete, use a natural pressure release for 10 minutes; carefully remove the lid.

Allow your salsa to cool completely; store in your refrigerator or freezer. Bon appétit!

Per serving: 83 Calories; 0.4g Fat; 18.8g Carbs; 3.2g Protein; 10.1g Sugars

797. Perfect Mini Cheesecakes

(Ready in about 40 minutes | Servings 4)

Ingredients

4 ounces cream cheese
1 cup cake flour
1/3 cup powdered sugar
1/4 teaspoon ground cinnamon
1 teaspoon vanilla extract
1 cup heavy cream, cold
1 ½ teaspoons baking powder
1/4 teaspoon ground cardamom
1 egg
1/2 cup honey
1/4 almond milk
A pinch of salt

Directions

In a mixing bowl, thoroughly combine the flour, baking powder, salt, cardamom, cinnamon, and vanilla.

Then, gradually add in the egg, honey, and milk. Mix to combine well. Now, spoon the batter into silicone cupcake liners and cover them with foil.

Place 1 cup of water and a metal trivet in your Instant Pot. Lower your cupcakes onto the trivet.

Secure the lid. Choose the "Manual" mode and cook for 25 minutes at High pressure. Once cooking is complete, use a natural pressure release for 10 minutes; carefully remove the lid.

While the cupcakes are cooking, prepare the frosting by mixing the remaining ingredients. Frost your cupcakes and enjoy!

Per serving: 497 Calories; 17.8g Fat; 77g Carbs; 9.8g Protein; 48.5g Sugars

798. Indian Masala Sauce

(Ready in about 30 minutes | Servings 4)

Ingredients

1 cup plain coconut yogurt
2 ripe tomatoes, pureed
4 cloves garlic, chopped
1 teaspoon Garam Masala
1 teaspoon cayenne pepper
1 bell pepper, seeded and chopped
1/2 teaspoon turmeric powder
1 teaspoon coriander powder
1 (1-inch) piece fresh ginger, peeled and grated
1 bird's eye chili, minced
1 cup vegetable broth
2 teaspoons olive oil
1 onion, chopped
Sea salt and ground black pepper, to taste

Directions

Press the "Sauté" button to preheat your Instant Pot. Add the oil and sauté the onion for about 3 minutes or until tender and fragrant.

Now, add the garlic, ginger and peppers; continue to sauté an additional minute or until they are aromatic.

Add the spices, tomatoes, and broth.

Secure the lid. Choose the "Manual" mode and cook for 11 minutes at High pressure. Once cooking is complete, use a natural pressure release for 10 minutes; carefully remove the lid.

Afterwards, add the coconut yogurt to the inner pot and stir to combine. Serve with chickpeas or roasted vegetables. Enjoy!

Per serving: 206 Calories; 17.2g Fat; 12.2g Carbs; 4.1g Protein; 6.1g Sugars

799. Giant No-Flip Pancake

(Ready in about 40 minutes | Servings 4)

Ingredients

1 cup all-purpose flour
4 tablespoons butter, melted
1/2 teaspoon vanilla extract
1 cup canned blueberries with syrup

5 eggs
1/4 teaspoon kosher salt
1/2 teaspoon cinnamon powder
1 ¼ cups milk

Directions

Place 1 cup of water and a metal trivet in your Instant Pot. Line the bottom of a springform pan with parchment paper; grease the bottom and sides of the pan with melted butter.

Mix the eggs, milk, flour, salt, cinnamon, and vanilla until everything is well combined. Now, spoon the batter into the prepared pan. Lower the pan onto the trivet.

Secure the lid. Choose the "Manual" mode and cook for 30 minutes at High pressure. Once cooking is complete, use a quick pressure release; carefully remove the lid.

Serve garnished with fresh blueberries and enjoy!

Per serving: 399 Calories; 19.8g Fat; 42.3g Carbs; 13.1g Protein; 17.5g Sugars

800. Perfect Homemade Bouillon

(Ready in about 45 minutes | Servings 8)

Ingredients

2 tablespoons olive oil
A bunch of fresh parsley
2 onions, sliced
2 carrots, sliced
2 bay leaves
2 sprig fresh rosemary

1 cup white wine
1 lemon, sliced
2 celery ribs, sliced
1 teaspoon mixed peppercorns
1 tablespoon salt

Directions

Add all ingredients to the inner pot of your Instant Pot. Add cold water until the inner pot is 2/3 full.

Secure the lid. Choose the "Soup/Broth" mode and cook for 30 minutes at High pressure. Once cooking is complete, use a natural pressure release for 10 minutes; carefully remove the lid.

Discard the vegetables. Bon appétit!

Per serving: 55 Calories; 3.4g Fat; 1.6g Carbs; 0.1g Protein; 0.6g Sugars

14826590R00129